The Uses of Social Investment

Edited by
Anton Hemerijck

OXFORD
UNIVERSITY PRESS

OXFORD

UNIVERSITY PRESS

Great Clarendon Street, Oxford, OX2 6DP,
United Kingdom

Oxford University Press is a department of the University of Oxford.
It furthers the University's objective of excellence in research, scholarship,
and education by publishing worldwide. Oxford is a registered trade mark of
Oxford University Press in the UK and in certain other countries

First Edition published in 2017
Impression: 1

Published in the United States of America by Oxford University Press
198 Madison Avenue, New York, NY 10016, United States of America

British Library Cataloguing in Publication Data
Data available

Library of Congress Control Number: 2016952212

ISBN 978–0–19–879048–8 (hbk.)
       978–0–19–879049–5 (pbk.)

Printed and bound by
CPI Group (UK) Ltd, Croydon, CR0 4YY

Preface and Acknowledgements

This volume took shape as a consequence of a number of truly fortunate, professionally satisfying and intellectually rich, tidings. In the year 2013, when OUP published my *Changing Welfare States* monograph, a series of critical articles were published bringing to the fore shortcomings to the social investment perspective that I defended in the conclusion of the book. One of them, with the most provocative title, *What Use is Social Investment?* came from Brian Nolan (2013). As my writings (with colleagues) were implicated in these articles, essays, and book chapters, I felt the urge and obligation to write a review on the so-called critics of social investment. This, then, should include a rejoinder on how to bring more theoretical nuance, methodological clarity, and political credibility to the social investment approach in welfare state research, while taking on board some of the justified criticisms levelled against social investment research and policy advocacy. As I was recently appointed Centennial Professor of Social Policy at the London School of Economics and Political Science (LSE), a part-time fixed-term appointment, established on the occasion of the 100th anniversary of the LSE with few strings attached except for research, I decided that 'social investment and its critics' would become my main academic preoccupation for my time at LSE.

After stepping down as Dean of the Social Science Faculty of the Vrije Universiteit Amsterdam in January 2014, I was granted a half-year sabbatical at the Collegio Carlo Alberto, now part of the University of Torino, in Moncalieri. During my stay at the Collegio, I presented my first assessment of the criticisms levelled against social investment and profited greatly from the constructive comments of Margarita Esteves-Abe, Manuela Naldini, Stefano Sacchi, Chiara Saraceno, and the students in the MSc programme 'Social Change and Public Policy' that participated in my course. I took the 'state-of-the-art' review I was working on to Switzerland for the international conference 'Assessing the Social Investment Strategy' that I co-organized with Giuliano Bonoli and Bruno Palier for IDHEAP (Swiss Graduate School of Public Administration), NCCR LIVES (Swiss National Centre of Competence in Research—Overcoming Vulnerability: Life Course Perspectives), and the Institute of Social Sciences of the University of Lausanne, 10–11 April 2014.

The idea of a volume on the 'uses of social investment' further crystalized when, back in Montcalieri, I was approached by Miro Beblavy from CEPS Brussels with the good news that I had some money left to spend for the NEUJOBS FP7 research project, funded by the European Commission (grant number 266833), that I participated in with my research group of the Vrije Universiteit. The catch was that I should come up with a proposal on how to productively use the leftover funding in sync with the purpose of the NEU-JOBS programme on future European labour markets. It took me less than a second to tell Miro that I wanted to organize a workshop, entitled 'Social Investment and Its Critics'. I immediately sent letters of invitations to some of the more vocal critics and sceptics of social investment, because without their participation, the workshop would be a non-starter. All replied practically overnight that they would be more than happy to travel to Amsterdam for the gathering. A volume was now in the making thanks to the timely intervention of Miro and the extended funding from the European Commission, for which I am extremely thankful.

The autumn of 2014, spent at LSE, was entirely devoted to making the Amsterdam workshop happen. I wrote the background document for the workshop and a prospectus for OUP. LSE proved to be the perfect breathing ground for my second take on social investment and its critics to mature. I am ever so grateful for the luxurious hospitality granted to me by the Department of Social Policy, and especially by David Lewis, as head of the department, his successor Stephen Jenkins, and Timo Fleckenstein, my closest intellectual ally in the Department of Social Policy, together with Jane Lewis and David Soskice for supporting my appointment as Centennial Professor of Social Policy. I cannot wait to have the present volume launched at LSE as a token of my gratitude to the Department and the School for my Centennial stay.

The Amsterdam workshop took place on 15 and 16 January 2015 in the beautiful building of the Vakbondsmuseum (trade union museum), called De Burcht (The Stronghold), originally designed and constructed by the famous Dutch architect Hendrik Petrus Berlage in 1903 for the Trade Union of the Diamond Workers, the first professionally run union organization in the Netherlands. Although the decorative surroundings of De Burcht contributed positively to the atmosphere of the encounter between social investment proponents, sceptics, empiricists, and critics, organizing a two-day workshop with the intent of true intellectual engagement was no sinecure. I was lucky to have the assistance of an extremely talented and logistically astute assistant in the form of master student Milanne Mulder. I am grateful for her unwavering help before, during, and after the workshop when many accounts (financial ones) still needed to be settled. Next to Milanne, Gijs van der Starre and Jonathan Zeitlin are also to be credited for making the workshop a huge success, as it was organized under the auspices of ACCESS EUROPE, a collaborative research institute of contemporary European studies, jointly hosted by Vrije Universiteit Amsterdam and the University of Amsterdam (UvA), that Jonathan and I founded in 2013, with Gijs as managing director.

After the workshop I spent most of my working hours chasing chapters, giving comments on various drafts with suggestions, mostly for cuts, while making individual contracts ready for the publisher. This took much longer than the initial half-year that I anticipated, but ultimately with fifty (co-)authors altogether contributing to this volume, in hindsight, this is no real surprise.

The introductory 'state-of-the-art' chapter on 'Social Investment and Its Critics' and the concluding essay on 'The Uses of Affordable Social Investment' bear the stamp of extraordinary intelligent friends and collaborators with whom I have worked on welfare state research throughout the years. As the book project evolved, I should cite in particular Giuliano Bonoli, Brian Burgoon, Bea Cantillon, Colin Crouch, Verena Draebing, Maurizio Ferrera, Timo Fleckenstein, Franca van Hooren, Jane Jenson, Lane Kenworthy, Kees van Kersbergen, Ab Klink, Marc van der Meer, Moira Nelson, Bruno Palier, Charles Sabel, Stefano Sacchi, Menno Soentken, Matthias Stepan, Frank Vandenbroucke, Babara Vis, and Jonathan Zeitlin. Although they do not bear responsibility for the arguments developed in the two bookend chapters of the volume, I can safely say that, without their perceptive and invaluable counsel over the years, on empirical conjectures, theoretical panache, and methodological nuts and bolts on social investment, the overall thesis on the progressive, admittedly uneven, social investment turn across the globe, would have been less persuasive. For this they deserve deep gratitude. Lest I forget, I am further indebted to the two anonymous referees of Oxford University Press, and of course my OUP editor Dominic Byatt who immediately took a liking to the project when I first consulted him in the summer of 2014.

Back in Amsterdam, the newly merged Department of Political Science and Public Administration at the Vrije Universiteit provided the perfect setting for editing the manuscript, for which I thank Head of Department and fine colleague Willem Trommel. Over the past half year, the book was assembled with the help of a truly superb research assistant, Simon Vydra, a former MSc student of mine. Simon helped me devise final revisions, while making sure tables and figures were not overlooked in the process. I am enormously thankful for his extraordinarily generous support in both practical and substantive matters over the tail end of the project. And ever so glad that Simon now has a Phd position at Leiden University to work on social investment and Big Data.

My wife Emke and our daughters Lieke and Meike, often suggested alternative pastimes and better things to do over the weekends than for me to write, edit, and respond to the emails of contributors. In the end, the three of them did not push too hard. But soon, now that I reside in Fiesole, overlooking Florence, they want to see 'returns' for what they think of as their social investments in this volume.

And right they are!

Rotterdam/Fiesole
December 2016

Table of Contents

Part 1. Introduction

Part 2. Limits to Social Investment

Part 3. Social Investment Endowment and Extensions

Part 4. Social Investment Assessment: Conceptualization and Methods

Part 5. Comparative Social Investment Experience

Part 6. EU Social Investment Advocacy

Table of Contents

List of Figures

List of Figures

List of Tables

List of Abbreviations

ALMPs	active labour-market policies
BMI	body mass index
CATI	computer-assisted telephone interviewing
CCT	conditional cash transfers
CDU	Christlich Demokratische Union
CEO	chief executive officer
CSR	country-specific recommendation
CWS	comparative welfare states
DGB	Deutsche Gewerkschaftsbund
DG EMPL	Directorate General for Employment
ECB	European Central Bank
ECE	early childhood education
ECEC	early childhood education and care
EITC	Earned Income Tax Credit
EMU	Economic and Monetary Union
ESF	European Social Fund
ESPN	European Social Policy Network
ESPROSS	social protection expenditure, current, by function, gross and net
ESS	European Social Survey
ETBs	education and training boards
EU	European Union
EU-IMF	European Union–International Monetary Fund
EU-SILC	European Union Statistics on Income and Living Conditions
EYC	Early Years Curriculum
FTE	full-time equivalent
GDP	gross domestic product
HDI	Human Development Index
ICT	information and communications technology

List of Abbreviations

IDB	Inter-American Development Bank
IEG	Independent Evaluation Group
ILO	International Labour Organization
IMF	International Monetary Fund
INVEDUC	Investing in Education in Europe: Attitudes, Politics and Policies
IPC-IG	International Policy Centre on Inclusive Growth
IR	inequality ratio
ISSP	International Social Survey Programme
JAF	Joint-Assessment Framework
LIS	Luxembourg Income Study
MBM	market basket measure
MIFAPRO	Mi Familia Progresa
MIP	Macroeconomic Imbalances Procedure
MoU	memorandum of understanding
NEETs	not in education, employment, or training
NESC	National Economic and Social Council
NGO	non-governmental organization
NSR	new social risks
OECD	Organisation for Economic Co-operation and Development
OMC	open method of coordination
OMT	outright monetary transactions
PIAAC	Programme for the International Assessment of Adult Competencies
PISA	Programme for International Student Assessment
QE	quantitative easing
RDD	random digit dialling
SGP	Stability and Growth Pact
SI	social investment
SIA	social investment approach
SII	social impact investment
SIP	Social Investment Package
SIWS	social investment welfare state
SMEs	small and medium-sized enterprises
SOCX	Social Expenditure Database
SPC	Social Protection Committee
SPD	Sozialdemokratische Partei Deutschland

SPPM	Social Protection Performance Monitor
SWDs	Staff Working Documents
TFEU	Treaty on the Functioning of the European Union
TTIP	Transatlantic Trade and Investment Partnership
UI	unemployment insurance
UK	United Kingdom
UNDP	United Nations Development Programme
UNESCO	United Nations Educational, Scientific and Cultural Organization
UNFCCC	United Nations Framework Convention on Climate Change
UNICEF	United Nations Children's Fund
US/USA	United States of America

List of Contributors

Evelyn Astor Policy Officer working on social policies at the Directorate-General (DG) Employment, Social Affairs and Inclusion at the European Commission.

Jean-Claude Barbier Professor of Sociology and Emeritus National Center for Scientific Research (CNRS) Researcher at the University of Paris.

Iain Begg Professorial Research Fellow at the European Institute, London School of Economics and Political Science.

Sonja Bekker Assistant Professor of European Governance and Social Policy at Labour Market Institute ReflecT, Tilburg University, the Netherlands.

Giuliano Bonoli Professor of Social Policy at the Swiss Graduate School for Public Administration at the University of Lausanne. Switzerland.

Brian Burgoon Professor of International and Comparative Political Economy at the University of Amsterdam, where he is Academic Director of the Amsterdam Institute for Social Science Research (AISSR).

Marius R. Busemeyer Professor of Political Science at the University of Konstanz, Germany.

Bea Cantillon Professor of Social Policy and Director of the Herman Deleeck Centre for Social Policy at the University of Antwerp.

Colin Crouch Professor Emeritus of the University of Warwick and external scientific member of the Max Planck Institute for the Study of Societies at Cologne.

Johan De Deken Associate Professor at the Department of Sociology at the University of Amsterdam and is affiliated to the Amsterdam Institute for Advanced Labour Studies (AIAS).

Verena Dräbing Consultant in the field of policy evaluation and PhD student in the Department of Political Science and Public Administration at Vrije University Amsterdam.

Maurizio Ferrera Professor of Political Science, Faculty of Political, Economic and Social Sciences of the University of Milan.

Timo Fleckenstein Associate Professor in the Department of Social Policy at the London School of Economics and Political Science.

Lieve Fransen Senior Advisor at the European Policy Centre (EPC) and former director at DG Employment Social Affairs of the European Commission.

List of Contributors

Silja Häusermann Professor of Political Science at the University of Zurich, Switzerland.

Anton Hemerijck Professor of Political Science and Sociology, European University Institute (EUI), Florence, and Centennial Professor of Social Policy, London School of Economics and Political Science (LSE)

Jane Jenson Professor of Political Science at the University of Montreal, a Senior Fellow in the Successful Societies Program of the Canadian Institute for Advanced Research (CIFAR), and a Fellow of the Royal Society of Canada.

Yuri Kazepov Professor of International Urban Sociology at the University of Vienna.

Lane Kenworthy Professor of Sociology and Yankelovich Chair in Social Thought at the University of California, San Diego.

Jonas Kraft PhD student at the Department of Political Science, Aarhus University, Denmark.

Soohyun Christine Lee Lecturer in Comparative Politics in the School of Politics and International Studies at the University of Leeds.

Margarita León Associate Professor at the Autonomous University of Barcelona (UAB) and a Senior Researcher in the Institute of Government and Public Policies (IGOP) of the same university.

Daniel Mertens Postdoctoral Researcher in the Political Science Department at Goethe-University of Frankfurt am Main, Germany.

Nathalie Morel Assistant Professor in Political Science, at Sciences Po, France.

John Myles Emeritus Professor of Sociology and Senior Fellow in the School of Public Policy and Governance, University of Toronto.

Moira Nelson Assistant Professor of Political Science at Lund University, Sweden.

Alain Noël Professor of Political Science at the University of Montreal, Canada.

Brian Nolan Director of the Employment, Equity and Growth Programme at the Institute for New Economic Thinking, Oxford Martin School, and Professor of Social Policy at the Department of Social Policy and Intervention.

Rory O'Donnell Director of Ireland's National Economic and Social Council (NESC).

Bruno Palier Co-Director of the Laboratory for Interdisciplinary Evaluation of Public Policies (LIEPP) and CNRS Researcher at Sciences Po (Centre d'études européennes).

Joakim Palme Professor of Political Science at the Department of Government, Uppsala University.

Sigrid Quack Professor of Sociology, University of Duisburg, Essen.

Costanzo Ranci Professor in Economic Sociology at the Polytechnic of Milan.

Deborah Rice Postdoctoral Researcher in Political Science, University of Oldenburg, Germany.

Charles Sabel Maurice T. Moore Professor of Law, Columbia Law School, New York.

Johan Sandberg Senior Lecturer in Sociology, Lund University, Sweden.

Chiara Saraceno Former Professor of Sociology at the University of Turin and Research Professor at the Wissenschaftszentrum Berlin (WZB). Presently Honorary Fellow at the Collegio Carlo Alberto, Turin.

Günther Schmid Director Emeritus Labour Market Policy and Employment at WZB.

Martin Seeleib-Kaiser Barnett Professor of Comparative Social Policy and Politics at the Oxford Institute of Social Policy and a Professorial Fellow at St Cross College, University of Oxford.

Menno Soentken Postdoctoral Researcher, Faculty of Social Sciences, Erasmus University, Rotterdam.

Damian Thomas Senior Policy Analyst at NESC, Ireland.

Franca van Hooren Assistant Professor in Political Science, University of Amsterdam.

Kees van Kersbergen Professor of Comparative Politics at Aarhus University.

Wim Van Lancker Postdoctoral Research Fellow of the Research Foundation Flanders (FWO), affiliated with the Herman Deleeck Centre for Social Policy at the University of Antwerp in Belgium.

Frank Vandenbroucke University Professor at the University of Amsterdam, Herman Deleeck Professor at the University of Antwerp.

Gerlinde Verbist Senior Researcher at the Herman Deleeck Centre for Social Policy and Lecturer at the Faculty of Social Sciences of the University of Antwerp.

Marc Vothknecht Policy Officer at the European Commission's Structural Reform Support Service.

Anne Wren Research Associate of the Institute for International Integration Studies at Trinity College, Dublin.

Jonathan Zeitlin Distinguished Faculty Professor of Public Policy and Governance, Department of Political Science, University of Amsterdam. Scientific Director of the Amsterdam Centre for Contemporary European Studies (ACCESS EUROPE).

Part 1
Introduction

1

Social Investment and Its Critics

Anton Hemerijck

1.1 The Social Investment Turn

Over the past decade, the idea of social investment gained considerable purchase in scholarly debates and policymaking environments, emanating from
the Scandinavian heartland of social investment to other European countries,
including Germany, the Netherlands, Austria, and the United Kingdom,
together with Slovenia among the newer member states of the European
Union (EU). The social investment turn, however, is not conscripted to
Europe. In Australia and Canada, the debate on social policy reform is increasingly couched in terms of investment in human capital and families with
children (Banting and Myles 2013; Smyth 2015). Most conspicuous perhaps is
the social investment drive in the less developed welfare regions of Latin
America, including Brazil, Argentina, Chile, and Uruguay, and East Asia, including South Korea, Taiwan, Singapore, and Taiwan (Peng 2011; Huber and
Stephens 2012; Morel, Palier, and Palme 2012c; Esteves-Abe, forthcoming).

Strongly supported by the Organisation for Economic Co-operation and
Development's (OECD's) work on education, families and inequality and the
World Bank's recent 'inclusive growth' priorities, over the 2000s, a fairly
coherent 'epistemic community' gained considerable sway in international
organizations and policy think tanks (Jenson 2010). A recent endorsement of
the idea of social investment can be read into President Barack Obama's 2015
State of the Union address, promising better access to high-quality early care
and education as a 'must-have' for middle-class American families, forcefully
explicating that: 'It's time we stop treating childcare as a side issue, or a
women's issue, and treat it like the national economic priority for all of us'
(Obama 2015). Perhaps the most assertive embrace of social investment of late
has come from the EU with the launch of the Social Investment Package for
Growth and Social Cohesion (European Commission 2013d) on 20 February

2013. In the Social Investment Package (SIP), the Commission counselled EU member states to focus on welfare reform to 'prepare' individuals, families and societies to respond to the new risks of a competitive knowledge economy, by investing in human capital and capabilities from early childhood through old age, rather than in policies that simply 'repair' damages after moments of economic or personal crisis. The idea of social investment is not new. Building on the pioneering work of the Dutch Presidency of the EU in 1997, calling attention to 'social policy as a productive factor', social investment ideas became part and parcel of the Lisbon Agenda, launched in 2000, with the ambition to turn Europe into the 'most competitive and dynamic knowledge-based economy in the world, capable of sustainable economic growth and more and better jobs and greater social cohesion' (European Council 2000).

In the academic debate, welfare reform dynamics have in recent years increasingly been couched in reference to the rise of a new social investment approach (SIA), transcending earlier conceptualizations of the post-war demand-oriented Keynesian welfare state and its supply-side market-liberal successor, subscribing to a negative view of welfare provision as distorting optimal (labour) market allocation. In their seminal stock-taking study *Towards a Social Investment Welfare State*, Morel, Palier, and Palme (2012c) prefer to talk about an 'emerging' policy paradigm, one that is not fully established in actual social policy practice, but that—in ideational terms—signals a significant departure from the dominant neoliberal market-oriented welfare paradigm of the 1980s and 1990s.

After Giuliano Bonoli's *The Origins of Active Social Policy* (2013) and my own monograph *Changing Welfare States* (2013) supplied evidential support for an incipient social investment turn across the EU in recent years, a prominent stream of critical studies on social investment have appeared bringing a number of limitations of the perspective to the scholarly debate; doubts have been raised with respect to claim of the superiority of 'active' social investment over 'passive' social insurance spending (Nolan 2013). Feminist scholars have disapproved of the gullible 'economization' of female labour force participation and dual earner families, based on a highly biased norma-tive objective of gender equality (Chapter 4, this volume). Probably the fiercest critique is that social investment is plagued by perverse 'Matthew Effects', with the middle class disproportionally benefiting from social investments at the expense of the worse off, in correspondence with the proclamation that 'unto every one that hath shall be given' in the Gospel of Matthew (Cantillon 2011; Chapter 5, this volume). Then there is the pessimistic thesis that discre-tionary social investments will irrevocably be outflanked and left defeated by austerity reform for many years to come (Mertens and Streeck 2011; Chapter 6, this volume). The critics have raised justified warnings against some of the exaggerated expectations of social investment manifestos and research for this project, warranting a considerate rejoinder, particularly in the light of the social aftershocks of the global financial crisis of mass unemployment and rising inequality.

The principle objective of *The Uses of Social Investment* volume is to investigate, through a collective effort by a wide range of academic and policy experts, the theoretical underpinnings and methodological caveats, empirical incidence and challenges, intended socioeconomic effects and unintended consequences, organizational design and political dynamics, of social investment oriented policy reforms, before and after the onslaught of the global financial crisis. One of the key questions this book will try to answer is the question whether it remains far-fetched to talk about a fully-fledged social investment shift in *policy paradigm*, understood as a coherent set of ideas, relating *causal understanding* of social risk change and effective policy responses, the *political mobilization* behind legitimate priorities of social risk mitigation, together with a *governance structure* that allows welfare policy-making to be conducted in an internally consistent fashion (cf. Hall 1989, 1993). By so doing, the volume aspires to improve our understanding of the conditions under which social investment ideas and policy reform endeavours have emerged, diffused, and proved robust in a wide range of settings across the globe; and vice versa, what institutional, political, economic, and organizational barriers have made it difficult to enact social investment oriented welfare reform in times, especially, of fiscal acute. By inviting the most important critics of social investment and its assertive advocates in welfare policy research, the scene is set for an endeavour of engaged discord over theory-building, causal inference and methods, and policy advocacy and criticisms, to deepen our knowledge and understanding of current welfare state performance and opportunities for alternative welfare state futures.

The purpose of this chapter is to introduce the social investment perspective, by reviewing its ideational emergence, merits, and limits in substantive portent, theoretical conceptualization, and methodological operationalization in four steps. First, Section 1.2 returns to the intellectual roots of social investment perspective by revisiting the landmark publication *Why We Need a New Welfare State* (Esping-Andersen et al. 2002), in the light of new ideas and recent empirical findings. Section 1.3 then turns to the main criticisms that have been levelled against social investment advocacy. Triggered by the critique, and also inspired by cumulative empirical endowments of social investment policy diffusion, Section 1.4 puts forward a theoretical framework of three interdependent and complementary welfare functions of social investment: (1) easing the 'flow' of contemporary labour-market and gendered life-course transitions; (2) raising the quality of the 'stock' of human capital and capabilities; and (3) maintaining strong minimum-income universal safety nets as social protection and economic stabilization 'buffers' in ageing societies, that subsequently serves a semi-structured background perspective to the majority of the individual contributions to the volume. Section 1.5 is devoted to the methodological challenge of identifying interdependent social investment policy mixes, empirically tracking social investment reforms, and associating such reforms to the promise of timely 'returns' on social investment in terms of socioeconomic well-being. Next, Section 1.6 shifts focus from social investment 'policy analysis' and the empirical assessment of 'returns' to the 'political analysis' of the social investment turn, as it conjures up the thorny dilemma of legitimating short-term pain in return for long-term gains. At face value, the political management of intertemporal trade-offs in times of fiscal austerity, accelerated demographic ageing, and rising political populism, seems insurmountable. Section 1.7 closes the introduction by outlining the structure of the rest of the volume.

1.2 *Why We Need a New Welfare State* Revisited

The notion of social investment emerged in political and academic discourse after the mid-1990s on the wing of the ambition of modernizing the welfare state and ensuring its long-term sustainability, in the face of demographic ageing, by making social policy systems more employment-friendly (Ferrera, Hemerijck, and Rhodes 2000; Jenson and Saint-Martin 2003; Morel, Palier, and Palme 2012c; Hemerijck 2013). First, surprisingly, it was the OECD in 1996, at the time still wedded to the market-liberal and welfare-state-critical Washington Consensus, who organized a conference focused on rethinking social policy in terms of positive economic output. The EU followed suit, and under the Dutch presidency in 1997, the term 'social policy as a productive factor' was coined, focused on exposing the neoliberal misconception that social policy interventions go at the expense of economic competitiveness (Morel, Palier, and Palme 2012c). These ideas were subsequently anchored in the EU's Lisbon Agenda of 2000 for social policy guidance in the knowledge-based economy, creation of better jobs, and greater social cohesion.

The philosophy and policy theory underpinning the SIA was given explicit impetus with the publication of a collective book by Gøsta Esping-Andersen, Duncan Gallie, Anton Hemerijck, and John Myles, *Why We Need a New Welfare State* (2002), commissioned by the Belgian Presidency of the EU in 2001. The central argument of *Why We Need a New Welfare State* was that the staying power of male-breadwinner employment-based social insurance increasingly fostered suboptimal life chances for large parts of the population. Esping-Andersen and colleagues contended that Europe's welfare states faced a genuine—paradigmatic—'Gordian knot' of how to sustain a deep normative

nt to social justice while aspiring to create a robust and competitive
-based social market economy. In terms of policy theory, *Why We
Welfare State* took issue with male-breadwinner social insurance
r job-protection dysfunctions, on the one hand, and, on the other,
eral myth that generous welfare provision inevitably implies a loss of
efficiency, harking back to the formulation of a 'big trade-off'
equality and efficiency, a dilemma coined by the American economist
un (1975) in the 1970s. Both neoliberal welfare retrenchment and
eadwinner employment-based social insurance are ill-suited to meet
t-industrial challenges of the knowledge economy and dual-earner
ood. According to Esping-Andersen and colleagues the economic sus-
lity of advanced welfare states hinged on the number and productivity
of future employees and taxpayers. On this reading, welfare reform should
contribute to mobilizing citizens' productive potential in order to mitigate
the novel risks of atypical employment, long-term unemployment, in-work
poverty, family instability, and labour-market exclusion, resulting from obsolete skills and dual-earner care obligations, consistent with widely shared
normative aspirations to decent work for everyone, gender equality, and capacitating service provision as the foundations of solidarity in a competitive
knowledge economy. The policy analysis of *Why We Need a New Welfare State*
was based on five important intellectual innovations in social policy research,
touching respectively on: (1) the changing nature of social risks; (2) a novel
assessment of the carrying capacity of the welfare state; (3) the imperative of
evaluating welfare provision from a dynamic life-course perspective; (4) the
intimately related dimension of family demography and gender role change;
all inspired, finally by (5) an updated normative conception of 'capacitating'
social justice.

1.2.1 Social Risk Change

Esping-Andersen and colleagues underscore how important socioeconomic
changes have since the 1990s fundamentally altered the nature of social risks
facing citizens and families in advanced welfare states. Under moderate economic growth levels, fiscal pressures have increased, not least because of greater
capital mobility and intensified European economic integration. In addition,
population ageing and declining fertility, together with a trend towards early
retirement of baby-boomers, severely burdened pension systems. Rapid technological change and accelerated economic internationalization have meanwhile reduced the demand for low-skill work in advanced economies. While
the shift towards post-industrial labour markets has opened up job opportunities for women, deindustrialization has also reduced the number of steady
lifetime jobs and increased job precariousness for both women and men.

Changing family structures and gender roles, with longer education spells, later childbirth, lone parenthood, high rates of divorce and remarriage, have created new tensions between careers and family life. As a consequence, rising levels of female labour-market participation have raised new demands for the provision of social care, especially for young children and the frail elderly.

Many academic experts concur that mature welfare states have increasingly been confronted with a range of so-called 'new social risks', varying from rising old-age dependency, high unemployment of low-skilled and older workers, insufficient social security coverage, precarious employment, human capital depletion due to rapid technological change, retraining needs, youth and long-term unemployment, increasing levels of early school dropout, greater family instability and single parenthood, and unsatisfactory work-care-family reconciliation, especially for working mothers (Huber and Stephens 2001; Castles 2004; Armingeon and Bonoli 2006; Hobson 2014; Gallie and Russell 2009).

With the return of mass unemployment since the onset of the financial crisis, the dichotomy of 'new' and 'old' social has manifestly broken down. This, however, does not invalidate social investment policy prerogatives, as Colin Crouch infers in Chapter 34 of this volume. According to Job Kvist the importance of the social investment perspective is that it addresses the 'old' risks of unemployment in 'new' ways (2015). Quintessentially, Charles Sabel underscores that the risks of the life course and the labour market have become less predictable and therefore less insurable in a strict actuarial sense. Uncertainty or non-actuarial risk makes it impossible to say who should pay how much to sustain a social insurance pool sufficient to cover actual losses. For example, if the risks of unemployment are seasonal or cyclical, funds can be reserved to cover regular spells of unemployment. But if unemployment is structural, caused by radical shifts in product design, production technology, or market trends that permanently devalue existing skills, unemployment insurance no longer suffices (Sabel et al. 2011; Sabel 2012). In order to mitigate the non-actuarial risks of atypical employment, long-term unemployment, in-work poverty, family instability, and labour-market exclusion, resulting from obsolete skills or deficient care support, surely a wider preventive portfolio of policy provisions is imperative alongside traditional social insurance. For this reason, *Why We Need a New Welfare State* urged for 'social investment' renewal aimed at resilience over the family life course, with the eradication of child poverty taking pride of place.

1.2.2 *The Welfare State's Carrying Capacity*

In the heated debate about the future of the welfare state, often two political positions feature in the foreground. On the one hand, most economists tend to focus on cost-containment measures required to face the challenge of demographic ageing in the area of pensions and health. On the other hand, many welfare state sociologists and political scientists continue to focus— equally narrowly—on the redistributive functions of social policy for different classes and the politics of sharing of the costs associated with supporting those in need. *Why We Need a New Welfare State* radically shifts the analysis away from cross-sectional distributive cost impact of social policy interventions here and now towards the more dynamic dimension of how social policy interacts with fertility, education, and labour supply, in a manner to support the future tax base. Central to the analysis is an assessment of the long-term 'carrying capacity' of the welfare state by enhancing aggregate productivity and employment as the means to securing well-being and life chances, including the fundamental argument that economic insecurity and unequal opportunities incur considerable waste of valuable human capital and economic growth.

In his contribution on the intergenerational contract in *Why We Need a New Welfare State*, Myles (2002) introduced a simple cost-benefit equation for any sustainable pension system, a formula that can be generalized for the welfare state at large.

Costs of welfare support =

$$\frac{\text{Number of welfare recipients}}{\text{Number of paid workers}} \quad \text{X} \quad \frac{\text{Average consumption of welfare recipients}}{\text{Average productivity of workers}}$$

Why We Need a New Welfare State advocates, following Myles, a fundamental policy reorientation from the 'numerator' to the 'denominator' of the welfare equation, by explicitly posing the question of how social policy interventions can contribute to higher employment and future improvements in overall productivity and economic growth and prosperity in times of ageing populations. The fiscal resources for welfare provision are ultimately generated by productive workers. A larger, more productive, and less socially scarred workforce is the main funding base of the welfare state's costly but potentially productive social spending. As a consequence, investments in tomorrow's taxpayers as future productive workers loom large in the social investment argument: investing in children, through high-quality education and affordable childcare, are critical means to achieve a sustainable welfare state, they boost the denominator side in the above equation.

Under post-industrial conditions of rising non-standard employment, the category of 'paid workers' represents enormous heterogeneity, ranging from part-time work, temp-agency work, fixed terms contract, (temporary) short-time work, and self-employment. Today, not all 'paid' workers in effect contribute to the welfare state's carrying capacity: the new phenomena of German mini-jobs, British tax credits, and other kinds of wage subsidies and in-work benefits for the working poor, across a host of advanced countries, epitomize new categories of paid workers supported by the welfare state at particular points in time (Schmid 2011). Augmented employment heterogeneity, however, does not deny the truism of the 'denominator' imperative of raising productive labour-market inputs. In the wake of the financial crisis, the growth of new forms of employment had gained further momentum.

Finally, the critical emphasis on the welfare state's 'carrying capacity' in *Why We Need a New Welfare State* cannot be read as a one-sided argument dismissive of traditional minimum-income protection and social insurance. Writing at the early stage of the Lisbon Era, Esping-Andersen and colleagues strongly criticized Third Way policy advocacy for its unduly selective belief that 'activation may substitute for conventional income guarantees. This may be regarded as naïve optimism, but, worse, it may also be counterproductive. (. . .) [T]he minimization of poverty and income insecurity is a precondition for any effective social investment strategy' (Esping-Andersen 2002: 5).

1.2.3 *The Life-Course Perspective*

Why We Need a New Welfare State addresses the changing nature of social risks by focusing explicitly on the life-course dynamics of citizens' life chances. As life-course dynamics have become increasingly erratic, as a consequence of more frequent labour-market transitions and family change, individuals face multifarious risk of damaging their human capital base, potentially causing scarring effects onto successive stages of the life course. People are particularly vulnerable: (1) when they move from education into their first job; (2) when they have children; (3) when they—almost inevitably—experience spells of labour-market inactivity; and, finally, (4) when they move to retirement. Over such transitions, people are prone to vary their labour-market engagement, depending on labour-market opportunities and policy supports for work–life balance. Unlike traditional social security, based on compensation and mitigation through income support 'here and now' after social misfortune has struck, social investment policies aim at preparing rather than repairing, focusing on the roots of social problems and emphasizing prevention rather than cure, hence the focus on ex ante service support for children and families and investment in human capital and capabilities throughout the life course. To be sure, absent possibilities of externalizing child and elderly care, rising numbers of female workers face 'broken careers' and postponed motherhood, resulting in lower fertility, which in turn intensifies the ageing burden.

From a life-course perspective, the distinction between welfare recipients and productive workers in the cost-benefit welfare equation, explicated above, breaks down, or rather turns into a life-course risk-pooling arrangement, instead of a redistributive bargain. Throughout their lives all citizens—at various stages—rely on welfare provision for education, pensions, health care, family support, and other episodes of inactivity for various reasons. Although much of the political debate is often couched in terms of a schism of 'them' and 'us', between those who benefit from the welfare state and 'hard-working' citizens who pay for it, twenty-first-century social reality is entirely different. School-age youngsters become workers, ill citizens will return to the labour market after recovery, and the majority of unemployment benefit recipients, under normal economic conditions, return to work, thereby resuming their contribution to the welfare state's 'carrying capacity' and contribution to the economic pie (Hills 2014).

1.2.4 *Gender Role Change and Family Demography*

Closely related to the emphasis on the welfare state's carrying capacity and the life-course perspective in the light of intrusive social risks change, *Why We Need a New Welfare State* squarely put the changed role of women and families at the heart of social diagnosis and policy resolution. Female emancipation and lifelong career aspiration call for a 'new gender contract'. It is imperative to recast the nexus of work, welfare, and family. The new gender contract should address two challenges: (1) make parenthood compatible with a life dedicated to work and career; and (2) create a more egalitarian equilibrium between men's and women's lives. To counter life chance disparities at an early age, Esping-Andersen and colleagues (2002) advocated quality preschool childcare services in conjunction with other policy interventions to enable more parents—and especially mothers—to engage in full-time employment, thereby contributing to rising employment while helping young kids to a 'strong start' in life, which will help them to be successful in work, health, and family life later on. Alongside guaranteed childcare, paid maternity and paternity leave should also be considered as a social investment.

As changes in education, as well as the expansion of the service sector, and changing social expectations and normative aspirations, have resulted in a significant increase in women's employment over the past decades, balancing care responsibilities and employment careers has grown in importance for both women and men and, as a consequence, for employers and policymakers (Hobson 2014). Given the fact that female participation is critical to sustaining the welfare state in ageing societies and that parenting is crucial to child development, twenty-first-century policymakers have good reasons to want to support robust families by helping parents to balance work and family life. For this reason, Esping-Andersen and colleagues strongly underlined the need for much greater gender equality in labour markets and households. However, most likely, women continue to do the majority of domestic care work, and flexible employment is gender biased, as women use part-time employment far more than men to help them combine work and care. Part-time employment with poor wages and benefits, irregular working hours, low job tenure, absence of training opportunities and promotion prospects continue to marginalize women in the labour market in many countries. A particularly worrying trend is the rise of marital homogamy in the new era of high female employment with highly educated and dual-earning couples doing well and low-skill and low-work intensity households falling into poverty. With rising levels of female employment there are fewer women who can be called upon to do more informal—and typically unpaid—care for increasing numbers of frail elderly. From a social investment perspective, it is crucial to recalibrate labour market regulation in a more age-sensitive and gender-friendly direction in order to enhance social participation of older adults. At the end of the day, policy innovation is not sufficient to bring about gender equity; women-friendly policies must be accompanied by wider attitudinal change in support of a more even-keeled sharing in household chores and care time between mothers and fathers.

1.2.5 Capacitating Social Justice

Finally, at the heart of *Why We Need a New Welfare State*, in more normative terms, lies a reorientation in social citizenship, away from *freedom from want* towards *freedom to act*, prioritizing high levels of employment for both men and women as the key policy objective, while combining elements of flexibility and security, under the proviso of worklife–family reconciliation arrangements and a guaranteed adequate *social minimum* serving citizens to pursue fuller and more satisfying lives. Rather than stressing the promotion of (income) redistribution as a basis for social justice, the normative claim behind social investment rests more on concrete needs and capabilities for social participation and inclusion. While distributive fairness remains a key value orientations, a more demanding understanding of solidarity has meanwhile taken root, recommending to enrich the ideas of 'distributive fairness' of John Rawls and with those of the 'capability approach' of economics Nobel Laureate Amartya Sen (1985, 2009) and Martha Nussbaum (2001) (see also Chapter 13, this volume). Following the normative logic of capacitation, entitlements and services should enable individuals to act as autonomous agents to allow multiple choices between different employment and family statuses according to shifting preferences and circumstances during the critical transitions over the life course. The diversity of social risks, the emergence of the non-actuarial risks of a competitive knowledge economy, the gendered life-course contingencies of modern familyhood, thus call for an important normative 'contextualization' of the 'rights-based approach' to social citizenship, in which the delivery of social rights are dependent on the quality take-up, and responsiveness of the social services that are essential to the vindication of social rights (de Búrca 2010).

1.3 Social Investment Critics

As the social investment perspective moved from the periphery to the centre of the (European) social policy debate, in recent years important critical studies on social investment have been published, bringing a number of unsettling limitations of the SIA to the scholarly debate. I broadly identify seven lineages of social investment critics, many of which will be further elaborated on in the rest of this volume. What now follows is a summary *tour d'horizon* of the most striking conceptual, empirical, normative, and methodological apprehensions, including reservations about the political viability of a fully-fledged social investment turn.

1.3.1 *Questioning Social Investment as a Welfare-Friendly Growth Paradigm*

In one of the most considerate, insightful, and constructive critical reviews of the social investment perspective, entitled 'What's the Use of "Social Investment"?', published in the *Journal of European Social Policy* in 2013, Brian Nolan raises a number of concerns about social investment as an economic policy paradigm with progressive employment and equity outcomes. Although he recognizes the significant proliferation of social investment ideas in policy debates and academic discourse, he remains unconvinced that the social investment perspective can be presented as an overarching policy paradigm to underpin strong employment-friendly economic growth. Nolan's critique is both empirical and analytical. Empirically, proof of the positive economic effects of social investments policy, he argues, is far from robust. Nolan believes that social investment policy analysis has not progressed much beyond the work of Nobel Laureate James Heckman on the microeconomic positive returns on early childhood education and care (ECEC). From a concise literature review on the relationship between economic growth and the role of state in mainstream economics, he concludes that there is also no consensus about the relationship between social policy and economic performance. Even if robust statistical correlations were on offer, it would be difficult to uncover the underlying causal mechanisms between welfare states and economic performance. In this respect, Nolan points to major analytical shortcomings in studies, using the OECD Social Expenditure Database (SOCX), which distinguishes between 'compensating' and 'investment' spending (Nikolai 2012), or between 'old/compensatory' and 'new/investing' spending (De Deken 2013; Vandenbroucke and Vleminkx 2012), or between 'compensating' and 'capacitating' social spending (Hemerijck 2013). Such distinctions, according to Nolan are problematic and misleading, as generous unemployment benefits cannot simply be understood as merely 'passive' or 'compensating': they often serve as an important precondition for productive job search and thus protect valuable human capital. More normatively, Nolan worries that social investment advocates, defending social policy as a 'productive factor' on the narrow economic grounds of 'returns', are likely to incur 'collateral damage' to traditional social policy legitimation based on the squarely normative commitments of social justice, fairness, need, equality, and social citizenship.

1.3.2 Restrictive Scope of Social Investment Life-Course Interventions

Social investment policies essentially add up to a supply-side strategy with a strong policy focus on life-course dynamics and gendered labour-market transitions and the mitigation of 'new' social risks'. For Colin Crouch and Maarten Keune (2012), new social risks policy diagnosis and the scope of policy interventions to ease labour-market transitions in post-industrial economies are far too narrow. As a supply-side strategy, social investment cannot serve as a substitute for effective macroeconomic management in times of depressed demand. Moreover, a fair number of activation reforms, enacted since the 1990s, have in effect reinforced the 'new social risk' of insufficient social security coverage by making eligibility and entitlement subject to far stricter conditionality requirements (Clasen and Clegg 2011). New social risks and the critical return of the old social risk of high youth and long-term unemployment and growing income and wealth polarization and social exclusion, according to Crouch and Keune, need to be tackled both from *within* the labour-market and family life-course nexus and from the *outside*. Tough austerity measures, in the context of already record high unemployment levels in many countries, easily invoke recessionary consequences, diverting economy from its optimal long-term growth path. According to Crouch (Chapter 34, this volume), the resurgence of mass unemployment and rising inequality do not per se weaken the social investment imperative. What is needed is a more 'consolidated' (old and new) social risk management, which inevitably is going to be costly, as it implies reconsidering policies beyond active social investment priorities, including minimum wages, collective bargaining, taxation, macroeconomic monetary and fiscal policy, and financial regulation, which all critically impact on the viability of the welfare state under twenty-first-century capitalism.

1.3.3 Social Citizenship Utilitarianism and Its Gender Bias

'Social policy as a productive factor', 'social returns' from care and educational 'investments', 'active social policy', 'employment-friendly welfare reform', 'capacitating social services', and the 'dynamic welfare state' are frames that have made considerable headway in the social policy debate over the past decades. Altogether they conjure up an image of a strong economic rationale behind social investment reform, potentially giving way to a rather narrow and utilitarian political discourse of undervaluing the care needs of citizens and families in immediate distress, and, by implication, undermining established social rights of citizenship, based on the solidaristic imperative of social protection for the weakest in society as an inalienable political right. There is a normative tension between overcoming social deficits through proactively unleashing human potential, creating opportunities through capacitation, through training or care servicing, on the one hand, and caring for citizens who cannot be easily empowered and capacitated due to disability, illness, and old age, on the other. To the extent that social risks can be better addressed in a 'growth-friendly' rather than 'growth-reducing' manner, so much the better, but framing some spending as 'investment' and—explicitly or implicitly—the remainder as 'consumption', as Nolan writes, 'puts the cart before the horse'. Similarly, critical feminists, like Chiara Saraceno (Chapter 4, this volume), raise concerns about the social investment understanding of social progress in terms of singularly promoting female employment growth and boosting fertility rates to financially support ageing populations in the name of gender equality, thereby delegitimizing family and mothers' caring roles as valuable activities in their own right (Jenson 2009; Saraceno and Keck 2010).

1.3.4 *The Staying Power of National Welfare Regimes and Dualization Adversities*

Welfare states are different in terms of policy design, economic development, political orientation, and cultural traditions. Welfare policy legacies are strong, persistent, and often quite reform-resistant. Successful adaptation to the exigencies of structural change largely depends on the intelligent use of prevailing policy settings. There are no easy answers to policy emulation, either from the vanguard of Nordic social investment or, for that matter, from the heartland of Anglo-Saxon neoliberalism. This sobering thought, advanced by Jean-Claude Barbier (Chapter 3, this volume), does not imply that it is per se impossible to take advantage of foreign reform experiences, but it does dampen naïve reform enthusiasm based on 'best practice' social models without regard for home-grown institutional conditions. According to Bruno Palier and Kathy Thelen, continental welfare regimes are particularly prone to processes of downward *dualization drift* instead of upward social investment recalibration (Palier and Thelen 2010). On the other hand, the preservation of generous social insurance and job protection coverage for a shrinking core of labour-market insiders at the expense of increased precariousness and high economic insecurity for outsiders, begs the question of how long dysfunctional male-breadwinner welfare systems with dualized cleavage structures can be maintained. Is there no escape from the dualization trap in continental welfare regimes? These pertinent questions are explored in Chapters 20, 21, 26, and 31, in this volume. I hasten to add that the political scientists studying processes of dualization do not find fault in the social investment perspective per se. To wit, Bruno Palier is a leading social investment advocate in France.

1.3.5 *Social Investment and Perverse Matthew Effects*

Probably the fiercest empirical critique is from Bea Cantillon (2011), who has come to argue that the social investment paradigm is plagued by perverse 'Matthew Effects', with the middle class disproportionally benefiting from social investments at the expense of the worse off. It has been shown that many of the interventions that aim at helping disadvantaged people gain a better position in society are de facto taken up more by middle-class individuals and families (Ghysels and Van Lancker 2011). Childcare services, for instance, are used more frequently by higher-income, dual-earning parents. In addition, low-educated persons are less likely to participate and benefit from training programmes. Some forms of activation may force disadvantaged individuals into low-quality jobs with little help in improving their life-course prospects. By prioritizing 'work first', activation policies may also push women into already highly feminized jobs, reinforcing gendered labour market segmentation and the existing gender gaps (Lister 2004; Dobrowolsky and Lister 2008; Ingold and Etherington 2013). These findings beg the question of the (re-)distributive portent of employment-centred social investment reform best positioned to counter the intergenerational reproduction of poverty (Cantillon and Van Lancker 2013; Pintelon et al. 2013). Has the shift to social investment policy priorities contributed to rising inequality, causing 'new' Matthew Effects, of the poor giving to the rich, after the Gospel of Matthew (Merton 1968)? According to Giuliano Bonoli, Bea Cantillon, and Wim Van Lancker (Chapter 5, this volume), there are good reasons to believe that 'new' social investment in-kind services, much less so than traditional cash-benefits, tend to flow to work-rich households and families. In Chapter 19, Kees van Kersbergen and Jonathan Kraft observe an incipient process of 'social investment' upgrading and social protection 'de-universalization', especially in Sweden and Denmark, whereby policies originally directed towards the poor and disadvantaged (unemployment insurance, social assistance) have been cut, while social services enjoyed also broadly by the middle class (e.g. education, health, training and support for working mothers) have expanded, suggesting a Matthew Effect in welfare states where broad political support for both 'passive' social protection and 'active' social capacitation has originally been very strong. No wonder that Bonoli, Cantillon, and Van Lancker are worried, in Chapter 5, about the potential 'crowding-out effects' of minimum-income protection provision by social investment reform in times of post-crisis austerity.

1.3.6 *The Uphill Politics of Social Investment in Times of Austerity*

The Great Recession and its fallout have created an entirely new austerity context for welfare state futures, posing critical hurdles for social investment reform opportunities. Although a social investment reform agenda is premised on the idea of simultaneously improving economic efficiency and social equity, social investments do not come cheap, certainly not in the short term. The budgetary context that has emerged in the aftermath of the global financial crisis seemingly leaves little room for an assertive reallocation from old to new social risks categories. In a dark reinterpretation of Paul Pierson's seminal writing (2001) on the 'new politics of the welfare state' as the politics of the status quo, Mertens and Streeck (2011) advance the thesis that discretionary social investments will most likely be outflanked and left defeated by acute reform for many years to come. This predicament conjures up the current state of play in the EU. The SIP, based on forward-looking social policies to 'prepare' individuals and families to respond to the changing nature of social risks in the competitive knowledge economy, was published in the wake of a major overhaul in EU fiscal surveillance—the Six Pack, Two Pack, and the Fiscal Compact—enacted after the Eurozone sovereign debt crisis of 2010. This raises the question of whether Europe's new macroeconomic governance regime is supportive of the social investment imperative. Reinforced fiscal austerity, underwritten by heterodox outright monetary transactions (OMT) and quantitative easing (QE) interventions by the European Central Bank (ECB) to counter deflation, continues to be based on the widespread belief that generous social provision inescapably 'crowds out' economic growth, a conviction that currently seems to trump an assertive EU social investment turn. How long can the schizophrenic posture of the European Commission as the 'social investment cheerleader', on the one hand, and the 'fiscal austerity headmaster', on the other, informed by contradictory policy theories, be sustained? This question is addressed from different angles in Chapters 27, 28, 29, and 30.

1.3.7 *Squaring the Methodological Circle of Social Investment Inputs, Outputs, and Outcomes*

Beyond these substantive critiques about the limits, biases, unintended consequences, and adverse effects of social investment, social investment research is riddled with methodological ambiguities. Take the examples of the Matthew Effect, conjectured by Cantillon as the result of *too much social investment*, and *dualization drift* dynamics resulting from *too little social investment* master-minded by insider-biased political interests. Aggregate *outcome indicators* are not particularly well suited for the testing of actual *policy performance*. More-over, trying to assess policy change in terms of outcomes here and now easily glosses over the imprint of incubation time lags, as yesterday's reforms often take a decade to exhibit observable effects. For some social investment policies, like early childhood education, the prospective payback time runs up to a generation. Gross expenditures on various social policy categories are often used as a proxy for *policy outputs*. Whereas Frank Vandenbroucke and Koen Vleminckx (2011) divide total expenditure by the number of benefit recipi-ents, Wolfgang Streeck and Daniel Mertens (2011) analyse social investment spending on education, family support, and active labour-market policy, entirely in percentages of gross domestic product (GDP), without regard to macroeconomic conditions and demographic variation in relevant policy clienteles, giving rise to different conclusions. Given the recent status of social investment policy analysis, empirical research is still in infancy, as Lane Kenworthy writes in Chapter 7 of this volume. Traditional social policy research on redistributive social policy interventions, based on easily manage-able pre- and post-tax comparisons, the kind for which Bea Cantillon and Brian Nolan are renowned, has a strong track record precisely because there are long-term series on relative poverty and income inequality available. On the other hand, comparing income inequality trends, before and after taxes, can be prob-lematic because baseline comparisons of pre-tax and pre-transfer labour market outcomes are very much influenced by what the welfare state does in terms of services, like education, housing, health care, and training policies (Esping-Andersen and Myles 2009). To capture how welfare states affect and respond to changes in income inequality, we need methodologies that focus on the interaction effects of income transfers, taxation, employment regulation, and social services. The methodological conundrum of social investment policy analysis runs deep for a variety of reasons, related to: (1) the multifaceted character of social investment as it involves a broad mix of differentiated and complementary policy instruments; (2) the importance of fortuitous and adverse policy interactions; (3) the multiplicity of effects and implications, understood as 'returns' from social investment for the socioeconomic well-being for different groups in society; and, finally, (4) the challenge of assessing an effective 'discount rate' of social investment across different time lines (long, medium, and short term). Any effort to methodologically gauge social invest-ment's returns, as Brian Burgoon forcefully argues in Chapter 14 of this volume, ultimately faces a dilemma of *relevance* and *rigour*: *relevance* in the sense of identifying aspects of social investment and its implications that apply to what policymakers and publics want to know about social policy reform; and *rigour* in the sense of measuring social investment and its implications in a way that support social-scientifically solid descriptive and causal inferences about social investment and its returns.

The seven lineages of critical concerns and caveats to social investment research and policy practice will be elaborated and debated throughout the volume. The remainder of the chapter replies to some of the early social investment criticisms that can be addressed on the basis of the recent research and evidence, bearing especially on the issues of theoretical conceptualization, methodological progress and the elusive politics of social investment reform.

1.4 Towards an Institutional Perspective: Stocks, Flows, and Buffers

The emphasis on the 'productive function' of social policy stands out as a distinguishing feature of the social investment perspective with an explicit focus on helping both men and women balance earning and caring together with a deliberate preventative orientation towards 'early identification' and 'early action' targeted at the vulnerable risk groups. The social investment perspective strongly advocates the regenerative and promotional side of social policy, including education, health, childcare, parenting and family services, lifelong learning, and long-term and elderly care, based on a general diagnosis that many of these not-for-profit policy provisions, which are key to high productivity knowledge economies, that have suffered tremendously from underfunding since the 1980s.

In essence, social investment is an encompassing strategy of developing, employing, and protecting human capital over the life course for the good of citizens, families, societies, and economies. Based on previous work (Hemerijck and Vandenbroucke 2012; Hemerijck 2013, 2014, 2015), three central interdependent social investment policy functions can be distinguished: (1) raising the quality of the 'stock' of human capital and capabilities over the life course; (2) easing the 'flow' of contemporary labour-market and life-course transitions; and (3) maintaining strong minimum-income universal safety nets as income protection and economic stabilization 'buffers' in ageing societies. The taxonomy of 'buffer', 'stock', and 'flow' social investment functions have to be viewed interactively, as 'institutional complementarities', to borrow a concept from the Varieties of Capitalism literature (Hall and Soskice 2001), seen through the lens of the life-course contingencies of modern familyhood, consistent with widely shared normative aspirations of work for everyone, gender equality, and capacitating service provision as the foundations of solidarity in the competitive knowledge economy.

1.4.1 *Stocks*

An overriding function of social investment policy is to strengthen people's skills and capacities, in order to prepare them for addressing life-course contingencies and improving their future life chances and prospects. The 'stock' function is linked to present and future productivity, and is directed towards 'capacitating' interventions enhancing and maintaining human capital or capabilities over the life course in ageing societies. This includes ECEC, general education, post-secondary vocational and university training, and lifelong learning. Given the fact that children make up the future workforce, investing in better education and affordable childcare will ultimately foster higher levels of productivity and employment when the ageing predicament reaches its pinnacle. As such, the 'stock' function of high-quality human capital and capabilities is social investment par excellence. It is linked to future productivity, and is directed towards 'capacitating' interventions enhancing and maintaining human capital or capabilities over the life course in ageing societies and knowledge economies. The first Programme for International Student Assessment (PISA) report (2000), explicitly framed the OECD's engagement with education in terms of social investment, by stating: 'The prosperity of countries now derives to a large extent from their human capital and the opportunities available to their citizens to acquire knowledge and skills that will enable them to continue learning throughout their lives.' Early childhood education has been shown to have a significant positive impact on improving children's chances of finishing their studies and finding employment, and avoiding risks such as delinquency and drug abuse (Heckman 2000). Labour-market activation programmes and high-quality systems of vocational training, education, and lifelong learning arrangements best ensure long-term employability and high employment participation (Hemerijck 2013).

1.4.2 *Flows*

The 'flow' function is directed at making the most effective use and efficient allocation of labour resources over the life course in support of high employment participation of both genders. The priority is to (re)integrate school-leavers, the unemployed, parents (especially mothers), older workers, and the disabled back into the labour market and provide assistance during vulnerable transitions (when more permanent labour-market exclusion is a real threat). The social investment function of labour-market 'flow' should therefore not be mistaken for one-dimensional labour-market deregulation as an effective recipe to improve labour allocation. The 'flow' function has to be understood in terms of helping to bridge critical life-course transitions from schooling to the first job, over the stressful times of building a career while raising children, taking up additional training and partaking in lifelong learning to prepare for later adult life, also while caring for frail elders, and so on. More than ever before, the vast majority of workers will have a succession of different jobs, intermingled with parenting/childcare, further study and training, and possibly joblessness. In a continuing quest for 'work–life balance', each successive life-course transition shapes successive stages; good transitions beget better transitions; and bridge failure increases the problem load on subsequent transitions. The road to high employment levels is therefore not paved with maximum labour-market flexibility or the neoliberal mantra of 'making work pay'. The social investment 'flow' imperative is to 'make transitions pay' through the provision of 'active securities' to address more volatile employment and life-course transitions, as the best way to ensuring sustainable and long working careers and, by implication, adequate pensions after retirement (Chapter 9, this volume). This requires the normalization of part-time work, with basic pension rights attached, but also family-friendly employment regulations.

1.4.3 Buffers

The 'buffer' function in the conceptual taxonomy aims both at securing income protection and at securing economic stabilization. This what Nicholas Barr (2001) has referred to as the 'piggy-bank' or 'consumption-smoothing' function of the welfare state. Adequate minimum-income protection is a critical precondition for an effective social investment strategy, as income 'buffers' help to compensate and mitigate social inequity at the micro level and thus provide the necessary financial security for people to develop their human capital while at the same time stabilizing the business cycle at the macro level. This kind of 'Keynesianism through the back door' is still practised today, as we have seen from the disruption of the 2007–10 financial crisis. The challenge is how to organize social security so as to offer adequate income support during near-inevitable spells of labour-market transition and associated inactivity (because of unemployment, training, and family caring leaves) over the life course. Social security has the function of supporting and protecting people when they face involuntary exclusion from the labour market. Typically, unemployment benefits provide people with an income as they look for jobs, and social assistance does the same when they are unemployed for a prolonged period, while also supporting those who, for whatever reason, cannot participate in the labour market. By and large, social security pools risks and redistributes employment contributions and tax revenues through benefits to those outside the labour market. Of critical importance are conditions of access, levels of benefit, and the duration of income protection, together with activation incentives and services. Generous universal benefits of short duration provide most adequate motivation and income support during job search and care, and retraining spells, underpinned by strong incentive-reinforcing activation measures and services (Nelson and Stephens 2012). As such, capacitating social services are not intended to replace social insurance. Universal social security that supports labour-market transitions, raises human capital, and provides effective social protection is fully compatible with the goals of social investment.

1.5 Institutional Complementarities and Life-Course Synergy Effects

In actual policy practice, there is significant functional overlap between the policy functions of 'stocks', 'flows', and 'buffers' (De Deken, 2014; Chapters 11 and 16, this volume). The three social investment policy functions all affect, in one way or another, the quality and quantity of labour supply. For example, early childhood development and care contributes to three objectives: parental employment 'flow', and, by implication, improved household income 'buffers' and reduced chance of poverty, and also an investment in the future human capital 'stock' of current cohorts of children. On the opposite end of the policy spectrum, passive minimum-income protection provides 'buffers' and financial security for those in-between jobs, allowing benefit recipients to 'flow' to more prosperous economic sectors, while enabling them to maintain and protect their human capital 'stock'. The three social investment policy functions are not only intertwined; they probably provide the best returns under a policy mix that deliberately 'aligns' and 'bundles' all the three functions together in varying combinations across the life course.

'Stock', 'flow', and 'buffer' overlap and reinforcements (and also mismatches and incompatibilities) essentially come in two varieties: institutional complementarities and life-course synergies. Life-course synergy effects pertain to the potential of escalating improvements of individual life chances with social investment policy supports harbouring positive 'knock-on' effects over time. The notion of policy complementarity refers to the 'goodness of fit' in policy design across the policy functions of 'stocks', 'flows', and 'buffers' in prevailing welfare policy portfolios. To illustrate how social investment provides positive returns, Table 1.1, distinguishes, on the horizontal axis, consecutive life-course stages of toddlers, children, young adults, adults, and older adults, and the complementary policy functions of 'stocks', 'flows', and 'buffers' on the vertical axis, based on an extensive literature review (see Hemerijck et al. 2016). In subsection 1.5.1, I briefly expand on the two dimensions of institutional complementarity and life-course synergy effects.

Table 1.1. 'Stocks', 'flows', and 'buffers' during the life course

	Toddler	Child	Young Adult	Adult	Older Adult
Stock	Universal and good-quality ECEC promotes cognitive development and social integration (Schindler et al. 2015; Heckman 2006). Also reduces poverty (Solga 2014) and intergenerational transfer of poverty (Chapter 10, this volume).	Good-quality primary and secondary education further promotes cognitive development. This translates early development into skill acquisition (Cunha et al. 2006; Burger 2010).	Secondary education and vocational education and training further promote skill acquisition and support high admission rates in tertiary education.	Training programmes increase and update the stock of individuals. Fitting labour-market placements then prevent skills deterioration, as skills cannot be stored and deteriorate if not used (Gangl 2006).	Training programmes and lifelong learning contribute to an up-to-date set of skills, a higher exit age, and employment prospects in older candidates (Jenkins et al. 2003; Taylor-Gooby, 2014; Brunello et al. 2015).
Flow	Good-quality ECEC fosters cooperation between parents and teachers (flow between home and childcare/preschool) for better development (Taylor et al. 1998).	Inclusive education allows for the necessary preparatory classes and interventions to smooth early transitions (e.g. preschool to school) (Broekhuizen et al. 2016).	Apprenticeships, good secondary and tertiary education, and vocational education and training ease the education–labour-market transition, especially when well coordinated at multiple levels of government (Busemeyer 2015).	ALMP promotes fast return to labour market (Martin and Grubb 2001) and unemployment benefits reduce job and skill mismatch (Chapter 11, this volume). Family policy allows a reconciliation between having children and being in full-time employment (Nieuwenhuis, Need, and Van Der Kolk 2012; Esping-Andersen 2015b).	Further training and development allows for higher employment prospects (Knuth 2014), higher exit age, and, consequently, a better pension (Hobson 2014; Schmid 2015).
Buffer	Living in a stable household with a low risk of poverty allows for proper nutrition and development (Bradley and Corwyn 2002).	Living in a stable household with a low risk of poverty fosters lower school dropout rates (Harding 2003) and better early development (Bradley and Corwyn 2002).	Solid minimum wages enables working students to live sustainably, improves labour mobility, and contributes to productivity growth (OECD 2015c; Esping-Andersen 2015b).	Minimum wage, unemployment benefits, and earned income tax credits form a robust safety net. Family benefits or increasing normal benefits based on number of children can positively affect fertility rate (Gauthier 2007).	Either minimum wage and unemployment buffers, or a sustainable pension (Hobson 2014; Schmid 2015).

1.5.1 *Institutional Complementarities*

Positive returns in terms of economic growth, employment opportunities, and (child) poverty mitigation, depend on 'goodness of fit' between complementary and interdependent policy provisions, including high-quality childcare, parental leave arrangements, training, education, and activation services, alongside adequate (universal) minimum-income protection. There is a double or even a triple dividend at play. Quality childcare services, alongside effective parental leave arrangements, supported by appropriate tax and benefit incentives and active labour-market policies (ALMPs), enable more parents to engage in gainful employment ('flow'), creating additional job opportunities, especially for mothers, while adding to the revenue bases of social protection ('buffer'), and, last but not least, helping their offspring to a 'strong' human capital start in life ('stock') (Esping-Andersen 2009). It should therefore come as no surprise that high female employment participation is correlated with above OECD average fertility (future 'stock' and 'flow') under universal access to childcare, formal leave arrangements, and additional family cash transfers. Likewise, generous unemployment insurance 'buffers' of short duration allow beneficiaries time to search for a new employment ('flow') commensurate with their qualifications ('stock'), while at the same stabilizing family income with positive effects on children's future learning capabilities ('stock'). The Danish 'flexicurity' model is renowned for the institutional complementarities of labour-market flexibility ('flow'), generous unemployment benefits ('buffers'), and human-capital oriented activating labour-market services ('stock') (Madsen 2014). Likewise, high investments in lifelong learning, active labour market policy, vocational training, and flexible retirement provision are associated with higher older worker employment participation and a higher average exit age (Hemerijck 2013).

Ex negativo, there is the *problematique* of 'institutional *in*-complementarity', of policy provisions that might be incompatible with each other. This predicament has been brought to the fore by the OECD (2015a) report *In It Together: Why Less Inequality Benefits All*. According to this report, one of the main transmission mechanisms between inequality and growth is human capital development. While there is always a gap in education outcomes across individuals with different socioeconomic backgrounds, this gap is particularly wide in high inequality countries, with disadvantaged households struggling to gain access to quality education for their offspring, which eventually is likely to provoke high rates of early school-leaving at a price of low across-the-board employment. Higher inequality in parental incomes tends to imply higher inequality of life chances of the children of low-income families. To achieve greater inequality of opportunities without tackling increasing inequality in outcomes will be very difficult (OECD 2015a: 27). In short, good 'stocks' develop in the context of strong 'buffers'.

One cannot turn a blind eye to the negative, unintended, and perverse side effects of generous social security benefits of long duration: that is, undermining work incentives and raising the tax burden. Selective employment-centred male-breadwinner social insurance 'buffers' contribute to high gross wage costs and reinforce a political preference for early labour-market exit, resulting in high levels of inactivity and a fiscally overburdened social insurance system. Restrictive employment protection with classical job security for insiders constrains labour-market 'flow' and employment growth. Similarly, a deeply anchored ideology of familialism not only prohibits female employment participation, but also worsen existing gender (pay and career) inequalities, including obstacles to early childhood human capital 'stock' development, which in turn frustrates future productivity, and, possibly through a 'low-fertility trap', is likely to exacerbate the ageing burden in pensions and health care. Isolated social investment policy innovations, without taking into account institutional (in)complementarities, can be counterproductive and extremely costly. A good example is childcare reform. Many continental European countries have expanded childcare provision to increase female employment. Yet in many cases such expanded services were not accompanied by reforms of employment protection, insider-biased unemployment insurance, and contribution-based pension systems, making childcare expansion costly, indeed privileging middle-class families, while failing to raise employment among less skilled and lower-paid women (Van Lancker 2013).

It should also not be forgotten that digressive job insecurity depresses domestic demand through unnecessary precautionary savings on the part of precarious workers and their families. Not extending social security entitlements to zero-hour contracts and other employment arrangements is bound to lead to problems of social security coverage in a manner that undermines the future effectiveness of safety-net 'buffers' in the future. Disentangling positive and more adverse effects across 'stock', 'flow', and 'buffer' policy provision is a sine quo non for effective social investment cost-benefit analysis.

1.5.2 Cumulative Life-Course Synergies

A good example of a 'life-course synergy effect' is the mitigation of child poverty through universal minimum-income 'buffers' and early childhood 'stock' development as a basis for further social and cognitive development, capacitating children to subsequently learn better and achieve better results in primary, secondary, and even tertiary education (Cuhne and Heckman 2007), with the ultimate 'knock-on' effect of better employment opportunities and more positive returns from further training later in life, including the competencies to manage volatile life-course transitions. Life-course synergy effects, like institutional complementarities, cannot be taken for granted, as inappropriately managed transitions can dampen the positive cumulative effects of earlier supports. High-quality ECEC, not leveraged in follow-up primary and secondary education policies because of early selection or class-biased school segmentation, is more likely to incur high school dropout rates. Moreover, people that 'fall through the cracks' even under well-designed policy packages, in the case of a deep economic crisis, will inevitably require individualized assistance in returning to education or the labour market, in order to counter further skill erosion and pre-empt long-term scarring effects.

1.5.3 *Towards a Social Investment Life-Course Multiplier*

By bringing the theoretical notions of institutional complementarities and life-course synergy effects together, it is now possible to stretch the social investment argument to its limits by conjecturing a 'life-course multiplier' of well-being, employment, and social protection also across generations (Figure 1.1).

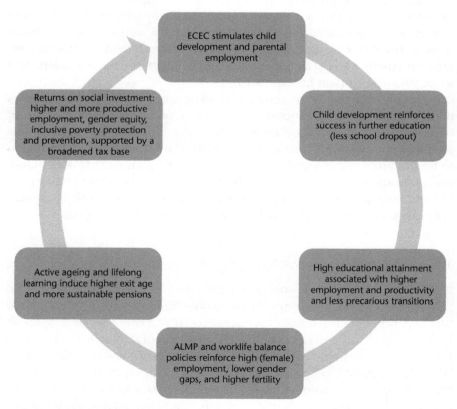

Figure 1.1. Social investment life-course multiplier

This is surely an audacious conjecture. For the ideal-typical social investment life-course multiplier to produce favourable outcomes in terms of high employment in adulthood, lower (long-term and youth) unemployment, high educational attainment and skill development, gender equity, and more earnings and income equality, all the three functions of 'stocks', 'flows', and 'buffers' need to be intimately aligned. However, for every step in the life-course multiplier there is pretty good evidence. With more disadvantaged children having access to quality education from an early age on, overall levels of education attainment are ratcheting up, resulting in higher aggregate labour productivity and upward social mobility at higher levels of employment. The more parents and especially mothers work, securing income and their position in the labour market, the broader the tax base, and also the higher the birth rate. One-and-a-half to two-earner families by and large use extra household income to ease chores of work–life balance, by relying more on public and private services, thereby creating extra jobs, further boosting economic output. Over the more mature phases of the life course, lifelong learning and healthy ageing policies help secure older worker employment participation, resulting in an overall high exit age, with the long-term consequence of lower outlays for early retirement, pensions, and health care. *Ex negativo*, the social investment multiplier lowers the costs of unemployment, underemployment, skill atrophy, social exclusion, family dysfunction, and crime. Figure 1.1 is presented in terms of a circle and not a line, for the reason that the conjectured life-course multiplier underscores how social investment returns are transmitted across generations. If children are cognitively stimulated and do not start out their lives in poverty, they are less likely to be poor in adulthood and more likely to be employed in productive jobs, with the effect that their offspring will not grow up in poverty, which gives an extra boost to tax revenue and thereby a stronger funding base for costly but beneficial social investment.

By explicating a social investment multiplier function as a working hypothesis to be further explored and tested empirically, there is an argument to be made to nuance the general conjecture made by Jon Kvist, taking heed of the work of economics Nobel Laureate James Heckman, that social investments are inevitable confronted with decreasing rates of returns over the life course (see, for instance, Kvist 2013, 2015). My apprehension is that Kvist's reasoning about falling rates of return from social investment policy inputs focuses too narrowly on human capital 'stocks', without due recognition of the importance of 'buffers' and 'flows' in the competitive knowledge economy characterized by a progressive destandardization of the life course and employment patterns. The notion of decreasing social investment returns holds for early education, but falls apart when applied to other social investment policies, such as ALMPs, the returns of which arguably not only peak in adulthood and late adulthood, but are more contingent on the state of the economy, and the availability of relevant institutional complementarities and capacitating rehabilitation services.

A sobering caution is that there is no optimal policy mix, as welfare systems are always in flux, and more important, that each country needs to elaborate its own policy package of 'buffer', 'flow', and 'stock' policies, depending on prevailing social, economic, and institutional conditions. The devil is in the detail of policy design and institutional complementarities. As such, social investment empirical analysis relies heavily on empirical data and case-by-case comparisons with a keen eye on the 'fine' structures of complementary policy portfolios and the overall institutional balance between policies that allows different social professionals to work together to achieve higher socioeconomic returns.

In the aggregate, the case-by-case comparative approach to social investment 'institutional complementarities' and 'life-course synergies' does allow for a critical review of the neoliberal 'negative' economic theory of the welfare state, which theoretically rules out effective social risk management beyond enforcing stringent labour-market discipline. Especially, the critical role of capacitating social policy carries important weight to what the political economists Torben Iversen and Ann Wren (1998) have termed the 'trilemma of the service economy'. The gist of it is that, with the shift from an industrial to a service economy, in the shadow of accelerating economic internationalization, it has become inherently more difficult for welfare states simultaneously to attain the triple goals of budgetary restraint, earnings equality, and job growth. Governments may pursue any two of these goals but no longer all three at the same time. Within a tight budgetary framework, private employment growth can be accomplished only at the cost of wage inequality. If wage equality is a prime objective, employment growth can be generated only through the public sector, at the cost of higher taxes or public borrowing (Iverson and Wren 1998: 508). As international competition and technological innovation restrict job creation in the exposed (mainly manufacturing) sector, employment growth in advanced economies may be achieved either in well-paid public services, thereby undercutting budgetary restraint, or in low-paid private services, whereby earnings equality is sacrificed. Iversen and Wren's trilemma is rooted in the so-called Baumol cost disease, named after the American economist and Nobel Laureate William Baumol (1967). The Baumol disease conjectures that productivity improvements in labour-intensive welfare services—health, education, and family care services—consistently lag behind productivity gains in more competitive industries. When public service pay increases follow wage developments in the more dynamic capital-intensive private sector, low productivity services become relatively expensive. In other words, externalization and professionalization of (for example) care provision, from the family to the public sector, conjure up a significant handicap for competitive adjustment. The social investment perspective indirectly questions the general validity of the Baumol predicaments (see also Chapter 8, this volume). Consider public health care: even if surgery is publicly financed, timely intervention allows an incapacitated worker to go back to work sooner, thereby creating extra output at less cost (Atkinson 2015: 121). Based on the available evidence of competitive welfare states, aligning service-intensive welfare provision compatible with robust public finances, high employment rates, and lower long-term unemployment, at lower relative poverty and earnings equality, we can no longer ignore the indirect contribution of employment-intensive public services in health and education to productivity growth in the dynamic private sector by providing firms with high-quality human capital inputs. The same indirect logic from public investments to private returns applies to parenting services and active labour-market policies. In other words, the Baumol cost disease and the service sector trilemma are not predetermined: like Matthew Effects and dualization drift dynamics, they are empirical variables, depending in large measure on the policy mix of institutional (in)complementarities at hand.

1.6 Politics of Social Investment Reform in Times of Post-Crisis Austerity

As documented by a growing body of literature, social investment reforms have taken place in many countries since the mid-1990s across the globe (see, for instance, Barrientos 2008; Palier 2010; Peng 2011; Bonoli and Natali 2012; Morel, Palier and Palme 2012c; Banting and Myles 2013; Bonoli 2013; Hemerijck 2013; Taylor-Gooby 2013). A broad indication of this overall trend can be seen in the fact that total spending on social services has steadily increased across the OECD over the past twenty years, while spending on cash transfers has remained flat (Richardson and Patana 2012; for the 1990s, cf. also Kautto 2002). It is generally recognized that European welfare states have, with varying degrees of success, upgraded their social investment character the most in a global context. Alongside retrenchments, there have been deliberate attempts to rebuild social programmes and institutions and thereby accommodate welfare policy repertoires to the new economic and social realities of the knowledge-based economy. With respect to *social insurance* and *assistance*, most countries today preside over universal minimum-income protection programmes, coupled with 'demanding' activation and 'enabling' reintegration measures, targeting labour-market 'outsiders' such as young, female, or low-skilled workers (Clasen and Clegg 2011). The area of *employment policy* saw a considerable increase, from the 1990s onwards (Bonoli

2013), alongside social security activation, in spending on ALMPs, and training and education servicing to improve life-course employability. With respect to *labour-market regulation*, several European countries have moved towards a greater acceptance of flexible labour markets, with new elements of security introduced for labour-market outsiders, governed by more flexible employment relations (Schmid 2008). For *pensions*, financing problems due to population ageing and lower growth have prompted the reversal of the trend towards early retirement policies, together with initiatives to promote longer and healthier working lives. A key shift has been the growth of (compulsory) occupational and private pensions and the development of multi-pillar systems, combining pay-as-you-go and fully funded methods, with relatively tight (actuarial) links between pension benefits and contributions, with a view to factoring in life expectancy (Ebbinghaus 2011). *Family policy*, covering childcare, parental leave, and employment regulation, and work and family life reconciliation policies, has experienced a profound upgrade in both scope and substance (Orloff 2010). Rather conspicuously, at subnational levels, driven by significant devolution in public administration, there has been a strong drive towards the provision of integrated, customized, capacitating service provision, often targeted at vulnerable groups with multiple problems in the areas of employment provision, skill rehabilitation, social assistance, family services, housing, and health and child policy, with professionals from different policy fields working together in multidisciplinary teams (Sabel 2012).

The European social investment turn has been uneven, variable, and, in terms of process, rather truncated. With their tradition of high-quality childcare and high employment rates for older workers, the Nordic countries continue to display the strongest social investment profile, but we also observed significant reform in the Netherlands (social activation), Belgium (support for dual-earner families), France (minimum-income protection for labour-market outsiders), the United Kingdom (fighting child poverty), Ireland (much improved education), and Spain (negotiated pension recalibration) in the period leading up to the financial crisis (Hemerijck 2013). Noteworthy is the German experience, round the turn of the century deemed as the 'sick man of Europe'. Confronted with dire fiscal difficulties in abiding by the Stability and Growth Pact (SGP), the contentious Hartz reforms of welfare retrenchment and labour-market deregulation ultimately broke the ice. In their wake, the archetypical Bismarckian welfare state decisively moved in the direction of social investment. Within the span of less than a decade, the Merkel governments adopted a parental leave scheme, providing strong incentives for women to return to work and for fathers to also take up care leave, significantly expanded childcare for under-3s, and finally introduced the right to childcare (Fleckenstein 2011; Chapter 20, this volume). While the Merkel II government constitutionally committed Germany to maintain a balanced budget in 2010, education and research were exempted from budget cuts.

Does the progressive social investment reform momentum suggest that we are likely to see more social investment reform in the near future in Europe and beyond? Not quite. For the European context, a timely survey on recent social investment reforms across Europe, compiled by the European Social Policy Network (ESPN), continues to identify important social investment progress across a broad range of countries, including Austria, Belgium, Germany, France, the Netherlands, Slovenia, and the Scandinavian countries, and catching-up processes in the United Kingdom, Spain, Portugal, Ireland, Hungary, Poland, and Slovakia. More worrying is that Greece, Italy, Romania, Bulgaria, and the Baltic States are falling behind, not least because of the reinforced austerity-retrenchment drive since 2010. Moreover, the ESPN observes backlashes in social investment policy innovation in a number of social investment vanguard countries, including Finland and the Netherlands, which are enacting pro-cyclical budget savings on childcare and family services, disproportionately affecting vulnerable families, with the likely long-term effects of lower levels of female employment, and higher human capital erosion and rising child poverty (Bouget et al. 2015). The Brussels-based think-tank Bruegel confirms that countries confronted with fiscal austerity record a noticeable generational shift in public expenditures, away from spending on families with children towards older cohorts, with the result of higher levels of youth unemployment and child poverty, and lower enrolment in preschool education and care (Hütti, Wilson, and Wolff 2015). This finding is also consistent with spending evolutions on public education across Europe, analysed by Frank Vandenbroucke and David Rinaldi, recording dramatic cuts in education spending in countries falling under fiscal surveillance by the troika of the ECB, the International Monetary Fund, and the European Commission, or memoranda of understanding (MoU), and excessive deficit surveillance between 2011 and 2015. Only a handful of EU member states have kept up pre-crisis education spending levels (Vandenbroucke and Rinaldi 2015; Chapter 29, this volume). The upshot of these trends is that the after-shocks of the Great Recession are creating new cleavages both between and within countries. Generous European welfare states in good fiscal shape have found the road to social investment the means to compete in the global knowledge-based economy. On the other hand, for a number of Eurozone welfare states, who require a 'capacitating' impulse the most, the social investment message is decidedly lost. Their crippled public finances essentially coerce them into a 'race to the bottom' scenario of price competition, low wages and welfare standards, un(der)employment, and widening inequities between the old and the young. Slashing active labour-market and lifelong education and social services, we know from the recent OECD and World Bank reports on 'inclusive growth', critically erodes job opportunities for men and women in the long term and thereby further thwarts their capacity to shoulder the impending age burden in pensions and health care.

Welfare state change is a work in progress, leading to patchwork mixes of old and new policies and institutions. Unsurprisingly, the process of welfare state change remains incomplete, resulting from the institutionally bounded and contingent adaptation to the challenges of family and gender change, adverse demography, the fiscal austerity aftershocks of the Great Recession, and how such conditions play out in the political process. The political support structure of social investment remains something of an enigma, which is perhaps why Nathalie Morel, Bruno Palier, and Joakim Palme continue to refer to social investment as an 'emerging' rather than an established policy paradigm (Morel, Palier, and Palme 2012c). Whereas the post-war welfare state of the industrial era was supported by a clearly demarcated class compromise between organized labour and capital in parliamentary and societal arenas, the cleavage structure of social investment is more elusive (Bonoli and Natali 2012). A fair number of political scientists are therefore rather sceptical about the political power of social investment ideas to take root, especially in times of post-crisis austerity (Häusermann 2010; Streeck and Mertens 2011; Breunig and Busemeyer 2012; Chapters 31 and 33, this volume). Allegedly, 'new social risk' groups of children, part-time working women, jobless youths, the low-skilled, and the frail elderly, do not add up to a coherent cleavage for effective political mobilization (Taylor-Gooby 2013). A fundamental point in Häusermann's theorization is that the alignment of actors is likely to be very different across different dimensions of reforms, what she calls the 'multidimensionality of post-industrial reform politics'. But as long as core social insurance programmes remain bound up with strong insider-interest constellations, social investment reforms are easily sacrificed in favour of more constrained status-quo-biased welfare reforms (Palier and Thelen 2010).

Perhaps the most profound political obstacle to the diffusion of social investment—well explicated by the path-breaking monograph *Governing for the Long-Term: Democracy and the Politics of Investment* by Alan Jacobs (2011)—concerns its *intertemporal character*, requiring longitudinal trade-offs to be made. Any kind of politics of investment suggests a willingness on the part of reformers to forego current consumption in order to be able to reallocate resources to programmes whose expected returns to be achieved in the future that will make everyone better off. In times of austerity, as Paul Pierson (2001) argues, social investments provide very few short-term electoral rewards for politicians facing negatively biased electorates. Beyond loss-averse electorates and status-quo-biased interest group polities, another reason why social investment is not conducive to effective mobilization bears on the causal uncertainty of prospective social investment returns. The timeframe for outlays in early childhood to pay off in terms of higher employment and productivity is nearly two decades. The predicament of causal uncertainty is further complicated by the political risk of policy reversal as the chain between current pain and future gain lengthens. Reforms enacted today by incumbents can be easily overturned after the next election, long before social investment reforms carry benefits. Finally, the overly complex policy analysis behind social investment, from the concern for 'carrying capacity', the focus on gender and the life course, and the critical importance of the complementary functions of 'stocks', 'flows', and 'buffers' in policy design, is not easily translated into an appealing ideological narrative for meta-policy welfare paradigm change.

But is reform immobilism resulting from insider veto-player resistance to change, together with hard-wired policy legacies, really what requires explanation? The empirical record from before the onslaught of the Great Recession is, I would argue, rather one of gradual social investment diffusion, beginning with isolated initiatives for vulnerable groups, followed by an increasing awareness of important policy interaction and life-course synergies, igniting, in turn, an accelerated development of more comprehensive and better integrated approaches, backed by considerable social investment agenda-setting from the European Commission, eventually leading to a plateau of country-specific social investment institutional equilibria. As such, the rise of the SIA is a prime example of what Wolfgang Streeck and Kathleen Thelen (2005) have coined 'gradual but transformative' institutional change in response to the changing policy environment.

Although social investment reform is premised on the idea of simultan-eously improving economic efficiency and social equity, social investments do not come cheap. Will the political centre, together with the European Commission, under the helm of Jean-Claude Juncker, be able to transcend the austerity reflex and counter the populist tide, by opening a genuine policy space for an ambitious and credible social investment strategy, and thereby rise to the occasion to become reliable guardians of a more 'caring' EU? There are no 'quick fixes', given the asymmetric overhang of sovereign debt crises.

1.7 Outline of the Volume

The economic turmoil and social distress the world has experienced over the past decade has called into question many issues of past socioeconomic policymaking, from supranational macroeconomic management to domestic welfare provision. After 2009, policy attention focused on immediate crisis management. Many governments pushed through social retrenchment and labour-market deregulation, as if the welfare state was the main culprit behind the most severe economic crisis since the 1930s. Recently, academic experts and policymakers have started to devote more attention to proactive social reform, harking back to the ideas of social investment developed in Europe around the turn of the century. As experts and practitioners are testing new theories and seeking novel policies, so does this volume on the uses of social investment. Do the social aftershocks of growing inequality, mass unemployment, and deep intergenerational social disadvantage create a reinvigorated opportunity to reconfigure the welfare state more assertively along the lines of social investment? Can we observe a rebalancing of inclusive welfare provision along the policy functions of upgrading human capital 'stock', easing the 'flow' of gendered labour-market and family life-course transition, while developing more inclusive income safety-net 'buffers' required to survive in an ever more competitive global knowledge economy? And to what effect? Is social investment really a 'magic bullet'—does it work and under what conditions? Can unintended side effects be corrected or are there weaknesses inherent to the concept of social investment? All of these open questions with significant policy relevance challenge social science research in answering them, but this may require novel theoretical perspectives and alternative methodologies, beyond traditional cross-sectional social policy analysis and political economy research with their primary focus on distribution.

With the above questions in mind I approached close to fifty leading experts in social policy across the disciplines of economics, law, political science, and sociology to write a short and focused chapter on various aspects of social investment—both critical and more complementary—from a comparative perspective. Beyond academic experts, I also invited a very small selection of policy advisers who have worked on the reinvigoration of social investment over the past decade. The theoretical perspectives, methodological approaches, empirical assessments, and critical viewpoints collected for the volume, do not add up to the definitive social investment reader. What I have strived for with this collection of thirty-five contributions is to produce a broad and highly variegated intervention in the ongoing debate about inclusive welfare provision and social policy research in an era of austerity. There is no ambition to have the last word on social investment. Raising critical questions, suggesting improvements in theoretical conceptualization and methodological operationalization, expanding the repertoire of diverse social investment experiences across different layers of policymaking and the globe, together with their successes and pitfalls, is what the volume has in store for the reader.

By deliberately stopping short of advancing a convergent collective view on social investment, out of the exchange of ideas over consecutive draft contributions, editorial feedback, and mutual correspondence between authors, which began with a two-day workshop organized in Amsterdam on 15 and 16 January 2015, to my surprise, a truly interconnected set of arguments, based on available evidence, emerged. Perspective, assessment, emphasis, method, inference, and judgement continue to differ, but I am certain that the overarching intellectual engagement that I have experienced over the past two years in putting the volume together will be communicated to the reader. While it is gratifying to the editor to discover a high degree of inter-connection among the contributions, there remains the problem of sequential presentation of the contributions in book form. The content that I decided upon remains arbitrary, but there is logic to it. The volume is divided into eight parts, having started with the current introduction meant as a 'state-of-the-art' review of the 'social investment and its critics' debate.

Next, Part 2 contains five critical reflections on the limits of the SIA from a variety of social science perspectives. The first intervention of Brian Nolan (Chapter 2) underscores the pitfalls in bridging social investment policy analysis and political advocacy. Jean-Claude Barbier, in Chapter 3, is more concerned with how prevailing, rather narrow, economic conceptions of social investment pose a threat to social protection provision as the basis of social citizenship. Chiara Saraceno then, in Chapter 4, raises concerns over the gullible endorsement of gender equality in social investment policy analysis and advocacy singularly in terms employment growth and higher fertility rates at the expense of family care as a valuable activity in its own right. The pertinent critique of perverse Matthew Effect provoked by social investment reforms is central to Chapter 5, by Giuliano Bonoli, Bea Cantillon, and Wim Van Lancker. Daniel Mertens closes Part 2 with Chapter 6: an assessment that a fully-fledged strategy of inclusive social investment is unlikely to survive in a post-crisis era of dire fiscal austerity.

Part 3, entitled 'Social Investment Endowment and Extensions', brings together a variety of academic experts who have, through their theoretical, empirical, and more normative publications, progressively shaped our understanding of the rise of the SIA in the face of structural change and the crisis. In Chapter 7, Lane Kenworthy reveals trajectories of proactive and reconstructive reform in various affluent nations in the direction of social investment, with supportive evidence of employment growth coupled with low levels of relative poverty. By revisiting, and in part revising, the service economy 'trilemma', Anne Wren, in Chapter 8, identifies public investment in university, school, and early childhood education as critical to an inclusive and sustainable knowledge-intensive service economy. For labour-market economist Günther Schmid, in Chapter 9, critical life-course and labour-market transitions require a *Gestalt*-change from unemployment insurance towards a system of employment insurance. In Chapter 10, Margarita León examines the intimate link between social investment policy analysis and the expansion of child policy, the trade-off in coverage and quality of childcare provision, and the increasing differentiation between preschool education for children aged 3 and above. By using the Swedish welfare state as an example, in Chapter 11 Verena Dräbing and Moira Nelson bring (lifelong) education back into the remit of comparative welfare state studies, anchored in a theoretical understanding of institutional complementarities across the policy functions of life-course skill acquisition and once-acquired skill protection, supported by active labour-market policy reintegration, resulting in more and better jobs at less skewed levels of inequality. In Chapter 12, on 'capacitating social services' aimed at early identification and social risk mitigation, Charles Sabel, Jonathan Zeitlin, and Sigrid Quack underline how, in a rather piecemeal manner, the costs and benefits of social investment are clarified through processes of social policy devolution and bottom-up local initiatives, with good results in the areas of older worker activation and youth care provision. In the final chapter of Part 3, Chapter 13, devoted to social justice, Nathalie Morel and Joakim Palme address the relevance of the 'capabilities approach' of Amartya Sen as a normative framework social investment policy analysis and for developing indicators for assessing social outcomes of how different complementary welfare arrangements support or hinder agency and capabilities.

Part 4 addresses the conceptual and methodological challenges that are inherently bound up with the study of the empirical assessment of the 'rates of return' on social investment, given its intertemporal horizon and its multidimensional character in policy scope. In Chapter 14, Brian Burgoon compares such aggregate measures with analysis of individual panel data in order to seek out how active labour-market provisions relate to passive unemployment insurance in terms of employment and income security, with a clear indication that complementary policy interventions seemingly do mitigate Matthew Effect perversities. Chapter 15, by Iain Begg, examines how social investment can best be assessed from an economic standpoint and draws particular attention to aspects that prove contentious. Next, in Chapter 16, Johan De Deken develops a typology that goes beyond the first-generation conceptualization of social investment, based on a dichotomy between 'compensation' and 'investment', by differentiating between social investment policy categories to allow for better use of the OECD SOCX for assessing cross-national and longitudinal social investment policy change. In closing Part 4, Gerlinde Verbist, in Chapter 17, takes up the issue of measuring the employment and inequality effects of publicly provided services in childcare and education to indicate critical gaps in knowledge for a proper assessment of such services in the framework of social investment policy strategies.

Part 5 is comparative in focus, highlighting the particular and varying social investment policy evolutions in different welfare systems, informed by some of the theoretical and methodological insights of earlier chapters. Together, the contributions to Part 5, by employing the functional triad of 'stocks', 'flows', and 'buffer' social investment policy provisions, add up to a rich contextualization of reform trajectories from a social investment perspective, revealing deliberate attempts to align various social policies behind a social investment impetus, alongside retrenchments and abrogated reforms because of stiff political opposition, before and after the economic crisis. Part 5 starts off with a contribution from Jane Jenson, in Chapter 18, on the ideational evolution of social investment policy advocacy by the World Bank and the OECD as they have both come to embrace new understandings of 'inclusive growth', and the critical role of human capital investment and conditional cash transfers in fighting poverty and inequality. In their assessment on recent developments in the Scandinavian heartland of social investment, Kees van Kersbergen and Johannes Kraft, in Chapter 19, observe that while the social investment welfare state remains popular, recent reforms have made the Nordic model less universal than it used to be, especially when it comes to traditional social safety-net buffers. In Chapter 20, Martin Seeleib-Kaiser reveals significantly progressive family policy transformation in Germany, consistent with the SIA, layered alongside the workfare-oriented Hartz reforms. For the case of the Netherlands, Menno Soentken, Franca van Hooren, and Deborah Rice, in Chapter 21, find a more ambivalent reform trajectory whereby the assertive Dutch social investment turn since the 1990s has been put on hold by budget cuts after the crisis which hit the Netherlands particularly hard, given its large and exposed financial sector. In Ireland, not unlike the Netherlands, the crisis forced massive fiscal consolidation, which, according to Rory O'Donnell and Damian Thomas in Chapter 22, has triggered reform in state services with social investment potential in activation, training, lone parents, and childcare. From across the Atlantic Ocean, Alain Noël reports in Chapter 23 of a rather unexpected social investment turn in Quebec with considerable success in increasing labour-market participation, limiting the rise of inequality, and reducing poverty since 1990s, at a time when the Canadian federal government moved away from social investment. Also in South East Asia, social investment has moved up the policy agenda, according to Timo Fleckenstein and Soohyun Christine Lee (see Chapter 24). The South Korean welfare state especially has experienced a far-reaching transformation, including the expansion of family policy to address the post-industrial challenges of female employment and low fertility. In Latin America, conditional cash transfers are intimately tied to school attendance, health, and human capital upgrading; however, Moira Nelson and Johan Sandberg, in Chapter 25, find severe gaps in effective social service delivery for a comprehensive approach to social investment to take shape in Latin America. The Italian experience, which brings us back to Europe in closing Part 5, is not dissimilar from the Latin American experience, in the sense that critical mismatches between childcare policies and female employment, between regional training and apprenticeship policies, and between labour regulation and activation, not only thwart an effective Italian social investment impetus, but, according to Yuri Kazepov and Costanzo Ranci in Chapter 26, are indeed associated with perverse Matthew Effect social outcomes.

Part 6 is devoted entirely to the social investment agenda-setting role of the EU. In their contribution (Chapter 27), Evelyn Astor, Lieve Fransen, and Marc Vothknecht outline the core dimensions of the SIA that the Commission has sought to take forward in their policy guidance in member states' policy reform endeavours; the aim being to help deliver on the EU's overall objective of upward social convergence. Similarly, in Chapter 28, Sonja Bekker reports on the European Semester experience thus far, by revealing how country-specific recommendations progressively promote social investment reforms which are consistent with the principles laid out in the Lisbon Treaty. In Chapter 29, Frank Vandenbroucke is less sanguine on the recent social investment track record of the EU, especially when it comes to the core dimension of human capital 'stock': data on education spending show that Europe is divesting rather than investing. Vandenbroucke calls for a renewed 'overlapping consensus' for making real progress on core social investment priorities, including a pivotal role for the EU in fostering social investment progress. Also Maurizio Ferrera, completing Part 6 of the volume with Chapter 30, opines that the EU is hamstrung by its ambivalent role in social investment agenda-setting while prioritizing fiscal austerity in its macroeconomics, and argues that a more focused attention on 'capacity' at the subnational and grass-root levels should be mustered.

What about the politics of social investment? Does social investment reform implicate entirely novel class, cleavage, and intergenerational compromises, or is social investment policy change a far less trying political endeavour of backing and aligning ongoing welfare recalibrations? This is the subject matter of the penultimate Part 7 of the book. Silja Häusermann and Bruno Palier, John Myles, Marius R. Busemeyer, and Colin Crouch all render different interpretations of the intertemporal political predicament of legitimating social investment reform. Häusermann and Palier, in Chapter 31, underscore how social investment reform is contingent on existing social policy legacies and related adjustment pressures, but that ultimately effective social investment reform coalitions come in two varieties, between the educated middle classes and either business or working-class interests. By taking a more intergenerational perspective, Myles points out, in Chapter 32, that economic conditions under which post-war policymakers were able to invest heavily in the future-oriented public goods of education and health care, undergirded by an extraordinary tolerance for high taxes, no longer obtain. As the cohort of the millennials born after 1980 have to prop up the funds for twenty-first-century social investments, while also bearing the cost of their ageing parents, the political space for social investment reform today is severely conscripted. Busemeyer, on the other hand, in Chapter 33, finds significant evidence of the willingness to pay for more educational investments by means of higher taxes. However, popular support drops once citizens are confronted with cutbacks in more traditional social security provision. In his contribution to Part 7, Chapter 34, Crouch intimates that as the rise of xenophobic populism and welfare chauvinism of preserving social protection for natives by excluding migrant and other outsiders, based on an economic agenda of protectionism, threatens open markets, economic elites on the right side of the political spectrum may be persuaded by a more assertive and expensive social investment strategy, in coalition with social democracy, to sustain global trade and also help to forestall the breakup of the European project.

Part 8 ends the collection with a concluding chapter that is in no way intended to provide a synthesis of the positions and arguments made over the previous thirty-four chapters. In so far that it does serve a distinctive purpose as a concluding essay, it focuses on what I have learned throughout the volume about the 'uses' of social investment for twenty-first-century welfare provision.

Part 2
Limits to Social Investment

2

Social Investment

The Thin Line between Evidence-Based Research and Political Advocacy

Brian Nolan

2.1 Introduction

Social investment has come to play a major part in debates about the role of social spending and the future of welfare states in Europe, in part because it has significant appeal to rather different audiences. Social investment is seen by some proponents as an emerging paradigm, setting out the preferred institutional structuring for the welfare state, towards which the (more or less fundamental) restructuring of existing institutions and policies should be directed (see, for example, Vandenbroucke, Hemerijck, and Palier 2011; Hemerijck and Vandenbroucke 2012; Morel, Palier, and Palme 2012c; Hemerijck 2014). Combining that desired end-point with a set of measures designed to get from here to there represents a social investment strategy for the welfare state (of which the Social Inclusion Strategy adopted at European Union (EU) level is one example) around which political advocacy can organize. The social investment perspective is also advanced as offering an innovative analytical framework for thinking about social policy, which entails making a clear conceptual distinction between forms of social spending which can be regarded as 'investment' and others which cannot. Social policies and spending patterns can then be analysed empirically through this lens, for example to compare the composition of spending across countries or its evolution over time, and identify countries as more or less focused on social investment at a point or over time.

This chapter argues that there is some degree of mutual reinforcement but also some tension between these various functions of the social investment perspective. We bring this out by questioning whether the distinction between social 'investment' and other social spending is robust conceptually and empirically, whether social investment can credibly be presented as the paradigm most likely to underpin robust economic growth, and whether the narrowly economic 'investment' rationale is the most productive way to frame and advance the debate about the future direction of social policy.

2.2 Is Social Investment a Robust Concept and Analytical Framework?

A central plank of the social investment perspective rests on its capacity to provide an innovative, robust, and useful conceptual and analytical framework for thinking about social policy. This entails making the conceptual distinction between forms of social spending which can be regarded as 'investment' and ones which cannot, and elaborating on this distinction in concrete terms to provide an analytical framework, allowing social policies and spending patterns to be examined empirically. Recent studies employing such a framework to compare the composition of spending across countries or over time include Vandenbroucke and Vlemincx (2011), Nikolai (2012), and De Deken (2014). We focus first on concerns about the conceptual distinction and then (related) ones about empirical application.

The central question from a conceptual perspective is how meaningful and robust is the distinction between 'social investment' and other forms of social spending? In economic theory, investment is spending on goods which are not consumed but are to be used for future production—such as factories and their machinery. No one would wish to allocate scarce resources to producing such capital stock for its own sake since that does not add to utility or contribute to well-being directly, investment instead representing postponed consumption in order to enhance productive capacity in the future. Social expenditure, by contrast, while it may or may not influence productive capacity in the future, generally makes a direct contribution to current individual utility or well-being in the period it occurs. So most social spending is not then purely 'investment' in the standard sense that economists traditionally have used the term.

However, since Mincer (1958) and Becker (1964), mainstream economics has also embraced the concept of 'human capital' on the basis that enhancing capacities and skills, notably through education and training, increases future productive capacity. From this perspective, education and training also represent a form of 'investment' with a quantifiable return in terms of extra output/income available to the individual and to society. The complication, though, is that education also clearly has consumption benefits to the individual, in terms of enjoyment of and fulfilment from the educational process itself. These direct benefits in terms of utility or well-being are generally ignored in empirical studies employing the human capital model to explain the demand for education and its impact on production, but that does not make them any less real or significant. So the distinction between 'investment' and 'consumption' is rather less clear-cut once one focuses on the productive capacity of workers. It is not then hard to argue that at least those forms of social spending conventionally grouped under the 'active labour market' umbrella, which are closely linked to education and training, can also be seen as 'investment' in human capital.

More broadly, though, thinking of labour as a factor of production whose productivity is not purely determined by innate abilities and the capital stock with which they are combined opens up a Pandora's box conceptually. As Pigou wrote in 1928, 'up to a point, consumption is investment in personal productive capacity' (Pigou 1928: 29). At least some spending by the individual on food, clothing, and so on, counted unambiguously as consumption in national accounting terms, clearly also has a potential return in terms of worker productivity. In the same vein, the recognition that the health and physical capacity of the workforce can play a crucial role in productive capacity helped to motivate health-focused interventions going back to the birth of modern welfare states, encompassing both provision of health care and public health measures such as provision of clean water and sanitation. The same could be said of unemployment insurance, helping to keep up the individual's nutritional intake and physical strength while he or she seeks alternative work so that they are still productive when they succeed. Even old age and disability pensions can be (and would on introduction have been) seen as allowing unproductive workers to exit the labour force and thus not act as a drag on industrial productivity and restructuring. Central planks of the welfare state target and support current consumption, but have also always been seen as influencing the productive capacity of the workforce into the future. It is very difficult to think of a form of social spending that is purely investment, without a substantial element of current consumption—as clearly recognized by T. W. Schultz in his highly influential 1961 *American Economic Review* paper 'Investment in Human Capital'.

Recent efforts to distinguish the social investment component in social spending, such as Vandenbroucke and Vlemincx (2011), Nikolai (2012), and De Deken (2014), bring out that allocation of specific forms of social spending is particularly problematic—family benefits and long-term care, for example, would generally be seen as more passive than active in nature, but also facilitate labour force participation by those who would otherwise be in family care work. More fundamentally, though, with a definition of 'investment' broad enough to include anything that might facilitate higher labour force participation or contribute (directly or indirectly) to the health and productive capacity of the workforce, what is it legitimate to exclude? Most income transfer programmes for those of working age that are 'passive' in nature have some investment element—certainly short-term insurance-type income supports that allow job search to be continued until a good 'match' is found. Longer-term income support may also contribute to maintaining unemployed workers' physical capacity, while even income replacement for those who are not likely to work again due to incapacity may facilitate working by other family members. Retirement and old-age pensions are generally seen as purely compensatory in this context, but this ignores the potential for dynamic interaction between labour force composition, capital investment, and the overall productive capacity of the economy. Exit from the labour force of older workers may lead to greater investment by firms in new plant, equipment, and technologies, and greater productive capacity for the economy. The fact that it is extremely difficult to work through the dynamic effects of different types of social spending on the productive capacity of the economy makes thinking in terms of a clear distinction between 'consumption' and 'investment' even more problematic.

2.3 Social Investment, Growth, and Employment

As a paradigm, proponents see social investment as offering the social component of an overarching economic and social model in which economic growth, and/or employment, can be fostered. Looking backwards, a substantial literature on the determinants of economic growth at the aggregate level has failed to produce a consensus about the role of the state more generally, much less welfare state institutions and spending specifically. Much of the research literature on the determinants of economic growth, as exemplified by Barro (1991) and Glaeser and colleagues (2004), includes both developing and developed countries and while 'institutions' are often found to be significant these are often framed very broadly. In studies concentrating on Organisation for Economic Co-operation and Development (OECD) countries, welfare institutions and spending are often ignored or captured crudely (see, for example, Bassanini and Scarpetta 2001). In any case, studies based on such aggregate indicators/evidence face major difficulties in establishing robust statistical correlations, and even more in ascribing them to underlying causal mechanisms. Most obviously, it may be poor economic performance that leads to high welfare state spending, rather than vice versa, and pooling time-series with cross-country data does not adequately address this central problem. The impact of social spending on economic activity can be expected to depend on the specifics of the programmes involved, so analysis based on a single aggregate spending variable or limited set of institutional variables is not likely to be particularly illuminating. Valuable sets of detailed institutional indicators are now available, but the institutional features they capture have not been reliably shown to affect aggregate growth rates. Findings from this type of analysis should in any case be taken as more suggestive than conclusive.

The argument for the social investment paradigm sometimes focuses instead (or as well) on employment, either as an end in itself or as a way of underpinning growth. Nelson and Stephens (2012), for example, use the pooled time-series/cross-section approach to assess the impact of a range of institutional and spending variables on employment, and conclude that short-term unemployment rates, sickness insurance, day care spending, education spending, active labour-market policy, and average years of education all have significant positive effects on total employment levels. What they term 'high-quality employment' is also examined by them as a dependent variable. So the economic performance standard that the social investment paradigm is set by its proponents needs to be clarified: is it to be seen as the most growth-friendly of available models, or is it to be assessed primarily in terms of employment levels and 'quality'? Conclusions with respect to employment, or even 'high-quality employment', do not necessarily translate into more economic growth, and there have been alternative paths to achieving economic growth in the past.

The case for the social investment paradigm rests heavily on the argument that in the new knowledge-based economy a skilled and flexible labour force is the key motor for growth, with social investment then central to producing such a labour force. It is not obvious, though, why even in such a changing environment economic growth could not be achieved via selective intensive investment in the highly skilled minority who will occupy the 'quality' jobs and drive aggregate productivity and economic growth, with a hollowed-out middle and many in much less-skilled poorly remunerated employment—which is how critics would characterize the neoliberal model or recent experience in the United States (US). The nature of that economic growth might not appeal in terms of social outcomes, and one could certainly claim that social investment will produce economic growth that is societally preferable, but that is a different argument.

Another plank in the evidence advanced in favour of social investment draws on evaluation-type micro studies focused on the various elements of the strategy, such as active labour-market policies and early childcare and education. Some such studies (notably Heckman 2006, on investing in early childhood) have been highly influential, but others have cast a colder eye on substantial parts of the active labour-market agenda. The evidence base on which the case for the social investment paradigm must rest is evolving, and aggregating up from the (limited) examples of specific schemes or interventions that perform well in evaluations in their own specific country and institutional setting to a coherent and convincing overall paradigm is extremely challenging.

2.4 Social Investment as a Platform

A core concern underlying the development of the social investment perspective is that social spending is under threat, exacerbated by the widely held notion that it is 'unproductive'. Social investment is seen as offering a potentially powerful platform from which to argue for the critical role of social spending in underpinning productive capacity and economic growth, in the face of alternative ideological perspectives and demands for 'retrenchment' across the board (Morel, Palier, and Palme 2012a). To serve this rhetorical or advocacy function in a political sense, the social investment perspective clearly needs to have some 'purchase', to resonate with key audiences. However, success in injecting the language of social investment and social policy as a productive factor into the mainstream of EU and in some cases national policy debate has not been matched by evident engagement of those predisposed by conventional frameworks of economic analysis to view social policy as redistribution of the economic 'pie' rather than potentially contributing to it. Diagnosing why is a complex matter that needs in-depth investigation, with a wealth of potential contributory factors that include political and sociological as well as intellectual. A stronger evidence base could help in engaging that audience, but is unlikely to suffice.

One must also think about the price being paid in attempting to engage with 'standard economics' on its own ground. The 'return' involved in deciding whether social spending is construed as 'investment' is taken to be an economic one, whether framed with reference to economic performance loosely defined, aggregate output, productive capacity, or employment. This is a narrow and potentially hazardous way to frame the potential return from social spending. The social investment strategy in implementation has been criticized as potentially or actually ignoring today's poor as spending is rechannelled to activation from income support (see, for example, Cantillon 2011; Barbier, 2012). More broadly, should social spending be assessed in terms of economic rather than social 'returns'? Social spending is primarily designed to address social needs; one would want to maximize the extent to which that is done in a 'growth-friendly' rather than 'growth-reducing' manner, but framing some social spending as 'investment' and—explicitly or implicitly—the remainder as 'consumption' puts the cart before the horse, runs the risk that economic impact will be seen as the dominant consideration, and could serve to skew choices about social spending. One could argue that capital spending on, for example, hospice care towards end of life, would generate a very substantial social return over a long period, and in that sense should surely qualify as 'social investment'. This goes well beyond a matter of terminology to the basis on which core social choices are made. A significant risk with the social investment perspective is that it masks the normative basis on which such social choices need to be made, giving the impression that they 'fall out' from an economic analysis. One can certainly make the case for a shift in resources from the retired to children on the basis of one's assessment of the current situation of these groups in at least some rich countries and what constitutes distributive and intergenerational equity, but the values and preferences involved need to be clearly articulated and to the fore rather than underlying an apparently technical argument.

It may, of course, be argued credibly that the impact of social spending on economic performance crucially affects the capacity to maintain social spending into the future and thus attain social goals; the implications need to be carefully thought through and reflected in the argument advanced. Where a clear choice exists between framing social spending directed towards a particular end—for example, supporting the living standards of working age people unable to find paid work—in a way that is growth-enhancing versus growth-reducing in a dynamic perspective, then there is every reason to favour the former. Where, though, does this leave us in terms of core choices between supporting the living standards of retired versus working age people, older versus younger unemployed, or early childhood education versus health care for the elderly? The economic return from these types of social spending will vary widely: is that relevant to choices about them, and if so how? At the very least, it is a legitimate concern that emphasizing the potential economic return from certain forms of spending in contrast to others could distract from the centrality of value-based choices in this arena.

2.5 Conclusions

The notion of 'social investment' has come to play a major part in debates about the role of social spending and the future of welfare states in Europe, and various aspects of its interpretation and application are examined in depth in this volume. This chapter has sought to raise some issues and concerns that need to be addressed about the concept and the way it is employed if it is to play the role that proponents hope for. It differentiated between social investment as a paradigm and strategy for social policies and spending, as a conceptual base and analytical framework, and as a platform for political engagement in both a narrow and broad sense. It argued that the conceptually distinguishing forms of social spending that can be seen as 'investment' from others that cannot, is problematic in theory and application, that the claims for the strategy and its evidence base need to be elaborated, and that framing debate in terms of a narrow economic argument runs the risk of obscuring normative choices and the broader case for social spending. This is intended to contribute to clarification and debate about the notion of social investment and the most useful way to employ it, towards which this volume is directed.

3

'Social Investment'

With or Against Social Protection?

Jean-Claude Barbier

3.1 Introduction

In the early stages of the building up of a renewed agenda for the social investment approach, I was invited by Yuri Kazepov and the journal *Sociologica* to contribute to a special symposium dedicated to Anton Hemerijck's 2013 book and my critical assessment of the social investment approach was written as a comment to his introductory chapter that was still in a preliminary stage (Barbier 2012). In order to try and live up to the high standards set out for the seminar for which this chapter was written, I wish to start my contribution by raising again conceptual issues, in the hope of making questions I mentioned in 2012 clearer while at the same time taking into account the new research Hemerijck and others have synthesized since. In a second step I will go directly to explaining my main contention, that is, that there are indeed two ways of envisaging the social investment approach today: *with* or *against* social protection. The first one is conceiving of the social investment approach as accompanying existing social protection; here, we need to devote serious consideration to what social protection actually is, and the mainstream English expression 'welfare state' will not be sufficient for this purpose. The second way is devising the social investment approach as a vehicle to destroy social protection and to help make Mario Draghi's remark come true, according to whom the European social model 'is already gone' (*Wall Street Journal*, 24 February 2012). After meeting some mainstream economists, I became convinced that fans of this second solution are more and more numerous. With my final reflection, I will try and evaluate what the chances are that this second possibility will materialize eventually: one can perhaps find an answer to this question in examining a notion closely related to social investment (SI), namely 'social impact investment' (SII), which has gained increasing currency in social policy today in Europe.

3.2 Conceptual Issues: Political and Scientific Notions of Social Investment

Sociology often finds its origin in political struggles and controversies among actors of social protection; these are indeed continually engaged in reforming it as social protection without reform would be a contradiction *in adjecto*. The social investment approach is, first and foremost, a political notion that reformers use more often than scientists. However you take it, it expresses an act of valuation: it presupposes investments in the 'social' which are valued and preferable to 'non-investments' deemed to be things of the past, to be reformed or even discarded. Yet, while fully admitting our own *Wertbeziehung* (value relationship) to the objects of our research, we social scientists must remain faithful to the Weberian principle of objectivity and value- (axio-logical) neutrality. This is why our vocation (*Beruf*) is first about making clear how one can rightly and consistently, as rigorously as possible, craft concepts out of the mainstream circulation of political notions. This is, how-ever, not an easy task; and it is especially hard in the context of the complex and overlapping structure of European fora where ideas are contested, adopted, and circulated, at the level of the EU and in various national settings. Indeed, scientific forums cannot be insulated from the functioning of policy communities fora, and, most damagingly, from political communication ones. The term SI has always been entirely normative, of course, as was a very analogous notion, the 'enabling state', coined by Neil and Barbara Gilbert (Gilbert 1995). Nathalie Morel, Bruno Palier, and Joakim Palme (2012c) were indeed right in acknowledging the similarity of both approaches. Maurizio Ferrera also recently recalled that, in the 1990s, the idea of social policy being an investment, 'was not presented as an alternative to the neoliberal perspec-tive, but as an enriching and coherent expansion: social policy was to be valorized (while modernized) because it was an important "productive fac-tor"' (Ferrera 2013: 6). The idea was also in line with research by Robert Boyer, who stressed the importance of health care and education investments for growth in late capitalism societies (Boyer 2002). In this respect, 'social' invest-ments are no new phenomena. Nevertheless, as we write in 2016, we keep experiencing important difficulties to construct SI as a genuine social science concept (*Begriff*). Especially in its 2013 'Social investment package (SIP)' (European Commission 2013d) while quoting A. Hemerijck several times, the European Commission used ambiguous language that we can start from in order to help delineate clearer concepts by contrast; its imprecision concerned both the terms used and their definitions.

The first regrettable feature of the communication was that it used indiscriminate vocabulary as if all notions meant the same thing. They perhaps do from a certain mainstream economic perspective, but they don't when it comes to really defining what social protection is about: 'social policies' does not equate to 'public spending on social policies' or 'public budgets for social policies'; it does not equate to 'social protection systems', nor 'welfare states' or 'welfare systems'; it does not equate to 'social services'. Only from a functional economic perspective could all these terms be used interchangeably. Indeed, understanding social protection conceptually is needed to determine whether there is a credible meaning for social investment. The second feature of the communication's approach is that it oscillates between three modes of defining SI. The first is listing a number of areas, like childcare, education, and so on. The second is to fall back on mainstream economic analysis of 'functions of social policy', that is, macroeconomic stabilization, redistribution, and allocation. The communication alters these classic functions: stabilization is kept but social protection is assimilated to redistribution and social investment is introduced as allocation (European Commission 2013e). The third approach uses the classic 'human capital' theory: social investment is investing in human capital, starting from early childhood. To what extent the three definitions are compatible with one another is not explained in the communication, and the heart of the confusion lies with the very articulation of social investment and social protection. After his 2013 book, Anton Hemerijck has brought new research to the discussion in his preliminary paper 'The Uses of Social Investment' (2015), distributed ahead of the Amsterdam seminar. How can we consider his argumentation today and contrast it to the Commission's confusing approach?

3.2.1 *Welfare State Reforms in Need of a Theory of the State*

Hemerijck states his basic conception of social investment as:

> The SI approach to welfare reform focuses on policies aimed at preparing individuals and societies to respond to the new risks of a competitive knowledge economy, by investing in human capital and capabilities from early childhood through old age, rather than in policies that simply 'repair' damages after moments of economic of personal crisis. (Hemerijck, Chapter 1, this volume: 4)

However, when one wants to define (and measure) what is SI and how to distinguish it from what is not SI, the distinction ordinarily opposes 'compensating' and 'investment spending', and the definition conundrum is only displaced but not solved; this links up to the former quantitative estimates made, including in the documents published by the Commission and in earlier research by Nicolai (2012). Hemerijck indeed acknowledges that his research 'continues to face difficulties in identifying and empirically tracking particular policy mixes and reform packages that manifest a social investment approach as distinct from other kinds of welfare efforts' (2015: 4).

More fundamentally, Hemerijck rightly contends that we need a 'theory of the state', suggesting the problem be approached through 'functions'. Whether this is a way of building a 'theory of the state', he does not fully explain. The three 'functions' he develops as typical of an SI approach (see Chapter 1, this volume) are: 'easing the flow of contemporary labour market and life course transitions', 'raising the quality of the stock of human capital and capabilities', and 'maintaining strong minimum income universal safety nets as social protection and economic stabilization buffers'. If the state appears as 'provider of services', this hardly provides a 'theory of the state', and one does not clearly see the link between the provider of services and the system of social protection, which is nowhere reduced in Europe to simple 'safety nets'. Hemerijck's recurring insistence on the limits of unemployment insurance ('traditional unemployment insurance can no longer function as an effective income reserve buffer between jobs' (Hemerijck 2012b: 52)) and on the necessity of 'universal safety nets' as 'buffers' also does not say how the system of social protection is considered: will social insurance still be part of its future? As for the 'flows' function, the very limited contribution of so-called 'activation policies' to the performance of social protection before the crisis, and even worse, after its start, is also a problem for treating them as a model to imitate: the least one can say is that such policies have been fundamentally ambiguous. I showed elsewhere in detail that the example of the French *Revenu de solidarité active* proved an utter disaster (Barbier 2011; Comité national d'évaluation 2011). Finally, one should note that Hemerijck advocates a modest stance: not an entire overhaul of the system of social protection, nor a single encompassing paradigm, 'the social investment perspective has come to be viewed as a container concept for the emergent recalibrated social policy paradigm with an important dimension of recognition in intellectual circles, administrative silos, and political arenas' (2015: 2). All in all, the new research developments about SI strongly advocate thinking again about what are the systems of social protection—these deeply complex and embedded institutions at the national level.

3.3 Social Protection and Social Investment

As the title of this chapter implies, there are two ways of envisaging SI. A first way is possible, that will be privileged here: considering SI as an innovative political intervention, a general reform strategy applied to existing European systems of social protection. A second way nevertheless exists, which has its roots in radical neoliberal economics: SI is a tool to destroy social protection systems by breaking up their holistic consistency into 'targeted', 'conditional', 'simple', 'temporary' 'programmes' that should be assessed individually on the basis of their 'social impact'; in this latter sense, as we will see in this section, social investment is reduced to SII, which with the Social Investment Package (European Commission 2013d) abundantly deals. If one leaves aside the SII choice for the moment, the credibility of SI strategies appears intrinsically linked to conserving large parts of the systems of social protection they intend to reform. The problem is not only to select areas where innovation is possible, it is also to design adequate circumstances for introducing this innovation into the existing systems. All sorts of questions then arise: will social insurance be compatible with SI? What balance will exist between universal and targeted benefits? Will there be unconditional benefits or support? And so on and so forth. Hence, conceptualizing existing welfare states is a crucial task.

At first glance, welfare states are only hazardous conglomerates, and indeed their eventual design and their constant reform are rarely the result of intentional design. In effect, as we have shown in previous works (Barbier 2008, 2013), national social protection systems are more than improbable combinations of social services. They, first, are social systems, articulating together macro-social mediations between the various orders of social activity (Théret 2002). These systems (institutional forms) closely relate the family, politics (among which is the state), and the economy. Empirically and everywhere, they combine private insurance, fiscal redistribution, and family solidarity. Beyond differentiations based on the proportions allocated to social insurance, social assistance, and non-profit provision of services, which vary from one country and historical period to the next, social protection unifies each national society. As Stephan Lessenich once justly remarked: 'Der demokratisch-kapitalistische Wohlfahrtsstaat ist die Staatsform unserer Zeit, die politische Ordnung der Gegenwartsgesellschaft—und es wird dies bis auch weiteres auch bleiben' ('the democratic capitalist welfare state is the form the state takes today, the type of political order of contemporary society, and it will stay as such in the future' (our translation from Lessenich 2003: 419). Social protection hence corresponds to a form of the state. Despite the wishes of so many neoliberal partisans, the welfare system is embedded in crucial economic, political, and individual elements (which determine the stability and the legitimation) of social life in Europe. Despite this undoubtedly being the case today, it might not remain so due to the profound transformations societies are experiencing. SI strategies cannot but heed that reality carefully.

Secondly, a social protection system is not to be equated with the state only (this is why the term 'welfare state' or the close French equivalent 'État social' (often mistranslated as l'État providence, a French equivalent of the 'nanny state', Barbier 2013) are partially inadequate qualifications). The same fact explains why, in his pioneering study of the German welfare state, Jens Alber (1986: 4) noted that German scholars often preferred the term 'social market economy' to the term 'welfare state'. The economy in question implies a constellation of actors that interact with the welfare state, at the national and at the European levels (trade unions, non-governmental organizations (NGOs), and the third sector, social security institutions, local communities, etc.). Some of these still enjoy a special protection under European law, inasmuch as they are not submitted to the overwhelming rule of market competition. Thirdly, social protection is not only a macro-system; it is linked to the individual status in society of citizens who are still wage earners in Europe. For them, modern social protection has given birth to another institutional form, a genuine social nexus closely interwoven with the wage-earner nexus (Boyer 2004). Social protection is first and foremost a collective institution, the roots of which echo the first use of the very term by Karl Polanyi (1957). All in all, social protection is a system that combines macro-relationships and the relations of individual citizens to the state, the economy, and the family. Fourthly, all systems of social protection are today national, and their European layer has remained marginal even at the moment when supranational governance by the European Central Bank (ECB) and the Commission have imposed their hegemony. Any significant welfare reform (social protection reform) happens in the context of a given polity, is associated with a given bounded territory, and is politically determined by the political community and the political institutions of the particular nation, with prerequisites of identification and reciprocity (Barbier 2013).

Social protection did not acquire its modern meaning until the turn of the nineteenth century. The expression itself was not currently employed in French until the second half of the twentieth century, and the term 'social protection system' (*système de protection sociale*; *Soziale Sicherung System*) did not become commonplace until the 1990s (French people preferred to call it 'Sécurité sociale', Germans 'Sozialstaat'). During the histories of the European nations, a variety of systems was built through the invention of national-specific institutional 'compromises', as the regulation economists stress (Boyer 2004). The common 'promise' made, according to Roosevelt in 1934, was 'security' (*sécurité*, *Sichereit*), 'the security of the home, the security of liveli-hood, and the security of social insurance' (Kaufmann 2003: 81), but actual-izations were immensely diverse from the foundation stages, and they still are, because of their constant reform and constant renegotiation among social groups, classes, and interests in the context of polities which have remained national. Hence the concept we suggested of national systems of social protection (Barbier and Théret 2009). Despite its strong capacity for inspiration,

T. H. Marshall's concept of 'social citizenship' always disregarded a diversity that, nevertheless, groups together the invention of social rights by the French Revolution in the late eighteenth century, the invention of social insurance in Germany, and so on and so forth. Finally, systems of social protection have another defining characteristic: they are historically based on rights, and these rights—today very much contested—are the crucial traces of a political substance that no economic analysis can ever reduce to a set of equations or functions. Social protection guards not only against the negative effects of the social division of labour, but also against those of the division of society into governing and governed (by establishing legitimate rights over state tax resources, which must be honoured by governments), and, finally, against those of the sexual division of domestic tasks (by guaranteeing specific social rights to women). Hence, if it is to be a consistent and sustainable strategy for the future, social investment cannot but find its insertion into the variegated national logics of these systems of social protection. It can be envisaged as a complement, a development, a continuation by new means.

3.4 Social Investment in the Future?

The hegemonic economization of analysis, and of social activities, tend to oversimplify the basic understanding of our institutions today in Europe. As Hemerijck has noted (2014), mainstream economic literature caricatures that 'welfare provision' is unsustainable and that it is only adequate for 'welfare dependent minorities' or manipulated by 'insider political mischief'. On the basis of these analyses, a second approach to social investment is promoted. With dire constraints put on social budgets, privatization and social business initiatives are promoted as simplistic alternatives to the highly complex systems of social protection. It is easy to see the influence of such a trend in the very content of the 2013 Communication of the Commission; it is tailored to the new needs of private funders who look for the application of traditional private management tools onto the activities of social protection, and especially social services. In this they are helped in important ways by the systematic economization of European Union (EU) law (Barbier and Colomb 2012). Hence, an alternative project for SI is the reconfiguring of all systems of social protection, including pension and health care—their core—into 'simple, conditional and targeted' programmes limited in duration and subject to the evaluation of their social return on investment. SII is the second way: social investment against social protection. It can bring with it a very serious potential of destruction of the complex and highly sophisticated systems of social protection with their historic anchors in the family, in politics, and in economics. In order to prevent this potential from damaging societies, social investment partisans should be aware of the importance of the balance accomplished in history, and sociologists should scrutinize in detail the state and the dynamics of social forces in nations and in Europe. For social protection systems, the last word still belongs to voters in national polities, but the role of ideas circulating at the European level is immensely important.

4

Family Relationships and Gender Equality in the Social Investment Discourse

An Overly Reductive View?

Chiara Saraceno

Gender awareness and acknowledgement of changing family arrangements are certainly a distinctive feature of the social investment discourse (Jenson 2009), in so far as one of its practical and intellectual drivers is the changing behaviour of women and the weakening of the male breadwinner model that underpinned the post-war welfare state. The main focuses, however, are on how to support women to enter and remain in the labour market, rather than how to support a change in men's roles within the family; on how to invest in children overcoming their parents' (mostly mothers') educational deficits, rather than on how to allow time to care and develop relationships. Viewed from this perspective, the social investment approach (SIA) embraces what Fraser (1997) called the 'universal breadwinner' model of social citizenship: a far cry not only from her 'care parity' model (where care giving grants access as such to social rights and some income), but also from her 'universal caregiver' model (where both women and men can combine care and paid work). The citizen envisaged by the SIA is first and foremost a paid worker, either in actuality or (when a child) in the making. It is the stereotypical male worker model that is being promoted rather than the worker and carer model (Daly 2011; Lewis and Giullari 2005). In this and other ways, it also implicitly devalues all unpaid activities that are not easily included in a human-capital-enriching approach. Finally, social investment supports a partial defamilization of women and children, through work–family conciliating policies, early childcare, and education. But it also accepts that women will retain the main responsibility for unpaid family work.

4.1 The Shifting Symbolic Balance in the Work–Family Conciliation Construct

The 'family' in the social investment discourse occupies an ambivalent position. It is the locus of changes that have undermined the male breadwinner model through marital instability and through women's (particularly mothers') increasing labour force participation. These changes are represented both as 'new social risks' that justify the new policy approach and as opportunities, instruments even, for this new approach. Thus, the 'new social risks' represented by the weakening of the male breadwinner model and marital instability force more women into the labour force to protect themselves, their children, and indeed their families from the risk of poverty, at the same time enlarging the tax base as well as the pool of available human capital. However, more women, and particularly more mothers, in the labour force open up the 'new risk' of a care deficit, both with regard to young children and frail older people in an increasingly ageing society. This requires a functional turn whereby work–family conciliating policies are placed at the forefront of social policies, so as to enable parents and adult children to participate in the labour force despite having dependent family members (see also Knijn and Smit 2009). Having mothers in paid work not only requires but also legitimizes having children in early education services. Offsetting the 'care deficit' for the frail through non-family provision, however, cannot be easily translated as a social investment opportunity and is therefore only a necessary 'buffer' (to use Hemerijck's terminology).

In this perspective, social investment frames family policies mainly as labour-market policies. This certainly offers a strong basis for advocating generous childcare services as well as parental leaves. But it also implicitly frames the family as an, albeit necessary, constraint on (women's) labour force participation that policies should reduce. The obverse—how to better accommodate paid work to the needs of the family and the right not only to care but also to enjoy one's own family—has a much more limited space in the social investment perspective. Furthermore, the need (and constraint) to have time for the family is conceived as concerning only women, in so far as, in Hemerijck's words, they are the ones who bear the main responsibility for this side of life. It is true that, in their influential 2002 work, Esping-Andersen and colleagues explicitly advocated greater gender equality within households and in the labour market. But, in the same book, Esping-Andersen was much more explicit concerning the advisability of a 'masculinization' of the female life course. He saw the obverse as a good idea in principle but difficult to realize (2002: 94–5; see also Esping-Andersen 2009: 80, 90). In this reduced perspective, the availability of parental leaves for fathers, rather than an acknowledgement of their right to family life and time, appears to be instrumental in freeing mothers from part of their caring duties, so that they can return earlier to work. The idea of the right to care for both men and women, fathers and mothers, which had, to a large degree, inspired the extension to fathers of the right to parental leave, particularly in some of the Nordic countries (Leira 2002), risks being overshadowed by the employment first imperative, and by a narrow construction of work–family conciliating policies as purely instrumental—to push or pull more women into the labour force, while not discouraging fertility.

As Mätzke and Ostner (2010) argue, the reframing of family policies as employment-friendly policies also marginalizes other important dimensions of family policies, in particular the acknowledgement of both the cost of children and the financial and non-financial value of care. Such marginalization has particularly negative consequences for households with modest economic means, where the balance between income and number of family consumers is particularly fragile; it thus exposes such families to the risk of in-work poverty, in the absence not only of a second earner but of children-linked transfers (Marx and Nolan 2014; Bothfeld and Rouault 2015). These are also the households where having a second earner is more difficult, either because of the combination of heavy family duties and low education and skills for the mother, or because they are single-parent, mainly single-mother, households.

There is also something else that is troubling in the emphasis of the social investment proponents on the virtues of women's employment: the implicit devaluation of care and relational work as valuable in its own right. In a social investment frame, such work becomes valuable when it is moved into the—public or private—market, as employment; that is, when it is effectively defamilialized. What remains in the private and unpaid sphere of the family is at best a necessity, at worst a constraint, an activity with no value in itself. There is no 'right to care', only the right to take time off paid work to perform a necessary task. Unpaid family care is treated not as an individually and socially meaningful activity, but, rather, as a necessity that cannot be avoided if the society wants both to maintain an adequate level of fertility and have more women in the labour force. Feminist scholars do argue that care (and housework) is work and may not be simply defined as the 'labour of love' assigned by definition to women in the family. They also, however, argue that paid and unpaid care is a crucial human activity and relationship, the value of which should be acknowledged in its own right (see, in addition to Fraser 1994; Knijn and Kremer 1997; Kittay 1999; Leira and Saraceno 2002; Nussbaum 2002; Fine and Glendinning 2005). In the exclusively paid work-oriented SIA, instead, women with family care responsibilities risk being left with (unpaid) work and responsibility that, if not quite stripped of all value, are totally secondary to the societal priorities of human capital and employment. Consequently, the need to receive care, as small children or as frail adults, which has always been a weak social right (Leira 2002), is also further weakened; those who provide it, as unpaid family members or as paid (mostly women) workers, are under-valued and, when doing it for pay, underpaid. We are a long way from the idea that care giving and receiving should be considered as an autonomous entitle-ment to social citizenship, as argued by many feminist analysts.

4.2 An Unfinished Revolution *Pour Cause*?

The SIA certainly makes a strong case for the valorization of women's human capital in the labour market and the economy, paying attention not only to participation but also wages and career opportunities. According to this approach, women's, and particularly mothers', labour force participation not only increases the pool of available human capital in an ageing society but, by increasing the tax base, also contributes to the increased social expenditure required by the SIA itself, as well as increasing labour demand (Esping-Andersen 2009; Hemerijck 2013). This is a nice argument to use when advocating for better support for women's equal opportunities in the labour market: more than men's, women's employment pays for itself. It is an argument, however, as Jenson (2009), among others, observes, that stops well short of advocating equal opportunities and equality for women both in the household and in the labour market. While Hemerijck takes as given that women will continue to be the main responsible person for unpaid family work, and therefore will also continue to be concentrated in part-time jobs and in discontinuous careers, Esping-Andersen (2008, 2009) also takes for granted that women will continue to earn less than men. Morel, Palier, and Palme (2012b) make no more than a passing mention of this as an unsolved problem. Thus, gender awareness notwithstanding, the actual gendered work-ing of both the family and the market in constraining women's opportunities is not the object of the SIA, either at the analytical or at the policy advocacy level (see also Lewis's 2010 critique of Esping-Andersen's (2009) 'incomplete revolution' argument). I would not go as far as Jenson (2009: 427) in arguing that 'Declining attention to equality of condition or even equal opportunities for women and men is a hallmark of the social investment perspective.' I would say, rather, that it is not one of its core concerns and goals.

In order not to be purely instrumental, women's employment should be supported for the sake of women themselves. This, however, means that one must 'make' (paid) work pay not out of necessity, but because it is a meaning-ful, well-remunerated, and acknowledged activity that leaves time also for other relationships and activities that one values. As things stand, while even highly educated women continue to experience gender discrimination in their careers, even in social-democratic, gender-egalitarian Sweden (e.g. Bihagen and Ohls 2006), many jobs offered to low-skilled women are low paid and far from being 'capacitating'. Precisely for this reason they are argued as being a cheap means for the full deployment of the human capital of better-educated women (and men). It may be worth noting in passing that the SIA says nothing about what happens to those men and women who are stuck in the many low-skilled, low-paid jobs which will still be necessary in techno-logically developed societies. Are they to be considered second-rate citizens because their human capital has little market value?

Issues of social class come up also in the case of the evaluation of parenting/mothering. Depending on their own human capital, parents, and specifically mothers, are seen as either an asset or a liability with regard to their children's human capital formation. Thus, while it may be good policy to allow well-educated mothers (and fathers) to have time to spend with their children as a form not only of individual but also social investment, allowing the same to low-educated mothers and fathers may appear as a risk from the perspective of the children's human capital. Such mothers should, rather, be encouraged to spend more time outside the household, in the labour market. This suggestion is particularly explicit in some of Esping-Andersen's work (see e.g. 2009 and Lewis's 2010 critique). Highly educated women should focus on employment since their human capital is an asset that should not be lost to society's development and financial returns. But, when mothers, these women are also instrumental first for 'producing' potentially high human capital children and, second, for developing this same human capital. They are therefore torn between opposite demands on their time by societal expectations (not to mention their own desires). The assurance that early childcare has, in the case of their children, a 'neutral' effect on cognitive development may be reassuring in so far as it promises no damage. But it may leave one wondering whether cognitive development is all there is in a child's experience and in a parent–child relationship. This last question is, of course, pivotal also for poorly educated mothers. But in their case the social investment discourse contains an additional devaluation: their adequacy as mothers is questioned because of their deficits in developing their children's cognitive skills. They should rather focus on becoming proper (co-)breadwinners in order to offer financial security to their children, 'freeing' them to attend enriching child-care and education services.

Investing in children, particularly those who are most disadvantaged, is, of course, important from a social justice and not only from a human capital perspective. Inequality among children, as well as in their life chances, because of family origin is the greatest injustice. Thus, universal early education is a crucial stepping stone in building social citizenship. It does not, however, need be framed in terms of compensating children for their parents' (mothers') inadequacy and ignoring other—caring, emotional, belonging—needs that children have, both within as well as outside their families (see also Lister 2003; Saraceno 2011). Nor should investment in children hide and legitimize a failure to address the socially structured inequalities that constrain their parents' opportunities and capabilities.

The 'one best model' that seems to underlie the social investment proposal with regard to women, and particularly mothers, actually hides strong inequalities, not only in life chances, but also in a differential evaluation of the societal worth of what different groups of women do.

4.3 Concluding Remarks

In the SIA's image of family and gender relations, it is possible to find arguments to pursue some of the changes in family and gender arrangements that have long been on the feminist agenda. Yet, the way these changes are argued for seems too instrumental (for other goals) and too unidimensional. Encouraging women's employment and supporting work–family conciliating policies are extolled more in the service of enlarging both household income and the tax base, rather than for allowing women to develop their own capabilities. While more gender equity in the labour market and in the household might be an outcome, this is neither planned for, nor particularly valued. Furthermore, the incorporation of women into the labour force occurs at the cost of devaluing other non-market-oriented activities, such as care, thus also halting, if not reverting, the process of critical revision of the (male) adult worker model. It was this model that, in recent decades, underpinned the requests for more 'time to care' and more work–family balance for men as well as women. The alternative vision of the worker *and* carer model is totally absent from the SIA.

Such unidimensionality is not only simplistic but also hides inequalities—between women and men, but also among women and among men. It also underplays tensions at the micro level between the imperative to reproduce—biologically and cognitively—human capital, therefore investing in having and raising children, and to be in employment as much as possible.

In contradistinction to Jenson (2009), who has argued that the SIA is favourable to girls but does nothing for adult women, I am at once more cautious in seeing nothing in the approach for adult women and less optimistic in finding it unmistakably favourable to girls. It is simply that girls, like boys, are the target of an investment in human capital. Thus they are better equipped in education and skills to compete with men in the labour market. Yet, as long as a radical re-visioning of gender arrangements in the labour market and in the household is neither a policy programme nor a strong guiding idea, these young women, as they grow older, will continue to experience a tension between putting their human capital to use in the labour market and having children and investing (also) in loving and caring relationships. As the experiences of their mothers and older sisters show, it is not enough to be as qualified as, or even better than, men. Having family responsibilities continues to divide the opportunities of men and women even in the societies that are closest to the ideal model underpinning the SIA.

5

Social Investment and the Matthew Effect

Limits to a Strategy

Giuliano Bonoli, Bea Cantillon, and Wim Van Lancker

5.1 Introduction

According to social investment logic, social policy in contemporary welfare states should not only provide a buffer for protection against the occurrence of social risks, but should focus at least as much on raising the *stock* of human capital and easing the *flow* of labour-market integration, to borrow Hemerijck's (Chapter 1, this volume) analytical framework. Raising the stock and easing the flow should particularly benefit disadvantaged, low-income people, since they are often not in employment and are dependent on cash benefits.

Since welfare states operate under the strain of permanent austerity, looming large is the matter of efficiency of social spending. Labour-market integration is regarded not only as a superior way of achieving income protection and social inclusion at the individual level, but also as an indispensable feature of 'productive' social policy systems, as higher employment levels decrease benefit dependency and contribute to sound public finances, hence to the future sustainability of the welfare state itself. The prime channel to achieve this ideal of social inclusion through labour-market participation is long-term investment in human capital, beginning in early life (Hemerijck 2012a).

The argument we put forward in this chapter is pretty simple at face value. *If* social spending on human capital and active labour-market policies benefits first and foremost the middle- and the higher-income groups at the expense of lower-income groups, a social investment strategy will not deliver on its promises to bestow upon disadvantaged people the skills to succeed in the labour market in the short term, and to contribute to sound public finances in the long term. On the contrary, it could widen the gap between the have and have nots, and induce an adverse distribution of social spending (Cantillon 2011). The phenomenon that social policies benefit middle and higher-income groups has been designated a Matthew Effect, a term coined by the great sociologist Robert K. Merton (1968) in a reference to a verse in the Gospel of Matthew: 'For unto every one that hath shall be given, and he shall have abundance: but from him that hath not shall be taken away even that which he hath' (Matthew 25:29, King James translation). In popular discourse, this is often succinctly summarized as the rich get richer, the poor stay poor. A Matthew Effect has been empirically observed in many domains of social life. Herman Deleeck was among the first to investigate who actually benefits from government expenditures on social policy measures. Based on data from the 1970s, Deleeck, Huybrechs, and Cantillon (1983) found that Belgium's then universal child benefit system, designed to compensate all families for the costs of child rearing, actually disproportionally benefited middle- and higher-income families. Children were entitled to child benefits up to age 18, unless they continued to study, in which case eligibility was extended to age 25. The Matthew Effect occurred because: (1) the number of eligible children increased with income; and (2) children from high-income families were overrepresented in higher education. Belgian policymakers had, of course, never intended to implement a child benefit system that benefited the rich; the occurrence of the Matthew Effect was an unintended consequence of the interplay between policy design and the social structure of families with children. Deleeck, Huybrechs, and Cantillon (1983) showed that similar mechanisms were at play in social housing, pensions, health care, cultural participation, and education. Julian Le Grand sketched a similar picture of welfare-service use in the United Kingdom: the better-off were found to make disproportionate use of public and social services such as education, housing, health care, social care, and transportation (Le Grand 1982). Since then, Matthew Effects have been identified in a diverse range of social policy fields, including education, health care, infant mortality, career longevity, early-childhood intervention, social security, housing, and childcare (e.g. Van Lancker 2014 for an overview).

There are good reasons to believe that social investment policies will be plagued by Matthew Effects as well. For instance, in order to increase labour-force participation, policies to combine work and family life are indispensable. Obviously, such policy will benefit those already participating in the labour market in the short term. This means that spending will benefit the middle- and higher-income groups. The underlying rationale, however, is that others will follow suit and that social spending on work-related policies will benefit the most disadvantaged, at least in the longer term. However, if job growth does only partially benefit work-poor households, as has been the case in many countries in recent decades (Corluy and Vandenbroucke 2014), work-related social spending will tend to accrue permanently to middle- and higher-income groups. Due to the underlying inequalities in the labour market, spending on human capital and active labour-market policies might induce greater social inequality in the long term. Such unintended consequence of the Matthew Effect is the exact opposite of what is intended by advocates of social investment spending.

In the next sections, we will investigate whether human capital policies such as childcare and higher education, and active labour-market policies, are prone to Matthew Effects, and how such mechanisms can be explained and remedied. We conclude by discussing the implications of the Matthew Effect for pursuing a successful social investment strategy.

5.2 Human Capital Investment: Early Childhood Education and Care

Children are key to any successful investment strategy, not only because the sustainability of the welfare state hinges on the number and productivity of future taxpayers, but also because inequalities in childhood pose a real threat to the accumulation of human capital and are the root cause of unequal opportunities in the labour market and later life. To quote Esping-Andersen in his highly influential contribution on this issue, a child-centred investment strategy *'must be a centre-piece of any policy for social inclusion'* (Esping-Andersen 2002a: 30). The linchpin of such a strategy is the provision of high-quality early childhood education and care (hereafter 'childcare'). The idea is that childcare services not only help to achieve social inclusion through the labour market, by allowing mothers of young children to engage in paid employment and balance their work and family duties, but also further the accumulation of human capital of children by providing them with a high-quality and stimulating environment. Both dimensions should be particularly beneficial for children from disadvantaged backgrounds, ultimately breaking the inter-generational chain of poverty.

The whole idea of mitigating social inequalities in early life and reducing child poverty through childcare services is built on the assumption that: (1) the provision of childcare services will increase parental (maternal) employment, hence increasing family income (*direct impact on poverty*); and (2) being enrolled in high-quality childcare services is beneficial for disadvantaged children in terms of cognitive and non-cognitive development, hence improving school readiness, which will in turn increase later labour-market opportunities (*indirect impact on poverty*). This means that, in particular, disadvantaged children should be enrolled in formal childcare services. After all, they often live in

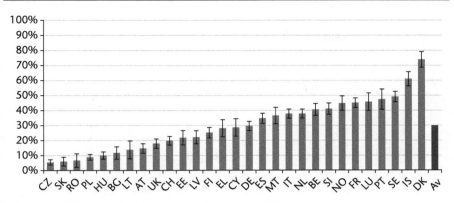

Figure 5.1. FTE formal care use, children aged 0–2, 2011

Note: The graph presents a full-time equivalent (FTE) measure of care use in order to take into account differences in the intensity of care use (i.e. hours of attendance per week). See Van Lancker (2013) for more information.

Source: Own calculations on EU-SILC 2011. Ireland is not included in the EU-SILC 2011 UDB.

families with low work intensity and they have the most to gain in terms of child development. If there is a Matthew Effect in childcare services use, government investment in childcare may not only fail to mitigate social inequalities but may even exacerbate them, because the better-off children are able to enhance their existing advantage through the benefits of childcare while the children who would benefit most are excluded.

Figure 5.1 shows the average full-time equivalent (FTE) measure of formal use for all children below the age of 3 in the EU27 + Norway, Island, and Switzerland. The disparity in formal care use between countries is enormous, ranging from more than 70 per cent of FTE in Denmark and 60 per cent of FTE in Iceland to barely 5 per cent in the Czech Republic, Slovak Republic, and Romania. Sweden, Portugal, Luxemburg, France, and Norway are also high-coverage countries with FTE use around 45 per cent.

Let us now turn to the social distribution of care use. To gauge the social stratification of care use, families with young children (defined as families with at least one child below the age of 6) are divided into five income groups (quintiles) for each country and the mean FTE formal care use of children living in low-income and high-income households is compared. Figure 5.2 presents for each country an inequality ratio (IR), that is, the mean FTE care use among children living in the highest-income family (fifth quintile) divided by the mean care use among children living in a low-income family (first quintile). An IR of 2 thus means that children from high-income families are enrolled in FTE childcare twice as much as their counterparts from low-income families, while an IR of 1 represents an equal distribution of care

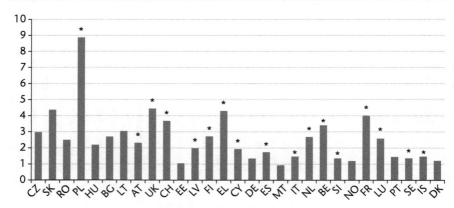

Figure 5.2. Inequality ration (Q5/Q1), FTE formal care use, children aged 0–2, 2011
Source: Own calculations on EU-SILC 2011. Ireland is not included in the EU-SILC 2011 UDB. Chi² test: * p < 0.05.

use. Exercises in which we have calculated IRs based on the educational level of the mother yield similar results (e.g. Van Lancker 2013).

Figure 5.2 shows that FTE formal care use amongst young children is socially stratified in the majority of countries. There are only three countries that achieve high levels of formal care use in which the difference in childcare use between children from low-income and high-income families is not significant: Denmark, Portugal, and Norway. We cannot discern a significant difference in Czech Republic, Slovak Republic, Romania, Hungary, Bulgaria, Lithuania, Estonia, Germany, and Malta as well, but none of these countries satisfy the condition of high levels of use. Moreover, the lack of significance might be due to the extremely low levels of care use in some of these countries and should not be interpreted as a result of organization of their childcare.

No single European country reports significant higher levels of care use for children from low-income families compared to their higher-income counterparts, suggesting that childcare services are not targeted towards disadvantaged children in any of these countries. The magnitude of the inequality is particularly striking in countries characterized by low levels of overall FTE care use, such as Poland, the United Kingdom, Switzerland, and Greece, while usage is more equal in countries reporting higher levels of FTE care use, such as Sweden, Iceland, Slovenia, and Italy. Indeed, the inequality ratio (IR) decreases as average usage goes up (r = −0.46). Nevertheless, some of the high-use countries report wide gaps between income groups: Belgium (IR: 3.4), the Netherlands (IR: 2.7), and France (IR: 4) are cases in point. In the case of Belgium, this amounts to 64 per cent of children from high-income families enrolled in formal care compared to only 19 per cent of children living in low-income households. In France, the situation is even more dramatic: an average FTE care use of 45 per cent (see Figure 5.1) conceals usage rates of 18 per cent for low-income children compared to 71 per cent for high-income children. Portugal and Denmark ensure equal participation in formal childcare at high levels, while Sweden (IR: 1.4) and Iceland (IR: 1.5) come close to equal outcomes. However, here too the inequalities are not negligible (60 per cent vs 44 per cent in Sweden and 72 per cent vs 49 per cent in Iceland). Such inequalities are clearly detrimental to the whole idea of social investment.

5.3 Human Capital Investment: Higher Education

A second pillar of social investment in human capital concerns higher education (Nikolai 2012). It is assumed that investing more in higher education will lead to increasing labour force participation. As a matter of fact, the Organisation for Economic Co-operation and Development (OECD) has calculated that having a tertiary degree in a knowledge society yields long-term economic gains at the individual (in terms of earnings) as well as the societal level (in terms of benefits foregone). It concludes that, today, 'most individuals need to go beyond upper secondary education' (OECD 2012b: 2).

Few have argued against the 'persistent inequality thesis' of Shavit and Blossfeld (1993) however. Roughly summarized, they show that educational expansion has not reduced the impact of social origin on educational attainment. The middle- and higher-income groups reap the benefits from investment in higher education. It is true that Breen and colleagues (2009) found, *contra* Shavit and Blossfeld, a widespread decline in educational inequality in the first two-thirds of the twentieth century in eight European countries. Importantly, however, the decline took place 'for the most part during a relatively short period of around 30 years in the middle of the century, between the oldest cohort (born 1908–24) and the second youngest (born 1945–54 and thus *in the educational system during the period 1950–75*)' (Breen et al. 2009: 1514). The general picture subsequently is one of stasis. It is also true that the Scandinavian welfare regimes have been more effective than others. However, as recently pointed out by Esping-Andersen, it is not clear 'whether this was produced by the education reforms or by other factors, such as more income equality and less poverty' (Esping-Andersen 2015b: 128). In the same vein, Erikson and Goldthorpe asserted that:

> Educational expansion and reform alone should not therefore be expected to serve as very effective instruments of public policy at creating greater equality of opportunity in the sense of 'a more level playing field'. Complementary efforts to reduce inequalities of condition, and especially class inequalities in economic security, stability and prospects, will also be required. (Erikson and Goldthorpe 2002: 42)

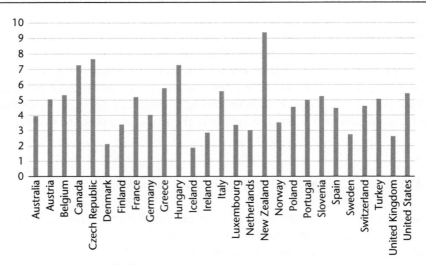

Figure 5.3. Likelihood of entering higher education for young people by parental educational level

Note: Likelihood is the ratio of the odds of being a student in higher education by educational level of the parents.

Source: Own calculations on the basis of OECD (2012b). Thanks to Matt Breunig for the inspiration.

Recent OECD data allow us to investigate the social gap in participation in tertiary education. Figure 5.3 shows the likelihood of participating in higher education for 20–34 year olds with parents with higher education, compared with 20–34 year olds with parents with low levels of education. Despite significant cross-country differences, no country succeeds in equalizing access to higher education. Even in the best-performing countries, Denmark and Iceland, young people with higher-educated parents are twice as likely to be enrolled in higher education compared with young people with low-educated parents. In other OECD countries the social gap is enormous, ranging from five times as likely in Belgium, Austria, France, Greece, Italy, Portugal, and Slovenia, to over seven times as likely in the Czech Republic and Hungary.

In an illuminating paper, Solga (2014) finds that, for a social investment strategy to work, high levels of education need to be open to as many people as possible, plus equality of outcomes in education will be necessary. The persistent Matthew Effect in today's higher education systems demonstrates that such an ideal is far from being reached in most countries.

5.4 Active Labour-Market Policies

Active labour-market policies are a highly relevant area in relation to our research question. They constitute a key component of an inclusive social investment strategy, since they are, by definition, targeted towards disadvantaged non-working individuals, such as the long-term unemployed, social assistance recipients, and so forth. Often, labour-market programmes are explicitly targeted at some disadvantaged group, like training for unskilled workers or job subsidies for older unemployed people. In this respect, we can expect active labour-market policies (ALMPs) to be relatively immune to Matthew Effects. On the other hand, it may also be the case that, within the overall disadvantaged target population, it will be the least disadvantaged who will be most likely to benefit from these policies, for two reasons.

First, many of the interventions that go under the rubric of ALMPs require some capabilities in the first place. This is clearly the case with job-related training, which may require a fair command of the local language and some cognitive or non-cognitive skills (see e.g. Heckman, 2000, 2006). Pre-existing abilities may also be a requirement for benefiting from other interventions, such as employment programmes. Since these in general require a minimum of productivity and a behaviour compatible with the expectation of organizations to be deployed, individuals with poor social and non-cognitive skills may be excluded from participation in these programmes too.

Secondly, since the ultimate objective of ALMPs is to put jobless people into jobs, those who implement them may anticipate the selectivity of the labour market. Firms must be selective when recruiting, and this is the main reason why some disadvantaged individuals find it particularly difficult to re-enter the labour market. Now, given the fact that firms are selective, it may be the case that ALMP institutions and/or street-level bureaucrats anticipate labour-market selectivity and allow participation in ALMPs only to jobless people who can be seen as promising in terms of labour-market re-entry. In other words, a case worker may decide that it is not worthwhile to send an older, long-term unemployed migrant to training, because his or her chances of getting a job, even after having completed training, seem very slim.

On the basis of this discussion, it seems clear that, on a theoretical basis, it is rather difficult to make clear-cut hypotheses with regard to the presence or absence of a Matthew Effect in ALMPs. As a result, it seems appropriate to turn to empirical analysis. There are very few studies on the issue of access biases in ALMPs. However, it is possible to obtain valuable empirical evidence from the very numerous evaluations of labour-market interventions. In fact, these studies in general describe the participant population and compare it to the eligible population. By looking at these simple comparisons, we can quickly ascertain whether disadvantaged people are over or underrepresented in the programmes.

Fabienne Liechti has explored the issue of the Matthew Effect in this literature (Liechti 2015). Her findings are intriguing. First, there is no clear direction in the access bias. Depending on the programme and on the definition of disadvantaged people used, the weakest are sometimes underrepresented (Matthew Effect) or overrepresented. However, when looking more closely at these access biases, one can uncover some variation. First, a Matthew Effect is stronger against migrants than against the low skilled. Why this is the case is unclear, but it may have to do with the fact that knowledge of the local language is required in order to participate in some programmes.

Looking at the different programmes, in job search assistance interventions one sees a slight overrepresentation of the low skilled and a stronger under-representation of migrants in the relevant programmes. In employment programmes, one finds a similar picture: low-skilled individuals are overrepresented and migrants underrepresented in these interventions. Things are different with regard to private sector wage subsidies. In this case both putatively disadvantaged groups (the low skilled and migrants) are clearly underrepresented. This result is probably an effect of labour-market selectivity, since in order to benefit from this programme one needs to find a job. Finally, in relation to training, one finds again contrasting results, with both positive and negative access biases in different programmes and for different groups.

The available evidence suggests that probably both effects we assumed earlier in this section are at play. Policy design favours a positive bias for disadvantaged people, but then other forces counteract it so that the overall result is sometimes a negative access bias for the most disadvantaged. A German study on access to a training programme designed for unskilled unemployed people is instructive in this respect (Fertig and Osiander 2012). The analysis of who the participants are reveals all sorts of biases. In relation to some easily observable features, the authors highlight a positive bias: East German, migration background, a foreign diploma, several episodes of unemployment, and no formal qualification. This seems consistent with the declared intention of the programme, that is, to reach unskilled disadvantaged jobless people. But then the authors uncover a negative bias in relation to characteristics that are not so easy to observe for the case workers: partners without a job, fewer than a hundred books in the household, weak locus of control, bad health, on social assistance, little employment over the last five years.

This combination of positive and negative biases can help us make sense also of what we see in the field of ALMPs. The impression is that there are two contrasting forces: a policy intention to reach disadvantaged people on the one hand, and the Matthew Effect on the other, motivated by insufficient capabilities and, possibly, anticipation of labour-market selectivity. The overall result of these contrasting forces is unpredictable. What is clear, however, is that the policy intention to reach the most disadvantaged is severely limited by Matthew Effects. Arguably, this is one of the reasons why employment growth does not benefit all households equally: whereas before the crisis the working age population without work has fallen continuously, the share of households with no working age member in employment remained fairly stable. The unequal distribution of jobs over households is strongly associated with marital selection and individual characteristics such as education, origin, and region (Cantillon 2011; Corluy and Vandenbroucke 2014).

5.5 Discussion: How to Ensure the Future Success of Social Investment?

More than a century of historical, sociological, economic, and psychological research leaves little doubt as to just how determining social, economic, and cultural contextual factors are for one's life chances. In their seminal work, *The Constant Flux*, Erikson and Goldthorpe (1992) showed that there is a high degree of constancy and commonality in social stratification (as measured in terms of father–son class mobility).

Some have called into question the structuring impact of social class in modern societies (e.g. Clark and Lipset 1991; Lee and Turner 1996; Pakulski and Waters 1996; Scott 1996). Beck (1992), for example, argues that we have evolved to a so-called 'risk society', characterized by greater as well as more diffuse social risks. However, 'bad' social risks such as unemployment, low work intensity, and illness continue to be significantly socially stratified, including (though to a lesser extent) in countries that are considered good examples when it comes to effectuating great(er) social equality. The existence of strong father–son social gradients for social risks that are statistically likely to induce poverty—particularly unemployment, low work intensity, ill-health, and low pay—has been demonstrated time and again (e.g. Feinstein 1993; O'Neill and Sweetman 1998; Cappellari and Jenkins 2002; Pintelon et al. 2013). Social class is also observed to influence the duration of poverty spells (Whelan, Layte, and Maître 2003; Dewilde 2008; Biewen 2009), while risky life events clearly do not trigger identical poverty effects for different social classes (Vandecasteele 2010). Moreover, compelling evidence has been found to support the view that stratification patterns are, by and large, the same across welfare states, be they Scandinavian, Anglo-Saxon, or continental European (Pintelon et al. 2013). Clearly, then, social background is an overwhelmingly important factor. The universal nature—in terms of both space and time—of the gravity of social class calls for moderation of expectations with regard to the impact of social investment (Cantillon 2014).

While it is true that most social investment advocates emphasize that social investment and social protection are two sides of the same coin and that social investment cannot thrive without some degree of old-fashioned social protection (and vice versa), we observe a decline in redistributive capacity of European welfare states over the past decades (e.g. Cantillon et al. 2014). This is associated with downward pressures on benefits for work-poor households and with a shift to spending on services which are less redistributive than cash spending (Verbist and Matsaganis 2014). Concomitantly, in many countries we observe an increase in inequality and poverty, especially in the long-heralded Scandinavian welfare states. This happened for various reasons, and social investment should not necessarily take the blame for this. It does mean, however, that the reality in which social investment policies take root is one of increasing class differentials. This is highly important, because tomorrow's opportunities are determined by today's distribution of resources (Corak 2013). Or, in Esping-Andersen's words: '"equality here and now" is very much a precondition for equality of opportunities (and vice versa)' (2015b: 127).

Even though many European countries can do much more in remedying Matthew Effects and investing in social investment policies, the social investment strategy in itself has inherent limits to furthering social inclusion because it relies on policies where the outcomes are strongly tied to the underlying class structure and social inequality. In Chapter 1, Hemerijck acknowledges that social investment policies, like any other policy that impacts on economic processes, 'creates redistributive winners and losers here and now and over time'. Yet the presence of Matthew Effects in the actual functioning of social investment policies may imply that the 'losers' will be the same, disadvantaged people in the short as well as in the long term. Therefore, cushioning policies raising the stock and easing the flows with a social protection buffer is not enough: a social investment strategy can only flourish in the fertile soil of a more equal distribution of incomes.

6

The 'New Welfare State' under Fiscal Strain

Austerity Gridlocks and the Privatization of Risk

Daniel Mertens

6.1 Introduction

Examining the impact of austerity on social investment has something ironic to it. With its aim to reconcile efficiency and equity, the social investment approach (SIA)—in theoretical terms—sets out to tackle the long-standing tension of the capitalist welfare state between accumulation on the one hand and social and political legitimacy on the other. Yet it seems that this tension itself has put social investment under severe pressure as fiscal crises have become a permanent condition for contemporary European societies (O'Connor 1973; Streeck 2014). The surge in public indebtedness after the financial crisis, and the subsequent troubles in the Eurozone periphery to refinance these debts, have led to an austerity consensus among elites that has imposed harsh constraints on public spending, including social investment. At the same time, the pro-cyclical nature of current austerity measures in many countries has undoubtedly exacerbated the need for social investment policies as unemployment and poverty rates have climbed and birth rates have decreased. Proponents of the SIA were quick to identify the challenges that are associated with these developments, but remain fairly optimistic about the long-term adjustments in Europe that involve the re-embedding of the neoliberal polity and economy (Hemerijck and Vandenbroucke 2012; Kersbergen and Hemerijck 2012; Hemerijck 2013). In this chapter, however, the analysis of the politico-economic dynamics of austerity regimes, more firmly set in place with the latest political changes within the Eurozone, suggests a bleaker scenario. Recent history indicates that fiscal consolidation episodes not only come with unduly social costs but in the end do not even spur additional social investment. What is more, the overriding impetus of fiscal austerity entails the danger of privatizing risks under the umbrella of social investment. Against this background, the chapter argues that, for the SIA to be progressively successful, it needs to voice a stronger critique of the fiscal orthodoxy underlying the current austerity consensus in the European Union (EU). Even though it might claim to develop counteracting potential by promoting 'the balancing of flexibility and security' (Petmesidou and Guillén 2014: 296), materializing this potential would require it to counter any neo-liberal appropriation of the approach that makes social investment seem easily compatible with a leaner state and legitimizes retrenchment of 'traditional' or consumptive social spending—as far as this distinction is applicable (Morel, Palier, and Palme 2012b; see Chapter 32, this volume).

6.2 Social Investment in the Age of Permanent and Acute Austerity

The contention that social investment is under major fiscal strain in many European countries must seem obvious for any observer of the current political economy. Nevertheless, the limits to social investment set by pre- and post-crisis austerity are more severe and complex than is usually acknowledged. For the main part these limits have to do with the fact that the institutional obstacles for allocating resources to new spending grow when fiscal conditions tighten and political pressure to balance the budget mounts up. Pierson's well-known notion of an 'age of permanent austerity' that has come about by the slowdown of accumulation, the maturation of welfare states, and population ageing (Pierson 1998, 2001) rests very much on this dynamic. Key here is that, in the face of stagnant tax revenues, 'immovable objects' in the budget—such as pensions and, increasingly, debt services—constrain the fiscal room to manoeuvre and thereby the capacity to confront new social risks with innovative expenditure programmes. Moreover, because legislation, organized interests, and electoral constituencies make specific budgetary positions more inert than others, rather discretionary or 'soft' types of spending are more prone to retrenchment. Both mechanisms entail difficulties for the SIA because social investment is, in many regards, new, innovative spending and, at the same time, less designed as entitlement spending that can count on organized interests to prevent its own curtailment. For instance, with regard to budgetary politics, pension expenditure is much more difficult to retrench than job creation programmes (see, in a similar vein, Breunig and Busemeyer 2012).

It is true, indeed, that '[s]ome policy legacies are better able to incorporate social investment innovations than others' (Hemerijck and Vandenbroucke 2012: 203), which helps to explain country variation in the degree social investment policies have taken hold over the past decades. But it is empirically less clear if the expansion of, for instance, family policies and educational programmes really were compatible with stringent budget consolidation. When comparing aggregate social investment spending in Britain, Germany, Sweden, and the USA between 1980 and 2007, it becomes apparent that a significant increase in social investment as a share of gross domestic product (GDP) was only achieved in Britain under New Labour and at the expense of a balanced budget (Figure 6.1; for a detailed discussion see Streeck and Mertens 2011, 2013). While Germany and the USA showed, by and large, stable spending, it was the Nordic poster child Sweden that cut back social investment as a share of GDP most heavily after it had confronted its worst crisis in the early 1990s and taken the road of fiscal consolidation. Even though it managed to maintain relatively high spending levels, it is a prime example of how fiscal crises can become turning points in welfare state development and how spending cuts are the weapons of choice in order to calm financial markets and regain investor confidence (Wenzelburger 2011; Haffert and Mehrtens 2015).

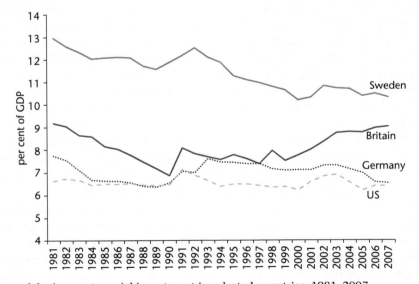

Figure 6.1. Aggregate social investment in selected countries, 1981–2007

Note: By following O'Connor's (1973: 97ff.) classical definition of social investment our data include R&D spending. For reasons of clarity this figure is adjusted for spending on ALMP, which nonetheless does not alter the trends identified.

Source: Streeck and Mertens (2011); based on OECD databases.

The definition and measurement of aggregate social investment, however, create problems of their own, as is discussed throughout this book. An obvious caveat is that they do not distinguish by types of benefits, nor do they consider the qualitative changes that may lie underneath such aggregates. Most importantly, separating mandatory from discretionary, investment-related spending items in national budgets sometimes is a crude endeavour (Chapter 16, this volume). Nevertheless, for the time being, it can serve as a heuristic to further investigate the relationship between social investment and fiscal austerity. This becomes particularly important when proponents of social investment policies conceive strict deficit reduction as a crucial step to win back fiscal capacity. The stance that new leeway opens up for governments to take an active role in social protection and investment once the public deficit is eliminated is what Haffert calls the 'progressive consolidation view' (Haffert 2015; Haffert and Mehrtens 2015).

The problem with this view is that it is not met by the recent history of fiscal consolidations. In particular, over the past three to four decades only a few Organisation for Economic Co-operation and Development (OECD) countries managed: (a) to achieve a budget surplus; and (b) to keep it for several years over the business cycle, mostly around the mid-1990s: Australia, Canada, Denmark, Finland, New Zealand, and Sweden. Since most of the consolidation efforts happened on the expenditure side, social investment spending—in line with Pierson's reasoning—was either reduced or at most maintained in the five years before the budget was balanced. Once the surplus had been achieved, only New Zealand steered significantly more money into education, family, and research and development (R&D) objectives. While Denmark increased its spending on education and Australia and Canada allocated more resources to family policies, overall social investment as a share of GDP drifted below earlier levels. While all countries reduced spending on active labour-market policy (ALMP) as a result of rising employment, Finland and Sweden cut spending in this area beyond policy demand, which contributed to social investment decline most pronouncedly in these two countries. What is especially noteworthy here is that, when controlled for unemployment and demographic factors, social investment still lags further behind than one would expect from a progressive effect of fiscal consolidations (Haffert 2015: 114–27). Therefore, the average record of social investment in really existing fiscal consolidation periods is rather bleak (Figure 6.2).

The main obstacle for social investment to substantially increase in surplus periods lies in the fact that the governments in surplus tend to use their improved fiscal position for tax cuts instead of new policy initiatives, and thereby further a general reduction in the size of the state. This observation corresponds nicely to the finding that shrinking public investment—as in physical infrastructure—over the past decades has taken place as 'collateral

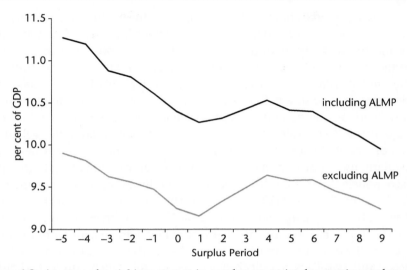

Figure 6.2. Average of social investment in surplus countries, by year in surplus
Note: Average includes Australia, Canada, Denmark, Finland, New Zealand, and Sweden.
Source: Data from Haffert (2015); based on OECD databases.

damage' of a general downsizing of the interventionist state (Keman 2010). Indeed, major consolidations—particularly when enacted as 'cold showers'— have always put the highest burden on investment spending, not on consumption, for reasons of differential rigidity (Blöchliger, Song, and Sutherland 2012). What should alarm proponents of the SIA, however, is that the decrease of fiscal flexibility that has been noted for the age of permanent austerity does not simply disappear when surpluses are achieved. The achievement of prolonged surpluses rather rests on a profound transformation of the fiscal regime, its ideas, institutions, and interests, into what can be called a 'surplus regime' (Haffert and Mehrtens 2015) or 'consolidation state' (Streeck 2015). What such consolidations have in common is that: (1) most political parties in a country make themselves parties of fiscal responsibility (ideas); (2) political majorities come about for passing new fiscal rules and a stricter budgetary framework (institutions); and (3) business and financial markets are able to exert pressure on governments to fulfil their demands for repayment and reduction of public debts (interests) (Posner and Sommerfeld 2013; Haffert 2015; Streeck 2015). These transformations make it extremely difficult to return to a more expansionary policy stance that would allow a greater leeway for social investment.

Of course, there is no general law to these observations and it should be highlighted that fiscal soundness does not preclude social investment per se, but rather its spending-based variety. It still stands that activation policies have gained ground in many countries, apart from spending restrictions, and on an organizational or programme level (Hemerijck 2013). Different pathways in the austerity-investment nexus do occur, but politico-economic dynamics that underlie recent budget consolidations are, overall, detrimental to the implementation of progressive policies (Blyth 2013). What makes the current situation so dire is that the institutional obstacles social investment confronts in the permanent austerity-ridden nation state have met an ever more constraining mode of governance on the supranational level under conditions of acute austerity. The priority macroeconomic adjustment, and particularly fiscal restraint, have taken over social investment and other progressive policies in post-crisis Europe is evident. By all accounts, the long-term outlook of the Europe 2020 agenda and the subsequent Social Investment Package (SIP) lag substantially behind various initiatives to restore—or to establish—budgetary balance in member states, with regard to both precedence and instruments available. For instance, the EU Fiscal Compact, the Six-Pack, and Two-Pack significantly expand on the deficit criteria laid out in the Stability and Growth Pact (SGP), now demanding fiscally unsound countries to be on an 'adjustment path' in order to forego sanctions (which are also easier to implement). Moreover, the conditionality of the memoranda-led policy interventions in Southern Europe has enforced austerity, among others, by giving the Troika (EU, ECB, and IMF) veto power over national fiscal policy. Tighter rules as well as stricter enforcement of these rules have subsequently led to deep cuts in the 'old' and the 'new' welfare state in 'programme countries', while simultaneously constraining future fiscal expansion across Europe (see e.g. Radice 2014; Arestis and Sawyer 2015; de la Porte and Heins 2015; Pavolini et al. 2015; Theodoropoulou 2015). These tendencies can be seen perfectly as a continuation of the regime shift outlined in this section which entails the quasi-constitutionalization of austerity. For instance, in 1990 only seven countries had legally anchored spending ceilings combined with sanctions or debt targets. In early 2009, the number of countries had increased to eighty (IMF 2009). In the case of the EU, social investment might additionally be hampered by the resistance of single member states to expand the community's fiscal capacity, as, for example, persistently displayed by the German policy stance (Schelkle 2012a).

As Arestis and Sawyer (2015: 116) aptly remind us, '[i]t is fiscal policy, which can be differentiated across countries to address the idiosyncratic economic [and social] problems of each country'. Narrowing the fiscal room to manoeuvre for member states while at the same time delegating the macroeconomic management of the Eurozone to the European Central Bank (ECB), therefore aggravates the gridlocks of pre-crisis austerity for social investment in the current setting. The counteracting ideas put forward by proponents of the SIA, such as creating social investment bonds or relaxing conditionality in exchange for social investment initiatives (Hemerijck 2014a; Chapter 30, this volume), are pragmatic responses, but in no way alter the mode of governance that has the 'fiscal discipline' rule supreme. The underlying tensions of resource allocation in capitalist democracies that pursue spending-based consolidations are unlikely to dissolve this way. After the crisis, the gap between export-led and credit-led economies within the Eurozone has grown, both with regard to social investment spending and socioeconomic performance (see e.g. Kvist 2013; Hemerijck 2014), which makes it difficult generalize these objections. But at the same time it underlines the necessity to dissent with the austerity consensus and its politico-economic dynamics present in pre- and post-crisis Europe.

6.3 From Austerity Gridlocks to Risk Privatization?

Despite the argument in Section 6.2, the overriding impetus of austerity has clearly not eliminated social investment as a policy objective, as is evident in the SIP. Furthermore, different countries may find different avenues of promoting human capital formation or bringing people back into work, depending on their institutional trajectory and their economic position. But with fiscal considerations overshadowing social investment initiatives, policymakers have to find ways to make such initiatives compatible with budgetary restraint, for example by increasing the share of private funding in programmes or by offering loans for private spending on social investment objectives. In both ways, governments can respond to rising demands for social investment without burdening the public purse. Thus, social investment may become private investment in specific cases, and the widespread increase of user financing in areas such as childcare is a case in point (van Kersbergen and Hemerijck 2012: 481). There are distributional problems associated with this trend that are different to those that are commonly attributed to social investment (see e.g. Chapter 5, this volume). Fiscal consolidations in themselves are usually regressive as they burden labour and particular dependent households more than capital (Ball et al. 2013), but the dimension added here is that austerity-led social investment shifts costs and risks on to households that are, in different ways, equipped to cope with them.

The rationale of this shift is already present in what has been termed 'asset-based welfare', and entails the promotion and facilitation of debt-financed housing, private pension insurance, or credit-as-welfare schemes in order to enable households to confront social risks with a minimum of collective intermediation (Hacker 2004; Crouch 2009; Krippner 2011; Hay 2013). This description fits the Anglophone economies best, but the SIA's emphasis on prevention and capabilities has led observers to stress the general policy alignment of asset-building with social investment (Midgley 2005; Jenson 2009a). What we can observe on the ground is that the growing importance of financial intermediaries and tools in welfare state arrangements (see e.g. Schelkle 2012), as well as the growth of private provision, control, and financing of welfare (Hills 2011), applies equally to policy areas that are part of the SIA. A glimpse at two core concerns of the SIA—human capital formation and employment activation—illustrate the assumed links between austerity, household finances, and social investment.

6.3.1 *Human Capital Formation*

In the area of education, private funding has traditionally been rather marginal since the majority of students attend public schools, but in pre-primary schooling, tutoring, and particularly tertiary education, the mobilization of household finances to supplement or replace public services has increased markedly (Eurodyce 2012). According to OECD data (Education and Training Statistics, extracted on 9 January 2015), the increase in private funding of tertiary education has outpaced public funding between 2001 and 2011 in twenty out of twenty-four countries, most significantly in Austria, Denmark, Germany, Italy, Portugal, and the UK. The overall stagnation of public spending on education has been noted repeatedly (e.g. Nikolai 2012), but what has mainly shifted financial burdens on households is the parallel rise in tuition fees. This trend can be observed in an increasing number of countries, and in some instances households have closed the financing gap by turning to student loans and private credit markets. This in turn has been reinforced by austere governments across the OECD, which, since the mid-1990s, gradually changed their student support schemes from financial aid and grants to loans. In other words, 'cost-sharing' in higher education has become a global reform pattern in the early twenty-first century (Usher 2005; Johnstone and Marcucci 2010; Vossensteyn et al. 2013; Soederberg 2014).

6.3.2 *Employment Activation*

Another concern of the SIA is how welfare states can help non-working people (back) into employment. Various initiatives in job creation and other ALMPs have been discussed and evaluated extensively over the past decades, but what is striking with regard to a new public–private mix in the age of financialization is the promotion of self-employment via microfinance. Especially under the header of the Europe 2020 strategy, the expansion of micro-lending to the unemployed in Europe has been praised, as delivering a reduction of (youth) unemployment as well as contributing to financial and social inclusion (EIF 2012: 6). Within the past decade, and driven by the financial crisis, the number and value of loans alike have increased dramatically, mostly directed to people living below the poverty line or in long-term unemployment (EMN 2014). While micro-lending initially grew in the transition economies of Central and Eastern Europe, it has gained prominence in Germany, Italy, the Netherlands, and Spain, for instance, as a novel activation tool largely managed by private financial institutions. What is crucial here is that micro-lending has been legitimized as a budget neutral social policy innovation. As Italy's former Minister of Foreign Affairs, Giulio Terzi, tellingly stated during his term, microfinance can 'help contain public spending by contributing to the reduction of social buffers, the cost of which rises in times of recession' (Ministero degli Affari Esteri 2013).

Both instances of austerity-led social investment contribute to the goals the SIA envisages such as increased employability and labour-market participation, but the role of the state here is to encourage private investment and establish an appropriate framework instead of taking on the investor role. This means that households and individuals carry: (a) the investment risk, which rests on the possibility that their investments do not pay, for instance because of dim economic and labour-market conditions; and subsequently (b) the default risk, which stems from the personal credit-financing of education and micro-businesses and which in turn increases with higher unemployment. Lower-income households, such as the long-term unemployed targeted by micro-lending, in particular, usually struggle with their investor role (Erturk et al. 2007), making austerity-led forms of social investment highly problematic. In other words, both instances contain the privatization of risks, which the consolidation state is not able or willing to carry. There are, nevertheless, doubts if these examples are representative of a trend or rather the ugly children of social investment marrying neoliberal financialization. Certainly, both developments are currently small in scale and remain fragmented across countries, but as far as the very notion of investment helps legitimizing lopsided cost- and risk-sharing in the consolidation state, they deserve critical attention and discussion.

6.4 Conclusion

Following one of fiscal sociology's key premises whereby the public budget is the manifestation of a social order, budgetary politics will decisively shape the future of social investment. As shown, the recent history of fiscal consolidations in the OECD economies provokes a rather dim outlook. Spending-based adjustments and the use of budgetary surpluses for tax decreases set strict limits on the expansion of social investment as far as it depends on reallocating scarce resources. With the socially disastrous transformation of permanent austerity into acute austerity in post-crisis Europe, social investment has been subjected, quasi-constitutionally, to the goal of balancing public budgets. While social investment spending is now urgently needed in many countries to buffer the impact of the recessionary spiral and to improve living conditions in the long and short term, it becomes equally prone to privatization policies: austerity-led social investments demand a higher share of cost- and risk-sharing from households and individuals than might be justifiable in terms of equity. These policies account for a fraction of social investment for the time being, but they may continue to serve as viable policy alternatives as long as budget consolidation rules supreme in Europe. In capitalist societies one can per se be wary about the idea that investments will pay out for everyone, but even if the SIA sticks with it, a more progressive and equitable mode of European welfare state integration seems incompatible with austerity.

Part 3

Social Investment Endowment and Extensions

7

Enabling Social Policy

Lane Kenworthy

The social investment approach to social policy emphasizes skill development and facilitation of employment alongside the traditional focus on provision of income to people not in employment. Policy tools include early education, improved K-12 schooling, affordable and good-quality universities, active labour market programmes (training, retraining, job placement), accessible lifelong learning, mentoring and other individualized assistance to those who need it, paid parental leave, encouragement of flexible work scheduling, and public employment.

All affluent nations have been moving in the direction of social investment (Morel, Palier, and Palme 2012c; Hemerijck 2013). The Nordic countries were the first movers. Much of continental Europe has begun to join in. Even in the United States, long a proponent of expecting employment but providing little support for it, policies such as early education, paid parental leave, college affordability, a higher wage floor, and a more robust employment-conditional earnings subsidy are now squarely on the agenda in a number of states and are gaining interest among national policymakers.

Should we promote employment? Does social investment work? Which policies and policy configurations are most effective? How should we pay for it?

7.1 Promoting Employment

Some believe social policy should aim to reduce people's reliance on employment. This sentiment is understandable. The need for a pay check can get us stuck in careers that divert us from more productive or rewarding pursuits. Paid work can be physically or emotionally stressful. It can be monotonous and boring. It can be alienating. Some jobs require a degree of indifference, meanness, or dishonesty towards customers or subordinates that eats away at one's humanity. Perhaps most problematic of all, work can interfere with family life.

Yet employment has significant virtues (Ferrera, Hemerijck, and Rhodes 2000; Scharpf and Schmidt 2000; Esping-Andersen et al. 2002; Kenworthy 2004, 2008; Layard 2005). It imposes regularity and discipline on people's lives. It can be a source of mental stimulation. It helps to fulfil the widespread desire to contribute to, and be integrated with, the larger society. It shapes identity and can boost self-esteem. With neighbourhood and family ties weakening, the office or factory is a key site of social interaction. Non-employment tends to be associated with feelings of social exclusion, discouragement, boredom, and unhappiness.

Just as important, in countries that have made commitments to pensions for their elderly, health care for all, and assorted other services and transfers, there is a need for additional government revenue. Some can come from raising tax rates, but that has become a tall order in a world with mobile capital. Increasing the share of the population in paid work can help to ensure the fiscal viability of a generous welfare state. It provides an increase in tax revenues without requiring an increase in tax rates. High employment eases the fiscal crunch another way too, by reducing the number of people fully or heavily reliant on government benefits.

If employment is worth promoting, what kinds of jobs should we foster? My answer: all of them, including low-end service positions. Manufacturing jobs have been declining steadily for decades, and that is almost certain to continue. Even if we do a superb job with schooling, high-end services won't employ everyone. Imagine a high-skill, high-employment economy of the future with 85 per cent of the working-age population in paid work. Suppose 65 per cent complete university and end up in high- or middle-paying service jobs. That optimistic scenario still leaves 20 per cent in other jobs. A few will work in manufacturing or farming, but for the rest we need low-end services.

Some favour minimizing low-end service jobs. One way to do that is to set the wage floor at a very high level, perhaps supplemented by heavy payroll taxes, in order to reduce employer demand for low-end positions. Another possibility would be to offer an unconditional basic income grant at a level generous enough to reduce the supply of people willing to work in a low-paying job.

I don't think that's the best way to proceed. As we get richer, most of us are willing to outsource more tasks that we don't have time or expertise or desire to do ourselves: changing the oil in the car, mowing the lawn, cleaning, cooking, caring for children and other family members, advising, educating, organizing, managing, coaching, transporting. And improved productivity and lower costs abroad will reduce the price we pay for food, manufactured goods, and some services, leaving us with more disposable income. So we'll want more people teaching preschool children, coaching and mentoring teenagers, helping adults find their way in the labour market or through a midlife career transition, caring for the elderly, and so on, and we'll be better able to purchase such services. If there is demand for these services and a supply of people willing to perform them, why discourage them? Low-end service jobs can be especially valuable for the young and immigrants, two groups who tend to struggle in the labour market.

If a low-end service job pays a modest wage, that need not mean a person's income also is low. A subsidy such as America's Earned Income Tax Credit (EITC) or the UK's Universal Credit (formerly Working Tax Credit) can boost household incomes while simultaneously encouraging employment.

For some, a low-end service job might be a career. Others will want it to be merely a stepping-stone. Government can help ensure that people have the capability to move up, via health care, early education, elementary and secondary schooling, lifelong learning opportunities, retraining, job placement assistance, special services for the mentally or physically disabled, language assistance for immigrants, targeted programmes for the young and the elderly, assistance with transportation, and help in organizing formal job ladders.

Mobility between jobs need not be confined to upward moves. It's very difficult to predict at age 18 or even 22 what kind of interests and capabilities you will have at age 35 or 50. Policy should facilitate people's ability to change job, occupation, or entire line of work at various points in the life course, even if the switch is simply to something different, rather than something better. This calls for counselling, mentoring, and perhaps several sabbaticals (every adult, not just parents of new-born children, should have access to several one-year paid leaves). It also means eligibility for pensions, unemployment insurance, sickness insurance, parental leave, holidays, and other non-wage benefits should be contingent on employment, but not on the particular job or employer you have.

If most people are expected to be in employment, policy also ought to improve the quality of work life. Low-end service jobs may offer limited mental stimulation or opportunity to participate in decision-making, and some are stressful. There is a limit to the amount of stimulation that some of these jobs will ever be able to provide, but most could do better, and we should try to figure out how and to push firms in that direction. Indeed, we should aim to improve working conditions in all jobs, rather than assuming that higher-skilled, better-paying positions automatically have decent work quality. I like the idea of an auditing procedure whereby government sets outcome standards for work conditions, leaves it up to firms to decide how to meet the standards, and monitors their efforts to do so.

Finally, policy ought to limit the degree to which job inequality spills over into social inequality and segregation. We want a society that is modestly rather than severely unequal. Jobs inevitably come with inequalities of status. If they also have profoundly unequal pay, this can easily spill over into social segregation and inequality of respect. Policy should push against this. Neighbourhoods should be designed or redesigned to encourage class mixing. Parks, beaches, libraries, and public transport ought to be attractive to all. And we might do well to consider a mandatory year of national service to ensure that everyone gets an experience of genuine social mixing as they embark on adulthood.

7.2 Does Social Investment Work?

Does a social investment strategy boost employment? Figure 7.1 shows employment rates in the rich longstanding democracies in 1989 and 2014. (A proper assessment would include employment hours, but we lack cross-nationally comparable data.) The figure includes the working-age population as a whole (age 25–64) and three groups among whom employment has tended to be comparatively low—prime-working-age women, the near-elderly, and the least-educated. Nearly all countries have higher employment rates now than they did twenty-five years ago, despite just recently emerging from the deepest economic crisis since the Great Depression. Moreover, Sweden, Denmark, and Norway, consistent practitioners of social investment since the 1970s, tend to be at or near the top in employment. While we don't know for certain how much of the common employment rise or the Nordic countries' success owes to social investment, these patterns suggest grounds for optimism that a social investment strategy can help (see Rueda 2015 for a different conclusion).

A second criterion favoured by many in assessing social investment is relative poverty. The relative poverty rate is, in effect, an indicator of income inequality between households in the middle (median) and lower parts of income distribution (Kenworthy 2011a). The hope is that social investment will produce larger employment increases in households at the bottom than in the middle, yielding larger growth in household income.

This is asking a great deal, as it isn't clear why social investment programmes would boost employment more in low-income households than in middle-income ones. Moreover, an array of economic forces—new technology (computers and robots), globalization, heightened product market competition in domestic services, increases in low-skill immigrants—have been putting downward pressure on wages at the low end (Bailey, Coward, and Whittaker 2011; Cantillon, Collado, and Van Mechelen 2015). In the period leading up to the 2008 economic crisis, as more countries were embracing social investment, relative poverty rates did not tend to fall (Cantillon and Vandenbroucke 2014).

Yet that doesn't mean household incomes were stagnant. In many countries, particularly the Nordics, lack of improvement in relative poverty rates

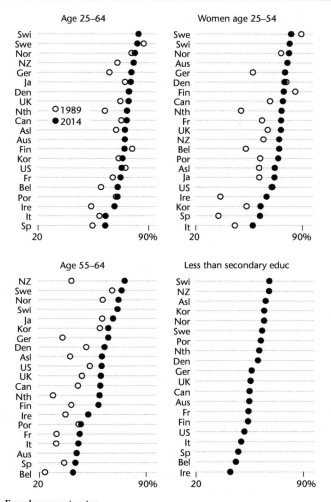

Figure 7.1. Employment rates

Note: The year 1989 is the earliest business-cycle peak year for which data are available for nearly all countries. 'Asl' is Australia; 'Aus' is Austria.

Source: OECD.

was a product of incomes at the low end rising but at roughly the same pace as incomes in the middle (Kenworthy 2011b, 2015a, 2015c). Relative incomes didn't improve, but absolute incomes did. It also bears noting that the Nordic countries have the lowest rates of material hardship, a broader indicator of living standards (Kenworthy 2015b).

Since the early 1990s, policymakers have worried that there is a sharp trade-off between high employment and low or modest inequality. A high wage floor and generous government benefits, in this view, reduce employer demand

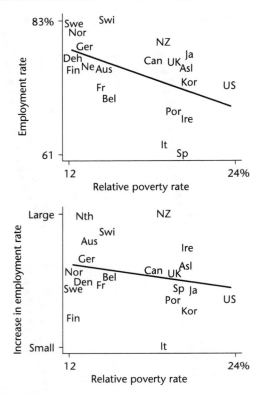

Figure 7.2. Jobs with equality

Note: Years 1979 to 2013. In the first chart, the vertical axis is the employment rate for persons aged 25–64 in 2013. In the second chart, the vertical axis is change in the employment rate for persons aged 25–64 between 1979 and 2013, adjusted for starting level. The relative poverty rate is the share of persons in households with an income (adjusted for household size) below 60 per cent of the country median, averaged over the period from 1979 to 2013. 'Asl' is Australia; 'Aus' is Austria. In the first chart, Denmark and the Netherlands occupy the same position.

Source: OECD; Luxembourg Income Study.

for workers at the low end of the labour market and reduce the incentive for benefit recipients to enter paid work (OECD 1994). A decade ago the cross-country evidence suggested that egalitarian institutions and policies might indeed have some adverse impact on employment, albeit not a large one (OECD 2006a; Kenworthy 2008).

A decade later there is greater cause for optimism. Figure 7.2 shows that countries with lower relative poverty rates have tended to do as well or better than their less egalitarian counterparts in achieving a high and rising employment rate.

It's worth noting in particular the employment performance of the United States. The USA has pursued a 'market liberal' approach to employment growth: a low wage floor, very limited labour market regulations, relatively stingy government benefits, comparatively low taxes, steady deregulation of product markets, and limited support for retraining, job placement, and work–family balance. Up to the turn of the century the 'great American jobs machine' was comparatively successful; the USA was among the rich world's leaders in raising its employment rate. But fifteen years later, America's employment record looks quite mediocre. Part of that is due to the 2008–9 crisis and its aftermath. But the problem began earlier. The period after the 2001 recession featured feeble job growth, and by 2007, the peak year prior to the crisis, the US employment rate had not yet recovered to its 2000 level (Kenworthy 2011c). A number of affluent nations with comparatively egalitarian institutions have been more successful than the United States at achieving and maintaining a high employment rate.

Another outcome of interest is economic growth. Does social investment increase growth? Part of the rationale for use of the term 'investment' is to emphasize that social investment expenditures can improve the economy's productive potential. This is achieved by increasing the share of people in employment or by increasing their productivity, or both (Morel, Palier, and Palme 2012b).

Social scientists have very little understanding of what contributes to faster medium- and long-term economic growth in rich democratic nations. Apart from catch-up (countries that start behind tend to grow faster), the evidence points to hardly any consistent growth boosters. What little evidence we have on social investment's impact on economic growth isn't supportive. Apart from Norway, which because of its oil wealth isn't useful in drawing inferences, the Nordic countries haven't averaged faster growth over the past generation than other affluent countries. So either they weren't executing the social investment strategy correctly, or they were and the resulting faster economic growth was offset by their other policies and institutions, or the comparative evidence so far does not support the claim that social investment boosts economic growth. I lean towards the third of these interpretations.

Even the theory behind social investment as growth-enhancing is questionable, as Brian Nolan (2013: 462) has pointed out:

> The case for the social investment paradigm rests heavily on the argument that the world is changing rapidly so that in the new knowledge-based economy a skilled and flexible labour force is the key motor for growth, with social investment then central to producing such a labour force. It is not obvious, though, why even in such a changing environment economic growth could not be achieved via selective intensive investment in the highly skilled minority who will occupy the 'quality' jobs and drive aggregate productivity and economic growth, with a hollowed-out middle and many in much less-skilled employment or not working.

What, then, is the verdict on social investment's impact? The evidence for the world's rich countries over the past generation is supportive of hopes that social investment can boost employment and facilitate its coupling with low relative poverty. It offers less reason for optimism about boosting economic growth or reducing relative poverty.

7.3 What Policies and Policy Configurations are Most Effective?

Suppose we embrace employment as a key aim of social policy and social investment as a useful strategy for promoting employment. We then need to know what policies to use. Should early education be universal or targeted to the poor? Should paid parental leave be for one year or three years? Should it include a 'daddy quota'? Should there be a statutory minimum wage? If so, how high? What is the best mix of carrots and sticks for social assistance recipients reluctant to enter or re-enter paid work? Should low market income be supplemented by an employment-conditional earnings subsidy? Is individualized assistance more helpful in the early years, the K-12 years, or later in the life course? What is the right balance between employment protection for workers and flexibility for employers? And so on.

Many of these questions don't yet have clear-cut answers. Getting the policy details right requires experimentation, adjustment, and learning from best practice. And since countries vary in political structure, economic institutions, culture, and in many other ways, optimal policies and policy combinations may well vary too.

7.4 Will Social Investment Be a Complement to Social Protection or a Substitute?

Finally, will social investment programmes be paid for by new revenues or by reallocating funds from 'old-risk' social programmes such as pensions, unemployment compensation, sickness insurance, social assistance, and the like? Some governments may be pushed towards substitution by fiscal constraints or by difficult-to-avoid increases in expenditures on big-ticket programmes such as health care and pensions (Cantillon 2011a; Streeck and Mertens 2011; Vandenbroucke and Vleminckx 2011). For others, such as centre-right or 'Third Way' centre-left governments, substitution might be the preferred path (Palme and Cronert 2015).

To avoid the substitution scenario, social investment proponents ought to forthrightly advocate for the social investment plus social protection approach and admit that it may require tax increases. They also would do well to encourage balanced budgets during economic upswings and to aggressively promote improvements in public-sector efficiency.

8

Social Investment and the Service Economy Trilemma

Anne Wren

8.1 Introduction

In 1998, Torben Iversen and I argued that, as a result of de-industrialization, governments faced a new trilemma—or three-way choice—between the policy goals of employment creation, equality, and budgetary restraint, such that at most two of these policy goals could be pursued successfully at the same time (Iversen and Wren 1998). In this chapter I will review the trilemma argument; describe what has changed since the article was written; and outline a potential role for social investment in enabling governments to reduce the starkness of the distributional trade-offs that the transition to a service economy presents.

8.1.1 *The Trilemma of the Service Economy*

In Iversen and Wren (1998), we argued that differences in the characteristics of production between manufacturing and services meant that governments were likely to face new kinds of distributional choices as de-industrialization forced an increased reliance on service sectors as the principal engines of employment growth. The argument went like this. In the golden age of industrial expansion in the 1950s and 1960s, technological advances, Fordist rationalization of production, and the exploitation of economies of scale, facilitated strong productivity growth in manufacturing sectors. Given high price and income elasticities of demand for a range of new consumable manufactures, the labour-saving effects of productivity increases in these sectors were compensated for by expansions in demand and employment resulting from falling prices and rising real wages.

In this context, as famously argued by Rehn and Meidner (Meidner 1974; Rehn 1985), egalitarian wage policies, linking wages across high and low productivity sectors, could have positive effects on employment creation. Cross-sectoral wage linkages had the effect of restraining real wages in the high productivity sectors in which dynamic expansion was taking place, providing an additional boost to demand; at the less productive end of the market meanwhile, relatively high wages forced businesses either to innovate to increase productivity or to fail, but the overall impact on the economy was a shift in resources towards the more dynamic sectors, especially when supported by active labour market policies.

Starting in the 1970s, however, rapid de-industrialization associated with changing consumer tastes and preferences, technological change, and increased competition from developing countries, has led to an increased reliance on service sectors as the chief engines of employment growth in the world's most developed economies. This is problematic because, as pointed out by Baumol many years ago, in many areas of services, in which face-to-face interpersonal interaction is an important component of production, the capacity for productivity increases is low (Baumol 1967). Good examples to think through here are childcare or nursing. It is hard to think of ways in which the numbers of young children or hospital patients cared for by an individual can be increased, without a decline in the quality of the service. This logic applies to a very broad range of social, educational, and personal services.

Our argument was that, under these conditions, the effect of egalitarian labour market institutions on employment could be the opposite of that predicted by Rehn and Meidner. Demand for a range of consumer and personal services tends to be highly price elastic because of the possibility of substitution through the household (we built on evidence in Appelbaum and Shettkat 1995, 1999). Given a low capacity for productivity growth in these sectors, however, it becomes particularly important to keep relative wages low, in order to generate a demand expansion based on the high price elasticity of demand. Since egalitarian wage-setting institutions tend to keep wages in these less productive sectors relatively high therefore (because they link them to developments in more productive sectors), they can have the effect of constraining employment expansion.

We argued that, as a result, governments in services based economies faced a 'trilemma' or three-way choice between the policy goals of employment creation, equality, and budgetary restraint (Iversen and Wren 1998). Creating large numbers of jobs in low productivity private service sectors, would, for the reasons described, necessitate trade-offs in terms of equality. For governments that remained committed to the simultaneous pursuit of equality and employment creation, an alternative, public sector route to employment creation existed, but the expansion of public service employment would, of necessity, entail higher levels of public spending and taxation. If governments operating in egalitarian wage-setting environments were not willing to engage in and finance public employment expansion, however, they faced the prospect of increasingly low levels of employment creation in a context of de-industrialization.

At the time of writing, in the late 1990s, the paths that countries were pursuing in response to the trilemma appeared to align closely with their dominant welfare state ideologies. Liberal regimes, for the most part, had pursued a strategy of reducing levels of protection on the wages of lower paid workers, and had witnessed significant increases in employment in low productivity private services sectors, and in inequality. In social democratic regimes, high levels of wage equality continued to be accompanied by high levels of public service employment, and taxation. In some Christian democratic regimes, like Germany, high levels of wage equality combined with a very small public service sector, resulted in levels of service employment creation that overall remained very low in comparative terms.

In subsequent years, as the pressure on labour markets stemming from the de-industrialization process has increased, almost all countries have moved in the direction of further market liberalization. As Thelen (2014) describes, however, liberalization trajectories, and their implications for equality, have varied significantly across different socioeconomic regimes. In some of the continental regimes, and especially in Germany, the continued protection of the rights of core workers, while allowing the size of the significantly less regulated market for 'atypical' workers to grow, has resulted in the development of heavily dualized labour markets, and sharply increasing inequality. In line with the trilemma argument, these developments have been associated with an expansion in employment in low productivity services in Germany in the past decade in particular. They have also been associated, however, with rates of inequality equalling or surpassing those of the UK since the mid-2000s, with the German d5/d1 ratio (at 1.84) surpassing that of the UK (at 1.82) in 2005 for the first time in recent history (OECD 2014a). In contrast, the strategy of 'embedded flexibilization' pursued in social democratic countries, has paired market promoting labour market reforms with policies aimed at protecting the most vulnerable workers—and with significant investments in active labour market policies in particular. While this strategy has been associated with increasing inequality at the lower end of the earnings distribution in some Scandinavian countries (like Denmark) levels of inequality in these regimes still remain low compared with those in Germany and the UK, for example, and in Sweden in particular have remained relatively unchanged since the early 1990s.

8.2 The ICT Revolution and High Productivity Services Sectors: Implications for the Trilemma

Over the past two decades also, however, the economic environment has changed in ways that have broader implications for the trilemma argument. In particular, the revolution in information and communications technology (ICT) has significantly enhanced the capacity for productivity increases, and for international trade, in certain areas of services. Trade was an important component in the Rehn–Meidner model because it allowed specialization in the high value-added production that could sustain high wages. And in our original article we noted that the starkness of the trilemma could be reduced where ways could be found to increase rates of productivity growth and trade in services, so that high value-added service sectors could begin to replace manufacturing sectors as the engines of growth and employment.

The new technology cannot, of course, substitute for those aspects of services that require face-to-face interpersonal interaction (cutting someone's hair, feeding a child, dressing a wound, for example). And, as a result, in the types of social, personal, and consumer services described in the previous section (in which this kind of human interaction is an important component of production) the diffusion of ICT, and its ability to enhance productivity, have been limited. For the same set of reasons these sectors are subject to significant natural barriers to trade, and remain largely untraded internationally.

In contrast, however, in areas of services in which face-to-face interpersonal interaction is a less essential characteristic of service provision, the diffusion of the new technology, and its impact on productivity have been marked. It is well established that ICT has significantly impacted on productivity growth in those sectors in which its diffusion has been greatest (Stiroh 2002; Triplett and Bosworth 2004; Jorgenson, Ho, and Stiroh 2005; Bosworth and Triplett 2007; Corrado et al. 2007), and, as the data in Table 8.1 indicate, some service sectors have, in fact, been at the forefront of this process. From the table we can see that the contribution of ICT capital to the growth of value-added in business services, financial intermediation, and post and telecommunications over the past three decades has been highly significant when compared to its contribution in a range of services in which the face-to-face component of provision is more important (for example, hotels and restaurants, retail trade, public administration, education, and health and social work, and other community social and personal services), and in most traditional manufacturing sectors.

Table 8.2, meanwhile indicates that these patterns correspond with higher rates of productivity growth in the ICT intensive services group (finance, business services, and transport, storage and communication) than in their less ICT intensive service sector counterparts (although it is important to

Table 8.1. Contribution of ICT capital to value-added growth by sector (percentage points)

	Level 1981	Average 1981–2007
Agriculture		
Agriculture, Forestry, and Fishing	0.025	0.059
Manufacturing Sectors		
Food Products, Beverages, and Tobacco	0.203	0.283
Textiles, Leather, and Footwear	0.057	0.129
Wood and Wood Products	0.146	0.185
Paper, Paper Products, Printing, and Publishing	0.445	0.607
Chemicals, Chemical Products	0.182	0.357
Rubber, Plastics	0.194	0.237
Basic Metals, Fabricated Metal Products	0.175	0.238
Electrical, Optical Equipment	0.487	0.608
Transport Equipment	0.255	0.298
Other Manufacturing	−0.027	0.199
Service Sectors		
Wholesale Trade	0.578	0.675
Retail Trade	0.342	0.410
Transport and Storage	0.245	0.429
Post and Telecommunications	**2.297**	**1.974**
Real Estate	0.373	0.539
Other Business Activities (including renting of machinery and equipment)	**0.799**	**1.049**
Construction	0.076	0.156
Hotels and Restaurants	−0.094	0.263
Financial Intermediation	**1.366**	**1.477**
Public Admin. and Defence	0.354	0.400
Education	0.146	0.220
Health and Social Work	0.131	0.201
Other Community, Social, and Personal Services	0.416	0.502

Note: Data from EU-KLEMS database, excluding Canada, Cyprus, Korea, Estonia, Greece, Latvia, Lithuania, Malta, Poland, Portugal, and Slovakia due to data availability.

Source: Wren (2013).

Table 8.2. Rates of productivity growth, services, and manufacturing, 1990–2004

Sector	Productivity Growth (Average, 1990–2004)
Manufacturing	2.20%
Hotels and Restaurants	1.21%
Wholesale and Retail Trade	1.32%
Other Community and Social Services	0.91%
Education	1.54%
Health	1.92%
Public Administration and Defence	1.57%
Transport and Storage, Communications	2.01%
Financial Intermediation	3.23%
Business Services	3.68%
Whole Economy	1.66%

Source: Wren (2013). Own calculations based on data from the Groningen Growth and Development Centre database.

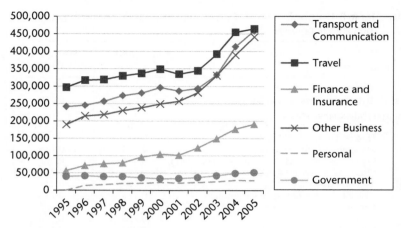

Figure 8.1. Cross-sectoral comparison of rates of expansion in service exports

Note: Data from OECD EBOPS database. Total exports, OECD countries 1994–2005 (modes 1 and 2, value in $US).

Source: Wren (2013).

recognize that the issue of productivity measurement in service remains controversial (Triplett and Bosworth 2004)).

And it is also no accident that this same set of sectors has witnessed a significant expansion of trade in recent decades (see Figure 8.1). In areas of provision where face-to-face human interaction is a less important component of production, the ability to digitize information and instantaneously transmit it across the globe greatly reduces the natural barriers to services trade (Sauve 2001; Freund and Weinhold 2002; Levy and Murnane 2005; Blinder 2007).

These 'dynamic' service sectors (Wren 2013) are thus more ICT intensive, more heavily traded internationally, and have a greater capacity for productivity growth than their less dynamic counterparts, in which face-to-face human interaction is a more important component of production. Potentially, therefore, they have the capacity to replace traditional manufacturing sectors as the primary engines of economic output and employment growth, thus reducing the starkness of the distributional trade-offs embodied in the trilemma. Expansion and growth in dynamic services obviously has direct effects on employment in the sectors in which it occurs. It can also, however, have indirect effects on employment in other, less dynamic sectors. Demand for many types of social, personal, and consumer services is income, as well as price, elastic (Kongsrud and Wanner 2005; Kalwji et al. 2007). Increased income from dynamic service sector expansion therefore allows for the possibility of a parallel expansion in these less productive sectors, without relying so heavily on relative wages and prices in these sectors remaining low. In other words, successful expansion in high productivity service sectors can reduce the starkness of the trade-off between the policy goals of employment creation and equality that is faced by governments in post-industrial economies. It can also, clearly, reduce the burden on individual taxpayers associated with the maintenance of larger public services sectors: in other words, it can render the 'social democratic' response to the trilemma more sustainable in a context of de-industrialization. I will argue in Section 8.3, however, that there is evidence to suggest that dynamic service sectors have skill requirements that differ significantly from those of manufacturing, and that the adaptation of education and training regimes to meet these new requirements may thus require significant social investment.

8.3 Social Investment and Dynamic Service Expansion

Any strategy for employment creation in high productivity service sectors must focus critically on the issue of skill formation, since the evidence suggests that the skills required for expansion in these sectors differ significantly from those that were important in the manufacturing golden age. As the data in Table 8.1 indicate, dynamic service sectors are the most ICT intensive of all economic sectors. This is significant for skills policy, since it is by now well established empirically, that ICT and college-educated labour are complements in production (see, for example, Autor, Levy, and Murnane 2003; Goos, Manning, and Solomons 2010; Michaels, Natraj, and Van Reenan 2010; Acemoglu and Autor 2011). As Autor, Levy, and Murnane (2003), point out, the new technology is highly effective at performing routine tasks which can be specified by stored instructions—even where the required programmes are highly complex (for example, bookkeeping or clerical work). As a result it acts as a substitute for labour in performing these tasks, which are typically carried out by workers at medium-skill levels (those with secondary, or some (but not complete) college education). It is less effective, however, at performing non-routine cognitive tasks requiring 'flexibility, creativity, generalized problem solving, and complex communications' (Autor, Levy, and Murnane 2003: 5) (what Hall and Soskice (2001) would describe as high-end general skills), rather it serves to complement the skills of the (typically college-educated) workers who perform those tasks. Faster access to more complete market information, for example, may improve managerial decision-making, but it cannot substitute for that decision-making. Since technology is a complement to, rather than a substitute for this type of human capital, therefore, investment in the new technology increases the demand for college-educated labour.

Successful expansion in ICT-intensive service sectors, therefore, is reliant on the existence of an adequate supply of workers with tertiary-level skills. In this regard, the skill requirements of the current era of service expansion differ significantly from those of the era of industrial expansion which preceded it. In the 1950s and 1960s, Fordist industrial expansion was associated with an increased demand for labour at low to medium skill levels—and was particularly notable for the existence of complementarities in production between low- and high-skilled industrial labour (see, for example, Wallerstein 1990). In contrast, successful expansion in high-end service sectors requires up-skilling, and increasing the numbers of workers receiving high quality tertiary education. There are few complementarities to low-skilled labour and they tend to be substituted out over time.

This underscores, of course, the importance of ensuring effective investment at the tertiary level, and also in facilitating tertiary enrolment and access. Recent research indicates, however, that it also implies a critical role for investment in schools-based learning beginning as early as the pre-primary level, since education at this level is increasingly regarded as a key determinant of tertiary outcomes—especially for children from lower-skilled households (see, for example, Cuhne and Heckman 2007; Heckman and Jacobs 2010).

So how well equipped are existing welfare production regimes to meet the skills demands of the service economy, and what are the implications for equality of the adaptation of skills regimes? The USA, in particular, has been relatively successful thus far at producing large numbers of high-quality college graduates. However, the private sector route to tertiary investment pursued in the USA, and other liberal regimes like the UK, in recent decades has had negative consequences in terms both of equality and efficiency. First, it is reliant on high levels of wage inequality that incentivize individual investment in (increasingly expensive) education (Ansell and Gingrich 2013; Wren 2013; Busemeyer and Iversen 2014). Second, it has resulted in an unequal distribution of skills and, given the increasing cost of private education, there is a high risk that this distribution will be replicated across generations (Duncan and Murnane 2011).

Finally, there is some evidence to suggest that in spite of the incentives for private investment existing in these regimes, overall levels of educational investment have been insufficient. Goldin and Katz (2008), for example, cite a failure of the US education system to provide an adequate supply of college-educated workers to keep pace with technological change, as one of the primary causes of the increase in inequality in that country at the end of the last century, while Wren, Fodor, and Theodoropoulou (2013) find that even in the highly decentralized wage setting environments found in liberal regimes, increases in public investment in school- and college-based education can have significant positive effects on employment in dynamic service sectors. As the data in Table 8.3 show, in the USA, and even more so in the UK, levels of tertiary enrolment fall well below those of Sweden.

The countries of Central and Northern Europe face a different set of challenges as regards educational policy. Here high levels of coordination in wage bargaining ensure higher levels of wage equality. One effect of this though is to reduce the incentives for private individuals to invest in higher level skills—since the relative rewards to such investment are substantially smaller. In these regimes, then, there is a risk of a shortage in the skills on which expansion in high-end knowledge intensive services relies, unless the government steps in to subsidize them (see Iversen and Soskice 2010, 2013; Ansell and Gingrich 2013; Wren, Fodor, and Theodoropoulou 2013).

In the social democratic regimes of Scandinavia, of course, this is what governments have traditionally done—providing high levels of investment in school- and college-based education all the way from the pre-primary to the tertiary level, which have resulted in high levels of tertiary enrolment (see Table 8.3). And this has facilitated the expansion of high-skilled employment in high-end service sectors (Wren 2013; Chapter 11, this volume). This strategy has several potential advantages in terms of equity. It does not rely on the existence of wage-premia for highly skilled workers to induce investment in higher level skills. It can facilitate greater equity of access to tertiary education—in the first place because that education is publicly financed, but also because the public financing of education for school-aged, and, even more critically pre-primary, children has knock-on effects on levels of equity in tertiary outcomes for children from different social backgrounds (see Heckman and Jacobs 2010). Finally, investment in early childhood education and care removes some of the costs of caring from women, increasing levels of equity between men and women in terms of access to labour markets, and facilitating women's labour force participation and employment.

Meanwhile, some continental European countries—like Germany—have traditionally combined high levels of coordination in wage setting with lower

Table 8.3. Variations in educational investment strategies

	Tertiary Enrolment (2007)	Total Investment in Tertiary Education (% GDP) (2005–10)	Public Investment in Tertiary Education (% Total) (2005–10)	D9D5 Ratio (2005–10)	Employment in Knowledge-Intensive Services (% Working-Age Population) (2005–10)
USA	65	3.12	42	2.33	30
UK	55	1.81	53	1.98	33
Germany	34	1.46	82	1.74	26
Netherlands	60	2.06	75	1.76	34
Sweden	73	2.12	89	1.66	34

Source: OECD and Brady, Huber, and Stephens (2014).

levels of public investment in tertiary and schools-based education, and levels of tertiary enrolment are relatively low (see Table 8.3). In the past, of course, as Hall and Soskice (2001) have influentially argued, this formed part of a highly effective educational strategy in which large proportions of the workforce participated in apprenticeship-based vocational training regimes which equipped workers with strong, firm, and sector-specific skills and formed the basis for comparative advantage in core areas of industrial production (for example, capital goods). The question, however, is whether this strategy remains sustainable in an era in which employment expansion increasingly relies on exploiting the complementarities between ICT and college-educated labour. Even in Germany, the archetype of the successful apprenticeship-based political economy, the proportion of workers employed in high-skilled industrial jobs has declined from 28 per cent in 1970 to 17 per cent in 2004, with a similar decline (from 31 per cent to 21 per cent) for medium-skilled workers (Wren 2013). The strategy pursued in the Netherlands, where high levels of investment in ICT and schools- and college-based education have been associated with high levels of highly-skilled service employment, stands in sharp contrast here (see also Wren 2013).

8.4 Conclusion

Thus the expansion of high productivity, ICT-intensive, traded service sectors may offer the promise of reducing the starkness of the service economy 'trilemma', but cross-national experiences suggest a potentially important role for social investment as governments manage the task of adapting the skills of the workforce to meet the needs of this economic transition.

Where high productivity service sectors emerge to replace declining industrial sectors as the engines of growth and employment, the constraints of the trilemma are relaxed along two dimensions. First, since the demand for many types of social and consumer services is income elastic, rising real incomes should facilitate the expansion of demand for and employment in these sectors without relying so heavily on keeping relative wages (and prices) low: in other words, the tightness of the trade-off between equality and employment growth in low productivity service sectors is reduced. Second, the income generated by high-end service expansion makes any level of public service provision more affordable in relative terms: in other words, the tax burden of the simultaneous pursuit of the goals of equality and employment creation is reduced.

Liberal (market-based) and social democratic (social investment-based) approaches to education and training have both been quite effective in developing workforces with the skills required for successful expansion in dynamic service sectors. These two strategies differ significantly, however, in their implications for inequality—in ways that partly mirror the original trilemma. Liberal regimes like the UK and USA have eschewed an integrated social investment approach to the problem of skill formation, and have relied instead on high levels of flexibility in wage setting, and highly inegalitarian wage structures, to incentivize private investment in education at all levels. This strategy has proved quite successful in providing highly skilled workers for expanding dynamic services industries, but at a cost of stark and growing inequities in educational and labour market outcomes.

The social democratic investment-based strategy, on the other hand, combining 'buffers' (Chapter 1, this volume) in terms of protections on the wages of low wage workers, with investment in the 'stock' (Chapter 1, this volume) of human capital from early childhood provision right through to the tertiary level, is associated simultaneously with higher levels of equality in educational and labour market outcomes, and higher levels of public spending to finance the pursuit of these goals. It's important to emphasize, however, that there are critical differences in the economic context described here, in which the ICT revolution has increased the feasibility of a growth strategy based on expansion in high productivity traded services sectors, and that considered in the original trilemma argument, in which the potential for this kind of expansion remained limited. This difference is important because, as is evidenced in the current context, public service sector expansion not only has direct effects on employment creation in public services sectors, but also, critically, can have important indirect effects (via skill formation) on the capacity for expansion in their high value-added private service sector counterparts. These effects reduce the tax burden on individuals and firms associated with a given level of spending on public service provision—hence reducing the starkness of the distributional trade-offs associated with the social democratic response to the trilemma, and increasing its economic (and arguably political) sustainability.

9

Towards Employment Insurance?

Günther Schmid

9.1 Introduction

The question mark in the title has been deliberately chosen. Of course, employment cannot be insured: full employment, that is, work for all to earn decent living wages has to be ensured through prudent monetary, financial, and economic policy, supported by labour market policy smoothing the efficient allocation of labour. However, we have to find an answer to the increasing risks of volatile income due to changing working times and varying limitations of employability over the life course. Unemployment is only an extreme case of these risks.

Over the life course we are confronted with various transition risks that endanger a full individual labour income: transitions from school to work become more and more critical, reflected in increasing youth unemployment, and skills—once acquired—do not hold for the whole life; transitions of changing working times in enterprises have to be managed; transitions from old to new technologies require risky restructurings that many firms cannot shoulder alone; starting a family with children is a far-ranging transition during any working life, which severely limits an individual's labour market capacities; obligations to care for ill or frail relatives from time to time require a smart transition management; the same holds true for people's increasing wishes for variable leisure times, especially in their mature years.

How to deal with those risks? Can we include them in existing unemployment insurance (UI) as already partly realized during the last decades, for instance in the form of part-time work or training allowances? Or can we get rid of these complications of coordinating work and life once and for all through an unconditional basic income for everybody? In the following I will argue for the first option, and I will suggest—despite the fuzzy terminology—to envisage a system of employment insurance because unemployment is only one of the serious labour income risks in the modern labour market. Thinking in terms of life-course risks has the additional advantage of keeping an eye on the links between various social insurance schemes, in particular on the link between employment and old age insurance.

The argument will be introduced by elaborating on the increasing variety of labour market risks (Section 9.2); considerable emphasis is then put on theoretical arguments for the inclusion of risks beyond unemployment into the social security system (Section 9.3); the third step delivers good practices or opportunities for including new risks into an extended system of UI (Section 9.4); the chapter concludes by re-emphasizing two essential elements for the paradigmatic shift towards employment insurance: making transitions pay and making the market fit for workers (Section 9.5).

9.2 Increasing Labour-Market Risks through Labour-Market Flexibilization

The flexibilization of the labour market goes on, and with this the increase of related labour market risks. In the second half of the twentieth century the regular working time was forty hours combining the eight-hour day with the five-day week. Moreover, unlimited or open employment relationships were the rule and men earning a living for the whole family were the role model. The fight for the thirty-five-hour week, for instance by the IG Metall trade union in Germany during the 1980s, was only an intermezzo. The average working time for full-time workers is back to a level of at least forty-one hours per week; however, this employment relationship is not the norm anymore.

Overtime is still the classic instrument for flexible working time; however, we observe an increasing share of unpaid overtime and for many modern employment relationships the borderlines between homework and labour market work become fuzzier. 'Irregular' working times like *shift-work, night-work, Saturday and Sunday work* are the rule for at least a quarter of employees. The increase of *part-time work* is almost endemic: in Germany, each second woman works less than thirty-two hours a week, and this trend is even spreading among men: one in ten men works part-time in Germany. *Temporary work,* either in the form of temp-agency work or fixed-term works contracts, is on the rise, especially among youths: about 40 per cent have a time-limited contract. *Own-account workers* make up an increasing share of the self-employed, many of them working up to eighty hours a week.

Thus, the delimitation of working time over the life course is on the rise in almost all developed countries. Yet the differences are huge and depend on the size of labour force participation (especially of women) and the kind of labour market institutions. There is strong evidence that 'flexible' jobs correlate with employment protection (Schmid 2011: 193). An international comparative perspective also shows that the share of involuntary part-time drops with the height of part-time work: involuntary part-time is far below 10 per cent in the two countries with the highest part-time rates (Switzerland and the Netherlands); in countries with low part-time rates like Bulgaria, Romania, and in the Mediterranean area the share of involuntary part-time is far beyond 50 per cent (Berkhout, Heyma, and Prins 2013). Furthermore, EU member states with high economic growth rates and elevated gross domestic product per capita display a high share of risky flexible employment relationships. Although this does not justify a causal reference, it suggests that risky flexible employment relationships might be a precondition for dynamic and prosperous economies (Schmid 2011).

What conclusion can be drawn from this stylized evidence? Companies obviously need greater flexibility—internal, external, numerical, or functional: the volatility of orders increases; new technologies have to be introduced; individual client preferences have to be accommodated; the work organization has to be made adaptable and linked to international networks. Workers need increasingly more time for family work, for care requirements of elderly relatives, for preparing vocational upgrading or change, for the increasing wealth of cultural events. The board of the largest—and still male-dominated—trade union in Germany, IG Metall, was surprised by the results of a representative survey: four out of five members wish to have temporarily the opportunity to reduce their working time to attend to their children or frail relatives (IG Metall Vorstand 2014). Moreover, young adults are more and more challenged to gain work experience with different employers. The risks related to such flexible employment relationships are alarming: declining real wages with little social protection, higher risk of unemployment, or extremely volatile income.

9.3 Why Should these New Social Risks Be Covered by Social Insurance?

Why should transition risks during the life course beyond involuntary unemployment be covered by social insurance? Currently we seem to experience the opposite: in almost all European member states insurance related benefits decline, even for the unemployed (Clasen and Clegg 2011). On the other hand, the 'German job miracle'—for instance—is to some extent the result of a successful inclusion, namely the coverage of declining income due to short-time work in recessions through the UI system (Schmid 2015: 84–6). Some countries also started to include training assistance covered by UI in labour market policies not only for the unemployed, but also for the re-employed to make their jobs more sustainable. Furthermore, activation measures for lone parents, for example, proved only effective so long as their support also covered childcare issues. Finally, so far all countries have failed to successfully 'activate' people with health problems or disability (Martin 2014: 27–8). The main reason for this failure is that conventional activation measures do not tackle the lack of capabilities related to the employment of these target groups—for instance, the required adjustment of workplaces to the work capacities of these people. In such cases, the activation slogan has to be reversed: rather than making workers fit for the market, the market has to be made fit for the workers (Gazier 2007). In other words: rather than requiring the individual to be 'adaptable' to changing market conditions, the new employment contract requires that employment practices be adapted to the circumstances of the individual (Deakin and Supiot 2009: 28).

From the perspective of social insurance theory (e.g. Barr 2001; Schmid 2008: 213–31, 2015), several reasons are apparent for an inclusion of risks into an extended UI system, which means not just providing basic income security through means-tested flat-rate payments, but status-related replacements of acquired wage income:

- First, individual and wage-related benefits can be calculated much easier and fairer than means-tested flat-rate benefits for which all household-related income streams have to be assessed. The German Hartz-IV system can be taken as an example of how complicated and costly means-tested procedures can be.

- Second, due to the property right established through wage-related and targeted insurance contributions, social insurance benefits are better protected against discretionary political decisions than benefits relying on general and not targeted taxes.

- Third, the incentive for social insurance benefits to work is stronger than for means-tested and (usually) flat-rate benefits, not least due to the entitlement effect because only formal and regular employment relationships ensure this re-entitlement.

- Fourth, the macroeconomic stabilization impact of wage-related replacements is higher than of means-tested and usually lower benefits.

- Fifth and so far neglected, positive externalities have to be considered, for example reducing deadweight losses from loan default, expanding access to credit (Hsu, Matsa, and Melzer 2014) and reducing cut-throat competition between workers in depressed labour markets (Lalive, Landais, and Zweimüller 2013).

- Sixth, research even shows that jobless people covered by UI remain healthier and more self-confident than jobless people without UI or only means-tested benefits (Schmid, 2008: 140–3).

A further general argument in favour of the insurance principle has to be added: any insurance induces potentially two behavioural responses: opportunism and trust. On the one hand, people tend to consider the insurance as a business deal—an investment for which they want something back, with a considerable value added and as soon as possible; in the opportunistic case they even tend to exploit the deal by inducing themselves the risky event either through careless conduct or fraud; this is the well-known *moral hazard* conjured in particular by mainstream economists. It is evident that such opportunistic behaviour requires control, in the case of unemployment insurance an effective public and/or private employment service.

However, often neglected, is the other possible behavioural response, that is, the willingness to consciously take the risk under the assumption of fair redistribution if the opportunities (chances) related to risk-taking do not succeed but fail; in other words (calculated) risk-taking on the basis of trust into security by solidarity. So, the other side of the coin is *innovative hazard*: if people can trust solidarity, they are more willing to take risks, for instance, the risk to invest in firm specific human capital (which reduces other job opportunities in the labour market), or the risk of investing into further training or even retraining (with unknown as well as uncertain returns), or the risk of voluntarily changing jobs (often connected with lower wages and unknown career opportunities). So, an extension of UI into a system of employment insurance has to be seen as a potential investment into more calculated risk-taking among a majority of workers (Sinn 1996; Bird 2001).

Against this argument, mainstream economists still tend to underestimate or even reject the investive function of (un)employment-related insurance. It is, however, a great mistake to view unemployment benefits as only a 'passive' transfer. Properly designed wage replacements are not only a fair compensation for people who become unemployed through no fault of their own but are also an 'active' investment in their productive job search. Evaluation studies—even from the Organisation for Economic Co-operation and Development (OECD)—demonstrate that unemployed with generous wage replacements in the first six to nine months find more productive jobs (higher wages) than the unemployed not covered by UI or covered only by means-tested benefits (Acemoglu and Shimer 2000; Gangl 2003). More importantly, these jobs are more sustainable and thus mitigate revolving-door effects, that is, leaving the benefit system and returning soon or entering another benefit system such as health or disability insurance (e.g. Tatsimaros 2006).

In contrast to the potential of an extended system of UI we observe diminishing returns of 'passive' as well as 'active' labour market policies. The last recession (2008/9) in particular reduced the stabilization impact of social policy in general and UI in particular (Clasen and Clegg 2011; European Commission 2013c). Most alarming, however, is the result of some recent comparative studies which clearly indicate the discouraging effects of recent labour market reforms on the innovative side of risk-taking: European labour markets did not become more dynamic despite deregulation, liberalization, or unprotected flexibilization. Related to Germany, for instance, it has been discovered that overall labour turnover declined from 8 to 6.5 per cent after the Hartz reforms despite the 'German job miracle' and that job tenure increased despite an increase in 'flexible' employment. The German labour market has become less efficient in reallocating workers as a result of intimidating labour market reforms that stifled risk-taking labour market behaviour (Giannelli, Jaenichen, and Rothe 2013; Knuth 2013). Moreover, the disciplining workfare policies in the majority of European welfare states did not only reduce transfer payments and thereby the stabilization impact of effective (consumer) demand but also diminished the dampening impact of activation policies on wage inequality (Rueda 2015). A vicious circle has been put in motion: wages at the top level increased due to decreasing competition among medium and high skilled workers, and wages at the low end or at the entry level decreased due to higher competition among low skilled or less experienced workers; lowering wages at the entry level again discourages labour mobility, which reduces labour market dynamics, and so on.

9.4 Which New Risks should Be Included in an Extended (Un)Employment Insurance?

Which life-course risks beyond unemployment should be included in an extended system of UI? Looking back to the brief overview of new social risks, it is in particular the spread of *part-time work* which entails not only high labour market risks (low wages, low probability of upward careers) but also the risks of low social protection in old age. Because part-time employment is mainly a female phenomenon, these risks are carried predominantly by women in an unjustified way. The main reason for part-time work is the reconciliation of family and occupation, especially during the rush hour of the life course between the ages of 30 and 50 years. In the meantime, however, part-time became economically suboptimal: the 'human capital' of women, which increased tremendously during the last decades, remains underutilized.

So far, most developed welfare states in Europe have reacted with some kind of wage-related parental leave allowances, partly compensated for either by health insurance, by special parental leave insurance (Sweden), general taxes (Germany) or subsidized individual saving accounts (Netherlands). Most of these systems still provide few incentives to equally share the parental risks between women and men. An average weekly working time of thirty-two hours for both parental partners during the family phase would be a solution.

One possible way to support such an option during the life course would be the inclusion of this risk of reduced employment capacity in a way analogue to short-time work covered by UI: the income loss induced by reduced working time could be compensated for by part-time unemployment benefits. Such an insurance benefit would also be helpful with care for frail elderly relatives which, for example in Germany, in three-quarters of cases is still provided within the family and again predominantly by women.

Temporary work, either in the form of temp-agency work or fixed-term contracts also contains high risks in terms of low wages and high probability of becoming unemployed. On the other hand, such employment relationships contribute to the required higher flexibility of the economy both on the demand side as well as on the supply side Most established UI systems have not yet been adapted to this new world of labour, as long-term employment relationships are still the underlying norm. In Germany, for instance, twelve months of regular employment within the last two years are required before entitlement to UI benefits. Many temp-agency workers or workers in fixed-term contracts do not jump over this benchmark when they become unemployed although they contributed to the UI-system. An extension of the two-year benchmark or reduction of the required length of the employment relationship would help. Furthermore, contributions to the UI system could be made contingent to the risks they are covering (following the principle of internalizing the risks), and the same holds true for wages and contributions to other wage-related social security systems (health and old age insurance).

The growing number of *own-account workers* among the self-employed is another source of social risks not yet properly covered by devices of collective risk management. Therefore, many take shelter in individual strategies of risk management, for instance through combining dependent wage work with risky self-employment. Part-time own-account work is in particular widespread among women, but unfortunately little information is available about the flows between inactivity, self-employment, dependent-employment, or a combination of all. An exception is a Swedish study which shows that most people enter self-employment by engaging first in combinatory work. Three 'transitional motivations' might explain this astonishing pattern: first, supplemented utility maximization, which means attaining psychological utility from self-employment by retaining at the same time economic security from dependent wage work (balancing flexibility and security on an individual level); second, providing a hedge against the potential risk of unemployment; third, reducing uncertainty associated with entry into self-employment or exit from self-employment (Schmid 2011: 196–7). Although little is known about the long-term consequences of these individual risk management strategies, anecdotal evidence clearly indicates that they often do not secure sustainable employment careers and in particular not the social protection in old age.

We also don't know how many more people would take this risk if a stronger social safety net would be available. What we know for sure is that unemployment is an important driver to take the risk, which however is not the best motivation ensuring a competitive and sustainable start-up.

A system of employment insurance could support or complement individual risk strategies related to self-employment in various ways. First, through virtual unemployment benefits, that is, by maintaining entitlements to UI-benefits until it is clear whether the start-up was successful or not; second, by including self-employed and own-account workers into the employment insurance system through mandatory contributions that might, at the beginning, be subsidized and should be made flexible, that is, conditional to the volatile income streams inherent in such forms of employment; third, through capitalization of UI benefit entitlements to compensate to some extent for the lack of capital at the beginning of start-ups; fourth, through professional counselling services provided by the public employment service. Finally, a universal (or citizenship-based) basic income security in old age as provided, for instance, in the Netherlands, Sweden, and Switzerland would effectively complement the collective element of managing these risks related to self-employment and own-account work.

Last but not least, the life-course risk of lacking or eroding skills and competences is a widening area of underdeveloped risk management. Remaining in our stylized fact-sheet framework, empirical evidence clearly shows that being low skilled implies having a high incidence and probability of being in and remaining stuck in a high-risk 'flexible' job: the low-skilled are correspondingly heavily underrepresented in insurance coverage (Schmid 2011: 179). It is also a well-established fact that St Martin's principle also holds true in continuous education and vocational training (Schmid 2015: 84–6). Many reasons explain this pattern and together build a structural blockade which is difficult to overcome: capital market restrictions, poaching or free-riding; mobility restrictions (especially for people with family obligations); the uncertainty of returns related to education and training investments both on the employer and employee side; and eventually information asymmetries.

This chapter is not the place to get through all these barriers (see Schmid 2015: 84–6). Space here allows only to argue on the plausibility level that including these risks into an extended UI system would help to manage these risks in a more efficient *and* equitable way. If we look on countries with high levels of continuous education and training, in particular for low-skilled and mature aged workers—Denmark, Sweden, and the Netherlands, in particular—we already find elements of social insurance inclusion: contributions of employers using temp-agency work into targeted training funds (the Netherlands), part-time training schemes, on-the-job training schemes, wage subsidies financed by the labour market training fund (Denmark), extension of UI-benefits conditional on participation in education or training programmes (Denmark), career transition agreements financed through collective funds and supported by the UI system (Sweden).

9.5 Conclusion

Many of the new labour market risks go beyond unemployment for which UI was once established. This development has been going on for a long time and, as a matter of fact, many countries have already adjusted to this situation by extending the spectrum of risks included into their social insurance—within or complementing their UI system. In this chapter I have argued that it is high time to go a step further. There is a need for a strategic shift from simply insuring unemployment towards a system of employment insurance that covers risks beyond unemployment, in particular risks related to critical transitions over the life course: transitions between full-time and part-time work, transitions between one occupation and another, transitions between care work and gainful employment, transitions between full work-capacities and partial work-capacities. Many of these transitions can or could be organized within stable employment relationships, thereby avoiding the exclusionary tendencies of non-standard employment. However, if it comes to breakdowns of this relationship either through external shocks, through mismanagement, or simply through individual misfortune or changing preferences, a broader set of income security than full-time unemployment benefits has to be provided.

This paradigmatic shift requires, first of all, a shift from stocks to flows (see Chapter 1, this volume). In other words, what is needed is a *career orientation* which strives for *making the most critical transitions pay* during the life course through securing the related income risks. One promising example is public support of lifelong learning, especially (but not exclusively) for the low-skilled. The benefit to society would be enhanced mobility, in particular in the form of mobility chains that open up new ports of entry for outsiders. Other examples related in particular to 'flexible' jobs like part-time, own-account work, and temporary jobs have been mentioned. Modern insurance theory not only hints at possible distorting effects of insurance through *moral hazard* but also to positive risk-taking innovations that can be a wellspring of economic dynamism and prosperity.

The second essential element for the required paradigmatic shift is to overcome inequalities and risk aversion through *capacity building*; for instance, through stepping stones (e.g. subsidized employment targeted to the specific life course risks, or conditional or virtual unemployment benefits); through enhancing general knowledge, competences, and skills over the life course; or through reasonable adjustment of workplaces, in other words: *through making the market fit for workers*. In this perspective, not only unemployment benefits but also any benefits maintaining and enhancing employability have to be considered as 'active' and not as 'passive' security. In other words: as an *investment* in the job search capacity of individuals, the matching capacity of the labour market, the employability of the 'labour force', the quality and productivity of work, and—last but not least—as an investment into the sovereignty of individuals over their life courses.

10

Social Investment and Childcare Expansion

A Perfect Match?

Margarita León

10.1 Introduction

Early childhood education and care (ECEC) has come to the forefront of policy discourse and action as part of a wider attempt to recalibrate developed welfare states through a social investment perspective in childcare and education services. Converging socioeconomic and demographic trends underpin discourse and action in this field, putting the question of who looks after the children at the centre of public debate and policy innovation. This 'politicization of childhood' (Jenson 2008) has become a major topic in emergent social policy paradigms (Esping-Andersen et al. 2002; Jenson 2010; Bonoli 2013).

By emphasizing equal opportunities in life rather than life outcomes, the underlying goal becomes that of 'preparing rather than repairing' (Morel, Palier, and Palme 2012c), which to a certain extent resembles Hacker's (2002) advocacy for pre-distribution. In this chapter I will firstly present the main challenges and dilemmas that have given a prominent place to early years education and care within the social investment paradigm. The chapter will then briefly echo certain controversy in relation to the policy directions that investing in children might take. Finally, reflecting on Hemerijck's framework, the chapter analyses expansion and institutional diversity in ECEC to claim that whilst there is a visible trend towards increasing spending and coverage in ECEC provision in most European Union (EU) and Organisation for Economic Co-operation and Development (OECD) countries, the appropriate complementarity of stocks (labour market integration), flows (human capital gains), and buffers (securing income protection for vulnerable families) will differ under different institutional, economic, and cultural conditions.

10.2 Investing in Early Years and Its Critics

Research from as disparate disciplines as neuroscience, psychology, economics, politics, sociology, and social policy has come together to prove positive links between investment in ECEC and female labour force participation; fertility dynamics; children's opportunities in life; and productivity imperatives in the knowledge-based economy.

Lack of adequate institutional support to the reconciliation of work and family life usually acts as a deterrent to the participation of women in the labour market and to having children. Women who anticipate a high conflict between the spheres of employment and family life are either less likely to be employed or to 'resolve' the conflict by not having children (Brewster and Rindfuss 2000; Gauthier 2007; Esping-Andersen 2009; Kamerman and Moss 2009; Boje and Ejnraes 2011; Budig, Misra, and Boeckmann 2012; Drobnic and León 2014). There is also a range of cross-discipline research which finds that early childhood is a key period in life when opportunities related to human capital are developing. Investment in ECEC seeks, from this point of view, to 'level the playing field' by minimizing the 'accident of birth' to break the intergenerational transmission of inequalities and ensure that children from different socioeconomic and ethnic backgrounds have access to primary social goods. To the extent that the second demographic transition is widening social class disparities in children's resources, investing in ECEC as a way of compensating for the loss of parental resources of the more disadvantaged children and their impact on children's cognitive development and educational achievement becomes a more pressing goal (McLanahan 2004; Esping-Andersen 2009). In addition, the European Strategy for Cooperation in Education and Training—ET 2011 (Urban et al. 2011)—emphasizes those strong connections between productivity and investment in early age. Making a radical switch with traditional literature in the economics of education, scholars such as Heckman, Pinto, and Savelyev (2013) contend that rather than cognitive knowledge, it is non-cognitive traits, such as motivation, self-esteem or leadership, mainly configured in our early years, which determine our productivity capacity later in life. In this way, the interactions between care, education, and the economy shape the debate on care for the young ones. This is also in line with Sen and Nussbaum's (1993) capabilities approach in that access to good quality education and availability of policies to ease the work–family conflict both become a precondition to achieve agency (Hobson 2014).

The scale of the challenge has thus pushed many national governments and international agencies to rethink welfare protection for children and families from either developed or developing countries. There is now a widespread consensus that Fordist family policies are ill-prepared to confront these challenges and that enhancing human capital, capacitating women whilst at the same time securing income protection for vulnerable individuals, are now key goals. International organizations (see, for instance, Starting Strong OECD reports) have played a key role in framing the ideological contours of the social investment perspective on ECEC providing for common solutions to shared problems.

This evidence is, nonetheless, confronted with different interpretations. To begin with, views as to whether ECEC attendance may have compensating effects for children's development are somehow mixed (Anderson et al. 2003). The assessment of publicly funded comprehensive preschool programmes for children aged 3 to 5 at risk of poverty in the USA, for instance, seems to be inconclusive. The limited focus on short-term cognitive measures appears to be inadequate for drawing conclusions about their long-term impact on the wellbeing of children. In their meta-analysis of sixteen studies, Anderson and colleagues (2003) conclude that even though ECEC interventions improved the cognitive and non-cognitive abilities of children who used the provision, which signals subsequent economic, social, and health success, they could not come to any clear conclusions as to the key features of effective and efficient programmes. In a similar vein, research assessing the benefits of early formal schooling does not seem to reach clear causations (Sharp 2002). Some other studies suggest that children require a minimum level of support from the home environment to benefit from higher quality care (Vandell et al. 2010; Anders et al. 2012). For example, conditional transfers that grant cash benefits to low-income households on the condition that parents invest this money in their children's education and health have been found to be successful in empowering families to provide favourable environments for child development, as can be observed in some Latin American countries (see Chapter 25, this volume). From a more critical perspective, scholars pertaining to the new sociology of childhood, often echoing Bourdieu's critical theory, denounce the uncritical embracing of the liberal logic that arguments in favour of ECEC expansion can encapsulate. The focus on children's agency allows these authors to link discourses and debates around ECEC with broader questions of universalism/particularism and structure/agency (James and Prout 2005; Graham, 2011). The predominance of 'investment' and economic rationales in some key arguments in favour of ECEC expansion (especially from the part of international bodies such as the OECD, World Bank, or the EU) reveals for some an understanding of early years' education as an instrumental means to productive gains through high returns on investment and macro-economic growth. By doing so, some authors would argue, it strips education of its social and psychological meaning for the individual child, ignoring the other key function of education in developing into mature and engaged citizens that can articulate their demands and participate in democratic society (Aubrey 2008).

Furthermore, the 'social investment' premise generates important trade-offs and tensions under conditions of permanent austerity in welfare states (Pierson 1996, 1998). The 'austerity turn' since the onslaught of the global financial crisis in 2007, with its 'collateral effects' on social spending, is an economic doctrine at odds with the social investment philosophy. In other words, the interconnections between macroeconomic, fiscal, employment, and social policies are so strong that a well-intended social investment message will face a wall rather than a window if confronted with the pressures for balanced budgets and deficit reductions endorsed by austerity politics (see Chapter 1, this volume). Therefore, the integration of apparently competing paradigms, that is, between market deregulation and social investment policies or between compensatory and preventive welfare, is a puzzle worth exploring (see Cantillon and Van Lancker 2013, and Chapter 5, this volume, for the 'Matthew Effect' risk of investing in childcare).

Nevertheless, this simultaneous change in the paradigm governing childcare and a common trajectory in the transformation of ECEC in Europe and around the globe is taking place, departing from very different starting points in the different countries. The common set of ideas, benchmarks, and policy prescriptions regarding ECEC at EU and OECD levels points towards a shared trajectory of policy change, although the appropriate complementarity of stocks, flows, and buffers differ under different macro and meso conditions. Developments have not been uniform regarding both the pace of transformation and the specific path taken (Oberhuemer 2010; Morgan 2012; Eurydice 2013; León 2014). Certainly, at the level of intervention and implementation of the policy paradigm, the actual expansion of ECEC (and, crucially, the way in which it expands) as part of a wider social investment approach, depend on a number of 'varieties' of cultural, political, and economic structures embedded within institutions that conform to the different welfare-regime types and that are pretty much anchored at the nation state and even subnational levels. As a consequence, different patterns and determinants of ECEC developments are to be expected cross-nationally and cross-regionally. Moving one step further, where comparative social policy analysis and policymaking meet, it is well known that welfare efforts in one direction do not necessarily produce the expected results. As a matter of fact, the virtuous intentions behind new social policies are seldom achieved to full effect. The relevant question then becomes: how do specific policies perform in reaching the anticipated outcomes?

When we move beyond assessing increases in spending in the early years to evaluate aspects related with quality of provision and content, an array of central issues are at stake: from preschool entry age, length of schooldays, and balance between free play and structured curriculum, to expertise and requirements of staff, the public/private welfare mix, and the complementarity between ECEC provision and other work–family reconciliation and care-related policies (parental leaves, cash for care, and working time arrangements in particular). Section 10.3 considers both quantitative and qualitative changes in early years' education and care in a number of countries. As a general trend, the shift from an assistential approach to childcare to a more educational focus, particularly for children aged 3 and older, has implied in most countries an improvement with regard to universal access and conditions of the service. In this respect, a significant degree of convergence in preschool provision is observed. Distinctive 'models of care' are, however, prevalent for formal and informal arrangements for very young children.

10.3 Diversity in ECEC Developments

Figure 10.1 shows that, as an overall trend, public spending in ECEC has increased in most countries although a high degree of cross-country variation remains. Several OECD countries have recently invested strongly in public financing of ECEC, commencing from very low levels. Still very few nations reach the target of 1 per cent of gross domestic product (GDP) as set up by the United Nations Children's Fund (UNICEF) with the clear long-term exception of Denmark. The 2008 financial crisis has in some European countries slowed down the incremental path of the early 2000s. This is particularly the case of Italy and the UK. In others, however, the economic downturn has not affected this growth even in countries with severe cuts in public spending such as

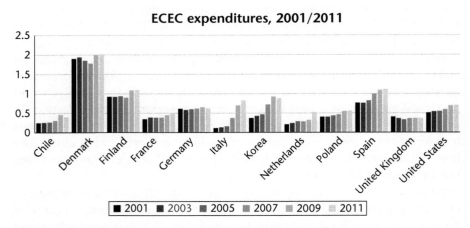

Figure 10.1. Expenditure on early childhood education and care

Source: Own elaboration from OECD family database—Indicator PF3.1—<http://www.oecd.org/els/family/database.htm>.

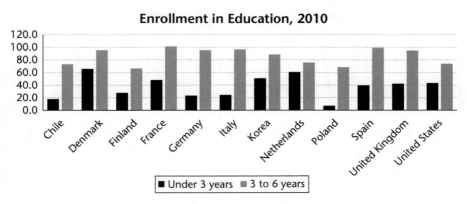

Figure 10.2. Enrolment in education

Spain, indicating a certain level of recalibration in welfare policies (León and Pavolini 2014). The extent to which quality aspects are being compromised in the long run by through-the-back-door retrenchment measures such as cuts in personnel, worsening pay conditions, or increasing staff/child ratios remains to be tested.

The 'investing in children' new blueprint might follow only to a certain extent the pathways of welfare regime classification. Two designs in opposite ends are usually identified by the literature, that is, the social-democratic approach where investment takes on mainly the supply side to facilitate access to a high quality system, to the liberal one where emphasis is placed on the demand side following choice-driven criteria whilst the supply side is usually left to the market. In between these two poles, a myriad of policy solutions is found and regime-types are somehow hard to identify (Mahon 2013). As shown in Figure 10.2, an increasing dividing line in ECEC provision in most countries is the separation between preschool attendance for children aged 3 and older and childcare services for the under 3s.

In countries such as Germany, Great Britain, Spain, and, to a certain extent, also Italy, improving ECEC for older children (just below school entry age) is altering, in a way, one of the founding stones of the Conservative, Liberal, and Mediterranean welfare states. States are adopting a much more proactive role in their responsibility towards children. By increasing state funding, regulation, and resources on expanded preschool years, the gap between non-compulsory but mostly universal educational provision and purely child-care services for smaller children has widened in most countries. This fact calls for more nuanced interpretations of what appears as straightforward expansionary trends. Differences in the form of provision according to children's age can be seen in Table 10.1. It affects from the definition of rights and

Table 10.1. ECEC institutional design in several European countries

Country	Organization & Governance		Providers & Funding		Access	
	0–3	3–6	0–3	3–6	0–3	3–6
Denmark	Crèches & Childminding. Responsibility of Ministry of Interior and Social Affairs.	Kindergarten 3+ Aged-integrated centres (0–6) Børnehaveklasser (preschool). Responsibility of Ministry of Interior and Social Affairs (3–6). Preschool (Børnehaveklasser) responsibility of Ministry of Education	Majority of provision is public (70 per cent). Private (non-profit) providers highly subsidized by the municipality (around 70 per cent of the costs). Preschool is part of the education system and fully funded by the state.		Universal entitlement to childcare provision Enrolment: 66 per cent.	Universal. Full-day provision. Preschool has been compulsory since 2009. Enrolment: 91 per cent.
Germany	Kinderkrippe (infant/ toddler centre). ECEC within the child and youth welfare sector. Federal Ministry for Family Affairs, Länder and municipalities share regulatory responsibilities; municipalities organize and manage funding of 0–6 ECEC.	Kindergarten.	Public funding in 0–3 is very limited. Around 2/3 of under-3s are in private non-profit (mostly religious) organizations but subsidized by the state. Around 1/3 of under-3s use municipal provided organizations. High regional disparities between East and West.		No legal entitlement. Very diverse forms of provision. Demand met by private care, Tagesmütter (care in private homes). Enrolment: 18 per cent. Regional variation western Länder (10 per cent), eastern (41 per cent).	Universal entitlement for at least four hours a day. In most states, free provision. Enrolment: 93 per cent.

Spain	Educación infantil/ Guarderías (crèches). Ministry of Education, Regional Gov. and Municipalities.	Educación Infantil (Universal Infant Education) (3+). Ministry of Education and regional governments.	Public funding is limited. Mainly private or externalized public services. High regional disparities.	Full state funding for 3+. The state assigns the budget to the regional governments.	No legal entitlement. Enrolment: 37 per cent.	Universal entitlement, but not compulsory. Enrolment: close to 100 per cent on a full-time basis.
England	Nurseries/ childminding. Department for Education, regulated by the national agency Ofsted	Early Years Curriculum (EYC) (3+).	Public sector involvement for specifically designed services. Voluntary sector services publicly subsidized; private sector services are fee-paying.	EYC universal entitlement for all preschool children (3+) to fifteen hrs/week in any EYC setting. Full state funding for 4+.	No legal entitlement. Enrolment: 41 per cent.	Universal and voluntary entitlement for 4+. Enrolment (4–6): 93 per cent.

Note: Categories for enrolment correspond to 2008 (OECD 2008, family database).

Source: Own elaboration from León, Ranci, and Rostgaard (2014b: 46–8).

responsibilities, to governance, private sector involvement, and enrolment rates (León, Ranci, and Rostgaard 2014a). For younger children the emphasis continues to be placed on the care dimension of the provision, and thus the definition of the quality criteria and/or standards for ECEC (qualification requirements of staff for instance) is usually weaker than in preschool provision. The mixed economy of welfare is also much more convoluted in childcare for the under 3s. Furthermore, the working conditions of preschool teachers are in most countries equivalent to primary school teachers in terms of pay, career promotion, and working time, resulting in higher standards of professionals and a much lower staff turnover when compared with carers in childcare services (León, Pavolini, and Rostgaard 2014b: 52). This wider cross-national variation and lower degree of standardization on services for very young children is a main reason for many organizations to advocate for the integration of ECEC into mainstream educational systems (see, for instance, European Commission 2011a, 2011b).

10.4 Conclusion

The social change embodied in relocating the care and education of very young children from families to different forms of collective provision involves a policy change of considerable magnitude. To the extent that we are still at the problem definition stage (Mahoney 2012) and that ECEC seems to be in a privileged position with regard to future directions of welfare states and social spending, research devoted to clarify narratives, goals, processes, and outcomes are needed. Different institutional and policy legacies lead to complexity and diversity (Streeck and Thelen 2005) and, hence, on rare occasions, a perfect match between a policy problem and a corresponding solution can be identified. An interesting question then becomes how do complex sets of institutional diversity, including here the framing force of norms and values (Schmidt 2008, 2010) coincide to provide for specific outcomes? In this sense, in the field of early years' education and care there might be opportunities for change-generating actions, in Streeck and Thelen's terms (Streeck and Thelen 2005). Following on from Hemerijck's 'flow', 'stock', and buffers' framework, I have argued in this chapter that whilst there is a visible trend towards increasing spending and coverage in ECEC provision in most EU and OECD countries, the extent to which investment in early childhood education is able to serve the multiple purpose of better parenting and work/family balance (as 'flow'), raising human capital (as 'stock'), and securing income protection of families (as 'buffer') is dependent on the quality-related aspects of the provision on the one hand, and on the complementarity of other closely related social policy mechanisms on the other. The path for institutional innovation in the case of preschool is more clearly drawn and fits within the spirit of the social investment paradigm. The gains of service attendance for infants and very young children are, however, less convincing, and public intervention has been much more modest and thus the room for cross-country variation is much wider. It is in this latter case where the set of encompassing policies addressing children's needs, work/family balance conflicts, and families' well-being are particularly relevant.

11

Addressing Human Capital Risks and the Role of Institutional Complementarities

Verena Dräbing and Moira Nelson

11.1 Introduction

This chapter elaborates on how to address human capital risks throughout the life course and therefore promote social investment. The chapter determines that only a comprehensive social investment approach (SIA) can truly address the challenges that exist in accumulating and preserving human capital. The necessity to be comprehensive arises not only from the inability of any particular policy to address all risks at all times. In a more fundamental sense, the effectiveness of any given policy depends on the existence of the other social investment policies in place.

To flesh out our argument, we employ the concepts of 'buffer', 'stock', and 'flow' (Hemerijck 2012a, 2015) which express the different ways that social investment policies address risks associated with human capital: stock facilitates skill acquisition; flow enables smooth transitions, thus reducing the risk of skill atrophy due to labour market absence; and buffer ensures stable income streams, thus protecting health, improving skill matching, and promoting innovative risk-taking. Having reviewed the ways in which social investment can function, we introduce the concept of institutional complementarity to discuss the relationship between the stock, flow, and buffer functions of social investment. In order to substantiate our resulting claim that a comprehensive SIA is most effective, we examine the relationship between three sets of social investment policies and related employment outcomes, including a more targeted discussion of the Swedish case as an example of a comprehensive approach. We conclude by reflecting both on the contingencies underlying institutional complementarities and the political feasibility of a comprehensive SIA.

11.2 Investing in Human Capital over the Life Course

The view of human capital as a productive factor is the lynchpin of the SIA. The Organisation for Economic Co-operation and Development (OECD) defines human capital as 'the knowledge, skills, competencies embodied in individuals that facilitate the creation of personal, social and economic well-being' (OECD 2001: 18). Beyond skills and knowledge, human capital is often defined to include health (Schultz 1961), since being healthy is a precondition for all other activities. The concepts of stock, flow, and buffer elucidate the different functions of social investment (Hemerijck 2012a, 2015) and we narrow in on how these functions address human capital risks throughout their life course. To begin, being able to function in society, for example as a student or job-seeker, depends necessarily on a certain level of physical and psychological health; health in turn derives largely from gaining the financial means to fulfil basic needs such as food, shelter, and social integration. In addition, financial resources are necessary to support a comprehensive job search and encourage people to take the risks involved in *inter alia* starting a business or earning another degree (see Chapter 9, this volume). When social investment policies provide income protection and therefore buffer, they are capacitating people to participate in these activities (Hemerijck 2015: 248). Without buffering, health declines, households slip into poverty, workers accept jobs below their skill level, and investments are not made due to a necessarily myopic focus on day-to-day living.

Beyond health, human capital can be thought of more directly in relation to the production process as the skills and knowledge workers bring to their job. Acquiring this form of human capital is a long-term process, whereby basic cognitive skills enable the acquisition of other skills such as literacy and so on. In this way, human capital acquisition can be seen as a dynamic and cumulative process (Heckman 2000). This understanding of human capital corresponds to the stock function of social investment, which refers to policies that invest in the skills and knowledge of a person. To the extent that education policies at various stages of the life course fail to deliver quality education or individuals fail to advance in and cannot re-enter the education system, skill acquisition does not occur and human capital stock remains underdeveloped.

Moreover, once skills and knowledge have been acquired, they cannot be stored in a warehouse like many types of physical capital. Rather, skills tend to atrophy, or deteriorate, if they are not used leading to scar effects (Gangl 2006) and such non-use is endemic in periods of labour market absence. The risk of skill atrophy is addressed when policies smooth labour market transitions or enable flow. This is accomplished by making the most efficient use and allocation of labor resources over the life course in support of high levels of labor market participation, the reintegration of school-leavers, unemployed, parents and especially working mothers with important unpaid care and parenting responsibilities, older worker, and the disabled, during precarious transitions.   (Hemerijck 2015: 248)

Buffering may indirectly enable flow by improving job matching, though it can arguably undermine flow if job-seekers hold out for jobs that no longer exist. In this way, flow is more geared towards aligning the interests of workers with the needs of the market. Without policies that facilitate flow, individuals face high and growing difficulties finding suitable jobs, become stigmatized as long-term unemployed, or exit the labour market entirely.

It remains a pressing question how to go about capacitating these functions of social investment in practice. A first step involves specifying policies that advance the stock, flow, and buffer functions of social investment. The literature recommends the following types of policies:

- Education policies (e.g. early childhood education and care (ECEC), primary, secondary, tertiary, lifelong learning)
- Select labour market policies (e.g. active labour-market policies (ALMPs), short-term unemployment benefits)
- Poverty alleviation policies (e.g. social assistance, housing benefits)
- Employment-centred family policies (e.g. ECEC, parental leave)

These policies have been found to bolster employment and employment in good jobs in particular (Nelson and Stephens 2012). Moreover, the literature expounds on how these policies often function in tandem with each other (Esping-Andersen 2002; Nelson and Stephens 2012; Huber and Stephens 2015). Section 11.3 draws on the concept of institutional complementarity in order to flesh out the interdependencies between these policies and their associated functions.

11.3 Designing a Social Investment Approach and Institutional Complementarities

Complementarity in the most basic sense refers to a 'relationship or situation in which two or more different things improve or emphasize each other's qualities' (Stevenson 2010: 356). With respect to stock, flow, and buffer, one may speak of there being institutional complementarities to further emphasizing any particular function due to the enduring reliance on each function over the life course. The cumulative nature of skill acquisition means that investing in the stock of young children magnifies the effect of policies for older children and so on (Cunha et al. 2006). In turn, both buffer and flow protect human capital investments such that promoting each function in earlier periods boosts the effectiveness of promoting each respective function at later points. Complementarities also arise as a matter of policy design, whereby individual policies complement each other by addressing different risks.

Complementarities also exist *between* the buffer, stock, and flow functions (De Deken 2014; Hemerijck 2015). Buffering policies can be seen as setting the stage for skill acquisition, or stock. Financial security enables people to initiate educational investments and to maintain the healthy lifestyle necessary to attend school (Huber and Stephens 2015). Ensuring a steady income stream also improves flow by enabling people to conduct a thorough job search, thus raising their chances of finding a suitable job (Hughes, Peoples, and Perlman 1996). Further, by raising human capital stock, workers gain the know-how and skills to both manage their health and navigate complex labour markets (Fugate, Kinicki, and Ashforth 2004), thereby promoting buffer and flow, respectively; the returns to flow also increase if human capital stock is greater. The nature of the complementarities within and between buffer, stock, and flow are summarized in Table 11.1.

Table 11.1. Institutional complementarities within and between buffer, stock, and flow

How ↓ complements ➡	Buffer	Stock	Flow
Buffer (e.g. social assistance, social insurance)	• *Provides financial security at an earlier time point, which improves the effectiveness of buffering at later time points* • *Provides financial security after social risks where other buffering policies do not*	• Provides financial security necessary to uphold health and thus participation in school and work • Provides financial security necessary for innovative risk-taking	• Provides financial security necessary to uphold health, thus enabling people to adjust to change and find work–life balance • Provides financial security necessary for a successful job search • Provides financial security necessary for innovative risk-taking
Stock (e.g. investments in public education, retraining programmes for the unemployed)	• Provides skills and knowledge on how to both live healthily and save for risky situations	• *Provides skills and knowledge that complement other earned skills and knowledge* • *Provides skills and knowledge that facilitate the learning process*	• Provides skills and knowledge on how to enter competitive and changeable labour markets
Flow (e.g. job-seeker assistance, day care)	• Facilitates transitions that secure market income and thus requalify workers for social insurance	• Facilitates transitions into school or work where training may occur	• *Facilitates transitions in situations where other flow policies do not*

131

There exists a rich literature from comparative political economy that lends insights into the nature of institutional complementarities (Crouch et al. 2005). The level of analysis remains a matter of debate: do complementarities operate at the systems level or rather at the level of a given policy? Does complementarity imply mutual dependence, whereby the one part influences the functioning of another, or simply similarity? Are complementarities inherent or rather do they depend on context and develop over time as the result of political processes? The Varieties of Capitalism approach, for instance, suggests that coordination problems may arise in promoting stock and flow simultaneously because of commitment problems between workers and employers (Hall and Soskice 2001). Various regulations and institutions are necessary to address these problems.

Recent socioeconomic transformations suggest that the complementarities within and among stock, flow, and buffer are particularly pronounced in today's context. The increased importance of employment levels to other social and economic objectives such as poverty and growth draw attention to factors that support employment, among which human capital policies are of key importance. The rise of the knowledge economy increases the level of skills and knowledge required for labour market participation (Nelson 2010), thereby raising the salience of accumulating and preserving human capital. Tertiary education and lifelong learning are particularly important to encourage the expansion of high value-added services (Chapter 8, this volume). Moreover, population ageing underscores the importance of labour market participation for the sustainability of the welfare state. Rising dependency ratios increase the urgency to capacitate labour market entry to ensure the future tax base (Bongaarts 2004). In this way, the particular gains to be reaped from promoting the complementarities detailed in Table 11.1 depend on the particular salience of human capital in today's context.

In order to substantiate the claim that there are gains to promoting complementarities within and between stock, flow, and buffer, Section 11.4 takes an empirical perspective. In particular, correlations between sets of social investment policies and related employment outcomes are plotted in order to enable a discussion of these policies' stock, flow, and buffer functions and their effectiveness.

11.4 Gauging Institutional Complementarities

Capacitating the stock, flow, and buffer functions of social investment simultaneously addresses human capital risks and therefore bolsters employment. This section takes on the task of evidencing this claim by considering available samples of advanced industrialized countries. Figures 11.1, 11.2, and 11.3

correlate policy mixes representing investments in stock, flow, and buffer policies with employment outcomes. Figure 11.1 examines the relationship between social investment policies and quality employment. From there, the analysis turns to how the stock, flow, and buffer functions of social investment policies work together to address the needs of two particular risk groups, mothers and the low-skilled. Available data on policies from earlier periods are included and averaged so as to capture the full range of policies taken up by those in the labour force today. The 'Swedish Model' is often seen as exemplary (Esping-Andersen 2009; Morel, Palier, and Palme 2012a; White 2012) because of its strong emphasis on human capital investment and reconciliation of work and care policies, and more detailed information is provided on the Swedish case.

To begin, social investment policies are expected to promote high quality employment by building up and protecting human capital through their stock, flow, and buffer functions (Hemerijck 2015). Figure 11.1 plots education-related expenditures against employment in knowledge-intensive employment, understood as quality employment because such jobs involve higher workplace autonomy and wages (Nelson and Stephens 2012). The marker size reflects the level of the short-term unemployment replacement rate.

Before interpreting the figure, it is useful to elaborate on the expected functions of the included policies. ECEC, public education, and ALMPs raise the stock of the (future) workforce by promoting skill acquisition. Unemployment insurance buffers income streams, therefore allowing workers to maintain a decent standard of living and conduct in a thorough job search. These policies also promote flow since their duration is limited; ECEC too promotes flow by occupying children and therefore enabling parents to return to their jobs.

Figure 11.1 reveals a positive relationship between education-related expenditures and knowledge intensive employment. Sweden reveals the highest level of investment in skill acquisition. In addition to high investment in skill acquisition, Sweden and Denmark also share relatively high short-term unemployment replacement rates; to some degree the Netherlands and then France also demonstrate this propitious combination. The remaining countries demonstrate noticeably lower investment in one or both types of policies.

Turning to Sweden, the extent to which Sweden invests in stock is evident foremost in terms of overall public educational expenditure (6.8 per cent of GDP in 2011 compared to an OECD average of 5.6 per cent) (OECD 2014d). This difference can be explained by investment in tertiary education. Tertiary education is free of charge and 65 per cent of students in post-secondary education received study grants or loans in 2010 (Statistics Sweden 2013), resulting in quite equal opportunities to access education.

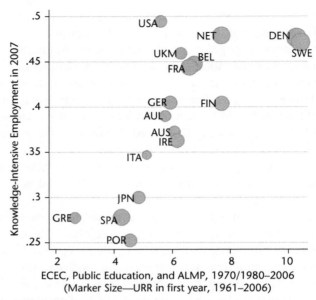

Figure 11.1. Boosting high-quality employment through stock, buffer, and flow

Source: All data comes from the Comparative Welfare States (CWS) data set (Brady, Huber, and Stephens 2014). Knowledge-intensive employment (kis2e) is measured as the percentage of the labour force. The x-axis is a composite measure of ECEC, public education at all levels, and ALMP expenditures, all as a percentage of gross domestic product (GDP) summed and averaged from 1970 (for education) or 1980 (for ALMP and ECEC) (or earliest available) to 2006. The markers are weighted by the one-year unemployment replacement rate.

High investment correlates with high attainment across all social groups. Those with at least upper secondary reached 91 per cent for women and 86 per cent for men in 2012 (Statistics Sweden 2014: 29). The Swedish school system tries to increase equality by offering compulsory schooling from age 7 to 16 (Eurydice 2014) in a non-selective system: first choices for school types are at the age of 16 and prior class selection is not performance-based (OECD 2014b). Although overall school quality and inequality resulting from free school choice received criticism (Skolverket 2012; EU Network of Independent Experts 2014; OECD 2014b), Sweden does manage to decrease inequality in outcomes across students of different backgrounds to a comparably strong extent (Skolverket 2012; OECD 2014b). School-based vocational training dominates, yet in 2008 apprenticeships have been introduced on the upper secondary and post-secondary level to smooth the school-to-work transition (Statistics Sweden 2013).

Investing in stock continues after workers have left school and entered the labour market. Sweden has a long tradition of high investment in ALMPs (Bonoli 2012). The job guarantee programme offers 16–24-year-olds unemployed for more than three months, support and training in the form of needs assessments, work experience placements, internships, financial support for start-ups, and access to education and training (Eurofound 2012). The focus of ALMPs for 15–24-year-olds is mostly on labour market services and less on training (Statistics Sweden 2013), thereby exhibiting a strong emphasis on the flow function.

The Swedish unemployment insurance scheme buffers by upholding basic health standards and capacitating workers to forego bad job offers, and promotes flow by limiting the duration of such policies. Over time, eligibility criteria to second pillar schemes have been tightened and conditionality has increased earning, suggesting a shift from flexicurity towards workfare (Bengtsson 2014). Such a shift highlights tensions between the buffer and flow functions. Decreasing generosity increases pressure on individuals to accept job offers, therefore increasing flow, but, past a certain point, relaxing the buffer function leads to poverty, poor health, and skill atrophy, as people are forced to accept jobs below their skill level and with low wages.

Beyond expanding good jobs, social investment is also purported to help disadvantaged groups, such as mothers and the low-skilled, to become employed at all. Policies that help parents combine work and family, such as ECEC and generous parental leave, raise mothers' employment (Nelson and Stephens 2013). These policies can also be seen to fulfil the stock, flow, and buffer functions: ECEC invests in human capital stock of children, both ECEC and parental leave enable parents to re-enter the labour market, either by providing alternative carers or legitimating short periods of labour market absence, and parental leave buffers by providing income-related transfers.

Figure 11.2 demonstrates that countries which provide generous parental leave and invest strongly in ECEC experience higher employment of mothers with 3–5-year-olds. Denmark, Finland, and Sweden stand out here in terms of their policy mixes and employment outcomes.

Turning to the Swedish case, childcare plays a major role in building the human capital stock of children and improving the flow of parents back into the labour market. Sweden provides a pedagogical curriculum for childcare services for children from the age of 1 (European Commission/EACEA/Eurydice/Eurostat 2014a) and the Swedish student–teacher ratio in pre-primary education in 2012 was below the OECD average (six compared to fourteen) (OECD 2014). Beyond high quality, regulation around opening hours and participation costs facilitate access for all social groups. Municipalities are legally obliged to provide childcare services for children aged 1 to 6 (EU Network of Independent Experts 2014). Opening hours of childcare and after-school care are in line with thirty-five hours full-time employment on work days (Plantenga and Remery 2013). Childcare and after-school care fees are income-dependent and capped (EU Network of Independent Experts

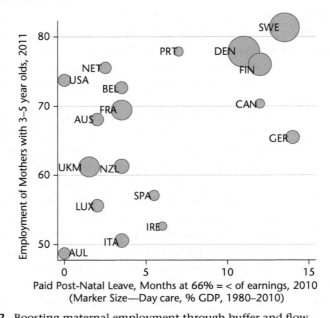

Figure 11.2. Boosting maternal employment through buffer and flow

Source: Data on maternal employment come from OECD family database. Data on paid post-natal leave generosity come from the Parental Leave Network. The size of the circles are based on spending on day care as a percentage of GDP from 1980 (or earliest available) to 2010 and the data come from the OECD social expenditure database.

2014). Swedish childcare enrolment rates are among the highest in the European Union (EU) (Eurydice 2014): 49.3 per cent for children aged 1, 88.5 per cent for children aged 2, and 93.1 per cent for children aged 3 (EU Network of Independent Experts 2014).

Swedish parental allowance offers flexible and gender equal arrangements to parents at relatively high replacement rates (80 per cent of previous earnings) (Statistics Sweden 2014). Parents may stay at home 480 days (Statistics Sweden 2014), which can be taken in blocks over several years, leading to a better reconciliation of work and care.

Besides mothers, the low-skilled also represent a disadvantaged group which stands to benefit from social investment policies. Figure 11.3 plots minimum income protection (the x-axis) and ALMP (the size of the markers) against the employment rate of those with a low level of education. Minimum income support plays a buffering function by helping to maintain health and social integration, whereas ALMPs uphold stock and flow functions by investing in human capital and facilitating transitions, respectively.

Figure 11.3 reveals a positive relationship between minimum income and the employment of those with low education; contexts with high levels of minimum income also tend to invest somewhat more in ALMP. As discussed

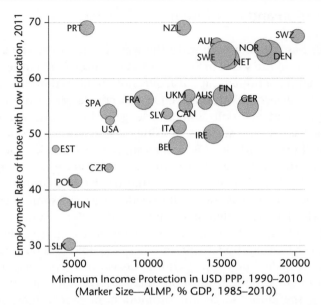

Figure 11.3. Boosting employment of those with low education through buffer, stock, and flow

Source: Low educated refers to those with less than upper secondary education and comes from *Education at a Glance* (OECD 2014b). Minimum income protection is the summary measure from the SaMip database (Nelson 2009) that includes social assistance, child supplements, housing supplements, refundable tax credits, and other unaffiliated policies. Exchange rates and purchasing power parity used to harmonize the SaMip data come from EUROSTAT and the OECD. The circles are weighted by total ALMP spending between 1985 (or earliest available) and 2010 as a percentage of GDP (OECD).

under Figure 11.1, there are relatively fewer people with low education in Sweden compared to other countries, which can be tied to the high investment in human capital stock. Moreover, most of the low educated are actually employed in jobs that require an upper secondary education, which demonstrates the high degree of learning that takes place on the job (Statistics Sweden 2005).

Drawing on Figure 11.3, social assistance and ALMPs in Sweden can be understood to address the challenges faced by those with low education. A comparative study classifies Sweden as a 'citizenship-based but residual assistance' regime (Gough et al. 1997), which combines both average extent and inclusion/exclusion with generous benefits (Gough 2001). The prominence of social insurance explains the only average extensiveness of social assistance. In recent years, the generosity of social assistance benefits has declined significantly (Kuivalainen and Nelson 2012) along with spending on ALMPs. Yet while the collective principles of the Swedish welfare state have weakened since the heyday of the 1950s, not least when considering the present challenge of integrating migrants, Sweden still performs well in international comparison.

11.5 Discussion and Conclusion

This chapter has drawn attention to the way in which the stock, flow, and buffer functions of the social investment state reinforce each other. Given the cumulative nature of human capital acquisition, policies that invest in human capital 'stock' are necessary throughout the life course. Moreover, since acquiring and applying earned skills and knowledge in the labour market depends on fulfilling basic needs such as housing, and navigating complex labour markets, the 'buffer' and 'flow' functions support the 'stock' function. There are other ways in which these three functions reinforce each other, as elaborated on in Table 11.1. These complementarities were examined empirically with a more focused discussion of the Swedish case. To summarize the findings, contexts that promoted stock, flow, and buffer simultaneously were found to exhibit superior employment outcomes. The case study of Sweden illuminated how various policies promoted stock, flow, and buffer in practice. The discussion spelled out how spending on various types of policies translated into human capital acquisition and preservation; importantly, more than simply spending, successful promotion of stock, flow, and buffer depends on coherence between policies and how they are implemented.

Whereas the empirical section suggested clear rewards for promoting institutional complementarities, it remains another question whether countries can muster the political will to enact reforms necessary to realize these complementarities. Considering the rich literature on institutional complementarities draws attention to the contextual nature of complementarities and suggests challenges in realizing them in practice. As discussed in Section 11.3, many of the expected gains to promoting stock, flow, and buffer derive from recent transformations, such as a shift towards post-industrial societies, low fertility rates, high divorce rates, and increasing economic competition. It remains to be seen how further socioeconomic changes, not least trade patterns and migrant flows, influence the complementarities between stock, flow, and buffer.

The literature on institutional complementarities also suggests that political compromises undergirding institutional complementarities require considerable time and manoeuvring to develop. Entrenched interests and various collective action and coordination problems are likely to hinder any automatic political response to the changing context. In this way, potential gains to promoting stock, flow, and buffer simultaneously do not necessarily suffice to build winning coalitions in favour of reform. Realizing a social investment welfare state is therefore likely to depend on policy entrepreneurs who skilfully communicate the socioeconomic benefits of social investment and manage to wrestle together a winning coalition in favour of reform.

Proponents of a strong version of complementarity predict that the social investment state, once established, should maintain a stable equilibrium. Increasing returns to existing institutional structures should make change difficult (Pierson 2000). At the same time, the Swedish case demonstrates considerable reform over the past few decades, despite having developed a quite extensive social investment state already by at least the 1960s (Bonoli 2012). These developments suggest a need for continuous adaptation to ongoing socio-economic change and perhaps deliver the lesson that realizing the economic rewards to institutional complementarities is ultimately a political struggle.

12

Capacitating Services and the Bottom-Up Approach to Social Investment

Charles Sabel, Jonathan Zeitlin, and Sigrid Quack

12.1 Introduction

There is a new emphasis in social welfare policy—so emphatic as to amount to a shift in paradigm—on prevention of harm rather than the palliation of its effects. A crucial component of this new social investment paradigm is the provision of capacitating social services aimed at the early identification of problems and at equipping an ever more diverse citizenry to surmount the increasing uncertainty they face in the labour market and the life course. Because the risks associated with uncertainty cannot be precisely foreseen, they are uninsurable in an actuarial sense. To respond to these non-actuarial risks, such capacitating services must be tailored to the needs of individuals and groups, typically by bringing together and continuously adjusting bundles of assistance from different policy domains (e.g. educational, psychological, and family services in the case of learning disabilities, or mental health, substance abuse, housing, childcare, and training services in the case of unemployment).

Investments are justified by their returns, and returns are calculated by weighing the cost of present expenditures against future gains. In the case of social investment, this would require a careful assessment of costs and benefits. But whose costs and whose benefits? Social investment is an investment in a public good, and therefore to be decided democratically. The returns might be expected to accrue to voters and politicians of the future rather than the demos of the present. For these reasons, it could prove difficult to mobilize sufficient political support for the paradigm shift even when experts agree on the advantages of doing so.

Seen this way, debate about social investment resembles discussion of climate change. Here too the effort has been focused on an ex ante, top-down assessment (by the United Nations Framework Convention on Climate Change (UNFCCC)) of the costs of the global harm (as a proxy for benefits foregone). In the absence of precise knowledge of the costs of climate change mitigation, debate has focused on the allocation of costs between rich and poor countries and between the richer generations of the future and the poorer generations of the present (with the gap between the two measured by highly controversial estimates of the discount rate) (see Sabel and Victor 2015).

But this comparison should give pause. The debate about climate change has been stalemated for two decades (at least until the recent Conference of the Parties 2015 directed attention towards more piecemeal solutions). Uncertainty about the costs of lowering emissions exacerbates the bargaining problem of their allocation. The bargaining problems heighten uncertainty as key parties must fear the reactions of counterparts who cannot meet their commitments. When it is unknown which commitments can be fulfilled and others' response if some are not, it is no surprise that bargaining among parties with sharply different interests is cautious to the point of paralysis.

If this is the future of social investment, only the most dogged optimist can claim that it has one. In this chapter, we argue that conceiving of the paradigm change in social welfare as a comprehensive and concerted investment is misguided. It obscures more feasible piecemeal approaches which, with an important proviso, are closer to the reform strategies that the principal actors are already or can be expected to be pursuing. In this approach, costs are not established ex ante and centrally, but rather are clarified through parallel practical efforts actually to provide capacitating services in particular domains. Reform coalitions are similarly not formed ex ante, through comprehensive bargaining, but rather developed on the fly, as initial successes demonstrate cost feasibility and generate in the short and medium term beneficiary clienteles. The crucial proviso is that decentralized efforts to move in the direction of social investment are carefully monitored, so that dead ends are rapidly identified, corrigible programmes are rapidly improved, and successes, where general, are generalized. Current debate in climate change urges a similar reorientation and points to examples where this approach has succeeded.

Willy-nilly, this is actually the trajectory of reform of social welfare systems in many places. It is proving impossible to design and establish by legislation or administrative rule comprehensive systems for providing capacitating services. In part, this is because it is difficult to specify the roles and responsibilities of members of integrated service teams ex ante in detail without limiting the very autonomy that the actors at various levels in the reformed systems will need to respond to novel and changing circumstances. These difficulties are exacerbated by the existing fragmentation of administrative responsibilities: vertically between national states, provinces or regions, and municipalities on the one hand; and horizontally between service providers from different policy domains on the other. Uncertainties about the division of labour in an ideal system are thus compounded by disputes over jurisdiction in the current one. But while this fragmentation frustrates efforts at unified and comprehensive solutions, it virtually guarantees that there will be many spaces for experimentation with different approaches to the provision of capacitating services. And this proliferation of alternatives—provided again that the structures for pooled evaluation of experience are put in place—can be an invaluable asset not a liability. In sum, the natural way of thinking about the transition to social investment is counterintuitively unlikely to succeed, and that what looks like a messy fall-back position—a concession to political and administrative reality—could actually be the starting point for a more promising strategy.

Similar arguments apply to the creation of the institutional complementarities on which the success of social investment depends. To ease successful transitions or 'flows' from one life phase and situation to another depends on increasing the 'stock' of adaptive skills, but actors will only be able to learn what is needed to increase adaptability if they are 'buffered' through social assurance and the provision of support services from the shocks and stresses that threaten to overwhelm them. It might seem that the success of capacitating institutions will therefore depend on the prior existence or simultaneous co-creation of complementary buffering institutions, thereby exacerbating the burden of the ex ante investment coordination problem. Though we focus in what follows on demonstrating the feasibility of piecemeal solutions to the problems of design, cost, and coalition politics of capaciting services, we point as well to some preliminary evidence that the problem of institutional complementaries can be addressed piecemeal as well.

12.2 The Intertemporal Problem in Social Investment

The introduction of capacitating services in many settings is likely to require politically painful shifts of resources from old to new programmes and/or tax increases, each of which imposes concentrated costs on particular social groups. Hence the need for what Alan Jacobs (2011) calls a 'politics of the long term'.

Jacobs is right, we think, to insist that these kinds of transformative reforms cannot be based on precise calculations of cost and benefits or detailed specifications of causal mechanisms, as in traditional business investments. The long-term consequences of transformative reforms are too uncertain, the causal chains involved too complex to permit 'anything approaching comprehensively rational calculation' of their expected utility. Hence policymakers typically rely on ideational frames and mental models—'simplified mappings of key causal relationships' in a given sphere—to fill informational gaps and assess the long-term outcomes of proposed reforms (Jacobs 2011: 53, 57). Once policymakers are convinced of the advantages of transformative reforms, Jacobs argues, they must then try to overcome potential opposition either through 'hyper insulation' of the reformers from veto players and electoral competition—a cabal of the far-sighted and publicly minded—or through inclusive negotiations with a wide range of societal interests—a grand coalition (Jacobs 2011: 58–69).

In Section 12.3, we want to underscore, in agreement with Jacobs, that knowledge of costs and benefits and causal mechanisms in areas like social investment and the provision of capacitating services is much more likely to be the result of the reform process than its precondition. But we want to argue in addition that the emergence of transformative coalitions in support of such investments is also more likely to occur piecemeal, as reform proceeds, rather than through the ex ante concertation of experts or an encompassing initial bargain.

12.3 The Limits of Ex Ante Calculation and Coalition Building for Comprehensive Reform

Consider first the limits to the possibility of ex ante calculation of the costs and benefits of comprehensive reform. We have a number of powerful indications that capacitating services are effective and affordable, and we have some knowledge of how such adaptive learning organizations operate, but we simply lack—and cannot be expected to soon obtain—credibly detailed knowledge of aggregate costs and benefits, let alone their exact distribution in time and among social groups.

A critical case in point is the Finnish education system, widely admired because of the country's exceptional performance in the Organisation for Economic Co-operation and Development (OECD) Programme for International Student Assessment (PISA) tests of 15-year-olds' proficiency in reading, mathematics, problem-solving, and scientific knowledge (Sahlberg 2011). One of the keys to this success is the provision of special education services to some 30 per cent of Finnish students, a much higher proportion of the school population than in other OECD countries (Sabel et al. 2011; Sabel 2012). More than two-thirds of these students receive short-term special needs instruction in standard classroom settings, often several times during their school career, with the aim of addressing particular learning problems and continuing with the normal course of study. A second crucial mechanism is a collegium within each school which at least annually reviews the treatments provided to each student. Finland's very high ranking in the league tables of international performance on the PISA tests is largely due to the outperformance of the lowest quintile of Finnish students, and it is of course these students who are the principal beneficiaries of the special education programme. This Finnish system is, moreover, plainly affordable in that Finland's costs per pupil are about one-third less than in the USA or Denmark, whose PISA results, especially for the lowest quintile, are substantially inferior.

The Finnish school system can therefore be read as a general vindication of the attractiveness and feasibility of social investment. It is, moreover, representative of a broader class of experimentalist institutions that use 'learning by monitoring' rapidly to address novel situations: by setting framework goals, authorizing front-line units or workers to pursue those goals by the means most appropriate to their context, and then monitoring the results so as to eliminate failures early and generalize successes when they show promise of being broadly applicable (Sabel 2006).

But it is a long way from this kind of general understanding of the organization of capacitating service provision, and its improvement through ongoing review of its own performance, to anything like knowledge of the precise causal mechanisms—exactly which sequence of treatments are effective in which cases or what is the right balance of disciplinary knowledge and further training in particular cognitive problems for effective special education teachers—that lead from the unreformed condition to future gains. Note that the Finns themselves, despite their direct experience of success in special education, have had difficulty in transferring the model of customized capacitating services to the closely related field of labour market activation.

The Finnish example and the use to which it has been put in international discussion suggest that it is more prudent—against the backdrop of a general understanding of the problem of providing capacitating services and promising approaches to doing so—to invest in the capacity to learn from and improve one's own efforts rather than accumulating more and more inevitably incomplete knowledge of what works.

As the reference to the climate change debate has already suggested, the difficulties in establishing precise costs and benefits make it all but impossible to address the problem of establishing coalitions for intertemporally extended bargains through either of the modes that Jacobs suggests. A shift to capacitating services will, in addition to complementarities between buffers, stocks, and flows, require reform of schools, vocational training, public health, child welfare, social assistance, elder care, and the police—core institutions of not just the traditional welfare state but the modern state generally. Is it possible to marshal evidence to persuade voters to support a one-off, comprehensive—and, given its scope, irrevocable—programme of change? Or at the other extreme, is it possible to imagine a small group of experts insulated somehow from public opinion and inside veto players deciding rationally on such a momentous shift?

But as with the clarification of costs and benefits, here too there is a piece-meal alternative. It seems mistaken to assume that in the case of a shift in social welfare paradigms the costs are all short term, while the benefits accrue only in a remote future. In the case of successful job training programmes, measurable benefits are evident within months or a very few years after the start of the programme, even if a full assessment takes longer. In the case of successful public school reform, there are tangible short-term benefits in improved test scores, decreases in dropout rates, and stabilization of the school environment, which in turn facilitates further reform. As we know from the history of many innovations in service provision, such as the US Post Office, or to take an organizationally more complex example, the Farm Extension Service, incipient programmes often build their own clienteles, generating coalitions of current beneficiaries and those who seek to enjoy similar kinds of benefits (Carpenter 2001). Returning for a moment to the climate change comparison, the introduction of capacitating services is more like mitigating the harm of black soot—which has immediate and local benefits as well as very long-term general ones—than like mitigating the emissions of greenhouse gases where the effects are overwhelmingly long term and general.

In sum, it is neither possible nor necessary to assemble ex ante the kind of information needed to make a compelling case for the paradigm shift in social services, nor all the more is it possible to build a coalition or cabal armed with such information that can be the political engine of reform. The messy solution of learning rapidly from experience is in fact the rational one, with the persistent proviso that initiatives are actually organized to learn from what they themselves and others do.

12.4 The Bottom-Up Approach in Action: A German Example

A study of the German federal labour-market activation programme 'Perspective 50plus' by Matthias Knuth (2014) and colleagues (Knuth, Stegmann, and Zink 2014) provides a compelling example of how given the failure of centralized hierarchical control, decentralized experiments can lead to the creation of capacitating services that are both more effective and less costly than standard treatments. The key, Knuth and his colleagues argue, was a governance architecture that allowed rapid pooling of local experience at both the regional and national levels.

The backdrop to the Perspective 50plus programme was the Hartz IV Reforms, which abolished traditional unemployment assistance (the follow-on benefit available upon exhaustion of unemployment insurance entitlements) by combining it with social assistance as a new, universal, tax-funded, means-tested, and flat-rate minimum income benefit. But as social assistance systems had been the responsibility of the municipalities, the new benefit created jurisdictional conflicts, and contrary to the government's intentions, the result was fragmentation, not unification, of Germany's public employment services. Following a ruling by the German Constitutional Court, a complex compromise was reached: in three-quarters of the country's territorial units, joint job-centre facilities to administer minimum income benefits were established by the municipalities and the regional branch of the Federal Employment Agency (Bundesagentur für Arbeit), with 'unified management and integrated processes but separate staff and responsibilities'; while in the other quarter of the country, these benefits are administered by the municipalities alone, even though most of the financial resources come from the federal budget (Knuth 2014: 243–4).

Established amidst this confusion in 2005 for a ten-year limited period, the Perspective 50plus programme took for granted the impossibility of establishing hierarchical control. The programme's immediate goal, linked to the federal government's 'work longer' agenda, was to bring older recipients of minimum income benefits back into (stable) employment. Because the Federal Ministry of Labour and Social Affairs has no legal powers over the municipalities, participation of the new joint jobcentres in the programme was voluntary, offering the latter an opportunity to develop specific strategies adapted to their labour market situation. Jobcentres could freely combine different instruments and spend the financial resources allocated to them as they considered appropriate. They had to commit to quantified outcome targets, measured in terms of rates of participants taking up jobs and remaining in employment for at least six months, with soft but consequential sanctions in case of underperformance. An important element of the programme was that local jobcentres had to partner with each other to form so-called employment pacts coordinated by regional units, which came to play a key role in monitoring the pacts' performance against the quantitative targets and promoting mutual learning between local jobcentres. A central Programme Management Agency, run by an independent non-profit organization, was responsible for reviewing and auditing proposals, advising both jobcentres and the ministry, organizing regional and national knowledge transfer conferences, facilitating peer exchanges, maintaining an inventory of good practices, and developing a monitoring and reporting database capable of tracking the experience of individual participants. Although the pilot programme started out with only 93 out of 438 jobcentres, it soon gained nationwide coverage, with 421 jobcentres and 34 per cent of the target group of elderly long-term unemployed involved by the end of 2012 (Knuth 2014: 246).

The results of the Perspective 50plus programme provide clear evidence that decentralized experimentation with the provision of capacitating services accompanied by coordinated arrangements for monitoring and rapid learning from local experience can produce superior employment outcomes at lower costs than standardized profiling and activation practices. At the core of the programme were tailored solutions for the individual needs of the older unemployed, often combining counselling, training, and provision of health services with unconventional solutions for transport and other problems. Many jobcentres established dedicated 50Plus teams of case workers, sometimes also including personnel from external service providers. Additional staff were recruited to keep caseloads of case workers lower than in standard operations. Such customized and integrated social services are typically considered an expensive solution, but the evaluation of the 50plus programme yields a strongly positive assessment of its effectiveness and cost-efficiency. Although many members of the Perspective 50plus target group combined multiple labour market risks (low education, long-term unemployment, and health problems), its relative success compares positively with the standard placement approach for matched groups operated by jobcentres outside the programme. The proportion of participants who took up employment increased from 26 per cent in 2008 to 35 per cent in 2012, while the spending per job placement was 11 per cent lower. Almost 70 per cent of those taking up a job, or 23 per cent of all programme participants, remained in employment for at least six months, compared to only 19 per cent in standard active labour market programmes for the same age and benefit group (Knuth 2014: 251–2).

Drawing on experiences from a range of such pilot programmes, including other projects directed towards young people and women returning to work as well as Perspective 50plus itself, the Bundesagentur für Arbeit introduced a new counselling concept in its services for recipients of unemployment benefits (starting in 2009) and basic social assistance (since 2012) (Bundesagentur für Arbeit 2015: 36). By offering a comprehensive further training programme for employment-oriented case management and guidelines for the development of integrated, often interdisciplinary teams that combine the skills necessary to address complex customer profiles in collaboration with a variety of external partners, the Bundesagentur für Arbeit aspires in its Agenda 2020 to diffuse positive lessons from such bottom-up experiments with capacitating services on a nationwide basis (Bundesagentur für Arbeit 2014).

12.5 A Dutch Prospect

Recent reforms of social welfare provision in the Netherlands, motivated in part by the persistent failure of a personal care voucher system, set the stage for similar and even more far-reaching developments, while also suggesting the possibility of a bottom-up, piecemeal solution to the problem of establishing institutional complementarities. As of 1 January 2015, responsibility for youth care, elder care, and social support for persons with disabilities (understood broadly as an incapacity to participate unassisted in active social life) was devolved to the municipalities. The general thrust of the reforms is straightforward: to shift from curative to a preventive approach to services and from fragmented to integrated service provision, as well as, to the extent possible, to localize services in the sense of making them geographically proximate to users and to increase reliance on local social and professional networks. A focal point is the creation of *wijk* or neighbourhood teams, organized around the official government goal of 'one family, one plan, one case manager'. These teams are composed of social workers and specialists in related fields who act as the portal for a large share of the issues involving at-risk children and families, providing early intervention, references to other specialists when necessary, and continuing support when appropriate. Notably, teams include specialists on personal finance and housing to assist stressed individuals and families stabilize their situations so that they can both take advantage of therapeutic possibilities and make use of the appropriate educational and vocational programmes. Put another way, the composition and activities of the *wijkteams* suppose that, for the range of issues for which they are responsible, the problem of complementarities can and probably must be addressed locally—through discretionary tailoring of various programmes to the needs of particular cases—before they have to be addressed at the level of systematic reform.

But that's where clarity ends. Core administrative problems remain unresolved: whether the members of the *wijkteams* should be municipal employees or employed by private contractors; what authority *wijkteams* have over the agencies that actually provide services in the more difficult cases where the team itself can't resolve matters; and who will have access to what kind of information within this more networked system (van Arum and Schoorl 2015).

Already, however, cities like Rotterdam have created some fifty such *wijkteams* and are working energetically to restructure specialized services—for youth with deep psychosocial problems, for situations involving domestic violence or child abuse—so that these both support and are supported by the new *wijkteams* (Gemeente Rotterdam 2014). Developments there are a microcosm of developments in the Netherlands and advanced welfare states more generally: the stakes are so high that the parties are making serious efforts to learn rapidly enough from decentralized experiments under fragmented conditions to make them work.

12.6 Conclusion

But even assuming that there are piecemeal solutions to the problems of designing and realizing social investment generally, background conditions might limit the settings in which such solutions are practicable. By way of conclusion, we consider the most general of the possible restrictions and suggest why that it may not be so restrictive after all.

By definition, bottom-up solutions are only feasible when national states permit decentralized initiative and experimentation. This might limit bottom-up solutions to federal systems—such as Germany—or national systems with traditions of local or municipal autonomy, as in the Nordic countries. But there are two qualifications to this general restriction. The first concerns inconspicuous endowments for decentralization which escape official classifications. The Netherlands, which, as we have seen in this chapter, is one of if not the boldest practitioner of the bottom-up strategy, is standardly characterized as a centralized or unitary state, not a permissive one tolerant of decentralization. There are likely many other countries that have little-noticed institutional and political reserves that can permit decentralization. Second, and perhaps counterintuitively, the widespread current political logjam may favour local experimentation. Political gridlock means that urgent programmes are formulated as framework goals to which subnational units consent on condition that they be granted substantial autonomy in implementation. Such developments are especially marked in the USA, where there is talk of a shift in the direction of executive federalism as reflected in legislation that openly authorizes state-level experimentation (Bulman-Pozen 2015). To the extent that this is so, continuing gridlock itself helps create conditions that favour bottom-up solutions, and bottom-up solutions help address the otherwise apparently intractable problems of a concerted shift to social investment.

13

A Normative Foundation for the Social Investment Approach?

Nathalie Morel and Joakim Palme

The growing importance of the concept of social investment has generated controversies around a host of issues: views have diverged about the content of the concept as such and its implementation in policy instruments, as well as the intended and unintended effects of social investment policies. This is what usually happens to contested concepts as different interests and ideologies try to capture them. In this case it is reinforced by the fact that the concept emerged in different contexts at fairly similar points in time. While there might be some advantages with ambiguous concepts in terms of mobilizing different interests around a common policy agenda (cf. Palier 2005), we find it problematic from a scholarly point of view because it makes rigorous analysis difficult. To make some advancement in the debate, the goals of social investment have to be clarified. In other words, the normative foundations of the policy agenda have to be laid down. We hope that this can pave the way for future discussions about the appropriate policy instruments as well as for meaningful analyses of impacts of applied policies with regard to goal performance.

While the social investment perspective appears to have become a new policy paradigm in Europe, this perspective and the policies implemented in its name have also been subject to some important critiques, regarding the outcomes of these policies, but also regarding the very principles on which the social investment perspective seems to rest. In many ways, these critiques raise the issue of the redefinition of the aims and principles of social policy and of the underlying social contract which the social investment perspective entails. The strongest critique relates to social investment's productivist view of social policy. Here, the argument is not only that social investment suffers from a one-sided emphasis on economic returns, but also that social investment entails a certain instrumentalization of social policy: the latter is intended to turn citizens into self-reliant, productive actors rather than to decommodify them or to enable them to flourish as (non-productive) individuals (Lister 2003; Saraceno 2015). Another core critique relates to the distributive principles of social investment policies, and the lesser focus it appears to place on poverty alleviation (Cantillon 2011).

Empirically, these critiques get some apparent support: indeed, it seems fair to say that the social dimension of social investment, and the social cohesion aims of the European social investment strategy as embodied in the Lisbon Strategy, have been paid lip-service both in terms of policy developments but also in academic research where a focus on economic indicators has tended to prevail when measuring policy outcomes.

In Morel, Palier, and Palme (2012b), we had argued that one of the problems with social investment is that it was an incomplete paradigm because different understandings of social investment co-existed in Europe, with the liberal version dominating over the social-democratic understanding. Here we would like to come back to this issue, but take it a step forward by trying to better specify the goals and normative underpinnings of what can meaningfully be termed social investment. In doing so, we would like to re-embed the social investment perspective in the broader debate about social citizenship and social progress.

13.1 Beyond Economic Growth: Social Investment and Social Progress

A core element of the social investment perspective is its emphasis on human capital. Investing in human capital from early childhood is understood as crucial to future economic growth and as an important element in reducing the intergenerational transmission of inequalities. Part of the ambiguity of the social investment approach (SIA) lies in the fact that this focus on human capital investment finds its inspiration in the works of economists as diverse as James Heckman and Amartya Sen. Heckman has made a powerful case for investing in early childhood education, by calculating the economic returns over the long run for society of such investments. Such an argument has also forcefully been put forward by eminent social investment proponents such as Esping-Andersen in *The Incomplete Revolution* (2009). This economic rationale has proven to be a powerful argument for 'selling' social investment, not least in countries where early childhood education and care services had long remained underdeveloped.

There are good reasons to go beyond such an economistic view of human capital investment, however, and here Amartya Sen's human capabilities approach seems particularly useful for conceptualizing the social returns of social investment and embedding social investment in a broader debate about social citizenship and social progress. Indeed, Sen takes issue with the prevailing limited understanding of the concept of human capital which tends to concentrate on the agency of human beings in augmenting production possibilities, arguing instead for a broader human capability perspective which values additional roles for human capital as well (Sen 2001: 296). While not discarding the value of human capital for economic growth, he reminds us that the benefits of education go beyond enhanced commodity production, to include the capacity to communicate, argue, choose in a more informed way, and increase the ability and freedom to shape one's life. Investing in human capital through education, he argues, may also improve the quality of public debate, an important dimension in the promotion of democracy and citizenship. In this way, human capital investments carry the potential to bring about not just economic change, but also social change (Sen 2001: 296). For Sen, there is

> [a] crucial valuational difference between the human capital focus and the concentration on human capabilities—a difference that relates to some extent to the distinction between means and ends. The acknowledgment of the role of human qualities in promoting and sustaining economic growth—momentous as it is— tells us nothing about why economic growth is sought in the first place. If, instead, the focus is, ultimately, on the expansion of human freedom to live the kind of lives that people have reason to value, then the role of economic growth in expanding these opportunities has to be integrated into that more fundamental understanding of the process of development as the expansion of human capability to lead more worthwhile and more free lives.   (Sen 2001: 295)

By reminding us that 'human beings are not merely means of production, but also the end of the exercise' (2001: 296), Sen helps to refocus the debate on the issue of social citizenship and societal progress.

The concept of social citizenship has been incredibly influential on the social policy literature. One important reason is that T. H. Marshall (1950) embedded social policy in a broader discussion of the social rights of citizens and how that relates to other aspects of citizenship, that is, democratic development. It also provides a story of how social policy is part of societal progress by making the same degree of civilization possible also for the poor that would otherwise be reserved only for the rich. It is, furthermore, about the abatement of social class and similar bases for creating division of welfare among citizens (Kap and Palme 2010).

The SIA can be anchored in a social citizenship agenda if it conforms to the underlying goal dimensions of not only alleviating poverty but also putting the abatement of fundamental social and economic inequalities on the agenda (cf. Marshall 1950). This is, moreover, about seeing social policy as a way of enhancing political citizenship by increasing possibilities for active participation. Finally, the way in which the social citizenship agenda was spelt out by Marshall provided an agenda for enhancing civilization and, in our view, societal progress. For the SIA this may seem as a tall agenda. In what follows we outline some important normative building blocks that will need to be further elaborated.

13.2 Equality of What? A Multidimensional and Agency-Oriented Approach

The normative claims behind social investment go beyond redistribution, to emphasize the role of capacitating services to foster individual capabilities for self-development and social and economic participation. But while current views of social investment tend to put forward a view of social justice that limits itself to promoting inclusion by equalizing the chances of participating in the market through the provision of different services (that invest in early childhood education, that enable parents and especially mothers to participate in the labour market, that offer lifelong training opportunities, and so on), Sen's capabilities approach emphasizes the role of both resources (that include both monetary resources and services) and conversion factors (the institutional framework and the framing of the socioeconomic context) in developing capabilities and supporting the agency of individuals in achieving a 'flourishing life'.

A number of scholars have tried to assess social policies from a capabilities approach, essentially in the field of employment policy (Salais 2003; Dean, Bonvin, and Vielle 2005; Bonvin and Farvaque 2006; Bonvin 2008; Orton 2011), but also for analysing work–life balance policies (Hobson and Fahlén 2009; Hobson 2011; 2014), two central fields of intervention for the SIA. In the field of employment policy, proponents of a capabilities approach have usefully highlighted the need to go beyond the notion of 'employability', which stresses the individual's responsibility in becoming 'employable', to highlight instead the importance of the framing of the socioeconomic context. This indicates that the state probably has a stronger role to play to create favourable macroeconomic conditions for employment growth and to ensure that jobs are available that match the supply of labour. As Bonvin and Farvaque have argued, the capabilities approach 'implies the shaping of the social context in order to make it more professionally and socially inclusive' (2006: 127).

This also points to the role of institutional complementarities to ensure both the social returns on investments, but also the economic returns. Following Hemerijck (2015), we can distinguish between the 'stocks', 'flows', and 'buffer' functions of welfare states. For instance, if we take the example of unemployment, the poverty risks associated with inadequate social insurance benefits may erode the social capital of benefit recipients undergoing spells of unemployment and/or sickness, thus jeopardizing the investments in human capital ('stocks'). Moreover, generous unemployment benefits not only help to secure transitions ('flows') on the labour market, making individuals more willing to take risks, they also ensure that individuals do not fall into a negative spiral of debt and poor health with detrimental effects on both their human and social capital. Coupled to effective employment services, generous insurances are more likely to ensure that the person can find a satisfying job, thus contributing to both economic productivity and social inclusion. Thus, it would be a mistake to see social insurance, social services, and social investments as alternative approaches. There is in fact a lot to suggest that they complement each other and have the potential to create synergies. The role of these complementarities has, in fact, traditionally been part of the social-democratic Nordic model, but its importance has been disregarded in the Third Way approach of social investment, where the focus has been more squarely on human capital investments but not on income security ('buffers') (see also Andersson 2007).

With respect to work–life balance policies, which are central in supporting 'flows', Hobson (2011) has explored Sen's capabilities approach, highlighting how his framework opens the way for two evaluative spaces, one designed for the analysis of a set of dimensions for the potential of individuals to achieve quality of life (their capabilities set); while the other is a normative framework for evaluating institutional forms and policies that promote an individual's capability to achieve it. In Section 13.3, we outline how these macro and micro spaces could be further integrated.

13.3 Measuring Social Returns on Social Investments

There are obviously good reasons to formulate the goals of the SIA in capability terms, a concept of welfare that is multidimensional and aimed at increasing the freedom of individuals, and not only freedom from want but also agency in more general terms. However, a basic assumption in this approach is that the unit of observation is the individual. Two things need to be added and emphasized in this context. One is that individual welfare is often dependent on institutional resources (collective; public or private). The other is that there are potential societal returns of a favourable development of individuals, particularly if we consider the social relations that the individual engages in, that is, the social capital. Whether this contributes to social trust and social cohesion is an open question certainly worth exploring but is beyond the realm of the present contribution.

Since the different dimensions of well-being are possible to influence, a resource-oriented approach is interesting from a policy point of view. However, a problem is that very few valid indicators of institutional resources have been developed despite the fact that a resource perspective on individual well-being invites us to see that public policies and other collectively based institutions, whether on the market or in the civil sphere, may serve as potential institutional resources.

Sen's (1985) view is that we approach equality with a multidimensional approach and in freedom terms this means that the direct observation of welfare is not possible, unless we know how individuals actually have chosen to live their lives. The capability approach is essentially a conceptual framework but it is emerging as an agenda for engagement in empirical research and policy evaluations (cf. Sen 2009; Hobson 2011). The capability approach has been tremendously important and continues to inspire scholars in different parts of the academic world, as well as actors in the world outside academia. In terms of measurement it has also had some obvious imprints. The most important is the Human Development Index (HDI) that is applied by the United Nations Development Programme (UNDP). In Europe, the open method of coordination (OMC) process also bears some imprints of the capability approach, notably in the social inclusion chapter. Yet there is a gap between the strong theoretical influence and the more modest direct implications for empirical research. This has probably to do with the conceptualization of welfare: 'capabilities' and 'functionings' are not directly observable. This warrants us to be more measurement oriented.

There are alternatives ways of progressing with what can be justifiably labelled as a 'capability approach'. The 'social indicator movement' is a good starting point. Perhaps an even more useful example is the Nordic 'level of living approach', which operationalizes different capability dimensions in what appears to be a reasonably straightforward and measurable way. Following Johansson (1970), this approach is—instead of talking about 'capabilities' and 'functioning'—using 'resources' multidimensionally and 'scope for action' to capture the agency dimension (Palme et al. 2003): the individual's command over resources in terms of health, education, employment, work conditions, social relations, political influence, as well as income and other economic assets are all important means for the possibility of controlling and consciously steering one's own life. An important feature of the level of living approach is that it sees welfare 'resources' as potentially able to influence policies. From a social investment perspective it is essential to sort out in which way policies can have an influence over the level and distribution of these 'resources' as well as for the 'scope for action', and ultimately the welfare of individual citizens.

An important aspect in Sen's thinking is that when we move to the societal level and want to inform policymaking, political priorities should be guided by political deliberations about how to rank various dimensions of welfare. This opens it up for countries to express their own preferences about what to prioritize. For the European Union (EU), it is, of course, a particular problem to deal with such a process. The multilevel framework appears new and not explored in this context. It is, however, beyond the scope of the present contribution to do this.

13.4 Conclusion

The welfare state has been described as a normative arrangement based on the idea of a social contract, with claims involving justice and fairness that go beyond issues of economic efficiency and effective insurance. The normative foundation of welfare provision has traditionally been about social justice between classes; more recently the social justice discussion has included new dimensions such as gender and generations (Chapter 1, this volume). While principles for just institutions could be derived from philosophical principles, it is impossible to avoid value judgements about what constitutes a good society. In contemporary discussions about how societies should be evaluated, John Rawls (1971) and Amartya Sen (1985) figure prominently. While Rawls has formulated a theory of justice, Sen is preoccupied with more concrete comparisons of equalities and individual freedoms in different societies. Do we have to choose between justice and equality if we are looking for a normative foundation for the SIA? We argue that the SIA suggests that there are good reasons for reconciling the two perspectives.

Rawls's (1971) *A Theory of Justice* offers three interesting notions around the concept of justice: the veil of ignorance, openness of institutions, and the difference principle. Kangas (2000) shows that it is perfectly possible to subject at least Rawls's first two to principles of empirical analysis in ways that are relevant for the social investment perspective. Kangas uses country comparison of income inequality and poverty over the life course as way of constructing a choice situation behind the 'veil of ignorance': in what country (read: institutional conditions) do you want to be born, given your knowledge about the poverty risks? The institutions that produce inequalities in human and social capital could also be empirically analysed and compared with regard to their openness. This kind of empirical analysis follows in the vein of Rothstein's (1998) analysis of universal social policy institutions.

The discourse around public policy in ageing societies can also contribute to a redefinition of the very idea of social justice. The sustainability issue raised by changes in population structure demands a shift away from understanding fairness in terms of static Rawlsian income equality towards a perspective that incorporates an explicit life-cycle and intergenerational perspective.

In line with the 'capability approach' of Amartya Sen, it furthermore necessitates an understanding of fairness as a right and an obligation to support the needs of each, so as to enable all to flourish. It can hence be argued that at the normative heart of the social investment strategy lies a reorientation of social citizenship, away from a compensating freedom from want logic towards the capacitating logic of freedom to act (Chapter 1, this volume).

Can the capabilities approach hence provide us with a normative framework for the SIA? The answer is both yes and no. It appears that the capability approach can contribute to a conceptual framework which can provide directions for policy designs and priorities as well as an evaluative framework for analysing institutional forms and policies that promote individual capabilities (so yes). Still, if we take Sen seriously, we should recognize that his approach suggests that there are no given answers to what a good society is or should be. How we prioritize different dimensions of welfare should be subject to democratic deliberations and may thus differ over time and between countries (so no). This is why the normative foundations can only be preliminary and should always be open for democratic discussions. Such a discussion can be helped if we have good data about how individual capabilities and performance of different socioeconomic institutions develop (cf. Kohl 2011).

Finally, we want to put social investment in a perspective of societal progress, which requires a genuine life-cycle perspective and an intergenerational approach. This is about recognizing that individuals have the potential to accumulate various kinds of assets over the life cycle and that it is further possible to transfer various kinds of assets over generations. The transferability of different kinds of capital is providing a perspective and understanding of what can be labelled societal progress in a Kantian sense. If social investment is in need of an overarching purpose, perhaps societal progress is a more open and better guiding star than social cohesion and a (theoretically) just society. Progress of society is different from seeing social change in evolutionary terms because it opens up for intentions, and hence values and conflicts to play a role (Offe 2011). Here we are in agreement with Offe's and Sen's critique of Rawlsian 'transcendental institutionalism' as being an encompassing blueprint of a just society that is neither available nor even desirable.

Part 4

Social Investment Assessment: Conceptualization and Methods

14

Practical Pluralism in the Empirical Study of Social Investment

Examples from Active Labour-Market Policy

Brian Burgoon

Debate about the wisdom of a SIA to welfare-state reform takes place not only on theoretical but also empirical terms, with respect to the character and implications of social investment reforms of welfare states. For instance, scholars and policymakers debate how labour activation affects economic well-being, based on how various measures of training policies and of employment activation affect the income, employment, and economic security of particular countries or groups. For this or any other aspect of the social investment debate, what stands as 'empirical evidence' ranges from evocative empirical anecdotes to randomized controlled experiments, focused on a few or on many countries or individuals, and using varied methods and philosophies for discerning trends, contrasts, and causality. The result is that scholars and policymakers base their convictions on very different kinds of empirical information, making it easy for them to talk past, rather than to, one another—in full conviction that they have the most rigorous or relevant empirical evidence on their side.

The present chapter provides guidance to navigating this empirical landscape by clarifying both the major challenges and distinct empirical approaches to understanding social investment's implications, or returns. As we shall see, empirically capturing the character and consequences of social investment poses distinct challenges to empirical researchers—more than applies to debates about other welfare reforms. The distinct challenges are threefold: the multifaceted character of what 'social investment' is thought to mean; the multifaceted implications of social investment in terms of varying aspects of well-being for varying groups; and the complex policy interactions associated with institutional complementarities or clashes in how social investment policies affect well-being. All three challenges, the chapter argues, create major tensions between relevance and rigour in empirical inquiry into social investment.

To keep the discussion tractable, the chapter will articulate these challenges and empirical solutions to them with illustrative reference to a particular slice of the social investment debate: if a policy cluster is associated with social investment, in this case active labour-market policies (ALMPs) that pose 'Matthew Effects', it should then promote labour-market efficiency and employment at the expense of rising poverty for vulnerable groups. Such an illustration should clarify the daunting empirical challenges we face and the myriad choices we must make to empirically gauge the wisdom of social investment. The discussion and illustration of the challenges, however, culminate in the chapter's main aim, to plea for pragmatic and pluralist empiricism in debating social investment. Such empiricism entails keeping conceptual contributions rooted in a methodologically self-conscious empirical study of social investment, but in a way that values multiple and complementary evidentiary approaches, and in a way that is pragmatic in using rough empirical information where data limitations, the prerogatives of particular audiences, and complexity in social investment's implications demand it.

14.1 The Perennial Challenges and Choices

Some empirical challenges to understanding the wisdom of social investment reforms are generic and perennial: challenges that apply to empirical debates about the character, pay-offs, and pitfalls of any specific feature of welfare reform—or, for that matter, of any public-policy treatment. With social investment, as with all other bodies of policy reform, we need valid descriptive measures of the policy interventions/treatments of interest. We also need valid and relevant measures of outcomes of interest, say economic growth or poverty reduction, for society as a whole or for particular societal groupings. And we need strategies to make valid and relevant claims about how a given intervention affects a given outcome. Particularly this last task—gauging whether a policy move has causal implications for a particular outcome—is something that opens enduring challenges with respect to epistemology (commitments as to what we can hope to know) and methodology (commitments as to *how* we can know what is knowable).

Taking studies of the nature and implications of ALMPs as but one example of the social investment debate, contributors (also in the present volume) meet these perennial challenges with varying choices across the full gamut of epistemology and methodology. We see single, detailed historical case studies chronicling the introduction and effectiveness of particular policy interventions (Sabel et al. 2011). We see cross-country qualitative historical comparisons (Morel, Palier, and Palme 2012c; Hemerijck 2013). And we see quantitative studies of various hues, from descriptive-statistical comparisons of aggregate country-level experiences (Hemerijck 2013); to more inferential-statistical analyses of observational data on national or individual-level experiences (Nelson and Stephens 2012; Rovny 2014); to quasi-experimental analysis of observational data (Heckman, LaLonde, and Smith 1999; Verbist, Roggeman, and De Lathauwer 2007; Dolfin and Schochet 2012); to experimental approaches using randomized controlled trials (Ashenfelter 1987; Hagglund 2007). Even within the narrow sliver of this scholarship focused on ALMPs' effectiveness we see enormous diversity and discord in the findings. For instance, a meta-study of some 200 inferential-quantitative studies of ALMPs' implications for employment and income found views to satisfy all political perspectives, though all variants of quantitative study tended to find particular value added of training and job-search provisions, as opposed to public-employment schemes, in reducing unemployment (Card, Kluve, and Weber 2010; Kluve 2010). The diverse findings are apparent because they examine different aspects of ALMP, in different settings, with respect to different groups and aspects of economic well-being, for different time periods. But as a general matter, the findings resting on the more controlled experimental end of the methodological spectrum tend to get higher marks for rigour, with randomized controlled experiments being the gold standard in judging the wisdom of a particular intervention.

14.2 Multifaceted Character of Social Investment

Several features of debate over the wisdom of social investment, however, complicate empirical research into that wisdom. The first such complicating feature is that the policy interventions understood to manifest 'social invest-ment' reforms vary substantially and lie in the eyes of many beholders, often seen as entailing combinations of policies that bundle and cut across distinct policy treatments and familiar social-policy categories. There are, to be sure, usual suspects in 'social investment' policies, such as services (as opposed to transfers) tiered towards activation, towards combining work with family, towards lifelong learning. However, in many recent conceptions of social investment approach (SIA), including that proposed by Hemerijck in Chapter 1 of this volume, a SIA need not exclude or undermine, and indeed should include, maintenance of more passive and compensatory provisions (EC 2013b; Hemerijck 2013). Even focusing on the usual suspects, however, the SIA involves a combination and clustering of very different parts of the welfare state. Indeed, this is part of what is meant by social investment entailing institutional or policy complementarities.

This multiplicity in what social investment is creates major challenges for empirical analysis. Understanding the implications or returns of social investment, such as for employment, might involve a very specific intervention/treatment or it might be about a somewhat more aggregated conception like training or employment services, or an even more aggregated conception like ALMP, or still broader conception like all unemployment-related provisions (e.g. ALMP plus unemployment insurance). The problem is that each conception might offer a distinct, offsetting or complementary, description of the degree of social investment effort of a given country at a particular moment. And just as important, each conception might have offsetting or complementary implications for the economic well-being of a given political economy.

Figure 14.1 provides a heuristic illustration of the problem. It shows a radar diagram based on ten dimensions of social policy. On the right-hand of the radar (right of the dotted line) are five dimensions corresponding to frequently used conceptions of social investment effort, and on the left-hand side five measures of more compensatory interventions, all within the broad categories of labour-market policies, old-age assistance, and family assistance. For the former, rightward half of the radar, the social investment measures are: total ALMP spending, training spending, employment administration/job-relocation spending, maternity/paternity spending, and childcare-services spending. For compensatory measures, serving principally 'buffer' functions (to use Hemerijck's language from this volume), we graph unemployment insurance, employment protection, family subsidies, old-age subsidies, and early-retirement subsidies. The unemployment-focused indicators are measured

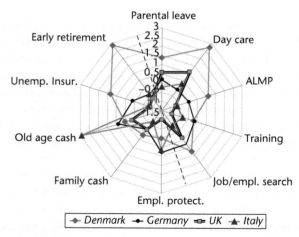

Figure 14.1. Selected indicators of social investment and compensatory policy effort

as a share of gross domestic product (GDP), weighted by the country's unemployment rate. The other dimensions are measured as a share of GDP. The scaling of these dimensions, further, is standardized based on values from the full spectrum of the twenty-three Organisation for Economic Co-operation and Development (OECD) countries 1960–2009 sample from which the data are drawn. This reveals the skew of Denmark, the UK, Germany, and Italy across the selected social policies presumed to be more or less manifesting social investment.

This simple snapshot suggests that countries often considered to be the most or least focused on social investment vary depending on one's conception or clustering of policies thought to manifest social investment. From this simple, limited snapshot, Denmark has the most generous social-policy effort in both social investment and compensatory terms, with a modest skew to social investment policy efforts. Italy, on the other hand, has the greatest compensatory skew with respect to old-age transfers and employment protection, in contrast to modest effort on the social investment dimensions. Germany and the UK are less obvious middle-ground settings. Most importantly, the full ordering across these four important countries is different for all different conceptions of the social investment provisions—for instance, whether one focuses on a part or combination of the parental leave, on day-care services, or on ALMP effort. Indeed, even within the category of ALMP, we see a different country ordering across the training and job-search/relocation components of ALMP. Hence, divining which countries are doing more with respect to social investment is obviously a complicated matter that requires the various clustering and unclustering of welfare state policies.

And if mapping social investment policies and reforms themselves pose empirical challenges, then a greater challenge is an empirical estimation of the causal *implications* of such policies and reforms relevant to the promise and pitfalls of social investment. The multi-component clustering of social investment puts real limits on what kinds of research designs are meaningful: who cares if some, very specific policy intervention, say a particular training provision, is more or less effective as shown by some experimental design, if what matters is the cluster or combination of that policy plus other training provisions? And yet, data may not allow experimental or even quasi-experimental analysis of the broader clustering of policy, such as 'ALMP effort' generally.

14.3 Multiplicity of 'Returns'

A second major empirical challenge is that the outcomes thought relevant to the returns, promises, or pitfalls of any given conception of social investment are themselves multiple: multiple with respect to aspects of well-being; and multiple with respect to the particular groups whose well-being is gauged. Both kinds of multiplicity in outcomes show up in recent scholarship, also where one might expect and find that a given social investment intervention yields benefits for the relatively privileged in a polity, but at the cost of lower income and higher economic insecurity for a polity, particularly for those who are less privileged already (Cantillon 2011). Such is the most obvious face of the putative 'Matthew Effects' of social investment reforms. Indeed, a particular social investment intervention may play out well for the income, employment, and life chances of some groups, while undermining those for others—along income, sector, class, education, gender, or ethnic lines. Attention to social investment's implications for poverty and income distributions may be as important as employment and growth—as is a central claim in Hemerijck's conception of social investment's 'stock', 'flow', and 'buffer' functions for a society and across various societal cleavages (see also Chapter 17, this volume).

The key empirical implication is that our analysis requires attention to a wide array of possibly complementary or offsetting outcomes and for an array of different groupings. Wealth may well get traded off for employment, or the less-educated and older workers may fare more poorly than younger educated ones. Finding this out requires diversely targeted analyses. In the ALMP context, for instance, it requires attention to how one or another conception of ALMP effort or treatment influences not just employment and income generally, but the chance of poverty for at-risk groups.

An example of such an analysis is Rovny's (2014) study of individual-level income data for eighteen OECD countries, to gauge whether ALMP spending (as a share of GDP, weighted by unemployment rates) correlates with poverty of at-risk groups with respect to combinations of gender, age, and education. Her findings are that ALMP tends to correlate with *lower* poverty risk for such groups, net of a range of individual and aggregate controls, and does so more strongly than more passive labour-market interventions like unemployment insurance. Figure 14.2 captures the aggregate cross-section scatterplots of this finding, with respect to less-skilled, older working-age males (55–64). The left-hand panel does so with respect to Rovny's data for eighteen OECD countries in 2005, and for the OECD accounting measure of 'ALMP' spending. The right-hand panel replicates this pattern using new data for all twenty-eight European Union (EU) countries, for a longer and more recent period, 2003–12, using the Eurostat measure of ALMP spending (focused on training, relocation assistance, and employment incentives).

More detailed analysis, of course, should consider the possibilities that such a negative correlation is spurious, dissolving once one looks at the individual level across time, controlling for endogeneity, omitted-variable bias, or selection-into-treatment. The European Union Statistics on Income

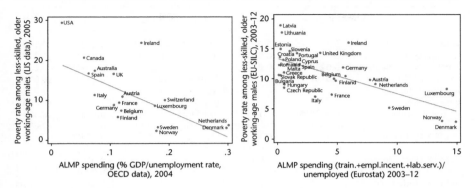

Figure 14.2. ALMP and poverty among less-skilled, older (55–65) males
Sources: LIS 2014 and OECD (left-hand panel); EU-SILC 2014 and Eurostat 2015 (right-hand panel).

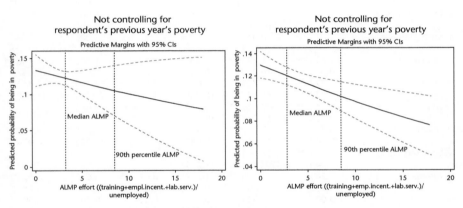

Figure 14.3. Predicted effects of ALMP on incidence of poverty among older less-educated males (aged 55–64)

and Living Conditions (EU-SILC) and Eurostat data allow us to get some purchase on such issues, where we can consider various model specifications, including matching techniques, and track the developments of particular individuals over time (as EU-SILC is a true panel for four-year intervals). Two such specifications show that the relationship between ALMP and poverty for older and less-educated working-age males may not be as straightforward as the aggregate scatterplots suggest. Figure 14.3 shows the marginal effects of ALMP effort on the probability that respondents in this at-risk category enter into poverty—with both models including a range of individual and country-year controls (see models (1) and (4) of Table 14.1). The left-hand side is a model that does not control for a respondent's previous year's condition of poverty, and here the relationship is not statistically significant at the 95 per cent confidence level (note how the upper and lower confidence

Table 14.1. ALMP and risk of poverty among less-skilled males (aged 55–64)

	(1)	(2)	(3)	(4)	(5)	(6)
ALMP spending per	−0.017	−0.023	0.213***	−0.046***	−0.025	0.103
unemployed	(0.018)	(0.018)	(0.059)	(0.017)	(0.019)	(0.070)
Total social expenditures	−0.073***	−0.071***	−0.043***	−0.045***	−0.044***	−0.023
(minus ALMP)	(0.014)	(0.014)	(0.016)	(0.014)	(0.014)	(0.016)
ALMP X Total social			−0.010***			−0.007**
expenditures			(0.003)			(0.003)
Part-time work	0.851***	1.158***	0.851***	0.595***	0.915***	0.595***
	(0.061)	(0.084)	(0.061)	(0.098)	(0.134)	(0.098)
ALMP X Part-time		−0.130***			−0.134***	
		(0.026)			(0.040)	
ALMP X Unemployed		−0.000			−0.050**	
		(0.015)			(0.024)	
ALMP X Student		−0.005			−5.915	
		(0.136)			(1,817.151)	
ALMP X Disabled		0.006			−0.039*	
		(0.013)			(0.020)	
ALMP X Retired		0.036***			−0.007	
		(0.013)			(0.019)	
ALMP X Military		43.242			0.000	
		(110307.2)			(0.000)	
ALMP X Home-maker		0.012			−0.006	
		(0.037)			(0.057)	
Unemployed	1.494***	1.493***	1.492***	1.138***	1.269***	1.136***
	(0.041)	(0.057)	(0.041)	(0.067)	(0.092)	(0.067)
Student	1.777**	1.791	1.833**	2.358**	37.599	2.442**
	(0.732)	(1.178)	(0.730)	(1.157)	(12,176.134)	(1.162)
Retired	−0.141***	−0.229***	−0.140***	−0.114**	−0.093	−0.114**
	(0.038)	(0.051)	(0.038)	(0.057)	(0.076)	(0.057)
Disabled	0.420***	0.399***	0.417***	0.207***	0.316***	0.199***
	(0.047)	(0.061)	(0.047)	(0.074)	(0.095)	(0.074)
Military service	3.534***	−521.344	3.398***			
	(1.249)	(1327585.497)	(1.251)			
Home-maker	1.281***	1.236***	1.279***	0.679***	0.667*	0.676***
	(0.136)	(0.207)	(0.136)	(0.245)	(0.356)	(0.245)
Age	−0.009*	−0.009*	−0.009*	−0.007	−0.006	−0.006
	(0.005)	(0.005)	(0.005)	(0.009)	(0.009)	(0.009)
Bad health	0.222***	0.225***	0.223***	0.162***	0.163***	0.164***
	(0.015)	(0.015)	(0.015)	(0.024)	(0.024)	(0.024)
Married	−0.450***	−0.449***	−0.450***	−0.320***	−0.318***	−0.320***
	(0.033)	(0.033)	(0.033)	(0.053)	(0.053)	(0.053)
Household size	−0.164***	−0.165***	−0.165***	−0.082**	−0.080**	−0.082**
	(0.023)	(0.023)	(0.023)	(0.034)	(0.034)	(0.034)
Other inactive	1.264***	1.267***	1.262***	0.885***	0.882***	0.882***
	(0.064)	(0.064)	(0.064)	(0.106)	(0.106)	(0.106)
Poverty (t-1)				3.088***	3.089***	3.086***
				(0.042)	(0.042)	(0.042)
Constant	−0.180	−0.188	−0.749	−1.664***	−1.773***	−2.111***
	(0.478)	(0.472)	(0.485)	(0.618)	(0.618)	(0.639)
Year dummies	Yes	Yes	Yes	Yes	Yes	Yes
Observations	60,619	60,619	60,619	35,581	35,581	35,581
Countries	27	27	27	27	27	27
Chi-square	3064	3101	3081	6231	6227	6246
Log-likelihood	−20333	−20308	−20324	−8803	−8793	−8801
Robust standard errors						
in parentheses						

*** p<0.01, ** p<0.05, *p<0.1

intervals do not retain negative slopes throughout the ALMP distribution). But the right-hand model *does* control for such previous poverty, and reveals a statistically significant poverty-reducing effect of ALMP. As this latter model captures over-time dynamics and modestly addresses selection-into-treatment, it is likely the better model. But the important point is that both specifications, and in fact a range of alternative specifications (see Table 14.1 for the full estimation results and interactive specifications with sources of individual risk), show no significant, direct 'Matthew Effect', where one might expect ALMP to correlate positively with poverty of this at-risk group. This example, of course, may also suffer from serious threats to inference, most obviously because the data do not measure whether particular individuals directly draw on ALMP programmes.

But the example, mainly, reminds us of how much empirical analysis of ALMPs' implications needs to carve-up and recombine not just the policy treatments themselves, but also the landscape of implications for various aspects of well-being (e.g. relevant to stocks, flows, and buffers) and for various societal groupings. Such is a daunting task, indeed, only imperfectly possible with the available data—certainly should one want to examine the relevance of broad policy clusters for a range of countries and years.

14.4 Social Investment Policy Complementarities and Clashes

A third major empirical challenge distinct from the social investment debate is perhaps the most fundamental: that key social investment reforms (components or combinations) may interact, be complementary, or clash with one another, in their implications for well-being. The highlighting of putative complementarities by many scholars is not just an expression of the importance of bundles rather than individual components of policy reform (the first challenge emphasized in Section 14.2); it is also an assertion that one component of social investment's implications may depend on, or causally interact with, another component of welfare policy. A commonly cited example is that the implementation of ALMPs that promote or reward employment by parents may bear fruit for employment or income only where suitable childcare services are in place that allow newly trained parents to combine work with family. Similarly, concern about possible 'Matthew Effects' not only involves expectation that a particular feature of social investment might favour well-being with respect to some groups, at the expense of other aspects of well-being of other groups; it is also a concern that social investment reforms may hollow-out more compensatory or redistributive features of welfare states and/or undermine the effectiveness of those latter features.

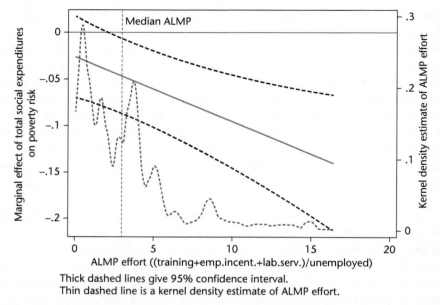

Thick dashed lines give 95% confidence interval.
Thin dashed line is a kernel density estimate of ALMP effort.

Figure 14.4. Predicted conditional effect of total social expenditures on poverty among older less-educated males (aged 55–64), across the range of ALMP.

Such interactions pose a large challenge to empirical analysis, requiring research designs that are substantially more complicated than the exploration of direct effects as summarized above so far. Sticking with the ALMP example, we might want to know how and whether ALMP alters or moderates the effect of other, redistributive features of the welfare state on poverty risk. One specification of such an analysis, summarized in Figure 14.4, models empirical interaction between ALMP and all other welfare spending (the latter measured as spending on all social expenditures as a share of GDP, minus spending on programmes in the ALMP measure). For the particular at-risk group being analysed, that interaction turns out to be statistically significantly *negative* (Figure 14.1 is based on the model with a respondent's previous year's poverty status, model (6) in Table 14.1). This means that ALMP correlates more strongly negatively, in a poverty-reducing direction, for those living in years and settings with more generous total social spending. And more to the point of Matthew Effects, the model shows that total social spending has, likewise, a stronger negative correlation with poverty—that is, more poverty-reducing effects—when at-risk respondents are in settings with more generous ALMP. Figure 14.4 captures this latter interaction by plotting the predicted effect of total social expenditures (the coefficient and confidence intervals) on the vertical axis, as a function of variation across the full sample spectrum of ALMP effort. The more generous ALMP in place, the more poverty-reducing is the effect of total welfare expenditures. This pattern suggests the opposite of a Matthew Effect—more a story of institutional complementarity between ALMP and the more general buffer-generating properties of broader social spending.

Such interaction may not hold up should one consider other (better) data and modelling specifications, or for that matter other clusters of social investment, other aspects of well-being for other at-risk groups. But understanding how ALMP, as one face of social investment, influences the poverty of this one at-risk group requires exploration of this and other kinds of interactions—for instance with other key components of total social spending used in the example and Figure 14.4. Such interactions are complex but studiable, crucial to debating the wisdom of social investment.

14.5 Conclusion: Coping through Practical and Pluralist Empiricism

In sum, empirically understanding the wisdom of social investment reform presents policymakers and scholars with distinct challenges beyond the perennial difficulties of estimating social-policy impacts: we face multi-faceted components and policy bundles thought to constitute 'social investment'; we face multi-faceted conceptions of implications or returns, given the many offsetting features of well-being for varied groupings of and within a given polity; and we face complex interactions of putative policy complementarities or clashes in how a given conception of social investment affects a given conception of well-being. These challenges very much complicate how we navigate the many epistemological and methodological paths to measuring social investment's promise and pitfalls. They pose major dilemmas between relevance and rigour, a dilemma that is more severe than for other debates about social policy and welfare reform. In this dilemma, the more one does to get a control on the empirics—for instance, the more one focuses on data that allow valid inferences about how a discrete policy treatment affects a given aspect of economic well-being—the more one is forced to ignore the multiplicity of social investment, the multiplicity of implications, and the complexity of interactions connecting them. Sticking with the ALMP empirical example, we should recognize the major limits to the data and analysis offered above but recognize just as sharply the limits of the alternatives. Clarifying how ALMP affects poverty might be more rigorous with a focus on individual take-up of a more particular slice of ALMP in policy space, time, and national experience; but such a focus would thereby overlook the broader category 'ALMP', and make it impossible to explore the range of countries and policy interactions that might be crucial to a more holistic understanding of this ALMP face of social investment.

171

This dilemma between rigour and relevance could be a recipe for despair or, worse, relativism. Some might believe that the empirical challenge is simply overwhelming, should one want to meet the highest standards of descriptive and causal inference about social investment and its implications. There are simply too many policy features, combinations, interactions, implications, and empirical groupings to keep track of. The practical limits of existing data availability only exacerbate the burden. We lack, for instance, enough detailed information on policy take-up by individuals for the range of policy interventions associated with social investment, and certainly not for the multiple countries and groupings—and certainly not for the longer time periods, spanning decades or even generations, for individuals or countries whose well-being or suffering is to be understood. Many scholars faced with such a burden may call for discussing only the narrowest of slices of social investment. Other scholars or policymakers might respond to the same empirical challenges and dilemma with the opposite response—a methodological relativism that sees any person's anecdote or scatterplot being no better or worse than any other person's focused quasi-experimental regression analysis on individual panel data. Such a response throws-in the empirical towel and abandons the social investment debate to conceptual speculation.

A better response is to debate the wisdom of social investment in a way that confronts the above challenges with a *pluralist and pragmatic empiricism*. Such empiricism, here, asserts the centrality of empirical analysis to the debate, as virtually any claim about the wisdom of social investment is, in the end, an empirical claim—requiring some empirical traction. The empirical traction one seeks, however, must recognize the very imperfect external and internal validity of inferences that any given empirical approach can support, even the most controlled observational or experimental work. This is what social investment's heightened dilemma of relevance and rigour demands of all scholars.

The complexity of the social investment debate also calls for *pluralism* in this empiricism, one that recognizes the complementary value added of different empirical approaches, and calls for empirical studies that work in concert with, are conscious of, other evidence. This means becoming familiar with at least the broad lines of empirical approaches and findings along the epistemological and methodological spectrum referred to in Section 14.1. Experimental-oriented methodologists should read and care about the findings of process-tracing historical case studies; those working with anecdotal information about particular case experiences should read and care about the worries and findings of the econometricians. Indeed, a given slice of the debate is likely best carried out with explicit reference to multiple empirical approaches—case histories supplemented by aggregate quantitative overviews and rigorous micro-level studies of narrow policy implementation.

Finally and most importantly, the social investment debate should be carried out by pluralist empiricism that is also *pragmatic*. Research into the wisdom of social investment should recognize the urgency of the debate, requiring social-scientific reflection now, not in a hundred years. And given the challenges and dilemma highlighted in this chapter, research must accept that for major aspects of the debate, for some audiences, and with very real data limitations, we have no choice but to rely on ready, sometimes more rudimentary, empirical designs to learn or say what we can and must about the empirical record. A rich historical case, or even an evocative anecdote or simple scatter plot, can convince when regression analysis or experimental trial do not, and may be all we have to work with for important parts of debate over social investment's promise or pitfalls.

15

Social Investment and Its Discount Rate

Iain Begg

Identifying policies as 'social investment' implies that they are qualitatively different from social outlays as a form of consumption. Investment implies spending intended to generate a future return, rather than being consumed immediately. For private investors, the rate of return on an investment has to be sufficient to offset the costs of tying up resources and there is an entire literature devoted to techniques for investment appraisal, building on simple concepts such as net present value, the rate of return, or shareholder value. Public investment, in principle, can be analysed with much the same tools and many governments use reference values for deciding whether or not to undertake a particular investment project, or to rank potential projects.

However, whereas a private business will focus predominantly on financial returns, perhaps making some allowance for strategic investments with less readily predictable results, but potentially transformative effects on commercial prospects, public investment decisions often also have a normative dimension, favouring projects that fulfil a wider political or social purpose. Cost-benefit analysis is, therefore, used to extend financial analysis, entailing decisions about the weight to accord to different social aims.

With constrained public spending, advocates of social investment need strong arguments to convince hard-nosed finance ministers to allocate more resources. This chapter tries to make explicit how social investment can best be assessed from an economic standpoint, drawing attention to aspects which may prove contentious. Recognizing that there will be ambiguity about whether a particular form of social spending is genuinely investment, this contribution asks whether social investment can be appraised in much the same way as other forms of investment, private or public, what the basis for measurement should be, and how to carry out the calculation. It also considers whether an investment perspective makes sense in decision-making on social policy orientations.

15.1 What is Meant By Investment?

From an economic perspective, the distinction between investment and consumption is conceptually robust, though possibly complicated by the notion of durable goods that have both consumption and investment characteristics. A theatre ticket is used up as soon as it is consumed, but a car or a personal computer delivers benefits over an extended period. The answer in accountancy terms is to provide for the depreciation of the asset. A continuum between investment and consumption, rather than a dichotomy, also characterizes several forms of social spending.

Standard cost-benefit analysis calculates a monetary value for the return on an investment, taking into account flows over time and allowing for preferences about how to value costs or benefits accruing to different individuals of groups. Normative considerations can, therefore, be built into the calculation by assigning weights to such groups or using benchmarks based on assumptions. A person–hour saved by a transport improvement could be valued in any number of ways, such as the mean or median wage of a representative worker, or (if it is leisure time), a so-called shadow price representing the average value of leisure. While invariably complex and contentious, the estimation itself is straightforward once the relevant parameters are agreed.

Social investment ought to be amenable to this approach. If, as Nolan (2013) argues, normative goals such as poverty relief or enhanced care for the elderly should be given greater weight in decision-making, they can readily be factored into a cost-benefit calculus, even though conceptual complications and awkward empirical problems must be anticipated. First, for many social investment measures, it can be tricky to link the investment spending to outcomes, especially those occurring far in the future. The causality may be blurred by other determinants. Second, investing in preschool children today may well raise their employability as adults and have the long-term social benefit of systematically lowering unemployment, but will it be possible to separate that effect from secondary education or other factors? Third, the norms behind values assumed for key parameters in the estimation may be obscure. The fact that social investment is conceived of as a package of measures or even as a policy paradigm, accentuates the difficulties in inferring causality.

There is then a question of to what should the investment be compared. Social investment is portrayed as an alternative means of setting priorities for welfare state spending, implying a trade-off between, for example, outlays for capacitating services and income support, or between better care for the elderly and childcare that activates parents. As Nolan (2013: 466) puts it, 'this goes well beyond a matter of terminology to the basis on which core social choices are made'.

15.2 What is an Appropriate Discount Rate?

Because many of the consequences of social investment only materialize in the longer term, the justification for making social investments will be crucially affected by the discount rate chosen. As in assessing action to prevent climate change, future costs and benefits have to be scaled down by discounting them, and to take into account the cumulative results of longer-term effects; Dasgupta (2008) explains the diverse ways of doing so.

The basics of discounting future net benefits were established long ago in the pioneering work of Ramsey (1928). His approach was to apply a discount rate for future consumption, while also recognizing that future generations will be wealthier, so that the marginal benefit to them of consumption foregone today will be low because the incremental amount will be small relative to a much bigger total. The topic has attracted substantial attention from a wide range of leading economists over the years as the reasoning has become more refined, often employing complex mathematical proofs.

The simple formula for the discount rate is given by the equation:

$$rt = d + egt$$

where the consumption adjusted discount rate rt is the sum of the inter-temporal discount rate d and a term reflecting the growth of consumption. In the latter term, gt is the annualized growth of consumption and e is the elasticity of the marginal utility of higher consumption. If future consumption is expected to grow rapidly, then the marginal utility deriving from an investment today will be small and the second term will be larger, justifying the social planner in taking less account of future benefits. If, however, future consumption does not grow (a zero or negative value for gt) then the discount rate would fall.

The debates around this formula are many, particularly in recent work on how to allow for the many uncertainties and very long time-scales associated with climate change, prompted by Stern's (2006) use of a very low discount rate. Critics, such as Nordhaus (2007), argued that Stern's advocacy of invest-ment now relied on an unreasonably low discount rates and should be closer to market rates, a stance rebutted by Stern (2015). The latter argues that market-based discount rates are prone to be unreliable for various reasons and may be wildly misleading for assessing the long-term effects associated with climate change. If future growth is volatile, which might arise if costs or benefits arise at different times, then an average consumption growth for gt would be less appropriate.

Lack of knowledge about (very) long-term outcomes could justify a lower value for d, while Dasgupta (2008) argues that there is no real basis for estimating probabilities when the time scale is measured in centuries. In some jurisdictions, a declining discount rate is therefore used for longer-term outcomes to capture this phenomenon. The time frame here is centuries rather than the decades over which social investments might be discounted, making it arguable that social investment be accorded special treatment.

Clearly, some forms of social investment yield rapid and more certain benefits. Examples include policies aimed at activation, whether in the form of childcare that enables parents (especially women) to return to the labour market or support that raises the employability of discouraged workers. Appraising such policies is not always simple, but there are well-tried techniques which make allowance for complications such as deadweight (where the outcome would have happened without the policy intervention) or displacement (where the gain for a beneficiary is at the expense of someone else).

15.3 Coping with Uncertainty around Outcomes

Similarly difficult issues arise over how to deal with uncertainty about the outcomes of social investments and the associated risks that the returns envisaged will not arise. As explained by Arrow and colleagues (2014) there is a growing inclination to apply a markedly lower discount rate for distant and uncertain effects, although there is also a view that the prevailing market rate of interest should be the basis.

According to Arrow and Lind (1970) governments differ from private agents because they are able to pool risk and can absorb uncertainty better than a private investor, leading the public sector to opt for different time and risk preferences. However, they point out that by doing so, more optimal private investment may be displaced. Their analysis identifies circumstances in which a public investment yielding a lower rate of return than a private investment may still be justified if the risk associated with the latter more than offsets the difference in return. The reason is the risk-pooling that the public sector is able to do, although this assumes that all the benefits accrue to the public in aggregate. If, however, some risks are to individual costs or benefits, then the risk cannot be pooled to the same extent and the net benefits should be reduced accordingly or different rates of discount applied.

Neumayer (2007) argues that both Stern and his critics were too preoccupied with the discount rate and should, instead, have focused on the irreversible loss of natural capital. A parallel could be drawn with the potential erosion of social cohesion if too little investment occurs to build up social capital. However, even if Neumayer's view is correct in relation to climate change, it may to harder to show that social capital loss is likely to be irreversible, because it would imply a wide-ranging breakdown of society.

Does any of this help in assessing social investment? A simple answer is in two parts. First, there is no compelling reason to doubt the applicability of the principles underlying discounting to social investment. Second, however, the approach to adopt in dealing with the very evident uncertainties around the extent and timing of the future net benefits of social investment needs debate.

15.4 The Assets from Social Investment and their Distribution

What are the assets generated by social investment? A direct answer is a combination of human and social capital. Investment in training should lead to enhanced human capital, while certain other forms of social intervention can boost social capital. Some social investments 'enable'—examples are childcare which allows parents to work or adequate transport—and those which 'activate' by helping to match available workers with jobs, or to upgrade their skills. Early childhood intervention is presumed to endow the recipients with capacities that will both raise their potential (human capital) and contribute to greater social cohesion (social capital). The eventual pay-off is lower future social costs because the costs associated with unemployment of higher social exclusion fall. In combination, the different strands of social investment raise the stock of productive workers.

Both the nature of the investment and the return it generates are open to dispute. Nolan (2013) finds that nearly all forms of social spending simultaneously have both investment and consumption characteristics. For example, he cites education as something which enhances human capital, and thus has investment attributes with long-term societal benefits but also something which pays off immediately for the individual. In parallel, should the objective of a social investment be to boost aggregate growth or jobs, or some more qualitative outcome? Many of the advocates of social investment claim that unless the whole package is in place, the results will be disappointing rendering appraisal still more complicated, although a similar argument can be made about constructing a transport network as opposed to individual bridges and roads. The obvious economic concept to apply in this context is that of externalities. Within a package, the external benefits of specific policy measures will be higher than in an ad hoc approach.

There are clearly many uncertainties in this narrative and the distribution of benefits is likely to be uneven, so that following the reasoning of Arrow and Lind (1970), some allowance for this uncertainty (which diminishes the net present value of the investment), should be made. Benefits and costs, as well as risks on either side do not necessarily accrue to the same individuals and will rarely be evenly spread. Moreover, benefits of public investment tend to accrue to individuals while costs fall on the public sector. If, in addition, the public sector that bears the risk, then it is bound to be pooled among a broad range of tax-payers or welfare recipients, but if risks fall on individuals, the effects could be much more concentrated. Equity considerations suggest giving more weight to the poor, notably in resort to discount rates.

There is some ambiguity about who ultimately benefits from social investments. For some, the public sector stands to gain considerably in the longer term, albeit with substantial uncertainty. For example, where future employment rates are increased or demands on social protection systems reduced, a future generation will benefit from the investment made today.

A further issue is what crowding out of passive income support implies for standard economic analysis of poverty or inequality. Here, a counterfactual has to be taken into account. European societies accept a responsibility for the well-being of the poor, and define poverty in relative, not absolute, terms. To this extent, an economic case for social investment can be made on distributive grounds, and not just on the basis of the efficient allocation of resources. Pre-emptive investments (instilling capacity in the individual or society to confront risks), curbs the need for redistributive payments (as compensation for different social contingencies). Thus, to the extent that social investment favours groups other than the most deprived, the criteria for justifying it will be more demanding. As Mosher (2015) observes, education is a form of spending that, by spreading opportunity, is able to foster equality, countering the tendency for new, skill-based technologies to aggravate inequality. Mosher focuses on the accumulated stock of education, rather than indicators of annual spending and, by so doing, indirectly makes use of an investment concept.

Education is widely, if often uncritically, regarded as an unambiguous benefit, yet the evidence on outcomes (see, for example, the evidence and references cited by Mosher 2015) suggests considerable variation in the relationships between levels of spending, attainment of basic qualifications, incomes, and job prospects (for an overview, see Solga 2014). Iversen and Stephens (2008) suggest that the effectiveness of education will be conditioned by the societal model, which could mean that the returns from social investment vary depending on the national context.

Some critics of the activation strand of social investment point to wider concerns about the distributive effects of the policies, notably where they favour the already privileged (the 'Matthew Effect', examined in Chapter 5, this volume) or lead to the phenomenon of 'churning' in which those supported go through a succession of schemes without ever making the transition to 'regular' employment. From an economic perspective, both sorts of criticisms can be accommodated.

A retort on distribution is that cost-benefit analysis does not preclude assigning relevant weightings to capture benefits accruing to different recipients. Outcomes may well 'less-deserving' recipients and by-pass the worst-off, but that is not in itself to be deplored. The role of the 'benevolent social planner' at the core of welfare economics is to maximize aggregate social welfare, even if subject to various normative constraints such as limiting poverty or too much inequality. Hence, if certain policy initiatives do too little for certain groups, the answer is not necessarily to reject the initiatives but to adopt complementary policies.

Criticisms of ineffective activation policies are, in principle, much easier to accommodate. Studies in countries with long-standing activation policies shed light on the features that have proved to be unsatisfactory: in Sweden, for example, Calmfors, Forslund, and Helmström (2002) argue that when used on a large scale, active labour market policies become less effective in promoting employment. Although such policies appear to reduce unemployment, they also reduce 'regular' employment, partly because the workers supported on active labour-market policy (ALMP) schemes displace others, while as an answer to youth unemployment, ALMP had disappointing results. What is crucial in this regard is to distinguish between flaws in policy design and the validity of the policy goals. Like any form of investment, social investment will represent a good use of public funding only if that rate of return is high enough compared to alternative uses of the resources. However, a complementary way of looking at the social investment approach (SIA) is to consider what would happen if it were not implemented. Defining a counterfactual is always difficult, especially when the policy change is extensive, but there are bound to be repercussions if the contingency the policy is designed to meet is dealt with by other means. Three alternative welfare-providing institutions can substitute for public policies, all of which have strengths and weaknesses compared with the SIA:

- The market, either through private insurance arrangements or by employers directly taking over the costs of boosting capacities similar to those envisaged in the social investment model. While easing pressure on the public purse, a potential shortcoming is to polarize access to risk management, engendering inequality.

- Not-for-profit, non-governmental charity organizations which offer support, often in a form that reflects their priorities or values, rather than those of the assisted individuals, implicitly imposing conditionality. Such support is valuable in many countries, but can result in the priorities of the donors over-riding those of society.

- The family which, by supporting its members, often acts as the 'social investor' of last resort, but which also has to make compromises in order to fulfil this role, such as withdrawal from the labour market.

15.5 Social Impact Investment

The term social investment is also used to describe private investments which yield a social return, a phenomenon which has grown in significance as a result of the squeeze on public finances. According to Wilson (2014) the investors in question fall into two groups: those she describes as 'impact-first' who seek to support worthy organizations that cannot generate an adequate rate of return on their own; and the 'financial-first' traditional investors who nevertheless want to achieve a social impact. This sort of investment (increasingly also known as 'impact investment') has been connected with an increased incidence of social enterprise as a form of corporate organization. Although there is only limited common ground with the notion of social investment covered in this book, some insights for assessing returns on the investment can be gleaned.

One is that there are conflicting views on whether the social element of the return is unavoidably at the expense of the financial return. Wilson (2014: 29) observes that there is evidence that the social and financial return can be positively correlated but 'it is not easy to prove' because of a 'lack of clear metrics and data'. Part of the problem is that the social element of the return is hard to measure. She also notes that while some investors are prepared to accept returns below the market rate, others still expect returns that reflect risk-adjusted market conditions.

Another insight is that innovative financial instruments are being used to fund social/impact investment. Bonds mobilizing private capital have been placed on the market, including those such as social impact bonds which are designed to achieve a stated social outcome, but in which the public sector only pays if the outcome is realized. As explained by Wilson (2014: 18), these bonds use private investment 'to pay for interventions, which are delivered by service providers with a proven track record. Financial returns to investors are made by the public sector on the basis of improved social outcomes. If outcomes do not improve, then investors do not recover their investment.' Also significant is that they have typically been applied for preventative purposes, suggesting a further link with the SIA examined in this book. A specific requirement for some social projects is to overcome the initial financing hurdle, a solution to which has been the creation of catalytic funds (Wilson 2014) to help in creating management capacity. In addition, the transferability of approaches between member states of the European Union (EU) cannot be taken for granted. It may be that some of the innovations emanating from this model could help to advance social investment as a welfare state model.

15.6 Policy Considerations

Is economic analysis simply incapable of coping with the political case for social investment? At one level, a clear answer is 'no'. Given that economics is the analysis of scarcity, the principles deployed to allocate resources should not make any distinction between investment labelled as 'social' from any other form of investment or, indeed, consumption. What is evident, however, is that there are formidable obstacles, theoretical and (more so) empirical, to arriving at a consensus on a methodology for appraising social investment.

There is, first, the question of causality. The logic of social investment is appealing but largely intuitive, because it makes the case that over the life course, early intervention will create greater resilience to social risks. However, it takes for granted that future social risks can be identified and allowed for, even though part of the genesis of the SIA is, precisely, that 'old' welfare provision was ill-equipped to deal with new social risks. If risks such as unemployment or social exclusion are correctly identified, an associated question is whether a clear chain of causality can be established. In this context, the social investment is effectively an insurance contract in which paying the premium today is expected to protect against a future contingency.

The second difficulty is that there are problems in valuing the benefits themselves. Put crudely, what is the value to society of having an additional person in employment or socially included? The counter-argument that it is impossible to put a price on human dignity leads nowhere, because all societies have to choose in some way. A hard-headed finance minister, trained to say 'no' often, has to consider not just the choice among social policy objectives, but also between social policy and other demands. Moreover, there are always other ways of alleviating social risks: is it better, for example, to alleviate poverty today by direct income transfers than by a long-term preventative strategy? There will unavoidably be a distributive dimension to the answer to this question.

Difficult choices arise about how to value outcomes from social investment that delivers far into the future. In the climate change debate, there is a logic behind the low rate of discount advocated by Stern (2015) for the very long term, in defiance of the more orthodox position that there should not be special pleading. The challenge to social investment is to formulate a similar case; without it, the net benefits will often prove inadequate to justify the investment. A related political economy challenge is how to deal with winners and losers. Opposition to change will, typically, be vocal from those who expect to lose from a change, whereas those expected to benefit will maintain a low profile.

Such an asymmetry will be more pronounced if there are concentrated, tangible losses, possibly in the short term, in contrast to dissipated and uncertain gains in the future. The notion of buffers, as explained by Hemerijck (Chapter 1, this volume), which also form part of the Social Investment Package (SIP), providing support for individuals during periods of transition (notably from and to employment) may be one means of addressing these political economy challenges. An economic analysis can provide rigour in appraising social investment, notably by highlighting some of the tensions between allocative and distributive considerations, but will always have to be tempered by political realities.

16

Conceptualizing and Measuring Social Investment

Johan De Deken

Section 1 of this chapter develops a typology of social investment that seeks to go beyond a conceptualization based on a mere dichotomy between 'compensation' and 'investment' by analysing these policies in terms of the kind of capital that is invested in and the targeted population. It also discusses some of the conceptual limitations of the approach. Section 2 is dedicated to operationalizing the concept, focusing on the input side of the policy process. It discusses what one can and cannot do with social expenditure by allocating the different policy branches that the Organisation for Economic Co-operation and Development (OECD) distinguishes in its Social Expenditure Database (SOCX) social expenditure database within the proposed typology. It concludes by discussing a series of methodological problems of interpreting cross-national and longitudinal variation in spending patterns to qualify the observed changes.

16.1 Conceptualizing Social Investment

The reproduction of society and the labour force has always been one of the central goals of welfare state intervention. The social investment approach (SIA) can be seen as an attempt to justify social policy interventions not merely in terms of their capacity to compensate for misfortune at the expense of burdening the economy, but as a productive factor that can boost the performance of that economy. This emphasis on economic sustainability is related to a concern with the possible deterioration of the ratio between the productive capacity of the active population and the welfare needs of the inactive population. As such the approach is intimately intertwined with the emphasis on activation in social and labour market policies and with various calls to use welfare state interventions to enhance skills and human capital. In this respect it shares some of the aims of neoliberal reform and neoconservative reform agendas. But what is distinct about the SIA is that it seeks to accomplish activation through other means than employment forcing instruments, and that it is concerned with limiting inequalities when promoting skills and human capital. One could see it as an egalitarian variant of productivist social policy paradigms, in which the return on investment is a productive labour force that participates in the private for-profit sector of the labour market. In order to emphasize the social nature of the approach, social investment has been associated with 'new' risks as opposed to 'old' ones; with unpredictable risks (or uncertainty) as opposed to (actuarially) predictable risks. In order to further legitimize the effectiveness of the approach, social investment is claimed to be an ex ante form of policy intervention as opposed to ex post, and as capacitating recipients rather than merely compensating them. Originally the paradigm distinguished two major kinds of social investment: measures that seek to expand the capabilities of individuals to be employed by raising the quality of the 'stock' of labour market participants (to use Hemerijck's language from Chapter 1, this volume); and measures that expand the opportunities to be employed by easing the 'flow' of contemporary labour market and life-course transitions.

16.1.1 *Fostering Individual Capabilities*

The measures that seek to enhance individual capabilities for employment can be further differentiated between three groups that target a different population:

(1) the existing stock of labour market participants who have lost their job (the unemployed) or their capacity to be employed (those who have become work incapacitated);

(2) the existing stock of labour market participants who still have a job, but who might need to be up-skilled or retrained in order to continue to be employable;

(3) the stock of future labour market participants who have not yet (children and adolescents) or never have been employed (e.g. home makers).

Policies that fall under the first category are not only those forms of active labour-market policies (ALMPs) that Bonoli (2011) has termed 'human capital investment' (various forms of retraining) and 'employment assistance' (placement services, counselling, job search programmes, job subsidies), but also unemployment insurance (as opposed to unemployment assistance) as an instrument to reward past investment and slow down its depletion (Estevez-Abe, Soskice, and Iversen 2001).

Measures that fall under the second category include employment protection regulations as an incentive for both employers and employees to invest in specific non-portable skills (Busemeyer 2009; Streeck 2011); unemployment insurance as an incentive for employees to invest in skills (Estevez-Abe, Soskice, and Iversen 2001); short-term maternity or parental leave (the effect of which is similar to that of the short-term impact of unemployment insurance); and policies that seek to promote 'life-long learning' in the workplace.

Measures that result in the third category include childcare in so far it improves the cognitive skills of children (in particular of those with a disadvantaged background); investments in primary, secondary, and tertiary education; measures that facilitate school-to-work transitions (like an institutionalized apprenticeship system); and some active labour market programmes targeted at adults who never were employed (such as home makers).

16.1.2 Expanding Employment Opportunities

The second kind of social investments are policies that attempt to increase the productive labour force by expanding job opportunities and easing life course transitions. This can be done through job creation in the public sector in the form of an expansion of public services (e.g. education, care) or through the active labour market programmes that Bonoli (2011) refers to as 'occupation'). It can also be done by creating jobs in the private sector by granting subsidies for work that suffers from a 'cost disease', by granting subsidies and tax exemption to employers who are willing to recruit hard to place job seekers; or by the demand side effect of service vouchers schemes. A third category of measures that improve the opportunities to be employed focus on the 'flow' function of life-course transitions. They include the socialization of care responsibilities including the supply side-effects of affordable childcare liberating parents, elderly care and care for the disabled to liberate carers, as well as the supply side-effects of service vouchers schemes. Finally, one can also improve employment opportunities by fostering the development of weak ties (Granovetter 1973) for those entering the labour market (the main example being here the network effect of apprenticeship systems, but some 'occupation' type of labour market policies were also expected to have this effect).

16.1.3 Integrating Compensatory Measures into Social Investment

Recently, the proponents of social investment have recognized that a shift towards social investment does not have to be implemented at the expense of compensatory forms of welfare state provision, but rather can play the role of institutional complementarities (see Chapter 11, this volume). It remains a bit unclear to what extent policies with a 'buffer' function are considered to be an integral part of social investment policies, or merely a set of traditional forms of welfare state intervention that form a 'critical precondition for an effective social investment strategy' (Hemerijck 2015: 248). We have already pointed out that some compensatory measures (e.g. unemployment insurance) may induce a 'stock' function (e.g. skill investment), even if they by and large have a 'buffer' function (Burgoon in this volume discusses more at length this problem of multiplicity).

16.1.4 *Limitations of the Social Investment Strategies*

In its emphasis on empowering individuals by fostering their individual capacities, the social investment paradigm tends to underplay the positional goods nature of individual human capital investments. As Fred Hirsch has pointed out, 'what is possible for the single individual is not possible for all individuals—and would not be possible if they all possessed equal talent', leading him to conclude that 'if everyone stands on tiptoe, no one sees better' (Hirsch 1976: 5–6). By emphasizing the fostering of individual capacities social investment strategies ignore power asymmetries in the labour market and fail to improve the labour market position of all labour market participants as a whole. Social investment, especially of the sort that seeks to strengthen the human capital of the individual, runs the risk of fostering competition among isolated individuals in a free market entailing hidden costs for themselves. Single individuals might end up being better off, but even if all market participants possess equal talent they are likely to continue to be excluded from opportunities. To some extent there is an overlap between the notion of freedom and opportunity of some variants of social investment and neoliberalism, in their emphasis of individual opportunities and their rejection of collective forms of advancement such as the decommodifying effect of unemployment and other forms of social insurance, and of employment protection legislation, that collectively improve the power balance in the labour market to the benefit of job employees. Rather than reducing people's exposure to the market, welfare state intervention must ease their adaptation to it (Crouch 2015). The individual becomes responsible for ensuring his or her employment by seeking forms of training and education to improve his or her human capital 'stock' and making use of the 'flow' provisions that facilitate his or her labour market and life-course transitions.

A second limitation of the SIA is that it tends to privilege employment in the private for-profit sector of the economy. The possible benefits of job creation schemes in the public sector, or of public sector expansion, is generally looked upon with scepticism. The underlying argument seems to be that this kind of employment cannot be expected to restore the economic sustainability of the welfare state (as it involves an additional burden on public finances, rather than generating additional tax revenue)—in essence adding to the nominator rather than the denominator of Myles equation of the cost of the welfare state (Myles 2002). 'Occupation'-type of ALMP is often not considered a genuine form of productive employment and is also held to be ineffective in bringing jobless people back to the productive labour market (Martin and Grubb 2001).

On the other hand, the Nordic countries that are often considered as leading the way in social investment strategies also tend to have very large public sector employment, in particular in areas such as health care and social care. Moreover, the apparent successes in keeping unemployment benefit caseloads down in those countries is to a significant extent related to the extensive use of public sector job creation programmes (De Deken and Clasen 2011: 311).

16.2 Measuring Social Investment

There are basically two ways one can try to measure the extent to which countries have embarked on the social investment path. On the one hand one can try to measure policy outputs and seek to develop policy performance indicators. On the other hand one can evaluate a possible shift in policy regime by examining input variables.

16.2.1 Output Variables

One can distinguish three kinds of output indicators. A first kind focuses on changes in the employment performance of a country, measured as the labour force participation rate. Using it as a benchmark for assessing employment success is marred with a series of methodological problems such as converting jobs into full-time equivalent, delimiting the labour force (e.g. how to deal with very important cross-national differences in work incapacity benefit recipients, early retirement, incidence of quasi-self-employment covering the true extent of the number of persons out of a job). Labour force participation rates also tell us little about the quality of employment that might result from the investment. Does increased labour force participation really lead to an overall increase in the productive output of an economy so that it is better equipped to meet the challenges of an ageing society or has it merely become a goal in itself and merely reflects the promulgation of jobs with limited added economic or social value? Labour force participation rates also say little about the quality of employment from the perspective of those who are employed: a lot of the job growth of the past two decades was in the form of precarious forms of atypical work that provided little if any security or job satisfaction. If the output of social investment policies is to be measured as increasing labour force participation, the measurement should take on board those quantitative and qualitative qualifications.

A second set of output variables measures social investment in terms of the reduction of poverty and inequality. Those variables are a useful complement to the first group of output variables as they might tell us something about the darker side of a strategy that seeks to reduce unemployment and boost employment at any cost. As activation policies and a sobering of the benefit system often lead to a proliferation of precarious work, they are also responsible for an increase in poverty amongst the working classes and of inequality within the labour force. Supplementing the assessment of changes in employment performance by changes in poverty or inequality allows for a better evaluation of the quality of the returns of social investment (Cantillon and Vandenbroucke 2014).

A third set of output variables that allow us to measure the effectiveness of social investment policies consists of benefit caseloads. To the extent that one of the main stated aims of the SIA is to trigger a policy shift from ex post remedies that address the consequences of being out of work towards ex ante prevention of people from becoming dependent on a transfer income, this should be reflected in a reduction of the caseload of working age benefits (De Deken and Clasen 2013).

16.2.2 *Input Variables*

Turning to the input side of the policy process, one can analyse cross-national and inter-temporal differences in policies by examining expenditure patterns. In such an analysis spending patterns are used as a proxy for institutional architecture of a welfare state. It builds upon the dictum of Rudolf Goldscheid (introduced to the Anglo-Saxon world by Joseph Schumpeter) that 'the budget is the skeleton of the state stripped of all misleading ideologies'. Even if among the advocates of social investment, it is increasingly claimed that social investment should not necessarily go at the expense of 'compensatory' or 'non-investment' forms of social protection, it is unlikely in an era of 'permanent austerity' that one can simply expand social spending. Hence the kind of resource competition that is inherent in the fiscal sociology of Goldscheid seems inevitable and justifies to some extent a disaggregated analysis of the structure of social expenditure. Such became possible ever since the OECD (and Eurostat) started to publish expenditure data broken down according to functional categories. The main challenge, though, is to link theoretically relevant policy categories that we identified in Section 16.1 to the administrative branches that are used in the databases of the OECD or Eurostat.

Earlier attempts to measure social investment on the basis of expenditure patterns opted for a rather basic dichotomous distinction between 'compensatory' and 'investment' (Nikolai 2012) or 'old' and 'new' forms of social spending (Vandenbroucke and Vleminckx 2011).

Nikolai's (2012) study limited itself to juxtaposing what it considered to be two exemplary expenditure items for each of these two categories. The category 'compensatory' programmes only included spending on old age and survivor pensions and spending on 'passive' labour market policies (consisting of unemployment compensation and early retirement). This left out important functionally equivalent programmes such as work incapacity schemes. The 'investment' category, on the other hand, included spending on family benefits (that included childcare as well as family benefits and maternity or parental leave schemes); spending on ALMPs; and spending on primary, secondary, and tertiary education. Some spending categories that could be quite important from a social investment perspective, such as elderly care, were left out of the analysis.

The (2011) study of Vandenbroucke and Vleminckx seeks to adopt a more comprehensive approach that tries to allocate most of the administrative spending categories of the OECD. Their 'old' spending category includes health care, old age and survivor pensions, and all cash benefits for the working age population (ranging from work incapacity benefits over compensation for the unemployed to income maintenance schemes and family benefits). Their 'new' category consists of parental leave schemes, elderly care, childcare and pre-primary education, and ALMPs, as well as primary and secondary education (though not tertiary education). The strength of their approach is that they initially keep the various components of their two main categories as subcategories, so that before they are amalgamated some correcting factors can be applied: thus spending on pension and care for the elderly is corrected for the share of the population over 65; and spending on childcare and pre-primary education is standardized between countries for the share of the population under the age of 5 (and a similar procedure is used to render spending on primary and secondary education comparable). But even though they also correct spending on ALMP for the incidence of unemployment in a country in a particular year, they decided not to do so for spending on unemployment benefits or on other working age benefits.

Given the conceptual complexity of social investment policies, it may be preferable to go beyond dichotomies that are merely amalgamating the OECD spending categories. This is what Table 16.1 tries to do by allocating the administrative policy branches that the OECD uses to theoretically relevant aspects of social investment (raising the quality of 'stock' of human capital and easing 'flow' of transitions of labour market participation)

Table 16.1. Linking social investment aspects to spending categories

Compensating Exit ('Buffer')	Fostering Individual Capabilities ('Stock')			Expanding Opportunities ('Flow')	
	Existing Participants		Potential Participants	Public Sector Employment	Private Sector Employment
	Out of Work	In Work			
- old-age pensions	- integration	- unempl. insur.	- childcare	- childcare	
- survivor pensions	- EmAs ALMP	- maternity leave	- pre-primary educ.	- care for elderly and frail	
- incapacity benefits	- HuCa ALMP	- parental leave	- primary educ.	- occup. ALMP	- wage subsidies
- early retirement		- paid leave	- secondary educ.		- serv. vouchers
- social assistance		- reintegration	- tertiary educ.		
- unempl. assistance		- HuCa ALMP	- EmAs ALMP		
			- HuCa ALMP		
	Ambiguous Categories *- health care* *- housing benefits* *- family benefits* *- long-term unemployment insurance* *- long-term maternity leave* *- sickness benefits*				

Note: 'EmAs' refers to Employment Assistance. 'HuCa' refers to Human Capital.

and juxtaposes them to one category of non-investment forms of social spending that only compensate exit from the labour market (and hence only perform a 'buffer' function without complementing the social investment functions).

16.2.3 Caveats of Using Spending Data

16.2.3.1 SPENDING ITEMS WITH MULTIPLE FUNCTIONS

A first problem that becomes obvious is that it is often hard to unambiguously allocate all the OECD spending branches unambiguously to a theoretically relevant aspect of social investment. Some administrative categories entail policies that have multiple functions. Thus spending on childcare can be seen as an instrument enabling women or parents to pursue a labour market career; but the very same spending item can also be seen as contributing to fostering the capacities of children as future labour market participants, as well as creating employment in the care sector. Moreover, there are forms of spending that have both an ex ante investment and an ex post compensation function attached to them. Hence there will be many proponents who would probably also feel very uncomfortable with allocating a social investment function to unemployment insurance (in contrast to unemployment assistance and social assistance), and maternal, parental, or general leave schemes.

191

Secondly, there are policies that do not translate into recorded spending. Some forms of social investment do not have a price tag attached to them that shows up in the OECD accounts. Mandatory policies such as statutory sickness pay are generally not recorded. Regulatory policies such as employment protection legislation may be costly but do not appear at all in the OECD accounts. An institutionalized system of apprenticeships that spreads the costs between the apprentice, the employer, and the state, will at best partially show in spending on secondary education. Moreover apprenticeships again have both a capacitating (skill-enhancing) aspect and an enabling dimension (fostering a network of 'weak ties' necessary to get a job).

16.2.3.2 PUBLIC AND MANDATED PRIVATE VERSUS VOLUNTARY PRIVATE

To the extent that a country relies upon compensatory spending that is formally considered 'voluntary private', it may (compared to other countries) appear to have gone more along the path of social investment than is actually the case (this is a major problem for compensatory transfers such as pensions, work incapacity, and early retirement benefits).

16.2.3.3 THE DIFFERENTIAL COMPOSITION OF 'COMPENSATORY' BENEFIT PACKAGES

Whereas in some countries unemployment compensation consists solely of unemployment insurance, other countries supplement the benefits from this administrative category with money from other areas of expenditure such as family benefits and housing benefits, that are considered neither investment nor compensatory. Some countries finance a sizeable part of their long-term care under the banner of general health care, whereas other countries have developed a separately registered spending item for this.

16.2.3.4 GROSS VERSUS NET SPENDING

So far the OECD database does not allow for a disaggregated analysis of net social spending. Countries differ significantly in the extent to which they tax the recipients of cash benefits. Because those transfers form the bulk of compensatory social spending, cross-national differences in direct taxation may lead in a particular country to an over- or under-estimation of the relative importance of social investment. But also cross-national differences in indirect taxes can lead to distortion in a comparative analysis. In countries with high consumption taxes, the state claws back a substantial part of social transfers. Because most of the services that are provided in the context of social investment are taxed at a reduced rate or not taxed at all, the importance of social investment, if measured in gross figures, might end up being underestimated.

16.2.3.5 FISCAL WELFARE

The OECD database only haphazardly records various forms of fiscal welfare. Some countries rely much more than others on tax breaks with a social purpose that are functionally equivalent to cash benefits (e.g. child tax allowances). The same is true of the use of fiscal measures to stimulate the provision of private cash benefits (e.g. private pension plans) or private services (e.g. childcare). Finally an increasing number of countries make use of in-work tax credits to facilitate labour market entry of problematic outsiders. Again the costs of such programmes is not recorded as social spending.

17

Measuring Social Investment Returns

Do Publicly Provided Services Enhance Social Inclusion?

Gerlinde Verbist

17.1 Introduction

The social-investment strategy aims to sustain the knowledge-based economy, which 'rests on a skilled and flexible labour force, which can easily adapt to the constantly changing needs of the economy but also be the motor of these changes' (Morel, Palier, and Palme 2012c: 1). Capacitating services are a key instrument in this strategy, as they help in creating a 'healthy, well-educated and more productive and mobile work force' (European Commission 2012b: 177). High levels of spending on services are often seen as an indicator of commitment to social investment. It is undeniable that services constitute an important part of government social spending in most countries (see Figure 17.1). Spending on publicly provided services corresponds to around 13 per cent of gross domestic product (GDP) on average across the thirty-four Organisation for Economic Co-operation and Development (OECD) countries, which is more than spending on cash social transfers (12 per cent). There is considerable cross-country variation, ranging from close to 8 per cent of GDP in Turkey to around 20 per cent in Denmark and Sweden. Services expenditures consist mainly of health care (6 per cent on average) and education services (5 per cent). Outlay on 'other services' mainly consists of spending on care to the elderly and to families; it represents a smaller share than the two major categories, but also shows large variation in spending across countries. The Nordic countries in particular appear here to be services-intensive, also in this group of 'other services'. There are indications that spending on social services as a share of GDP is on the increase over the past decades (see e.g. Kauto 2002; OECD 2008, 2011).

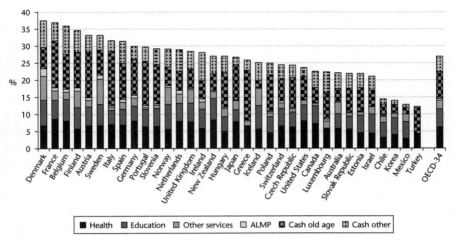

Figure 17.1. Public expenditure for in-kind and cash transfers, as a percentage of GDP, 2011

Notes: Countries are ranked by decreasing order of total public social expenditures. Education spending for Greece, Luxembourg, and Turkey refers to 2015. Spending on Active Labour Market Policies (ALMPs) cannot be split by cash/service breakdown and is hence given separately. 'Education' refers to public spending on education institutions. 'Cash old age' includes old age and survivor spending. 'Cash other' refers to spending on incapacity benefits, family benefits, unemployment benefits, and other social areas.

Source: OECD SOCX for expenditures other than education; OECD (2014b) *Education at a Glance 2014* for Education expenditures.

This goes along the lines that Esping-Andersen and colleagues (2002: 4) advocated in terms of changing welfare state architectures in Europe, stating,

> [A]s the new social risks weigh most heavily on the younger cohorts, we explicitly advocate a reallocation of social expenditures towards family services, active labour market policy, early childhood education and vocational training, so as to ensure productivity improvement and high employment for both men and women in the knowledge-based economy.

Preparing individuals for the knowledge-based economy and increasing their employability are central themes in social-investment rhetoric. But, interestingly, despite the fact that social inclusion is also part of this rhetoric, a key book on social investment (Morel, Palier, and Palme 2012c) hardly discusses the poverty and inequality effects of services or other instruments in the social-investment paradigm. It is rather assumed that a well-implemented social-investment welfare state will be egalitarian by increasing employment. The underlying assumption of the social investment strategy is that advantages will be found at two levels: namely an increase of economic efficiency and employment, as well as a reduction in inequality and poverty (Nolan 2013).

However, the focus on investment and work risks relegating the distributive aspect to the background (Cantillon 2011). For services, this is to some extent understandable, as they do not have inequality reduction as their primary aim. But as social inclusion is to be enhanced through a social investment strategy, it is important to study the distributive properties of services.

Opposing views have been expressed regarding the inequality impact of services. Le Grand (1982: 137), for instance, claimed that '[p]ublic expenditure on health care, education, housing and transport systematically favours the better off and thereby contributes to inequality in final income', while Esping-Andersen and Myles (2009: 654) state 'that services are generally redistributive in an egalitarian direction, albeit less so than are cash transfers'.

Gauging the distributive characteristics of services is difficult, as they do not only affect net disposable incomes, but also shape market incomes. A typical example is how service-intensive Nordic welfare states have defamiliarized caring responsibilities for children and the elderly, resulting in virtually identical employment rates for men and women. Consequently, the Nordic countries have low child-poverty rates even before social benefits are taken into account. Ignoring these indirect effects of publicly provided social services on the distribution of market incomes risks seriously misjudging their real distributional impact (Verbist and Matsaganis 2014).

17.2 Distributive Impact of the In-Kind Benefit of Capacitating Social Services

Studies try to gauge the impact of services on inequality in different ways. A first indication can be given by looking at correlations between spending levels on services (e.g. as a share of GDP) and inequality levels over countries (see e.g. Busemeyer 2014 for vocational education). Given the complex interactions between spending on sources, and especially the fact that the impact of services on social inclusion can only be measured over a longer time span, this can only provide a rough indication. We come back to these long-term effects in Section 17.3.

Another way to study the redistributive impact of services is incorporating in-kind benefits from social services into the income concept. Most empirical studies on cross-national differences in the levels of inequality and poverty use cash incomes only. As more than half of social spending in OECD countries is provided through non-cash benefits in the form of services such 'cash-income-only' studies miss an important part of welfare state efforts. Especially given the wide variety across countries in their relative share of cash and in-kind spending, this might give a misleading picture of redistributive outcomes. Both in-kind and cash transfers impact on living standards inequality, so a measure that includes these in-kind benefits is theoretically superior to the more conventional cash-income measures (Callan, Smeeding, and Tsakloglou 2008; Canberra Group 2011).

Incorporating the value of publicly provided services in household income is challenging as it raises a range of methodological issues regarding allocation, valuation, and taking account of corresponding needs through equivalence scales (see e.g. OECD 2008, 2011; Aaberge, Langørgen, and Lindgren 2010; Aaberge et al. 2010; Verbist, Förster, and Vaalavuo 2012).

The first issue relates to the allocation of these benefits across individuals: who are the beneficiaries to whom the value of public services is attributed? The literature distinguishes the 'actual consumption approach' and the 'insurance value approach' (see e.g. Marical et al. 2008). The actual consumption approach allocates the value of public services to those individuals actually using the service; it can hence only be applied if actual beneficiaries can be identified. This approach is typically used in the case of education (Antoninis and Tsakloglou 2001; Callan, Smeeding, and Tsakloglou 2008) and childcare services (Matsaganis and Verbist 2009; Vaalavuo 2011; Van Lancker and Ghysels 2012). For health care, most empirical studies use an insurance value approach, imputing the value of coverage to each person based on specific characteristics (such as age and sex). It is based on the notion that what the government provides is equivalent to funding an insurance policy where the value of the premium is the same for everybody sharing the same characteristics and also incorporates the value of access to this type of service (Smeeding 1982; Marical et al. 2008).

The second issue refers to valuation, which is very difficult for publicly provided services, as these services are provided outside market settings, and so there is no market price mechanism at work. In the literature, the standard practice is to value the in-kind benefit deriving from public services at their production cost, meaning that its measurement is based on the inputs used to provide these services rather than on the actual outputs produced (see e.g. Smeeding et al. 1993; Aaberge and Langørgen 2006; Marical et al. 2008). This means, however, that it does not necessarily reflect the user's valuation of the service. Another problem with using the production cost is that it does not take account of the quality and efficiency in services provision.

Finally, there is the issue of taking account of the corresponding needs. Equivalence scales are commonly used in distribution analyses to take account of economies of scale resulting from the fact that needs of a household grow with each additional member in a non-proportional way. But as some types of non-cash income may have associated needs that are unmeasured in usual equivalence scales, using a cash-income equivalence scale when non-cash income components are included in the income concept may give rise to a 'consistency' problem (Radner 1997). Service-related needs do not necessarily depend on economies of scale as captured by a standard cash-income equivalence scale, and may therefore require an alternative approach. Recent studies that experiment with such alternatives are Aaberge, Langørgen, and Lindgren (2010), Aaberge and colleagues (2010), Paulus, Sutherland, and Tsakloglou (2010), and Verbist and Matsaganis (2014).

Over the past decades the number of studies investigating the first-order redistributive impact of social services has grown considerably (for overviews, see e.g. Marical et al. 2008; Vaalavuo 2011; Verbist, Förster, and Vaalavuo 2012). These studies differ in terms of country coverage as well as types of services studied. Pioneering work was done by Smeeding (1977, 1982), who investigated the poverty impact of in-kind food, housing, and medical-care benefits in the United States. The outcomes of the various national studies are not directly comparable to one another due to differences in methodology and data; but in general it appears that these services have an inequality-reducing effect. International comparative evidence is on the increase, starting with Smeeding and colleagues (1993), who study the distributive effect of health care, education, and public housing in seven countries (Australia, Canada, the Netherlands, Sweden, United Kingdom, United States, and West Germany), using the LIS (Luxembourg Income Study) data for years between 1979 and 1983. Garfinkel, Rainwater, and Smeeding (2006) supplement this analysis by using more countries and more recent LIS data (2002 or earlier). More recent evidence is presented in Paulus, Sutherland, and Tsakloglou (2010), who investigate the inequality effect of the same three services in five European Union (EU) countries, as well as in OECD (2008, 2011), which present the widest country coverage. OECD (2008) investigates for fifteen OECD countries the inequality impact of the three services that have received most attention in the literature: public health care, education, and housing (for more details, see Marical et al. 2008). OECD (2011) extends the analysis both in terms of number of countries (twenty-seven OECD member states) and types of services, as it also studies childcare and long-term elderly care (for more details see Verbist, Förster, and Vaalavuo 2012). The outcomes of these studies all go in the same direction: including the value of publicly provided social services has a considerable equalizing effect on income distribution. Inequality reduction through services is important: on average across the countries considered in OECD (2011), the Gini coefficient is reduced by about one-fifth when moving from cash to extended income. Even though this is less than inequality reduction through cash transfers (which is about one-third), it is still considerable (OECD 2011; Verbist and Matsaganis 2014). For all countries health care and education services are by far the most important contributors to inequality reduction; the impact of early childhood education and childcare (ECEC), long-term elderly care and social housing is much smaller, mostly because their size is much more modest.

We now illustrate this with empirical material from OECD (2011) on the distributive impact of education and ECEC services. As investment in human capital and family policy as a productive factor are essential ingredients of the social investment strategy, these two categories stand out as its most direct manifestations. For education, the distributive impact is likely to vary across education levels, so we present results separately for compulsory (here defined as the total of primary and lower secondary education) and tertiary education.

Figure 17.2 gives the distribution of the in-kind benefits from education and ECEC over equivalized cash income quintiles. Total expenditures tend to go slightly more to lower incomes than to the top groups (see Panel A). The first quintile receives on average 21 per cent of all education expenditures, compared to 18 per cent in the fifth quintile. Compulsory education, however, is somewhat more oriented towards the lower incomes (Panel B), while the reverse applies for tertiary education (Panel C). This follows from the fact that pupils in compulsory education tend to be more concentrated in the lower parts of the income distribution. The position of these children in the income distribution is closely related to how successful countries are in combating child poverty, either by changing market income through high employment or by well-designed tax-benefit policies. These outcomes confirm the better performance in this domain of the Nordic countries, and the challenges other countries face to better protect children against income poverty and social exclusion (see e.g. Gornick and Jäntti 2012). Outcomes for tertiary education services are quite different, largely because the distribution of participants in higher education is different. We also observe much more cross-country variation, with very progressive patterns in the Nordic countries and very pronounced regressive patterns in, for example, Estonia and Mexico. In Denmark, Norway, and Sweden the bottom quintile accounts for around half of the participants in higher education. These participation patterns reflect socioeconomic differences that are important in terms of access to higher education, as well as institutional differences in, for example, affordability, the structure of earlier levels of education, and so on. The Nordic countries are characterized by accessible and affordable tertiary education institutions translating in high enrolment rates (Vaalavuo 2011). The interpretation of these outcomes is, however, complicated as many students live away from their parents in the Nordic countries and are thus classified as a separate household. Due to their low incomes, students are often concentrated in the poorest 20 per cent of the population. This partly reflects cultural differences, but is from a poverty perspective also partly an artefact: students living away from their high-income parents have temporary low incomes during their student years, but the literature on the returns to education indicates that in the earnings distribution their probable position later will be towards the top (Callan, Smeeding, and Tsakloglou 2008). But even when

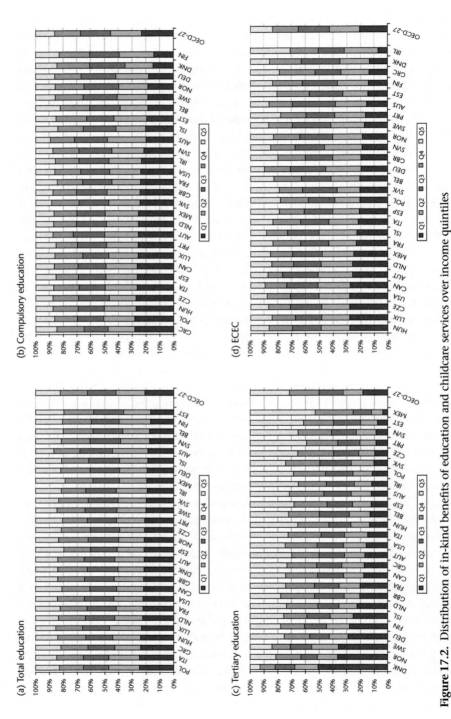

Figure 17.2. Distribution of in-kind benefits of education and childcare services over income quintiles

Source: Verbist et al. 2012.

Note: Countries are ranked in decreasing order by share of in-kind benefits in the bottom quintile (Q1).

controlling for this artefact, Sweden and Norway still have the most equal distribution of tertiary education expenditures (Vaalavuo 2011).

Also the distribution of ECEC services exhibits considerable heterogeneity across countries with more pro-poorness in countries like Hungary and Luxembourg and a clearly regressive pattern in, for example, Ireland. In contrast to compulsory education, where almost all children of that age group are in school, the pattern is also driven by differential use of ECEC services. In most countries, children in higher-income households are more likely to be enrolled in public ECEC facilities than those in lower-income households (see Table 17.1). The difference between childcare and pre-primary education is relevant in this context: for the youngest age group (0 to 3 years) enrolment is much more stratified along socioeconomic lines, with dual-earner couples (and hence higher incomes) making relatively more use of childcare (Förster and Verbist 2012; Van Lancker 2013). For children aged 4–5 years, pre-primary education is much more widespread, with often very high enrolment rates when getting closer to the age of compulsory schooling. An important

Table 17.1. Actual ECEC beneficiaries as a share of potential beneficiaries (children aged 0–5), by income quintile

	Q1	Q2	Q3	Q4	Q5	Total
AUS	33.0%	35.0%	50.8%	39.3%	42.4%	40.1%
AUT	38.1%	44.7%	46.6%	42.8%	47.7%	43.2%
BEL	54.2%	69.9%	71.6%	75.7%	79.0%	69.2%
CAN	30.9%	32.9%	29.2%	27.5%	26.3%	29.8%
CZE	44.1%	45.6%	46.9%	40.0%	40.7%	43.8%
DEU	65.8%	59.9%	67.9%	61.0%	57.1%	62.8%
DNK	80.1%	80.4%	86.0%	86.8%	84.6%	83.8%
EST	56.1%	48.0%	54.2%	53.3%	48.4%	52.0%
ESP	64.7%	66.4%	66.9%	68.0%	72.7%	67.6%
FIN	42.2%	45.2%	55.2%	69.5%	66.1%	54.0%
FRA	63.4%	56.9%	63.4%	63.2%	70.8%	63.0%
GBR	33.7%	38.8%	45.7%	52.2%	53.1%	43.0%
GRC	33.2%	37.6%	38.1%	50.8%	43.8%	40.7%
HUN	53.0%	52.2%	54.9%	57.2%	55.7%	54.2%
IRL	15.1%	26.7%	31.5%	31.4%	43.0%	28.9%
ISL	59.3%	70.4%	67.4%	74.6%	66.8%	66.8%
ITA	55.3%	57.4%	57.4%	57.4%	68.9%	58.5%
LUX	52.2%	63.3%	64.3%	63.3%	75.6%	61.6%
MEX	15.2%	15.9%	16.2%	15.5%	16.1%	15.8%
NLD	66.2%	64.8%	66.8%	69.1%	85.5%	69.4%
NOR	48.6%	57.2%	60.2%	58.9%	67.6%	57.5%
POL	17.4%	17.2%	20.6%	24.5%	31.5%	21.8%
PRT	46.5%	45.3%	54.8%	68.1%	68.3%	56.2%
SWE	70.6%	70.6%	72.6%	70.0%	69.6%	70.9%
SVK	29.3%	33.4%	56.1%	42.4%	64.8%	43.2%
SVN	56.2%	64.1%	62.0%	57.7%	62.7%	60.4%
USA	29.6%	27.7%	29.5%	28.8%	28.5%	28.9%
OECD-27	46.4%	49.2%	53.2%	53.7%	56.9%	51.4%

Source: Förster and Verbist (2012).

element in this context is that pre-primary education is in general free of charge, while parents have to pay a fee for childcare use. Even though in many countries these fees are income-dependent in order to limit the private cost of childcare for low-income families, the use of childcare is still often biased towards higher incomes.

17.3 Employment and Long-Term Inequality Effects of Publicly Provided Services

So far we have only discussed first-order distributive effects of publicly provided services. But services (as well as cash transfers) also have other effects, relating to behavioural reactions and long-term impacts. Trying to study second-order distributive effects of public policies empirically is, however, a hazardous task because finding a pre-government counterfactual is problematic (Jesuit and Mahler 2010): we do not know what the distribution of market income would be without cash and in-kind transfers. The few studies that try to take account of such second-order effects (e.g. Jesuit and Mahler 2010; Doerrenberg and Peichl 2014) concentrate on cash redistribution only. Nevertheless, second-order effects due to services merit further attention as they are at the heart of social investment strategy. We therefore think it is important to try to grasp these second-order effects, and we now turn to consider short-term and long-term second-order effects of education and ECEC services.

In the short term, education services can often have negative effects on labour supply. As the public provision of education stimulates participation, these participants obviously cannot spend their school time on the labour market. There is little question that primary and secondary education in the longer term consistently increase labour supply, so not surprisingly these types of education are heavily subsidized in almost all OECD countries and are to a large extent compulsory. They provide the human capital that society deems to be the absolute minimum to be attained. The expectation that job training programmes would have similar positive effects is not corroborated by empirical evidence. The vast literature on evaluating such programmes shows only modest gains in terms of labour supply and earnings (Currie and Gahvari 2008). It is argued that this is due to the fact that these programmes are often too short and too superficial to generate a more substantial impact (Lalonde 1995).

How education services impact on income inequality in the longer term is difficult to assess, and until now hardly any studies have undertaken this difficult task, mainly due to conceptual and methodological limitations, and lack of information. Exceptions are Sylwester (2002) and Bergh (2005). By combining data on public education spending between 1960 and 1969 with changes in Gini inequality indicators for later years, Sylwester (2002) demonstrates that a country with higher education expenditures (as a share of GDP) has lower income inequality in later years. Bergh (2005) then shows that this equalizing effect is entirely due to public spending on primary and secondary education. The effect of public higher-education expenditures, in contrast, is either not significant or even negative. Intuitively, one would expect higher public spending on tertiary education to lead to higher enrolment rates and subsequently lower income inequality. Bergh and Fink (2008), however, show that if public subsidies raise the incentive to enrol in tertiary education, this in the first instance increases inequality if the group enjoying the wage premiums associated with higher education is small. As enrolment increases, this effect will become less and eventually will be egalitarian.

For childcare services, Currie and Gahvari (2008) assert that they have short-term positive effects for the parents, in particular for young mothers. Childcare services reduce the relative price of childcare and should facilitate employment of parents, especially mothers. The European Commission (2009) reports evidence from country studies according to which the availability of childcare facilities intensifies mothers' labour-market participation rates. On the basis of a literature review, however, they conclude that there is little empirical evidence that these positive short-term effects will offset the deadweight loss associated with the tax system. Moreover, if the use of childcare is biased against vulnerable socioeconomic groups (such as low-skilled mothers), then investment in ECEC will not necessarily be inequality-reducing (Van Lancker 2013). One may expect larger long-term effects than short-term ones, as these services may limit potential losses in future earnings stemming from longer career interruptions. But stimulating maternal employment is not the only channel through which childcare services could foster social inclusion in the longer term. They also aim to enhance school readiness of children, in order to have a positive impact on human-capital formation of young children and their potential wages later in life. There is empirical literature that offers some support for the idea that in-kind transfers to children may be productivity-enhancing in the long term (for an overview, see Karoly, Kilburn, and Cannon 2006). Early-intervention programmes can be effectively equalizing, as they support the most vulnerable groups (Esping-Andersen 2008). Various studies demonstrate that the quality of childcare provision is an important condition in order to derive beneficial effects from preschool programmes (for an overview, see Esping-Andersen et al. 2012). A comparison of programmes in Denmark and the United States indicates that investment in high-quality services is of itself insufficient (Esping-Andersen et al. 2012). This should be connected to the quality of the subsequent school system, parental leave arrangements, and broader welfare programmes (Van Lancker 2013).

The long-term effects of both education and childcare services may provide a justification for the more paternalistic arguments that are traditionally seen as underpinning the provision of public services over cash transfers. Provision in kind steers families towards education and childcare, which might not be the case if the value of these provisions was given in cash to families. According to Currie and Gahvari (2008: 1), such paternalistic arguments become more powerful

> when the intended recipient of a transfer program is a child but the transfer goes to parents. Parents may not take full account of the utility of their children when making decisions or they may neglect to factor in externalities. For example, suboptimal spending on children's education may lead not only to poorer individual prospects, but also to slower future economic growth.

17.4 Conclusion

In current policy discourses 'social investment' in human capital, is increasingly seen as the way forward in bringing about structural and sustainable social progress. What can we expect from social investment policies if our concern is with inequality and poverty? Even though services are a key instrument of the social-investment strategy, this issue is often neglected by researchers and policymakers often. This also relates to the many methodological challenges if one wants to assess both first- and second-order distributive effects of services. Interestingly, when bringing together empirical literature on this topic, it is clear that services matter for making societies more egalitarian. Taking the example of compulsory education, empirical outcomes from both a first- and a second-order perspective are unequivocal: this type of investment in children is good for reducing income equality. Probably the compulsory character is of high importance here. Empirical evidence on tertiary education and ECEC services tells a different story, with a variety of experiences across countries. In most countries these two types of services are more socially stratified, with often relatively more beneficiaries towards the top of the income distribution. Consequently, simply increasing spending on these services will not be enough to foster egalitarianism, as the wider social context is also very important. Crucial parameters, such as access, availability, and quality of the services, need to be considered and integrated into the analysis and in the policy perspective; this, however, poses conceptual and methodological challenges for future research.

Part 5

Comparative Social Investment Experience

18

Developing and Spreading a Social Investment Perspective

The World Bank and OECD Compared

Jane Jenson

In the mid-1990s, the practice of international organizations involved in social development began to cohere around new ideas, including social investment. Their concern with 'flow', 'stock', and 'buffers' generated child-centred strategies and investment in human capital to ensure economic growth and social development. International organizations played key roles in the development and diffusion of social investment perspectives, with the objective of breaking the intergenerational cycle of disadvantage by investing in the human capital of the next generations. They did not always, however, prescribe the same policy instruments, because they stressed different routes to achieving social development. For the Global South, international organizations endorsed the instrument of conditional cash transfers (CCT) to allow very poor families to invest in children's health and education, a stock-plus-buffer strategy. For the North, they recommended early childhood education and care (ECEC) to ensure human capital development and the labour market activation of parents (and other adults), a stock-plus-flow strategy.

In addition, as regions converged around precarious/informal labour markets, low wages, high poverty, and transformed families, the observation that international organizations working in both North and South shared the policy objective of breaking the intergenerational cycle of disadvantage was by no means only the result of diffusion from the 'developed North' towards the 'developing world', as had been the common direction of movement in the decades after 1945. Ideas and practices moved from South to North as well.

The analysis of this chapter begins when international organizations working in the North and South were both challenged to identify an appropriate strategy for alleviating some of the human costs of the structural adjustments that many of these same international organizations had promoted in the 1970s and 1980s. For the World Bank (and regional banks) and for the Organisation of Economic Co-operation and Development (OECD), by the mid-1990s the costs of sponsoring structural adjustments were visible, in the form of high poverty rates even among the employed, child poverty, and—at the societal level—threats to social cohesion.

This chapter documents the emergence and deployment of the social investment perspective by the World Bank and OECD beginning in the mid-1990s, and indicates several points of commonality and intersection while also tracking differences in the two strategies.

18.1 The World Bank: A Social Investment Perspective after the Washington Consensus

The role of international organizations in shaping social policy in the Global South has been summarized this way: 'Developing countries is an international practice. The agencies engaged in this practice include . . . international intergovernmental organizations, such as the organs of the United Nations and the World Bank, many of which have been expressly set up to resolve various development problems' (Gore 2000: 789). These international organizations also have significant resources. Not only can they endorse 'avant-garde' social knowledge; they can also distribute resources to ensure implementation of their preferred practices (Clemens and Kremer 2016).

Development practice has changed over time. The 1980s was the decade of structural adjustments and the Washington Consensus, a list of tough neoliberal prescriptions for the Global South (Gore 2000: 789–90). Then beginning in the mid-1990s several key actors struggled over policy directions, creating space for new policy thinking. United Nations Children's Fund (UNICEF) led the charge for 'development with a human face', thereby moving 'child poverty' significantly higher on the agenda of 'development problems' (Jenson 2010: 68–9; also Mahon 2010: 174–5). Exposure of the limits of market fundamentalism and the failures of the Washington Consensus (by among others Joseph Stiglitz, a Bank vice-president and senior economist at the time) encouraged recalibration of the World Bank's position. For example, its 1997 World Development Report signalled a shift in the 'development establishment's' thinking about states and markets (Evans and Rauch 1999: 748). The 2005 World Development Report consecrated a decade-long move away from all-encompassing and univocal formulae (such as the ten injunctions of the Washington Consensus) to an approach in which 'the emphasis is on the need for humility, for policy diversity, for selective and modest reforms, and for experimentation' (Rodrik 2006: 974).

This policy rethink coincided with the development of what we now label the social investment perspective (Jenson 2010). If market fundamentalism had failed and a single global formula was no longer effective, there was policy space for meso-level strategies and honed interventions such as Dani Rodrik endorsed. They might also rest on the conviction that social welfare spending and growth were complementary, not contradictory (Hall 2007: 155). A perspective with its own convincing analysis of the intergenerational transmission of poverty and proposed instruments for eradicating it could make headway (Hall 2007: 152).

By the mid-1990s the key themes of the social investment perspective were in place as were ideas about instruments for improving the stock of human capital and for stabilizing buffers, including attention to breaking intergenerational cycles. *Investing in People: The World Bank in Action* (World Bank 1995) was published to lay out explicitly the Bank's approach to human development. Overseen by the Directors of the Education and Social Policy Department and the Population, Health and Nutrition Department, the 1995 document's child-centred approach anchored its very definition of investment: 'Investing in people means helping people invest in themselves and their children. It means empowering households, especially poor households, to increase the quantity and quality of investments in children. For people to break the cycle of poverty and improve their lives, they must have access to adequate social services . . . ' (World Bank 1995: 3).

The perspective's origins in these units of the Bank technocracy meant education was designated a driver of development, and increased human capital the objective. Another document from the same World Bank group was prefaced this way:

> The key words in today's development economics are 'human capital'. More and more emphasis is being placed on investments in education, health, and nutrition as a means of bettering the lives of people in developing countries. There is now enough theoretical and empirical evidence to indicate that both public and private investments in people contribute significantly to economic growth and the alleviation of poverty.   (Psacharopoulos 1995: v)

The image of a 'cycle of disadvantage' was already present: 'Also of great concern is the self-perpetuating cycle of illiteracy, illness, inadequate nutrition, high fertility, and slow economic growth common in developing countries. As this chapter explains, that cycle can be broken by effective investments in health, nutrition, population, and education' (World Bank 1995: 11).

This mid-1990s focus on investments in human capital as grounding for human development also contained an innovation. 'Education' would from now on encompass early childhood education (Psacharopoulos 1995: 15; World Bank 1995: v, 56–7; Jenson 2010: 65). The Bank's policy entrepreneurs drew on research that displayed efficiencies for their investments by improving school readiness (via preschool and health) and by supporting disadvantaged groups as well as allowing siblings (older sisters for the most part) to remain in school and enhancing parents' work–family reconciliation (World Bank 1995: 19; Mahon 2010: 176–7, 180).

As early as 1995, in other words, we can observe the three key themes that compose the social investment perspective: a preoccupation with education and human capital, including early childhood education; a child-centred orientation in which children are already creating the future; ensuring individuals' success is beneficial for the community as a whole, now and into the future (Jenson and Saint-Martin 2006: 434). In this early version of the social investment perspective there were also expectations that investments would increase equity and social justice for adult women. This gender sensitivity would later fade from the Bank's social investment perspective. A main analytic claim throughout continued to focus on children: that 'investments in girls' education have significant benefits for future generations' (World Bank 1995: 7).

Beginning in the late 1990s a new policy instrument began to dominate efforts to achieve the pay-offs of investments in early childhood development and to battle poverty, including its intergenerational transmission. This was the conditional cash transfer (CCT). By 2015 all Latin American countries had at least one CCT and between 2008 and 2010 the number of cash transfer programmes in Africa went from twenty-one to thirty-seven (Hall 2015: 89). They are a key policy instrument about which the Human Development network of the Bank deploys both vast amounts of social knowledge, expertise, and large loans (Clemens and Kremer 2016: 57, 59).

CCTs emerged as a policy innovation in the 1980s in several Latin American countries (Fiszbein and Schady 2009: 35). But in 1997 Mexico created the CCT which we now associate with the social investment perspective. At the time there were fifteen different food subsidy programmes, much disliked by technocrats in the Mexican finance ministry. The new programme, PRO-GRESA (later Oportunidades) was pushed through by economist Santiago Levy, Undersecretary of Expenditure in the Ministry of Finance. He reduced food subsidies and convinced the administration to adopt his preferred position of targeting the very poorest and imposing co-responsibility (that is, conditionality) (Teichman 2008: 453).

The World Bank quickly joined the CCT bandwagon, offering technical expertise and funding for the extension of these instruments across Latin America (Clemens and Kremer 2016: 59). They were explicitly described as tools of social investment. The World Bank's much-cited report on CCTs rehearses all of the arguments about CCTs as social investments, particularly in the human capital of children (Fiszbein and Schady 2009: 11). While Bank technocrats continued to praise the Mexican CCT, primarily because it had been designed to provide reliable evaluation data, the version that was standardized and diffused owed more to the Brazilian Bolsa Família that imposed lighter conditions and used a much less neoliberal discourse (Ancelovici and Jenson 2013).

The World Bank was the main actor in the certification and diffusion of CCTs as a policy instrument within the social investment perspective, but other international organizations also spread them enthusiastically. The Brazil-based International Policy Centre on Inclusive Growth (IPC-IG) of the United Nations Development Programme (UNDP), for example, has been another key diffuser of knowledge about CCTs, in Africa and Lusophone countries (Ancelovici and Jenson 2013: 307).

Prioritizing CCTs had important consequences for how the social investment perspective unrolled over time. CCTs address child poverty and child development as well as poverty. 'Flow' concerns about labour market participation are minimally addressed. Conditionality is detached from parental employment; income is the only measure to determine access. Thus the Bank's considerations of employment (and social policies associated with it, such as pensions) use another analytic frame, while women's employment and gender equality is handled by a separate unit in the large organization that is the World Bank, the Gender and Development unit.

The social investment perspective, with CCTs and ECEC as popular policy instruments, has now been incorporated into a new paradigm about development in the Global South. 'Inclusive growth' has displaced the narrower pro-poor paradigm (Jenson 2015). Buffer-like notions underpin calls for a social protection floor and the policy instruments, especially CCTs, of the social investment perspective are components of this approach in Latin America, Europe, and Asia (Hasmath 2015). Proponents of inclusive growth eschew narrow or fundamentalist approaches, preferring an 'ultra-pragmatic approach to development policy practice' (Hasmath 2015: 4), a vision consistent with the World Bank's conversion to experimentation and policy diversity described in this section (Rodrik 2006).

18.2 The OECD: Quick Off the Mark but Poorly Coordinated

The OECD is an important international organization but lacks a key resource of the Banks (and many others working in the Global South). It can be propositional but does not deliver programme funding and support. The OECD analyses and assesses a wide range of policy areas and provides evaluations of national experiences within a comparative perspective. It can make quite specific recommendations to governments that follow from its analytic and policy preferences, but it cannot enforce them (Mahon 2009: 183–4). The exclusively propositional role of the organization has been important in two ways with respect to its involvement with a social investment perspective: it could move early and make a significant intervention; and it could shift its analytic lens elsewhere with ease. As it moved towards social investment, the OECD also focused on stock (human capital). But in contrast to the Bank, it spotlighted issues related to flow out of and into the labour market.

The OECD first took up social investment for a reason similar to that of the World Bank. It was concerned about the social and political costs of its own and others' commitment to structural adjustments. Having been in the 1980s and early 1990s a fervent proponent of labour-market interventions shaped both by neoliberal critiques of post-1945 welfare states and by commitments to market fundamentalism, the OECD by the mid-1990s had become concerned about social cohesion, convening a major conference in December 1996 on societal cohesion in the era of globalization. The OECD's work on social cohesion was explicitly linked to social investment: 'By shifting from a social expenditure to a social investment perspective, it is expected that considerable progress can be made in transforming the welfare state' (report of the 1996 conference, quoted in Jenson and Saint-Martin 2003: 84). The OECD began to 'speak social investment' and deploy the premises that we now assign to this approach at the same time as the World Bank was doing.

Another 1996 high-level conference, Beyond 2000: The New Social Policy Agenda, concluded with a call for a 'new framework for social policy reform', labelled a social investment approach (SIA) to state action: 'The challenge is to ensure that return to social expenditures are maximised, in the form of social cohesion and active participation in society and the labour market' (OECD 1997: 5–6). The report also called for a framework to deal with 'social problems which are not being properly addressed' (now labelled the new social risks) and new policy instruments (OECD 1997: 4–5). The article in the *OECD Observer* summarizing the meeting deployed many of the keywords now used by the social investment perspective. Social policy should be 'pre-emptive and preventative' and, in the face of the new social risks, should be 'underwriting social investment helping individuals to get (re-)established in the labour market and society' in part because 'the main risk that families now face is that their children will not be able to establish themselves in careers' and in part because these challenges are leading to a demographic challenge in which fertility is falling (Pearson and Scherer 1997: 9, 7). In his introduction to the same *OECD Observer*, the Secretary-General called for 'enhancement of human capital through wise investment strategies in education, health and social security', language strongly reminiscent of the World Bank's 1995 document (cited in Section 18.1) that had just appeared.

After this initial intervention about modernizing social policy, and countering new social risks, the OECD proceeded to undertake significant work on a key policy instrument of the social investment perspective, ECEC. Two units worked on the issue. The first was the Education Policy Unit that focused on early childhood education and was responsible for the Starting Strong series of three publications (Paananen, Kumpulainen, and Lipponen 2015: 693ff.) The second and most influential of these projects was the *Babies and Bosses* series organized by the Directorate of Education, Employment, Labour and Social Affairs, that had earlier been a strong proponent of the idea that social policy is costly because it brakes growth (Mahon 2010: 181–2). These studies were part of the OECD's move towards the position that social spending can support growth. Beginning in 2001 and as the titles signal, they focused on reconciling work and family (Mahon 2009: 192ff.).

These *Babies and Bosses* reports almost exclusively developed the labour-market 'flow' component of the social investment perspective. For example, the argument laid out in the synthesis report was that leaves and childcare services encourage parental employment, and parental employment limits poverty. Human capital fell out of the frame, while ECEC's potential contribution to child development is mentioned but very briefly and not as a priority (OECD 2007: 127–68). Over time the focus on quality in early childhood education in the Starting Strong analyses also significantly declined, with a 'discursive break' between the second (2006) and third (2012) documents (Paananen, Kumpulainen, and Lipponen 2015: 699, 702).

Work on schooling also took off for the OECD in these years and education was framed as a 'priority' of the 'modern knowledge economies'. But ECEC was not always included under the education rubric (OECD 2006: 4 and *passim*). The OECD did not, in other words, systematically extend its definition of 'education' back to early childhood, as is the practice of those promoting the social investment perspective and as the World Bank and other development international organizations had already done by 1995.

With respect to labour-market activation and support for employment, the OECD has always played a major propositional role. Since the *Jobs Strategy* of the mid-1990s it has promoted elimination of so-called structural blockages to employment. This is a 'flow' strategy like the reconciliation agenda of *Babies and Bosses*. Beyond that, the social investment perspective on poverty is quite invisible in recent work on 'activation strategies' (OECD 2013a). This 2013 publication does not mention the key notion of the social investment perspective, the intergenerational transmission of disadvantage, while the report also critiques one of the favourite social investment buffers, income supplements or work-first payments (Jenson and Saint-Martin 2006: 447). The criticism is that they do little to increase the income of the poor (OECD 2013a: 15–16). In other words, the focus on 'poor families' by the mid-2000s had shifted to spotlighting the effects of growing inequality and judging instruments by their capacity to reduce inequality (OECD 2013a: 12ff.).

The recent take-up of the 'inclusive growth' frame, applied as well to activation strategies, has led the OECD to discuss and even recommend CCTs as an instrument for inclusion, alongside other measures that will address the needs of a variety of vulnerable groups (OECD 2013a, 2014a). In line with its long-standing priority of improving labour-market flow via activation, the OECD even reconfigured the policy representation of CCTs, labelling them examples of 'activation and social protection', although the very summary provided of the Mexican, Brazilian, and Chilean instruments shows they are basically buffers delinked from employment (OECD 2013a: 19). Thus, following the categorization used in the Global South, CCTs are classified as a form of social protection, while the definition of 'activation' is broadened to cover much more than labour market participation by individuals. For example, 'activation is the combination of policy tools that provide support and incentives for: i) job search and job finding; ii) productive and rewarding participation in society; and iii) self-sufficiency and independence from public support' (OECD 2013a: 8). Only by using this definition can a CCT become an 'activation' instrument.

This framework for activation does not use the social investment perspective announced two decades ago. The analytic logic is different, stripped of an intergenerational analysis or a human capital focus and being agnostic about the link to employment. Thus, while the OECD remains an international organization leading the way for many social and economic issues, as its work on inequality has most certainly done (OECD 2011), it is no longer leading an integrated social investment perspective for the OECD world or globally.

18.3 The Current State of Play

International organizations travel on their ideas. They must also react to new challenges and address their failures and they are not immune from the effects of past policies when they do so. The two organizations examined in detail in this short chapter had, in particular, to respond both to the shortfalls of their commitment to structural adjustments in the 1980s and 1990s and later to the fall-out of the great crisis that began in 2007.

Both the World Bank and OECD responded to the first challenge by turning to what we have labelled a social investment perspective, emphasizing investments in human capital and adopting an intergenerational policy vision. Each focused, however, on only two of the three possible social investment functions: stock-plus-buffer for the Bank and stock-plus-flow for the OECD.

The perspective appears to have implanted itself more firmly in one international organization than the other. The ideas of the social investment perspective resonated with existing Bank framing, especially human capital as support for growth, and with its mission to fight poverty via human development (Clemens and Kremer 2016). This framing quickly attached early childhood education to the concept of childhood development. Then the Bank prioritized a policy innovation: the CCT to fight poverty in the present and its transmission into the next generation. The OECD's story is different. Its enthusiasm for social investment arrived early and identified ECEC as a key policy, as part of its attention to labour-market flow. The perspective never took off in an integrated fashion, however. Directorates and units continued to pursue their work with varied analytic frameworks, even within the education sector.

In the crisis, both the Bank and OECD also had to respond. The first did so by reinforcing its commitment to the favoured policy approach and tools. The OECD in contrast shifted towards the innovative position of blurring boundaries between rich, poor, emergent, and developing countries. Its analysis of inequality covers much more than the OECD world. Its commitment to the inclusive growth framework means it can propose its members familiarize themselves with policies and instruments developed in the Global South, such as CCTs, while it positions itself to speak to the world:

> Social tensions are visible across the globe. Citizens throughout the world are taking to the streets to voice their concerns and demands. . . . It is imperative to find solutions that foster economic growth in a more inclusive manner, where the gaps between the rich and the poor—not only in terms of income, but also in other dimensions that matter for people—are less pronounced, and opportunities, as well as the 'growth dividend', are shared more equally. (OECD, n.d.)

It can also, then, adopt the vocabulary used by other international organizations for decades: the 'go social' dimension of the inclusive growth strategy is now described as 'investment in people', the same trope the World Bank used in 1995 when it designated its move away from the Washington Consensus as 'investing in people'. But the OECD relies very little on the concepts of the social investment perspective to do so. It has moved on from poverty, even its intergenerational transmission, to seeking strategies to limit inequality. As critics of the social investment perspective have long told us, other perspectives are needed if the goal is to increase equality.

19

De-universalization and Selective Social Investment in Scandinavia?

Kees van Kersbergen and Jonas Kraft

19.1 Introduction

Scandinavian welfare states are characterized by universalism in benefits and services, a distinctive prominence of policies that facilitate human capital formation, and high levels of spending, taxation, and income redistribution that produce the lowest levels of income inequality in the Organisation for Economic Co-operation and Development (OECD) world. The universal welfare state clearly stands out when it comes to social investment policies and the associated social and economic performance, particularly because of its strong focus on raising the quality of the 'stock' of human capital and capabilities. In addition, the Scandinavian welfare states have been able to follow the social investment path, whilst avoiding to a large extent the main pitfalls or drawbacks that have been associated with social investment in other countries.

Will Scandinavia be able to maintain this path and uphold its widely praised qualities and performance? Scandinavian universalism has had huge positive feedback effects on popular support for the encompassing welfare state. Hence, the welfare state's fate depends upon the extent to which universalism continues to be the underlying moral and political principle of social policy, particularly inclusive social investment policies. Recent developments in social policy, however, cast doubt on universalism's prospects. While the welfare state remains broadly popular, a series of reforms have made the welfare state much less universal than it used to be.

Here we first describe the role of social investment in the universal welfare state to highlight its distinctiveness. We then clarify how the self-reinforcing feedback loops of the universal welfare state explain its social and political support foundation and robustness. Third, we turn to rising inequality, de-universalization, and 'selective social investments', and present empirical observations that challenge the conventional wisdom on the Scandinavian welfare state. The heyday of the universal welfare state may not be over, but some trends can ultimately undermine universalism and with that the very basis of the welfare state's popular support base.

19.2 Universalism and Social Investment

Scandinavian countries have been practising social investment policies long before the term was invented and became popular in research and European Union political discourse (Morel, Palier, and Palme 2012a; Nolan 2013). The ideas of social policy as a productive factor and social policy as investment rather than an economic cost go back to Alva and Gunnar Myrdal's social engineering approach (Etzemüller 2014). They developed the idea that to fight the decline of fertility and increase the quality of Sweden's population (in short, to solve the 'population question'), 'productive social policy' would promote the productivity of the economy and improve the quality of the population (Andersson 2005; Morel, Palier, and Palme 2012a; Hort 2014).

The early introduction of social investment in Scandinavia and its subsequent development make the Nordic welfare states stand out. Figure 19.1 shows Scandinavian government spending on three social investment policies—education, family benefits (OECD 2015c), and active labour market programmes—in comparison with Anglo-Saxon, Central European, and Southern European countries. The distinctiveness of Scandinavia clearly comes to the fore. Between 2005 and 2009, average spending on education, families, and active employment initiatives was 11 per cent of gross domestic product (GDP) in the Nordic welfare states, while elsewhere this was only 7–8 per cent of GDP. This unique pattern does not only show up for the 2000s, but can be traced back as far as the data allow us to go. In the 1995–9 period, for instance, Nordic governments used close to 6 percentage points more of national income on social investment than governments in the other country groups. For the late 1980s, the difference was smaller, but still approximately 2 per cent of GDP.

Not only do Scandinavian welfare states spend much more on investing in their citizens, public services financed by the government are also widely used. Table 19.1 shows the enrolment rates of formal childcare, preschool educational programmes, and of youth education, that is, policies widely accepted as crucial to social investment. The Scandinavian countries (except Finland) top the enrolment charts for Western democracies and lie well above the OECD average. Denmark has a particularly high level of enrolment in formal

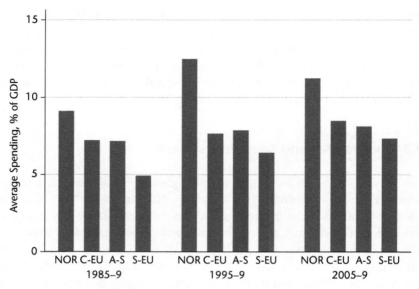

Figure 19.1. Public spending on education, family benefits, and ALMP

Note: NOR (Nordic countries): Denmark, Finland, Norway, Sweden. C-EU (Central European countries): Austria, Belgium, Germany, Luxembourg, Netherlands, Switzerland. A-S (Anglo-Saxon countries): Australia, Canada, Ireland, New Zealand, United Kingdom, United States. S-EU (Southern European countries): France, Greece, Italy, Portugal, Spain.

Sources: Education spending from World Bank database (2013), family and active labour market policies spending from OECD (2013b).

Table 19.1. Enrolment in childcare and educational services

	Formal Childcare (under 3 years old)			Preschool Programmes (3 to 5 years old)			Youth Education (20 to 29 years old)		
	2003	2007	2010	2003	2007	2010	2003	2007	2010
Denmark	56.1	65.7	65.7	89.3	91.3	94.1	31.9	38.2	38.4
Finland	21.3	25.0	27.7	–	–	73.0	40.4	43.0	41.7
Norway	29.5	47.3	54.0	82.5	92.8	96.2	28.6	29.9	29.4
Sweden	44.1	46.7	46.7	82.4	89.9	92.9	34.5	34.5	36.5
Central Europe	18.3	33.0	36.5	74.7	79.9	84.0	21.0	22.5	25.5
Anglo-Saxons	24.5	34.6	36.8	78.6	80.7	76.5	26.0	24.8	25.3
Southern Europe	14.8	30.8	33.7	84.9	84.1	85.7	21.9	21.9	26.0

Note: The table shows the share of persons enrolled in childcare and education for particular age groups. Missing data for formal childcare: all years (Canada, Switzerland); 2003 (Australia, USA, Italy). Preschool programmes: 2003 and 2007 (Ireland, Australia, Canada, Netherlands). Youth education: 2003 (Canada).

Source: OECD (2005, 2015b).

Table 19.2. Labour force participation rates across country groups and decades

	1985–9		1995–9		2005–9	
	Women	Total	Women	Total	Women	Total
Nordics	75.2	79.9	73.9	77.9	75.8	78.6
Central Europe	46.9	62.3	59.3	69.7	66.9	73.7
Anglo-Saxons	59.4	72.0	64.7	73.5	69.4	75.9
Southern Europe	47.0	62.8	52.4	64.2	60.6	69.3

Note: The labour force participation rate is the share of persons between 15 and 64 years of age in the labour force.
Source: OECD (2015f).

childcare provided for children under the age of 3, whereas Finland has a very high share of persons aged between 20 and 29 enrolled in educational programmes. Norway and Sweden similarly perform well in all three categories. Worth noting is that enrolment has increased over time and, in some areas, continues to do so.

The widespread consumption of these public services illustrates the universal traits in the Scandinavian social investment approach (SIA). A vast majority of citizens use and enrol in government programmes that facilitate skills formation and prepare children and students for future jobs and employment. The outcome of this clearly surfaces when looking at key labour market participation indicators. Table 19.2 depicts labour market participation rates for Scandinavia and the other three groups. Again, the Nordic countries stand out as having the largest labour force measured as a share of the total working population. Not only does the public provision of childcare, education, work–life balance initiatives, and active employment policies provide people with the skills to work, they also free up time to participate in the labour market. This has been especially conducive to female labour market participation. Table 19.2 clearly illustrates that even though there is some catching-up effect over time, nowhere does female labour market participation come even close to the Scandinavian level. Furthermore, the universal social investment strategy contributes to a more equal distribution of skills and opportunities. In part, this explains the low poverty levels and income inequality that universal welfare states have experienced across decades (see Figure 19.2).

19.3 The Political Robustness of the Universal Welfare State

This overview shows that: (1) comparatively speaking social investment has been a feature clearly distinguishing the Scandinavian welfare state from other types; (2) this defining characteristic has been robust and has become even more pronounced over time, at least until very recently. As Rothstein (1996,

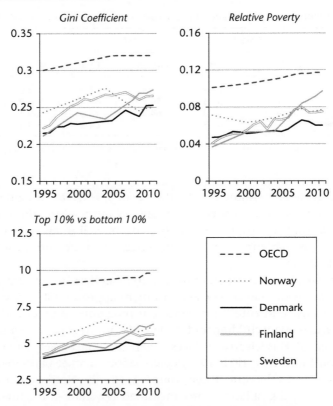

Figure 19.2. Inequality and poverty in Scandinavia and the OECD, 1995–2011
Source: OECD (2015c).

1998) has demonstrated, the political institution of the universal welfare state has strong moral strengths and consequences that are beneficial to its political sustainability. The relative staying power of the universal welfare state with social investment stems from the mutually reinforcing moral and political logic that underpins both its interests-based social and political support coalition and its norms-based popular legitimacy.

First, the welfare state exists for all citizens, regardless of class, occupation, income, or gender. Rothstein (1996: 112) spells out the normative principle as follows: 'If there is no obvious reason against, all citizens should be treated equally by the state. If there are burdens to be shared (e.g., taxes) or goods to be distributed (e.g., health care), they should be equally shared.' Once in place, this principle of universalism forces those who favour more selective policies and services in a politically defensive position, because they somehow would need to defend the unequal treatment of citizens.

Second, universalism accords legitimacy to the welfare state by overcoming potential doubt about abuse of power and fairness in implementation of social policies. Universal social policies and services do not suffer from the delegitimizing kind of bureaucratic discretion problems in implementation associated with selective and means-tested policies. If the universal welfare state 'is to treat different individuals differently, it must be the *specific* situation of the individual (sickness, age, unemployment, etc.) that determines the concrete meaning of "equal concern and respect" and not the *general* situation of the individual (status, wealth, power)' (Rothstein 1996: 113–14, emphasis in original).

Third, the universal welfare state is less vulnerable than selective systems to violations of the fair share principle. Misuse of provisions and fraud are more likely when needs are to be tested than when benefits and services are provided universally as a social right. This too has beneficial consequences for the universal welfare state's legitimacy.

Universalism's principles of equal treatment, equal concern and respect, and fair shares therefore accord the universal welfare state a unique moral and political infrastructure that produces a positive and self-reinforcing feedback loop from social policies to political support, back to social policies, and so forth (see Fage Hedegaard 2015). The key political feature is that the middle class is included, both as a contributor and as a receiver, in the social and political coalition that supports it. Universalism also straightforwardly implies income redistribution, even in the absence of progressive taxation, simply because while every individual receives the same, higher income groups pay a larger absolute sum of money than the lower income groups (Rothstein 1998: 147ff). In addition, the universal welfare state is not only generous in its benefits and allowances, but also 'service heavy' in that over the life course it offers a wide range of social services, which can be seen as investments with very high rates of social returns (Kvist 2013, 2015b).

Social investment and income redistribution obviously create a high level of equality of outcome in the income and skills distribution and with that— money and education being the most important instrumental goods that can overcome inequalities of opportunity (Fishkin 2014)—a very high level of social mobility. There is a strong relationship between income inequality and intergenerational earnings elasticity (how much a son's earnings depend on parental earnings), with Scandinavia standing out as having the lowest income inequality and the highest mobility (lowest elasticity) (Corak 2013: 82). Sweden is slightly off here: it has the highest level of equality, but mobility is lower than in the rest of Scandinavia. This is explained by the fact that Sweden, unlike Norway and Denmark, has always had a more rigid and closed upper class (Björklund, Roine, and Waldenström 2012), while wealth inequality is comparatively speaking very high (Jantti, Sierminska, and Smeeding 2008; Esping-Andersen 2015).

This is the 'common wisdom' on the Scandinavian welfare state, namely that universalism and social investment are two components of the same political-normative sequence that generates broad support for the welfare state and on practically all social indicators (particularly income equality) produces outcomes that are socially and economically superior compared to systems that are much less encompassing and more selective. Moreover, the broad consensus has made welfare state renovation and adaptation to changing internal and external challenges to the Nordic model a manageable political task (Dølvik et al. 2015).

19.4 A Trend towards De-universalization?

In the more recent period things have started to look slightly differently. Some trends could indicate a change of direction in the SIA. Recent studies suggest that the welfare state is fundamentally changing and that the transformation can best be characterized as a move away from universalism. There is a decline of universalism and inclusive social investment, measured as rising selectivity in social policy and seen as an effect of tighter eligibility criteria, more targeting, and privatization. Similarly, focusing on outcomes, there are signs of de-universalization, measured as rising inequality and poverty and understood as an effect of direct retrenchment and policy drift (Lindh 2009; Kuivalainen and Niemelä 2010; Kenworthy 2011b; Kvist and Greve 2011; Andersen 2012b; Brady and Bostic 2013; Harsløf and Ulmestig 2013; Marx, Salanauskaite, and Verbist 2013; Béland et al. 2014; Greve 2014; Kildal and Kuhnle 2014; Van Lancker and Van Mechelen 2014).

Let us start with inequality. Even though the universal welfare state comparatively speaking remains a haven of income redistribution (the OECD Gini-coefficient hovers around 0.32, the Scandinavian one around 0.26), income inequality in the region generally has been on the rise in the last decades (see Figure 19.2). There is some interesting intra-Scandinavian variation, where Norway's inequality (measured as Gini-coefficient and the top 10 per cent versus bottom 10 per cent) first jumped ahead and then was brought back to comparable Scandinavian levels between 2004 and 2009. The most recent data (2010–11) indicate further increases in inequality (Sweden and Norway) and stabilization (Denmark and Finland).

Another indication of de-universalization relates back to the Myrdals' idea of solving 'the population question'. To them, an ageing population and lack of fertility were central threats to society and a central problem to be solved through social engineering, that is, direct public investments with expected high social returns. However, when we look at current fertility rates (number of children per woman), many of the Scandinavian countries are actually

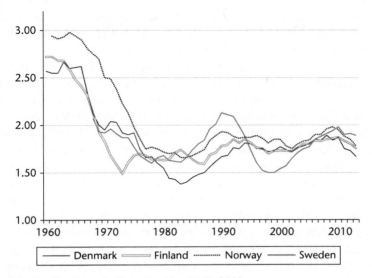

Figure 19.3. Fertility rates in Scandinavia, 1960–2013
Source: Eurostat (2015).

increasingly underperforming. Over the last ten years, fertility rates have been dropping substantially in Denmark, slightly in Norway and Finland, and have only increased a little in Sweden. To insure a stable population development, a country needs a fertility rate of 2.07 (Kvist 2013: 100). In 2013, the fertility rate was only 1.67 in Denmark, 1.75 in Finland, 1.89 in Sweden, and 1.78 in Norway (Eurostat 2015). Of course, these rates are probably somewhat affected by the slowdown in economic growth since 2008, but the numbers clearly indicate a general tendency too (Figure 19.3).

Scandinavian countries still have the highest fertility rates, but falling fertility rates across Scandinavia may be a first warning sign that this is about to change. The slowdown has already become a concern in public discourse (e.g. Andersen 2012a; Hansen 2014), and we observe that several of the social investment policies that underpin the 'Nordic fertility regime' (Andersson et al. 2009) are now being reformed. The tendency is most evident in Denmark that has recently experienced a vast amount of welfare state reforms, including changes in childcare programmes. As part of an economic recovery package in 2010, for instance, the centre-right government supported by the populist right-wing Danish People's Party introduced a cumulative ceiling on child cash benefits (Finansministeriet 2010). The reform was de facto directed towards immigrant families and implied that most families with more than two children would reach the ceiling quickly. However, because many ethnic-Danish families with three children were also affected, the reform was reconfigured so that most three-child families no longer were included under the

223

benefit ceiling. Further, the 2010 reform package limited government subsidies to fertility treatment, to which approximately 8 per cent of new-borns in Denmark owed their lives in 2010 (Sundhedsstyrelsen 2012).

The centre-left government that took office in 2011 repealed the Danish childcare benefit ceiling, but replaced it with a means-tested version in 2012. As of 2014, Danish high-income families now only receive a reduced cash benefit (Finansministeriet 2012; Kvist 2015a). Similar de-universalization tendencies might also be present in reforms of Swedish childcare services. Since the 1990s, Swedish municipalities have increasingly delegated child-care provision to private actors, as a result of which the share of private care providers has reached a high 20 per cent today. Even though quality differences have not emerged, private providers are especially popular among middle-class, highly educated parents (Béland et al. 2014: 749).

In general, increasing privatization poses a threat to universalism because it tends to create divides between social groups and challenges the quality of public services. We observe privatization tendencies in both the Danish and Swedish educational system. The proportion of 15-year-old students attend-ing private schools increased 10 percentage points from 2003 to 2012 in Sweden (OECD 2014c). In the late 1980s and 1990s, the Swedish school system underwent decentralization and privatization reforms, which included trans-ferring employer responsibility for teachers from the central to the municipal level and increasing citizens' choice between private and public schools (Klitgaard 2008: 491–2; Busemeyer 2014: 88). Such reforms can best be viewed as an attempt 'to cater to the interests of the middle class, which demanded more opportunities for choice in education' (Busemeyer 2014: 88). In Denmark we observe a similar tendency. The share of pupils in private schools has increased from 12.1 per cent in 2000 to 16.5 per cent in 2014 (Økonomi- og Indenrigsministeriet 2015). Finland has seen a slight increase in public school enrolment shares, whereas no significant change is detected in Norway (OECD 2014c).

Not only has the share of pupils in private schools increased, there are also rising differences in the performance of private and public schools. There is a rising mathematical performance gap between private and public schools in Denmark and Finland (and to some extent in Sweden), caused by socio-economic factors (OECD 2014c). On top of this, there is a general fall in pupils' skills in all Nordic countries (Egelund 2012; Halleröd 2015).

Finally, one of the major recent challenges to the universal welfare state has been the increasing inflow of immigrants (Pettersen and Østby 2013). In regard to eligibility, we witness increasing welfare chauvinism—more so in Denmark than elsewhere—that directly or indirectly is excluding immigrants from welfare benefits. The ceiling on childcare cash benefits serves as an example here. Generally, there is evidence of indirect yet systematic welfare chauvinism in Danish labour market policies between 2001 and 2011 (Careja et al. 2015).

The exclusion of immigrants is also present in public services. Looking at performance in upper secondary schools in Scandinavia, it turns out that— both among girls and boys—immigrants as well as descendants of immigrants have higher drop-out rates than the rest of the population, reinforcing the risk of social exclusion (Pettersen and Østby 2013). The immigrant bias in the use of social investment-related services starts at a very early age. In Denmark, (non-Western) immigrants are less likely to send their children to public childcare institutions. Even though the gap has been closing for children above the age of 3, profound differences in the use of public childcare institutions between non-Western immigrants and ethnic Danes still exist. In 2014, 90 per cent of 2-year-old children with ethnic-Danish parents were enrolled in public childcare, whereas only 80 per cent of 2-year-old children of non-Western immigrants were enrolled. Disturbingly, the enrolment share was even smaller for third-generation descendants (Denmark Statistics 2014: 119).

19.5 Conclusion

In the Scandinavian self-image, the universal social investment model is part and parcel of the Nordic model. Although this model is continuously challenged, its adaptive capacity and distinctive qualities are considered to be unique and worth maintaining. The final report of a pan-Nordic research project on the viability of the Nordic model (NordMod) concludes: 'Their adaptive capability has kept the Nordic countries near the top of most international rankings, with social outcomes that set them apart from other groups of countries, albeit to a lesser extent than previously' (Dølvik et al. 2015: 137). The viability of the model depends on whether the Nordic countries will be able to continue on the high employment, high productivity, broad consensus-based, inclusive, egalitarian, all-encompassing, and social investment-oriented route that has been so distinctive. There are various routes open for the future and which direction will be taken depends on political choice in the face of increasing challenges.

We agree with these conclusions and we have pointed to some observable empirical trends that indicate changes in some of the fundamental components of the Nordic model: rising inequality, de-universalization, and more selective social investments. Such developments have one thing in common: they ultimately imply the risk of destabilizing the—until now—self-reinforcing moral and political support base of the universal welfare state and, with that, its social investment orientation.

Ultimately, this could result in an increased dualization in the Nordic societies. While Scandinavian social investments have so far prevented deep insider–outsider divisions, de-universalization could be a first step towards segmented labour markets and family structures. Without universal and inclusive policies, there is breeding ground for a divide between a privileged group of insiders and a less privileged group of outsiders with poorer job opportunities, higher risk of poverty, and with a lack of social and political integration.

20

The Truncated German Social Investment Turn

Martin Seeleib-Kaiser

20.1 Introduction

Traditionally Germany has been categorized as the archetypical conservative welfare state (Esping-Andersen 1990), a categorization not systematically questioned in much of the comparative welfare state regime literature (for a review see Ferragina and Seeleib-Kaiser 2011). For many scholars Germany was largely stuck and unable to reform its coordinated market economy and welfare state arrangements at the turn of the twenty-first century, due to a large number of veto points and players and the dominance of two 'welfare state parties' (Heinze 1998; Schmidt 2002; Kitschelt and Streeck 2003; Leibfried and Obinger 2003). More recent research has highlighted a widening and deepening of the historically institutionalized social protection dualism (Emmenegger et al. 2012; Seeleib-Kaiser, Saunders, and Naczyk 2012), whilst at the same time emphasizing significant family policy transformations, which can be considered as partially in line with the social investment paradigm (Bleses and Seeleib-Kaiser 2004; Seeleib-Kaiser 2010). This chapter sets out to sketch the main policy developments and aims to identify political determinants of social policy change in Germany.

20.2 Methodological Considerations

Esping-Andersen (1990) identified the work–welfare nexus as the core dimension of institutional welfare state arrangements and suggested using the concept of decommodification. Subsequently, he added the concept of defamilialization to assess the care–welfare nexus (Esping-Andersen 1999). Within welfare state research we often focus on either of the two domains or tend to compare entire welfare states. However, as the various social policy domains can follow different reform trajectories and specific (social) policies can determine politics (Lowi 1972; Seeleib-Kaiser 1993; Kasza 2002), we need to take into account a broad array of social policies to be able to assess and explain policy changes. In addition, taking into account both domains is of key importance if we want to scrutinize the three main functions of social policies, that is, easing the 'flow' transitions over the life-course, improving the 'stock' of human capital and maintaining robust social protection as economic stabilization 'buffers', as outlined by Hemerijck (2015).

I suggest focusing on family policy, pensions, and unemployment insurance, thereby covering 'old' and 'new social risks' (Bonoli 2007). Reforming family policy from a largely transfer-intensive approach towards a more 'active' policy is seen as a cornerstone by those advocating for social investment and activation policies (Bonoli 2013). Pensions and unemployment insurance have been key programmes included in Esping-Andersen's (1990) seminal work and the construction of the decommodification index; more recently both programmes have been identified as being in need of reform or even retrenchment as they focus on 'compensation' instead of on social investment, which has become a dominating paradigm in European social policy analysis (for a critical review of the social investment literature see Nolan 2013; Chapter 2, this volume).

Furthermore, we need a clear reference point to be able to assess welfare state change and continuity. The ideal-typical classification of welfare state regimes introduced by Esping-Andersen (1990, 1999) relies on data from 1980, a point in time at which, according to Danforth's (2014) longitudinal analysis— including a broader array of institutional and outcome variables—welfare regimes have become salient.

20.2.1 Policy Developments

Although historically the German welfare state was based on a relatively strong social protection dualism, clearly differentiating between outsiders (the poor) and insiders (workers) (Leibfried and Tennstedt 1985), Leisering (2009) has argued that the German welfare state embarked on a route towards 'quasi-universalism'; political actors hoped that the social assistance scheme would truly become residual (Giese 1986). As highlighted by Alber (1986) poverty reduction was a main aim of the political actors in developing the German welfare state during the post-Second World War era. Low unemployment rates and benefits of social insurance schemes linked to rising earnings indeed resulted in low poverty and inequality by the early 1980s (Seeleib-Kaiser 2014). Family policy continued to be transfer heavy and aimed to support the family as an institution, as part of a strong male breadwinner model (Lewis 1992).

The 1980s can be characterized as a transition period for the German welfare state that saw some retrenchment, re-commodification, and very minor recalibration. Subsequently, the German welfare state did not seem to deviate much from the ideal-typical Conservative welfare state with a clear focus on the male breadwinner, despite showing first signs of disintegration, which were said to lead to a 'two-thirds society' (Glotz 1985; Offe 1991).

The expansion of the West German welfare state to the eastern parts of the country as part of the unification process constituted a critical juncture with respect to the arrangements insuring against the risks of unemployment and old age. The political decision not to significantly increase the subsidies from general taxation for the two social insurance schemes meant that inevitably social insurance contributions would skyrocket, which they did until the early 2000s, and the only alternative to stop this development would be to implement significant policy changes (Seeleib-Kaiser 2016). The pension and labour-market reforms of the early 2000s reversed the road to 'quasi-universalism' and once again reinforced the institutional dualism, differentiating between social protection insiders and outsiders. Social protection insiders can be defined as individuals, usually workers in standard employment relationships (labour market insiders), covered either through comprehensive statutory social protection or by statutory entitlements, complemented or supplemented by private/occupational social protection to a level that maintains living standards. Outsiders are defined as the (working) poor that would have to rely on modest (largely means-tested) public provision, primarily intended to ameliorate poverty. In the realm of pension policies we saw a partial privatization of the social insurance scheme with the consequence that in the future only pensioners with additional occupational or private pensions will a have a potential income sufficient to maintain the achieved living standard. With regards to the risk of unemployment, only short-term unemployed receive an earnings-related unemployment benefit, whilst the long-term unemployed and former atypical worker, who do not meet the eligibility criteria, have to rely on a means-tested benefit (Seeleib-Kaiser, Saunders, and Naczyk 2012). These reforms clearly limited the 'buffer' function, or automatic stabilizers, of the German welfare state.

By contrast to policy developments in the domain of 'old' social risks, family policies have seen a more or less continued expansion since the late 1980s. The most important reforms in the 1980s and 1990s included the introduction of parental leave with a maximum duration of three years; the introduction of childcare credits into the statutory pension scheme; the entitlement to days off from work to care for dependent sick children; and the introduction of an entitlement to publicly provided or subsidized childcare for children from 3 to 6 years of age. Although these incremental reforms each only changed a very small element of the strong German male-breadwinner model, in their sum they laid the foundation of the more transformative

229

reforms to come. These reforms included the introduction of an earnings-related and gender-neutral parental leave benefit (capped at a maximum of €1,800 per month) for the duration of twelve months (with an additional two 'partner' months), and a significant expansion of childcare provision for children between the ages of 1 and 3. Since August 2013, every child above the age of 1 is entitled to a place in publicly provided or subsidized childcare (Seeleib-Kaiser 2010; Fleckenstein 2011). As will be further explicated in the following section, these reforms clearly aimed at furthering the functions of improving the transitions between work and family (flow) as well as maintaining and improving the stock of human capital.

20.3 Explaining Policy Change

How can we explain these policy changes? Based on the veto player theorem (Tsebelis 2002) and the large number of veto players (Katzenstein 1987; Schmidt 2002) we would not have expected any comprehensive social policy reform in Germany. Within the comparative welfare state literature, power resources and partisanship have been identified as key variables determining social policy outputs and outcomes (Korpi 1983; Esping-Andersen 1990; Huber and Stephens 2001; Brady 2009), whilst the Varieties of Capitalism literature (Estévez-Abe, Iversen, and Soskice 2001; Mares 2003) has argued that the generous social protection system, especially with regard to the risk of unemployment, in Germany can be partly explained by the support of organized business and their interest in workers acquiring specific skills.

The key social policy reforms since the late 1990s and early 2000s, however, have not followed any of these theoretical propositions, as the high number of veto players did not block reform, a Social Democrat-led government significantly retrenched the statutory unemployment and old-age insurance schemes and a Christian-Democratic minister within a 'grand coalition' enacted major family policy reforms. Whilst the reforms of the unemployment and pension schemes prima facie might be explained by the role of 'insider actors' in achieving welfare state reform (Rueda 2007; Palier and Thelen 2010), the reforms within the domain of family policy definitely did not follow the politics of 'dualization'. As highlighted by Naczyk and Seeleib-Kaiser (2015) unions acted as consenters within a bounded policy space in the domain of old social risks. Various reasons might have muted the public opposition of organized labour against the reforms implemented by the Social Democrat-led coalition government in the early 2000s. Firstly, from the perspective of the unions there was no viable alternative to the Red–Green government—any other coalition would have potentially enacted even more far-ranging policy reforms. Secondly, political strikes are constitutionally banned in Germany, limiting the actions available to unions. Nevertheless, the Hartz IV legislation created a massive conflict between the Social Democratic Party and the Unions, which was described by the former party secretary, Peter Glotz, as the most 'severe crisis' in the relationship between the party and the unions (cited in FAZ 2004).

If the insider/outsider theory has only limited power in explaining the welfare state changes, how can we explain them? Elsewhere I have highlighted the importance of ideas and interpretative patterns in explaining welfare state reform in Germany (Seeleib-Kaiser 2002; Bleses and Seeleib-Kaiser 2004; Seeleib-Kaiser and Fleckenstein 2007). As I will show in the following, the interpretative patterns promoted by employers have become hegemonic over time. The Christian Democratic Party (CDU) and the Social Democratic Party of Germany (SPD) largely accepted the employers' interpretation to reduce costs, which was embedded in the larger political discourse about the declining international competitiveness of German companies in the 1990s and early 2000s. Although Social Democrats and Greens initially were very sceptical about the argument advanced by employers and the then Christian Democratic–Liberal coalition government, they eventually accepted that social insurance contributions had to be stabilized, if not reduced. The debates on globalization were strategically interwoven with arguments emphasizing the need for more personal responsibility, private provision, and market reliance. These interpretative patterns guided much of the labour market and pension reforms of the late 1990s and early 2000s (Seeleib-Kaiser 2001). Whilst globalization 'mandated' a reduction in social insurance contributions and can thus be characterized as a 'causal belief' (Goldstein and Keohane 1993), which was used as an ideational weapon (Blyth 2001), supporting families and providing them with more 'choice' emerged as a new dominant interpretative pattern and was shared by the mainstream political parties by the 1990s. Nevertheless, substantial opposition against a more employment-oriented family policy initially continued to persist within the CDU. Eventually, the ideational support by the employers' organizations to develop a more employment-oriented family policy was crucial for the reforms enacted by the Christian Democratic-led 'grand coalition' government in the early 2000s (Bleses and Seeleib-Kaiser 2004; Fleckenstein and Seeleib-Kaiser 2011).

Starting in the 1980s, and more forcefully since the 1990s, employers have actively pushed for a more dualized social protection system, while unions have supported a more universal approach (Naczyk and Seeleib-Kaiser 2015). Within the realm of social protection in old age, employers emphasized the necessity to reduce costs of the public pension system, starting in the late 1980s and more forcefully in 1990s, as the high costs were said to be undermining the competitiveness of German firms (Seeleib-Kaiser 2001; Brosig

2014: 272–7), eventually acting as protagonists for significant benefit reductions and comprehensive changes of the system (Hegelich 2006). Employers' associations more or less unconditionally promoted the idea of expanding private and occupational pensions on a voluntary basis to partly 'compensate' for the benefit reductions in the statutory scheme (Deutscher Bundestag 2000). The German Trade Unions (Deutsche Gewerkschaftsbund (DGB)) opposed the proposed benefit reductions and claimed that it was possible to maintain the public guarantee of the achieved living standard within the statutory pension system (DGB 2000). Within this debate the functions of 'flows', 'stocks', and 'buffers' have played no significant role, as the debate was clearly centred around the question whether the relatively generous pension scheme could be maintained (or not) in an era characterized by economic globalization and demographic decline.

In the realm of unemployment insurance, the employers' associations forcefully argued for a significant retrenchment of the unemployment insurance scheme since the 1990s (cf. Murmann 1995) and called for limiting the maximum duration of unemployment insurance benefit receipt from thirty-two months for older workers to twelve months. They argued that the main goal of social policy reform must be the reduction of social insurance contributions, that is, costs, while at the same time it was necessary to increase the incentives for the unemployed to take up jobs (FAZ 1997). In the words of its Chief Executive: 'It is still the case that it may be more beneficial for a skilled worker [*Facharbeiter*] to receive unemployment or social assistance than to take up work' (Berliner Zeitung 2002, author's translation). The DGB opposed the reduction in duration of benefit receipt and emphasized a similar logic to that expressed by the Varieties of Capitalism approach, whereby comprehensive unemployment protection had a positive effect on skill formation. Furthermore, they argued that from an international comparative perspective Germany did not have a very generous unemployment insurance regarding benefit duration, as the maximum duration was significantly longer in Denmark, France, and the Netherlands. In short, the unions demanded that the system be kept unchanged (DGB 2003). It is interesting to note that the function of the unemployment insurance benefit as an automatic stabilizer (or economic stabilization buffer) was no longer part of the justification repertoire; moreover, employers focused on highlighting the disincentives created by the existing unemployment benefit system and the need for a reformed scheme to improve the 'flow' from unemployment to employment. The DGB unsuccessfully argued for the existing scheme, as it would positively contribute to skill formation, that is, contribute to improving the human capital stock.

Within the domain of family policy a new interpretative pattern had emerged during the 1980s and 1990s, whereby families needed more support.

Core to the interpretative pattern was the concept of parental 'choice', which included an expansion of measures to improve the reconciliation of family and work (Bleses and Seeleib-Kaiser 2004). After the Red–Green coalition government had lost the 2005 elections and a new grand coalition government was formed, the Christian Democratic Family Minister Ursula von der Leyen accelerated the speed of reform towards an employment-oriented family policy. Von der Leyen used ideational leadership (Stiller 2010) and 'brute' political force effectively to push through these reforms against opposition from the conservative wing within the CDU, its Bavarian sister party and parts of the Catholic Church (Seeleib-Kaiser 2010). She argued that a reformed family policy would have a positive impact on fertility, improve human capital formation through early childhood education, and provide mothers with more and better opportunities to re-enter the workforce after a short parental leave. Framing the reform policy as a 'necessity' to improve the fertility rate as well as to ensure the long-term stability of the economy and the social security system was in line with the interpretative patterns put forward by the employers. Organized business emphasized that it would be greatly beneficial if mothers returned quickly to work after giving birth, as long-term leave policies would lead to a de-qualification of parents. In 2005, the President of the German Employers' Association stated: 'Based on the increased scarcity of skilled employees, we can no longer forgo the potential of highly qualified women and mothers' (FAZ 2005). The peak employers' association BDA (2008) supported the policy of expanding childcare provision, including the planned introduction of an entitlement to childcare for children older than 1 year in 2013, as part of their strategy to promote employment of skilled women, thereby providing vital ideational and political backing for the 'modernizers' within the CDU (Seeleib-Kaiser 2010). It is clear that in the political debates leading to the reform of family policy the functions of improving the 'flow' transitions between family responsibilities and employment as well as skill formation and skill retention played a key role.

Although the employers were clearly the protagonists in the process of reinterpreting the interpretative pattern within the domain of old social risks, the political parties had to accept it before policy change could be enacted. After many years opposing the interpretative pattern, the Social Democrats and Greens finally accepted it during their tenure in government, whereby it became dominant, if not hegemonic. The story with regard to the changing interpretative patterns within the domain of family policy differed somewhat. Initially the Social Democrats had developed an interpretative pattern, whereby an employment-oriented family policy was beneficial, if not crucial, for the success of the German economy in an era of skill scarcity, which was eventually accepted by the modernizers within the CDU (Seeleib-Kaiser 2010; Fleckenstein 2011). But only once the employers had signed up to the new interpretative pattern for an employment-oriented family policy, had it the potential of becoming dominant, as it provided support for the modernizers within CDU.

20.4 Conclusion

This chapter has highlighted the need to take a long-term perspective when analysing policy continuity and change. German unification constituted a critical juncture, which eventually put the country on a path to transformational change in the domains of pension and unemployment policies. Once the decision not to significantly increase general taxation, but to fund German unification in large part through the social insurance schemes had been taken and was widely accepted by the political parties, benefit cutbacks, and, ultimately, comprehensive reforms of the pension and unemployment insurance became inevitable, as the rapidly increasing social insurance contributions were widely perceived to place pressure on the competitiveness of German companies. Reforms were perceived to be inevitable, as otherwise the German export-oriented economy would become uncompetitive. Similarly, employers constructed the need for an employment-oriented family policy as inevitable, as companies were in need of skilled female workers in an age of demographic change.

As has been shown throughout this chapter, dominant ideas and interpretative patterns justifying social policy can change and are reinterpreted over time. Ideas and causal beliefs are core to understanding continuity and change, as a changed social construction and a reinterpretation of the economic costs and benefits of social policy have provided the causal legitimation for the transformation of the German welfare state. The empirical analysis of the political discourse and the interpretative patterns has unveiled that German employers no longer seem to require generous public unemployment or pension programmes for skill formation and retention, as highlighted by the Varieties of Capitalism literature, but have identified the potential pool of skilled female workers as core to the long-term success and sustainability of the German economy. A new politics for the market has emerged that effectively combines elements of dualization and social investment.

21

The Impact of Social Investment Reforms on Income and Activation in the Netherlands

Menno Soentken, Franca van Hooren, and Deborah Rice

21.1 Introduction

Among the continental welfare states, the Netherlands was the first to move into the social investment direction (Hemerijck 2002; Nikolai 2012; ESPN 2015). Yet as Hemerijck (2015 and Chapter 1, this volume) points out, social investment is not a substitute for protection, and adequate minimum income protection 'buffers' are a critical precondition for an effective social investment strategy. How can we understand this multidimensional nature of social investment in a social investment vanguard state such as the Netherlands? To what extent is minimum income protection a guaranteed buffer, along the development of flow arrangements, also for those people that do not have acquired paid employment? How can capacitating services support transitional labour market flows for precarious groups in society? In this chapter we assess the buffer and flow dimensions of the social investment state for two typical new social risk groups which are both likely to be in a precarious income position: early school-leavers and lone parents. Early school-leavers are (by definition) low-skilled and not well prepared to find durable employment in the knowledge-based economy and typically do not have sufficient social insurance coverage. The latter also applies to lone parents, who have a high risk of welfare loss due to difficulties with reconciling work and family life.

In Section 21.2 we assess the buffer function in terms of minimum income protection for the two social risk groups by applying an 'at-risk household-type model'. Within both risk groups, we simulate different income situations including working full-time (at minimum wage), working part-time, and being unemployed. More specifically, for each situation we calculated the net disposable income, which includes gross income from wages, social security benefits, tax credits, health-care allowance, child benefits and childcare benefits, minus taxes, social security contributions, health insurance costs, and childcare costs. Income data were gathered through archival records, governmental websites, and documents of municipalities. We have chosen not to include housing costs, housing benefits, and mortgage interest tax deductibility in the calculations, since there is a large dispersion of housing costs depending on geographical location as well as a large dispersion of benefits and tax deductions depending on the type of housing arrangement. The income situations are simulated for the years 1995, 2007, and 2012. The data show that the buffer function of the welfare state for the two risk groups out of work has declined in the last decade, particularly for early school leavers. On the other hand, the buffer function, in terms of minimum income protection, for those risk groups that have acquired paid employed has significantly improved. The critical question thus becomes, how and to what extent risk groups without work are supported to (re)enter the labour market through labour market flow arrangements.

This question is answered in Section 21.3. We assess the employment services offered by caseworkers to beneficiaries of the Dutch social assistance scheme. Here we focus on social assistance recipients because our risk groups are not likely to have acquired a sufficient work history to qualify for unemployment insurance benefits. In the Netherlands, one must have had paid work for twenty-six out of the preceding thirty-six weeks in order to qualify for three months of social insurance benefits. Furthermore, a work history of at least four years makes one eligible for one month of social insurance benefits for each working year (maximum duration: thirty-eight months). We start by discussing the policy context in which caseworkers operate. By subsequently analysing caseworkers' choices and considerations, we reveal what happens in practice with social investment policy intentions. Are they indeed individually tailored and of good quality, that is, capacitating? Or are services more focused on increased sanctioning and work-first measures, that is, recommodifying? Information on the type of services offered is based on twenty-one semi-structured interviews conducted with managers and caseworkers responsible for implementing the Dutch social assistance scheme in seven municipal jobcentres in 2011 (Rice 2015).

21.2 The Dutch Social Investment Turn and Its Reversal?

After having been a passive conservative welfare state fostering low employment rates for decades, as of the early 1980s this started to change. While at first welfare state cutbacks and benefit reductions were the main policy tool, as of 1994 this was expanded to include a range of activation measures introduced by a Labour/Liberal coalition that proclaimed to pursue a 'jobs, jobs, and more jobs' strategy (Van Oorschot 2004; Kuipers 2006). In subsequent years, this coalition, among other things, introduced and intensified activation obligations for the long-term unemployed; introduced job-seeking requirements for lone parents receiving social assistance benefits; and it substantially lowered social assistance benefit levels for claimants aged 18 to 21. At the same time, the Labour/Liberal coalition made local governments responsible for the activation of social assistance recipients by matching the supply and demand of labour. The coalition also gave a great impulse to increase the availability of childcare services for working parents.

In the 2000s, further reforms were implemented along the same lines. Social assistance eligibility requirements were further restricted; municipal responsibilities and resources to activate social assistance recipients were expanded (Borghi and Van Berkel 2007). In 2005, a new Childcare Act reformed the Dutch childcare system. Income dependent childcare benefits became available for all working parents. For low-income families the childcare benefits covered a large share of real childcare costs (Van Hooren and Becker 2012). This new childcare act privatized the provision of childcare entirely. Parents receive childcare subsidies with which they can purchase a childcare place. Initially, the idea was that the state, employers, and families would each pay for one-third of total childcare costs, with employers contributing on a voluntary basis. Although the entitlement of employers' contributions was regulated in almost 90 per cent of collective labour agreements, in 2007, the government nevertheless decided to make employers' contributions mandatory and secured them by imposing a levy. As a consequence, parents now get an (income dependent) childcare subsidy directly and entirely from the state.

While many of these policy changes indicated a social investment approach (SIA) supported by substantial expansion of capacitating services, this expansion came to a halt in the late 2000s. Already in 2006 the budget available for local governments to finance labour reintegration services was reduced. More substantial budget cuts in active labour market policy followed in 2009 and especially after 2010, under a new centre-right government. Meanwhile, the income dependent childcare benefits were reduced especially for higher income groups. From 2004 onwards, and especially after the onset of the 2008 financial crisis, the indexation of child support was repeatedly suspended, meaning that the height of the benefit was not indexed for inflation and hence declined in real terms. For example, as a consequence of these policy changes, for a family with two children aged 10 and 14, the real value of universal child support decreased from 232 euros per month in 1995 (2012 prices) to 166 euros in 2012.

The Dutch social investment trajectory is in some ways comparable with its continental counterpart Germany (Chapter 20, this volume). Also in

Germany family policies have seen a more or less continued expansion since the late 1980s. Incremental reforms in the German male-breadwinner model laid the foundation of more transformative reforms that even overtook the Dutch reforms on the social investment ladder. Noteworthy is that while the social investment turn in the Netherlands came to a standstill after the onset of the 2008 financial crisis, German social investments, particularly in child-care and family policies, improved significantly (see Chapter 20, this volume).

21.3 Assessing Social Investment Buffers

As can be observed from Table 21.1, the net disposable income of an unemployed early school leaver aged 18 who has left the elderly home and depends on social assistance has decreased dramatically over the past two decades. This decrease is a direct result of the lowering of benefit levels for young social assistance claimants in 1996. This outcome is related to reforms in Dutch social assistance policy. Table 21.1 also shows that when working, the net disposable income of an early school leaver improved in real terms in the same period. Hence, as a result of social assistance restrictions, an early school leaver became crucially dependent on paid employment to be able to maintain an independent household.

Table 21.2 shows that the net disposable income of a lone parent having two young children, but without work decreased by 18 per cent in the period 1995 to 2007. This fall is associated with a decrease in the level of social assistance for lone parents from 90 per cent of the level received by a couple to 70 per cent. The increase in net income of this category between 2007 and 2012 is the consequence of the introduction of a new income-dependent child allowance. Meanwhile the net income of a lone parent in paid employment increased massively between 1995 and 2007. This is the result, primarily, of the 2005 Childcare Act.

In 1995, the cost of childcare was still higher than the income gained from working full-time at minimum wage. As a consequence, a lone parent working

Table 21.1. Net disposable income of a young single person aged 18; post-tax, post-transfer, euros per month in 2012 prices

	Net Disposable Income in Euros per Month			Percentage Change	
	1995	2007	2012	1995–2007	2007–12
Depending on social assistance benefits	551	141	155	−74	+10
Working 50% at minimum wage	580	613	645	+6	+5
Working 100% at minimum wage	1065	1195	1247	+12	+4

Table 21.2. Net disposable income of a lone parent with children aged 2 and 7; post-tax, post-transfer, and post-childcare expenditure, euros per month in 2012 prices

Income Situation	Net Disposable Income in Euros per Month			Percentage Change	
	1995	2007	2012	1995–2007	2007–12
100% employed at minimum wage, children attend full-time day care	667	1523	1600	+128	+5
50% employed at minimum wage, children attend half-time day care	905	978	1066	+8	+9
Dependent on social assistance benefits, children do not attend day care	1220	999	1120	−18	+12

full-time was financially worse off than when receiving social assistance. Due to the new income-dependent childcare subsidies introduced in 2005, by 2007, this situation was turned around and a full-time working lone parent earned considerably more than a parent receiving social assistance, also after deducting childcare costs. Besides much lower net childcare costs, tax credits for working (single) parents have also positively influenced the net disposable income of working lone parents. In conclusion, the Dutch income simulations for two new social risk groups suggest an increased income difference between those who manage to find paid employment and those who remain dependent on social assistance. Sharp social assistance reductions have basically forced early school leavers onto the labour market or back into education. Meanwhile, for lone parents it has become financially much more attractive to work because of cheaper childcare and beneficial tax credits. In other words, the data show that the buffer function of the welfare state for the two risk groups out of work has declined in the last decade, particularly for early school leavers. On the other hand, the buffer function for those risk groups that have acquired paid employed has significantly improved. The critical question thus becomes, how and to what extent these risk groups without work are supported to (re)enter the labour market through labour market flow arrangements.

21.4 Assessing Social Investment Flow Arrangements

Since the mid-1990s, local governments have been responsible for managing the administration of social assistance and related activation trajectories. Local governments have both legal and financial incentives to activate benefit recipients. The national government sets criteria for the sanctioning of non-compliant benefit recipients, which local governments have to implement (Van Oorschot 2004). At the same time, local governments receive fixed budgets for the provision of social assistance benefits and for labour market reintegration services. As a consequence, if fewer people rely on social assistance, the local government benefits financially.

In the early 2000s, municipalities were granted more possibilities and a large implementation discretion to offer also people with medical disadvantages or multiple social problems appropriate labour-market opportunities, sometimes in cooperation with health and care organizations (Kamerstukken II 2002–3, 28 870; 2007–8, 28 719). However, as we noted in Section 21.2, in the late 2000s, there have been a series of cuts in the budget available for activating services.

Hereafter we reflect on how case workers at the municipal level have dealt with both the demanding activation obligations and the more developmental approach towards 'difficult' clients in administering social assistance. At the end we discuss the impact of shrinking budgets available for activation.

21.4.1 *Employment Service Provision*

The first observation that emerges from the interviews is that case managers demonstrate a focus on stimulating active participation of young social assistance claimants in the labour market. Our interviews reveal that case managers have clearly tried to prioritize a capacitating approach. Our respondents indicate that when meeting a young client applying for a social assistance benefit for the first time, an individually tailored trajectory is started. This trajectory begins with assessing the claimant's capabilities and skills to engage in work, often coupled with a personality test and job profession test. According to case managers from different municipalities, the goal of the first intake is to motivate the young person to find suitable work or opt for further education instead of pushing young clients into just any kind of work. For young people already receiving social assistance benefits, sanctions are only applied when a person does not want to be available for work or education. However, the use of sanctioning (i.e. benefit cuts) is generally reconsidered when it does not contribute to the motivation of the client and when benefit cuts run the risk of further solidifying a young person's marginalization and social exclusion.

Also with regard to lone parents the priority of caseworkers is usually not to find paid work at any cost. Instead, the well-being of children is of central importance. Activation requirements are adapted and loosened when it becomes apparent that children cannot attend day care because of health issues or personality problems. Part-time work, even if it requires a social assistance top-up, is seen as legitimate if more care for children is needed. When clients are confronted with multiple problems (especially physical or mental health issues), caseworkers even have the option to issue a 'temporary waiver' from job-search obligations. Services to lone parents are generally individually tailored. If needed, caseworkers try to organize debt counselling, home visits, and contact with other institutions to help parents reconcile work and care for their children. Caseworkers also fulfil a mediating role to support the employment of single parents. For instance, if a parent cannot work more hours because children need to be picked up from school, the caseworker might arrange suitable day care. Alternatively, several caseworkers report to be willing to consult with an employer if increasing the number of working hours would be possible. In sum, case workers report to focus on activation only where possible, by offering the needed capacitating services.

21.4.2 *Effects of Budget Cuts on Service Provision*

Dutch case workers state that their support oriented at capacitation depends on the availability of a sufficient budget. The problem they experience is that national level policy changes with the aim of promoting capacitation are often accompanied by budget cuts. The assumption behind this is that activation will lead to decreased public expenditure on benefits. Yet the practical implication experienced by caseworkers is an undermining of the means to provide capacitating support. Several respondents reported in 2011 that due to ongoing budget cuts, local benefit regimes were made stricter, such as by introducing tighter sanctions or a waiting period before the commencement of benefit payments. Another consequence of the budget cuts has been that less (or less high-quality) services were being offered to social assistance clients. For example, wage subsidies were shortened or eliminated; the introduction of part-time activation trajectories was reconsidered; and one of the seven municipalities in which interviews were conducted even stopped granting personal reintegration budgets for which it had become renowned. Finally, many municipalities have begun to invest their service budgets primarily in clients where a return on such an investment (in the form of a job entry) can be expected. Further research should report to what extent the focus on the most promising clients affects the job opportunities of those groups who have a considerable distance to the labour market.

To conclude, it appears that caseworkers in the municipal Dutch social assistance system generally pursue a supportive path when assisting young benefit claimants and lone mothers, focusing on capacitating employment measures that are geared towards higher qualifications and/or quality work rather than quick labour market entry. However, the interviews also show that capacitating service provision is under high cost-pressure in the Netherlands, which runs the risk of a reinforced geographic fragmentation of service quality alongside a more restrictive targeting of service measures.

21.5 Conclusion

Our research has assessed two central elements of the social investment turn; the maintenance of adequate minimum income protection as buffer and arrangements to improve labour market flow. In terms of buffers, we found increasing differentiation in net income between people in paid employment and those who remain inactive. Our income simulation indicates that minimum income protection for work-poor households has declined. On the other hand, the income simulations also show increased buffers, in terms of minimal income protection, for those risk groups who engage in paid work, especially for lone parents with young children. In other words, when risk groups do find work they have a considerably better position nowadays than before the social investment turn. This lends some credibility to the proponents of social investment who argue that social investment policies can especially benefit the 'outsiders' by mobilizing the productive potentials of citizens (by including them in the labour market). It is indeed the case that the labour market participation of, for instance, single parents in the Netherlands almost doubled between 1996 and 2011 (CBS 2013). This implies that more single parents enjoy a relatively better living standard, and hence have increased their buffers in terms of household income, since the social investment turn in the Netherlands. Our research also points to the existence of comprehensive, individually tailored, and good-quality flow arrangements at the local level. The interviews reveal that capacitation of risk groups is an explicit aim of service delivery at the local level. Within the social assistance scheme, clients are offered individually tailored and integrated services and work is geared towards higher qualifications and/or quality work rather than quick labour market entry, which supports the social investment aim of enabling vulnerable groups to 'jump the trampoline'.

Yet, our interviews also suggest that capacitation was brought in jeopardy by recent budget cuts in the Netherlands. This may lead to the unfavourable situation (from a social investment perspective) that declining buffers are inadequately compensated by high-quality flow arrangements to help precarious groups into paid employment. Such a condition may produce socially selective 'Matthew Effects' where, in some cases, those facing fewer barriers to the labour market profit more than people who are at a relatively large distance from the labour market. Yet, this chapter shows that these Matthew Effects are a variable and not a given. Consistent with the findings of Sabel, Zeitlin, and Quack (Chapter 12, this volume), there is ample room for discretionary capacitating services at the local level. The interviews point out that initially, street-level rent-seeking has not been an issue and further devolution and decentralization of responsibilities is in principle consistent with the social investment turn. Only under the condition of tough austerity measures do case workers target measures and services especially to those groups with fewer labour market barriers. This points to a political contestation that determines the scope, character, and eventual outcomes of social investment policies. Further research should therefore pay attention to the impact of politics on the implementation of social investment policies. What are the conditions under which governments are prone to implement social investment policies, and when are they more likely to retrench such arrangements? Further research should also reveal whether the Netherlands is still the continental social investment vanguard as the crisis had adverse consequences for capacitating service provision.

22

Ireland

The Evolving Tensions between Austerity, Welfare Expansion, and Targeted Social Investment

Rory O'Donnell and Damian Thomas

22.1 Introduction

This chapter reviews the development of the social investment agenda in Ireland in the past two decades. First, it describes how Ireland's hybrid welfare regime was improved in the period of strong economic growth from the early 1990s to 2008. We explain how, during that period, a social investment perspective emerged as an overlapping consensus within social partnership. Section 22.4 summarizes social policy developments in the period of massive fiscal consolidation from 2008 to 2014. Finally, in Section 22.6 we discuss and interpret the evolution of social investment and the challenge of creating tailored capacitating services. There can be no simple overall conclusion on the trajectory and fate of the social investment agenda in Ireland. Significant elements of social investment are evident, but are not yet sufficiently supported by a focus on the organizational arrangements necessary for delivery of tailored services. There remain evolving tensions between austerity, the long-term trend of welfare expansion and important social investment initiatives, some of which remain targeted on disadvantaged areas.

22.2 Ireland's Welfare Regime in the Celtic Tiger Years

From the early 1990s to 2007, Ireland achieved strong economic and employment growth, closing the gap in living standards with its EU-15 neighbours.

From 1987 to 2008 a series of three-year social partnership programmes shaped economic and social policy, wages, and employment relations (O'Donnell, Adshead, and Thomas 2011). These were built on a central, if elementary, social investment foundation agreed between 1987 and 1990: that recovery from the crisis of the 1980s, and reduction of the debt/gross domestic product (GDP) ratio, required growth of the denominator though higher employment, participation, and productivity. Growth through the 1990s was characterized by improved competitiveness, increased labour force participation, fiscal balance and reduced public debt. However, after 2000 growth was increasingly fuelled by credit, over-expansion of construction and pro-cyclical fiscal policy (Barnes and Wren 2012).

The period of economic progress and social partnership saw significant improvement to Ireland's underdeveloped welfare system. Public spending on education, health, and other social programmes increased strongly while, given revenue buoyancy, taxes were also reduced. The value of the main welfare transfers was increased and universal Child Benefit and secondary benefits also increased significantly. By contrast, state spending on early childhood care and education remained low, reflecting divergent views on the importance and validity of female employment in achieving economic prosperity and social inclusion. Overall, Ireland's period of remarkable economic and employment growth was also a period of social progress, with increased social protection (providing stronger buffers), rising educational attainment (greatly enhancing the stock of human capital in each cohort of young people), and significant social promotion (easing flows into education and employment among the marginalized). The level of income inequality was broadly stable, though relatively high by comparison with other EU-15 countries. Policy developments confirmed that Ireland had a 'hybrid' welfare model, given the mix of means-tested, insurance-based, and universalist income support and service arrangements.

The 1990s also saw the establishment of a range of new local and community development entities whose task was to find innovative ways to support employment and participation in areas experiencing disadvantage. Some of these, such as the local partnerships, focused on labour market issues, broadly defined, both creating services (to enhance stocks of human capital and flows through difficult transitions) and adapting mainstream welfare instruments (to ease flows back to work and to better meet the income needs of disadvantaged families) (detailed account provided by Weishaupt 2011). Although a part of the agenda was *targeting* of resources on disadvantaged areas, these local entities also constituted an early initiative in *tailoring* services to the complex needs of individuals and communities. Indeed, there is evidence that the better local organizations created metrics, monitoring, and organizational arrangements of the kind discussed by Sabel, Zeitlin, and Quack in

Chapter 12 (Borscheid and Reid 2012). Later, there were further interesting initiatives of this kind in early childhood intervention, disability, mental health, and care of the elderly—initiatives which involved complementary action on stocks and flows. Though state-supported, and in some cases state-created, these entities and their social investment type experiments in tailored services were on a small scale overall and were largely parallel to the mainstream state services. Furthermore, although the mainstream services were better funded than ever before, most were not reformed and reorganized along social investment lines—that is, not configured to provide tailored services, nor focused on creating capacities that would assist participation and, as a result, not exploring institutional complementarities.

22.3 Social Investment as an Overlapping Consensus: The Developmental Welfare State

Despite the trajectory of fairly inclusive growth and increased public expenditure, the social partners were anxious to deepen the social dimension of Ireland's remarkable economic progress. Intense analysis and deliberation in the National Economic and Social Council (NESC) between 2002 and 2005, moved beyond a sterile, recurring debate about rival welfare regimes—universalist, insurance-based, and liberal—by converging on a social investment perspective.

The 2005 report, *The Developmental Welfare State*, adopted by consensus in NESC, proposed a different framework, arguing that each welfare system consists of three spheres: income supports (buffers), the provision of services (to enhance stocks and assist transitions), and a system of innovation to identify and address new needs (which can involve stocks, flows, and buffers). Although the agreed label was 'developmental welfare', its central argument undoubtedly reflected a social investment perspective: that a radical development of services—education, health care, child development and care, disability, eldercare, housing, transport, and employment services—was the most important route to improving social protection in Ireland. This, it was agreed, had a triple logic, both social and economic: supporting the increasing number of both men and women in employment, redressing the marginal position of socially disadvantaged groups, and according autonomy and respect to people with disabilities and in institutional care.

There was agreement that a life-course approach be adopted in fleshing out and delivering enhanced bundles of income, services, and innovative initiatives, and detailed discussion of institutional complementarities. While such services may be provided by the state or other organizations, it was argued that the majority of the population should use the same set of services. To achieve this, and to meet the diversity and complexity of individual needs, services would have to be more tailored. Reflecting both service quality and funding, the report proposed a system of 'tailored universalism'. There was also a strong emphasis on the organizational and institutional reform needed to ensure the delivery of tailored services at the front line.

The Developmental Welfare State (DWS) report reframed the debate on Ireland's welfare state and shaped the social partnership agreement negotiated in 2006, *Towards 2016: Ten Year Framework Social Partnership Agreement 2006–2015*. Although the agreement set out the ambition of 're-inventing and repositioning Ireland's social policies' (Department of the Taoiseach 2006) the main thrust of the DWS—the need for high-quality, tailored, services and 'participation packages'—had less influence on policy than the classificatory 'life cycle approach'.

To an extent this reflected a segmentation within social partnership and government; a progressive social agenda agreed between the partners and government was largely disconnected from the industrial relations bargain struck between the state and the public sector unions (O'Donnell, Cahill, and Thomas 2010). This, along with other dysfunctions in politics and policy, prompted criticism of the system of policymaking, bargaining, and implementation, and arguments for the adoption of a more ambitious public sector reform agenda suited to developmental welfare and activation (NESC 2002, 2005, 2011). But, as noted in Section 22.4, it took a massive crisis and collapse of social partnership to remove the blockages to a programme of public sector reform and reorganization.

22.4 Policy Directions during the Crisis and After

For a variety of reasons, both domestic and European, Ireland was hit particularly hard by the crisis which started in 2008 (Barnes and Wren 2012). There were five dimensions to Ireland's crisis—fiscal, economic, social, banking, and reputational (NESC 2009). GDP fell by 12 per cent between 2007 and 2009. Between 2007 and 2012 employment fell by 14 per cent, the largest percentage fall in the Organisation for Economic Co-operation and Development (OECD). The unemployment rate rose from 4.6 per cent to a peak of 15.1 per cent in late 2014. General government revenue shrank by approximately 20 per cent between 2007 and 2010. The scale of the banking crisis saw the Irish state undertake bank guarantees and recapitalizations on a much greater scale than other European countries (Barnes and Wren 2012).

Attempts by government and the social partners to agree a response failed in 2009, ending national level social partnership. In November 2010, Ireland entered a three year EU-IMF Programme of Financial Support that included further sharp fiscal retrenchment and reform aimed at labour market activation, fiscal sustainability, and financial regulation.

A new Universal Social Charge was introduced, increasing the insurance contributions of all employees, especially those on lower incomes. A combination of an imposed pension levy, the first ever cut in public service pay rates and a 10 per cent reduction in staff numbers resulted in the annual public service pay bill falling by almost 20 per cent.

While national social partnership ended in 2009, Government negotiated two multi-annual agreements with public service unions in 2013 and 2015. In pursuing fiscal consolidation and reform government committed to protecting the core budgets of social protection, health, and education. In terms of buffers, the weekly rates of core social welfare transfers were cut by 8 per cent between 2009 and 2011, conditionality was tightened and secondary benefits were reduced. A lower rate of Jobseeker Allowance was introduced for young people and later combined with a 'youth guarantee' on training and education. There were greater reductions in programme budgets, in areas such as special needs education, health, disability services, community development, and social inclusion. Indeed, as we discuss later in this section, these bore heavily on some of the innovative programmes and organizations involved in pioneering tailored services.

At the same time, there were policy developments that have a potential social investment character—in areas of childcare, services for the unemployed, training, lone parents, youth, and early child development. For example, the 2009 decision to create a universal free preschool year for children aged 3 years signalled an increased focus on state-supported services rather than income transfers or tax measures. The 2016 budget confirmed the move in the social investment direction, announcing the extension of free childcare for older infants and enhanced parental leave.

An important area of reform, set out in the European Union–International Monetary Fund (EU-IMF) Programme, was labour market activation. The need to move from a passive to a more active regime—in which income buffers would be more closely linked to education and training (stock enhancement) and job search (flows)—had earlier been articulated by national and international observers (NESC 2005a, 2011). In 2010, responsibility for the public employment service was transferred to the Department of Social Protection and in 2012 three services—the administration of benefits, the design and supervision of active labour market policies, and job matching and job placement—were merged in new Intreo offices. A separate new activation programme for the long-term unemployed, JobPath, was put out to tender and is delivered by two private sector companies. There was reform of the lone parent payment, reducing the duration of the categorical payment, and gradually moving lone parents onto the mainstream unemployment transfers and labour market supports. There was a major institutional reconfiguration in training and further education with establishment of a new Further Education and Training Authority (Solas) and regional education and training boards (ETBs) linking training and vocational education.

Daly (2015) suggests that the increased focus on activation of the unemployed is the most visible and advanced example of social investment in Ireland. There is, however, concern that there will be insufficient links between three elements: the new activation measures (driving flows by means of job search and, in some cases, sanction), education and training services to enhance employment prospects (stocks), and family and other policies (that create synergies between stocks, flows, and buffers to support both child development and female employment) (Sweeney, Barr, and Pyne 2014; Sweeney 2015).

Local partnerships and other non-governmental organizations (NGOs), that led the early experiments in tailored services, now receive funding under tighter, narrower, departmental mandates. In addition, local and community development has been put under the ambit of local government and together these changes have altered the landscape within which many local and social development organizations work. There is a view, echoed by many in the NGO sector, that increased centralization is reducing their autonomy to innovate, tailor, and bundle services in response to local conditions. If this transpires, it would limit the creation of synergies between stocks, flows, and buffers and institutional complementarities across the main social policy sectors. The government argues that the new arrangements will ensure more accountability, less duplication, and a greater focus on outcomes.

Another interesting development is the move to mainstream, or at least extend, the tailored capacitating approach to early intervention for young children. Through the ABC Programme, government is extending prevention and early intervention to thirteen selected areas—an approach that has a logic in stocks, flows, and buffers. These are also some initiatives to learn from and extend the earlier experiments in tailored services in the areas of disability and eldercare.

22.5 Assessing the Story of Social Investment in Ireland

As regards the trajectory of the social investment agenda in Ireland, we see the co-existence of significant social investment initiatives and factors that limit the development of the well-resourced tailored capacitating services that would characterize a general social investment turn.

In the period of economic growth from the early 1990s to 2008 Ireland enhanced its historically weak welfare state by increasing transfers, extending social protection to new groups, such as lone parents, and widening access to services such as health care and third-level education. These improvements in social protection—though fairly transfer intensive and not strongly universalist—were hardly at odds with a social investment approach (SIA). But nor did they exemplify it very distinctly. Indeed, the buoyancy of Irish revenue and employment in those years allowed the politics of welfare state expansion and tax reduction to co-exist. However, Ireland also took relatively early steps to innovate in the creation and delivery of tailored services (combining action on stocks, flows, and buffers to address problems of access to work, literacy, addiction, etc.); but these were targeted at particularly disadvantaged neighbourhoods and largely provided by a new set of state-supported local organizations parallel to the statutory system of welfare and social services. The best of these innovations certainly made progress towards capacitating services and creation of niche-level institutional complementarities across social policy domains; but the lack of sufficient support from, and reform in, intermediate-level public institutional structures, and clarity at the policy centre about the social investment thrust of Irish welfare state reform, meant that these innovations remained marginal.

Between 2002 and 2005, after a decade of growth and welfare expansion, there emerged an overlapping consensus on social investment as a guiding framework, in *The Developmental Welfare State* hammered out in NESC. This was adopted as the guiding framework in the ten-year social partnership agreement of 2006. But the ambitious social policy reform programme agreed between government and the social partners, as well as being weakly reflected in organizational reform, was soon undercut by the onset of the crisis.

Policy trends since the onset of Ireland's severe crisis also paint a complex picture. Despite unprecedented fiscal consolidation, the main welfare transfers, or buffers, were reduced only slightly. Indeed, research demonstrates that Ireland's relatively high social transfers lifted almost 40 per cent of the population out of poverty in 2011 and were effective in reducing poverty for all social welfare groups in the face of a huge fall in employment, income, and wealth (Watson and Maître 2013). If we hold the view that income transfers and services are complementary, then policy efforts to protect basic transfers at a time of massive fiscal consolidation should not be viewed as representing a turn away from social investment.

It is true that there were proportionately greater cuts in the programme budgets that supported some services—in areas such as community development, literacy, addiction, and disability—including those provided by the local partnership and NGOs. Indeed, because of budget reductions and tighter central control, these entities generally feel less able to innovate, tailor, and combine services than they did before the crisis. If these organizations were the leading edge of social investment experimentation from the 1990s until 2005, the emphasis swung towards state entities, and away from NGOs, in the wake of the crisis. Indeed, as noted in Section 22.4, there has been some movement to mainstream, or at least extend, the tailored service pilots in early intervention, disability, and eldercare.

Beyond protection of transfers, there were a number of policy actions which are, on the face of it, indicative of a social investment, activation-oriented, approach. One was the gradual extension of universal free preschool care. Another was the reform of the lone parent payment, gradually moving lone parents onto the mainstream unemployment transfers and labour market supports. A third was the reduction on the jobseekers assistance to those under 25, combined (belatedly) with the 'youth guarantee' on training and education. Much the most significant welfare reform was the merging of the unemployment payments system with counselling and other supports in new Intreo offices and the creation of a new parallel activation-oriented pro-gramme for the long-term unemployed, offered by private providers. As emphasized by Soentken, van Hooren, and Rice in Chapter 21 on the Nether-lands, the proof of the social investment pudding will be in the eating. The reforms mentioned will only take on a definite social investment character if enhanced services provided for children, lone parents, young people, and the unemployed are genuinely tailored and capacitating, thereby simultaneously enhancing stocks, flows, and buffers.

On this critical question it remains unclear whether the necessary organiza-tional structures and routines are being created at both the front line and in the agencies and departments that plan and coordinate services. Earlier steps in this direction were more evident in parallel local entities and in some of the NGOs than in the mainstream state system.

A feature of the crisis is that it unblocked reform and reorganization across state organizations. But the government's public sector reform agenda has, to date, focused more on central control of budgets and staff numbers, and strengthening of formal accountability procedures, than on devolution to the front line and the dynamic accountability that would underpin an SIA (NESC 2013). Some argue that reduced staff numbers make it harder than ever to provide tailored services.

Another qualification concerns the limited universalism in Ireland's approach to social protection. While child benefit and free childcare years are universal, in many areas there remains a reliance on means-tested access to state services and tax relief for use of private services. While social investment is not synonymous with universalism or publicly provided services, means tests and tax reliefs can weaken the drive for quality in public services and the cross-class coalition supporting social investment. They thus weaken the drive to enhance and exploit institutional complementarities across key social policy domains.

As in other countries, the Irish social policy environment continues to consist of range of parallel sectoral landscapes with weak interconnections and a limited focus on cross-sectoral learning. This prompts us to think about the relation between concrete, piecemeal, cases of organizations capable of tailoring and bundling services—which is a first litmus test—and the wider, more articulated, social investment agenda set out in Chapter 1 and explored throughout this volume. Chapter 12 (this volume) shows that while the social investment agenda cannot rely on a strong, wide, and enduring consensus, it seems to be progressing through the piecemeal welfare reforms underway in many states. The same chapter also underscores that decentralized efforts to move in the direction of social investment require careful monitoring, so that dead-ends are rapidly identified and corrected and existing programmes can be improved on the basis of regular learning feedback loops.

The Irish case prompts us to think also about the role of civil society engagement in social investment and tailored services. During the period of social partnership from 1987 to 2008, the need for tailored capacitating services for the long-term unemployed and disadvantaged localities was linked to support for capacity building, community and local development, spatial targeting, and the involvement of networks of NGOs and public bodies in the kind of 'new governance' that was much discussed internationally (NESF 1997). Since 2008, a combination of reduced participation, increased centralization, cuts in programmes, and other reforms have dramatically altered the landscape in which civic organizations operate. Although comprehensive reform of state entities was overdue, it is not clear if the reform programme actually pursued since 2008 has increased the prospect of creating organizations capable of tailoring, delivering, and continuously bundling capacitating services.

The Irish case confirms that we should not rely on the idea of transition from 'old' to 'new social risks' as the logic of the social investment perspective. Movement towards a social investment agenda over the past twenty-five years partly reflected new *norms* concerning long-standing *old risks*, such as disability, poverty, and marginalization, which were not protected in a social insurance model. Indeed, the agenda of capacitating services was not so much a case of *reforming* an existing state-based institutional infrastructure, but *building* entire service systems from scratch, in areas such as childcare, eldercare, and addiction (O'Donnell 2008, O'Donnell, Adshead, and Thomas 2011).

In Chapter 1, Hemerijck tentatively suggests two related political factors that have contributed to social investment's endurance during the current economic and financial crisis in Europe. First, social investment's recalibration of welfare policy places manageable demands on political leadership to build broad coalitions of support for inclusive welfare provision. Second, social investment relegitimizes the role of the state in supporting economic development and social progress after the global financial crisis. As Ireland moves into a new phase of economic growth, there is reason to believe that both of these political factors can contribute to a broad coalition in favour of an inclusive growth model. Indeed, the outcome of the February 2016 election is widely understood as demonstrating a popular wish for better public services rather than tax reductions. The political challenge is to use this to create a coalition capable of addressing the organizational challenges at the heart of a social investment agenda.

23

Social Investment in a Federal Welfare State

The Quebec Experience

Alain Noël

In his first House of Commons speech following his June 1997 re-election, Canadian Prime Minister Jean Chrétien explained that the time had come to 'invest in the future of our young people' (Chrétien 1997: 1625). Knowing his government was about to achieve a first budgetary surplus in almost thirty years, the prime minister announced a new, 'balanced approach of social investment and prudent financial management' (Governor General 1997: 1550). The social investment perspective had arrived in Canada (Saint-Martin 2000: 37). In line with other Organisation for Economic Co-operation and Development (OECD) centre-left governments, the Chrétien government turned its attention to social inclusion and began implementing reforms to improve opportunities for children and encourage labour market participation for all working-age adults (Jenson 2013: 55). The new National Child Benefit introduced in 1998 and the National Children's Agenda announced in 1999 constituted the core of this new orientation, 'the flagships' of a 'new era' (Jenson 2001: 120).

The results, however, proved uneven, in part because insufficient resources were invested, and in part because the federal government did not control all the political levers. The new children's benefits, for instance, were often offset by cuts in provincial transfers, so that overall there was 'a weakening of the redistributive role of the Canadian state' (Banting 2006: 430). Limited progress was also made in early childhood education, education, and training, clearly provincial competences. Altogether, concluded Keith Banting, Canadian governments proved keener to make work pay by restructuring and lowering the benefits of income security programmes than to invest durably in early learning, training, or education. Focused on a rather liberal reading of the new idea of social investment, they also tended to neglect the old imperatives of social protection, for those who could not work in particular (Banting 2006: 444).

After 2006, with the coming to power of Stephen Harper's Conservative Party, the very notion of social investment vanished (Banting and Myles 2016: 524–5). Some policy initiatives, such as the 2007 Working Income Tax Benefit, could be seen as consistent with the idea of social investment, but many other orientations, starting with the 2007 replacement of the new intergovernmental childcare agreements with a flat-rate transfer given to parents whether they used day care or not, were definitively not (Jenson 2013: 59). In 2014, the Harper government even introduced an income-splitting measure that only benefited high-income one-earner two-parent families, a choice that went directly against the idea of encouraging women's labour force participation (Battle 2015).

The country thus became more 'a poster child for retrenchment' than a social investment model (Banting and Myles 2016: 524). But Canada is a federal welfare state, where provincial governments play an important role. In the 1990s and 2000s, in particular, the most significant changes in taxes and transfers took place in the provinces (Frenette, Green, and Milligan 2009). Overall these changes increased post-tax inequality, but one province took a different road. While transfers to the lowest two income quintiles declined in most of Canada, they increased in Quebec, as the provincial government went ahead with ambitious and rather consistent social investment reforms (Boychuk 2013: 248–50; Noël 2013).

A federated state within a liberal welfare regime, Quebec did not have the most favourable institutional and political context to implement social investment reforms. Yet, in a few years between the mid-1990s and the mid-2000s, Quebec governments, headed in turn by the province's two main political parties, transformed substantially a number of social policies, and succeeded in increasing labour market participation, limiting the rise of inequality, and reducing poverty. By 2016, some of these achievements had faded, with respect to poverty reduction in particular, but the main social investment reforms appeared embedded and institutionalized.

The Quebec experience can thus be seen as an instructive case on the possibilities of social investment in a highly constrained, federal and liberal welfare state context. It underlines, in particular, the importance of social forces and political actors in bringing about unexpected changes, and points as well to trade-offs between the maintenance of established social programmes and the development of new ones.

Section 23.1 presents background elements on Canadian federalism, the Canadian welfare regime, and Quebec's own political trajectory. Section 23.2 provides a political account of Quebec's turn toward social investment, pointing in particular to the emergence of a new social pact following the 1995 referendum on sovereignty. Section 23.3 then examines the relatively positive outcomes of the new Quebec model, in light of the parallel evolution of the neighbouring province of Ontario. Section 23.4 discusses the limits and sustainability of these achievements.

23.1 A Provincial Welfare State

Quebec, of course, is not a country. It is a somewhat reluctant province within the Canadian federation, whose fate remains largely determined by decisions taken in Ottawa. At the same time, the Quebec government has more resources and autonomy than most federated states in the world. Indeed, few federations are as decentralized as Canada. First, the provinces exercise full legislative competence on most social policy questions, including health care services, education, training, social assistance, and social services, and on many aspects of family and pension policies, leaving only old-age security and unemployment insurance as sole federal social responsibilities. Second, provincial governments have the financial means to act autonomously because they collect themselves a large part of their revenues. In 2011, provincial own-source revenues amounted to 39.7 per cent of total tax revenues in Canada (Blöchliger and Nettley 2015). In Switzerland, the closest federation in terms of decentralization, canton revenues represented only 24.1 per cent of total tax revenues. The province's revenue-raising capacity also means they have a strong influence on taxation, a key instrument for redistribution. Third, federal transfers to the provinces, primarily to support social programmes and equalize fiscal capacities, are formula-driven and increasingly unconditional. The federal role in financing social programmes remains important, but it has become more open-ended than in the past, and policy differences among provinces have tended to increase (Banting and Myles 2013: 17; Boychuk 2013). In many policy domains, provincial government can act more or less as sovereign countries would. This autonomy has not produced strong divergence. A similar context, policy diffusion, and political emulation contributed to bring rather similar outcomes. Provincial autonomy, however, has made innovation and distinctiveness possible.

The welfare state that emerged in Canada after the Second World War was very much a 'liberal' one, with some elements of universalism (the federal old-age security programme and provincial health care programmes), important social insurance measures (unemployment insurance, the Canada and Quebec Pension Plans), and significant but rather stingy means-tested programmes (social assistance and social services). In 2014, Canadian public social expenditures as a percentage of gross domestic product (GDP) were at 17.0 per cent, compared to 19.2 per cent for the United States, 21.7 per cent for the United Kingdom, 28.1 per cent for Sweden, and 31.9 per cent for France (OECD 2016a). In 2011, the Canadian poverty rate, defined as the percentage of the population living with less than half of the country's median income (after tax and transfer) was 12 per cent, compared to 18 per cent for the United States (2012), 9.5 per cent for the United Kingdom, 9.7 per cent for Sweden, and 8 per cent for France (OECD 2016b). Low social expenditures and a high poverty rate are the hallmarks of the liberal welfare state (Brady 2009: 81–2).

As the only province with a French-speaking majority, and as a society that sees itself as a distinct nation, with its own institutions and a strong sense of identity, Quebec always stood apart (Bouchard 2013: 269). In fact, Canada has become a decentralized federation largely because Quebec has consistently resisted the impulse, strong in the rest of Canada, to further empower the central government (Noël 2008; Rocher 2009). For a long time, Quebec was a relatively poor region of Canada, marked by an entrenched ethnic/linguistic division of labour. Business was predominantly conducted in English and French-speaking Quebeckers, even when they were bilingual, remained disadvantaged. Such enduring ethnic cleavages can only be undone by a major social and political mobilization (Tilly 1998). This is what happened in the 1960s with Quebec's 'Quiet Revolution'.

The process started with the election in 1960 of a new Liberal government, after fifteen years of Conservative rule. The Lesage government initiated a series of reforms to fight corruption and improve the civil service, modernize and upgrade the education system, and open up economic opportunities for French-speaking Quebeckers. It also implemented important social reforms, to make possible the development of a modern welfare state. In six years, between 1960 and 1966, public expenditures tripled (Fortin 2011: 91). At the same time, trade unions and social movements fought for better working and social conditions, and for language laws that would change the balance of power in the labour market (Levine 1997). By the 1980s, the ethnic/linguistic inequality that long marred Quebec's labour market had been eliminated, and the province's lag in education and income also had been virtually erased (Fortin 2011).

The welfare state that emerged out of the Quiet Revolution was not radically different from that of other Canadian provinces. Quebec's successful efforts to catch up and undo an old ethnic and linguistic cleavage was unique, however, and transformative. It left French-speaking Quebeckers with a favourable attitude towards both equality and state intervention, and anchored Quebec politics around a somewhat left-of-centre consensus (Noël 2013). Quebec voters and political parties became profoundly divided over Quebec sovereignty, but remained rather united on social and economic questions. Until recently, for instance, no major party openly supported a pro-market, neoliberal agenda (Haddow 2015: 40). Quebec trade unions also became more powerful than elsewhere in the country, representing nearly 40 per cent of the workforce. While more difficult to measure and compare, the women's movement and a host of social movements also grew well-organized and influential. Quebec thus developed a somewhat more interventionist and redistributive version of the Canadian provincial welfare state, anchored in well-established patterns of cooperation between the state, business, and labour (Noël 2013).

23.2 The Social Investment Turn

In the 1980s and early 1990s, the Quebec government experimented with new types of interventions, developed in collaboration with a vigorous and autonomous third sector of non-profit, community organizations. Day-care services, for instance, were often provided by parent-controlled, non-profit, local organizations (Vaillancourt 2003). The magnitude of these innovations, however, remained limited and Quebec did not offer more childcare spaces than other Canadian provinces (Haddow 2015: 135). The major breakthrough came after 1995.

In October 1995, the government of Jacques Parizeau held a referendum on sovereignty and failed by a very narrow margin of 54,288 votes. This referendum was a watershed in Quebec politics. All social actors were involved, the participation rate was extremely high (93.5 per cent), and the negative result—and his own reaction to it—led to the immediate resignation of the premier. A setback for Quebec sovereignty, the referendum defeat was also a failure for a large left-of-centre coalition that included three political parties, most of the labour movement, and a broad array of community and social organizations. On the No side, which included most business associations, the near-defeat also came as a shock. When Lucien Bouchard assumed office as the new premier in January 1996, he had to mend important social divisions. 'Federalists had been scared', he noted in a recent interview, and 'Quebec was divided...There were wounds to heal' (Bouchard 2015: 27, author's translation). The economic and public finance context was also difficult. The unemployment rate stood above 11 per cent and the Quebec government faced a record high deficit, just as Ottawa had announced major cuts in transfers to the provinces (Noël 2013: 263).

Bouchard almost immediately convened a socioeconomic summit, to be held in two steps, first in March 1996 in Quebec City, and then in October in Montreal. The aim was to conclude a 'new social pact for Quebec', centred on deficit reduction and on labour market and social reforms conducive to a higher level of employment.

With strong trade unions and an organized business sector, Quebec had held such summits before, when the left-of-centre Parti Québécois was in power. The 1996 summit, however, was set in a rather dramatic moment, and it innovated by including representatives from the community sector. While it took some doing to bring in business leaders, explained Bouchard twenty years later, it was not difficult to convince union leaders, 'even though there was not much to gain for them'. We were 'friends', Bouchard noted, 'we had done the referendum campaign together'. As for the community sector, they probably appeared more foreign to Bouchard, but they had also been referendum partners and could help to 'broaden the consensus and avoid being trapped in the famous triangle of government, trade unions and business' (Bouchard 2015: 27, author's translation). The decision to include this fourth social pillar was probably foreordained. Indeed, in the spring of 1995, the Quebec's Women Federation had organized a highly successful march toward Quebec, to denounce women poverty and press demands for equality. The coalition that emerged in the process obtained important concessions from the government on the minimum wage, pay equity, and the social economy, and it became an important element of the Yes side during the referendum campaign. It simply could not be overlooked for the 1996 summit.

These community groups, recalled Bouchard, 'made us think' (2015: 27). They were ready to consider measures to reduce the deficit and increase employment, but insisted as well on efforts to promote equality and reduce poverty. Social investment as such was not on the initial agenda, but the configuration of forces created a favourable context for innovation by bringing in the preoccupations of perennial outsiders (women, the poor, the youth), alongside those of business and labour.

The general thrust of the summit was not so much to 'turn vice into virtue'—eliminating inequitable or inefficient programmes to fund new initiatives (Levy 1999)—but rather to agree on a trade-off whereby retrenchment efforts in traditional but costly social services (mainly health care and education) would be compensated by the adoption of new services and transfers, in favour of women, young families, and the poor. Budget cuts in the 'old' welfare state programmes would not merely serve the deficit reduction objective; they would also sustain the emergence of a 'new' welfare state, designed to enhance employment, equality, and income security for those less well served by existing programmes. Retrenchment was to go hand in hand with expansion (Hemerijck 2013: 48).

Years later, trade union militants and voices on the left were still railing against Bouchard and the severe cuts in health and education budgets that he imposed after 1996. In the process, however, a new Quebec model emerged, that would almost immediately become institutionalized, popular, and effective.

23.3 The New Quebec Model

The train of reforms adopted between 1996 and the beginning of the 2000s can be summarized under three headings: family policy designed to sustain early childhood development and facilitate work/family conciliation, labour market policies to make work pay and foster labour market integration, and poverty reduction measures.

The transformation of Quebec's family policy was undoubtedly the most spectacular and wide-reaching development. It included a strong investment to make regulated day-care spaces available to all parents at a modest daily rate, the introduction of a new universal and targeted family allowance, and the creation of a distinct Quebec Parental Insurance Plan, more generous than the existing federal programme, accessible to self-employed workers, and designed to offer paternity benefits as well. In terms of spending, the new family policy brought Quebec to a level comparable with that of Denmark and Sweden (Noël 2013). More significantly, as Jane Jenson argued, this policy moved 'against the current' by favouring the development of low-cost, universal, not-for-profit early childhood education centres and providing extra transfers to lone-parent families (2002: 309–10).

A number of reforms transformed labour market policies. Early on, in November 1996, a new law on pay equity established an institutional framework to correct gender-based discrepancies in earnings. This law was not merely symbolic. By 2006, the Quebec government had reached a comprehensive pay equity agreement with its own employees, and about half of the province's employers had also complied with the law's requirements (Noël 2013: 269). In Quebec at least, women's demands for equality were not entirely 'lost in translation' (Jenson 2009). This outcome, clearly, was a political achievement. In a recent testimony, then Minister of Employment and Social Solidarity and Minister for the Status of Women Louise Harel recalled that at the 1996 summit, business representatives sought in vain to convince the government to abandon its projected law on pay equity (Harel 2015). In 1997, the Quebec government also introduced a Public Prescription Drug Insurance Plan, still unique in Canada, to cover the medication costs of all citizens not protected by an employer's plan. One of the core objectives of this Plan was to facilitate the labour market integration of persons who relied on social assistance because it covered high medication costs. The minimum wage and labour market standards were also improved, and working income supplements were introduced. Finally, all active labour market policies were integrated within a new agency, Emploi-Québec, which offered active measures irrespective of whether a person was eligible for unemployment insurance, living with social assistance, or simply without benefits.

Third, measures to reduce poverty and social exclusion were also adopted, including an end to penalties for social assistance recipients who would not accept a given job or training programme, a gradual improvement of social assistance benefits, and the creation of new poverty monitoring and consultative agencies to advise the government.

These reforms were not cast explicitly in the language of social investment, but they corresponded closely to the approach's objectives of easing the 'flow' in labour market and life-course transitions, improving the 'stock' of human capital and capabilities, and maintaining social protection 'buffers' for the most vulnerable. Across the different reforms, there were also common principles or modes of operation: a predominantly universalist orientation, a preoccupation for equality, poverty reduction, citizen empowerment, a preference for public or non-profit mechanisms, and an explicit recognition of the role of community organizations and social economy enterprises. These orientations reflected the political equilibrium reached in 1996, when a left-of-centre party agreed on a new social pact with the province's main social actors, but they were sufficiently anchored to survive the coming to power of the more conservative Quebec Liberal Party in 2003.

What about the outcomes? Consider, first, family policy. The introduction of the new early childhood education centres in 1997 made an important difference. Figure 23.1 presents the percentage of 0–5-year-old children with a full-time or part-time centre-based childcare place in Quebec and Ontario (the largest province, long the industrial centre of Canada, and Quebec's

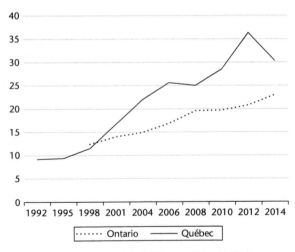

Figure 23.1. Percentage of 0–5-year-old children with a full-time or part-time centre-based childcare place, Ontario and Quebec, 1992–2014

Source: Friendly et al. 2015: 138.

immediate neighbour to the west, Ontario is the conventional reference in Quebec policy debates). Slightly behind Ontario in 1992, Quebec surged ahead after 1997, with a steadily increasing number of children enrolled in regulated childcare services. The gap between the two provinces would in fact be wider if we considered 0–12-year-old children, because Quebec schools routinely provided after-school childcare. In 2014, the percentage of 0–12-year-old children with a childcare space was 50.8 per cent in Quebec, compared to 17.7 per cent for Ontario (Friendly et al. 2015: 124). In 2014, the parents' median monthly fee for a toddler (between 1.5 and 3 years old) was C$152 in Montreal (or anywhere in Quebec), against C$1,324 in Toronto (Friendly et al. 2015: 129).

Figure 23.2 suggests cheaper and more accessible day-care services had an impact on the labour market participation of women at the age of having children. Significantly below the Ontario figure, the Quebec employment rate increased rapidly in the 1990s, to rise above that of Ontario in the 2000s.

The shift in labour market policy is harder to track because Canadian governments do not publish elaborate statistics in this respect. Two figures can nevertheless provide a glimpse of what happened after the mid-1990s. Figure 23.3 indicates that in real terms spending on active labour market programmes increased but not much and not for long, showing the limits of the new Quebec model.

Figure 23.4 shows that the employment situation nevertheless improved over the years, with a brief bump after the 2008 financial crisis. More importantly,

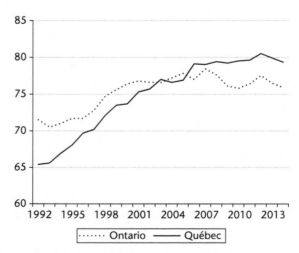

Figure 23.2. Percentage of 25–44-year-old women in employment, Ontario and Quebec, 1992–2014

Source: Statistics Canada (CANSIM 282–0002).

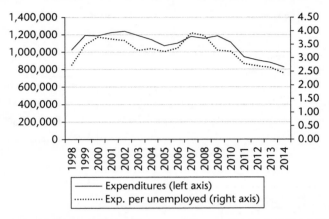

Figure 23.3. Active labour-market policy expenditures, Quebec, 1998–2014

Sources: Expenditures: Ministère du Travail, de l'Emploi et de la Solidarité sociale, *Rapport annuel de gestion*, Québec, MESS, 1998–99 à 2013–14; Unemployment data: Statistics Canada (CANSIM 282–0050).

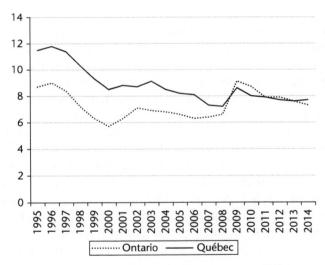

Figure 23.4. Unemployment rate, Ontario and Quebec, 1995–2014

Source: Statistics Canada (CANSIM 282–0002).

the gap with Ontario, almost 3 percentage points in 1995, practically disappeared. The number of persons relying on social assistance also decreased dramatically. At 11.5 per cent in March 1996, the ratio of social assistance recipients to the total population aged 0 to 64 was down to 6.4 per cent by January 2016, the lowest ratio in more than thirty-five years (Noël 2015: 135; Ministère du Travail, de l'Emploi et de la Solidarité sociale 2016).

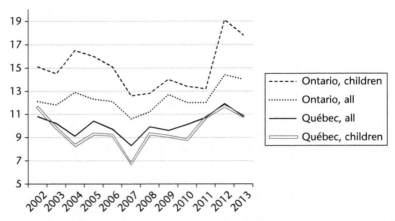

Figure 23.5. Poverty rate based on the market basket measure (MBM), all persons and persons below 18, Ontario and Quebec, 2002–13
Source: Centre d'étude sur la pauvreté et l'exclusion (CEPE).

Finally, the new Quebec model had some success in preventing the rise of inequality and reducing poverty. Figure 23.5 shows the evolution of poverty rates in Ontario and Quebec between 2002 and 2013, calculated on the basis of the market basket measure (MBM). The MBM is a new measure of poverty designed by the Canadian government, which is based on the cost of a defined basket of goods in each region. Because it takes into account regional variations in the cost of living, this is an excellent measure to compare provinces or cities within Canada. Three conclusions can be drawn from Figure 23.5. First, the starting point in 2002, when Quebec adopted a law against poverty and social exclusion, was close, but since then poverty has been consistently more important in Ontario. Second, in Ontario, the risk of poverty is more important for families with children, whereas the opposite is true in Quebec, thanks to more generous family policies. And third, both provinces were making progress against poverty until 2008, but lost most of their gains afterward.

Quebec's new social model made a difference, for women and for families in particular. It improved services and transfers to families, contributed to the growing labour market participation of women, helped close the historical Quebec–Ontario gap in unemployment rates, limited the rise of inequality in Quebec, and reduced the incidence of poverty, for children in particular. A number of studies have established empirically the connection between the province's new social investment policies and these positive results. Quebec taxes more, spends more, and obtains better redistributive results (Haddow 2013, 2014, 2015; Bernard et al., forthcoming).

23.4 Conclusion

The prospects for social investment seem less auspicious in liberal welfare regimes. Less generous and encompassing, these welfare states are not as solidly anchored in public opinion, and they appear more likely to meet post-industrial challenges with market-conforming policies, at the cost of greater inequality (Thelen 2014: 12; Van Kersbergen and Vis 2014: 178). Organized labour is weak and declining, and so are probably other collective actors (Hassel 2015: 238–44). Parties of the left also tend to be less competitive, or less able to forge working coalitions uniting the middle class with low-skilled workers (Iversen and Soskice 2015). The Quebec experience does not necessarily invalidate these claims. Indeed, with strong trade unions and social movements, a high level of taxes and public expenditures, and a some-what social-democratic consensus, Quebec stands as an outlier in North America (Noël 2013; Haddow 2014). All the same, the province's trajectory suggests that diverse avenues remain open, even in a liberal welfare state.

Questions can be raised on the limits and sustainability of Quebec's experience. Indeed, since 2003, Quebec has been governed by the right-of-centre Quebec Liberal Party—except for an eighteen-month interlude of Parti Québécois minority government—and many of the programmes put in place in the late 1990s and early 2000s have been incrementally downgraded. The Liberals, for instance, have gradually favoured the development of for-profit day-care centres; they increased the fees for middle-class families, and they are now reintroducing penalties for social assistance recipients. In the end, however, a good part of the social investment reforms of the last twenty years is now institutionalized and likely to be maintained.

These reforms still leave open many questions. Poverty, in particular, has been on the rise again in the last seven or eight years. This may be due to the inherent limitations of the social investment approach (SIA), which focuses more on families and on employment than on poverty as such (Cantillon 2014), or it could be attributed to the wavering commitments of right-of-centre governments. Another intriguing possibility is that the benefits associated with women's massive entry into the labour market are now largely spent (Nieuwenhuis et al. 2016). Whatever the case, Quebec, like other jurisdictions, will have to pay attention to those who were left out by the social investment turn, poor working-age persons that remain far from the labour market and live alone, without children.

24

A Social Investment Turn in East Asia?

South Korea in Comparative Perspective

Timo Fleckenstein and Soohyun Christine Lee

The welfare states of Japan, South Korea, and Taiwan were built by conservative elites to serve the project of late industrialization, and for this reason the East Asian *developmental* welfare state focused its resources on those who were deemed most important for economic development (especially, male industrial workers). Starting in the 1990s and increasingly since the 2000s, however, the developmental welfare state has experienced a far-reaching transformation, including the expansion of family policy to address the post-industrial challenges of female employment participation and low fertility rates.

In this chapter, we assess the transformation of the East Asian developmental welfare state, with a focus on family policy and special attention to the South Korean case, where we observed the most comprehensive policy expansion. In addition to public policies, we also discuss the importance of private social investment policies in the region. Private education expenditure, especially so-called 'shadow education', enjoys great prominence in East Asia, and therefore cannot be ignored when assessing social investment policies in the region.

24.1 The East Asian Developmental Welfare State

East Asian countries are latecomers in the development of welfare states. Social welfare provision developed in the context of late industrialization. At early stages of industrialization, social policy was considered incompatible with economic development, as development strategies pursued light, labour-intensive manufacturing, where pressure on labour costs left little room for social welfare provision. When the economic success of light-industry-driven development created labour shortages and corresponding pressure on wages, a shift in the developmental strategy towards higher-value-added heavy industry made economic development in the region and social policy compatible. The need for human capital investments for greater labour productivity and labour force stability provided the socioeconomic underpinnings for higher expenditure on education and training in particular, but also on health and enterprise welfare (Deyo 1992).

Whilst the language of social investment had not been used in this particular context for obvious reasons, social policy was viewed as an *investment* to facilitate economic development (especially through the boosting of *stocks*). The developmental welfare state literature and the related productivist welfare regime approach (Kwon 1997, 2005; Holliday 2000; Holliday and Wilding 2003b) highlight that social policy was used instrumentally and strictly subordinated to the imperatives of economic growth and rapid industrialization in order to catch up with the West. However, the developmental state was highly selective in its welfare efforts and investments, and it concentrated social welfare provision on the presumably productive parts of the population, especially skilled workers in large companies but also civil servants and the military. Looking at the coverage of early social insurance schemes (health care and old-age security), we find large parts of the population excluded (Kwon 1997). Not only social protection for more vulnerable members of society but also social care were not considered good investments but a burden on the economy (Holliday and Wilding 2003a). In other words, 'old' social investment policies in the region focused on male industrial workers in critical sectors, whereas labour market outsiders and especially women were largely excluded from social welfare provision. Thus, the highly dualized labour market translated into a dualized system of social protection, where *buffers* were not only weak but also incredibly selective. However, policy expansion in the aftermath of democratization not only included a growing share of labour market outsiders in social protection schemes (with the universalization of health care, unemployment protection, and old-age security) (Estevez-Abe 2008; Kwon 2009; Peng and Wong 2010), but also social care provision has experienced substantial growth since the second half of the 1990s.

24.2 Public Social Investment Policies and the Rise of Family Policy

The developmentalist logic was reinforced by a Confucian ethos, which shaped societies in the region. Confucianism ascribes great importance to the family and encourages a rigid division of gender roles, with the men as the 'natural' head of the family and its breadwinner, and with women as the provider of care (Won and Pascall 2004; see also Lewis 1992 on the male breadwinner model). Unpaid care work by women but also social protection through families based on the Confucian ideals of filial piety and family obligations (in particular, through intergenerational monetary transfers) (Jones 1993) allowed the developmental state prioritizing of economic over social development. Developmentalism and Confucianism were complementary to each other, and created a stable equilibrium (cf. Hall and Soskice 2001 on the notion of institutional complementarities).

However, not only democratization in the late 1980s and early 1990s providing bottom-up pressure for social policy expansion (Peng 2002; Wong 2004; Fleckenstein and Lee 2014) but also social changes destabilized the developmental state. As with Western countries, post-industrialization in East Asia was accompanied by a significant increase in female employment participation (Figure 24.1). Admittedly, overall female employment in the region (with the exception of Japan) is still somewhat lower than in Western Organisation for Economic Co-operation and Development (OECD) countries, but it is obvious that East Asia has embarked upon a similar trajectory. Interestingly, if one looks at full-time equivalent employment rates, one finds Korea (with 55.2 per cent in 2013) outperforming the majority of Western countries (e.g. UK 52.4, Germany 52.3, France 51.9, Netherlands 42.7, Italy 38.5, OECD average 50.1), pointing to a very low incidence of part-time employment in Korea (OECD 2016c).

At the same time, fertility has seen a dramatic decline in Japan, Korea, and Taiwan, recording fertility rates not only below the replacement rate but also

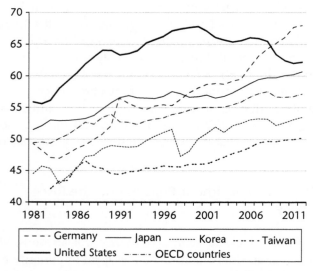

Figure 24.1. Female employment rates, 1981–2012
Source: OECD, Taiwanese Executive Yuan.

tailing behind most of the OECD world (Table 24.1). We also observe an extraordinary increase in divorce rates in the region (Table 24.2), in addition to the ever falling number of multi-generation households (Table 24.3).

Against these observations, it can be concluded that the Confucian family ideal has been eroding in the region, and that families are now under consid-erable 'stress'. In fact, the strong male breadwinner bias in Confucian ideology (Sung and Pascall 2014) has fuelled the rise of work/family conflicts. These developments have established the socioeconomic underpinnings for a greater role of the state in family affairs, as with Western countries (Esping-Andersen 1999; Lewis 2009). Improving *flows* and *stocks*, the expansion of family policies helping with work/family reconciliation in particular repre-sents the most prominent area of 'new' social investments in the region. Japan pioneered the expansion of childcare provision with the Angel Plan in the

Table 24.1. Fertility rates in Japan, Korea, and Taiwan

	1970	1980	1990	2000	2010
Japan	2.13	1.75	1.54	1.36	1.39
Korea	4.53	2.83	1.59	1.47	1.23
Taiwan	4.00	2.50	1.80	1.68	0.92
OECD	2.71	2.14	1.86	1.65	1.70

Source: OECD, Taiwanese Executive Yuan.

Table 24.2. Divorce rates in Japan, Korea, and Taiwan

	1971	1980	1990	2000	2005
Japan	1.0	1.2	1.3	2.1	2.1
Korea	0.3	0.6	1.1	2.5	2.6
Taiwan	0.4	0.8*	1.4*	2.4	2.8
OECD	1.2	1.7	2.0	2.4	2.3

Note: * Taiwanese data are from 1981 and 1991, respectively.
Source: OECD, Taiwanese Executive Yuan.

Table 24.3. Family types in Japan, Korea, and Taiwan

		1970	1980	1990	2000	2010
Japan	Nuclear Family	71.4	75.4	77.6	81.2	84.1
	Extended Family	17.3	17.8	16.6	13.6	10.2
Korea	Nuclear Family	71.5	72.9	76.0	82.0	82.2
	Extended Family	18.8	11.0	10.2	8.0	6.2
Taiwan	Nuclear Family	–	–	76.2*	76.2	76.0
	Extended Family	–	–	18.4*	17.0	15.3

Note: * Taiwanese data are from 1995.
Source: Japanese Statistical Bureau, Statistics Korea, Taiwanese Executive Yuan.

mid-1990s, in addition to the improvement of parental leave schemes and child allowances (Estevez-Abe 2008; Miura and Hamada 2014), and Korea and Taiwan followed the Japanese trajectory. Whilst family policy expansion in Taiwan has been somewhat limited compared to its two neighbours, Korea has outpaced the Japanese pioneer in more recent times (An and Peng 2015).

In Korea, new social investment policies entered the scene in the late 1990s during the first centre-left government of Kim Dae-Jung (1998–2003). Although the language of social investments was not adopted, Kim Dae-Jung's notion of 'productive welfare' largely complied with the social investment paradigm. Here, it is worthy to note that social policy was, for the first time, acknowledged as a government priority, and that productive social policy became a key objective of the Kim government, along with fostering market economy and democracy (Office of the President 1999). While social investment strategies in Europe are typically associated with the modernization of social democracy (and sometimes with adopting certain element of neoliberalism), in the Korean context new social investment policies represented a move away from pure developmentalism towards the embracing of social citizenship. Productive welfare was presented as a policy approach that 'goes beyond traditional passive welfare targeted at marginalised groups and pursues the active protection of rights to work', as it was described as a 'human-development-centred' approach to social welfare (Office of the President 1999: 23). Social services, education, and training were identified as key elements to facilitate 'human development'. In terms of family policy and social service expansion, the need to address increasing child poverty after the economic crisis of 1997/8 and to promote female employment was put forward as a rationale (Office of the President 1999: 59, 62). Children of low-income families could either receive free childcare (aged 5 plus) or some financial support (under the age of 5) (Ministry of Health and Welfare 2002). The delivery of childcare, however, was largely dependent on the private sector, as the government sought to increase childcare provision through deregulation. Obtaining government approval for the opening of childcare facilities was no longer required, and the number of private nurseries nearly doubled during the time of the government (from 6,538 centres in 1997 to 11,046 centres in 2002) (Ministry of Health and Welfare 2014). Improving care leaves, the duration of maternity leave was increased from two to three months, and care leave became available to fathers. The new paid parental leave, though, remained somewhat modest with a flat-rate benefit of ₩200,000 (approximately GB£120) (Ministry of Labour 2002b).

Putting these developments into perspective, however, it needs to be noted that social investment initiatives implemented during the government were 'dwarfed' by the scale of expansion in traditional income protection policies (that is the improvement of *buffers*), though still limited by European standards.

In order to tackle rising poverty, the government expanded the rather selective coverage of social insurance programmes and public assistance, and spending for 'traditional' social security programmes increased by 3.3 times from 3.7 to ₩12.3 trillion between 1997 and 2002, while the increase in social services spending, from ₩0.5 to ₩1 trillion, was much more modest (Ministry of Health and Welfare, 1997, 2002; Ministry of Labour 1997, 2002a). The East Asian financial crisis of 1997/8 revealed the vulnerability of the welfare-through-work system, when the availability of decent jobs that keep people out of poverty was quickly diminishing. Hence, despite the new prominence of social investment policies, traditional social protection was in practice prioritized during the Kim Dae-Jung government, especially in the face of the East Asian financial crisis exposing enormous gaps in Korean social protection.

In the second centre-left government under Roh Moo-Hyun (2003–8), social investment policies gained prominence, and we observe that the social investment perspective was explicitly adopted in key speeches and policy documents as a conceptual framework for social welfare reform. Following the president's independence day speech, in which he proclaimed 'to build a platform for sustainable growth through education and social investment' (Ministry of Health and Welfare 2006), the Welfare Minister Rhyu Shi-Min announced the government's adaptation of a social investment approach (SIA); with references to Anthony Gidden's work, and Head Start and Sure Start as policy examples among others. The thrust of the government's SIA was to 'increase personal potential and capability' through 'active investment in children as it would secure a high-quality labour force in the future' and 'promotion of female labour market participation through the socialisation of care'. To this end, the government intended to 'shift the focus of the welfare state from redistributing income by social insurance and public assistance to ensure fair opportunity by improving capability to participate in the market' (Ministry of Health and Welfare 2006). Later in the same year, underlining the investment orientation of social policy, the government published a comprehensive policy paper called 'Vision 2030', in which social policy was recognized as a pre-requisite of economic development: 'Economic policy and social policy are the two different sides of the same coin. We need a shift to a new paradigm which sees a virtuous circle between the two policy areas and to seek better coordination between the two' (Government of the Republic of Korea 2006: 13). Thus, whilst *flows* continued to enjoy great prominence, *stocks* started to receive greater attention during the Roh government.

The adoption of a social investment perspective did not remain rhetoric but entailed substantial policy change. Childcare benefits experienced an important expansion, making middle-class families eligible for financial support for the first time. Unlike its predecessor, which sought a market-driven increase in childcare services, the Roh government was committed to increasing public provision of childcare with the ambition of doubling the number of public childcare centres from 1,352 to 2,700 by 2010. The underlying rationale was to provide higher-quality services, which were better suited to children's human capital development. For private providers, to drive up the quality of care, the government introduced a new 'basic subsidy' covering up to one-third of childcare costs of all children between age 0 and 2 (Ministry of Gender Equality and Family 2006). Accordingly, between 2003 and 2006, the child-care budget increased fourfold from ₩235 billion to ₩1.04 trillion (from approximately GB£139 million to GB£614 million). The expansion of publicly subsidized childcare was expected to produce positive impacts on economic growth, and care services were identified as a new 'growth engine' with a considerable potential to create jobs for women (National Advisory Council of Economy 2007; see also Peng 2012b). Complementing childcare expansion, the eligibility of parental leave was relaxed to both parents with children under the age of 3, effectively doubling the total leave duration for a couple to up to twenty-four months. The parental leave benefit gradually increased to ₩500,000 (approximately GB£310) (Ministry of Labour 2008).

With the end of centre-left rule, social investment policies have lost in prominence in terms of public policy discourse with the language of 'social investments' disappearing by and large in key policy documents and speeches. The conservative Lee Myung-Bak government (2008–13) emphasized, in rather broad terms, the importance of 'investment for the future', and the current Park Geun-Hye government (from 2013) adopted a life course approach as a key framework for social welfare reform (Ministry of Health and Welfare 2010, 2013). Yet, the SIA of *stocks* and *flows* nevertheless con-tinued to inform government policy, and we observe a high level of continuity during conservative government leadership. Childcare benefits continued to expand until childcare became free for all families in 2013. In addition, further efforts were made to improve the quality of childcare and to enhance early education in childcare provision. A national curriculum for preschool children (*nurigwajeong*) was introduced, first for 5-year-old children in 2012 and then extended to 3- and 4-year-old children in 2013 with an aim to better prepare children for primary education. The introduction of a national curriculum was accompanied by greater financial commitment to childcare centres. Whilst the Lee government emphasized market provision, the current Park govern-ment ascribes greater importance to public childcare provision (Ministry of Health and Welfare 2013). Also, improving *flows*, parental leave experienced expansion with the introduction of earnings-related benefits at 40 per cent income replacement rate with a floor and ceiling, which effectively doubled the maximum amount of benefit to ₩1,000,000 (approximately GB£615). This change was accompanied by relaxed eligibility criteria, and parental leave benefit can now be claimed for children under the age of 6 with each parent having an entitlement of twelve months (Ministry of Employment and Labour 2012). Recent changes in legislation have doubled family policy expenditure between 2010 and 2013 (Ministry of Health and Welfare 2014).

Despite this significant policy expansion, it has been suggested that the human capital and employment orientation of family policy has been undermined by the introduction of a new, controversial homecare allowance for stay-at-home parents (effectively mothers) during the Lee government, and by its expansion to all preschool children regardless of family income at the beginning of the Park government (currently maximum ₩200,000 per month (approximately GB£120)) (Ministry of Health and Welfare 2013: 32). Not only does the homecare allowance discourage women's labour market participation, it also deprives children of early education opportunities outside the home (In-Kyung Kim 2012). Moreover, the Lee government strongly promoted part-time employment for women under the banner of 'flexi jobs', arguing that women with caring responsibility prefer part-time over full-time employment (Ministry of Gender Equality and Family 2011: 129). Whilst there might be a genuine preference for reduced hours amongst many women in Korea (as in other countries), it needs to be noted that part-time employment in Korea does not normally promote quality jobs but jobs at the periphery of the labour market. Thus, a strategy of boosting part-time employment can be thought of as reinforcing gender segmentation in Korea's dualized labour market.

The seemingly contradictory policy directions point to the fact that, under conservative governments, the socioeconomic rationale of childcare and family policy more broadly moved towards boosting fertility rates. Numerous surveys suggest that financial costs of raising children and the difficulty of reconciling work and family life are key reasons that discourage young people from having more children (Lee et al., 2005; Government of the Republic of Korea 2009). Dual-earner policies such as free childcare provision but also financial support for the family in the form of a homecare allowance—a general family support policy in Korpi's (2000) typology—are means of reducing the costs of having children. Thus, despite pulling women and children into different the directions of labour market and early education participation, both might be effective investments for increasing fertility rates.

24.3 The Rise of Private Social Investments in Korea

In addition to high public investments in education, the region displays great private education expenditure; that is investing in *stocks*. Significant private spending on higher education is not uncommon elsewhere (especially in the anglophone world), yet East Asia also has a long track record of extensive private, that is fee-based, tutoring, which provides supplementary instruction to students who are enrolled in the public school system. It has been described as a 'parallel education sector' (Dang and Rogers 2008: 161) but also as 'shadow education' (Bray 1999), as it mimics mainstream education. Although private tutoring is a 'global phenomenon', the extraordinary prominence of after-school education in East Asia can be linked to Confucianism, in which educational achievement is highly valued—not only for reasons of personal progression but also, more generally, to promote the social status of the student's family (Bray and Lykins 2012: 8). Japan is widely considered the pioneer in private tutoring, where students, typically in *jukus*, receive intensive supplementary education, particularly during school vacations (Dang and Rogers 2008: 163).

Korea followed the trajectory of its neighbour, and now shows an even greater extent of private tutoring. After-school education is commonly provided in *hagwons*, private learning institutes. There are nearly 100,000 *hagwons* in Korea, which employ more teachers than the public education sector and have become the largest employer of graduates in humanities and social sciences. Notably, we find a concentration of about 6,000 *hagwons* in the wealthy Seoul borough of Gangnam, where the strong presence of private institutes is considered an important driver in rising property prices (Bray and Lykins 2012: 29; OECD 2013b: 18). Whilst private tutoring was banned in the past during the authoritarian era, household expenditure for private tutoring has successively increased since democratization in the late 1980s and has become equivalent to about 80 per cent of public expenditure on primary and secondary education (Dang and Rogers 2008; Bray and Lykins 2012). In absolute terms, Koreans spent US\$17.3 billion on after-school education in 2010; this figure excludes extra-curricular activities such as music education and sports activities that are not directly related to the curriculum in mainstream education. Among the 15-year-olds, for instance, we find that about three-quarters of students receive after-school education, which is twice the OECD average (OECD 2013b: 18). In elementary schools, the participation rate goes up to almost 90 per cent (Bray and Lykins 2012: 5). According to survey data, excessive private spending for tutoring is driven by the desire to enter prestigious universities, whose attendance largely determines later life chances in Korea. Data also show that having fewer children raises parental expectations, and that parents are concerned about the quality of public schools. Parents also report a perception that their children would experience a disadvantage if they did not attend a *hagwon* (OECD 2013b: 19f.).

Private tutoring certainly contributes to the development of human capital (Bray and Lykins 2012: 2) and is considered incredibly important for the understanding of the extraordinary performance of Korean students in international educational assessment exercises, such as PISA (OECD 2013b: 18), yet excessive after-school education also presents some serious 'side-effects'. Private tutoring reinforces and amplifies existing social inequalities. Unsurprisingly, high-income families spend significantly more resources on after-school education, adding to the socioeconomic advantages of their children. We also observe an increasing gap in participation and spending since the 2000s (Bray and Lykins 2012: 16). These developments can be thought to have contributed to rising social and educational inequality since the democratization of the country. Hence, private tutoring has important implications for social cohesion.

Some private tutoring might have positive effect on children's well-being, as it can help young learners to cope with difficult material in school. It also, however, runs the risk of dominating the life of young people. In Korea, there is no question that 'education fever' (Seth 2002) dominates the lives of the majority of young learners of different ages. Against this background, it might not come as much of a surprise that Korea took the second last place of eleven countries in the Children's Society's recent pilot study of life satisfaction among 12-year-olds (The Children's Society 2014). As discussed earlier in this section, excessive household expenditure for after-school education is driven by parents' desire for great academic education of their children, and indeed Korea shows extraordinary enrolment rates in higher education. Nowhere else in the OECD can we see more young people entering tertiary education (OECD 2009). Whilst education expansion provided the growing Korean economy with skilled workers, the boom of higher education came at the expense of intermediate skills. Small and medium-sized enterprises (SMEs) in particular, which employ about 90 per cent of Korean workers, suffer from a lack of vocational skills and display low productivity. Hence, 'over-education' has caused a severe *skills mismatch*, in addition to low 'education premiums' for tertiary education by international standards (Park 2011). Hence, Koreans mobilize significant private resources for the education of their children, but these resources might not be allocated most efficiently from an economic point of view. This private over-investment in human capital (*stocks*), though, needs to be seen in the context of the dualized social protection and labour market, where career opportunities and lifetime income depend most heavily on your access to Korea's extremely hierarchical university system.

Korean policymakers show increasing awareness of the excessive nature of private tutoring and its negative side-effects, but only limited measures to contain after-school education were taken (notably, the requirement that tuition in *hagwons* needs to end by 10 p.m.). In its assessment of the Korean case, the Asian Development Bank concludes that 'Korean experience sounds a major warning to other parts of the region. It shows that, once shadow education structures and habits become entrenched, they are very difficult to change' (Bray and Lykins 2012: 71).

The burden of private education has been continuously identified as the key obstacle to having more children. The first national plan for low-fertility and ageing underlines that high private education expenditures, along with childcare costs, are a key reason behind fertility rate decline (Government of the Republic of Korea 2009). It is also reported that private education expenditure has a greater negative impact than childcare costs on the number of children that people want to have (Lee et al. 2005). The most recent wave of the Marriage and Birth Trend survey confirms the negative impact of private education expenditure on fertility, and suggested that fertility increase would not be possible unless the issue of private education was addressed (Kim et al. 2012: 148f.).

24.4 Conclusions

East Asian welfare states, with their historically strong bias towards productivism, have been redefined starting in the mid-/late 1990s with the expansion of employment-oriented family policy in particular. Whilst 'old' social investments are widely viewed as an instrumental means that promoted late industrialization in the region, 'new' social investment policies especially address the post-industrial challenges of female employment and ultra-low fertility rates. This transformation has received support across the political spectrum in Japan, South Korea, and Taiwan, with political parties of the left and right supporting family policy expansion (Estevez-Abe 2008; Tsai 2011; Fleckenstein and Lee 2014).

Social investment strategies in East Asia, in the realm of family policy, display considerable similarity with policy responses in Western OECD countries, where also the political left and right drove family policy expansion (see, for policy developments in the West: Lewis 2009; Fleckenstein 2010; Morgan 2013). These observations call into question the notion of 'East Asian exceptionalism' (cf. Peng and Wong 2010) that has dominated much of the literature on welfare capitalism in the region, as it questions the argument that recent changes in East Asia only readjust the developmental welfare state (Peng 2012b).

Despite some significant policy changes, important challenges remain in the region. Based on the Korean experience, it is suggested that the consolidation of social investment policies in the region ought to focus on 'quality' rather than 'quantity'. Whilst, admittedly, the quality of childcare provision and early education has slowly gained importance (i.e. the quality of *stocks*), it has been argued that social investment policies have prioritized the challenges of low fertility (i.e. the quantity of *stocks*) and women's employment (i.e. *flows*). Education and human capital did not feature as prominently, as educational achievement has already been high by international standards (Choi, Chung, and Chang 2014). However, low-quality services do not only inhibit take-up (especially amongst middle-class families, thus undermining some female employment participation), it is also known that early education yields particularly high returns making it an efficient allocation of resources.

In addition, policies ought to devote greater attention to the kind of labour market participation that is promoted through social investment policies. Women's jobs are largely found at the periphery of the labour market, where the quality of jobs is rather low (Peng 2012a). In fact, social investment policies facilitating social care jobs as a 'new growth engine' reinforce occupational segregation and highly dualized labour markets. Although Korean women display extraordinary educational attainment with near universal enrolment in tertiary education, this is not reflected in the labour market. Not only are employment rates of tertiary-educated women in Korea the lowest amongst OECD countries, we also find the widest gender gap (OECD 2012c). Hence, to make better use of women's human capital, employment-promoting family policies need to be complemented by a broader set of labour market and non-discrimination policies. A firmer focus on gender equality appears imperative.

Finally, the Korean experience shows that private social investments, especially shadow education, cannot be ignored by policymakers. Whilst private education expenditure has certainly driven up educational attainment, it does not only have a detrimental impact on equality and the well-being of many children, it also undermines the effectiveness of family policy in terms of raising fertility rates. Childcare expansion and the homecare allowance have reduced the costs of children, yet the financial pressure from private education has acted as a counter-measure. Hence, from an economic point of view, the taming of private social investment is not only vital for satisfying the country's vocational skills needs, but also critical for greater effectiveness of public social investment strategies as far as the aspiration of raising fertility rates is concerned.

25

Social Investment in Latin America

Johan Sandberg and Moira Nelson

25.1 Introduction

This chapter reviews the reach, limited success, and persistent barriers involved with social investment in the Latin American context. In particular, we aim to understand the viability of the social investment approach (SIA) in Latin America by focusing on the case of conditional cash transfers (CCTs) and the extent to which these policies fulfil the social investment functions of stock, buffer, and flow (Hemerijck 2013, 2015). While all three functions are critical to addressing human capital risks, there are various gaps in the ability of CCTs to fulfil these functions. Such gaps are not exceptional, insofar as any individual policy can only cope with a limited number of issues. Yet therein lies the relevance of institutional complementarities (see Chapter 11, this volume) and the importance of a comprehensive policy mix in order to fulfil all three social investment functions to a satisfactory degree. The discussion outlines ways in which to address the role of institutional complementarities in Latin America.

The chapter proceeds in three stages. In Section 25.2, social investments in the Latin American context are laid out and advancements in and barriers to social investment in Latin America are reviewed. In Section 25.3, the particular advantages and disadvantages to CCTs are reviewed. In Section 25.4, strategies for advancing the social investment agenda in Latin America are discussed.

25.2 Social Investment in the Latin American Context

The onset of the social investment turn can be observed in a rudimentary sense by looking at spending, coverage, and outcomes. Virtually every country in the region has increased social expenditures during the last two decades, on average up from 13.8 per cent of gross domestic product (GDP) in the early 1990s to some 19.1 per cent in 2013 (ECLAC 2014). CCTs constitute the central piece in Latin American countries' social investment strategy, covering more than 22 million families in 18 countries throughout the region (Cecchini and Madariaga 2011). The region has made significant progress in educational access to primary and secondary education, primarily through investments in infrastructure and teacher staffing. The proportion of people aged 15–29 with completed primary education has increased from some 60.5 per cent in 1990 to 94 per cent in 2012. In 2012, some 59 per cent had completed secondary education compared to 25.8 per cent in 1990. Finally, the proportion of people having completed tertiary education increased from some 4.4 per cent in 1990 to 10.0 per cent in 2012 (ECLAC 2014). However, adequate levels of learning have not accompanied increased access; United Nations Educational, Scientific and Cultural Organization (UNESCO) (2013) finds that about one-third of primary students and half of secondary students have not acquired basic learning in literacy and mathematics.

Most countries have also increased early childhood education and care (ECEC) (Staab 2010). Yet, enrolment of children aged 0–3 in centre-based day care remains low, ranging from 1.2 per cent in Guatemala to 26.1 and 35.1 per cent in Chile and Uruguay, respectively (Berlinski and Schady 2015). More progress has been made in preschool services where attendance rates have increased from 52 per cent in 2000 to some 69 per cent in 2012, to be compared with an average rate of 83 per cent among Organisation for Economic Co-operation and Development (OECD) countries (García da Rosa, Guadalupe, and Pozuelo 2015). However, in spite of recent efforts to increase day care and preschool attendance, spending on ECEC services and programmes made up less than 6 per cent of total social spending in 2012 (Berlinski and Schady 2015). Labour market policies have received less focus in Latin America. The International Labour Organization (ILO) (2013) encourages ongoing efforts of school to work transition, vocational training programmes, and second-chance educational programmes although it points out that these efforts are fragmented and coverage varies greatly across countries.

Social investments like CCTs, educational policies, and ECEC must be placed in a historical context in order to understand their particular role in a region where poverty reduction efforts have been found to form the very basis for social policy transformations during the last two decades (e.g. Barrientos, Gideon, and Molyneux 2008; Cecchini, Filgueira, and Robles 2014). Social investments gained foothold in the region at the end of the 1990s as countries struggled with adverse social situations brought on by decades of crises and structural adjustment (Birdsall and De la Torre 2001; Barrientos, Gideon, and Molyneux 2008): economic growth had in the 1980s and 1990s reached only half of that achieved between 1950 and 1970; over 40 per cent of Latin Americans were living in poverty; and the regional Gini index of inequality reached 0.52 in 1998 (Serra and Stiglitz 2008; Portes 2010). Public employment decreased significantly during the wave of privatizations in the 1990s and the informal sector generated 70 per cent of new jobs, leaving large segments of the population without social protection (Ocampo 2004; Barrientos 2009). As outlined by Jenson in Chapter 18, there has been a simultaneous redirection of social policy towards social investments in Europe and Latin America. Human capital investments were heavily promoted by international organizations and resonated with the widespread view in the region that Latin America's economic growth and development lag behind Asia's due to its human capital deficit (e.g. Birdsall, Ross, and Sabot 1995). However, Latin America's embrace of social investments does not stem from an articulate and coherent framework but is rather the result of ad-hoc responses to socioeconomic crises and an increased focus on breaking the intergenerational transmission of poverty through human capital accumulation among children and adolescents.

The poverty-centred focus of Latin America's social investment turn is evident in that programmes like CCTs were initially launched in direct response to crises, often forming part of structural adjustments. For instance, the evolution of Brazil's CCT programme from Bolsa Escola to Bolsa Família took place during a period of severe economic crises and structural adjustment reforms (IMF 2003). President Lula's government in effect highlighted the use of Bolsa Família to alleviate poverty in a 2003 letter of intent for standby credit to the International Monetary Fund (IMF 2003a). Mexico's Progresa programme was a direct response to the country's major macroeconomic crisis in 1994–5 (Levy 2006), and the World Bank funded its first CCT programme Familias en Acción in 2001 upon request from the Colombian government to alleviate poverty resulting from the worst economic crisis in the country's history and subsequent structural adjustments (World Bank 2001). Similarly, Uruguay launched Ingreso Ciudadano as an integral part of its Emergency Plan following the acute economic crisis in 2002 when the Uruguayan government received two stand-by credits from the International Monetary Fund (IMF) to weather the crisis (IMF 2002; Consejo Nacional de Coordinación de Políticas Sociales 2007).

Along with unprecedented economic growth, enhanced social assistance through programmes such as CCTs have led to a reduction in poverty rates from some 43.8 per cent in 1999 to some 28.1 per cent in 2013 (ECLAC 2015). However, social investments in Latin America face formidable challenges. Similar to the case of Italy presented in Chapter 26 in this volume, Latin American countries lack important structural and institutional pre-conditions. Much like Italy, public social spending in the region remains low while disproportionally favouring old age. Only some 13.8 per cent of public investments is earmarked to young people, in spite of the fact that the young make up over 26 per cent of the region's total population (ECLAC 2014). The lack of structural changes in spending undermines social investments in the face of pronounced infantilization of poverty where children are clearly overrepresented and where nearly 22 million young Latin Americans neither study nor work (ILO 2013). As in Italy, structural labour market problems persist where almost half of the working population have informal employment, in essence dividing social welfare along a dual structure of social insurance and social assistance (Cecchini and Martínez 2012; ILO 2013). Social investments have to date not altered dualized social policy systems but have rather included historically excluded groups in existing structures through selective targeting. Furthermore, a strong state is firmly rooted in the social investment imperative (Hemerijck 2013), and while most states assume increasingly larger roles in welfare and social policy systems, they remain characterized by institutional weaknesses, low taxation revenues, and limited administrative capacity (ECLAC 2010). Finally, social investments still lack a comprehensive framework and rather constitute a fragmented set of policies and programmes implemented in stand-alone fashion. As a result, investments in human capital are often lost due to lack of complementarities between policies that promote stock, buffer, and flow, and inadequate basic services. Existing gaps in social investments in Latin America are particularly well illustrated by the case of CCTs presented in Section 25.3.

25.3 Advances and Persistent Barriers: The Case of Conditional Cash Transfers

In earlier work, we have examined systematic reviews of existing impact evaluations and complement those with findings from recently completed field work in Uruguay and Guatemala in order to gauge the extent to which CCTs fulfil social investment objectives (Nelson and Sandberg 2016). The analysis finds that CCTs fulfil two objectives—poverty alleviation, which is related to the buffer function, and initial human capital investments, which are related to the stock. Evaluations clearly demonstrate that while beneficiaries do not exit poverty the programmes have significantly reduced poverty gaps in the short-term (e.g. Skoufias, Davis, and De la Vega 2001; Soares et al. 2007; Cecchini and Madariaga 2011). For instance, Fiszbein and Schady (2009) find short-term reduction in poverty gaps and moderate effects on poverty headcount in Brazil, Mexico, Ecuador, and Jamaica, while Amarante and colleagues (2009) find that Uruguay's programme has significantly reduced extreme poverty while only marginally impacting incidence rates.

Consumption effects demonstrate the degree to which cash transfers actually generate enhanced access to basic needs. In their study of evaluations conducted in seven countries, Kabeer, Piza, and Taylor (2012) consistently find strong evidence that beneficiaries increase consumption. These findings are corroborated by reviews presented by Independent Evaluation Group (IEG) (2011) and Adato and Hoddinott (2010) that also find beneficiary households to have increased consumption on health, education and food-related items. However, interviews with mothers in Montevideo, Uruguay, and the Lago Atitlán area in Guatemala reveal that cash transfers are too small to cover rising food prices and increasing out-of-pocket expenses for school supplies (Sandberg 2012; Sandberg and Tally 2015).

Beyond relieving poverty by providing income maintenance, CCTs are specifically designed to incentivize increased investments in human capital by making cash transfers conditional upon children attending school and health visits. This focus on human capital accumulation among children and adolescents is central to the programmes' objective to enhance skills among younger generations in order to break intergenerational transmission of poverty (Valencia Lomelí 2008; Fiszbein and Schady 2009; UNDP 2010). Several reviews of existing evaluations show that CCTs have had significant positive impact on school enrolment (Fiszbein and Schady 2009; Adato and Hoddinott 2010; Krishnaratne, White, and Carpenter 2013). However, De Brauw and colleagues (2015) find that while girls in the Bolsa Família programme increase their school participation, no such effect is found among boys. Evaluation studies also analyse CCTs' impact on health investments and reviews find mixed effects. Several studies find that the programmes increase health care visits (Adato and Hoddinott 2010; Gaarder, Glassman, and Todd 2010; IEG 2011; Ranganathan and Lagarde 2012; Glassman, Duran, and Koblinsky 2013). Yet, Fiszbein and Schady (2009) find no such effects, while others find merely weak effects on basic preventions and health outcomes (Gaarder, Glassman, and Todd 2010; Ranganathan and Lagarde 2012).

Beyond short- and medium-term effects on poverty alleviation and school enrolment, CCTs are expected to have long-term effects. First, CCTs are expected to simultaneously reduce chronic poverty transmitted across generations. However, this logic is founded on theoretical assumptions rather than on empirical evidence. In essence, CCTs' long-term effects are still largely unknown since most cohorts are still in school and have not yet entered the labour market. Most evaluations to date are therefore based on ex ante simulations and questionable assumptions pertaining to educational adequacy and future employment trajectories. Long-term effects of CCTs are generally assessed in terms of educational completion, skills acquired, health and nutrition status, and employment. There is in fact no conclusive evidence of CCTs having an impact on educational attainment, and while Fiszbein and Schady

(2009: 127) find some enhancement in cognitive development among the youngest children, no such effect has been found on learning among school-age children (e.g. Adato and Hoddinott 2010; IEG 2011; Krishnaratne, White, and Carpenter 2013). These poor outcomes could partly be explained by rather weak attachment to schools where, in spite of CCTs, over 50 per cent of adolescents in Latin America fail to complete secondary education (IDB 2013). Hence, while CCTs positively impact initial school attendance, the programmes' impact on human capital investments remains low since they fail to incentivize continued schooling.

CCTs are also expected to have long-term effects on health. Yet, studies on CCTs' long-term effects on investments in health find inconclusive evidence for both health and nutritional status, and outcomes are rather found to be dependent on various contextual factors (Ranganathan and Lagarde 2012; Glassman, Duran, and Koblinsky 2013). For example, De Brauw and colleagues (2015) find that the only health impact of Bolsa Família pertains to increases in body mass index (BMI) for age, while Adato and Hoddinott (2010) find that there are mixed nutritional effects among preschool children in Honduras, Brazil, Nicaragua, and Mexico. Similarly, the Inter-American Development Bank's (IDB's) (2011) impact evaluation of Mi Familia Progresa (MIFAPRO) in Guatemala finds positive effects on selected health indicators but insignificant impact on malnutrition.

Besides enabling consumption of basic goods, human capital investments in beneficiaries' education and health have been expected to lead to labour market insertion, thereby contributing to a break in intergenerational transmission of poverty. However, existing studies find weak links between CCTs and subsequent formal employment (Gonzáles de la Rocha 2008; Rodríguez-Oreggia and Freije 2012), while questioning whether there will indeed be enough jobs for employable beneficiaries once they graduate from CCT programmes (Adato and Hoddinnot 2010). The chief architect of Mexico's Progresa programme warns that without a significant growth in productive jobs, cash transfers will be needed indefinitely (Levy 2008).

Hence, in terms of social investment functions we conclude that CCTs are successful to some degree in buffering by alleviating short-term poverty though it remains questionable whether CCTs promote the buffer function enough to enable school completion and facilitate transfers into formal jobs. These policies' limited success in breaking the intergenerational transmission of poverty may be seen to result from CCTs' lack of emphasis on the stock function. Beneficiaries often do not complete their studies and as a case in point only 34 per cent of adolescents who actually remain in school acquire 'skills necessary for a productive life' (IDB 2013a). The need to improve the complementarities between buffer and stock functions can be seen when considering the incompatibilities between CCTs' twin objectives of relieving poverty and enabling skill investments (e.g. Handa and Davis 2006; Soares and Britto 2007; Teichman 2008). The vast majority of CCT programmes have established exit rules based on age rather than completion of educational cycles, overlooking the fact that children from vulnerable households in Latin America often have to repeat grades and are therefore inhibited from completing school at the stipulated age. Fieldwork in Uruguay indicates that age-based exit rules have adverse effects on secondary school retention; beneficiaries may drop out in anticipation of the age mark since they cannot afford secondary schooling without the cash transfers (Sandberg 2015). Furthermore, support of the stock and buffer functions may not reach full potential without support from policies enabling flow.

Yet blaming CCTs' limited realization of their long-term objectives on their insufficient stock function would be misplaced since these policies in themselves are not capable of enabling all forms of human capital investments. While incentivized demand for investments in education and health services may promote stock, further development in stock function is most likely dependent on supply-side factors (Fenwick 2014; Huber and Stephens 2015). For instance, students may not live near school and lack the money or access to transportation to travel to school. Schools may be underfunded, or lack sufficient infrastructure. They may be understaffed by underpaid teachers who provide inadequate levels of teaching and involve various social problems. Interviewed mothers in recently completed fieldwork in Uruguay reveal that they many times refrain from sending their children to school because of expensive bus fares, excessive violence at school, and an overall sense of low educational quality (Sandberg 2012). These findings are supported by recent household survey data from eight countries in the region showing that the main reason for school desertion among 13–15 year olds is 'lack of interest', followed by 'economic problems' (IDB 2013). Thus, the pronounced focus on incentivized behaviour on the demand-side disregards supply-side support necessary for optimal functioning of stock, flow, and buffer.

25.4 Advancing Social Investments in Latin America

Evident in our analysis in Section 25.3, CCTs make important social investment contributions. They are, however, inadequately supported by policies impacting before (e.g. ECEC and preschool), during (e.g. educational reforms to increase quality of teaching and learning), and after educational trajectories (e.g. labour market policies). This points to the vast importance of policy context in planning, designing, and implementing social investments. Programmes like CCTs have, to date, been implemented on the margins of existing welfare and social policy systems and the gaps discussed in Section 25.3 would no doubt require long-term structural and systematic changes in most countries (Cecchini, Filgueira, and Robles 2014). In theory, these gaps could be addressed in the short- and medium-term through a comprehensive SIA that ideally pursues three interrelated objectives. First, investments are needed to enhance quality of basic services to extract the greatest impact of social investments. Second, social investment policies like CCTs, ECEC, and educational policies should be closely integrated with health and education services to ensure complementarities between buffer and stock functions in order to maximize human capital accumulation. Third, complementarities between existing stock and buffer policies should be integrated with policies that perform the flow function to ensure that people in the region take on good jobs.

Such an approach would no doubt require significant increases in social spending, particularly to improve quality in public education and health systems. As a percentage of GDP, social spending on education reached on average only 5.0 per cent in 2013, while spending on social security and social assistance reached an average of 9.1 per cent. Health spending not only remains far below at some 4.2 per cent of GDP, but it has also increased the least (barely 1 per cent) during the last twenty years (ECLAC 2014). Moreover, several studies have raised concerns over social investments' potential crowding out of necessary investments in basic services (Hall 2008; Lavinas 2015). Such crowding out actually took place in Guatemala where the government continuously made line transfers from the Ministry of Education to fund the MIFAPRO programme and municipal councils in the country's rural areas were forced to withdraw funding for medicines in order to co-finance cash transfers to beneficiaries (Sandberg and Tally 2015).

Countries like Chile and Uruguay may have demonstrated a way forward in pursuing integrated systems approaches to social investments (Barrientos, Gideon, and Molyneux 2008). These countries pursue strategies that seek to organize and integrate services provided by health, education, and protection for families with children. It should, however, be noted that there are a myriad of policy contingencies as countries move from comprehensive plans to implementation of required cross-sectorial integration, not least coordination between different state institutions. For instance, Staab (2010) finds that while Chile's Crece Contigo certainly expands public ECEC, any levelling of opportunities is likely to be erased once children enter the country's segmented education system where quality is closely correlated with family income. Similarly, in the case of Uruguay, recently completed research finds that the country's CCT programme was in fact implemented without integration with educational policies and programmes, as outlined in the comprehensive Equity Plan. As pointed out by one of the members of the commission that designed the programme: 'we ended up with that which we did not want—a cash transfer pure and simple' (Sandberg 2015: 328).

In conclusion, social investments have certainly made an impact in Latin American social policy during the last two decades, not least through the region-wide adoption of CCTs. However, historic roles and fragmented applications of social investment programmes to alleviate poverty and socioeconomic exclusion have so far limited their impact. Going forward, future development of social investments in Latin America is likely to depend to a large extent on the political and administrative capacity of countries to both increase spending on and coordinate education, health, and labour policies. We argue that such coordination must be embedded in the view of social investment as a comprehensive policy approach, replacing current practices that only weakly couple the stock, flow, and buffer functions which are each fundamental to the SIA.

26

Why No Social Investment in Italy

Timing, Austerity, and Macro-Level Matthew Effects

Yuri Kazepov and Costanzo Ranci

26.1 Introduction

In this chapter the case of Italy is considered as *an extreme adverse case* for social investment policies. Not only is the country's social expenditure strongly targeted to compensatory policies with little room for a social investment strategy, but also the contextual conditions within which these policies might be implemented, are likely to produce ambiguous consequences: they are highly ineffective, and may even have unexpected negative impacts on both economic growth and equal opportunities.

Three recent social investment policies will be presented in order to show that their negative effects depend not only, nor necessarily, on the poor quantity and quality of such policies, but also, and basically, on the lack of specific structural and institutional pre-conditions: (a) childcare policies; (b) work–study programmes; and (c) apprenticeship. Our main general conclusion is that as these configurations are variable across Europe, the social investment strategy should be context-sensitive and tailored to the different structural and institutional configurations in order to be suitable and effective.

26.2 Social Investment in Italy: An Introduction to the Context

Social investment policies seem to have very little chance of being developed in Italy (Ascoli and Pavolini 2015). The structural composition of national social expenditure show that public financial expenses in family policy, education

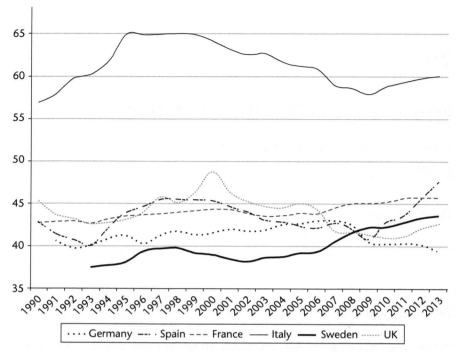

Figure 26.1. Trends in the share of expenditures for old age and survivors pensions over total social expenditures, main EU countries (1990–2013)

Source: on calculations on ESPROSS database (Eurostat, 2016), accessed 28 January 2016.

and active labour market policies are substantially lower and expenses in old age and survivors pensions are substantially higher than the Organisation for Economic Co-operation and Development (OECD) average (Nikolai 2012). According to Nikolai's analysis, Italy turns out to be a 'traditional compensatory welfare state' (Nikolai 2012: 110). Social protection expenditure, current, by function, gross and net (ESPROSS)-Eurostat data show that the gap in old age plus survivors expenditure between Italy and the other major European Union (EU) countries has become greater in the last two decades (Figure 26.1). At the same time, the trend in family and childcare expenditure has been so steady that since 2000 Italy has been overtaken even by Spain (Figure 26.2).

Besides childcare and family policies, the social investment approach (SIA) highlights the importance of education and training. These investments in human capital should be directly fostering competition and growth through ad hoc policies supporting the functional relation between education and the labour market, their coordination, and the 'synchronization' of demand and supply. The way in which this relation is established in Italy is highly

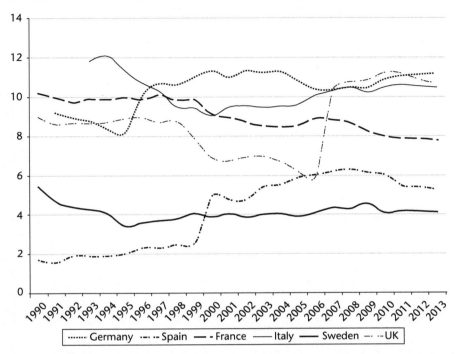

Figure 26.2. Trends in the share of family and childcare expenditures over total social expenditures, main EU countries (1990–2013)

Source: Own calculations on ESPROSS database (Eurostat 2016), accessed 28 January 2016.

problematic and—to some extent—also very ambiguous. Considering education, public expenditure is the lowest in OECD countries (thirty-second out of thirty-two countries; OECD 2013c: 4). Expenses are also quite unbalanced favouring primary schools rather than the tertiary level (annual expenditures for student are respectively 12 per cent higher than the OECD average and 30 per cent lower than the OECD average).

This situation is embedded in a labour market characterized by demand–supply mismatch that systematically pushes young people to the margins without institutional protection. Italy shares with Spain, Greece, and Croatia the highest unemployment rates for young people since the 1980s, which further increased after 2008. This picture is made even more dramatic by the fact that NEETs (not in education, employment, or training) present (2012) in Italy the highest figures (23.9 per cent) in Europe after Bulgaria (24.7 per cent) and Greece (27.4 per cent). This contextual picture is complemented by the fact that fixed-term contracts are almost the only option young people have to enter the labour market (Figure 26.3).

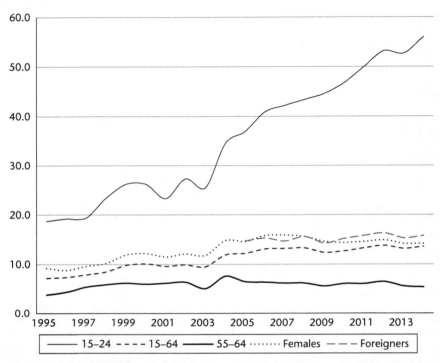

Figure 26.3. Temporary employees as percentage of the total number of employees, by sex and age (1995–2014)

Source: Own calculations on ESPROSS database/[lfsa_etpga] (Eurostat 2015), accessed 28 January 2016.

Labour policies were in the last few decades one of the most reformed policy fields in Italy (Sacchi and Vesan 2015). Many of these reforms attempted to embrace the SIA and covered issues like career guidance, training, apprenticeship (e.g. the so-called Pacchetto Treu in 1997), and work–study programmes (Law 53 in 2003). In 2014, a complex reform (Law 183)—evocatively named 'Jobs Act'— has determined a deep change in the labour market: lower constraints to dismissal for employers, a broader system of unemployment benefits, and a strengthening of active policy services in the event of unemployment have been introduced with the aim of increasing flexibility and fostering job creation.

These facts are the starting point of our chapter. Based on empirical research carried out in Italy about social investment policies developed in six major Italian cities (Ascoli, Ranci, and Sgritta 2015), we answer two specific questions:

1) What is the social and economic impact of social investment policies when they are implemented in a context like Italy, where there is little room to manoeuvre? Do these interventions achieve the positive results that are supposed to be obtained according to SIA?

2) Why are social investment policies so ineffective in Italy? Does this negative impact depend on the bad implementation of such policies or financial constraints due to the dominance of compensatory welfare programmes, or are there more structural and/or institutional mechanisms preventing these policies from being effective?

26.3 Social Investment Policies in Italy

26.3.1 *Childcare Policies*

Childcare services have a positive impact on employment even in Italy. Del Boca, Mencarini, and Pasqua (2012) found that attending a daily care service had positive impacts on educational attainments in high school and university, significantly increasing final scores. It has been estimated that an increase in the coverage rate of childcare services by 10 per cent at the national scale would produce a 13 per cent increase in the overall employment rate of mothers (Brilli, Del Boca, and Pronzato 2011).

Despite these results, the actual developments of childcare policies in the country substantially modify this positive outcome (Cerea 2015). Starting from a very late development of early childcare services in respect of other EU countries, in the past two decades Italy has witnessed a moderate growth as a result of minimal state financial supports and stronger investments by municipalities. In two decades the supply of childcare services doubled, up to a 12 per cent coverage rate at the national level in 2012 (Istat 2013). In spite of recent national austerity measures drastically cutting municipal budgets, childcare expenditures and coverage rates increased in the biggest cities in the country. In the period 2003–12 coverage rates increased by 11 per cent in Milan, by 15 per cent in Rome, and only by 3 per cent in Naples (Cerea et al. 2015). Financial investments in childcare increased by 27 per cent in Milan and Rome, and by 9 per cent in Naples. However, major territorial differences reflecting a historically deeply rooted north–south divide still exist: the coverage level for children aged 0–2 drops from 31 per cent in Milan to only 6 per cent in Naples.

Despite generally positive main trends, the growth in public supply did not necessarily mean that its impact on human capital developments and female employment was as positive as expected. The growth in supply of service was possible because it was privatized. While publicly managed childcare services have experienced a slight increase, publicly financed private services increased much more. In 2012 places provided by private services represented almost one quarter of the overall publicly funded supply at the national level (Ranci and Sabatinelli 2014), but the share in big cities is even higher. In Rome, private agencies manage 42 per cent of total childcare supply and in Milan they cover 39 per cent (Cerea et al. 2015).

The main reason for privatizing childcare services supply has been the chance to obtain a significant reduction in the costs of personnel. While educators in public services are hired on the basis of a national contract providing them with a good salary and security of employment, in private agencies more flexibility and lower costs are obtained through temporary contracts and outsourcing. In these agencies educators work more hours for lower salaries, with less continuity and lower career opportunities. In a word, growth in supply has been mainly obtained by worsening the working conditions in childcare services and consequently through a deterioration in the quality of services.

Furthermore, the impact of recent childcare policies on female employment has been much lower than expected. Recent research about the access to childcare services in 101 Italian big cities found out that already working mothers have clear priority over unemployed or temporarily employed ones (Gambardella, Pavolini, and Arlotti 2015; Pavolini and Arlotti 2015). Indeed, mothers' permanent employment gives children priority in the access to services in almost 100 per cent of municipalities, while unemployed (accepted in 78 per cent of municipalities), temporarily employed (accepted only in 36 per cent), and inactive (accepted in 30 per cent) mothers are significantly disadvantaged. Moreover, the level of income does not prioritize access. The overall impact is that poor households and low work-intensity households have no priority access to childcare services. Such a Matthew Effect (Abrassart and Bonoli 2014; Chapter 5, this volume) questions the capacity of childcare policies to activate a higher female participation in the labour market and reinforce the ambiguity of their impact.

To sum up, childcare services are still part of a 'secondary labour market' (Doeringer and Piore 1971), where wages and welfare benefits are much lower than in the primary market. As a consequence the increase in demand recently occurred was met only through a deterioration in the quality of services. Finally, if childcare services are surely instrumental in protecting female employment, they have not supported the activation of higher number of Italian mothers who do not participate in the labour market.

26.3.2 *Policies Fostering Work–Study Programmes*

Work–study programmes are relevant SI policies as they foresee—for pupils aged 15 years or older enrolled in upper secondary schools—several options, ranging from a period of time (approx. 120 hours/year) spent within firms for a short stage (70.9 per cent of cases) involving training on the job, up to more sophisticated experiments. In our research (Ascoli, Ranci, and Sgritta 2015) six regional case studies (Lombardy, Emilia Romagna, Marche, Latium, Campania, and Apulia) were carried out, which allowed a fine-tuning of the results of the official monitoring activity (Indire 2013a, 2013b).

In the school year 2012/13, 45.6 per cent of upper secondary schools (3,177 out of 6,972) used work–study programmes a method to strengthen the potential relationship with the labour market and to develop the required competences. A total of 11,600 projects have been implemented, out of which 87.1 per cent have been taken up by technical and vocational schools. A total of 227,886 students have been involved, accounting for 8.7 per cent of all upper secondary school students in Italy.

These quite impressive figures occur in a country like Italy characterized by great disparities among regions in terms of socioeconomic dynamism, institutional capacity, and effective networks of actors, which strongly influence the potential impact this measure has. The divide between those regions that adopted work–study programmes and those which did not is, for instance, very high. The range goes from Lombardy where more than 85 per cent of schools activated such a programme to Campania, where only less than 6 per cent of schools did (Indire 2013a: 39). This might be related to the different local/regional labour markets (with the highest rates of youth unemployment concentrated in the south of Italy), but also to the weaker networks schools have with external actors like employers' associations and firms and the different priorities the regional school offices might have. These relations are left to the goodwill of teachers and headmasters. Regional disparities became particularly evident after the autonomy of schools was approved in the 1990s and even enforced in 2000. Since then, the local dimension has become crucial, reinforcing—from the institutional point of view—existing socioeconomic territorial differences.

In this picture, public funding from the Ministry of Education covers almost three-quarters of the total invested resources while schools and regions cover 15–20 per cent. This is not enough to rebalance territorial inequalities. It is also surprising that only 1.1 per cent is funded by private bodies (enterprises) showing a limited commitment by employers. In other European systems their share is much higher and their co-management of the programme much more structured, favouring the demand–supply match. In the last few years resources have remained relatively stable with the consequence that—given the rising numbers of schools and pupils involved—the average number of hours rapidly declined from 224h/year in 2006/7 to 108h/year in 2011/12 (Indire 2013a).

The available data do not allow us to assess the impact of being involved in a school–work programme on the chances of entering the labour market. Proxies we calculated using different databases do not show relevant differences between those who participated and those who did not. Despite this disappointing result, we should not underplay the innovative potential of the measure, as it was one of the few attempts in Italy to implement a measure strongly coherent with the SIA.

26.3.3 *Apprenticeship: A Moving Target*

The apprenticeship system is potentially a highly coherent and important part of an SI strategy because it has a large training/educational component and it develops skills potentially important for a knowledge-based competitive economy.

In the mid-1990s the Italian apprenticeship system was a declining option because of the de-industrialization process. However, the need to adapt regulations to the new context, persisting high youth unemployment rates, and the difficulties of school-to-work transition initiated an intensive reform period. This framed apprenticeship schemes as the 'main entry into the labour market for young people' (art. 1.b. LN 92/2012) and included them as a key component in the Italian Youth Guarantee strategy.

The path towards a social investment-based apprenticeship system started in Italy in 1997 and has followed different steps. Age limits have been increased to 29, and also access after high-school graduation has been granted. Beyond traditional apprenticeship contracts (mainly targeted at young students who want to complete compulsory education by including a work-based experience in their curricula), an *advanced training and research apprenticeship contract* has been introduced addressing the needs of highly qualified people aged up to 29. As a consequence of such reforms, the number of apprentices started to rise again, increasing from 250,000 in 1997 to 650,000 in 2008, when the crisis also hit the apprenticeship system (Isfol-Inps 2013).

In spite of these interesting developments, research on the implementation of this new system (see Corradini and Orientale Caputo 2015; Villani 2015) has disclosed a basic contradiction which the recent crisis has made prominent: the lack of coordination between training/education and the labour market. Reforms only marginally considered the Italian socioeconomic structure or the deficiencies of the education system. Regions were expected to regulate, plan, and monitor the implementation of reforms and to support enterprises providing off-company training and education. A major role was also given to social partners, which had to define both professional profiles and training content. The result of these complex interactions was 200 different contracts within 20 different regional regulatory frameworks and about 800 professional profiles (Di Monaco and Pilutti 2012). Reforms reinforced the existing fragmented landscape of actors organized at different territorial levels with diverging agendas and often lacking the institutional capacity to adequately coordinate and implement multilevel governance arrangements, in particular in southern regions.

Take-up rates and the quality of apprenticeship have consequently remained at a very low level. In 2011, more than 80 per cent of all apprentices did not participate in training activities (Villani 2015: 18). Moreover contracts are relatively unstable: despite a foreseen duration of more than two years, more than 85 per cent of the contracts are interrupted before their foreseen end and nearly 50 per cent are interrupted within three months. These are often in seasonal jobs (hotels, restaurants) (Villani 2015). Although the figures have slightly improved in the past few years, the high interruption rates support the argument that apprenticeship contracts are systematically misused. Their training mission is subordinated to short-term labour costs saving strategies undermining the potential of the social investment strategy.

In order to prevent misuse as a form of cheap labour (OECD 2013c), the most recent reforms (LN 92/2012) have set limits on the access of employers to the system (apprenticeship is allowed only for firms that have hired 50 per cent of previous apprentices). However, the same reforms have relaxed the duration of apprenticeship contracts (six to thirty-six months) and training requirements (a training plan for apprentices is no longer mandatory; off-the-job training is reduced to 120 hours within three years; etc.) undermining its use as a measure for the transition from education to work. However, in spite of such incentives and 100 per cent tax relief given for every apprentice hired, the system has not off-set the substitution effect with other flexible labour contracts: apprenticeship contracts accounted for less than 3 per cent of new contracts compared to 68 per cent of fixed-term contracts in 2011 (Isfol-Inps 2012: 62).

These facts make the impact of apprenticeship reforms rather feeble and do not provide the most favourable ground for the development of SI strategies.

26.4 Social Investment in Italy: A Mission Impossible?

Understanding how social investment works in different contexts is crucial to grasping its impact. The functional link between human capital development, labour productivity, and demand for highly skilled professional services (Andersson 2007; Nelson and Stephens 2012; Wren 2013b) is often underplayed. In fact, despite a progressive global economic integration, there are still specific institutional and structural contextual conditions making this functional link peculiarly different across countries. These contextual conditions do not only set the frame for social investment development, but also alter what are supposed to be the socioeconomic and institutional 'virtuous' mechanisms on which the social investment strategy is based. To use Hemerijck's vocabulary (Chapter 1, this volume): not only are *buffers* promoting different types of social inclusion from country to country, but also *stocks* and *flows* are differently shaped across Europe. If it is expected that social investment is (or should be) a 'universal' or at least European-wide strategy, this differentiation should not only be acknowledged, but should also be part of the analytical architecture of the social investment approach, in particular when it comes to developing context-sensitive social investment strategies.

The Italian case shows the relevance of contextual factors (Kazepov 2008) in preventing social investment strategy from obtaining positive results. Data on welfare expenditures have already shown the overall weak capacity of welfare policies in promoting social investment in the country. Our analysis was focused on two 'virtuous mechanisms' that, according to Hemerijck, are supposed to work together to make a social investment strategy feasible and likely to produce a positive impact (Hemerijck 2013, 2015).

First, we investigated whether early education policies aimed at increasing de-familization of care and at supporting female employment were able to ease the *flow* of women towards the labour market. Indeed, in Italy persistent gender disparities in both the labour market and household organization have slowed down the growth of female employment in the last decades, making care/work reconciliation very difficult to achieve. The gender gap in the employment rates of persons aged 25–49 is in Italy almost double that in the other major European countries (Eurostat 2015): 0.28 in 2013, compared to 0.11 in Germany or 0.05 in Sweden.

In the last decade, increased social investments by the state and local administrations have produced a relevant progress in childcare expenditures and coverage rates, but have not effectively promoted higher female employment. In the time span 2000–13, improvements in the gender gap in the employment rate have been proportionally less than the equivalent trend in other European countries: the gap has been reduced by 32 per cent in Italy, while it has fallen by 64 per cent in Spain, 44 per cent in Germany, and 46 per cent in France (Eurostat 2015). Furthermore, improvement in tertiary education has been unable to reduce this gap: not only is the employment rate of women with tertiary educations lower than in any major European country (73.8 per cent in Italy vs 82.7 per cent as EU-25 average), but it has also been decreasing in the past decade (−4.8 per cent) more than the EU-25 average (−1.5 per cent) (Eurostat 2015).

The poor performance of childcare policy is due not only to limited financing, institutional inertia, and huge regional differentiation, but also to difficulties of this policy in overcoming quantity/quality trade-offs and in prioritizing the care/work reconciliation of women who are in a weaker position in the labour market. A Matthew Effect, depressing the activation utility of childcare policy, is therefore likely to be generated.

Second, we considered two policies based on investments in the human capital *stock* that are supposed to be able to increase employment and labour productivity: work–study programmes and apprenticeship policy. Both these policies are crucial for Italy as they potentially extend the supply of high-skilled labour offering more chances for the young to be integrated into the labour market. Indeed, Italy is characterized by a paradox: on the one hand, it is one of the European countries with the lowest tertiary attainment rate for 30–34-year-olds (20 per cent), quite distant from the Europe 2020 Strategy target (fixed at 40 per cent); on the other, the level of over-education of tertiary-educated workers aged 25–34 is very high: 19 per cent (Maestripieri and Ranci 2015). This situation has especially discouraged young people not only from entering the labour market but also from enrolling for education and training.

In this context, a social investment strategy would require a large-scale change in both public spending (improving the quality of educational programmes and widening access to tertiary education) and the occupational structure (supporting the growth of high productivity sectors). Unfortunately, both policy initiatives that we analysed demonstrated that they are unable to perform these tasks. Work–study programmes basically reproduced the huge territorial unbalance characterizing the labour market, concentrating most of the activity in the work-richest areas. Furthermore, there was no evidence that this policy was able to enhance the school–work transition of beneficiaries. On the other hand, apprenticeship policy was strongly limited by institutional fragmentation, and by a general misuse by private enterprises, which considered it mainly as a short-term labour cost-saving strategy rather than an opportunity for human capital investment. *Stocks* were therefore neither accumulated nor used for increasing productivity through this policy tool.

To sum up, social investment is generally considered as a supply-side political strategy aimed at meeting the demand for a high-skilled labour force arising from the most competitive, efficient, and internationalized economic sectors in a country. Our analysis, however, has identified that these policies are likely to fail in Italy, due to the lack of the contextual preconditions that must be in place in order to make this strategy feasible and effective.

We considered three aspects of such problem. First, while social investment strategy requires a functional interdependence between the education system and labour demand and a shared orientation towards high-skilled employment, in Italy structural disconnection between these two systems exposes human capital investments to the risk of over-education and poor economic returns, making policies aimed at supporting the production of *stocks* poorly convenient and not attractive. Second, policies aimed at creating more *flows* would require a relatively high level of gender parity within households and in the labour market to reduce the chance of Matthew Effects. However, in Italy the lack of pressures on the part of households and enterprises to increase female employment has contributed to preventing childcare policies from adopting activation goals. Finally, policies providing *bridges* to permanently include more people into the labour market, such as apprenticeship policy, are limited due to the dominance of enterprises reluctant to invest in human capital and leaning more on labour cost-saving strategies.

Should we conclude that social investment strategy does not work in Italy? This is not our main conclusion. Our diagnosis is that social investment policies are clearly ineffective in Italy because of the lack of policies complementing supply-side intervention with a more structural transformation of the Italian labour market. In such unchanged context, social investment strategies are likely to be ineffective, instrumentally used to perpetuate the existing situation, or even a Trojan horse to reduce welfare programmes. At the same time, the social investment approach is a challenge for countries, like Italy, that seem to be leaning towards a 'low road' to global competitiveness, based on labour-cost saving, low productivity, low remuneration of highly qualified labour force, and high flexibility without equivalent social protection. An ultimate failure of social investment policies would imply a general decline in the Italian economic system.

Part 6
EU Social Investment Advocacy

27

Social Investment for a Cohesive and Competitive European Union

Evelyn Astor, Lieve Fransen, and Marc Vothknecht

27.1 Introduction

Europe, like most other regions in the world, is faced with societal transformations such as ageing, potential future labour market shortages, changing family structures, evolving roles of women, scarcity of public resources, and the transformation towards an increasingly knowledge-based and globalized economy. These challenges have far-reaching implications for the sustainability and adequacy of European Union (EU) welfare states. At the same time, the protracted economic and financial crisis has increased social challenges as well as created further fiscal constraints. Fiscal constraints, however, should not be an obstacle for reforming towards social investment given the evidence that the countries that moved timely in the direction of social investment have weathered the crisis better.

The Social Investment Package (SIP) was a major step in the direction of guiding EU member states to reform their social protection systems to adapt to the challenges of the twenty-first century. The SIP put forward a policy framework that stresses the importance of investing in human capital from an early age, of ensuring equality in women's participation in the labour market and longer working lives, and of providing integrated social services and benefits enabling people to better cope with risks and key transitions across the life course. To achieve this, the SIP called for a more effective and efficient use of budgets for social policies, making use of social policy innovation for evidence-based reforms, and strengthening partnerships with all actors involved in the design and delivery of social policies, including the third and private sectors.

The aim of this chapter is fourfold: (i) summarize social policy development in the EU; (ii) reflect on the role of the EU in helping member states to reform and modernize their social protection systems; (iii) take stock of the recent progress in EU and Member States in this direction; and (iv) identify priorities and challenges to be addressed in the future.

27.2 The Development of Social Policies in the European Union

Social objectives have been a cornerstone of the European project starting with the Treaty of Rome, where the founders affirmed 'the constant improvements of the living and working conditions' as the essential objective of their efforts. Successive treaty changes have built on this early commitment and set out the Union's role to coordinate and guide member states towards achieving social cohesion and upward social convergence. Further, a social *acquis communautaire* has been developed in policy areas such as health and safety or gender equality.

By defining social protection as a productive factor important for the European economy, the Lisbon Strategy (2000–10) moved social and employment policies closer to the core of the EU agenda. In terms of governance, the Strategy led to the creation of Treaty-based committees in the employment and social fields and to the social open method of coordination (OMC) in which member states and the Commission worked together towards achieving common social objectives. The OMC focused on policy learning and knowledge transfer through benchmarking and peer review. However, at the end of the decade it became clear that limiting Lisbon's priorities had not improved the overall results of the strategy, as the levels of poverty, inequality, and social exclusion continued to remain high.

The Europe 2020 Strategy adopted in 2010 aimed at better responding to these challenges by providing an integrated framework for smart, sustainable and inclusive growth, underpinned by five mutually dependent and reinforcing targets and seven flagship initiatives. The Strategy recognized the need to move towards a better integration of economic, employment, and social objectives in the EU. In the social policy area, the Strategy set out quantified objectives to reduce poverty and social exclusion, boost employment, improve tertiary educational attainment, and reduce early school leaving.

As a response to the imbalances created by the financial crisis, and in parallel to the medium-term and integrated Europe 2020 Strategy, the European Semester process was created in 2010 in order to achieve 'a more integrated surveillance of economic policies'. Each spring, the Commission adopts country-specific recommendations (CSRs) after analysing the reform efforts and commitments made by each member state, which are then reviewed and endorsed by the Council. The legal base for adoption of CSRs (articles 121 and 148 of the Treaty on the Functioning of the European Union) is thereby linked specifically to employment and macroeconomic objectives, and not to the wider social objectives set out in the treaties. That being said, the European Semester has also been viewed as the main governance vehicle to support the achievement of the wider objectives of the Europe 2020 Strategy (European Commission 2014e), including the targets to reduce poverty and improve educational outcomes.

27.3 EU Policy Guidance towards Social Investment

The Europe 2020 Strategy set out an integrated agenda, but the development of comprehensive EU policy guidance on how to reform member states' social welfare systems and adapt them to the realities of the twenty-first century has followed later, notably through the White Paper on Pensions and the SIP.

The development of the Union's approach to social policies has largely been driven by the increasing recognition and understanding of the deeply integrated nature of social, labour market, and economic developments in its member states. Not least the financial and economic crisis proved the interdependence of EU economies as well as the great divergence in the capacity of national social protection systems to invest in and protect people when needed and respond to adverse economic shocks. With increasingly integrated economies and labour markets in the EU, the coordination of national policies cannot be limited to the macroeconomic and fiscal sphere, but needs to consider their interaction with and impact on social policies.

In the SIP, the European Commission stressed the important contribution of well-designed welfare systems to better functioning labour markets and competitive economies. Importantly, public (and private) spending on adequate social protection, human capital formation and maintenance, and social services is not considered mainly a cost weighing on public budgets and employers' business prospects. Rather, insufficient or ineffective social policies can manifest in lower educational outcomes, overall lower skill development, and a lower-quality and less-productive workforce. In consequence, this could have large negative economic and social spill-over effects in other member states and contribute to economic disequilibria in the EU.

However, the crisis and fiscal consolidation measures have, in some cases, come into conflict with social investment reform efforts. The European Social Policy Network (ESPN) has highlighted that fiscal consolidation has, in some member states, led to budgetary cuts for existing policies that aimed at strengthening human and social capital (Bouget et al. 2015). It has also led to the postponement or cancelling of new social investment policies, and the prioritization of passive short-term measures to protect people over more preventative, activating, and enabling measures. These trends are worrying also from an economic standpoint, as effective social policies are crucial in creating the supply-side conditions necessary for smart, sustainable, and inclusive economic growth, and to deliver on the promise of upward social convergence in the EU.

In view of increasing life expectancy, more people working more and longer will be key to ensure both the adequacy and sustainability of our social protection systems and to help foster economic growth. It is more crucial than ever to address the underrepresentation of women, young people, older workers, and people with low educational backgrounds or skill levels in the labour market.

A social investment approach (SIA) should thereby provide individualized support that facilitates participation in the labour market and society throughout life, combined with adequate income support when needed. This calls for a strong(er) preventive dimension and early interventions at different stages of life. One key example is early childhood education and care services, which have been shown to be important in improving the educational outcomes of children (in particular for those from disadvantaged backgrounds), improving their future employability, preventing poverty, and facilitating social participation later on in life (European Commission 2013a). At the same time as supporting children's development, these services, as well as long-term care services, are important in supporting parents and carers, especially women, to fully participate in the labour market.

Further, tailoring activating and enabling services to the needs of the individual increases the effectiveness of these services in helping people develop their skills and improve their potential to enter the labour market or increase their earnings potential. Moreover, ensuring that every young person receives a good quality offer of employment, continued education, or training (Council Recommendation 2013) can help avoid the detrimental 'scarring effects' of long-term unemployment or inactivity on young people's outcomes later on in life. The Youth Employment Initiative is providing financial support for the implementation of 'youth guarantee' measures, and constitutes a promising example of a SIA for a specific population.

Activating and enabling policies are most effective when joined up with adequate income support, which provides a buffer against the risk of poverty and social exclusion (Immervoll and Scarpetta 2012). However, progress in the member states towards comprehensive active labour-market policies (ALMPs) and the integrated provision of employment and social services has been slow and uneven (Bouget et al. 2015).

Reducing tax-benefit disincentives to work, reducing early exits to retirement, creating adapted and age-friendly working environments, and improving access to lifelong learning are important to ensure older workers' access to the labour market, help people to develop their skills and keep them updated, and make a contribution to the social and economic life (European Commission 2012b). Policymakers and social partners have increasingly recognized the need for better developed late career labour markets, and employment rates of older workers have risen significantly in a number of member states over the past decade. However, further dedicated policy efforts by member states are necessary to deliver on longer working lives in the future (European Commission and SPC 2015a).

Prevention, rehabilitation, and independent living arrangements can, likewise, help older people remain independent as long as possible and reduce/delay their need to call on long-term care. Improved access to long-term care services will thereby also help reduce involuntary labour market exits of (mostly female) older workers who take care of their relatives. Today, the way in which long-term care is treated in the social protection systems of member states varies greatly, notably in the relative weight assigned to formal and informal care. Whereas informal care provided by relatives plays a significant role in all member states, there are enormous variations in the degree to which affordable formal services have been developed and made available (European Commission and SPC 2014b).

Overall, social protection systems in the EU member states are characterized by a considerable heterogeneity in terms of their size, structure, and financing arrangements. As efficient and effective social protection systems require that different social policies are complementary to each other, the general architecture of the social protection system and the inter- and intra-generational allocation of resources need to be taken into account when designing social policy reforms. This includes the rebalancing between budgets where needed, and the identification of complementarities between policies to maximize their pay-off (e.g. income support and ALMPs) (European Commission and SPC 2015b). The institutional linkages between different social (and employment) policy areas thereby tend to be better developed in countries with a strong social investment orientation. However, social policies' reforms still tend to apply a piecemeal approach to specific policy fields without paying sufficient attention to the interplay with other policy areas (Bouget et al. 2015).

The efficiency and effectiveness of social benefits and services also depends on how they are implemented on the ground. Social policy innovations can help social policies or programmes do even more with equal or less resources, and address societal challenges in a more effective manner. They can also help to strengthen the evidence base for policy reforms through, for example, testing new approaches before scaling them up. Further, administrative simplification and the setting up of single entry points can help improve accessibility and hence the take-up of benefits and services.

Finally, efficient and effective implementation of social investment requires strengthened partnerships with the key actors involved in the designing and delivering of social policies and programmes (e.g. public authorities, third sector, social enterprises, and private sector). It is important to maximize the complementarity of efforts and ensure that we are all rowing in the same direction. Improving partnerships with the third sector, social enterprises, and the private sector can also help identify gaps and overlaps in policy interventions and foster innovation. Creating a favourable environment for these organizations to operate can therefore catalyse better social outcomes.

27.4 Supporting Member States Implement Social Investment

To support member states implement policy reforms towards a SIA, the Commission has reoriented its key instruments for supporting social policy. These include its governance instruments; financial support for policy reform, research, and innovation; capacity building support for third- and private sector organizations that are active in advancing social investment; and development of analytical tools/assessment frameworks to support evidence-based policy reform.

The Commission has increasingly called for policy reforms in line with a SIA in the framework of the European Semester. The policy priorities identified in the revised Employment Guidelines start reflecting a SIA and call for modernizing social protection systems to provide effective, efficient, and adequate protection throughout all stages of an individual's life. By focusing on specific policies, however, the need for integrated social services (e.g. through beneficiary-friendly single entry points) is given too little attention. Likewise, the SIA has been increasingly reflected in the country-specific analysis and guidance given through CSRs and accompanying analytical country reports, as evident from the increase of social investment-linked CSRs between 2011 and 2015. However, despite these positive steps, the Annual Growth Survey and CSRs still fall short of calling for systems-level reforms in the direction of social investment.

EU-funding instruments have also been reoriented to better support the implementation of social investment policies in the European Semester. The European Structural and Investment Funds, especially the European Social Fund (ESF), can be strongly supportive of the policy priorities of the SIP. The introduction of ex ante conditionality in the new financial period (2014–20) is expected to help target ESF funding to the key social and employment policy challenges highlighted in the European Semester. Whereas the ESF was largely focused on employment-related issues in the last financial period, at least 20 per cent of ESF funds are now earmarked towards supporting reform in the social policy field. However, the focus still remains on employment-related reforms and less on integrated social services. To further support reform implementation, 'investments' co-financed by structural funds can be exempted from deficit calculations as of January 2015, although the use of this clause is still to be seen.

The EU has also reinforced its partnerships with third-and private sector organizations. Notably, the Commission has established a four-year framework partnership to financially support EU-level social non-governmental organization (NGO) networks, which can support a SIA at national and local level and explain the available EU-level support tools to their members. EU-level framework partnership agreements also exist for EU networks active in the promotion of microfinance and social enterprise finance.

The Commission has made a leap forward in close cooperation with member states by developing tools to strengthen the analytical capacity to assess social investment policies. One important development in this regard is the tool for the multidimensional assessment of the efficiency and effectiveness of social policies (European Commission and SPC 2015b), which applies a macro-level perspective on the set-up of social protection systems in the member states and focuses on the complementarity of the social policy mix in place.

Further, the Commission has taken initiatives to support the analytical and methodological basis for the development of adequate minimum income provisions, which are a crucial element of comprehensive social protection systems. With the European Reference Budgets Network, the Commission has worked to develop high-quality comparable reference budgets to help member states improve the adequacy of income support measures. A shared framework and methodology, which is discussed by the Social Protection Committee (SPC), will facilitate to monitor whether minimum floors are sufficient to provide adequate buffers against risks when and if they arise.

27.5 Moving Forward

Taking stock, the EU has taken substantial efforts to support member states' policy reforms towards a SIA, and many member states have been reorienting their social policies in this direction. However, large differences still exist between member states' policy approaches and not all member states appear to be reforming their social policies in an integrated fashion. Moreover, the crisis and fiscal constraints appear to have in some cases complicated reform efforts.

In what follows, some key challenges in the implementation of social investment reforms are discussed. First, in line with the findings of the ESPN report on social investment, there is a need to further develop evidence on institutional complementarities for positive social outcomes. Some analysis already exists on the links between certain social policy measures: for instance, on the role of ALMPs and social assistance, or on well-designed parental leave schemes and accessible early childhood education and care. However, a stronger focus on the vertical integration across different levels of benefit and service provision is required.

Designing and delivering complementary policies depends in particular on the effective cooperation between the national, regional and local levels. In many member states, regional and local authorities have substantial autonomy in the formulation and implementation of social policies, especially in the case of services. Those responsibilities at different levels of government complicate efforts to ensure that benefits and services complement each other. Evidence on successful experiences in the close coordination of social policies both across policy areas and between different levels of government can serve as inspiration for policymakers.

More work also needs to be done on the complementarities between social policies on the one hand and employment, and economic and fiscal policies on the other. President Juncker has put policies that create growth and jobs at the centre of the policy agenda of the Commission, which does not only call for public and private investment to strengthen aggregate demand, but will crucially hinge on supply-side measures to mobilize the productive potential of citizens as well. A more integrated and balanced design of macro-level policies will therefore also require an increased recognition and understanding of the role that social policies play for employment, and economic and fiscal outcomes, and vice versa.

These inter-linkages should also be better reflected in the European Semester process. As highlighted in the Commission's Communication on the Mid-Term Review of the Europe 2020 Strategy, the Semester has, to a large degree, been focused on the macroeconomic stabilization needs and on crisis management and less on the longer-term integrated targets of the 2020 Strategy (European Commission 2014e). While social investment policies have been given more attention in the Semester process more recently, there is still a need to better reconcile the short-term and the longer-term policy priorities. Moreover, the enhanced competences in macroeconomic and fiscal governance following the adoption of the Stability and Growth Pact (SGP) (i.e. the Six Pack, Two Pack, and Fiscal Compact) have led to enforceability (through the potential of financial sanctions) of only those recommendations that address 'macroeconomic imbalances'. Despite the growing evidence that underperforming social policies (Eurofound 2012; Vandenbroucke, Diris, and Verbist 2013) can have macroeconomic spill-over effects, Macroeconomic Imbalance Procedure (MIP) recommendations in the area of social policy tend only to focus on projected spending increases of large expenditure items such as pensions, health, and long-term care. The lack of enforceability of the CSRs in the social field as opposed to MIP recommendations has also led to weaker incentives for member states to implement the EU social policy recommendations. As a result, member states' implementation of social policy reforms along the CSRs has been highly uneven, as demonstrated in the 2015 Country Reports.

EU-level social monitoring instruments have also yet to be adapted to reflect a broader assessment approach. Currently, the social indicators in the Joint-Assessment Framework (JAF), the Social Protection Performance Monitor (SPPM), and the Social and Employment Scoreboard look primarily at final outcomes and the protection aspect of social policies. This is troubling, as the focus of the SPC thematic surveillance and the Commission's social priorities in the European Semester are much influenced by recent trends in these indicators, which should therefore provide a comprehensive picture of all aspects of social policies.

Contingent on the further development of simulation and forecasting capacities in the employment and social field, microsimulation tools in particular could provide the basis for a more systematic assessment of intended reforms and their employment and distributional impacts. A better ability to model employment and social outcomes could also help align the short-term policy priorities identified in the European Semester with achieving the longer-term objectives of the Europe 2020 Strategy. More systematic evidence on the cumulative economic and social returns of social policies should also help assess the positive cross-border effects that social investment can have, as well as the negative 'spill-over' effects due to lack of investment, especially in view of the single market and the increasing mobility of European workers. Measuring the extent of these cross-border consequences of underinvestment in human capital would be helpful in better targeting EU policies and identifying the potential need for further EU-level action in the social field.

Another important question to consider is the benchmark that is chosen to assess member states' progress and set ambition levels for reform. Within the European Semester process, the EU average is often the common standard against which social outcomes are assessed. The EU average, however, does not necessarily represent a good performance, nor is it a suitable reference for member states with more advanced social protection systems. In order to avoid the risk of downward harmonization and to support upward social convergence instead, more ambitious targets could be defined based on country-specific potentials.

28

Can European Socioeconomic Governance Be Social Investment Proof?

Sonja Bekker

In recent years European Union (EU) socioeconomic governance has changed considerably. The creation of the European Semester has furthered integrated socioeconomic policy coordination, and stricter economic governance has aimed to improve compliance with debt and deficit rules. What room does the new governance architecture give to social investment? On the one hand long-term goals and Treaty norms support stock, buffer, and flow functions of social investment. On the other hand, the focus on public finances in the Stability and Growth Pact (SGP) limits options for investing in societies. This chapter shows that the flexibility within EU socioeconomic governance does not restrict social investment necessarily. It is the member state, however, that has an important role in promoting and developing social investment. Good national practices may then feed into the coordination process and challenge ideas on how to improve the EU's social and economic state.

28.1 New Socioeconomic Governance and the Options for Social Investment

Current EU socioeconomic governance takes place within the framework of the European Semester. It includes the Europe 2020 Strategy and the Macro-economic Imbalances Procedure (MIP) which both offer some scope for social investment. Europe 2020 formulates a range of social goals, such as the decrease of early school-leaving or the Flagship initiatives 'Agenda for new skills and jobs', which essentially mind stock and flow functions of social investment (see also Kvist 2013). It hosts most EU implementation activities in order to facilitate national progress. Europe 2020 monitors social investment policies and their outcomes, provides financial assistance via the European Social Fund, and streamlines governance and reporting (European Commission 2015). The MIP predominantly considers macroeconomic issues. However, recently it has been expanded to include social indicators (albeit auxiliary indicators), including reducing long-term unemployment and at-risk-poverty rates. Besides Europe 2020 and the MIP, the SGP is also part of the European Semester. This coordination mechanism may be seen as the most restrictive for social investment due to its emphasis on meeting debt and deficit targets. The implementation of the Six-Pack and the Fiscal compact has strengthened the SGP, and also the MIP may result in financial penalties for Eurozone countries (Bekker and Klosse 2013). The Europe 2020 Strategy has remained a soft coordination cycle. Thus, in case of conflicting messages stemming from either one of these coordination mechanisms, the message to reduce public expenditure has been communicated to member states with much more force than the message to reach social goals. Within this wider coordination setting, a general EU-level narrative to develop social investment seems frail (Ferrera 2016).

Nevertheless, the question whether European socioeconomic governance can be social investment proof is not a straightforward one to answer. The complexity inherent in the new governance system makes it difficult to pass a quick judgement that applies for all member states. As the governance process tailors evaluations to specific national challenges, the EU's policy recommendations vary considerably from country to country (Bekker 2015). The dissimilar room for social investment per member state is furthered by the different sets of rules applying to certain groups of countries. First, important distinctions are to be made between bail-out and non-bail-out countries. The financial assistance packages for bail-out countries were given on the condition of drastic cuts in social expenditure and major structural reforms, leaving little to no room for social investment (Clauwaert and Schömann 2012; Costamagna 2012; Doherty 2014; Kilpatrick and de Witte 2014). The conditional loans of these countries are not based on the SGP rules, however, and thus fall outside ordinary EU socioeconomic surveillance (Begg 2013). Secondly, rules differ for Eurozone and non-Eurozone countries, as only Eurozone countries may get a financial sanction when perpetually failing to meet the SGP or MIP rules. In theory, countries in good economic and fiscal state are in preventative surveillance, leaving them more room for social investment than countries in a corrective arm of coordination. Thirdly, the set-up of the socioeconomic governance process ensures that the process is open to changes in targets following revised economic or social circumstances. This makes the process and its targets not per se statically oriented to social investment or not. On the contrary, the options for social investment may differ from country to country and from year to year. It is therefore relevant to distinguish the quick crisis fixes from the long-term goals (Barnard 2014).

The Treaty is one of the sources to sketch the resilience of social goals, even though its norms could have been used much more strongly to advocate the role and function of social policies (Barnard 2014). The fundamental social goals in the Treaty largely match the stock, flow, and buffer functions of social investment. For example, Art. 3 of the Treaty on European Union sets the Union's goal at promoting the well-being of its peoples and at working towards a highly competitive social market economy, full employment, and social progress. In addition, the Union's goal is to combat social exclusion and discrimination, promote social justice and protection, guarantee equality between women and men, and further solidarity between generations, as well as protect the rights of the child. Similar norms may be found in the Treaty's Social Policy chapter, for instance Art. 151 Treaty on the Functioning of the European Union (TFEU) which refers to the European Social Charter and the Community Charter of the Fundamental Social Rights of Workers. Similarly, the horizontal clause, Art. 9 TFEU, arranges that the Union shall take into account a number of requirements in defining and implementing its policies and activities, among which 'flow' functions such as the promotion of a high level of employment, 'buffer' aspects of the guarantee of adequate social protection, and 'stock' components of the fight against social exclusion, and a high level of education, training, and protection of human health.

The austerity measures and structural reforms in the member states as well as the EU-level rhetoric of stricter economic governance seem to contrast with the Treaty goals. The question is whether social investment-contrasting developments have been the result of stricter regulations or whether perhaps other factors have played a role as well (see also the discussion in Zeitlin and Vanhercke 2014). From the perspective of regulations, the degree of causality between EU targets and national reforms could be questioned, at least for member states in good economic weather. Flexibility in judging the performance of countries has remained part of the process, including choices in cutting down on public investment (Micossi and Peirce 2014). Such flexibility includes national-level decisions on how to achieve the SGP targets (Lierse 2011; Begg 2013). Current regulations allow for lenient budgetary evaluations if a temporarily worsened fiscal position results from exceptional events outside member state control, for example, natural disasters or a severe economic downturn. Postponement of deadlines for deficit reduction is granted when weak economic performance hampers achievements, despite a member state's serious consolidation efforts (Micossi and Peirce 2014). Such postponement of deadlines was granted more than once in recent years, for instance, in the cases of the Netherlands, Poland, France, and Spain. In addition, Begg (2013) argues that whereas the SGP has been focused on austerity measures, new regulations, for instance, introducing the Fiscal compact, also refer to the EU's objectives of growth, employment, and cohesion. Although growth, employment, and cohesion might be a narrow interpretation of social investment, the collection of arguments mentioned makes it interesting to establish to what degree the EU has been advocating for growth, employment, and cohesion within the SGP cycle. Section 28.2 explores to what extent a growth and jobs perspective is present in the country-specific recommendations (CSRs) that stem from the most social investment-constraining coordination cycle: the SGP.

28.2 Country-Specific Recommendations Stemming from SGP Coordination

The following analysis encompasses all the CSRs that have resulted from SGP surveillance between 2011 and 2015. It explores to what extent these SGP-related CSRs offer space for social investment, even if in a narrow and indirect way. It moreover gives examples of the richer background information on which these CSRs are based, in order to show that the narrow message in the CSR in fact hides a richer evaluation that allows much more room for social investment. Overall, one may conclude that the 2011–15 SGP coordination addresses social policies, albeit often related to improving the sustainability and/or the efficiency of pension and the health care systems (Bekker 2015). A clear argument to develop social investment is lacking. Yet, some parts of SGP-related CSRs do relate to elements of social investment and give at least the impression that the SGP is not solely about seeking reduction of public expenditure. The clearest CSRs in this respect are the ones that combine the message to mind public expenditure with the message to spend more on certain growth areas. Such recommendations have not been given often: only twice in 2011 (BG, UK), 2012 (DE, UK), and 2014 (DE, CZ); and three times in 2013 (DE, LT, CZ). In 2015 SGP surveillance has not resulted in suggestions to spend more, although for example Germany did receive the recommendation to increase public investment in infrastructure, education and research, yet this CSR stemmed from the MIP.

A more frequent message was to avoid cutting expenditure or to minimize cuts in certain areas, with a peak in such policy advice of eight SGP-related CSRs in 2013. Gaining popularity are policies that are relatively cheap to implement: making the tax system support jobs and growth for instance by changing taxes from labour to consumption. Within the scope of the SGP such recommendations have not been given in 2011, but it was part of seven CSRs in 2014, albeit decreasing to three in 2015. Sometimes the SGP addresses quite specific social policy issues, including securing access to health care for vulnerable groups or combating the shadow economy. Yet, with the exception of the year 2013, SGP recommendations do not usually address issues that could be related to social investment. It thus seems that social investment perspectives are possible, even within the scope of the SGP, yet, always in a balancing act with meeting fiscal requirements. Ferrera (2016) found that the 2015 CSRs have become much less detailed and this partly explains why many countries no longer received specific messages to also mind jobs and growth. Another explanation is that in 2015, for the first time, new-style SGP surveillance did not result in a CSR for all of the member states. Germany, Luxembourg, the Netherlands, Slovakia, Slovenia, and Sweden did not get a CSR stemming from the SGP, and for these countries this opens up space for thinking in lines of social investment.

28.3 CSRs in their Context: More Views on a Potential Investment Approach

For all types of CSR it is relevant to view the underlying analysis to interpret their meaning. CSRs are not isolated messages but stem from extensive assessments of member state's socioeconomic progress as well as the impact of recent and future reforms. Such integrated evaluation and contextualized messages are part of the Commission's Country Reports (before 2015 these Country Reports were separated into Staff Working Documents (SWDs) and In-depth Reviews). These Country Reports contain ample examples of support for investing in society and citizens. Usually recommendations on investment are based on the MIP or Europe 2020 evaluations, however, not on the SGP. The background evaluations moreover show how interrelated social and economic issues are making a sole focus on SGP too narrow. Thus, although the broad analysis underlying the CSRs offers opportunities for social investment, these ideas get lost in translation into SGP-related CSRs. Only glimpses of social investment remain in part of some SGP-based CSRs for some countries. Examples are outlined in subsection 28.3.1.

28.3.1 CSRs Suggesting Spend More

In 2011 both the UK and Bulgaria received broad advice to prioritize growth-enhancing expenditure and in 2012 this advice was repeated for the UK. In 2012 Germany received a CSR with more specific information on how to spend its money: to enhance spending on education and research at all levels of government, and the 2013 and 2014 CSRs repeat this message. The 2013 and 2014 CSRs to the Czech Republic call to prioritize growth-enhancing expenditure to support recovery and improve growth prospects. Sketching the context of this message the European Commission (2014a) encourages the Czech Republic to end its period of restrained growth. A solution is to strengthen domestic drivers of growth, although minding public finances is considered relevant as well. The Commission also calls to make better use of EU funds and to remove obstacles that keep people away from the labour market. Such a message relates to flow functions of social investment. Indeed, the Commission analyses that in spite of the Czech Republic's comparatively high employment rate, some groups keep having difficulties in accessing the labour market, among which are women with small children, youth, older people, low-skilled, and disabled persons. The employment impact of mother-hood in the Czech Republic is one of the largest in the EU, due to limited access to affordable childcare and the limited take-up of part-time work. Moreover, education needs to be improved, and this relates to the stock function of social investment. Currently people's socioeconomic background strongly influences educational performance. Czech higher education has too limited resources whereas there is an increase in inflow. In addition, the overall quality of learning outcomes should be improved, as well as the labour-market relevance of graduates' skills. Thus, even within the SGP there are recommendations to countries to spend more money, and viewing the detailed background analysis, such CSRs at time stem from observations that relate to stock, flow, and buffer functions of social investment. Although social investment as such is not mentioned by the Commission, the CSRs, and especially the background analyses, give countries good arguments to develop social investment strategies.

28.3.2 Avoid or Minimize Cuts

While spending more money was not a message widely communicated to member states, the recommendation to avoid or minimize cuts in certain growth areas has been given more often. In 2011, Germany gets the specific message to pursue growth-friendly consolidation by safeguarding adequate expenditure on education and by enhancing the efficiency of public spending on health care and long-term care. As subsection 28.3.1 shows, after 2012 this recommendation changes in the message to spend more on education. The Netherlands is a noteworthy example of ongoing CSRs to not randomly cut budgets, yet to make careful choices. Four times in a row the Netherlands has been getting the CSR to ensure growth friendly and sustainable consoli-dation by protecting expenditure in areas directly relevant for growth: research and innovation, education and training. In reality, the European Commission (2014b: 7) sees adverse trends and calls this worrisome as well as potentially harmful to economic growth. For, although general Dutch government expenditure is bound to increase, expenditure on education is planned to fall from 19 per cent of total government expenditure in 2005 to 16.6 per cent in 2017. The Commission acknowledges that the total expenditure on education does not fully relate to the quality of spending, yet a deeper analysis of expenditure at school level shows that since the 1990s educational institutions have increasingly invested in buildings. In some regional education centres this has led to financial difficulties and cuts in expenditure, directly affecting the quality of education. Although perhaps only indirectly and partially addressing social investment concerns, also this type of recommendation gives member states a choice to at least not diminish expenditure on education.

28.3.3 *Other Social Investment Recommendations*

Also interesting for the social investment approach (SIA) is the category which may be labelled as 'other'. This category hardly has a common denominator. Recommendations vary strongly from country to country. For example the 2014 CSR to the UK suggests addressing the structural skills mismatches with a view to boosting growth. The SWD explains that in spite of the overall good labour market, the outcomes are less positive for young people. In addition, the UK has a shortage of workers with high-quality vocational and technical skills, thus contributing to a mismatch in the job market (European Commission 2014d). In Spain the growing poverty has been set higher on the agenda, and a small part of these concerns, health care accessible for vulnerable groups, was included in the 2013 and 2014 CSRs. Likewise, the Polish poverty rates are a concern and in 2013 and 2014 the country has received a CSR to improve the targeting of social policies, thus addressing buffer and flow functions of social investment. The SWD explains that Poland's social protection system is unable to reduce poverty sufficiently, as both the coverage and adequacy of unemployment and social assistance benefits is low (European Commission 2014c). At the same time spending on pensions is high. The real income per capita is relatively low and the statutory minimum wages are among the lowest in the EU. Finding a job is not always a solution to escape from poverty, as the in-work poverty rate is the fifth highest in the EU. Moreover, temporary and part-time job holders are much more at risk of poverty than those in permanent jobs. While Poland has been addressing this issue by increasing the minimum wage, the Commission says that the country overlooks poverty drivers linked to sectoral mobility, family support, and household work intensity and therefore social policies should be targeted better. Also directed to improve the position of vulnerable groups at the labour market is the 2012 CSR to the Czech Republic to reduce discrepancies in the tax treatment of employees and the self-employed, as self-employed are entitled to a significantly lower effective tax rate than employees and have less generous rules on tax deductibility (European Commission 2012a). It means that the system gives what the Commission calls 'perverse incentives' for employers to hire de facto dependent employees as self-employed (European Commission 2012a: 13). This moreover results in lower tax revenues for the public authorities. The Commission warns that relatively modest unemployment rates mask a shift of labour from regular employment to bogus self-employment as well as cuts in hours worked. It causes lower job security for households, which has an impact on confidence. Furthermore, a 2013 SGP-recommendation to Latvia addresses the position of vulnerable groups, and calls to further reduce the tax burden on low-income earners by shifting taxation to areas such as excise duties, recurrent property taxes, and/or environmental taxes. The aim of suggested reforms is to improve the employment opportunities of low-income groups and thus could be linked to flow functions of social investment.

28.4 Conclusion and Outlook

The EU seems neither to prominently promote social investment, nor to pose absolute obstacles to invest in economies and societies, at least not to all member states. Treaty norms set important social investment elements as an aim of the Union. Within the European Semester, especially the Europe 2020 Strategy develops arguments to invest in stock, buffer, and flow functions of labour markets and social policies. The SGP might be considered as the most social investment-restrictive governance mode of the European Semester. However, in spite its focus on meeting budgetary rules, it does not necessarily obstruct social investment initiatives. In its policy recommendations, the SGP has even suggested that some member states spend more on education or to reduce poverty.

Such room for social investment in socioeconomic coordination could be expressed much more clearly, however. Firstly, CSRs are only narrow summaries of broad and integrated socioeconomic evaluations. Much of the richness of the Commission's evaluations gets lost when summarizing it into CSRs. Moreover, a narrow focus on the SGP, which is after all only one of the socioeconomic coordination instruments, leads unnecessarily to a poor interpretation of proposals for policy reforms. The integrated background information in the SWD illustrates that the EU gives much more arguments for social investment than either the CSRs or the SGP suggest. That this message does not come across, is forgotten, or even suppressed by concerns of reducing public expenditure, shows that the different socioeconomic coordination mechanisms should be aligned better (see also Chapter 29, this volume). Treaty norms could be helpful in supporting the purpose of socioeconomic coordination and draw the attention back to obtaining the Europe 2020 goals. Not only should the balance between the social and the economic be restored, but the room for social investment across the different countries should be correspondingly aligned. Countries in corrective stages of economic coordination and countries in financial assistance packages should also have enough room to invest in societies and economies (Kvist 2013).

At the same time member states have not always fully used the available space to develop integrated and balanced socioeconomic policies. Member states could develop SI using the Commission's own argumentation in the broad evaluations of member state's socioeconomic policies. Moreover, they may use the flexibility in the socioeconomic governance process to argue for alternative approaches to restore jobs and growth. Some member states already develop such argumentation. For example, Poland argues in its national reform programme that investments in social infrastructure (e.g. education, health care, culture) is a means to unleash regional potential and to contribute to social inclusion. Good national practices, giving the Social Investment Approach (SIA) as a better alternative to austerity, may then feed into the coordination process and possibly lead to a stronger promotion of social investment at EU level.

29

Social Investment as a Policy Platform

A European Argument

Frank Vandenbroucke

Six years ago, Anton Hemerijck, Bruno Palier, and I published a paper, entitled 'The EU Needs a Social Investment Pact' (Vandenbroucke, Hemerijck, and Palier 2011). We did not present social investment as an easy panacea. Successful social investment presupposes a well-designed complementarity between 'developing human capital', by means of education, training, and activation and 'protecting human capital' by means of traditional instruments of social protection; both capacitating social services and adequate minimum income protection have to play a role. We also insisted that the social investment perspective had to be embedded in the European Union's (EU's) economic and budgetary surveillance.

Our call did ring a bell. In 2013, the European Commission launched its 'Social Investment Package' (European Commission 2013d). Obviously, a 'package' is not a 'pact'. The idea of a pact underscores the sense of reciprocity that is required: all member states should be committed to policies that respond to the need for social investment; simultaneously, member states' efforts in this direction—notably efforts by member states in a difficult budget-ary context—should be supported in a tangible way. When difficult reforms are necessary, there must also be solidarity in reform (Vandenbroucke and Vanhercke 2014: 91–5). In this contribution, I argue that our call for a truly reciprocal social investment pact is still highly relevant today; we are, alas, far removed from an effective common orientation on social investment in the EU. Despite my sympathy for social investment, I am wary about qualifying it as a fully-fledged analytical paradigm in the domain of the social sciences: social investment is a policy perspective that should be based on a broad consensus between people who may entertain certain disagreements on the level of their empirical and/or normative understanding of the social world. For that reason, I use the expression 'overlapping consensus' when I describe the nature of the social investment advocacy. I explain both the necessity to develop such a consensus across the EU, the role the notion of social investment can play in it, and my weariness about the understanding of social investment as a fully-fledged analytical paradigm in social science in Sections 29.1 and 29.2 respectively. In Section 29.3, I present summary data on education in the EU, showing that we are far removed from a true social investment perspective at the EU level. In Section 29.4, I conclude, by emphasizing that defenders of the social investment perspective need clear thinking about the role the EU has to play in this perspective.

29.1 Social Investment as a Policy Platform for the EU

To understand the relevance of the social investment argument to policy-making in the EU, one should revisit the fundamental goals that have been part and parcel of the European project since the Treaty of Rome of 1957. The founding fathers of the European project were convinced that market integration would allow the simultaneous pursuit of economic progress and social progress and cohesion, both within countries (through the gradual development of the welfare states) and between countries (through upward convergence across the Union). They optimistically assumed that growing cohesion between and within countries could be reached by supranational economic cooperation, together with some specific instruments for raising the standard of living across the member states (which were later brought together in the EU's 'economic, social and territorial' cohesion policy). Economic integration was to be organized at the EU level, and would boost economic growth and create upward convergence; domestic social policies were to redistribute the fruits of economic progress, while remaining a national prerogative. This belief was not proven wrong until the mid-2000s. Now, the experience of the crisis forces us to reconsider the question: how can the EU be a successful union of flourishing welfare states? Both on the left and the right of the political spectrum, despite conflicting views on the economic policy that is needed, many would argue that the crux is to restore growth by implementing the right kind of economic and monetary governance at EU level. My view is different: yes, it is essential to restore growth, which is mainly a matter of economic and monetary policy; but this short-term urgency cannot be isolated from the imperative to develop a social policy concept for the EU. I will not elaborate upon this concept here (see Vandenbroucke 2015), but for one important aspect: since human capital is the fundamental corollary of long-term developments in productivity, upward convergence in prosperity across the EU implies upward convergence in the quality of human capital.

For upward convergence, the main long-term stumbling block is the huge disparity in human capital across Europe. I insist on the qualification 'long term': the short-term stumbling blocks are of a different nature. Despite impressive progress in Spain, Italy, and Greece with regard to formal educational attainment, the four southern Eurozone countries remain outliers in the EU with a high percentage of the active population without upper secondary qualification. Admittedly, formal educational attainment is a superficial indicator of the quality of human capital and indicators on skill levels and educational outcomes should be added to the assessment; however, such indicators tell basically the same story. In countries like Spain and Italy the mean literacy score of the population as measured by Organisation for Economic Co-operation and Development (OECD) Programme for the International Assessment of Adult Competencies (PIAAC), is 10 per cent, lower than in the Netherlands, Finland, and Sweden: for a mean score, this is a considerable gap. The OECD Programme for International Student Assessment (PISA) results show an important disparity with regard to the quality of investment in human capital in today's youth, with weak average PISA scores for countries such as Romania, Bulgaria, Greece, and Slovakia; mediocre scores in Portugal, Italy, Spain, and a number of other countries; and relatively high scores in Finland, Ireland, the Netherlands, Estonia, Germany, and Poland. The PISA scores not only illustrate the particular deficit of southern Eurozone welfare states—compared to other Eurozone members—with regard to education; they underscore the huge education and skills agenda the whole EU is confronted with, since the human capital asymmetry also stretches beyond the Eurozone. In Section 29.3, I will focus on the education agenda in a narrow sense. However, developing our human capital is not just about education in a narrow sense; it requires a broad perspective, starting with family support, early child education and care (ECEC), activation and training for the unemployed, and lifelong learning for the whole workforce. A drive for excellence in education needs a broad framework of consistent policies, that is, 'social investment' as defined by Hemerijck in Chapter 1 of this volume.

Moreover, a drive for excellence in education also requires sufficiently egalitarian background conditions. Improving general education and skill levels is essential to economic growth and social progress, but it's not enough. The OECD's Education at a Glance (2014) shows that countries with fewer low-skilled adults and more highly skilled ones do better in economic terms than countries with similar average levels of skills but with larger differences in skills across the population. Greater access to education for people of all skill levels stimulates both economic growth and social inclusion. Access to education for the poor and lower middle class, in turn, depends on the quality of the income redistribution, as yet another recent OECD report shows: the OECD (2015c) analysis compares the education performance at different levels of inequality of three social groups—people whose parents come from high, medium, and low educational backgrounds—across three areas, namely education attainment, skills, and employment. It is no surprise to find that people from lower socioeconomic groups do less well in all three of these dimensions than people from higher socioeconomic groups. However, the OECD shows that, as inequality rises, the outcomes for people from lower groups decline even further. Admittedly, the causal link between students' success in education and their parents' income is complex; cultural capital is the main driver for the children's educational success (Diris and Vandenbroucke forthcoming). But in a cross-country comparison, the quality of the income redistribution does play a role. As the OECD puts it:

> It has long been popular to say that while there is no social consensus around the desirability of tackling inequality of outcomes, for example by redistributing wealth, surely we can agree that it is necessary to ensure that we have equality of opportunities—i.e. that all should have the same life chances, regardless of their initial conditions. (. . .) [However], [h]igher inequality of incomes of parents tends to imply higher inequality of life chances of their children. To achieve greater inequality of opportunities without tackling increasing inequality in outcomes will be very difficult.   (OECD 2015c: 27)

In a sense, this insight is not new. In *Why We Need a New Welfare State*, written at the start of the Lisbon era, Esping-Andersen argued:

> The Third Way may be criticized for its unduly selective appropriation of [Nordic] social democratic policy. (. . .) [I]t has a tendency to believe that activation may substitute for conventional income maintenance guarantees. This may be regarded as naïve optimism, but, worse, it may also be counterproductive. (. . .) [T]he minimization of poverty and income security is a precondition for an effective social investment strategy.
> (Esping-Andersen 2002: 5; cf. also Vandenbroucke and Vleminckx 2011)

Despite this caveat, in the course of the Lisbon era, social investment has come to be seen as a one-sided argument, dismissive of traditional concerns with income redistribution and social insurance (e.g. Cantillon 2011). The way the social investment argument was put forward, even by sophisticated defenders, may have contributed to this. For instance, when Hemerijck describes the new welfare state as a departure from the old social insurance welfare state and emphasizes the 'erosion of the effectiveness of the social insurance principle' (Hemerijck 2013: 38), he correctly points out that tackling structural unemployment requires capacitating services tailored to particular social needs; however, that does not diminish the need for adequate countercyclical unemployment insurance. In a similar vein, we need to maintain an insurance approach to provision for old age, in line with Myles' chapter on 'A New Social Contract for the Elderly' in *Why We Need a New Welfare State* (Myles 2002); there is still an important policy challenge in that respect in today's EU. In Chapter 34, this volume, Colin Crouch assertively underscores the need to advance a 'consolidated' old and new risks analysis, integrating capacitating and compensating policy interventions as complementary and not as rivals.

29.2 A Policy Platform or a Scientific Paradigm?

Crouch situates the social investment debate in the context of shifting con-flicts and alliances among social democrats, conservatives, and neoliberals. Broad alliances are needed indeed. Developing a basic consensus on the European social model and the role the EU has to play in it, is not a luxury anymore; it has become an existential necessity for the EU (Vandenbroucke 2015). The social investment perspective can provide a 'unifying policy con-cept' for the EU (Hemerijck and Vandenbroucke 2012), which fits well into such a basic consensus.

In Chapter 1, this volume, Hemerijck characterizes social investment as a 'policy paradigm'; the expression refers both to the 'cognitive understanding' of causal relations between policy efforts and outcomes and to 'political mobilization' behind policy priorities. I would add to this that there is a distinction between a policy paradigm, so conceived, and a fully-fledged analytical paradigm in the realm of science. The need for consensus-building is one of the reasons why I am wary about an understanding of the social investment perspective as a fully fledged, well-identifiable and definite scien-tific paradigm. Rather than convincing people, such endeavour may enter-tain persistent division in the scientific and policy community, which is counterproductive from the point of view of consensus-building. There are some fundamental issues which explain why the scientific community will not easily rally behind social investment as a scientific paradigm.

In the recent past, the classification of welfare states from the social invest-ment perspective was often based on a binary distinction between 'investment spending' (or 'capacitating spending') and 'non-investment spending' (or 'compensatory spending'). Some of the questions raised by Nolan (2013; Chapter 2, this volume) on the analytical robustness of that distinction are not easy to answer. The distinction is fuzzy; its fuzziness is not resolved by shifting from a dichotomous assessment to a conceptual continuum. But, then, is it really necessary to classify spending patterns in this way, if we aim to assess the actual developments in human capital across welfare states, and the policy efforts deployed to that end? Human capital can be measured by indicators on educational attainment and levels of skills. Policy efforts can be measured by public spending in education and related domains, by indicators on the quality and quantity of staff—that is, they can be measured by examining these policy domains as such, rather than their relative importance vis-à-vis other domains. As often, a 'thick' concept (the distinction between capacitating spending and compensating spending) is more difficult to handle than a 'thin' concept (human capital); in this case, the 'thick' concept may even be conceptually problematic.

Hemerijck rightly emphasizes the complementarity between policy domains. As much as it is important, this is, again, a thick concept which is difficult to apply operationally in empirical analysis, let alone to measure. It requires qualitative judgements by experts, which are inevitably subjective. The difficulty of this ambitious exercise transpires in the report on Social Investment in Europe, prepared by the European Social Policy Network (ESPN). This report aims to assess progress made in thirty-four countries in the direction of social investment. It thereby focuses on three areas: the extent to which the country's social policies have facilitated early childhood development, have supported the participation of parents (especially women) in the labour market, and have provided adequate, activating, and enabling support to those experiencing social and labour market exclusion (Bouget et al. 2015). This report contains a wealth of interesting data and observations. It also looks for complementarity or lack of complementarity in public policy. But, depending on one's personal view, one might take issue with some of the qualitative judgements made in the report. That is not in itself an indictment of the concept of 'complementarity', nor of the need for a holistic approach; but it signals a caveat with regard to the empirical potential of such rather thick concepts, notably with regard to the empirical precision with which they can be applied.

Simultaneously, the ESPN report contains facts that should disturb any policymaker who is sympathetic towards the core social investment argument: between 2008 and 2012 spending on families fell in twenty-one out of twenty-eight EU member states. Even allowing for demographic changes over this period, this is in stark contrast to an increase in spending in old age in twenty-six member states (Bouget et al. 2015: Annex 3, figure A5). The ESPN report frequently mentions negative outcomes not only in child and family policies, but also in social insurance and income support, active labour-market policies (ALMPs), education, elderly and long-term care, and access to health care. These conclusions concur with an OECD review on the basis of a relatively standard set of indicators: in eight of the nine European countries under examination (Germany being an exception) austerity packages affected families with children more than families without children (OECD 2015a: 124–5). That is not a sign of progress towards social investment.

It is therefore rather disturbing that the official Commission press release of 24 April 2015 painted a much rosier picture than the ESPN report itself. The report identifies 'four main ways in which a focus on fiscal consolidation and a failure to apply social impact assessments of policy changes have often laid to negative effects for the development of social investment policies' (Bouget et al. 2015: 12–13); the Commission press release mentions, in passing, that 'the crisis and fiscal constraints have, at times, complicated some Member States' reform efforts'. In Section 29.3, I present some additional simple observations with regard to education, which are prima facie also very worrying. Here, I want to stress that an important policy concept (complementarity), which is rightly presented by Hemerijck as part and parcel of the policy paradigm, does not readily translate into an operational concept applicable in empirical research, a fortiori, if one would wish to test it rigorously as a scientific paradigm. Hence, it seems safer to conceive of the social investment argument as a policy argument that acknowledges a number of empirical difficulties, uncertainties, and disagreements. If the social investment argument is to create a platform for European action, it should be based on an overlapping consensus between people who may hold different views on certain aspects of our scientific understanding of the world. If the impact of social investment policies in terms of social outcomes is to be tested empirically, we may prefer thin concepts (such as human capital) above thick concepts (such as capacitating social spending or complementarity): thin concepts may be easier to apply in empirical analyses and generate less controversy among scholars.

29.3 Instead of Upward Convergence, Poor Social Investment Will Generate Further Divergence in the EU

As indicated at the end of Section 29.2, I am less confident about the 'progress made' towards social investment in the EU than the official assessment now is. That is not to deny positive dynamics with regard to part of the social investment agenda as described by Hemerijck (2013) (for instance, the agenda related to women's employment) and in Bouget and colleagues (2015). However, from a social investment perspective, there are also shortcomings and setbacks. Education is a telling example.

The European Commission has developed a comprehensive agenda on education, training, and skills, and issued excellent recommendations on the modernization of education systems. However, this agenda does not carry sufficient weight at the highest levels of European political decision-making and in the setting of budgetary priorities. Figure 29.1 displays data on the evolution of public spending on education in real terms. The black bars compare, for each country, its public education spending in 2013 with its average spending over the years 2006–8 (deflated with the gross domestic

325

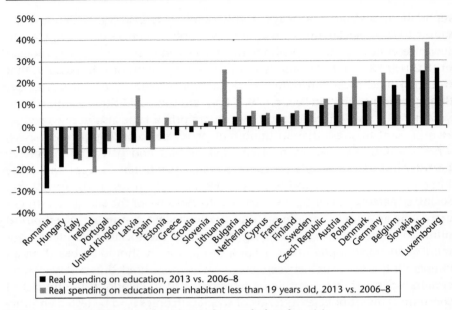

Figure 29.1. Spending on education before and after the crisis

Sources: Eurostat (public spending on education, general government), own calculations, data extracted on 29 February, 2016.

product (GDP) deflator): in eleven EU member states, real spending is now lower than it was, on average, in the years before the crisis. In Romania the decline is 28 per cent, in Hungary it is 19 per cent, in Italy 15 per cent, in Ireland 14 per cent, and in Portugal 12 per cent. Meanwhile, there was a significant increase in real spending, with an increase in education spending of 10 per cent or more in Poland, Denmark, Germany, Belgium, Slovakia, Malta, and Luxemburg. Obviously, demography plays a role: the grey bars in Figure 29.1 take demographic change into account, by calculating real public spending on education per inhabitant younger than 19 years old: per young inhabitant, real spending diminished 'only' by 17 per cent in Romania and 12 per cent in Hungary; in contrast, in Ireland real spending per young inhabitant diminished by 21 per cent. The effort in public education spending is spectacular in countries like Germany, Poland, and Slovakia, when taking demography into account. Some of the countries with spectacular increases in real spending had a relatively low level of spending relative to their GDP in the mid-2000s: they used the produce of economic growth in part to catch up on education spending. In contrast, one cannot say that countries that cut education spending drastically were 'big spenders' on education, when education spending is compared to GDP (not shown here). Some of the latter countries (like Romania) are also countries with poor results in the OECD's PISA tests of the skills of 15-year-old children. To avoid misunderstanding, I insist that the message is not that spending guarantees educational performance; but cutting spending is not a recipe for progress either. The take-home message emerging from this graph is a dramatic divergence in the real public effort for education, with drastic cuts in some countries that badly need to improve their educational performance.

29.4 Conclusion: A Matter of Common Concern, to Be Embedded in EU Economic and Budgetary Governance

Social investment is a unifying policy concept: a policy concept, which can be based on an overlapping consensus; a unifying concept, because it is very well-suited to inform the common orientation that is needed across the EU if we want to reconnect with the original inspiration of the European founding fathers. In this sense, my argument is Eurocentric. Obviously, it is not to say social investment arguments do not apply to non-EU welfare states. But this common orientation is so crucial to the future of the EU that it should be embedded, as a 'matter of common concern', in the EU's economic and budgetary governance. Without a credible link between budgetary and economic choices on the one hand, and social investment priorities on the other hand, both the legitimacy of the EU and the legitimacy of the social investment narrative are bound to crumble. Admittedly, embedding social investment priorities—understood in the encompassing and sophisticated way described by Hemerijck in Chapter 1, this volume—in economic and budgetary processes is not an easy task. Proponents of social investment as a unifying policy concept for the EU should consider this to be their most important intellectual and political challenge.

30

Accelerator or Brake?

The EU and the Difficult Politics of Social Investment

Maurizio Ferrera

30.1 Introduction

The promotion of social investment constitutes a complex challenge of recalibration for European welfare states, implying changes along three distinct dimensions: functional (resource shifts across life-cycle risks); distributive (resource shifts across social groups); organizational (resource and competence shifts across levels of government and forms of provision). Policy multidimensionality and complexity are however only one side of the challenge. Recalibration towards social investment raises daunting political problems as well, linked to the presence of explicit and extended intertemporal trade-offs. The rationale of social investment is to modernize social protection now (often through entitlement restrictions and 'cuts' to make room for new programmes) in order to reap collective benefits in the future: more capital goods (for example, greater skills), less social 'evils (for example, school dropouts), the reduction of compensatory/remedial expenditure (for example, unemployment or minimum income subsidies). The temporal mismatch between social investment reforms and their returns requires a degree of 'political patience' on the side of both current voters and incumbent politicians which is not readily available in contemporary democracies.

The European Union (EU) has been the main agenda setter in this field. As a political actor, the EU can take advantage of its relative insulation from domestic electoral processes and its technical expertise and delegated authority. It also has at its disposal sizeable funds that can co-finance national and, in particular, subnational policy initiatives. What use has the EU made of its persuasion and capacitation resources in promoting social investment? To what extent have EU actors (and especially the Commission) been able to recognize and exploit their potential for facilitation? This chapter will try to answer these questions.

30.2 Discursive Persuasion

Although the expression 'social investment' was formally and officially adopted only in 2013, with the 'Social Investment Package' (SIP) (European Commission 2013d), the EU had started to prepare the grounds for the new paradigm already in the mid-1990s and the social investment rationale informed the overall logic of the Lisbon strategy and of the 'social open methods of coordination (OMCs)' since their inception. Social investment has continued to play an important function in the overall framework which underpins the Europe 2020 strategy. At a general level, the first and obvious remark to be made is that the EU has been the discursive entrepreneur which has linked social objectives and programmes to the policy investment perspective.

In the last couple of decades, the European Commission has affirmed itself as the prime authority in the provision of reliable comparative data and as an important source for systematic and original policy analysis. Even though considerable analytical and empirical work still needs to be done in order to pinpoint and measure exactly what policy areas count as 'social investment' (De Deken 2014), a rich portfolio of quantitative indicators has been developed for monitoring social developments in a broad sense and for assessing the achievement of common objectives (Vanhercke and Lelie 2012; Barcevičius, Weishaupt, and Zeitlin 2014: 16–86). Within Council, the Employment Committee and the Social Protection Committee have made massive efforts, in their turn, to elaborate social indicators. The most important to date is the EU Social Scoreboard (also known as Scoreboard of Key Social and Employment Indicators), which is widely recognized as the best tool for communicating EU social outcomes. Important progres has also been made in terms of monitoring and evaluation, for example via the Europe 2020 Joint-Assessment Framework (JAF) and the Social Protection Performance Monitor (SPPM). JAF is an analytical tool for the analysis and evaluation of national steps implementing the employment guidelines of Europe 2020. The SPPM is focused on social inclusion, pensions, health care, and long-term care, and also includes a series of 'trends to watch' for an early detection of developments running against the Europe 2020 targets. The Commission has also started to move from retrospective to prospective analyses, enhancing its forecasting exercises, extrapolating possible consequences of policy actions and inactions and discussing them publicly. The rationale for emphasizing forecasts is, interestingly, that of sustaining future-oriented policies and politics within the member states: stressing the risks associated with inaction 'could be a powerful way to communicate the advantages of reforms and help governments that pursue modernization to get a dividend vis-à-vis their public opinion and voters' (EPSC 2015: 7).

What matters critically for the politics of the long term is persuasive evidence about the potential gains of policy investments and about causal mechanisms (Jacobs 2011). Evidence-based policymaking is inherently difficult and is typically exposed to epistemic traps. Nevertheless, policymakers and voters alike do need insights and epistemic resources to 'fill the unknowns', especially when confronted with a new approach. In the case of social investment, since the second half of the 2000s the Commission has made several efforts to move in this direction, by arguing in support of the social investment 'case' in a number of preparatory documents for the 2013 Package. The Policy Roadmap for the SIP's implementation (up to 2017) confirms the Commission's commitment to produce further evidence (European Commission 2015c).

All these efforts are undoubtedly commendable, but what can we say about their effectiveness—especially their political effectiveness? Systematic empirical evidence is unfortunately lacking. There are, however, some signals which allow for some initial speculation. First, we have the Commission's own view on the matter (EPSC 2015), according to which the arguments and evidence in support of social investment (and more generally the Europe 2020 Strategy) have mostly remained circumscribed to specialized expert arenas and have not 'delivered the expected degree of political influence'. In fact, while the prime objective of the social investment and Europe 2020 discourse was to create incentives for action and disincentives for inaction, 'results are mixed at best. It has been a strategy that solicited insufficient political buy-in.' (EPSC 2015: 2)

Secondly, we have a number of empirical signals from expert reports. According to a recent survey (European Commission 2015e), some policy changes in the fields covered by the SIP have been introduced in recent years, but the actual salience and use of the social investment discursive framework has remained very low: the social investment approach has made only modest inroads at the ideational levels. This lack of impact is depressing not only per se, but also considering that the 2013 social investment package recommended the Commission to 'focus on social investment and active inclusion in Country Specific Recommendations . . . in the framework of the European Semester' (European Commission 2013d: 22). After some timid signs in this direction during the 2014 cycle, in 2015 the Juncker Commission decided to drastically reduce the number of country-specific recommendations (CSRs) and to focus them essentially on macroeconomic and fiscal issues. Preliminary evidence shows that social messages have not been lost, but rather mainstreamed through the CSRs. Their visibility has however decreased, thus reducing the potential of CSRs for influencing national governments, indirectly facilitating policy investments and their politics (Vanhercke, Zeitlin, and Zwinkels 2015).

The third signal of political failure is the relatively marginal role played by social investment discourse in the party manifestos for the EP elections of 2014. According to a content analysis exercise, the top list of expressions used to discuss social issues included the following: health, discrimination, solidarity, equality, poverty, women (De Ruiter, Akerboom, and Steunenberg 2014). Only the Green and Liberal platforms made a marginal reference to social investment and briefly expanded on its agenda. The two main groupings—the European Popular Party and the Party of European Socialists and Democrats—refrained from even mentioning the concept.

30.3 Institutional Pressure and 'Capacitation'

In addition to evidence and arguments, the EU has tried to promote social investment through soft institutional pressures aimed at shaping national policy agendas and reform capacities. The OMCs and, more recently, the 'socialization' of the Semester have indeed prompted some policy adaptation and change towards the Europe 2020 targets through peer pressure, learning, discursive socialization/diffusion, and leverage (Barcevičius, Weishaupt, and Zeitlin 2014; Zeitlin and Vanhercke 2014) But such dynamics are slow-moving, ancillary in respect of the much harder macroeconomic and fiscal constraints within the Semester, and very sensitive to political and temporal contingencies.

A more significant instrument of institutional pressure has been the linkage between EU funds and the implementation of the SIP recommendations through the so-called ex ante conditionality. According to the rules adopted for 2014–19, in order to get funds, qualifying member states have to explicitly spell out the coherence of their stated goals vis-à-vis the thematic objectives of Europe 2020. For the European Social Fund (ESF) the focus is on employment, social inclusion, poverty, and anti-discrimination, as well as education (20 per cent of the ESF has been ring-fenced for poverty and social inclusion). The conditions to be met relate to effective policies being pursued, EU law affecting the implementation of the funds being transposed, and adequate administrative capacity being in place. The key point about ex ante conditionality is the possibility for the Commission to impose penalties. Failure to carry out the action plan leads to a suspension of EU payments. Ex ante conditionality shapes agendas and capacities in several ways. First, national authorities must develop adequate technical and epistemic expertise in order to meet EU conditions. Second, they may now appeal to a new external constraint for resisting pressures aimed at capturing 'horizontal' (i.e. present- rather than future-oriented) gains. Third, the involvement of the EU and the investment-oriented nature of ex ante conditionality in a multi-annual financial framework offers to national and local actor constellations a guarantee on the inter-temporal continuity of agreements and commitments.

The emerging evidence about the negotiations of Partnership agreements and Operational programmes shows some encouraging signs (European Commission 2015e). The main elements of the new cohesion strategy have been incorporated in national proposals. The shifts in terms of funding do correspond to the new EU priorities, especially as regards the ESF: investments in the fields of employment and social inclusion will absorb a larger share than in the previous programming period. The need to prepare for investment by fulfilling conditions in advance of programme implementation has been taken seriously.

Two caveats on the effectiveness of ex ante conditionality need mentioning. Firstly, its capacity to influence domestic policy choices is obviously limited to those member states which qualify for substantial Cohesion funds, mostly in Southern and Eastern Europe. As these member states also tend to be the laggards in terms of social investment recalibration, this element may turn out to be less a limitation than an indirect instrument for supporting the catching up of welfare laggards and shaping such process in terms of more social investment. Secondly, conditionality can be effective only to the extent that the underlying 'policy theory' is transparent, epistemically plausible (lest the cure be worse than the disease), sensitive to 'local' inputs and information, and subject to public scrutiny. This second caveat raises more problems than the first: EU's recommendations and prescriptions are often formulated as top-down, one size fits all instructions. In the long term, inappropriate conditionality might even create a divergence between 'constrained' and 'unconstrained' recalibration, with the latter benefiting from higher degrees of freedom in discovering the best policy investment trajectory through trials and errors and experiential learning from below.

From this brief overview, we can conclude that, overall, the agenda-shaping and capacity enhancing role of the EU—through soft and hard incentives—has been greater than its discursive role. There also seems to be, on the capacity front, more sensitivity and an evolving strategy on the side of the Commission. The Annual Growth Survey for 2016 underscored once again, for example, that EU funding will be deliberately used in supporting reform implementation, also by factoring the CSRs priorities into the programming of the European Structural and Investment Funds for 2014–20 (European Commission 2015a). Social investments are explicitly mentioned among the qualifying goals for national applications to the so-called Investment Plan for Europe. Even more significantly, in the wake of the Annual Growth Survey for

2016, the Commission has proposed the establishment of a Structural Reform Support Service 'with the objective of strengthening the capacity of Member States to prepare and implement growth-enhancing administrative and structural reforms, including through assistance for the efficient and effective use of the Union funds' (European Commission 2015e: 2).

30.4 Making the Case for Social Investment: Framing Mistakes

What factors may account for the less successful performance of the EU in terms of information and argument, compared to capacity? When the notion was originally launched in academic and policy debates, the Commission chose to stress the economic and productivist dimension of social investment: social investment as resources spent with a view to generating future benefits, actualized within a specified time frame and return rate. Through this choice, the Directorate General for Employment (DG EMPL) (the key social investment entrepreneur within the Commission) hoped to build a bridge towards the economic Directorate Generals and thus 'sell' them under new and more sophisticated guise the 'social policy as a productive factor' arguments of the past. With hindsight, such a choice has been counterproductive, as it prompted a more severe analytical and empirical scrutiny of the key theses of social investment on the side of the EU's economic staff. As underlined by Nolan (2013), 'social' investment does not quite fit with the concepts and theories used by economics when discussing the nature, functions, and preconditions of investment (as opposed, for instance, to consumption). A strict economic 'case' for social investment was not likely to persuade even potentially sympathetic economists. The problem is that economists are today the top policy advisors of political leaders, possibly the highest epistemic authorities within their entourages at both EU and national levels. If the social investment approach is not passing their test, it is unlikely to capture the attention of politicians.

A second framing mistake has been the presentation of social investment more as a strategic alternative rather than a complement to the traditional social protection approach and discourse. As has been underlined by various commentators—and in particular by Bea Cantillon (2011)—SI cannot be presented as a panacea for the manifold social problems and challenges of European societies, and it would be unreasonable to financially downsize or symbolically de-valorize certain established and key 'repairing' policies (e.g. for poverty reduction). The juxtaposition between a supposedly ineffective and outdated social protection, on the one hand, and the optimistic promises of social investment, on the other, has weakened the persuasion potential vis-à-vis many influential social scientists. More generally, if the economists' critique on the 'investment' component of the new paradigm has alienated the sympathies of market-oriented actors, the ambiguity of its 'social' component has in its turn alienated the sympathies of socially oriented actors. In the politics of policymaking and intellectual debates, social investment has started to fall between two stools.

The third weakness has been the failure to highlight and develop the 'social justice rationale' of social investment. The EU's policy discourse is notoriously couched in terms of descriptive neutrality and based on cognitive ideas related to pragmatic goals and policy instruments. This partly results from the Commission's institutional role as a (supposedly) impartial body pursuing common objectives. To a large extent, it also results from the predominance of economic thinking and mainstream economists among the Commission's policy staff. The two factors push the Commission to reason essentially in terms of functional necessities, efficiency gains, and policy effectiveness. An explicit focus on normative ideas is perceived as institutionally and scientifically inappropriate. It is also avoided for fear of raising risky conflicts and policy stalemates. The fact is, however, that no functional necessity can be identified or justified in a normative vacuum. And abdicating value analysis leads to biases that may be extremely pernicious precisely because they are not acknowledged (Tsakalotos 2005).

These three framing mistakes bear significant responsibility—I contend—for the underperforming effectiveness of social investment in the battle for ideas and for attention. This has had negative implications not only for the sphere of policymaking, but also for the wider sphere of EU politics. The 'weak political buy in' lamented by the Commission has not only affected top leaders and civil servants, but also the informed and educated public—who might have been a promising interlocutor of the social investment discourse.

30.5 Strengthening Capacity: The Unexploited Potential

The EU record on capacitation has been greater than on persuasion and framing. Nevertheless, the question may be raised whether the Commission has fully exploited the available potential, especially in mobilizing institutional and social actors and forging horizontal and vertical alliances favouring social investment. Sub-national governments, especially in the larger member states, are key players in place-based policy investments and thus a natural interlocutor of the Commission. To a large extent, social investment recalibration can be seen as a triadic political game in which each actor (sub-national, national, and supranational) entertains formal links and political relationships with the other two. Regions are of course formally involved in the allocation of the Cohesion funds. But the 'regional card' could be played more vigorously by the Commission in managing ex ante conditionality. Regions and local authorities are everywhere struggling with shrinking resources and rising needs. There is evidence that some national reforms have more or less deliberately generated an 'austerity localism' which, far from improving decentralized problem solving capacity, has instead reinforced or established new patterns of exclusion and distributive conflicts (Featherstone et al. 2012; Johansson and Hvinden 2016). Closer and more focused links (formal and informal) between the Commission and subnational governments could support the latter in claiming additional funds (or avoiding cuts) from their national governments, consolidating their institutional role and strengthening their position in the emerging system of EU social governance. Reversing the perspective, one could also argue that the Commission itself could benefit from stronger links in order to revise its top-down, target-based approach, engaging instead in a learning exercise 'from the bottom'.

In addition to the 'regional card', a lot more could be done in terms of capacity by playing the 'non-public actors' card. The last decade has witnessed an increasingly strong involvement of civil society organizations in service provisions. Empirical research has just started to explore such developments and to characterize their substantive agendas and achievements as well as their novel governance practices (Pestoff, Brandsen, and Verscheure 2012; Anheier and Krlev 2014). One indication of this literature is that the new generation of 'local welfare systems' does not mechanically mirror national welfare regime features, but operates according to its own distinctive logic, often with unexpected links with other (including cross-border) systems. This is interesting in at least two respects: (1) at the grass-root level Europe's social sphere is becoming less 'public' and less 'national' and is increasingly nested in wider vertical and horizontal networks; (2) local systems are becoming key arenas for novel solutions to social challenges. A strategic connection with the emerging protagonists of 'social innovation' (especially, but not exclusively, at the local level) could be a precious asset for advancing the social investment agenda. In many member states, interesting experiments outside the public sphere (in a strict sense) are currently under way. Such initiatives (which the Italian debate has dubbed *secondo welfare*) typically mobilize non-public resources which are made available by a wide range of economic and social actors: the social partners (often at the local/ company level through decentralized bargaining), territorial associations of various sorts, banks, foundations, philanthropic subjects, and so on. These actors are—typically—highly motivated to learn, and sensitive to empirical evidence and principled arguments. For the Commission, they could be precious interlocutors: their 'noviceness' makes them ideal targets for 'thick persuasion' (Checkel 2002).

30.6 Conclusion

Mario Monti is known for having often dubbed the EU as the 'trade union' which defends the interests of future generations. He mainly referred to fiscal discipline: by posing limits to public deficits and debts, the Economic and Monetary Union has foreclosed a perverse resource shift from the future to the present. Financing current consumptions (e.g. through pensions) by transferring their costs onto future workers or as yet unborn citizens was an unreasonable practice in which the member states indulged for too long in the past. But fiscal discipline is not enough. The interests of future generations must be defended today especially through investment policies. If the EU wants to be serious about future generations, social investment is indeed an 'imperative'. The EU can play a big role in responding to the imperative, but for moving in this direction three steps must be urgently undertaken: endorsing with more conviction the social investment paradigm; changing rules and putting in place the right incentives for member states to implement the necessary reforms; and providing national politicians with adequate framings for policy investments while supporting their capacity to push them through reluctant domestic political processes. The last step is the most difficult and yet the most delicate. By its very nature, democratic politics has problems in serving the long term. It requires a nudge: will EU authorities perceive this challenge and thus be able to effectively address it?

Part 7
The Politics of Social Investment

31

The Politics of Social Investment

Policy Legacies and Class Coalitions

Silja Häusermann and Bruno Palier

31.1 Introduction

As emphasized by Anton Hemerijck in Chapter 1, and reiterated in many other chapters in this volume, there has recently been a substantial amount of implementation of social investment policies in many different European countries (e.g. the expansion of childcare infrastructure in many continental welfare states such as Germany or Switzerland; Bleses and Seeleib-Kaiser 2004; Fleckenstein 2011; Häusermann and Kübler 2011; Hieda 2013), but also in Latin America (e.g. the promotion of cash transfers to the poor in Brazil or Mexico, which are conditional on the families sending their children to school or participating in health plans; Bourguignon, Ferreira, and Leite 2003; Soares et al. 2009) and South East Asia (Peng 2015; Chapter 24, this volume). The reforms in all these countries can and should be counted as part of the social investment agenda, because they all focus on higher employment and future improvements in overall productivity and economic growth and prosperity (Hemerijck 2015).

However, the turn to social investment is also highly diverse in terms of its functions and policy instruments. Hemerijck distinguishes three welfare functions of social investment (2015: 7): supporting the efficient use and allocation of labour resources over the life course ('flow'), enhancing and maintaining human capital ('stock'), and mitigating social inequity while at the same time providing automatic macroeconomic stabilizers ('buffer'). The different policy instruments implemented across the regions of the world serve these functions to varying degrees and in varying combinations: while social investment is, for example, strongly focused on fertility and female labour market participation ('flow') in South East Asia, it tends to take the form of the 'educational conditions' for the poorest in the conditional cash transfer programmes several Latin American countries have developed in the recent decades (combining 'buffer' and 'stock' functions), and it puts a strong emphasis on either labour market activation or childcare/early childhood education in Western Europe (targeting 'flow' and 'stock').

To understand why social investment ideas and policies have developed to different extents and in such different forms across countries, we need to study the *politics* of reforms. In other words, we need to explain why some functions of social investment are more prominent on a particular reform agenda, as well as who the political actors are who can successfully compromise and coalesce on stock, flow, and buffer policies. In our short contribution, we argue that *policy legacies* and *class coalitions* are key factors in this respect.

We will develop and briefly illustrate two claims regarding the politics of social investment. *First*, the social investment policy agenda of a country depends on the pre-existing institutional context in the form of *policy legacies*, because these legacies shape both the actual and the perceived challenges a country faces. In other words, legacies condition the problem perception and problem diagnosis that prevails in a country, and they set priorities in terms of the pursued social investment functions. *Second*, the political success of these (agenda-specific) social investment policy proposals depends on the availability of a political support coalition. Such a coalition does not need overall consensus or unanimity, as the politics of social investment—like all politics—are contentious, but the coalition needs to be broad enough. We will argue that the educated middle classes are the key supporters of social investment, and they can ally with either business interests or working-class interests to implement (parts of) a social investment agenda.

We will illustrate these two claims with reference to family policy and female labour market policy developments in three crucial cases of countries—France, Germany, and Switzerland—which share a problematic policy legacy when it comes to social investment, but differ regarding the problem diagnosis and the coalitional potentials and policy consequences.

31.2 Contextualizing Social Investment Politics

31.2.1 *Institutional Legacies and Reform Agendas*

Our first claim is that the content of a social investment *agenda* depends on the policy legacies specific to a political (country) context. The policy legacies of a country reflect the economic production strategy and related welfare state reforms a country has pursued in the past, and—by means of mechanisms of path dependency—the ensuing configuration of interests that are dominant politically.

To conceptualize how policy legacies are relevant for shaping a particular social investment 'policy theory' in a country, it is helpful to refer to the different *time horizons* of particular social policies: *immediate vs future distributive effects* (see Jacobs 2011; Hemerijck 2015; and Chapter 32, this volume, on the temporality of social investment and its consequences).

Investments by definition entail immediate costs and delayed returns, that is, mainly *future* distributive effects. Spending on education or early childhood education—even though also having immediate benefits for, for example, teachers and parents—are typical examples of such investments. Policies pursuing stock and flow functions are closest to this investment profile. The distributive effects of such policies, moreover, are more uncertain and more universal in character, as the precise amount of returns and the specific beneficiaries are difficult to identify. On the other hand, policy legacies entail *immediate* distributive effects when the distribution of both the costs and the benefits is clearly identifiable at the time of spending. The literature usually refers to this kind of policies as 'consumptive' and both traditional social insurance as well as minimum income protection ('buffer') are examples of it, even though both obviously also have long-term productivity-enhancing functions.

Countries have a specific policy legacy in terms of the *ratio* of welfare resources that is bound in policies entailing immediate vs future distributive effects, or—in other words—in policies immediately correcting market outcomes vs policies enhancing productivity. This legacy in terms of an investment/consumption ratio structures the relative saliency of policy functions in a country, the problem diagnosis/growth strategy, as well as the reform capacity (Beramendi et al. 2015; Hassel and Palier 2015). Functional 'problem pressure', such as low employment performance or high child poverty rates do not explain directly the type of problems policymakers perceive as relevant, the diagnosis they make of these problems and the solutions they will adopt. The specific institutional context acts as filter of exogenous pressures and leads to different problems for different types of welfare and production regimes (Iversen and Wren 1998; Scharpf and Schmidt 2000).

Figure 31.1 stylizes the profiles of such legacies in a two-dimensional space. Countries can be situated in this space of policy legacies, depending on the emphasis their welfare state has been putting on either of the dimensions.

Countries in the upper left quadrant (particularly the Nordic ones) build on a legacy of stock and flow, as well as universalist buffer policies. All three investment functions are likely to be on the radar of national elites. The main challenge, however, refers to the fiscal (e.g. tax levels) and social (e.g. migration) sustainability of simultaneously maintaining stock, buffer, and flow

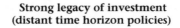

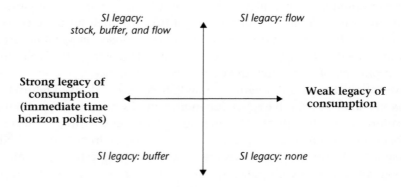

Figure 31.1. Institutional legacies and expected social investment agenda

policies universally. In these countries, the politics of social investment centre around the question *for whom* such an encompassing social investment strategy should be preserved (Lindvall and Rueda 2014). As shown in Chapter 19 in this volume, we indeed observe trends of a de-universalization of the Nordic welfare systems.

In liberal Anglo-Saxon countries and many countries of South East Asia, the policy legacy is relatively weak on consumption and stronger on productivity and activation (flow). The social investment strategy in these countries will be on securing minimum protection (buffer), as well as developing a growth strategy based on innovation and high-skilled services (like finance in UK or information and communications technology (ICT) in California or East Asia), thereby putting the question of skill development and education (how, by whom, to whom it should be provided in what quality) at the centre of a social investment agenda (stock). Achieving higher education is key for the upper middle classes in such countries with liberal labour markets.

On the bottom left side, countries that have relied more heavily on consumption policies generally do have effective minimum protection and automatic macroeconomic stabilizers (buffer), but they face the problem of declining employment rates, as employment in manufacturing shrinks and only few policy legacies are activation-oriented (mostly continental Europe). Given the unsustainability of mass employment in the manufacturing sector, as well as the prevalence of gendered new social risks, their social investment agenda centres on easing transitions into the labour market and generally increasing the labour-market participation of women (flow).

Finally, Southern European countries and Latin American countries generally have had a tradition of highly fragmented labour markets *and* welfare states. They tend to be only weakly productivity-oriented, that is, they have hardly any social investment legacy to build on. Despite clear functional pressure for a more productivity-oriented perspective, the actual social investment agenda in these countries remains comparatively very narrow, focused on some forms of outsider support and activation (flow and buffer). In the case of the Latin American countries still plagued by high levels of poverty, the buffer function of social investment is very important. The conditional cash-transfer programmes in Latin American countries such as Brazil, Mexico, or Chile are among the most visible examples of such a debate centred on investment in the poor. They might combine the 'buffer' with some form of 'stock' approach.

31.2.2 *Coalitional Potentials and Reform Outputs*

Our first claim referred to the historical contingency of *relative priorities* between buffer, stock, and flow on particular countries' social investment agendas. Our *second claim* refers to *reform-capacity*: the political success of social investment proposals that make it to the political agenda of a country will depend on the relative power of key political actors and their political interplay in terms of coalitional politics.

Who are the relevant actors in terms of social investment policymaking? Producer groups certainly contribute strongly to shape the reform strategy in a country and contribute to the diagnosis, since their focus is strongly productivity-oriented (Thelen 2014). Also, technocratic experts (oftentimes from international organizations) contribute to the advocacy of social investment in a country, because of their future-orientation (i.e. a naturally lower discount rate than politicians).

However, actual policy reform in a democratic context eventually depends on the presence of relevant social forces that are able and willing to support (a reorientation of) a policy. Such social forces are then mobilized and organized by—country-specific—collective actors (political parties or interest organizations, trade unions, etc.). Chapters 32 and 33 (this volume) both refer—theoretically and empirically—to the difficult intergenerational trade-offs the politics of social investment face. But most collective political actors mobilize *social classes* rather than age groups. Hence, thinking about support coalitions for social investment in terms of class coalitions makes sense politically.

Existing research argues and shows that the educated middle class is the strongest supporter of policies with distant and insecure returns, that is, investment policies (Gingrich and Häusermann 2015). Beramendi and colleagues (2015) give a number of reasons that might explain this: high education and productivity account for a lower discount rate, since needs are less immediate and employment prospects are relatively good in the post-industrial economy. In addition, the culturally egalitarian value profile of the educated middle class fosters support for the more universalist, insecure distributive effects of investment, not least in terms of gender. Finally, some degree of material self-interest also fosters support for extensive investments in different forms of education, training, and human capital formation, since these areas provide ample employment for the educated middle class (Kitschelt and Rehm 2014). In the developed world, the educated middle class is predominantly represented by the left parties (social democrats or green parties, depending on the country).

Even though the educated middle classes are the main supporters of social investment development, this class by itself is generally not big and strong enough to carry a policy reorientation to success. It is certainly true that the size of the educated middle class varies greatly across countries (depending itself strongly on the welfare state legacy, see Oesch 2015): in the Nordic countries, educated people in interpersonal service-occupations represent about a fourth of the workforce, whereas the same group remains way below 10 per cent in the Southern European countries, for instance (Beramendi et al. 2015). Hence, the 'natural' constituency supporting investment-oriented reforms is itself in part a consequence of the pre-existing institutional legacy, as claimed in Section 31.1, and this in turn obviously influences the opportunities for coalitions and reforms.

Nevertheless, there is a need for cross-class coalitions for actual policy change since the educated middle class is not big enough to carry alone a policy reorientation. We see two main class coalition potentials: a middle-class–business alliance on the one hand and a middle-class–working-class alliance on the other hand. The policy packages supported and adopted by these two alliances obviously differ, especially in terms of the accent they place on different functions of the social investment agenda. A middle-class–working-class alliance puts more emphasis on buffer than a middle-class–business alliance. In addition, class coalitions can combine stock, flow, or buffer policies with entirely distinct compensations and political exchanges, for example, with purely redistributive purposes or regressive income transfers that have no social investment function whatsoever. We will illustrate the diversity of policy outputs resulting from this coalitional constraint empirically in Section 31.3.

Theoretically, two key implications result from our two claims. First, the relative importance of buffer, flow, and stock policies differs strongly across countries, depending on the institutional legacies. The study of the politics of social investment cannot sensibly compare the identical catalogue of policies across countries to assess the extent of a social investment turn. The analysis of politics needs to start with the analysis of the agenda. And second, the politics of social investment are coalitional politics (Häusermann 2012). Hence, we cannot and should not study the politics of buffer, stock, and flow in isolation since they are likely to be part of broader political packages: the dynamics of class coalitions between the educated middle classes and potential allies may lead to seemingly contradictory or incoherent policy outputs, as well as to only partial implementations of social investment agendas.

31.3 Empirical Illustration: Family Policy Development in Bismarckian Welfare States: France, Germany, and Switzerland

In this brief contribution, we are obviously unable to provide empirical evidence for the effects of legacies and coalitional dynamics across all policy contexts. Rather, we want to discuss the empirical content of our two theoretical claims with respect to one key field of social investment—family policy—and three emblematic cases of countries: France, Germany, and Switzerland. With their familialist heritage, all three countries share a policy legacy that puts little emphasis on flow and stock in the field of family policy. Nevertheless, two of them—Germany and Switzerland—have in recent decades shown an explicit social investment turn in the field of family policy, especially with a stronger emphasis on the flow function. This turn, however, was supported by different coalitions between the two countries, which accounted for distinctive policy consequences. In France, by contrast, there was no discernible social investment turn in this field. In the following, we show briefly that these policy developments can only be understood through the combined effects of policy legacies and coalitional dynamics.

Both Germany and Switzerland share a very weakly developed investment legacy in the field of family policy. By the end of the 1990s, demographic worries, low female labour market participation and an increasing shortage of highly skilled workers have put the easing of family-labour market transitions (flow) high on the political agenda. Hence, in terms of social investment agenda, the two countries shared an acute focus on 'flow' policies among the investment-oriented elites. In Germany, however, the political class coalition supporting the expansion of investment-oriented family policy is based on a middle-class–working-class alliance between the electorates of the Social Democratic Party of Germany (SPD) and Christian Democratic Party (CDU)/ Christian Social Union (CSU) (see e.g. Morgan 2013; Häusermann and Zollinger 2016). Therefore, policies fostering labour market participation of women and support for external childcare (e.g. the reform of educational benefits in 2000, the extension of childcare infrastructure in 2004 and 2008, or the reform of parental leave in 2007) were consistently combined with purely consumption-oriented income transfers that pursue socially conservative, much more than 'buffer'-functions (in particular the at-home-care allowance introduced in 2012, but also the increases in traditional child benefits in 2001 and 2009). Expansion of immediate, consumptive transfers were the prize the Left had to pay to realize part of its social investment strategy in favour of medium- and high-skilled women.

In contrast, the Swiss work–care policy strategy was built politically on a middle-class–business alliance of support (given that the conservative Christian Democratic wing of working-class mobilization is much weaker than in Germany). This difference in the political class coalition shaped the form that social investment reforms took (see e.g. Häusermann and Kübler 2011; Häusermann and Zollinger 2014): an exclusive focus on 'flow', that is, female labour market participation incentives and childcare services (e.g. the introduction of maternity leave only for employed mothers for only fourteen weeks in 2004; subsidies for external childcare in 2003 and 2009; but an explicit rejection of tax credits for parents taking care of their children at home in 2013).

The comparison shows that both political alliances have contributed to a strong expansion of childcare services, but the overall social investment orientation—and thus eventually the policy outcomes—differ depending on the underlying coalition.

France presents a paradoxically contrasted situation. If one looks at outcomes, in terms of fertility rate, preschool coverage outside families, or female participation in the labour market, it seems—in terms of policy legacy—much closer to a social investment welfare state than many other Bismarckian countries. This may, however, be due less to an explicit social investment strategy than to an unintended effect of the policy legacy. The very same legacy today is preventing an explicit turn to social investment in France, such as turning to a dual earner model or to a more egalitarian investment in all children.

The French policy legacy stems from the late nineteenth century. At the time, there was a huge preoccupation about the low fertility of French families that led to traditional pro-natalist family policies favouring families with numerous children (adopted in the 1930s). Also, in the late nineteenth century, France elaborated its educational policy, as a pillar of the meritocratic Republic. These policies are leading to apparently good result in terms of fertility, childcare coverage, and female participation in the labour market. Outcomes are however much less satisfactory in term of full-time participation of women in the labour market (flow), and in terms of investment in children and youth (stock) as Programme for International Student Assessment (PISA) results for France show, or the high number of not in education, employment, or training (NEETs) in this country.

If Jane Lewis (1992) noticed that France has a 'nuanced' male breadwinner model, it was mainly because of the long-term existence of preschools ('école maternelle'), which were built not in a social investment spirit, but much more in order to educate as early as possible the future citizens of the French Republic. Indeed, even though childcare facilities (especially for children aged 3 to 6) have long existed in France, they were justified not so much by either the will to invest in human capital of young children (stock) or to allow mothers to work (flow), than to prepare good Republican citizens that were free from the influence of the (anti-Republican) Church. Part of this Republican model also means a very hierarchical and elitist school system, that continues to lead to dramatic failure rates amongst pupils (Chevalier 2016).

Family policies in France associate a strong pro-natalist stance with familialism. These characteristics have not been questioned recently (partly because of the mobilization of strong lobbies defending these familialist policies), and have so far prevented an explicit turn to social investment that would mean investing in all children (stock) and favouring women's full participation in the labour market (flow). Indeed, family allowances continue to be targeted to numerous families (no allowance for families with only one children: the investment in each child is not part of the policy, it is the *number* of children that continues to matter here). Parental leaves continue to be long (up to three years per child) and low paid, and are mostly taken by low educated mothers—France remains a country of 'free choice' (Morel 2007). Social benefits are still not individualized, and taxation continues to be based on household, hence hampering full-time employment for women. France continues to have a very elitist school system that prevents equal investment in all children, especially in secondary and tertiary education (Chevalier 2016). The defenders of the familialist policies as well as the defenders (and beneficiaries) of the existing school system all belong to the middle and upper classes, and are unwilling to switch to more egalitarian social investment types of policies. Both governing parties (socialist and moderate right-wing parties) who dominate in the French quasi-majoritarian electoral system, are trying to attract these electorates and would not dare to fiercely attack them head-on. It is thus unlikely that a shift towards explicit social investment would come from the two main parties. Changes may come either from small parties, such as the Greens, who are not unsympathetic to social investment, but whose principal policy concerns centre around other issues, like the environment.

Hence, relatively high levels of fertility and female labour market participation prevent France from becoming aware of a need for social investment. In addition, and related to the paradoxical effect of the policy legacy, the strong educational inequalities, as well as inequalities between men and women in the labour markets are not put on the political agenda, because there are no political coalitions able to raise these issues.

31.4 Conclusion

In this contribution, we have advanced two claims on the politics of social investment: social investment agendas differ depending on the policy legacies of a country, and social investment reforms depend on the availability of class coalitions supporting particular orientations and functions of social investment. This implies that analyses of the politics of social investment need to be context-specific in order to understand both the agendas and the policy outputs.

Our arguments entail a range of conclusions. First, there is not *one* social investment agenda, and there is not *one* social investment support coalition. In other words, social investment politics are *conditional*, not linear (it is not 'the stronger the left, the more social investment'), because the agendas differ and because policies have to be supported by political coalitions. The distinction between flow-, buffer-, and stock-oriented functions of social investment hint at this diversity of the social investment agendas, but the important thing is that these three functions—even though complementary—are unlikely to be developed jointly in particular contexts and their relative saliency is enshrined in policy legacies, rather than at the disposal of policy engineers.

Second, the politics of social investment is coalitional politics. Even though preferences at the level of citizens depend rather strongly on age, we argue that the actual politics of social investment largely consist in class politics, because collective actors mobilize in terms of class interests. Social classes, given their distinct socioeconomic status, have different discount rates and distributive preferences, both in the present as well as intertemporally. The educated middle classes cannot only afford a longer time horizon, they and their children are also more likely to harvest the distant fruit of investment.

Finally, since social investment politics is coalitional politics, social investment reforms may come in highly diverse, inconsistent, and contradictory forms. Not only will support coalitions compromise and coalesce around stock, buffer, and flow policies, but beyond these functions, there can be exchange between investment and purely consumption-oriented (possibly even regressive) redistribution. The political implication is that actual, coherent 'social investment turns' are unlikely. The implication for research is that we need to study the politics of social investment and social consumption jointly, not separately.

There are a number of factors that we have deliberately not integrated in our argument. A hard austerity constraint (see Chapter 6, this volume) would obviously create additional, exogenous constraints for social investment policies. Also, as stated by Anton Hemerijck in Chapter 1, assertive state capacity is required to secure and stabilize intertemporal bargains in both parliamentary and extra-parliamentary tiers of governance.

32

Three Challenges for the Social Investment Strategy

Investing in the Future, Taxes, and the Millennials

John Myles

32.1 Introduction

One reason I am attracted to the *new* social investment strategy is the fact that my generation—born in the 1940s and 1950s—were big winners from an earlier social investment spree, the one executed by post-war social reformers. *Post-war* investments in education and health care were massive by historical standards and my generation was the beneficiary. A key element in their approach was to break down traditional class barriers by expanding accessibility to post-secondary education. That was the magic bullet my professors were discussing in 1960 when I went to university. The new social investment model has changed the target group to very young children but to my ears, it has a familiar ring. Here, I raise three, somewhat neglected, challenges facing the contemporary version.

The first has to do with the future orientation of the social investment perspective (Jenson 2012: 66; Morel, Palier, and Palme 2012a: 6). By definition, social *investments* require policymakers and voters with patience and long-term time horizons (aka low discount rates) since they require foregoing some measure of current consumption in order to get long-term returns. In many cases the expected returns are unlikely to be realized for several decades. Hence, social investment requires lots of 'patient capital'. Like the Medici, many of the investors will be dead before their great cathedrals are completed. Will voters and policy elites be prepared to *wait?* Will they assume the risk?

Second, we are living in a very different policy environment from that of the sixties. Keynesianism was then in its heyday; policy elites believed taxation was good. They saw taxation as a tool not only to finance public services and welfare states but also as a tool to enhance economic efficiency. Against a background of strong economic growth, workers' pay packets rose year after year despite high levels of taxation. All that has changed as a result of tepid rates of economic growth and a revolution in tax doctrine since the 1980s.

Third, the fact that the cohorts born since 1980—the millennials—will be financing the social investment agenda seems to have gone relatively unnoticed in the literature. They are now in their twenties and thirties and are the de facto revenue source for any major new public investment over the next several decades. Pre-millennials are already 'ageing out' of both the labour force and the population. Hence, social investment advocates are placing big expectations on the millennials' financial shoulders, particularly in light of their responsibilities to pay for population ageing, to invest for their own retirement years, and to save us from global warming. Will they rise to the challenge?

32.2 The Problem of Time Horizons: Social Investment Requires Patient Capital

Today's publics and policy elites are much like the current generation of corporate chief executive officers (CEOs): they expect high short-term returns on their new 'investments'. Major social policy reforms, however, often require many years to mature, that is, 'patient capital'. As Pierson (2004: 90) highlights, major social reforms often produce slow moving outcomes where meaningful change in the dependent variable occurs only over the long term. The major reason is the demography of cohort replacement. Canadian pension reforms, for example, were basically finished by 1966 but big reductions in elderly poverty were not evident until the 1990s. Old age poverty rates declined rapidly from the mid-eighties on reaching Swedish levels of about 6 per cent by 1995. What had happened? It basically took thirty years for the 1965 Canada Pension Plan to mature. The first cohort to receive full benefits from the Canada Pension Plan turned 65 in 1976, the second cohort in 1977, and so forth; by 1995 most retirees were receiving full benefits and older cohorts had aged out of the population (Myles 2000).

Early childhood education (ECE) that has been so prominently featured in the social investment literature (e.g. Esping-Andersen et al. 2002) has the same temporal character. The promise is that more investment in early childhood education will produce a future generation of young adults better and, importantly, more equally equipped to function in a knowledge-based economy.

If we start investing heavily in 2-year-olds tomorrow, however, it will take a quarter of a century before we can expect measurable changes in the employment and wages of young adults. And it will take an additional several decades before the cohorts who missed out on our new programmes age out of the working age population.

Many of our initiatives in health, education, and welfare policy have characteristics of this sort. Smoking cessation and job training programmes are most likely to be successful among the young. Large population gains in longevity or employment will appear only slowly as older cohorts of smokers and the less skilled age out of the population.

New social investments in programmes with long time horizons require voters and policy elites with what the economists call 'low discount rates', a willingness to forego some significant share of current consumption in order to invest in projects whose benefits will only be realized in the distant future and may provide few or no benefits to those currently making contributions.

These examples illustrate an analytical problem that, following Alan Jacobs (2011), conventional welfare state theory has not addressed very much. The conventional approaches focus largely on point-in-time, redistributive politics—who bears the cost and who gets the benefits of welfare state expansion or retrenchment. The politics of public policy, however, is not just a struggle over *who* gets what but also over *when*, now or in the future (Jacobs 2011: 141).

Social investment advocates have a basic theoretical puzzle to solve. Under what conditions will the current generation make the social investment trade-offs required between current consumption and future well-being? As Jacobs (2011: 34) highlights, the standard assumption is that individuals typically place higher value on temporally proximate utility than on temporally distant utility. We are impatient investors. For political elites, impatience is systemically induced by the short-term time horizons of the electoral cycle. Nevertheless, he points out, there are also many examples of policy elites imposing large and substantial short-term costs on the electorate in order to enhance social welfare in the long term (Jacobs 2011: 36). Examples include recent shifts to funded pension systems, investment in infrastructure, and restriction of fishing quotas to replenish fish stocks.

My aim here is not to solve the puzzle but simply to put it on the analytical agenda. Under what conditions (and in which countries) can we expect the millennials and their political elites to make the inter-temporal trade-offs required to enhance their own futures and/or those of their children? Jacobs posits three necessary conditions for governments to choose long-term investments for which costs are absorbed in the short term. The first and most obvious is that governments will invest for the long term to the extent that they are electorally safe from retribution at the polls. You might think of this as the strategic component. The second involves a cognitive component, the problem of uncertainty that arises from the sheer complexity of long-term causal processes. Will investments in early childhood education today really provide the expected benefits in labour market outcomes twenty or thirty years from now? The third condition concerns the government's institutional capacity to enact the change. The key challenge here concerns the capacity to meet resistance from organized interests that would pay the costs of investment. Here, think about industry opposition to environmental regulations that require heavy investment in new technologies today in exchange for long-term environmental gains.

32.3 Where Will the Money Come From? The Revolution in Tax Theory and Slow Economic Growth

It is important to acknowledge that social investment advocates are asking the next generation to provide *additional* revenues to finance the welfare state. As Esping-Andersen (2002b: 5) argues, British Third Wayers were naïve to think that new investments in education, training, and activation could *substitute* for traditional income maintenance programmes. Cost-savings in traditional programmes (social assistance, unemployment insurance) may be realized as the social investment strategy matures but in the interim we are faced with a classic double-funding problem: the old trains have to be kept running until the new high-speed railways are in place.

New investments require new revenues and as Steinmo (2003) observes, policy elites have gone through a mass conversion on this issue since the end of the 1970s. The Second World War stimulated the growth of mass taxation and rising state revenues throughout the developed world. In most developed countries, revenues doubled as a share of gross domestic product (GDP) between 1930 and 1945. At the close of the war, there was an expectation that taxes would be rolled back to pre-war levels but that did not happen. As the logic of Keynesian economic management took hold, policy elites saw taxation policy as a tool for enhancing economic efficiency as well as providing revenues for health care, education, and income redistribution. Moreover, it was widely assumed that equity concerns should drive tax design.

All of that changed with the dramatic slowing of economic growth in the 1970s and the failure of Keynesianism, opening a political space for what might be called 'Hayek's revenge'. Beginning in the United States and the United Kingdom in the 1980s, newly ascendant doctrines insisted that the tax system should be concerned more with efficiency than with equity; that capital gains should be taxed at lower rates, if at all; that progressive taxes have disincentive effects; and that the tax mix should shift from income taxes to consumption taxes. In addition, fiscal elites became disillusioned with the idea of using tax incentives to achieve social and economic goals. As Steinmo (2003: 216) shows, tax policy experts on both the left and the right concluded that tax expenditures were simply 'giveaways to the rich and powerful'. Economic well-being would be enhanced by reducing the share of the public budget in the economy.

Anti-tax doctrine is a key part of the policy legacy we are leaving to the next generation and taps into other currents in public opinion: a general sense of risk adverseness and a decline of trust in government that has been ongoing for decades, particularly among the young (Dalton 2005). Tax aversion is particularly noticeable in the Anglo-Saxon countries where tax revenues as a percentage of GDP have fallen significantly since the end of the 1990s.

Policy paradigms do change of course. Two decades ago the Organisation for Economic Co-operation and Development (OECD 1994) was telling us that we faced a big trade-off between jobs and equality. A bit more inequality would be good for job creation. Now, the OECD (2015c) has concluded that high levels of inequality are bad for economic growth. Governments would be well advised to implement carefully designed policies to contain and to reverse the inequality surge. The question is whether the millennials can be weaned from the tax aversion and distrust of the public sector inherited from their elders.

32.4 Generational 'Luck' and the Millennials

I come from the infamous generation that entered young adulthood in the 1960s. I was born in 1943 in the shadow of Auschwitz and Hiroshima. Iron-ically, that made me part of what is no doubt the 'luckiest generation' in the twentieth century. In the post-war years my family was living through what was arguably the greatest economic boom in human history. I graduated from high school in 1960 just in time to take advantage of the great post-war expansion in university education. When we completed our degrees, jobs were plentiful. The 1960s was also a period of dramatic social policy innov-ation. In Canada, we got national health insurance and big expansions in public pensions, unemployment benefits, and social assistance.

My grandparents' generation, by contrast, had been much less lucky. Born in the 1880s and 1890s they lived through two world wars and the Great Depression with no welfare state. When the post-war boom came along, they were too old to take advantage. Because they had 'poor lives', old age was a virtual synonym for poverty in the post-war years. That's no longer the case— in part, a great success story for the post-war welfare state but also the result of generational luck.

There are two views of the next generation—cohorts born since 1980. On the one hand, they come from much smaller families and have had much more parental attention and parental economic resources at their disposal. Since they have few siblings, their inheritances when their parents pass away will be proportionately greater. They are certainly more highly educated than any previous generation. Their lifestyles and consumption patterns reflect the incredible technological revolution of the past thirty years. They would scoff at the puny black-and-white televisions that were the miracle of my childhood. Most significantly, young women have been the beneficiaries of the 'gender revolution' in education and employment since the post-war years (Goldin 2006). These gains have had a price however.

32.4.1 Postponed Adulthood

For my generation—the birth cohorts of high industrialism and today's retirees—the transition to adulthood occurred early in life. Industrial economies were relatively benign places for muscular young men and unmarried women, and from 1900 through the 1960s, the main age markers of reaching social and economic maturity fell decade after decade (Beaujot 2004). By the 1950s and 1960s, young adults were leaving home, getting married, and having their first child much sooner than any of the cohorts that had preceded them.

All that has changed. Since the 1960s, all of the age markers of social adulthood have been rising. Marriage and first childbirth now occur in the late twenties or early thirties. Marriage and fertility rates are down and large numbers of young adults are living with mum and dad into their twenties and thirties. Because of mum and dad, middle-class youth are not counted among the 'poor' since they have a roof over their heads, are well fed, and have access to the Internet. In lower-income households, in contrast, youth earnings have made a comeback as an important source of family finances (Newman 2012: 14).

The consequences of starting adulthood later have been compounded by shift in the age–wage distribution. Employment opportunities and entry-level wages have fallen. These developments, of course, vary across countries. In North America, both the cumulative earnings and the accumulated wealth of adults in their mid-thirties have fallen dramatically since the end of the 1970s. By 1999, the median wealth of young Canadian-born families (where the highest earner was aged 25 to 34) was down 26 per cent from 1984 (Morissette, Zhang, and Drolet 2002). And one shudders at the experience of young adults in Southern Europe.

Postponed adulthood is one reason we have made such little progress in reducing child poverty. While the social and economic life course has changed, biology has not. Because of biology, young adults (those under age 35) still comprise the vast majority of parents of our youngest children, and no social policy can change that.

32.4.2 *A Divided Generation*

But let's move on and imagine how the lives of our post-industrial thirty-somethings will evolve as they move through their working years towards retirement after 2050. As with any major change, there is good news for some and bad news for others.

The first cohort divide in a world of dual-earner families is between single-adult households with comparatively little labour to sell and those with two or more adult earners. While the earnings of young adults have been falling overall, family earnings for many young families have been rising because of higher female employment. By contrast, single-earner households—with or without children—are at greater risk and their numbers have been rising. Among the bottom quintile in the Canadian family income distribution, fewer than 10 per cent are currently living with a partner compared to 90 per cent in the top quintile.

The second divide that will persist over the working lives of the millennials has two sources: (a) the division between the educationally advantaged and disadvantaged; and (b) the multiplier effect of marital homogamy. Well-educated men and women tend to marry one another, forming families with high earnings and few risks of unemployment. Less well-educated couples tend to have lower wages and they are far more likely to experience periods without work. Marital selection based on education has risen and it is unlikely to abate. In the 1950s, there were few highly educated women to marry. The doctor married his nurse or his secretary. Today a male doctor is more likely to be married to another doctor, lawyer, or advertising executive.

While the rising *employment* of women has tended to reduce inequality, the rise in the correlation between husbands' and wives' earnings (earnings homogamy) has raised inequality (OECD 2015c: 221–6). In Canada, for example, the relationship between husbands' and wives' earnings looked somewhat like an inverted-U in 1980: women married to men in the lower middle of the earnings distribution had the highest earnings. By 2000, the relationship was monotonic such that the highest paid women were married to the highest paid men and the lowest paid women to the lowest paid men (Myles 2010). Morissette and Johnson (2004) show that while the growth in the earnings gap among *individual* workers with more or less education has been relatively modest in Canada, the corresponding gap in family earnings has risen substantially. Between 1980 and 2000, couples with two university graduates saw their average annual earnings rise by 14 per cent, to 22 per cent, while couples where both partners had high school education or less had stagnant or declining earnings. Putnam (2015) concludes that, in the USA, the growing economic divide is already evident in the growing social divide between the top third and everyone else in the next generation.

32.4.3 *Hidden in the Household*

Although Scandinavia appears to be an exception, elsewhere young adults are staying (or returning to) their parents' homes well into their twenties and thirties (Newman 2012). Is that a good or a bad thing? By my generational standards, leaving home at age 17 was initially frightening but quickly became a liberating experience. I can't imagine living at home into my twenties or early thirties. But, as Pope Francis says, who am I to judge?

There is an analogy between today's young adults and the elderly of the 1950s and 1960s. Because of their poverty, the elderly frequently moved in with their adult children. Since poverty is calculated on a household basis, they were no longer counted among the 'poor' so that a great deal of old age poverty was hidden in the household.

Today, the kids are living at home, often into their thirties, for much the same reason. Because we count 'poverty' on a household basis, they have become part of the invisible poor. Because of mum and dad, they have a roof over their heads, are well fed, and have access to the Internet. And based on recent accounts (Newman 2012), while many are experiencing post-adolescent stress, many others are quite content. They grew up in relative affluence by comparison to my grandparents and are well educated. So what's to worry about?

My most basic worry is about social waste or, in the language of the OECD (2015f:15), our 'squandered investment' in the education and skills of the next generation. By infantilizing our young adults, we are wasting their energy and talents. Young adults provided the energy, creativeness, and innovation that characterized the 1960s and 1970s, moving us forward. We often made dreadful mistakes. But the opportunity to make mistakes should never be taken away from any generation. The basic requirement of inter-generational justice is that we leave our children and grandchildren a world at least as good as the one we experienced, socially, politically, economically, and environmentally. Unwittingly, perhaps, the baby-boomers (and pre-baby boomers like me) are failing the next generation; not all of them, but many. I may be a victim of 'boomer nostalgia' since, according to Mintz (2015), our early transition to adulthood was something of an historical anomaly. If so, I am unrepentant so long as the challenges to social investment I have raised remain unresolved.

32.5 Conclusion

My main goal in this chapter has been to highlight three challenges to the social investment strategy and my list is undoubtedly incomplete. I confess, however, to being short on solutions.

I have indicated my scepticism about the potential of reallocating resources from so-called 'passive' welfare state cash benefits to finance new social investments in the short and intermediate terms. Kenworthy (2011b) demonstrates that cross-national differences in the income trajectories of the bottom decile continue to be almost entirely a function of 'passive' cash benefits, not social investment.

Although they may improve average capabilities, I also doubt that raising investments in education per se will solve the inequality problem because of pervasive 'Matthew Effects'. The main gains from higher education and training expenditures are likely to accrue to the most able and to the children of middle and upper income families (Cantillon 2014; Foley and Green 2015). I do see promise, however, in allocating (and reallocating) resources in favour of the less able in primary and secondary schools as well as in ECEC (see Chapter 12, this volume).

Restructuring post-secondary and post-graduate education to ensure earlier and higher-quality transitions into the labour market could also bring efficiency gains by reducing credential creep and years spent in schooling. Preparing students for the labour market is in line with the 'productivist' orientation of social investment advocates (Morel, Palier, and Palme 2012a: 2) but, I suspect, will meet resistance from a professoriate invested in the status quo. It took many years for medical schools to stop insisting on a classical education in Greek and Latin for entry.

Higher (and earlier) employment in well-paid jobs for young adults is the contemporary corollary of the post-war 'full employment' agenda. Although post-war reformers are often accused of creating 'passive' welfare states, the foundational thinkers such as Myrdal, Rehn, Keynes, and Beveridge agreed that a luxurious welfare state including compensatory social insurance was financially feasible only when most adult *males* were gainfully employed and paying taxes most of their lives. The gender mix of full employment has changed but not the intuition. Let's forgive the post-war reformers for their 'male-stream' version of the world and bring that intuition forward in time to enable the next generation to finance a social investment strategy.

33

Public Opinion and the Politics of Social Investment

Marius R. Busemeyer

33.1 Introduction

As the contributions to this volume impressively demonstrate, the social investment model has become a very prominent reference point in academic debates about the future of the welfare state in Europe and beyond. In order to become a politically viable project in the future, however, the transformation of existing welfare states towards the social investment model needs to be supported by large public majorities. Our knowledge about the 'politics' dimension of social investment, however, is rather limited so far, in particular with regard to the difficult topic of budgetary trade-offs between 'new' and 'old' social policies (Vandenbroucke and Vleminckx 2011). One of the main reasons for this lack of knowledge is that existing surveys of public opinion such as the European Social Survey (ESS) or the International Social Survey Programme (ISSP) do not include questions that would force respondents to make difficult choices between equally popular social policies.

This chapter presents new evidence from an original survey of public opinion in eight Western European countries gathered in the project Investing in Education in Europe: Attitudes, Politics and Policies (INVEDUC). In this survey, we asked European citizens for their support for increasing spending on different sectors of the education system as well as their willingness to accept cutbacks in other parts of the welfare state, if the social investment component would be expanded. In this chapter, I want to present some of the major findings of relevance for the political dimension of the social investment project. In general, my findings support the plausible expectation that increasing social investments is a popular policy. However, the data also show that citizens are much less enthusiastic about social investments if they would have to accept cutbacks in other parts of the welfare state.

The remainder of the chapter is structured as follows: in Section 33.2, I discuss some theoretical expectations with regard to the dynamics of public opinion on social investment. Subsequently, I will introduce the INVEDUC survey, followed by a more detailed presentation of major findings and a concluding discussion about the implications for the political viability of the social investment model.

33.2 Theoretical Expectations

Theoretical expectations about the dynamics of public opinion on social investment are actually more ambiguous than could be assumed. On the one hand, it could be argued that increasing social investments should be a very popular policy. Of course, this is to a large extent true for most social policies, since the ubiquitous public support for the welfare state has repeatedly been found to be a major factor preventing large-scale welfare state retrenchment (Pierson 2001; Brooks and Manza 2007). However, there are a number of reasons why social investment could be even more popular than other social policies. This is particularly true for the case of education, which is in many ways at the core to the social investment paradigm (Taylor-Gooby 2008: 4). Since expanding educational opportunities holds the promise to both contribute to mitigating social inequality as well as enhancing employability in today's globalized knowledge economies (Busemeyer 2014), Ansell (2010: 136) believes that the promise to support education is an 'archetypical crowd-pleaser'. As is argued by Bonoli (2013: 8), many social investment policies allow for 'affordable credit-claiming': expanding early childhood education (ECE), active labour-market policies (ALMPs), and family care policies are believed to be hugely popular with citizen-voters, because they help to address new types of social risks that have become more important in the past years, such as single parenthood, low skills, long-term unemployment, and long-term care for the elderly and disabled (Häusermann 2012). However, some social investment policies have the advantage that compared to traditional transfer and social insurance programmes such as pensions, passive unemployment benefits, or sick pay, they are less costly, that is, more 'affordable'.

On the other hand, however, promoting the transformation of existing welfare states towards the social investment model could be less popular than expected, in particular when difficult budgetary trade-offs are taken into account. Many policies in the social investment catalogue have a discretionary character, whereas the traditional social transfer and insurance programmes are based on legal entitlements. This is important, because in times of fiscal austerity, discretionary types of spending are easier to cut back (Streeck and Mertens 2011; Breunig and Busemeyer 2012) than entitlement-based programmes. In case of the former, policymakers can simply decide to lower the level of quality in service provision by 'stretching resources' (e.g. by increasing class size in schools or by hiring fewer teachers), whereas in case of the latter, politically costly legal changes are usually required. As famously argued by Pierson (2001) and others (Alber 1984; Brooks and Manza 2007), welfare state entitlement programmes create high levels of public support among the groups of beneficiaries who have come to depend on these benefits. If—as in the contemporary period of post-crisis austerity—no additional fiscal resources can be tapped, expanding social investment would require cut-backs in other parts of the welfare state, potentially triggering a public backlash.

Hence, in sum, it is an open question how deeply entrenched public support for the social investment agenda really is. Providing an answer to this question is crucially important in order to understand the political viability of the social investment paradigm, because it would help to identify potential political obstacles. Existing cross-national studies on the reform trajectories in European welfare states across the last decade or so show that not all welfare states have unambiguously moved in the social investment direction (Taylor-Gooby 2008; Vandenbroucke and Vleminckx 2011; Morel, Palier, and Palme 2012c; Bonoli 2013; Hemerijck 2013). On the one hand, our data on public opinion could reveal that the reluctance of some welfare states to move towards the social investment model is actually rooted in public preferences and attitudes. On the other, it could be possible to find that social investment is indeed as popular as many believe, which would then turn the focus towards the level of policymaking. If increasing social investment is popular, but still does not happen, we would expect to find particular political obstacles preventing the implementation of popular policies.

33.3 Measuring Public Opinion on Social Investment

Existing evidence from international surveys of public opinion suggest a high level of public support for social investment in general and education in particular. Figure 33.1 presents data on public opinion about increasing public spending on education from the ISSP Role of Government IV Module (2006). In this survey, respondents are asked whether they would 'like to see more or less government spending' in a range of policy areas, including education. Respondents are also reminded that an increase in spending 'might require a tax increase to pay for it'. But, except for this particular reminder, respondents

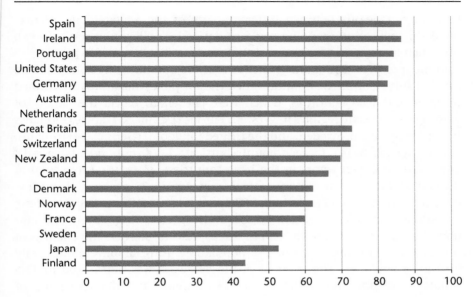

Figure 33.1. Public support for the government to spend 'more' or 'much more' on education

Note: Support for 'more' or 'much more' spending on education.

Source: ISSP Role of Government IV, 2006.

are not forced to make a choice between different spending areas. In Figure 33.1, I present the share of respondents aggregated at the country level who supported 'more' or 'much more' public spending on education, compared to those who preferred the same or less spending. The data show that increasing public education spending is supported by large majorities in many Organisation for Economic Co-operation and Development (OECD) countries. Surprisingly, public support for more spending is lowest in Finland—commonly regarded as a role model in education reforms—most probably because it is already at a high level in that country. Apart from Finland, spending increases are supported by majorities of 50 per cent or more up to huge majorities of more than 80 per cent in Germany, the United States, Portugal, Ireland, and Spain. Given these large majorities, it is surprising to find that actual levels of public spending in some of these countries have not moved much within the last decade. For instance, according to the most recent data from the OECD, spending (public and private) on educational institutions in Germany as a percentage of gross domestic product (GDP) only increased slightly from 4.9 per cent in 2000 to 5.1 per cent in 2011, which is still significantly below the OECD average of 6.1 per cent (OECD 2014c: 231).

One potential reason for this mismatch between public opinion and actual policy output could be that existing surveys do not fully take into account the budgetary trade-offs between different parts of the welfare state. Hence, increasing education spending could be a popular policy on a general level, but much less so once concrete distributional conflicts come into play.

In order to provide a (partial) answer to these questions, we conducted an original survey of public opinion on education policy most broadly defined in eight European countries, which were chosen to reflect the variety of existing welfare state regimes in Western Europe (Denmark, France, Germany, Ireland, Italy, Spain, Sweden, and the United Kingdom) (Gensicke, Hartmann, and Tschersich 2014). In each country, at least 1,000 respondents aged 18 and above took part (more in the large countries), amounting to a total of 8,905 observations. The response rate was on average 27 per cent, with a low of 20 per cent in Ireland and a high of 36 per cent in Denmark. The interviews were done using computer-assisted telephone interviewing (CATI), and random digit dialling (RDD) was employed in order to increase the chances of reaching the growing share of the population using mobile phones only instead of landlines. The conduct of the fieldwork was outsourced to TNS Infratest Sozialforschung. The dataset also provides two different kinds of weights, which are both used in the presentation of the descriptive statistics in Section 33.4. First, a design weight was applied in the case of landlines only to take into account different selection probabilities of individuals depending on the number of landlines per household and the number of potential interviewees in a given household; second, a selectivity weight was assigned that corrects for differences between the sample and the target population by referring to well-known stratification characteristics of the latter (using stratification variables such as age, gender, education levels, occupational status, regions, and employment status). A pre-test of the questionnaire was run in all eight countries in February/March 2014, with the main phase of fieldwork taking place between mid-April and end of May 2014. All interviews were conducted by native speakers.

33.4 Empirical Evidence

In the following, I will present data on two different aspects: first, how the support for public spending on education changes once respondents are made aware of existing budgetary trade-offs, and, second, how citizen-voters react when being directly confronted with hard distributional choices between social investment and social transfers.

Starting with the first topic, the survey contains the following quasi-experimental question. The full sample was divided into four equally sized groups and the assignment to one of these groups was entirely random. These four groups were asked for their support (on a five-point scale from strongly agree, agree, neither agree nor disagree, disagree, to strongly disagree) for the following statements:

Split 1: The government should increase spending on education.

Split 2: The government should increase spending on education, even if that implies higher taxes.

Split 3: The government should increase spending on education, even if that implies cutting back spending in other areas such as pensions.

Split 4: The government should increasing spending on education, even if that implies a higher public debt.

Figure 33.2 presents the estimated average levels of support for education spending including the 95 per cent confidence intervals across the four different groups and with the scale reversed, so that higher values indicate higher levels of support. As can be seen from the figure (and as is confirmed in pairwise t-tests), the differences in the estimated means are always statistically significant, which indicates that the framing of the question indeed matters. Once citizens are reminded of the budgetary implications of their expressed support for more education spending, this support drops.

In the framing without constraints, the mean level of support is 3.76, which implies that about 71 per cent of respondents are in favour of more or much more spending on education. Support for spending drops to 3.13 (48 per cent

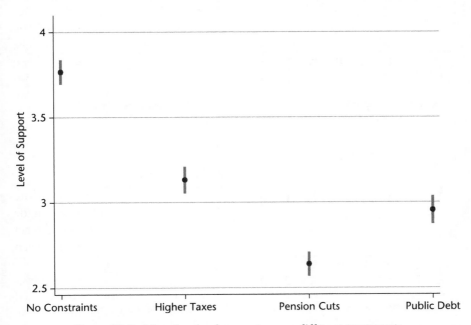

Figure 33.2. Mean levels of support across different treatments

of respondents demanding more or much more spending) when respondents are confronted with the fact that this would require higher taxes and to 2.95 (41 per cent demanding more or much more spending) when this would have to be paid for with higher levels of public debt. The largest drop in support for education spending, however, can be observed when citizens are confronted with the possibility of cutbacks in other parts of the welfare state, in particular pensions. In this case, support for spending decreases to 2.64, which is equivalent to a mere 26 per cent of the respondents demanding more or much more spending. These stark differences are remarkable in the sense that a seemingly solid majority of more than 70 per cent of respondents expressing support for more education spending is reduced to a rather small minority of 26 per cent, once they are confronted with the reality of cutbacks in other social policy programmes.

Figure 33.3 displays average levels of support grouped by the eight countries covered in the survey, which reveals some interesting potential feedback effects of existing welfare state regimes on patterns of public opinion. For

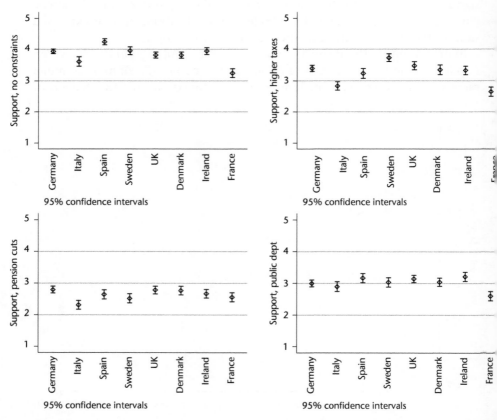

Figure 33.3. Mean levels of support across different treatments and different countries

instance, public support for education spending in France is conspicuously lower than in other countries, which already became apparent in Figure 33.1. In particular when reminded that higher spending on education would have to be financed with higher taxes or higher levels of public debt, support for spending increases drops precipitously, which might be a consequence of the dire state of public finance in this country. In Italy, in contrast, support for education spending drops furthest when respondents are confronted with the possibility that this would require cutbacks in pensions. Swedish citizens are in principle very much in favour of increasing education spending, even if that would require higher levels of taxes. Germans and Spaniards are equally positive about education spending increases (see also Figure 33.1), but seem to be less willing to accept trade-offs.

The survey contains another question that confronts respondents with the difficult trade-off between 'new' and 'old' social policies in an even more direct manner. This time the sample is not split into four, but in two equally sized groups. Again, assignment to the different groups is random. The first group is asked the following question:

What do you think about the following statement? To be able to finance more spending on education and families, the government should cut back on old age pensions and unemployment benefits.

In contrast, the second group is asked this question:

What do you think about the following statement? To be able to finance more spending on old age pensions and unemployment benefits, the government should cut back spending on education and families.

Again, responses to these questions were recorded on a five-point Likert scale (strongly agree, agree, neither agree nor disagree, disagree, strongly disagree).

The goal of these questions is to find out how citizen-voters react when faced with hard distributional choices, which in many ways are the kind of decisions that policymakers face nowadays in post-crisis Europe. The sample is split into two groups in order to find out whether citizens would be more willing to accept cutbacks in traditional social transfer programmes in order to finance social investment-style policies compared to the opposite trade-off.

The simple answer to this question is no. Table 33.1 presents the distribution of respondents across the different categories of the scale. The bottom row of Table 33.1 shows the mean level of support for spending increases is very similar. Although it continues to be statistically significant (as shown in an unpaired t-test), the magnitude of the difference is miniscule. Furthermore, compared to the questions discussed, average levels of support for spending increases—either on social investments or social transfers—drops precipitously once citizen-voters are confronted with trade-offs. The mean

Table 33.1. Trade-offs in spending preferences: social investment vs passive social transfers

	More Spending on Education and Families and Less on Old-Age Pensions and Unemployment Benefits		More Spending on Old-Age Pensions and Unemployment Benefits and Less on Education and Families	
	Per cent	Cumulative	Per cent	Cumulative
Strongly agree	1.60	1.60	1.14	1.14
Agree	9.66	11.26	6.68	7.82
Neither agree nor disagree	15.29	26.55	15.12	22.94
Disagree	43.37	69.92	49.62	72.56
Strongly disagree	28.44	98.36	25.20	97.76
Don't know/no answer	1.64	100.00	2.24	100.00
Overall mean (and standard deviation)	2.1115 (0.9857)		2.0685 (0.8867)	

Table 33.2. Disagreement with spending increases across different socioeconomic groups, share of respondents disagreeing or disagreeing strongly

	Old Age		Small Kids	
	Aged 65 and above	Aged below 65	Small kids at home	No small kids at home
More spending on social investment, less on social transfers	79.25 per cent	70.34 per cent	63.09 per cent	74.69 per cent
More spending on social transfers, less on social investments	77.13 per cent	76.19 per cent	76.15 per cent	76.52 per cent

level hovers around the value of 2, which is equivalent to the category of 'disagree'. Looking at the cumulative distribution of observations across the different categories, it can be seen that about 70 per cent of respondents either disagree or disagree strongly with spending increases. This roughly corresponds with the size of the minority who supported increasing education spending, even if would lead to cutbacks in pensions as discussed above.

Table 33.2 displays the share of respondents supporting spending increases within different socioeconomic groups. Here, I focus on individuals with small kids at home on the one hand (which would benefit from increasing spending on education and families) and individuals aged 65 and above as primary beneficiaries of pensions on the other. Of course, one could also add other beneficiary groups of social transfers, such as the unemployed.

The table reveals some interesting findings. First of all, increasing spending on social investment-style policies is more controversial than spending on social transfers. Expanding social transfer programmes at the expense of social investments is deeply unpopular across all groups, with more than 75 per cent of respondents voicing disagreement or even strong disagreement. The situation is somewhat different in the case of increasing spending on social investment policies. Not surprisingly, the elderly are more opposed to this (79.25 per cent) compared to the non-elderly (70.34 per cent). Furthermore, individuals with small children at home are significantly less opposed to spending increases on education and families financed by cutbacks in other parts of the welfare state compared to individuals without small children at home (63.09 per cent vs 74.69 per cent). However, this also shows that even this group of potential beneficiaries is by majority opposed to financing spending by cutting back other parts of the welfare state. In sum, this evidence shows that proposals to increase social investments might trigger particularly strong negative reactions from the beneficiaries of traditional transfer programmes, but also receive significantly more support from the new beneficiaries.

33.5 Conclusions

What are the main take-aways from this brief discussion of new empirical evidence on the public opinion of social investment? In general, there is good news and bad news for the political viability of the social investment paradigm. The good news is that the survey evidence clearly confirms that social investment policies, in particular education, are hugely popular with citizen-voters. Thus, expanding social investments should present an attractive opportunity for policymakers to claim credit. The bad news, however, is that public support for expanding social investments drops significantly, once potential trade-offs are fully acknowledged. When pressed, citizen-voters would maybe accept higher levels of taxes or public debt in order to finance additional spending, but they are particularly wary of cutbacks in other parts of the welfare state. Unfortunately, the reality in many countries in post-crisis Europe is that additional spending cannot be financed from new revenue sources but often requires exactly the kind of redistribution between different welfare state programmes that voters dislike. Therefore, promoting the social investment model holds enormous political potential on the one hand, but it also comes with a number of political risks on the other. In sum, proponents of the social investment approach (SIA) should be aware of the fact that its successful implementation most likely hinges on the ability of policymakers to pursue a balanced approach that strengthens the social investment pillar of the welfare state, while maintaining the social transfer pillar at the same time (Allmendinger 2009; Vandenbroucke and Vleminckx 2011).

34

Social Investment, Social Democracy, Neoliberalism, and Xenophobia

Colin Crouch

Anton Hemerijck comments that 'the social investment policy turn has not been associated with a ruptured economic crisis or pitched political struggle' and 'has generally been couched in non-partisan Pareto-optimal terms with economic and social progress advancing in tandem'. He draws attention to the appeal of different elements within the paradigm to both social and Christian Democrats, but also wonders 'whether the tranquil composure of the social investment paradigm is strong enough to withstand the novel economic context of austerity-biased E(M)U fiscal governance' (Hemerijck 2015: 254). These points bring out the poised position of the social investment welfare state (SIWS) between technocratic policy design and political conflict, and hint at an increase in the latter in the changed climate since the financial crisis of 2007–8. In the following I shall explore some aspects of this climate, together with other issues that question the technocratic emphasis of some SIWS discussions.

In addition to appealing to Social and Christian Democrats, the first appearance (outside Scandinavia) of the SWIS strategy also marked a constructive compromise between social democracy and neoliberalism, but it left too many social democratic needs unfulfilled. Any attempt at its renegotiation must deal with the fact that neoliberals today are more aggressive than in the late 1990s. However, the rise of xenophobic populism might persuade them of the relative attractiveness of a positive relationship with social democracy. A reformulated version of SIWS along Hemerijck's lines would be a fundamental part of such a relationship.

Two major forces are at work in European societies, which offer anything but 'tranquil composure'. One is the reinvigorated wave of neoliberal reform, which involves reducing protections from competitive forces across wide areas, especially in the labour market. Once the financial crisis had provoked the Eurocrisis, a phenomenon that had been caused primarily by financial deregulation was redefined as having been caused by social policy spending. A major failure of neoliberal policies paradoxically became a justification for strengthening them (Crouch 2011). The second force is the reaction of many working people to the disruption to life that globalization and deregulation bring, which is increasingly taking the form of xenophobic populism. Social policies of the kind associated with social and Christian democracy become the main victims of this clash between globalization and xenophobia. While the latter supports some forms of protective social policy, that is not its main aim, which concentrates on hostility to immigrants, the most visible and vulnerable manifestation of globalization encountered by working people. Social policies are often a major target of attack for right-wing populism, as immigrants and other 'undeserving' people can be depicted as the main recipients of social support, to the disadvantage of 'hard-working' natives who would, it is argued, be better off with lower taxes and less social policy. In the process the idea of a welfare state becomes detached from the concept of social citizenship, becoming instead the American idea of welfare as handouts to various non-deserving groups, almost a badge of non-citizenship.

There is therefore a triangular conflict among neoliberal globalization, xenophobic populism, and the social democratic (and to some extent Christian democratic) welfare state—the first two being on the attack, the last on the defensive. In some respects the sharpest conflict is between neoliberalism and xenophobia, since the former represents unfettered globalization, the free movement of all factors of production including labour, and the abolition of almost all protective safety nets. The populist movements oppose globalization, particularly the free movement of labour, are often protectionist, and sometimes seek to maintain social protection provided it is restricted to natives. In this perspective social and Christian democracy stand between the other two, representing support for free trade and free movement but with various kinds of social support. However, in some countries we see political alliances between neoliberalism and right-wing populism: the British Conservative Party, the US Republican Party, past Dutch and present Norwegian governments. This is a mutually incompatible combination. It can happen, partly because neoliberalism is an abstract, rather academic doctrine, not easily converted into mass democratic mobilization apart from a few slogans about lower taxes and less regulation. Neoliberals work behind the scenes, lobbying governments and international organizations outside the frame of democratic politics. When they need to make a wider public appeal it is usually articulated in alliance with the traditional right, which is why Christian democrats and other conservatives have often allied with them. But the traditional right is changing, with its moderate, largely Christian, component declining in favour of its nationalistic and xenophobic one; hence the growing potential of the oxymoron of neoliberal–xenophobic alliances.

Despite its internal contradictions, this is a highly powerful coalition, as it gains strength from its own negative consequences. The more that neoliberalism generates instability in people's lives, the more this can be blamed on 'foreigners' rather than on neoliberalism itself, creating popular support for the xenophobic part of the alliance. Far from suffering from the social instability it creates, neoliberalism is indirectly rewarded for it.

But there must be a serious question over the long-term viability of such coalitions. At what point does populism cease to concentrate its attack on immigrants and spread out to general protectionism and anti-globalization? In some cases, including the Front National in France and the current governing party in Hungary, that point has already been reached. In many other countries the confrontation will sharpen very considerably if the Transatlantic Trade and Investment Partnership (TTIP) goes ahead in any form. While in the longer term the comparative advantages that liberalized trade usually bring would benefit many parts of Europe and North America, this would only be after a long and disruptive process as whole industries and regional economies, particularly in Southern and Central Europe and some parts of the USA and Canada, entered crises of competitiveness, and collapsed. The serious problem of adaptation to the international economy now being experienced in south-west Europe would spread to several other regions. There would be considerable unemployment, disruption, and insecurity, which would likely increase the strength of right-wing populism. How far can neoliberals continue to share the political rewards that flow from association with this wave, rather than see their project become its eventual victim? At what point does a coalition with social democracy become more attractive to them? Was the shift in the Dutch government in 2012 from a neoliberal–populist coalition to a neoliberal–social democratic one just a minor reassembly of groups within a multi-party system, or did it presage a more substantive and general change that might be followed elsewhere? Both neoliberalism and social democracy are children of the Enlightenment, universalistic and modernizing forces. Or will there be countries where social democracy itself takes a nationalistic form? What would happen in Greece if European insistence on an uncompromising neoliberal solution to the country's crisis produces first a collapse of Syriza and then an amalgamation of a large part of Syriza's former support with the neo-Nazi New Dawn?

We have recently already experienced historical compromises between neoliberalism and social democracy, in the form of such 1990s 'Third Way' phenomena as Britain's New Labour, the German Social Democratic Party's (SPD's) Neue Mitte, the New Democrats in the USA, and more recently in Italy under the Renzi government. These movements all accepted a large part of the neoliberal market-making agenda, particularly in the labour market, but retained the social democratic welfare state, and completely resisted xenophobia. Its intellectual expression in labour and social policy terms can be found in the ideas of new social risks (NSR), flexicurity, and the initial forms of SIWS.

Behind these lay the fundamental implicit assumption of social democracy, that the expansion of markets is to be welcomed provided it is accompanied by public policy both to repair the disruption that markets cause and to provide the infrastructure that markets need if they are support high value-added competition rather than a race to the bottom. NSR analysis addressed this framework directly, with the essentially optimistic view that the nature of risks in workers' lives had changed since the basic problems of need and insecurity of twentieth-century industrial life had been addressed by the welfare state. More complex but also more positive risks confronted today's working population, which would enable money that had been spent confronting the old risks to be transferred to dealing with newer ones. The overall result would be an upgrading of the quality of the work force without increased net public cost.

Given the changed balance of class forces in post-industrial societies, this was possibly as good a compromise as the centre left could achieve; but for neoliberals it conceded too much. Since they have paradoxically emerged strengthened from the financial crisis, they are today less willing to accept compromise with organized labour or social democracy. The increase in public debt incurred by countries struggling with the crisis has been interpreted as justifying an intensified assault on social spending in general. The collapse of large parts of economies has supported calls to give all priority to restoring the strength of markets, at the cost of both the welfare state and policies for coping with environmental damage and climate change. One sees this dramatic change to the right in the conduct of the European Commission and European Central Bank (ECB), whose approach to the crisis in Greece, the other Southern European debtor countries, and Ireland has been for austerity and social retrenchment pure and simple. In Chapter 28 in this volume, Sonja Bekker shows that SIWS retains its place in the Europe 2020 project; but it remains at the level of bland general statements, and there is not a word of it in the conditions imposed on Greece. It seems that whenever a difficult issue arises it disappears from the agenda.

34.1 Revising and Reclaiming the SIWS Strategy

This is the wider political context in which the renewal of the SIWS should be seen. As formulated by Anton Hemerijck in Chapter 1, and supported by Frank Vandenbroucke and others, this renewal addresses many of the deficiencies of the original approach, while maintaining its position as a viable compromise offer to neoliberals, should these see that right-wing populism presents a bigger threat to their own project.

Based as they were on the pre-crisis period, initial NSR policies underestimated the degree of instability produced in the contemporary economy, and the consequent need for strong social-policy support if workers are to enjoy some protection from it. This is made more intense by the continuing growth of inequality. The very wealthy are taking an increasing share of consumption growth, leaving less to serve as a cushion against uncertainty for the rest of the population (OECD 2011a; Bastagli, Coady, and Gupta 2012; Förster, Llena-Nozal, and Nafilyan 2014). People respond by having increasing recourse to consumption credit, which brings the threat of a return of financial crisis. Meanwhile, social democracy is an even weaker force than it was in the 1990s, as its primary social support in trade unions has declined even further. Increasingly the social democratic labour movement finds itself drawn into protecting the interests of labour market 'insiders' rather than the working population in general (Beramendi et al. 2015; Rueda, Wibbels, and Altamirano 2015). Meanwhile, as other contributors to this collection make clear, the original SIWS strategy itself undermined universalism in various ways: it favoured those with personal resources over those without (the so-called Matthew Effect), and it privileged those who work over other members of society, challenging the role of the full-time parent.

If eventually they wish to return to a compromise with social democracy rather than that with the far right, neoliberals will therefore find that its terms have changed. The 'old' social risks are back and have disturbed expectations that there could be a major transfer of funds from old to new social policy. This does not weaken any of the arguments for SIWS; nor does the return of old social risks discredit the idea that there are new ones. We have to confront 'consolidated' old and new risks. This is feasible but expensive, requiring reaffirmation of the citizenship welfare state, not a restriction of it.

34.1.1 *Beating the Matthew Effect*

Countries with a strong social investment approach (SIA) remain economically successful, with lower levels of inequality than nearly all those that lack such policies—whether these be neoliberal cases like the USA and UK or the poor-quality welfare states of Southern and Central Europe. Although the arguments of Bea Cantillon, Kees van Kersbergen, and others in this volume that the SIWS approach has been accompanied by 'Matthew Effects' are valid and important, one cannot find counterfactual cases—that is, countries that have ignored SIWS and produced egalitarian societies with high levels of employment and high value-added products. The answer lies, as Bonoli,

Cantillon, and Van Lancker argue in Chapter 5, in ensuring that SIWS does not substitute for redistributive policies; rather, the more SIWS, the more need for the redistributive welfare state.

The case for SIWS, as Hemerijck makes clear, rests on the assumption that the economy will continue to create major opportunities for highly educated and skilled people. So far this has proved to be the case. Jan Tinbergen (1975) argued that there was a race in the labour market between technology and education: technology tended to destroy low-skilled jobs but to create opportunities for highly skilled ones; the question was whether education could keep pace with the change, producing enough people to take advantage of new up-market possibilities. So far the Organisation for Economic Co-operation and Development (OECD) considers that the race has turned out about even (OECD 2011a: 19–58): the number of jobs using high skills has increased at least as fast as the decline in the unskilled. But this optimism needs three corrections. First, a certain proportion of low-skilled jobs will always remain. It is the holders of these who suffer the negative consequences that is described in Chapter 5. Second, within the overall up-market move of the advanced economies there will always be major shock episodes, not just marginal adjustments with which equilibrium can cope, when major firms, industries, sometimes entire regional economies, collapse. These disturb the orderly adjustments of 'stocks, flows, and buffers', and should be expected to increase in frequency in the globalized economy. Eventually new and better activities should arrive to provide new opportunities in affected areas, but this can be a protracted process. In the meantime a population incurs major insecurity and possibly a move into poverty. This is when right-wing populism becomes a particular risk. Finally, we cannot assume that the Tinbergen race will continue to turn out so even. At least in some countries and regions the search for constant upgrading may be unsuccessful.

In all these cases, the protective welfare state continues to be necessary, partly to provide passive support, but also to give people the confidence to take risks when opportunities do occur, and to continue to consume and thereby support the economy.

The renewed SIWS project fully retains the original emphasis on the importance of paid work. It is consistent with the idea that the dignity and political power of people outside a small elite is rooted in the fact that their work is economically useful. This is contested by those who consider that work can be provided for all only under increasingly degraded conditions, and that we should explore such policies as a citizen's income, that contemplate some people not being required to work at all (Standing 2014). It is highly unlikely that such an approach would be accepted in a predominantly neoliberal age, but even if it were it would have negative implications. People dependent on a citizen's income would be highly vulnerable to drastic income loss should the political consensus that had introduced it change, as is likely.

Several contributors to this collection perceive that behind this issue stands a more fundamental one: the normative base of citizenship and the relation of SIWS to it. SIWS is consistent with the approach to citizenship that sees it, not as an abstract set of entitlements, but as something we enjoy because our society needs us. We contribute our labour power and skill, and it is in exchange for this that we proudly, not gratefully, expect various rights. This 'rights imply responsibilities' approach is sometimes seen as conservative, but this is an error. If rights do not have this kind of basis, they can quickly become seen as privileges that have been granted, whether by a ruling elite or by our fellow citizens, either of which might decide to remove them. The work-based concept of citizenship is characteristic of Nordic social democracy, and it acquires new importance in highly econo-mistic neoliberal societies.

If work has this centrality to citizenship, it becomes a highly important collective good. This is problematic, since it is requires a base in the market if it is not to become highly inefficiently organized. The collective good cannot be secured by the state just providing jobs, or nowadays even through Keynesian demand management. The state can, however, ensure that its activities do not hinder job creation in the market but instead provide incentives for it. It is, for example, important that forms of taxation like employers' contributions to social insurance do not give employers a disincentive to employ labour; contributions need to be based on turnover, not employment. The costs of job security need to be borne by the state rather than by employers, which for Southern European countries in particular means a move from employment protection laws (that throw the burden of workers' security on to the employer) to generous unemployment support and the SIWS agenda. It might have been acceptable for employment protection to be borne by employers when these were benefiting from protectionist walls maintained by governments, as in the major periods of post-war industrial development in Southern Europe and elsewhere; but in open labour markets it can become a major hindrance.

Tax credits for people in low-paid work and other elements in the agenda to combat Matthew Effects (see Chapter 5, this volume) are also important. These measures too imply a shift in the cost of supporting employment and wages from employers to the state. This must then be compensated by adequate general, not employment-related, levels of business taxation. The point is to facilitate a working population able to compete in open labour markets but with various forms of non-protectionist state support. The normative base of these is citizenship entitlements, not 'welfare handouts'.

34.1.2 *Paid Work and Parental Work*

This argument implies citizenship rights for those who are preparing to work, who are working, who would work if they were not sick or disabled, or who have worked until they are old. This does not include everybody. Chiara Saraceno, in Chapter 4, and others in this volume warn of negative consequences of this approach for parenthood. The pressure to be members of the paid workforce is causing some resentment among women in the Nordic countries who would prefer to be full-time mothers. Traditional Christian, in particular Roman Catholic, social policy always stressed the value of motherhood, and this has been part of its own distinctive critique of the values of capitalism and the market economy. These values have become unpopular during the current shared neoliberal and social-democratic agenda of eliminating the barriers to women's labour force participation, particularly because it has always been implicated in male domination. But this does not dispose of a serious argument.

I have framed this chapter as a search for a new compromise between neoliberalism and social democracy against a conservatism that is becoming xenophobic and potentially protectionist. I have implicitly assumed that other elements of conservatism, particularly religion, are in decline, at least in European societies, and can be ignored. But there are important babies in the conservative bathwater. One of them is the right of individuals and families not to have their lives dominated by the market, including the labour market. This has implications beyond our present concerns, but the place of parents (not just mothers) in the work-based model of citizenship is highly relevant. The SIWS agenda addresses this very directly with its emphasis on childcare, but needs to go further. Social policy must recognize the right of a parent of preschool children to be a full-time parent—helping to prepare the next generation of working citizens—and to receive public financial support, even if they have a partner in paid employment. Such rights have been recognized for mothers, and the idea of paid parental leave from work for limited periods is beginning to be accepted for fathers too. These policies need to be developed further.

34.2 Conclusion

I have placed the new stage in the development of SIWS policies that Hemerijck has launched in the context of the ongoing pattern of shifting conflicts and alliances among social democrats, conservatives, and neoliberals. The current form of that pattern has a reinvigorated, post-crisis neoliberalism and an aggressive xenophobic populist form of conservatism in an internally contradictory alliance against a defensive and weakened social democracy. SIWS belongs clearly to the social democratic family of policies, but it offers a shared agenda with neoliberalism, because of their shared acceptance of the priority of work, competitiveness, and globalization. One form of that compromise, during the Third Way period, enjoyed important successes; but it underestimated the need for broader welfare state policies in the turbulence of the global economy. We need to combat 'consolidated' old and new risks, with high unemployment support as well as active labour-market policy (ALMP). Capacitating and compensating welfare states are complementary, not rivals. The Third Way compromise with neoliberalism was less demanding, since NSR analysis assumed that the 'old' social risks had gone. They are back with a vengeance. Meanwhile, however, following the financial crisis many neoliberals have ceased to believe that they need compromises. For them to contemplate such a deal, they need to become concerned at the threat to their project posed by right-wing populism, and to accept that populations will not respond to major problems of adjustment as though they were depersonalized factors of production.

Part 8
Conclusion

35

The Uses of Affordable Social Investment

Anton Hemerijck

35.1 Social Investment at a Crossroads

From the early 2000s on, a good number of welfare state researchers have come down from the ivory tower of academia to advocate a new approach to welfare recalibration, based on a distinct shift in policy attention from ex-post social risk insurance to ex-ante risk prevention, to foster economic security and social inclusion in an era of rapid socioeconomic restructuring (Giddens 1998; Midgley 1999; Ferrera et al., 2000; Esping-Andersen et al. 2002; Taylor-Gooby 2004, 2008; Hacker 2006; Jenson and Saint-Martin 2006). The challenges of economic globalization, trade liberalization, skill-biased technological innovation and digitilization, family and gender change, the rise of the service economy, population ageing, fiscal austerity, economic crisis management, high unemployment, sluggish and imbalanced growth, increased poverty, inequality, and large-scale migration, affect (vulnerable) citizens through highly personalized life-course disruptions, for which there is no simple actuarially neutral solution. Twenty-first-century welfare provision, they argued, required multidimensional and highly integrated welfare policy responses, which allowed for 'tailor-made'—gender and life-course sensitive—'bundles' of capacitating social services, income benefits, and employment regulation.

This volume has taken the promises of the social investment approach (SIA) seriously by exploring its policy theory and underlying normative commitments, tracing its evolution in policy practice, analysing its positive and negative effects in terms of socioeconomic well-being, ranging broadly from employment, to labour productivity, gender equality, and relative poverty and redistribution, highlighting the role of international organizations in setting the social investment agenda, and making sense of the politics of long-term social investment in times of troubled economics and impatient politics.

Why did the idea of social investment rise and gradually mature before the onslaught of the global financial crisis? How do we identify and empirically trace particular policy mixes and reforms that manifest a social investment approach as distinct from other forms of welfare policy interventions? What do we know about the well-being impact of social investment policy innovation, its mission and hoped-for accomplishments, but also potential drawbacks of creating new forms of inequality and labour market dualization? Can such adverse side effects, brought to our attention by the critics of social investment, be corrected or are there inherent biases to the 'meritocratic' employment-centred and service-oriented social investment reform?

The fallout of the 2008 global financial crisis inadvertently begs a more cardinal question. Is the SIA really still relevant? The aftermath of the Great Recession has created a new austerity context that conspires heavily against costly social investments. Acute pro-cyclical fiscal consolidation is not the only hindrance to proactive social investment reform in the new hard times. The rise of national populist welfare chauvinism, attempting to preserve traditional social protection for native communities by excluding migrants and other outsider groups, is entirely incompatible with inclusive dual-earner family-friendly social investment recalibration. The years ahead will thus differ markedly from the decade leading up to the crisis when the social investment paradigm progressively gained intellectual and policy credibility, but not, I hasten to add, wholesale political support.

Immediately after the 2008 global credit crunch, policy attention concentrated, perhaps justifiably so, on fiscal crisis management. Thus far austerity politics has however not ignited a healthy recovery from the crisis. The social aftershocks of the economic crisis and austerity cuts reform have arguably been more disruptive. The world over has witnessed a sharp increase in employment precariousness, deepening the ongoing trend towards labour market polarization. Similarly, levels of household inequality and child poverty have continued to increase.

By the mid 2010s, many experts, especially those working at international think-tanks returned to reconsidering proactive social reform, inspired by the ideas of social investment introduced round the turn of the century, under the various guises of the 'active', 'enabling', 'pre-distributive', 'developmental', 'post-industrial', and 'dynamic' welfare state (Garfinkel, Rainwater, and Smeeding 2010; Morel, Palier, and Palme 2012; Bonoli 2013; Hemerijck, 2013; OECD, 2014; 2015; Garland 2016; Stoesz 2016).

Will the social investment paradigm resume pride of place in the debate on global welfare state futures? Can we expect a rebalancing of inclusive welfare provisions along the complementary policy functions of upgrading human capital 'stock', easing the 'flow' of gendered labour market and family life-course transitions, buttressed with inclusive income safety-net 'buffers', required to survive and prosper in an ever more competitive global knowledge economy? And to what effect: is social investment a 'magic bullet': does it bear socioeconomic fruit in hard times and can it sustain a more inclusive global economic order? Or, is it too late for social investment to step into the limelight again? Will the social investment comeback revert to marginality as the calls for deficit and debt reduction, based on the mantras of 'one-size-fits-all' balanced budgets, labour market deregulation, and disinflation, grow again louder? Or, alternatively, will negative side-effects further fuel national populism and welfare chauvinism in protectionist direction?

With these questions in mind I approached close to fifty leading experts in social policy from various disciplines, including economics, law, political science, and sociology, to write a short and focused chapter on various aspects of social investment—critical and more complementary. Over the previous thirty-four chapters, all participant contributors have been testing new theories and methods for improved academic insight and also for more practical policy answers—broadly from a comparative perspective. For the final pages of the volume, I will not venture to synthesize the many observations, inferences, and reflections. In so far as this final chapter serves the purpose of closing words, it focuses on what I take home from the preceding thirty-four chapters as the larger 'uses' of social investment. I distinguish between five of such uses of social investment.

The overarching first 'use' of social investment concerns its 'paradigmatic' bearings. Whether and to what extent does the SIA, as it evolved matured over the past decade, add up to a distinct policy paradigm for twenty-first-century welfare capitalism? An intimately related second 'use' of social investment relates to what extent new conceptual insights have inspired novel especially methodologies in social policy research, inspired also by critical receptions that often accompanies theoretical innovation. The second use relates to methodological innovation, in particular with respect to methodological approaches able to (dynamically) assess purported quantitative returns in socioeconomic well-being, in full recognition of the many caveats intrinsic to making prospective conjectures. Given the progressive, admittedly uneven, diffusion of the social investment policy priorities across the globe, a third 'use' bears on the practical ramifications, both intended and unintended, of social investment reform, here understood in terms of virtuous policy complementarities across the policy functions of 'stocks', 'flows', and 'buffers', including their governance prerequisites, as theorized in Chapter 1 of this volume. The politics of social investment and its discourse of 'capacitating' social justice represents the fourth use of social investment in its uphill battle against the fiscal austerity backlash and the rise of populist welfare chauvinism. Will social investment stand up to fiscal austerity and insider-biased welfare chauvinism, or is that hopeful guess overly naive? The fifth and final 'use' is geographically confined to the European Union (EU), the birthplace of social investment. After Brexit, the conundrum of economic imbalances between 'core' and the 'periphery' is likely to deepen the EU's legitimacy crisis. What are the prospects for aligning EMU governance and the SIA for an assertive inclusive growth strategy able to counter the economic imbalances unleashed by the crisis and further amplified by the EU's austerity reflex in recent years?

The articulation of these five 'uses' of social investment for the remainder of the final chapter is primarily meant to invite readers from academia and policy-making circles to take the social investment debate to a new level—no longer in terms of social investment advocates versus critics, but rather one of seeking a more nuanced and empirically grounded understanding of the kinds of integrated policy mixes of social protection, labour market inclusion, and human capital promotion, including relevant political-institutional support structures, for improving twenty-first-century life chances for all.

35.2 From an Aspirational Metaphor to a Coherent Policy Paradigm

It is fair to say that the social investment perspective has come to inspire welfare reform the world over since the 1990s, less so in terms of an overarching social investment master trend, but more as a search process triggered by disenchantment with neoliberal recipes of the 1980s and 1990s and the return to power of the centre left in many Organisation for Economic Co-operation and Development (OECD) countries and the growing political strength of the left in Latin America. In the process, the objective of economic security and social protection came to be redefined in terms of more encompassing human development strategies, whereby employment and human capital improvement were not be divorced from poverty alleviation and inequality mitigation. The broader human development ambition of the SIA, combining and integrating investments in human capital 'stock', 'flow' provisions to ease labour market transitions, and safety-net 'buffers' to protect against income and poverty shortfall, can be observed in welfare reform trajectories across many of the member states of the EU (Hemerijck 2015). Likewise, the Latin American example of cash-conditional income transfers (CCTs), complemented by educational and health care interventions designed to improve human capital and support labour market integration, are representative of the global shift of integrating 'compensating' to 'capacitating' welfare provision to bolster personal and familial resilience and mitigate the inter-generational reproduction of poverty and joblessness (Barrientos 2013).

Does the global trend towards more integrated and multifunctional welfare provision with the triple aim of strengthening productive capacity, enhancing employability, and reducing poverty in an integrated fashion add to a fully fledged social investment welfare paradigm shift? In some of the preceding chapters, notably Chapters 2 and 29, doubts continue to be aired as to whether one can speak of the SIA as a coherent paradigm, transcending earlier conceptualizations of the demand-oriented Keynesian welfare state of the post-war decades and the supply-side market-oriented neoliberal critique of the interventionist welfare state as distorting optimal (labour) market allocation, which ascended to hegemony in the 1980s and 1990s. Many other contributors, ranging from Lane Kenworthy (Chapter 7) to Günther Schmid (Chapter 9), Margarita León (Chapter 10), Verena Dräbing and Moira Nelson (Chapter 11), Charles Sabel, Jonathan Zeitlin, and Sigrid Quack (Chapter 12), Brian Burgoon (Chapter 14), Jane Jenson (Chapter 18), Martin Seeleib-Kaiser (Chapter 20), Alain Noël (Chapter 23), Timo Fleckenstein and Soohyun Christine Lee (Chapter 24), Evelyn Astor, Lieve Fransen, and Marc Vothknecht (Chapter 27), Maurizio Ferrera (Chapter 30), Silja Häusermann and Bruno Palier (Chapter 31), John Myles (Chapter 32), Marius R. Busemeyer (Chapter 33), and Colin Crouch (Chapter 34), do attach paradigmatic qualities to the SIA.

Taking heed of the seminal writings of Peter Hall on the political power of economic ideas, I ascertain a policy paradigm as an overarching set of ideas that brings the cognitive understanding of causal relations between policy efforts and outcomes and the political mobilization behind social and economic priorities together with the institutional structures that allow economic policymaking to be conducted in a coherent fashion (Hall 1989, 1993). A policy paradigm hereby specifies in unison how salient problems facing (policymakers) are to be perceived, what objectives are to be privileged and what sort of policy instruments have to be put to use to reach political objectives, and what kind of institutional capabilities are required to implement, administer, stabilize, and monitor policy progress. Once a policy paradigm is taken for granted, intellectual inertia naturally prevails. Any stable 'goodness of fit' between salient political premises and causal understandings of socio-economic reality inevitably imply blind spots for alternative causalities and competing priorities. With the passing of time, faltering policies may spark a novel search process for alternative solutions, whereby competing policy paradigms may gain credibility. Empirical backing and growing support in academia, however, is never sufficient for effective paradigm change. As we know from Hall, alternative policy theories only become relevant when they provide solutions to impending political problems. In the process of politicization, persuasive discourses and frames are often invoked to catch the public imagination about the issues at stake, and especially to delegitimize competing policy paradigms. Changing economic conditions, by altering policy outcomes indirectly modify power positions of relevant stakeholders, which can foster a political reorientation and steer policy in new directions— albeit not without significant resistance from the political carriers of still prevailing policy paradigms. To underscore the paradigmatic portent of the social investment turn, a comparison with the Keynesian-Beveridgean welfare compromise of the postwar era and its antithesis, the neoliberal critique on the interventionist welfare state, is perhaps in order.

35.2.1 *Antipodes of the Keynesian-Beveridgean Welfare State and the Neoliberal Critique*

The defining innovation of the modern welfare state was that social protection came to be firmly anchored on the explicit commitment to grant 'social rights' as positive freedoms to citizens in areas of human need and well-being. The overriding political objective was (male) full employment and universal social security in cases of unemployment, sickness, disability, and old age poverty. The Keynesian revolution in economic theory, based on an understanding of inherently volatile financial markets and the business cycle under industrial capitalism, exemplified how the political objective of full employment can be supported by countercyclical macroeconomic demand management and fine-tuning. In the event of a recession, comprehensive social insurance and adequate job protection, for which the 1942 and 1944 Beveridge reports gave the necessary policy ammunition, were to operate as automatic demand stabilizers, thereby protecting families from demand-deficient cyclical unemployment and economic hardship (Beveridge 1942, 1944). It is important to remember that the Keynesian-Beveridgean goal of full employment was conscripted to male breadwinners only. Post-war social security repertoires thereby reinforced traditional family structures, with women and children dependent on male employment opportunities and wages, and their deferred rights in sickness, unemployment, and old age insurance. The political narrative of the post-war welfare state compromise evoked the image of full (male) employment in a free society without 'want, disease, ignorance and squalor'. In the fortuitous event of (male) full employment, wage coordination between the social partners and the state was required to mitigate inflationary pressures in the post-war industrial economy.

If Keynesian macroeconomics was the brainchild of the Great Depression, the revival of neoclassical economic theory in various guises was the intellectual product of the crisis of stagflation, the malignant combination of cost-push price inflation, economic stagnation, and structural unemployment (Scharpf 1991). Economic cycles were to be understood as outcomes of exogenous shocks—the oil shocks of the 1970s being the clearest cases in point—combined with slow transmission through the real economy as the result of market rigidities, including labour market distortions related to welfare provision. From this perspective, unemployment became diagnosed as a microeconomic problem of supply-side 'hysteresis', and in particular low search intensity and poor motivation, because of deficient incentives produced by generous welfare provision and job protection legislation. In addition, strong 'insider–outsider' cleavages reinforced unfavourable employment chances for the young, women, the old, and the low skilled (Lindbeck and Snower 1988; Rueda 2007). In terms of macroeconomic management, policymakers were advised to introduce anti-inflationary monetary and rule-based fiscal policies to underpin micro-level supply liberalization (*structural reform*) for optimal labour market allocation in a more service-oriented economy. Closely associated with a 'market-distorting' view of generous welfare provision and rigid labour markets, there is the conjecture of low (public) service productivity, often associated with so-called 'Baumol cost disease' (Baumol 1967). When public service pay increases following wage developments in the more dynamic capital-intensive private sector, low productivity services become relatively more expensive. In effect, the welfare state, by trying to reduce inequality through a politics of income redistribution and public employment expansion, 'crowds out' private economic initiative reinforcing labour market distortions, leading to lower labour supply, less training, more net wage compression, higher unemployment among the old, the young, and the low-skilled, and secular stagnation, more generally. In short, generous welfare provision is inevitably besieged by what the American economist Arthur Okun coined the 'big trade-off' between equality and efficiency (Okun 1975). In terms of discourse, neoliberalism portrayed the Keynesian-Beveridgean welfare state as a 'nanny state', sapping all entrepreneurial initiative and personal responsibility from the free market economy. In defending the neoliberal turn, the image that 'there-is-no-alternative' to undistorted market competition reverberated strongly with conservative parties in the 1980s and 1990s, calling for welfare retrenchment, labour market deregulation, and public service privatization. Rich democracies should embrace higher level inequality as an imperative for competitiveness, but also for achieving full employment through flexible labour market self-adjustment.

35.2.2 *The Quiet Social Investment Paradigm Shift*

After the mid-1990s, in the span of a mere decade, the notion of social investment matured from an intuitively appealing metaphor of 'social policy as productive factor' to nothing less than a paradigmatic rethink of an active welfare state for the twenty-first-century knowledge economy, based on: (1) novel causal insights on how (old and new) social risks impact on life chances; (2) political objectives to be privileged; and (3) mutually reinforcing policy instruments and governance institutions best able to foster resilience and mitigate social vulnerability in knowledge-based economies with ageing societies.

With its emphasis on prevention of harm rather than compensating for damage done, the social investment policy paradigm is emblematically more *future-oriented* than the two antecedent paradigms. By privileging the 'preparing' of individuals, families, and societies to respond to the new risks of a competitive knowledge economy, by investing in human capital and capabilities from early childhood through old age, rather than through policies of post hoc 'repairing' damage after moments of economic or personal crisis, the social investment paradigm is fundamentally *preventative*. The Keynesian welfare state, by contrast, is principally *reactive*, coming into play in times of recession, until male full employment is restored. Neoliberalism, as an even more general theory, is in a sense *ahistorical*. Indiscriminate fiscal austerity and market-clearing product and labour regulation should prevail under all circumstances, irrespective of the economic cycle.

In the social investment perspective, full employment is no longer the ultimate policy goal per se. Rather, high levels of employment or raising labour force participation are required to service the 'carrying capacity' of active welfare states, so as to counter the intergenerational transmission of social disadvantage. In terms of *policy theory*, the social investment perspective takes issue with the neoliberal claim that generous welfare provision implies a loss of economic efficiency, by making a strong case for how productive social policy *'crowds in'* growth, employment, social protection, and, not least, fairness. There are many 'multiple dividends' or 'life-course multipliers' at work. Quality childcare services, alongside effective parental leave arrangements, supported by appropriate tax and benefit incentives and active labour-market policies (ALMPs), enabling more parents to engage in gainful employment without career interruptions, are representative social investment policy instruments. They improve the chances of finding jobs especially for mothers, thereby boosting household incomes, while at the same time helping their offspring to a strong start.

With its strategic concern with work–life balance and family reconciliation, the social investment paradigm radically transcends the *maternalist* bias in the Keynesian male breadwinner full employment welfare state and the *gender-blind* neoliberal critique of the post-war welfare state. However, there is a long way to go before *gender equity* is achieved. From a critical feminist perspective, Chiara Saraceno in Chapter 4 of this volume rebuts the instrumental focus on 'productive' employment as this indirectly delegitimizes non-paid family and maternal care as a meaningful activity, which in turn may undermine the necessity of more informal male parenting care. She also points to looming new dichotomies between deserving (e.g. children, the young) and undeserving (e.g. the old, the severely disabled, the 'inactivable') social investment clienteles.

Although the social investment perspective underscores the need for strong social security 'buffers', it deviates from the passive male-breadwinner social security portfolio of the mid-twentieth-century Keynesian-Beveridgean welfare state, singularly focused on ex post income compensation 'buffers' as important for aggregate demand stabilization and consumption smoothing, by underscoring the importance of 'stocks' and 'flows' in the gendered knowledge-based and high employment economy. Lifelong education, from early childhood education and care (ECEC), general education, vocational training, and adult learning, improves the quantity and quality of human capital and enhances employment opportunities as more people contribute to the welfare state's 'carrying capacity'. In the SIA, upgrading and up-keeping human capital can therefore not be divorced from poverty relief and basic economic security as a citizenship right. Social protection 'buffers' remain of central importance in mitigating economic hardship, but should be designed to ease labour market 'flow' and to smooth critical life-course transitions to mitigate the risk of skill erosion.

With neoliberalism, the social investment paradigm arguably shares a concern with the 'supply side', but is based on the more gendered understanding of labour market 'flow' and a far more positive theory of state, especially when it comes to human capital 'stock'. In the neoliberal paradigm, a perfectly deregulated labour market, unburdened with social protection 'buffers' is believed to set the right incentives for private economic actors to invest in their human capital 'stock'. In the social investment policy paradigm, education policy, from ECEC to primary, secondary, and tertiary education, vocational training, apprenticeship systems, and lifelong learning, is an integral part of the twenty-first-century welfare state. Chapters 10, 11, and 33 all underline how education policy harbours important consequences for life chances in terms employment and distributive outcomes, with ECEC laying the foundation for cognitive and social skill development, upward educational mobility, and lower school dropout rates. A decade of OECD Programme for International Student Assessment (PISA) studies strongly supports the conjecture that there is no trade-off between educational efficiency and equity: high numeracy and literacy rates can be achieved with educational policies that abide by the principles of equal opportunities and high-quality public provision, with the additional dividend of better employment opportunities for vulnerable groups.

By bringing lifelong education back into welfare state analysis, the SIA's a positive theory of state, gives ample credence to public policy and social service workers cross-cutting, aligning, and integrating the jurisdictions of 'stock', 'flow', and 'buffer' policy provision. In the social investment policy paradigm, welfare provision and social services in education, family support, health, and housing, may not incur immediate economic output, but are seen as critical social-infrastructural preconditions for employment, sustainable growth, and economic well-being. In the Keynesian welfare paradigm, the state operated singularly as a reactive economic 'shock absorber', protecting families from demand-deficient mass unemployment and economic hardship by dampening the business cycle, as a temporary intervention until economic and employment growth resumed. In the governance of the Keynesian-Beveridgean welfare state, moreover, national social insurance systems and employment services developed as clearly demarcated policy silos with hierarchically organized, administrative structures. The neoliberal theory of the state, put on the table after the recessions of the 1970s and 1980s, is utterly negative, assuming as a matter of fact that public officials and organized stakeholders are prone to 'rent-seeking' according to public choice models of collective action, principle–agent, and new public management theory.

The social investment policy paradigm also places the Baumol cost predicament in a different light. Publicly financed social investments may create extra private output at less public cost—in parenting services, education, ALMP interventions, and long-term care, for example. In an era of de-industrialization, expansion in these sectors is, according to Anne Wren in Chapter 8, essential to avoid the unappealing set of trade-offs between fiscal responsibility, employment creation, and equality, embodied in the service economy 'trilemma'. As a careful calibration of 'stocks', 'flows', and 'buffers' generates positive socioeconomic spillovers, governments have a vital role to play in financing, regulating, and monitoring multi-dimensional social investment progress.

In response to critical life-course transitions, 'capacitating social services', ECEC, ALMP, and long-term care services, are imperative for equipping and assisting individuals and families to mitigate the unforeseeable hazards they face, tailored to personal circumstances, alongside 'compensatory' social insurance provision. In Chapter 12, Charles Sabel, Jonathan Zeitlin, and Sigrid Quack underline how administrative capabilities that support the integrated provision of customized social services in post-industrial economies, including pre-school, activation programmes, parental leave, mentoring and parenting counselling, family-friendly employment regulation, and individualized assistance, trespass the functional silos of the Keynesian-Beveridgean welfare state edifice. Integrated benefit and 'productive' service delivery requires collaborative governance structures to help orchestrate mutually reinforcing provisions and ensure effective coordination and feedback learning across multiple layers of local policy execution and cross-sectoral social concertation. As the changing nature of social risks is no longer exclusively connected with unemployment but also with income volatility due to critical life-course transitions (in particular between family and care and formal employment), the need to extend unemployment insurance towards a system of "employment insurance" becomes evident, according to Günther Schmid (Chapter 9). Stronger and more continuous life-course connections between the interdependent policy functions of 'stocks', 'flows', and 'buffers' require novel monitoring feedback mechanisms for effective policy learning, as Sabel et al. also underscore. As such, the role of public policy in the social investment paradigm transcends the neoliberal obsession with 'level playing field' regulation. Social investment policy prerogatives are rooted in a far more 'contextualized' understanding of family demography, and life-course and labour market dynamics.

At the heart of the social investment paradigm, in terms of political discourse, lies a reorientation in social citizenship, away from *freedom from want* towards *freedom to act*, prioritizing high levels of employment for both men and women as a key policy objective, under the proviso of work–family reconciliation arrangement and a guaranteed adequate *social minimum* serving citizens to pursue fuller and more satisfying lives. Rather than stressing the promotion of (incomes) equality as a basis for social justice, normative claims behind social investment underline the basic needs and capabilities for self-development and social participation, reminiscent of the capability approach of Amartya Sen, as intimated by Nathalie Morel and Joakim Palme in Chapter 13.

The social investment shift in policy emphasis from income compensation for economic hardship to human development, in no insignificant measure, progressed on the wing of important policy reorientations prepared for by the OECD and the World Bank in the new millennium. While the World Bank came to endorse a "stock-plus-buffer" strategy around conditional cash transfers (CCT) to allow very poor families to invest in children's health and education, the OECD today recommends a "stock-plus-flow" strategy, centred on ECEC and parental labour market activation, as Jane Jenson recounts in Chapter 18.

35.2.3 *Lacking an Anchor in Hegemonic Economic Theory*

As both the mid-twentieth-century Keynesian-Beveridgean welfare state and the social retrenchment neoliberal critique of the modern welfare state were solidly anchored in hegemonic macro- and micro-economic theories, this naturally begs the question of what kind of macro- and/or micro-economic policy framework best suits the SIA. The first thing to underscore in this respect is that under both Keynesian 'demand management' and neoclassical 'supply-side' economics, social policy interventions, in theoretical terms, remained subservient to private economic production as the overriding engine of prosperity. In the social investment paradigm, ex ante preventive and proactive 'stock', 'flow', and 'buffer' policies are conclusively drawn into the 'productive function' of the competitive knowledge-based economy.

Building on different theoretical insights and empirical findings, produced by a diverse array of social science disciplines, the social investment paradigm is, in the second place, highly synthetic in character, and therefore does not lend itself to straightforward economic complexity reduction. By giving equal weight to 'stocks', 'flows', and 'buffers', and their combined institutional prerequisites, the social investment paradigm may therefore lack the parsimony of Keynesian macroeconomic demand management, neoclassical supply-side microeconomics, and rational expectation macro-economics. On the other hand, in more practical terms, social investment policy analysis does a better job in delineating critically important meso-level institutional prerogatives for achieving high returns from social investment by guiding policymakers towards fairly concrete, diversified, and integrated, policy mixes. To the extent that investments in social infrastructure of human capital, employment regulation, and social transfer are critical to sustainable growth, and, by contrast, austerity reflexes, based on an older understanding of market-based competitiveness, result in public under-investments, entrapping countries in low growth (and low tax) equilibria, there is a need to rethink mainstream welfare economics on this score.

Brian Nolan (Chapter 2) fears that by trying to justify social policy interventions in instrumental economic terms, the SIA may fall prey to a self-defeating venture of taking on mainstream economists on their own turf. Losing this battle will allow mainstream economists to continue to 'frame the debate' on social protection and welfare spending as a break on competitiveness to the detriment of the normative case for social policy in terms of social justice. I find Nolan's position unnecessarily defensive. To the extent that mainstream economists venture conjectures and recommendations that are increasingly difficult to corroborate—as their axiomatic models are ill-equipped to make sense of the empirical interplay of gendered labour markets, family demography, and the role of welfare provision in a life-course perspective—it is imperative for responsible and honest social scientists, including economists, to expose these anomalies and the theoretical inadequacies that prevent standard economics, both neoclassical and Keynesian, from seriously probing the productive contemporary portent of active welfare states in competitive knowledge economies and ageing societies. This is an academic endeavour in its own right. No less important, however, is to enlighten self-acclaimed practical policymakers, wedded to pre-existing policy beliefs, of the Pareto-optimal potential of social investment, based on the available evidence.

Notwithstanding, the distinct lack of a solid anchor in any kind of general macro- and/or micro-economic theory, admittedly, can be judged as an inherent weakness of the social investment policy paradigm in comparison to its antecedents. If we turn to recent publications of the World Bank and the OECD, we observe a rather surprising reappraisal in economic thinking, away from general 'pars pro toto' macro- and micro-economic theorizing towards attempts to conjecture progress in terms 'inclusive growth', understood as growth equitably shared across society, based on a broader concern for socioeconomic well-being in terms of human flourishing (Stiglitz, Sen, and Fitoussi 2009; see also Deeming and Smyth 2017). Inspired by the work of Thomas Piketty (2014), the OECD (2015) today abides by the conjecture that rising income and wealth inequalities since the 1980s in effect have been detrimental to economic growth. The notion of 'inclusive growth', it should be emphasized, embodies a policy agenda or platform rather than a novel theoretical economic synthesis. What is captivating to the 'inclusive growth' agenda is that it reasons from salient policy concerns, such as poverty reduction, human development, access to public services, and climate change, to economic growth, rather than the other way around. This explicit focus on the quality of growth is reminiscent of the era of the post-war welfare state compromise when economic policy priorities, including growth and fiscal balance, were embedded in the over- arching social priority of achieving full employment in a free society. The inclusive growth agenda, today endorsed by the OECD, United Nations, the World Bank, the International Monetary Fund (IMF), and the EU through the European Semester, summons a fortuitous epistemic support structure for the improved understanding of the productive role of social investment in family policy, labour market activation, health care and social housing, through qualitative policy analysis, away from the mainstream negative neoclassical trade-off between equity and efficiency, based on the premise of 'unproductive' public services. The new inclusive growth episteme could be a fertile environment for bringing together evidence from a wide range of social science studies, using multifarious methodologies, for addressing inequality, overcoming poverty, countering early school-leaving, fighting unemployment, and improving work–family balance, and thus probing new frontiers in welfare policymaking.

By bringing the positive role of 'capacitating' social services and the re-appreciation of social protection together under the roof of a richer and more contextualized—gender and life-course sensitive—understanding of policy making, it is indeed my contention that the SIA indeed adds up to nothing less than a quiet but fundamental paradigmatic rethink of the welfare state for the twenty-first-century knowledge-based economy that departs in fundamental ways from the policy theories, policy instruments, and methodological concerns of the preceding Keynesian-Beveridgean welfare state compromise and the neoliberal critique of the interventionist welfare state (see Table 35.1).

Peter Hall (1989), Colin Crouch (2011), and Vivien Schmidt and Mark Thatcher (2013) all remind us that old paradigms often prove remarkably resilient, even when they are under heavy attack during economic crisis conditions. This what John Maynard Keynes meant when he wrote the following famous passage in the conclusion of his General Theory: 'the ideas of economists and

Table 35.1. Three welfare policy paradigms

	Keynesian–Beveridgean Welfare State Compromise	Neoliberal Critique of Interventionist Welfare State	Social Investment Welfare State
Policy objective	Full employment and social citizenship rights to education, housing, health care, and unemployment, sickness and old age insurance	Non-inflationary economic growth and undistorted labour market allocation	Human development breaking the inter-generation reproduction of social disadvantage contingent of high levels of employment
Policy problem	Demand deficient unemployment and (old age) poverty	Stagflation, labour market hysteresis, and public sector cost-containment	Heterogeneous ('old' and 'new') life course and labour market risks in times of adverse demography
Economic structure	Industrial economy	Service economy	Knowledge economy
Policy theory	Volatile industrial and financial capitalism requires macroeconomic steering through counter-cyclical demand management and social insurance p against standard biographical social risks	Insurmountable "big trade-off" between equity and efficiency: generous benefits 'crowd out' private economic initiative through 'moral hazard', 'deadweight loss', 'collective rent-seeking' and 'Baumol cost disease'	Social investments 'crowd in' private economic initiative, growth and competitiveness through higher employment, improved human capital use and economic security over the life course
Policy instruments	Income-replacing benefits and (industrial) job protection, acting alongside macro-level discretionary fiscal and monetary policy as *ex post* 'shock absorbers' to restore macroeconomic balance and full employment	Benefit curtailment, labour market deregulation, service liberalization, and (public) pension privatization, undergirded by non-discretionary rules-based fiscal consolidation and hard currency monetary policy, *unswervingly* enforcing 'structural reform' imperatives irrespective of economic and social context	Capacitating social services and benefits mitigating (gender-sensitive) labour market and life-course contingencies *ex ante*, through lifelong human capital 'stock' enhancement, smoothing family-friendly labour market 'flow', supported by activating social security
Institutional prerequisites	Effective taxation, efficient social security administration, national accounting, and social partnership concertation to master inflationary pressures under full employment	Contracting out public services and new public management techniques to pre-empt organized interest rent-seeking and bureaucratic capture by 'distributive coalitions'	Effective provision of of personalized services and benefits in 'institutional complementarity' reinforcing life course synergies

Target population	Male breadwinners and (indirectly) dependent family members	Working age population and dependent pensioner cohorts	All age cohorts at critical life course transitions and personalized social needs, with an emphasis on (young) dual-earner households
Gender and family	Gender biased male breadwinner – female homemaker household division of labour	Allegedly gender neutral but in effect gender blind in modus operandi	Gender-equitable with a deliberate orientation on family and labour marker contingencies
Time horizon	*Short-term* macroeconomic 'shock absorption' demand management to mitigate unemployment, poverty and inequality to restore *medium-term* full employment equilibrium	General (and thus *ahistorical*) imperative to permanently enforce laissez-faire "level-playing field' equilibria through hard currencies, balanced budgets and market liberalization	*Future-oriented* preventative mixes of 'stock', 'flow' and 'buffer' policies to sustain the 'carrying capacity' of popular welfare state with explicit focus human development in times of need and transition
Relation to economic theory	Keynesian macroeconomic and actuarial economics	Neo-classical supply-side microeconomics, rational-expectations macroeconomics and monetarism, and public choice	Lacking an explicit anchor in economic theory because of knowledge economy complexity and differentiated institutional complementarities for 'crowding in' social investment wellbeing returns and 'inclusive growth'
Political discourse	Full employment in a free society without want, disease, ignorance and squalor (Beveridge)	TINA ('there-is-no-alternative') to privileging 'negative' over 'positive' freedoms as welfare interventions inadvertently set free societies on a 'road to serfdom' (Hayek). Market outcomes and associated levels of inequality have to be accepted as inevitable and fair in open economies.	Capacitating social justice and economic security for 'human flourishing (Sen) requiring fair redistribution for all (Rawls)

political philosophers, both when they are right and when they are wrong, are more powerful that is commonly understood. Indeed the world is ruled by little else' (1936: 383). A telling specimen of prevailing intellectual inertia is the speech that Angela Merkel gave at the 2013 World Economic Forum in Davos, wherein she dramatized the European predicament by underscoring that the European continent 'represents 7 per cent of the world's population, 25 per cent of the world's GDP and 50 per cent of the world's social spending', intimating that Europe's generous welfare states are a major drag on competitiveneess (Merkel 2013). On closer inspection, the EU's share of world welfare spending is under 40 per cent and in terms of per capita broadly in sync with the US and Japan. Moreover, the EU's share of global social spending is about to fall simply because developing economies in East Asia and Latin America are rapidly catching up (Begg et al. 2015). More erroneous in Chancellor Merkel's address is that the post-crisis competitiveness problems of the EU are caused by overgenerous welfare provisions. This simply does not stand up to empirical scrutiny, as four out of the ten most successful economies in the world in the Global Competitiveness Index of the World Economic Forum (2014) are among the most generous of EU welfare states, including Germany, with levels of social spending edging around 30 per cent of GDP. The social investment paradigm suggests that, for empirical reasons at least, we should also consider the causal arrow running in reverse, with proactive and generous welfare provision adding to the long-term economic success of countries like Germany, the Netherlands, Sweden, and Finland, both before and after the financial crash.

We will return to ponder the political clout of the SIA in a moment, but the ambivalent political endorsement of the social investment paradigm, in comparison to the two antecedent welfare policy paradigms, is that, historically, the social investment turn cannot be associated with an episodic economic crisis, on a par with the Great Depression of the 1930s and the Oil Shocks of the 1970s, that sealed the politicization of, respectively, welfare state expansion after 1945 and welfare retrenchment and labour market deregulation since the 1980s. The social investment paradigm shift, by comparison, conjures up a 'quiet revolution', as the outcome of cumulative policy reforms whose transformative portent matured over the long term (Hemerijck 2015).

35.3 From Paradigm Change to Methodological Triangulation

One of the important prerequisites of the establishment of any novel policy paradigm is proof of effectiveness in comparison to prevailing ideas. Research on social investment has made significant inroads into comparative welfare state research in recent years, especially with respect to qualitative policy analysis, and case comparisons on the relative merits of in-kind services, such as ECEC, parental leave, vocational training, and ALMPs, including studies on the politics of reform under which social investment provisions are layered onto existing, more passive, social security portfolios across different welfare regimes. This is important progress. There have also been various attempts to gauge what kind of social investment instruments best serve the purpose of employment and productivity growth. Are the long-term effects of ECEC more positive than the ALMP interventions? Like any notion of 'investment', the concept of social investment begs a question of measurable 'returns'. Equally important is the question of unintended effects: does social investment policy progress 'crowd out' resources for basic income protection and poverty reduction for those more difficult to activate and employ?

Despite improved knowledge on social investment reform and aggregate outcomes, relevant empirical inferences and theoretical conjectures have yet to be translated into methodological approaches that can do justice to the notion of social investment holding out a promise of measurable well-being 'returns'. Given the likelihood of temporal synergies, spillover interdependencies, and institutional interaction effects between the policy functions of 'stocks', 'flows', and 'buffers', novel methodological tools are warranted to better gauge current and future returns on social investment and the institutional prerequisites of effective social investment policy mixes. This methodological point carries enormous weight: where welfare budget allocation is merely informed by isolated trials and case studies, longer, interconnected, and cumulative well-being returns from effective 'stock', 'flow', and 'buffer' policy mixes, but also mismatches, will remain under-examined and, as a consequence, underdeveloped in policy practice, due to an ingrained reluctance to query alternative insights in an age of 'evidence-based' policy-making. It is imperative for research to single out 'virtuous complementarities' from 'malignant' or 'contradictory' interdependencies between services, benefits, and regulation. Unfortunately, the devil is in the detail of policy interdependencies. The SIA requires in-depth understanding of the interconnections between social services, benefits, and regulation, together with the (national and local) institutional conditions of delivery. Generous high quality childcare provision in highly regulated labour markets is a recipe for perverse Matthew Effects. A policy package of easy access to quality childcare and parental leave arrangements that can allow for equal sharing between mothers and fathers would sustain a higher level of employment with more subdued gender gaps. The unravelling of the temporal chain of social investment returns, the importance of understanding how stocks, flows, and buffer policies hang together, requires significant methodological innovation at multiple layers of inquiry, in order to reap the full potential of social investment policy analysis. The good news is that welfare state research has always been a breeding ground for interdisciplinary collaboration between sociologists, economists, demographers, and political scientists, using a wide variety of theories and methodologies, with a particularly fruitful and open-minded dialogue between quantitative and qualitative research (Amenta and Hicks 2010).

Because social investment policy pertains to multifaceted and interconnected interventions operating across various stages over people's life spans and at the policy level across functionally variegated domains, it fair to say that a unified methodological approach to social investment returns and drawbacks is a near impossibility. On the other hand, cumulatively, the social investment literature, including its critics, has produced a good number of 'grounded' testable claims with respect to employment, poverty, and productivity, and also spending dilemmas and Matthew Effects, exemplified by Bonoli, Cantillon, and Van Lancker (Chapter 5) of social investment policy provisions potentially undermining the more compensatory or redistributive functions of the welfare state. As such, it may be possible, depending on data-availability, to turn theoretical postulates into testable research methodologies.

As the social investment-oriented welfare states are distinctly service-intensive, there is, according to Gerlinde Verbist (Chapter 17), an overriding need to integrate social services in quantitative assessments of welfare performance. Doing so, however, may come at a price of less generalizable truths about welfare spending efforts and relevant socioeconomic outcomes as life-course synergies and institutional complementarities inevitably cloud the picture. A second complicating factor is that social investment, particularly early childhood development, is based on a general presumption that real rates of return to social investment only pay off after many years. Exactly because many of the consequences of social investment only materialize in the longer run, the justification for making social investments will be crucially affected by the choice of the so-called 'discount rate', as Iain Begg confirms in Chapter 15, which augurs in a host of additional methodological problems pertaining to making economic predictions. A third convoluting factor is that social investments in a world of heterogeneous social risks mean different things for different clienteles when it comes to age, skill, gender, ethnicity, and family situation. In other words, there is no optimal methodology at hand. But then methodologies are never perfect. The caveats listed here require differentiated research approaches and methodologies to studying the changing nature of social risks, the effectiveness of diverse policy mixes in risk mitigation in the short-, medium-, and long-term, and an assessment of how particular social risk groups fare under different economic and institutional conditions.

To lead the way out of the methodological conundrum, Johan de Deken, in Chapter 16, breaks with the simplistic conceptualization of social investment based on the dichotomy between 'compensation' and 'investment', by relating different policy branches that the OECD distinguishes in its Social Expenditure Database (SOCX) to the social investment functions of 'stocks', 'flows', and 'buffers'. De Deken concludes on the need for methodological layering, with macro correlational analyses to help supply interesting empirical puzzles, setting the scene for quantitative micro-level pooled-time series and panel data testing, to be complemented with more qualitative institutional studies looking into institutional complementarities and life-course synergies in concrete welfare regimes, including in-depth care analyses of capacitating services.

Brian Burgoon (Chapter 14) advocates joining-up existing quantitative and qualitative research methodologies in a multidisciplinary approach to gathering data and evidence, while maintaining high standards of scientific inference. His chapter compares aggregate measures with analysis of individual panel data (from European Union Statistics on Income and Living Conditions (EU-SILC)), tracking patterns of individual employment and poverty. By so doing, he is able to show how social investment reforms—such as active labour market provisions in relation to passive unemployment insurance—may help mitigate Matthew Effects, the conjecture that social investment in areas of ALMP and child and family policy tend to disproportionately privilege middle- and upper-class segments in the population. The available evidence on the positive returns of social investment in terms of employment and productivity is rather solid. The distributive promise of social investment in terms of breaking the intergenerational reproduction of poverty and inequality is contested by the Matthew Effect literature. To be sure, Matthew Effects preponderate in every branch of public policy. But it is definitely true that, in comparison to straightforward cash-transfers, more conditional social investment services, requiring an element of pro-active engagement by clients, are indeed more susceptible to the Matthew Effect conundrum. Brian Burgoon, rather surprisingly, finds quantitative support for the effect of ALMP on employment and productivity growth, thereby significantly contributing to the welfare state's 'carrying capacity'. But he also shows that ALMP positively contributes to fighting individual poverty for vulnerable groups both directly and indirectly, whereby Matthew Effects are seemingly mitigated. To be sure, childcare provision is more prone to Matthew Effects compared to passive family benefits. But the pertinent question is not whether or not formal childcare fails to mitigate social inequalities per se, but how different portfolios of 'stock', 'flow', and 'buffer' policies impact on employment and relative poverty. There is convincing evidence that childcare Matthew Effects prevail in Continental welfare regimes, where social security 'buffers' are more insider-biased and labour market 'flow' far less family-friendly than in Scandinavian welfare regimes (Ghysels and Van Lancker, 2013). More pertinently, there is no cross-national evidence that more compensatory social insurance welfare states, like France or Italy, are more egalitarian. Snapshot comparisons between social services and income protection are ill-equipped to make sense of the joint impact and interaction effect between 'stock', 'flow', and 'buffer' provisions. In conclusion, Matthew Effects are real, but, as Burgoon reveals, they can be alleviated, contingent on prevailing institutional complementarities across a wider range of capacitating services, employment regulation, and the particular design of income protection (see also Rovny 2014). Ambitious social investment policy repertoires seemingly strengthen rather than hollow out the poverty-reducing buffer functions of prevailing social safety nets.

I concur with De Deken and Burgoon that a multi-layered and theoretically informed methodology on social investment 'returns' and 'perversities', combining macro-correlation, micro-level quantitative, and qualitative institutional analysis in relation to socioeconomic outcomes and spending efforts, could make way for balanced assessment of potential trade-offs between social investment policies and objectives at the aggregate level, thereby offering a critical starting point of delving deeper into specific questions of institutional complementarities and capacitating social service delivery, which are crucial for understanding barriers and opportunities to social investment reform, and consequently economic and social returns.

The ultimate challenge is to triangulate quantitative-micro analyses of individual socioeconomic experiences and quantitative-macro analyses of country-year development with mid-range or meso-level qualitative institutional analyses of selected national and local experiences of how the social investment functions of easing the 'flow' of labour market and life-course transitions, and raising the quality of the human capital 'stock' and capabilities, buttressed by inclusive stabilization 'buffers' that actively support citizens through transitions, are reflected in the politics of country-specific reform trajectories and how they shape socioeconomic outcomes. Comparative institutional analysis, ideally, should include an assessment of the governance mechanisms of the delivery of integrated bundles of capacitating services in local settings in countries under study. Such mid-range comparative research holds significant promise of identifying the complex temporal interdependencies of 'stock', 'flow', and 'buffer' policies as intervening causal mechanisms that connect social investment efforts to outcomes, against the background of country-specific economic and demographic conditions and institutional capabilities.

The 'goodness of fit' and also 'misfit' in the multidimensional interplay of different social investment policy functions are brought out most convincingly in the comparative chapters on Sweden by Dräbing and Nelson (Chapter 11), the Netherlands by Soentken, van Hooren, and Rice (Chapter 21), Italy by Kazepov and Ranci (Chapter 26), Quebec by Noël (Chapter 23), South East

Asia by Fleckenstein and Lee (Chapter 24), and Latin America by Sandberg and Nelson (Chapter 25), most of which also touch on the Matthew Effect quandary.

If we wish to be able to account for and assess institutional complementarities, interaction effects, and life-course synergies in processes and outcomes, thereby taking social investment truly seriously, comparative welfare state researchers have to bite the bullet of interdisciplinary methodological innovation. By building further on prevailing interdisciplinary ingenuity and the already open methodological outlook in welfare state research per se, important advances in triangulating qualitative comparative case analysis and quantitative projections of macro and micro social investment costs and benefits can be foreseen with greater sophistication.

35.4 From Transformative to Virtuous Institutional Policy Complementarities

An important driver behind the emancipation and maturation of the social investment policy paradigm is that expansive European welfare states, facing demographic ageing at subdued levels of economic growth, have been hard pressed to develop policy strategies to raise levels of employment, of women and older workers in particular (Hemerijck 2013). This is apparent in measures to raise the official retirement age through active ageing, so as to keep older workers on the payroll, and expansions in early childhood care and paternal leave provision, to lure mothers into the labour market and have them bolster the 'carrying capacity' of comprehensive welfare systems. Evidently, total spending on family services, ECEC and ALMP, has steadily increased across the OECD over the past twenty years, while spending on cash benefits has remained relatively flat. According to Lane Kenworthy (Chapter 7) practically all affluent nations have been moving in the direction of social investment. Alongside retrenchments, there have been deliberate attempts to rebuild social programmes and institutions and thereby accommodate welfare policy repertoires to the new realities of the knowledge-based economy in ageing societies.

In terms of performance, the achievements of social investment vary across countries, as they rely on different policy mixes in addressing divergent socioeconomic problems. While there is no one-size-fits-all social investment policy package on offer, policy coherence between the welfare functions—'stocks', 'flows', and 'buffers'—seems imperative. From a life-course perspective, policies are effective only if the entire chain is maintained, from ECEC to lifelong training and active ageing. High unemployment benefits of short duration coupled with strong activation incentives and training obligations, supported by vigorous ALMP services, Verena Dräbing and Moira Nelson contend in Chapter 11, are successful in lowering unemployment and raising productivity in Sweden. Capacitating social services, according to Charles Sabel, Jonathan Zeitlin, and Sigrid Quack (Chapter 12), based on positive results in Germany and the Netherlands, have to be provided by highly competent, client-friendly, and professional frontline personnel. Where ALMP and early childhood development are intimately aligned they indeed foster better performance in employment, productivity, and poverty, as the Danish case, exemplified by Kees van Kersbergen and Jonathan Kraft in Chapter 19, makes clear. By contrast, expanding childcare without taking into consideration labour market barriers to female employment incur perverse Matthew Effects, as shown by the evidence collected by Giuliano Bonoli, Bea Cantillon, and Wim Van Lancker (Chapter 5). Working mothers hardly profit from family services in dualized labour markets. Likewise, Margarita León reveals in Chapter 10 that while there has been a progressive social investment turn in policy thinking and practice, in terms of delivery, issues of coverage and service quality in dual-earner family support structures have yet to be seriously addressed in many countries.

From a comparative perspective, the Nordic countries continue to display the strongest evidence for a Pareto-optimal solution to the knowledge-based economy, with rising levels of productive male and female employment participation over the life course, including a positive relationship between fertility and female employment, with falling unemployment, low inflation, and even budget surpluses. But while the Nordic countries continue to rank as the most egalitarian societies in the world, they are no longer the poster children of social investment.

By 2008, on the eve of the outbreak of the global credit crunch, social investment policy priorities were no longer the prerogatives the Scandinavian model. Ever since the mid-1990s, a notable number of Continental welfare regimes, such as the Netherlands (social activation), Germany (massive expansion of support for dual-earner families), and Austria (introduction of long-term care and nationwide harmonization of activating social assistance), have turned to social investment. But while Germany significantly upgraded its dual-earner family and childcare policy provisions, as shown by Martin Seeleib-Kaiser (Chapter 20), important ambiguities remain. German childcare provision is layered with a more traditional transfer, the so-called *Betreuungsgeld*, whereby parents can receive 150 DM per child and per month if they look after their children themselves and do *not* use childcare facilities. This is contrary to the logic of social investment and may engender quite regressive consequences for the cognitive and social development for children from more disadvantaged (migrant) backgrounds. Moreover, the so-called *Schuldenbremse* or debt brake, the agreement of the coalition to reduce public debt to zero, may in the near future require drastic reductions in social investment spending on education by the Länder, who are responsible for education, at a time when interest rates on public debt are extremely low. In addition, despite Germany's swift recovery from the economic crisis, job precariousness and record high levels of in-work poverty, has unfortunately sharpened labour market dualization.

While the welfare state remains popular in Scandinavia, reforms have made it much less universal than it used to be, as Kees van Kersbergen and Jonas Kraft remind us in Chapter 19. Rather worrying is that benefit programmes aimed particularly at the poor and disadvantaged have been cut, while services enjoyed by the middle classes have expanded, incurring unambiguous Matthew Effects. In the Netherlands, as the calls for budget consolidation became more intrusive, and after having bailed out a considerable number of too-big-to-fail Dutch international banks, welfare cuts also resumed pride of place. But in contrast, in Sweden and Denmark, work–life reconciliation, and child and long-term care policies were cut, testifying to a less robust commitment to social investment as Menno Soentken, Franca van Hooren, and Deborah Rice recount in Chapter 21.

In Great Britain, New Labour launched a successful attack on child poverty. Among the new member states of the EU, Poland, Slovenia, Hungary, and the Czech Republic significantly improved their family leave and childcare policies, while Estonia actively raised levels of educational attainment in the early 2000s. Meanwhile, also, other parts of the globe experienced significant social investment policy diffusion. The Canadian province of Quebec is perhaps the new poster child of social investment. Alain Noël documents in Chapter 23 how by the mid-1990s key political and social actors agreed on a new social pact with ambitious social investment reforms, which subsequently succeeded in increasing labour market participation, limiting the rise of inequality, and reducing poverty, rather surprisingly, given the broader context of a liberal national welfare regime.

In Latin America, there has been a significant expansion of cash-conditional transfer programmes, primarily designed to break the inter-generational transmission of disadvantage, by making income transfers to poor families contingent making sure that children attend school, documented by Johan Sandberg and Moira Nelson (Chapter 25). However, because Latin American cash transfer 'buffers' are immensely popular, this seems to make it politically difficult to strengthen the human capital 'stock' modernization impetus in a country like Brazil. In the Far East, and especially in South Korea, to counter low levels of female employment and low childbirth, steps have been taken to expand childcare and productive work–family reconciliation policies, from free childcare to long-term care expansion, as recorded by Timo Fleckenstein and Soohyun Lee in Chapter 24. On the other hand, the South Korean overemphasis on education may frustrate the expansion of more universal social security buffers. The Italian policy mix of stocks, flows, and buffers is remarkably incoherent, argue Yuri Kazepov and Costanzo Ranci in Chapter 26, with little cross-purpose policy coordination with, rampant youth unemployment, stagnant productivity, deep insider–outsider cleavages, and widespread Matthew Effects as a consequence.

Although the evidence base of social investment policy change (and non-change) and its associated socioeconomic returns, broadly understood, has become stronger with wider empirical bearing than originally anticipated in the 2002 publication *Why We Need a New Welfare State*, the comparative overview assembled for this volume also leads to a more sobering conclusion that social investment is no miracle policy paradigm. Matthew Effects can be redressed and labour market dualization countered, but the devil of social investment returns lies in the details of policy synergy and institutional complementarities. Dilemmas, trilemmas, and trade-offs are not givens. Rather, they constitute political challenges to reformers. This brings me to the fourth use of social investment: its politics.

35.5 Towards a More Assertive Politics of Social Investment in Hard Times

The SIA lacks political weight. Its elusive policy theory, from the mundane concern for the 'carrying capacity' of advanced welfare states and the intimate recalibration of employment relations, training, family services, and basic safety-net buffers, in a gender- and family-friendly manner, does not easily translate into an appealing ideological discourse for transformative welfare reform. In addition, the cleavage structure behind social investment policies is particularly transitory. 'New' risk groups of single parent, part-time working females, underage children, jobless youths, low skill, long-term unemployed, frail elderly, and migrants, do not add up to a coherent interest structure for effective social investment political mobilization (Bonoli and Natali 2012). Is there any interest in the political centre, from the greens to social democracy, Christian-democracy, and enlightened business elites and trade unionists, to construct an overlapping consensus behind assertive social investment? Based on the wealth of material presented in this volume, I would nonetheless like to end on a cautionary optimistic note on the rescue of the SIA from one-sided austerity politics and its populist backlash. As I wrote in Chapter 1 of this volume, the politics of social investment remains something of an enigma to many scholars. This is why Nathalie Morel, Bruno Palier, and Joakim Palme have referred to social investment as an 'emerging' rather than an established policy paradigm in their 2012 book (Morel, Palier, and Palme 2012).

The debate in this volume on the politics of social investment has been critically informed by the seminal study of Alan Jacobs, *Governing the Long Term: Democracy and the Politics of Investment* (2011), more in particular by the inter-temporal trade-off, inherent to any notion of 'investment', bearing on the willingness to forego current consumption in order to realize—often uncertain—future gains that would not likely materialize otherwise, such as better childcare, education and training, and savings for old age pensions. Silja Häusermann and Bruno Palier in Chapter 31 distinguish between investment vs. consumption-oriented policies and theorize tussle between them in the political process. John Myles (Chapter 32) soberly observes, more historically, that the conditions that enabled the generation of Beveridge and Keynes to invest in health care, education, and social security, funded by high taxes over a lengthy period of sustained economic growth, no longer hold. It seems therefore unlikely that reformist politicians, in times of fiscal duress when electoral 'negativity biases' toward present losses rule the day, would rally around integrated and inclusive policy mixes of improved work–life balance 'flow' in the labour market, universal minimum income 'buffers', and consistent attempts to raise the quality of human capital 'stock' from early childhood to vocational training and lifelong learning. Myles furthermore opines that the millennial cohorts, having to bear the costs of the new social investment impetus, are far more individualistic and economically divided than older generations, which does not bode well for a broad political consensus over social investment to come forth any time soon. Likewise, Daniel Mertens, in Chapter 6, underscores the limits that the post-crisis austerity context places on public social investments. More likely, private social investments will be fast forwarded (more private child care, more expensive student loans and private health insurance) accelerating a risk shift to households, disproportionately adversely affecting the more vulnerable segments of society.

While the jury is still out on the matter of the politics of social investment, the empirical observations exemplified in this volume do reveal that social investment reform has progressively taken root with positive results. Reorienting welfare provision towards social investment constitutes a complex political game, raising daunting dilemmas, even in the purview of Pareto superior outcomes. This begs the question of the coalitional dynamics behind effective social investment reform. Do social investment reforms require novel cleavages and intergenerational compromises before they can take effect, or is the politics of social investment a less trying endeavour of proactively codifying ongoing piecemeal social investment progress with assertive backing in domestic and supranational political arenas? To the extent that social investment reform takes place, we have to ponder policymakers and electorates as less myopic and less divided than commonly understood. In Chapter 33 Marius Busemeyer observes, based on a representative survey, that social investment policies are popular with electorates, but that voters do worry about the consequences of social investments for existing compensatory social insurance benefits. In Chapter 12, Charles Sabel, Jonathan Zeitlin, and Sigrid Quack argue that conceiving of social investment as a concerted decision to postpone consumption today in order to secure a better future for our children is misguided, because such a decision moment ignores the practical and incremental ways through which social investment reform comes about in various spheres of (local) policymaking, whereby costs and benefits are clarified over long-drawn-out reform trials and implementation efforts, rather than objectified ex ante. They show how social investment reforms in ALMP and youth policy are not so much the outcomes of comprehensive bargaining, but rather develop on the fly as social investment programmes gain efficiency and in due course create clienteles which in turn raise demands for policy integration and coordination. Social investment policies may not represent a powerful platform for ex ante political mobilization. However, once introduced, as the outcome of coalition agreements and ambiguous side-payments, and to the extent that they assume wide coverage, they do become important in electoral terms, by providing electoral support for the government parties that introduced them and forcing incoming coalitions not to renege on ex post social investment progress. This interpretation to a large extent explains social investment progress in Latin America, especially with respect to CCTs (Barrientos, 2013).

The multidimensional and multi-layered infrastructure of the welfare state, almost inevitably implicates that transformative social investment reforms take effect over long cycles of sequentially layered and interconnected parametric policy changes, driven by lateral spill-over effects, unintended consequences, and trial-and-error corrections, rather than through episodic and highly politicized meta-policy paradigm revolutions. As exemplified by many contributions in this volume, the empirical record from before the onslaught of the Great Recession has essentially been one of gradual social investment policy diffusion across the globe, beginning with isolated initiatives for vulnerable groups, followed by an increasing awareness of positive policy complementarities and life course synergies, accelerating, in turn, more comprehensive and better integrated approaches. How then do we explain piecemeal but nonetheless transformative social investment progress? My suspicion is that the political support basis for social investment reform is potentially broader, but at the same time more diffuse, than 'hard boiled' political scientists with their strong attachment to built-in status-quo biased constituencies, tend to believe. Against the premise of tough inter-temporal trade-offs, social investment reform does cater to short-term winners, in the form of more childcare places, better social and cognitive stimulus for youngsters, more generous family allowances, and improved activation and training provisions for the unemployed. Policymakers may worry about the belated returns of ECEC in terms of labour productivity, but their electorates— that is, parents—care deeply about education for their offspring. Moreover, social investment progress may even engender mutually beneficial synergies for both 'old' social insurance and 'new' social service clienteles. To the extent that social investment policy reform serves to raise (female and maternal) employment, this helps to ease cost-containment pressures on health care and pension provision as more people participate in labour markets and pay taxes and social contributions.

In comparative terms, there is ample evidence that social investment delivers better economic and social results than the prevailing alternatives of pro-cyclical austerity and populist, insider-biased, welfarism chauvinism in terms of employment, educational attainment, gender balance, and relative poverty. To the extent that austerity reform is the breeding ground of anti-establishment welfare right- and left-wing populism, there must be a tangible political interest for centrist political elites, committed to international cooperation (and European integration) to take social investment today very seriously indeed. The gravest threat to economic stability and political cohesion is when mass youth unemployment translates into permanent labour market hysteresis in rapidly ageing economies. If electoral safety is hard to come by in times of impatient populist politics, it seems opportune to foster coalitional safety on the basis of an assertive social investment platform. In the knowledge-based service economy, access to middle-class lifestyles critically depends on dual-earner families, generating additional pressures for childcare, income-support for single-earner households, and policies to help reconcile work and family life. Most citizens (especially younger cohorts) aspire to decent jobs, access to continuous training and education, quality child and elder care, and adequate pensions after their elongated working careers. Provided that social investment reform adds to overall productivity and employment growth in the long run through human capital development and an improved utilization of labour inputs across the life course, a social investment political discourse can be broadly framed in Pareto-optimal terms, which in turn opens up a far wider political space for coalition compromises and social investment political mobilization after initial steps in this direction have prepared the ground.

As such, social investment reform is compatible with a range of centrist ideological positions. For centre-left Social Democrats and the Greens and centre-right Christian and liberal politicians, with a primary interest in job creation and economic growth, the social investment paradigm harbours a wide array of policy solutions transcending the big 'equity-efficiency' trade-off. For Christian Democracy to support social investment, male-breadwinner principles have already given way to dual earner household priorities.

The belated but irreversible social investment turn in Continental Europe, beginning with the Netherlands in the 1990s, followed by Austria and Germany in the 2000s, can be interpreted as the product of political learning, triggered by significant losses in female votes for Christian Democrat parties (Korthouwer 2010; Fleckenstein 2011). Moreover, politicians wishing to break away from failed neoliberal orthodoxy, the social investment paradigm serves to positively re-legitimize the role of the state in the new (mixed) knowledge economy, driving up quality standards in family policy, education, and employment services, in support of a policy agenda of inclusive growth. After the dust of the social aftershocks of the Great Recession settles, converging family aspirations founded in decent work for everyone and 'dual-earner' capacitating care provision in reciprocity may become a new ticket of electoral success.

Despite widespread social and political discontent, the millennials in the recent US elections and the British referendum on the EU did not vote for Donald Trump in the US and neither for Brexit. But to the extent that populist parties successfully convey a nostalgic image of a native welfare paradise lost because of globalization and mass migration, mainstream parties face a serious uphill battle. That said, in the post-crisis context, social investment policy progress continues to bring out, finally, the feasibility of squarely positive political choices, based on a notion of capacitating social justice and solidarity, as an antidote to the demoralizing neoliberal 'there-is-no-alternative' and populist 'lost paradise' discourses. According to Nathalie Morel and Joakim Palme in Chapter 13, the philosophy of Amartya Sen is discursively instructive for thinking about how and which institutional 'capabilities' serve human flourishing. Surely, a political discourse of 'capacitating' social justice is definitely more persuasive than 'there-is-no-alternative' and 'lost paradise' pronouncements.

In conclusion, social investment reform may lack in ideological salience, but as it can be framed in less stark partisan and distributive terms, it may open up far wider political space for coalition compromises in times when traditional cleavages, electoral constituencies, and party families have weakened. Immediate gains in early childhood, female employment, improved work–life balance, and reduced levels of early school leaving, good medium-term outcomes in employment, educational attainment, and mitigated cost-containment pressures anchored in a normative discourse of 'capacitating solidarity', it is my contention that social investment reform actually places fairly manageable demands on political leadership to build broad support behind a social investment platform. For social investment policy to survive politically in the new hard times, it is my contention that it must break with the policy legacy of being the Third-Way 'handmaiden' to neoliberalism—wise to pursue when the economy expands, but forbidden when the chips are down, for which, in the European context in hindsight, the internal market and the 'one-size-fits-all' fiscal rules of the Maastricht Treaty hold much blame.

35.6 Squaring Social Investment Progress and Fiscal Prudence for Europe

The benign portrayal of cumulative social investment diffusion across the globe, with notable exceptions, was rudely interrupted by the onslaught of the global financial crisis. Nowhere has this predicament been more troublesome than in Europe, the birthplace of social investment. Seven years since the onslaught of the global financial crisis, EMU crisis management continues to be fraught with ambiguities. The posture of the European Commission has been remarkably schizophrenic. On the one hand, the Commission presented itself as the global social investment cheerleader with the launch of the 2013 Social Investment Package (SIP). But on the other hand, the Commission demands strict fiscal rectitude from its member states, as prescribed by the Six-Pack, Two-Pack, and the Fiscal Compact, and the Excessive Deficit Procedure, together with Troika bailout programmes, enacted in the wake of the Eurocrisis that shook the besieged continent in 2010. Indeed, the primacy of austerity very much relegated social investment reform—once more—to the world of fair-weather utopias. Thus far, intrusive fiscal consolidation has intensified problems of 'lowflation', private and public under-investment, and stagnant productivity, endangering the very objective—economic recovery—that the austerity reflex was meant to realize.

It is important to remember that the EU single market and single currency were masterminded at a time when the neoliberal consensus was riding high. The architects of the EMU thus believed that single currency and associated fiscal rules, layered on top of the internal market, would inescapably discipline participating EU member states to hold their 'wasteful' welfare states in check, by forcing them to adopt liberalizing 'structural reforms', including removing job protection legislation, benefit retrenchment, and pension privatization, in the hope of fast-forwarding market-conforming economic convergence (Jones 2013). In the process of European economic integration, the single market and the currency union have come to 'de-structure' national solidarity membership boundaries (Ferrera 2005), making national welfare states fundamentally semi-sovereign in operative modus operandi, requiring an important element of reorganization of social solidarity at the level of EU. Steps in this direction have been rather tepid, understandably so. In spite of the growing lip service paid to social investment ideas and policies, by centre-left governments in the late 1990s and early 2000s, the 'default' policy paradigm of welfare retrenchment, labour market liberalization, and fiscal austerity, anchored in the Maastricht Treaty, has continued to rule the day. Time and again, when there was an economic setback, the social investment impulse was relegated to the sidelines.

Particularly unsettling today, in hindsight, is that the austerity 'default' policy theory trumps any chance of social investment progress in EMU member states with high levels of public deficit and debt, arguably the countries that need a social investment impulse the most. The crippled state of public finances essentially coerces the Mediterranean economies into a 'race to the bottom' scenario of price competition, lower wages, and welfare standards, un (der)employment, and widening inequities between the old and the young. It is important to underscore that the lack of social investment reform in the EMU 'periphery' before the crisis is not simply a matter of deficient domestic reform ownership. The governance architecture of the single currency is also to blame. In hindsight, the uniform fiscal rules together with the one-size nominal interest rate policy of the European Central Bank (ECB) operated as a (Hartz) 'reform accelerator' in Germany, but as a 'reform tranquilizer' in Greece, Italy, Portugal, and, to a lesser extent, Spain. With the euro crisis, the wheels of fortune turned. In reasonably good fiscal shape, the Northern economies, blessed with good quality human capital 'stock', continued their upward social investment course, making way for even higher levels of productivity and female employment growth by enlarging and improved streamlining of the policy mix of 'stocks', 'flows', and 'buffers'. Germany experienced an unprecedented growth spurt, helped by low interest rates and an undervalued euro, triggering a swift reduction in unemployment. Spain, Italy, and Greece were plunged into a deep recession with record high (youth) unemployment. The euro crisis brought the incipient social investment turns in Portugal and Spain to a grinding halt as fiscal consolidation under the Fiscal Compact left no margin for social policy innovation in the face of massive hikes in unemployment and poverty. Mediterranean welfare states have been forced to slash active labour market and lifelong education and social services, actions that we know from the recent OECD and World Bank reports on 'inclusive growth', will, in the long run, critically erode job opportunities for men and women, resulting in intensified insider–outsider divisions, raising the spectre of a 'lost generation' at the heart of the EMU, potentially putting the long-term viability of the single currency at risk. Moreover, as more robust social investment reforms are foreseen for the 'core' EMU economies as they recover, while the EMU 'peripheries', hardest hit by the crisis, are—for the time being—prohibited from making much needed social investments, this is likely to enhance—rather than reduce—macroeconomic imbalance and divergence in the Eurozone, which may further undermine the viability of the single currency.

There is no denying that an assertive EMU social investment strategy in the context of today's fragile economic recovery and dire budgetary pressures generates tensions and trade-offs between different social policy preferences in the short term. And given the magnitude of the asymmetric overhang of the sovereign debt crisis, and—not to forget—the dismal trajectories of social investment (non-)reform in Southern Europe prior to the crisis, there are no quick fixes. But there is the political context to take into account. High (youth) unemployment, rising economic insecurity, in-work poverty and inequality, with growing shares of youths not in employment, education, and training (NEETs), have meanwhile significantly improved the political fortunes of radical anti-establishment populist parties from the xenophobic right and radical left. Politically, it is indeed questionable whether pro-cyclical austerity, underwritten by the heterodox monetary policy to counter deflation, will suffice to curb the rise of anti-EU populism and xenophobia. In Ireland, a more flexible political economy, on the other hand, and an initial intrusive fiscal consolidation also left little room for social investment innovation. On the other hand, in Ireland, a more flexible economy, where initially intrusive fiscal consolidation left little room for social investment progress; more recently that there have been important improvements in activation, training, childcare and lone parent support, as Rory O'Donnell and Damian Thomas writes (Chapter 22).

The pertinent question boils down to whether the current EMU governance regime can be truly supportive of the social investment imperative, or whether a new regime is called for. Evelyn Astor, Lieve Fransen, and Marc Vothknecht (Chapter 27), and also Sonja Bekker (Chapter 28), would probably answer 'yes' to the former. In Chapter 28 Sonja Bekker points to real social (investment) progress in country-specific recommendations (CSR) issued over the Europe 2020 semester cycle, thereby correcting the negative view of austerity trumping social investment tout court. More specifically, she reveals rather strong resistance on the part of domestic policymakers to follow through such social-investment-oriented recommendations in actual reforms. Maurizio Ferrera (Chapter 30) and Frank Vandenbroucke (Chapter 29) are far less sanguine. Ferrera uncovers an entrenched bias in EU institutions, especially with key economic policy analysts working for the Commission and the ECB, who in the past have completely ignored social investment evidence, simply because such positive economic news cannot be explained in their axiomatic worldviews of trade-offs and trilemmas for which there are allegedly no alternatives.

If countries that need a social investment impulse the most cannot pursue it because reinforced fiscal rules require uncompromising austerity for them, while economies in much better fiscal shape are progressively advised to upgrade their social investment portfolios, this will surely result in deeper socioeconomic divergence, with dangerous spill-over effects, undermining the viability of the EMU integration project. For this reason Jean-Claude Barbier (Chapter 3) fears that Draghi's prophesy of the 'long gone' European social model from 2012 is indeed near! As long as reinforced fiscal austerity, underwritten by heterodox outright monetary transactions (OMT) and quantitative easing (QE) interventions by the ECB to counter deflation, continues to be based on now defunct neoliberal economic beliefs, the prevailing EMU governance regime acts more as a 'brake' than as an 'accelerator' to proactive and preventative welfare reform, and innovation and diffusion, and the social investment agenda is lost to Europe.

The 'long' rejoinder to the European conundrum may, however, still be more positive. With the publication of the non-binding Social Investment Package (non-binding SIP), the intellectual genie of the social investment policy paradigm is out of the bottle, with solid evidence of 'capacitating' welfare provision enhancing dual-earner employment and skills levels, while mitigating the reproduction of intergenerational poverty. The folk wisdom that generous welfare provision inevitably 'crowds out' entrepreneurship, employment, and productivity growth, no longer stands up to empirical scrutiny. Also, the mantra of structural reform is past its prime. Social investment is no 'silver bullet' policy, as the Matthew Effect conundrum exemplifies. But compared to the post-crisis austerity reflex and welfare chauvinist populist nostalgia, social investment can build on a far better economic, employment, social, and gender track record. It should come as no surprise that global policy attention is shifting—evidence brought forth most notably by recent OECD studies showing that well-calibrated social investment policies 'crowd in' inclusive growth. The predicament of a fragile Eurozone recovery, high levels of (in-work) poverty and a deepening intergenerational divide, may open up a vista, contingent on effective social mobilization and adequate EU support, for more assertively anchoring a strong social investment commitment, based on positive empirical feedback, in future EMU economic governance.

Now that the euro is on safer (but not secure) ground, European policymakers should face up to the truly existential—economic, political, and social— challenge of mitigating social imbalances and asymmetries by forging a viable reform consensus that does justice to the political self-image of the EU, laid down in the 2009 Lisbon Treaty, as an inclusive 'social market economy'. The endorsement of a 'Social Triple A' for Europe in the so-called Five Presidents' Report (2015), followed by the public consultation on the 'European Pillar of Social Rights', initiated by President Jean-Claude Juncker in 2016, conjures up a breath of fresh air. It is high time to correct past mistakes by taking the social investment paradigm seriously indeed. Europe will only prosper politically and economically if it improves on its own social model, proud as it should be of the historical feats of inclusive welfare states and progressive regional economic integration, which are unparalleled in the world. But where economic stagnation prevails, high unemployment and rising poverty and inequality become the breeding grounds for xenophobic anti-EU populism, as Colin Crouch observes in Chapter 34. As political accountability continues to be bound up with widely cherished national welfare states, it is no wonder that harsh austerity reform, reinforcing economic insecurity, double-digit unemployment, and div-isive inequality, alongside additional failures to resolve the euro crisis, and the refugee and immigration crises and the Jihadist terrorist threat, are increasingly met with anti-establishment and EU-sceptic political mobilization, pressuring ruling governments to water down their commitments to European solutions. Because social investment reform is principally a 'supply side' alternative to the neo-liberal retrenchment-deregulation agenda, the Commission's recommitment to social investment in 2013 cannot substitute for effective macroeconomic management, especially not in times of depressed demand (Hemerijck and Vandenbroucke 2012).

For the EU, struggling with the political aftershock of the Brexit referendum in Great Britain, whose governments have been the most vocal critics of 'Social Europe', it is of truly existential importance to explicitly present itself as a 'holding environment' within which 'active' social-investment-oriented European welfare states can prosper. Can the fiscal rules and the European Semester process be amended for this purpose, in a manner to encourage member states to enact affordable social investment strategies, while maintaining the overall integrity of a rules-based budgetary framework? The task at hand is to formulate a conditional two-level reform agenda, based on an 'overlapping consensus', as Frank Vandenbroucke calls it, of making long-term social investments and medium-term fiscal consolidation mutually supportive, by incentivizing all governments to pursue credible budgetary discipline and social investment reform and to be effectively supported therein (Vandenbroucke, Hemerijck, and Palier 2011; Hemerijck and Vandenbroucke 2012). The challenge is to design a governance framework which contains a 'double commitment' to fiscal prudence in sync with the urgent need to ramp up social investment across the entire Eurozone economy and its interdependent, but nonetheless institutionally heterogeneous, semi-sovereign nations, for which a 'one-size-fits-all' approach will not suffice to correct and overcome economic imbalances. A different approach is in order. What is required is a transformative change in economic governance: away from a top-down welfare state 'disciplining device' towards a more positive 'holding environment' for developing, expanding, and sustaining social investment welfare states. In other words, the EU should supply a protective social policy shield that would allow domestic actors to be able to help themselves, a political space that the current institutional set-up does not allow for.

For the Eurozone, my preferred solution is to discount social investments from the deficit rules in the reinforced Stability and Growth Pact (SGP), in the area of lifelong education, in order to clear the necessary fiscal space for pursuing them in the context of the Europe 2020 Strategy, closely monitored through the European Semester in terms of appropriate alignments of 'stocks', 'flows', and 'buffers' under different economic and institutional conditions, thereby anchoring the SIA in the European Semester process, including appropriate socioeconomic indicators (Hemerijck 2016). Conditionally discounting public social investments from SGP criteria allows both for adherence to Eurozone fiscal rules and domestic welfare policy discretion, necessary for dedicated and long-term domestic 'social investment reform ownership'. This would incentivize peripheral and core economies alike to jointly pursue a social investment strategy, supported also by European Structural Funds and patient-capital financing by the European Investment Bank (EIB), with the added advantage of a more synchronized business cycle. A more ambitious approach would be to introduce a 'Golden Rule' that excludes public social investments from any restrictions on public deficits. I would prefer a more conditional approach whereby Eurozone countries would be allowed to make debt-financed social investments if they are able to plausibly conjecture well-being returns that may help expand the economy and increase the tax base in the long run. Explicitly granting fiscal space for manoeuvre (within bounds) to countries that experience social and economic imbalances would help secure sustainable financing for life course human capital development before the ageing burden reaches its peak.

Although human capital 'stock' exemptions from the rules of the SGP and Fiscal Compact, alongside monitoring the goodness of fit of country specific 'buffer' and 'flow' can be enacted without a major overhaul of the European Semester Process and the EMU governance framework, it is extremely important to the more assertive social investment turn to have ample political visibility. To this effect, it would be advisable to seal the discounting of social investment in EMU governance under the title of a Eurozone 'Social Investment Pact' that would strengthen the EU as a community of 'capacitating solidarity' and social citizenship, one that would allow active European welfare states and the single currency to prosper in tandem.

In the final analysis, I conclude that social investment is not lost for Europe. Both in domestic policy arenas and EMU governance procedures, it is my contention that social investment incentivizes significant scope ample scope for what Giuliano Bonoli (2012) has coined 'affordable credit-claiming' in the new hard times of weak and uneven growth and rising anti-EU popular disenchantment in the aftermath of global financial crisis.

Bibliography

Aaberge, R., and Langørgen, A. (2006). 'Measuring the benefits from public services: the effects of local government spending on the distribution of income in Norway'. *Review of Income and Wealth*, 52(1), 61–83.

Aaberge, R., Langørgen, A., and Lindgren, P. (2010). 'The impact of basic public services on the distribution of income in European countries', paper presented at Net-SILC Conference, Warsaw, March.

Aaberge, R., Bhuller, M., Langørgen, A., and Mogstad, M. (2010). 'The distributional impact of public services when needs differ', *Journal of Public Economics*, 94, 549–62.

Abrassart, A., and Bonoli, G. (2014). 'Obstacles to childcare services for low income families', paper presented at the XVIII ISA World Congress of Sociology, Yokohama, Japan, 13–19 July.

Acemoglu, D., and Autor, D. H. (2011). 'Skills, tasks and technologies: implications for employment and earnings.' In O. Ashenfelter and D. Card (eds.), *Handbook of Labor Economics*. Amsterdam: Elsevier, 1043–1171.

Acemoglu, A., and Shimer, R. (2000). 'Productivity gains from unemployment insurance', *European Economic Review*, 44(7), 1195–224.

Adato, M., and Hoddinott, J. (eds.) (2010). *Conditional Cash Transfers in Latin America*. Baltimore, MD: Johns Hopkins University Press.

Alber, J. (1984). 'Versorgungsklassen im Wohlfahrtsstaat: Überlegungen und Daten zur Situation in der Bundesrepublik', *Kölner Zeitschrift für Soziologie und Sozialpsychologie*, 36(1), 225–51.

Alber, J. (1986). 'Germany'. In P. Flora (ed.), *Growth to Limits: The Western European Welfare States since World War II*. Berlin and New York: Walter de Gruyter, 1–154.

Allmendinger, J. (2009). 'Der Sozialstaat des 21. Jahrhunderts braucht zwei Beine', *Aus Politik und Zeitgeschichte*, 45, 3–5.

Amarante, V., Arim, R., De Melo, G., and Vigorito, A. (2009). 'Family allowances and child school attendance: an ex-ante evaluation of alternative schemes in Uruguay', paper presented at the PEP-PMMA Conference, Cairo, 29 March–2 April.

Amenta, E., and Hicks, A. (2010). 'Research methods'. In F. G. Castles, S. Leibfried, J. Lewis, H. Obinger, and C. Pierson (eds.), *The Oxford Handbook of the Welfare State*. Oxford: Oxford University Press, 105–20.

An, M. Y., and Peng, I. (2015). 'Diverging paths? A comparative look at childcare policies in Japan, South Korea and Taiwan', *Social Policy & Administration*, 50(5), 540–58.

Anand, R., Mishra, S., and Peiris, S. J. (2013). *Inclusive Growth: Measurement and Determinants*, IMF Working Paper WP/13/135. Washington, DC: IMF.

Ancelovici, M., and Jenson, J. (2013). 'Standardization for transnational diffusion: the case of truth commissions and conditional cash transfers', *International Political Sociology*, 7(2), 294–312.

Anders, Y., Rossbach, H. G., Weinert, S., Ebert, S., Kuger, S., Lehrl, S., and von Maurice, J. (2012). 'Home and preschool learning environments and their relations to the development of early numeracy skills', *Early Childhood Research Quarterly*, 27(2), 231–44.

Andersen, J. G. (2012a). 'Det vil være en katastrofe at fjerne børnechecken', *Politiken DEBAT*, <http://www.politiken.dk>, accessed 14 October 2015.

Andersen, J. G. (2012b). 'Universalisation and de-Universalisation of Unemployment Protection in Denmark and Sweden'. In A. Anttonen, L. Haikio, and K. Stefánsson (eds.), *Welfare State, Universalism and Diversity*. Cheltenham: Edward Elgar, 162–86.

Anderson, L. M., Shinn, C., Fullilove, M. T., Scrimshaw, S. C., Fielding, J. E., Normand, J., Carande-Kulis, G. V., and the Task Force on Community Preventive Services (2003). 'The effectiveness of early childhood development programs: a systematic review', *American Journal of Preventive Medicine*, 24(35), 32–42.

Andersson, G., Ronsen, M., Knudsen, L. B., Lappegård, T., Neyer, G., Skrede, K., Teschner, K., and Vikat, A. (2009). 'Cohort fertility patterns in the Nordic countries', *Demographic Research*, 20, 313–52.

Andersson, J. (2005). 'A productive social citizenship? Reflections on the concept of productive social policies in the European tradition'. In L. Magnusson and B. Stråth (eds.), *A European Social Citizenship? Preconditions for Future Policies from a Historical Perspective*. Brussels: Peter Lang, 69–88.

Andersson, J. (2007). 'Solidarity or competition? Creating the European knowledge society'. In L. Magnusson and B. Strith (eds.), *European Solidarities: Tensions and Contentions of a Concept*. Brussels: P.I.E. Peter Lang, 293–311.

Anheier, H., and Krlev, G. (2014). 'Welfare regimes, policy reforms, and hybridity', *American Behavioral Scientist*, 58(11), 1392–411.

Ansell, B. W. (2010). *From the Ballot to the Blackboard: The Redistributive Political Economy of Education*. Cambridge: Cambridge University Press.

Ansell, B. W., and Gingrich, J. (2013). 'A tale of two trilemmas: varieties of higher education and the service economy'. In A. Wren (ed.), *The Political Economy of the Service Transition*. Oxford: Oxford University Press, 195–226.

Antoninis, M., and Tsakloglou, P. (2001). 'Who benefits from public education in Greece? Evidence and policy implications', *Education Economics*, 9(2), 197–222.

Appelbaum, E., and Schettkat, R. (1995). 'Employment and productivity in industrialized countries', *International Labour Review*, 134(4–5), 605–23.

Appelbaum, E., and Schettkat, R. (1999). 'Are prices unimportant? The changing structure of the industrialized economies', *Journal of Post Keynesian Economics*, 21(3), 387–98.

Arestis, P., and Sawyer, M. C. (2015). 'The Eurozone needs a complete make-over of its fiscal policies'. In A. Bitzenis, N. Karagiannis, and J. Marangos (eds.), *Europe in Crisis:*

Problems, Challenges, and Alternative Perspectives. Basingstoke: Palgrave Macmillan, 111–20.

Armingeon, K., and Bonoli, G. (2006). *Adapting Post-war Social Policies to New Social Risks*. London: Routledge.

Arrow, K. J., and Lind, R. C. (1970). 'Uncertainty and the evaluation of public investment decisions', *American Economic Review*, 60(3), 364–78.

Arrow, K. J., Cropper, M. L., Gollier, C., Groom, B., Heal, G. M., Newell, R. G., Nordhaus, W. D., Pindyck, R. S., Pizer, W. A., Portney, P. R., Sterner, T., Tol, R. S. J., and Weitzman, M. L. (2014). 'Should governments use a declining discount rate in project analysis?' *Review of Environmental Economics and Policy*, 8, 145–63.

Ascoli, U., and Pavolini, E. (eds.) (2015). *The Italian Welfare State in a European Perspective: A Comparative Analysis*. Bristol: Policy Press.

Ascoli, U., Ranci, C., and Sgritta, G. B. (eds) (2015). *Investire nel sociale. La difficile innovazione del welfare italiano*. Bologna: Il Mulino.

Ashenfelter, O. (1987). 'The case for evaluating training programs with randomized trials', *Economics of Education Review* 6, 333–8.

Atkinson, A. B. (2015). *Inequality: What Can Be Done?* Cambridge, MA: Harvard University Press.

Aubrey, C. (2008). 'Early childhood and care in England: when pedagogy is wed to politics', *Journal of Early Childhood Research*, 6(1), 7–21.

Autor, D. H., Levy, F., and Murnane, R. J. (2003). 'The skill content of recent technological change: an empirical exploration', *Quarterly Journal of Economics*, 118(4), 1279–333.

Bailey, J., Coward, J., and Whittaker, M. (2011). 'Painful separation: an international study of the weakening relationship between economic growth and the pay of ordinary workers'. Commission on Living Standards, Resolution Foundation.

Ball, L., Furceri, D., Leigh, D., and Loungani, P. (2013). *The Distributional Effects of Fiscal Consolidation*, IMF Working Paper 13/151. Washington, DC: International Monetary Fund.

Banting, K. (2006). 'Dis-embedding liberalism? The new social policy paradigm in Canada'. In D. A. Green and J. R. Kesselman (eds.), *Dimensions of Inequality in Canada*. Vancouver: UBC Press, 417–52.

Banting, K., and Myles, J. (2013). 'Introduction: inequality and the fading of redistributive politics'. In K. Banting and J. Myles (eds.), *Inequality and the Fading of Redistributive Politics*. Vancouver: UBC Press, 1–39.

Banting, K., and Myles, J. (2016). 'Framing the new inequality: the politics of income redistribution in Canada'. In D. A. Green, W. C. Riddell, and F. St-Hilaire (eds.), *Income Inequality: The Canadian Story*. Montreal: Institute for Research on Public Policy, 509–40.

Barbier, J.-C. (2008). *La longue marche vers l'Europe sociale*. Paris: PUF.

Barbier, J.-C. (2011). 'Activer les pauvres et les chômeurs par l'emploi? Leçons d'une stratégie de réforme', *Politiques sociales et familiales*, 104, 47–58.

Barbier, J.-C. (2012). 'Social investment, a problematic concept with an ambiguous past: a comment on Anton Hemerijck', *Sociologica*, 1, 1–10.

Barbier, J.-C. (2013). *The Road to Social Europe: A Contemporary Approach to Political Cultures and Diversity in Europe*. Abingdon: Routledge.

Barbier, J.-C., and Colomb, F. (2012). 'EU law as *Janus bifrons*, a sociological approach to "social Europe"', *European Integration online Papers (EIoP)*, Special Mini-Issue 1, EU Law, Governance and Social Policy, ed. J.-C. Barbier, 16(2), <http://eiop.or.at/eiop/texte/2012-002a.htm>, accessed 26 October 2016.

Barbier, J.-C., and Théret, B. (2009). *Le système français de protection sociale*. Paris: La Découverte, Repères.

Barcevičius, E., Weishaupt, J. T., and Zeitlin, J. (eds.) (2014). *Assessing the Open Method of Coordination: Institutional Design and National Influence of EU Social Policy Coordination*. Basingstoke: Palgrave Macmillan.

Barnard, C. (2014). 'EU employment law and the European social model: the past, the present and the future', *Current Legal Problems*, 67(1), 199–237.

Barnes, L., and Wren, A. (2012). 'The liberal model in (the) crisis: continuity and change in Great Britain and Ireland'. In N. Bermeo and J. Pontusson (eds.), *Coping with Crisis: Government Reactions to the Great Recession*. New York: Russell Sage Foundation, 287–324.

Barr, N. A. (2001). *The Welfare State as Piggy Bank: Information, Risk, Uncertainty, and the Role of the State*. Oxford: Oxford University Press.

Barrientos, A. (2008). 'Social transfers and growth: A review'. Available at SSRN 1538926. <https://ssrn.com/abstract=1538926>, accessed 14 December 2016.

Barrientos, A. (2009). 'Labour markets and the (hyphenated) welfare regime in Latin America', *Economy and Society*, 38(1), 87–108.

Barrientos, A. (2013). *Social Assistance in Developing Countries*. Cambridge: Cambridge University Press.

Barrientos, A., Gideon, J., and Molyneux, M. (2008). 'New developments in Latin America's social policy', *Development and Change*, 39(5), 759–74.

Barro, R. J. (1991). 'Economic growth in a cross section of countries', *Quarterly Journal of Economics*, 106(2), 407–33.

Bassanini, A., and Scarpetta, S. (2001). 'The driving forces of economic growth: panel data evidence for the OECD countries'. *OECD Economic Studies* 33(2), 9–56.

Bastagli, F., Coady, D., and Gupta, S. (2012). *Income Inequality and Fiscal Policy*, IMF Staff Discussion Note SDN/12/08. Washington, DC: IMF.

Battle, K. (2015). 'Renewing Canada's social architecture: child benefits in Canada, policy and politics', Caledon Institute of Social Policy, Ottawa, June.

Baumol, W. J. (1967). 'Macroeconomics of unbalanced growth: the anatomy of urban crisis', *American Economic Review*, 57, 415–26.

BDA (Bundesvereinigung der deutschen Arbeitgeberverbände). (2008). *Ausbau der Kinderbetreuung richtig und überfällig*. Berlin: BDA.

Beaujot, R. (2004). 'Delayed life transitions: trends and implications', The Vanier Institute of the Family, Ottawa.

Beck, U. (1992). *Risk Society: Towards a New Modernity*. London: Sage.

Becker, G. (1964). *Human Capital: A Theoretical and Empirical Analysis, with Special Reference to Education*. Chicago: University of Chicago Press.

Begg, I. (2013). 'Are better defined rules enough? An assessment of the post-crisis reforms of the governance of EMU transfer', *European Review of Labour and Research*, 19(1), 49–62.

Begg, I., Mushoevel, F., and Niblett, R. (2015). 'The welfare state in Europe – visions for reform'. In Bertelsmann Stiftung (ed.), *Vision Europe Summit. Redesigning European Welfare States – Ways Forward*, Gütersloh, 12–37.

Bekker, S. (2015). 'European socioeconomic governance in action: Coordinating social policies in the third European Semester', Paper series no. 19, Observatoire social européen.

Bekker, S., and Klosse, S. (2013). 'EU governance of economic and social policies: chances and challenges for social Europe', *European Journal of Social Law*, 2, 103–20.

Béland, D., Blomqvist, P., Andersen, J. G., Palme, J., and Waddan, A. (2014). 'The universal decline of universality? Social policy change in Canada, Denmark, Sweden and the UK', *Social Policy & Administration*, 48(7), 739–56.

Bengtsson, M. (2014). 'Towards standby-ability: Swedish and Danish activation policies in flux', *International Journal of Social Welfare*, 23(S1), S54–70.

Beramendi, P., Häusermann, S., Kitschelt, H., and Kriesi, H. (2015). *The Politics of Advanced Capitalism*. Cambridge: Cambridge University Press.

Bergh, A. (2005). 'On the counterfactual problem of welfare state research: how can we measure redistribution?' *European Sociological Review*, 21(4), 345–57.

Bergh, A., and Fink, G. (2008). 'Higher education policy, enrollment, and income inequality', *Social Science Quarterly*, 89(1), 217–35.

Berkhout, E.,, Heyma, A., and Prins, J. (2013). 'Flexibility @ work 2013: yearly report on flexible labor and employment'. SEO Socioeconomic Research and Randstad, Amsterdam.

Berliner Zeitung. (2002). 'Arbeitgeber unterstützen Gerster-Vorstoß', *Berliner Zeitung*, 6 March.

Berlinski, S., and Schady, N. (eds.) (2015). *The Early Years: Child Well-Being and the Role of Public Policy*. New York: Palgrave Macmillan.

Bernard, P., van den Berg, A., Plante, C., Raïq, H., Proulx, C., and Faustmann, S. (forthcoming). *One Regime or Many? Social Policy and Welfare Outcomes in Canada's Largest Provinces*. Toronto: University of Toronto Press.

Beveridge, W. H. (1942). 'Social insurance and allied services, presented to parliament as Command Paper 6404. Report by Sir William Beveridge [The Beveridge Report]'. HMSO, London.

Beveridge, W. H. (1944). *Full Employment in a Free Society: A Report*. London: Allen & Unwin.

Biewen, M. (2009). 'Measuring state dependence in individual poverty histories when there is feedback to employment status and household composition', *Journal of Applied Econometrics*, 24(7), 1095–1116.

Bihagen, E., and Ohls, M. (2006). 'The glass ceiling, where is it?' *Sociological Review*, 54 (1), 20–47.

Bird, E. J. (2001). 'Does the welfare state induce risk-taking?' *Journal of Public Economics*, 80(3), 357–83.

Bibliography

Birdsall, N., and De la Torre, A. (2001). *Washington Contentious: Economic Policies for Social Equity in Latin America*. Washington, DC: Carnegie Endowment for International Peace.

Birdsall, N., Ross, D., and Sabot, R. (1995). 'Inequality and growth reconsidered: lessons from East Asia'. *World Bank Economic Review*, 9(3), 477–508.

Björklund, A., Roine, J., and Waldenström, D. (2012). 'Intergenerational top income mobility in Sweden: capitalist dynasties in the land of equal opportunity?' *Journal of Public Economics*, 96(5–6), 474–84.

Bleses, P., and Seeleib-Kaiser, M. (2004). *The Dual Transformation of the German Welfare State*. Basingstoke: Palgrave Macmillan.

Blinder, A. (2007). 'How many U.S. jobs might be offshorable?' *World Economics*, 10(2), 41–78.

Blöchliger, H., and Nettley, M. (2015). *Sub-Central Tax Autonomy: 2011 Update*, OECD Working Papers on Fiscal Federalism, No. 20. Paris: OECD.

Blöchliger, H., Song, D.-H., and Sutherland, D. (2012). *Fiscal Consolidation: Part 4. Case Studies of Large Fiscal Consolidation Episodes*, OECD Economics Department Working Papers No. 935. Paris: OECD.

Blyth, M. (2001). 'The transformation of the Swedish model: economic ideas, distributional conflict, and institutional change', *World Politics*, 54, 1–26.

Blyth, M. (2013). *Austerity: The History of a Dangerous Idea*. New York: Oxford University Press.

Boje, T., and Ejnraes, A. (2011). 'Family policy and welfare regime'. In H. Dahl, M. Keranen, and A. Kovalainen (eds.), *Europeanisation, Care and Gender*. Basingstoke: Palgrave Macmillan, 77–93.

Bongaarts, J. (2004). 'Population aging and the rising cost of public pensions', *Population and Development Review*, 30(1), 1–23.

Bonoli, G. (2007). 'Too narrow and too wide at once: the "welfare state" as a dependent variable in policy analysis'. In J. Clasen and N. Siegel (eds.), *Investigating Welfare State Change: The 'Dependent Variable Problem' in Comparative Perspective*. Cheltenham: Edward Elgar, 24–39.

Bonoli, G. (2011). 'Active labour market policy in a changing economic context'. In J. Clasen and D. Clegg (eds.), *Regulating the Risk of Unemployment: National Adaptations to Post-Industrial Labour Markets in Europe*. Oxford: Oxford University Press.

Bonoli, G. (2012). 'Active labour market policy and social investment: a changing relationship'. In N. Morel, B. Palier, and J. Palme (eds.), *Towards a Social Investment Welfare State*. Bristol: Policy Press, 181–204.

Bonoli, G. (2012). 'Blame avoidance and credit claiming revisited', in G. Bonoli and D. Natali (eds.), *The Politics of the New Welfare State*. Oxford: Oxford University Press, 94–110.

Bonoli, G. (2013). *The Origins of Active Social Policy: Labour Market and Childcare Policies in a Comparative Perspective*. Oxford and New York: Oxford University Press.

Bonoli, G., and Natali, D. (eds.) (2012). *The Politics of the New Welfare State*. Oxford: Oxford University Press.

Bonvin, J.-M. (2008). 'Activation policies, new modes of governance and the issue of responsibility', *Social Policy and Society*, 7(3), 367–77.

Bonvin, J.-M., and Farvaque, N. (2006). 'Promoting capability for work: the role of local actors'. In S. Deneulin, M. Nebel, and N. Sagovsky (eds.), *The Capability Approach: Transforming Unjust Structures*. Dordrecht: Springer, 121–42.

Borghi, V., and van Berkel, R. (2007). 'Individualised service provision in an era of activation and new governance'. *International Journal of Sociology and Social Policy*, 27(9/10), 413–24.

Borscheid, M., and Reid, O. (2012). 'New skills for new jobs? Challenges in accessing the labour market for marginalised communities in north Dublin', *Irish Review of Community Economic Development Law and Policy*, 1(3), 75–97.

Bosworth, B., and Triplett, J. E. (2007). 'Is the 21st century productivity expansion still in services? And what should be done about it?', paper presented at the 2007 Meeting of the American Economic Association, Cambridge, MA.

Bothfeld, S., and Rouault, S. (2015). 'Families facing the crisis: is social investment a sustainable social policy strategy?' *Social Politics*, 22(1), 60–85.

Bouchard, G. (2013). 'Neoliberalism in Quebec: the response of a small nation under pressure'. In P. A. Hall and M. Lamont (eds.), *Social Resilience in the Neoliberal Era*. Cambridge: Cambridge University Press, 267–92.

Bouchard, L. (2015). 'Les fruits d'un sommet, 20 ans après. Propos recueillis par Michel Venne'. In A. Poitras (ed.), *L'État du Québec 2016*. Montreal: Institut du Nouveau Monde and Del Busso, 23–9.

Bouget, D., Frazer, H., Marlier, E., Sabato, S., and Vanhercke, B. (2015). 'Social investment in Europe: a study of national policies'. European Social Policy Network (ESPN). European Commission, Brussels.

Bourguignon, F., Ferreira, F. H. G., and Leite, P. G. (2003). 'Conditional cash transfers, schooling, and child labor: micro-simulating Brazil's Bolsa Escola program', *World Bank Economic Review*, 17(2), 229–54.

Boychuk, G. W. (2013). 'Territorial politics and the new politics of redistribution'. In K. Banting and J. Myles (eds.), *Inequality and the Fading of Redistributive Politics*. Vancouver: UBC Press, 234–55.

Boyer, R. (2002). *La croissance début de siècle*. Paris: Albin Michel.

Boyer, R. (2004). *Théorie de la Régulation, les fondamentaux*. Paris: La Découverte, Repères.

Bradley, R. H., and Corwyn, R. F. (2002). 'Socioeconomic status and child development', *Annual Review of Psychology*, 53(1), 371–99.

Brady, D. (2009). *Rich Democracies, Poor People: How Politics Explain Poverty*. Oxford: Oxford University Press.

Brady, D., and Bostic, A. (2013). 'Paradoxes lost and found: the dimensions of social welfare transfers, relative poverty and redistribution preferences', paper presented at ESPANET meeting, Edinburgh. Available at <http://federation.ens.fr/ydepot/semin/texte1314/BRA2014PAR.pdf>, accessed 21 December 2016.

Brady, D., Huber, E., and Stephens, J. D. (2014). *Comparative Welfare States Data Set*. Chapel Hill, NC, and Berlin: University of the North Carolina Press and WZB (Berlin Social Research Centre).

Bray, M. (1999). 'The Shadow Education System: Private Tutoring and Its Implications for Planners'. Fundamentals of Educational Planning Series, Number 61.

Bray, M., and Lykins, C. (2012). *Shadow Education: Private Supplementary Tutoring and Its Implications for Policy Makers in Asia.* Mandaluyong City: Asian Development Bank.

Breen, R., Luijkx, R., Müller, W., and Pollak, R. (2009). 'Non-persistent inequality in educational attainment: evidence from eight European countries', *American Journal of Sociology*, 114(5), 1475–521.

Breunig, C., and Busemeyer, M. R. (2012). 'Fiscal austerity and the trade-off between public investment and social spending', *Journal of European Public Policy*, 19(6), 921–38.

Brewster, K. L., and Rindfuss, R. R. (2000). 'Fertility and women's employment in industrialized nations', *Annual Review of Sociology*, 26, 271–96.

Brilli, Y., Del Boca, D., and Pronzato, C. (2011). *Exploring the Impacts of Public Childcare on Mothers and Children in Italy: Does Rationing Play a Role?* IZA Discussion Paper n. 5918.

Broekhuizen, M. L., Mokrova, I. L., Burchinal, M. R., Garrett-Peters, P. T., and Family Life Project Key Investigators. (2016). 'Classroom quality at pre-kindergarten and kindergarten and children's social skills and behavior problems', *Early Childhood Research Quarterly*, 36, 212–22.

Brooks, C., and Manza, J. (2007). *Why Welfare States Persist: The Importance of Public Opinion in Democracies.* Chicago: University of Chicago Press.

Brosig, M. (2014). *Problem Altersarmut: Reformperspektiven der Alterssicherung.* Frankfurt am Main: Campus.

Brunello, G., Fort, M., Schneeweis, N., and Winter-Ebmer, R. (2015). 'The causal effect of education on health: what is the role of health behaviors?' *Health Economics*, 25(3), 314–36.

Budig, M. J., Misra, J., and Boeckmann, I. (2012). 'The motherhood penalty in cross-national perspective: the importance of work–family policies and cultural attitudes', *Social Politics: International Studies in Gender, State & Society*, 19(2), 163–93.

Bulman-Pozen, J. (2015). 'Executive federalism comes to America', unpublished paper, Columbia Law School, August.

Bundesagentur für Arbeit. (2014). 'BA 2020: Answers of the Bundesagentur für Arbeit to Future Questions'. Nürnberg.

Bundesagentur für Arbeit. (2015). 'Geschäftsbericht 2014'. Nürnberg, March, <http://www.arbeitsagentur.de/web/wcm/idc/groups/public/documents/webdatei/mdaw/mjyz/~edisp/l6019022dstbai739095.pdf?_ba.sid=L6019022DSTBAI739098>, accessed 26 October 2016.

Burger, K. (2010). 'How does early childhood care and education affect cognitive development? An international review of the effects of early interventions for children from different social backgrounds', *Early Childhood Research Quarterly*, 25(2), 140–65.

Busemeyer, M. (2009). 'Asset specificity, institutional complementarities and the variety of skill regimes in coordinated market economies', *Socio-Economic Review*, 7(3), 375–406.

Busemeyer, M. (2014). *Skills and Inequality: Partisan Politics and the Political Economy of Education Reforms in Western Welfare States.* Cambridge: Cambridge University Press.

Busemeyer, M., and Iversen, T. (eds.) (2014). 'The political economy of skills and inequality', special issue of the *Socio-Economic Review*, 12(2), 241–3.

Callan, T., Smeeding, T., and Tsakloglou, P. (2008). 'Short-run distributional effects of public education transfers to tertiary education students in seven European countries', *Education Economics*, 16(3), 275–88.

Calmfors, L., Forslund, A., and Helmström, M. (2002). *Does Active Labour Market Policy Work? Lessons from the Swedish Experience*. CESIfo Working Paper no. 675. Available at: <https://papers.ssrn.com/sol3/papers.cfm?abstract_id=305360>, accessed 26 October 2016.

Canberra Group (2011). *Handbook on Household Income Statistics*, 2nd edn. Geneva: United Nations.

Cantillon, B. (2011a). *Disambiguating Lisbon: Growth, Employment, and Social Inclusion in the Investment State*, Working Paper 10-07. Antwerp: Herman Deleeck Centre for Social Policy, University of Antwerp.

Cantillon, B. (2011b). 'The paradox of the social investment state: growth, employment and poverty in the Lisbon era', *Journal of European Social Policy*, 21(5), 432–49.

Cantillon, B. (2014). 'Beyond social investment: which concepts and values for social policy-making in Europe?' In B. Cantillon and F. Vandenbroucke (eds.), *Reconciling Work and Poverty Reduction: How Successful are European Welfare States?* Oxford: Oxford University Press, 286–318.

Cantillon, B., and Van Lancker, W. (2013). 'Three shortcomings of the social investment perspective', *Social Policy and Society*, 12, 553–64.

Cantillon, B., and Vandenbroucke, F. (eds.) (2014). *Reconciling Work and Poverty Reduction: How Successful are European Welfare States?* Oxford: Oxford University Press.

Cantillon, B., Collado, D., and Van Mechelen, N. (2015). *The End of Decent Social protection for the Poor? The Dynamics of Low Wages, Minimum Income Packages, and Median Household Incomes*, ImPRovE Working Paper 15-03. Antwerp: Herman Deleeck Centre for Social Policy, University of Antwerp.

Cantillon, B., Van Mechelen, N., Pintelon, O., and van den Heede, A. (2014). 'Social redistribution, poverty and the adequacy of social protection in the EU'. In B. Cantillon and F. Vandenbroucke (eds.), *Reconciling Work and Poverty Reduction: How Successful are European Welfare States?* Oxford: Oxford University Press, 157–84.

Cappellari, L., and Jenkins, S. P. (2002). 'Who stays poor? Who becomes poor? Evidence from the British household panel survey'. *The Economic Journal*, 112(478), C60–C67.

Card, D., Kluve, J., and Weber, A. (2010). 'Active labour market policy evaluations: a meta-analysis', *Economic Journal* 120(548), F452–77.

Careja, R., Elmelund-Præstekær, C., Klitgaard, M. B., and Larsen, E. G. (2015). *Do Populist Right Wing Parties Matter? The Impact of Welfare Chauvinism on Public Policy*. Odense: University of Southern Denmark Press.

Carpenter, D. P. (2001). *The Forging of Bureaucratic Autonomy: Reputations, Networks, and Policy Innovations in Executive Agencies, 1862–1928*. Princeton, NJ: Princeton University Press.

Castles, F. G. (2004). *The Future of the Welfare State: Crisis Myths and Crisis Realities.* Oxford: Oxford University Press.

CBS (Centraal Bureau voor de Statistiek). (2013). Beroepsbevolking; kerncijfers naar geslacht en andere persoonskenmerken. Available at: <http://statline.cbs.nl/Statweb/publication/?VW=T&DM=SLNL&PA=71958ned&D1=0,6-11&D2=a&D3=0,16,18,21& D4=74-75&HD=161026-1606&HDR=T&STB=G3,G1,G2>, accessed 26 October 2016.

Cecchini, S., and Madariaga, A. (2011). *Programas de Transferencias Condicionadas: Balance de la Experiencia en América Latina y el Caribe.* Santiago: ECLAC.

Cecchini, S., and Martínez, R. (2012). *Inclusive Social Protection in Latin America: A Comprehensive, Rights-based Approach.* Santiago: ECLAC.

Cecchini, S., Filgueira, F., and Robles, C. (2014). *Social Protection Systems in Latin America and the Caribbean: A Comparative View.* Santiago: ECLAC.

Cerea, S. (2015). 'Introduzione. I servizi per l'infanzia nella prospettiva del social investment'. In U. Ascoli, C. Ranci, and G. B. Sgritta (eds.), *Investire nel sociale. La difficile innovazione del welfare italiano.* Bologna: Il Mulino, 33–43.

Cerea, S., Giannone, M., Salvati, A., and Saruis, T. (2015). 'I dilemmi del social investment nelle politiche locali per l'infanzia'. In U. Ascoli, C. Ranci, and G. B. Sgritta (eds.), *Investire nel sociale. La difficile innovazione del welfare italiano.* Bologna: Il Mulino, 75–99.

Checkel, J. T. (2002). *Persuasion in International Institutions*, ARENA Working Paper 02/14. <http://www.sv.uio.no/arena/english/research/publications/arena-working-papers/2001-2010/2002/wp02_14.htm>, accessed 26 October 2016.

Chevalier, T. (2016). 'Varieties of youth welfare citizenship: towards a two-dimension typology', *Journal of European Social Policy*, 26(1), 3–19.

Children's Society, The (2014). 'The good childhood report 2014', London.

Choi, Y. J., Chung, M.-K., and Chang, J. (2014). 'Uncomfortable compromise between developmentalism and welfarism? Politics of social investment in South Korea', paper presented at ISA World Congress, Yokohama, Japan.

Chrétien, J. (1997). 'Speech from the Throne; Resumption of Debate on Address in Reply', presented at 36th Parliament, 1st Session, House of Commons, Canada, 24 September, <http://www.parl.gc.ca/HousePublications/Publication.aspx?Language= E&Mode=1&Parl=36&Ses=1&DocId=2332707#LINK38>, accessed 26 October 2016.

Clark, T. N., and Lipset, S. M. (1991). 'Are social classes dying?'. *International Sociology*, 6(4), 397–410.

Clasen, J., and Clegg, D. (eds.) (2011). *Regulating the Risk of Unemployment: National Adaptions to Post-Industrial Labour Markets in Europe.* Oxford: Oxford University Press.

Clauwaert, S., and Schömann, I. (2012). 'The crisis and national labour law reforms: a mapping exercise', *European Labor Law Journal*, 5(1), 57–69.

Clemens, M. and Kremer, M. (2016). 'The new role for the world bank', *Journal of Economic Perspectives*, 30, 1, 53–76.

Comité national d'évaluation du RSA (2011). 'Rapport final, La documentation française', <http://www.ladocumentationfrancaise.fr/var/storage/rapports-publics/ 114000721/0000.pdf>, accessed 5 April 2015.

Consejo Nacional de Coordinación de Políticas Sociales (2007). *Plan de Equidad.* Montevideo: IMPO.

Corak, M. (2013). 'Income inequality, equality of opportunity, and intergenerational mobility', *Journal of Economic Perspectives* 27(3), 79–102.4.

Corluy, V., and Vandenbroucke, F. (2014). 'Individual employment, household employment, and risk of poverty in the European Union: a decomposition analysis'. In B. Cantillon and F. Vandenbroucke (eds.), *Reconciling Work and Poverty Reduction: How Successful are European Welfare States?* Oxford: Oxford University Press.

Corradini, S., and Orientale-Caputo, G. (2015). 'L'apprendistato in Italia'. In U. Ascoli, C. Ranci, and G. B. Sgritta (eds.), *Investire nel sociale. La difficile innovazione del welfare italiano*. Bologna: Il Mulino, 205–42.

Corrado, C., Lengerman, P., Bartelsman, E. J., and Beaulieu, J. J. (2007). 'Sectoral Productivity in the United States: Recent Developments and the Role of IT', Finance and Economics Discussion Series, Board of Governors of the Federal Reserve System (U.S), 24.

Costamagna, F. (2012). *Saving Europe 'Under Strict Conditionality': A Threat for EU Social Dimension?* LPF Working Paper No. 7, <https://ssrn.com/abstract=2230329 or http://dx.doi.org/10.2139/ssrn.2230329>, accessed 26 October 2016.

Council Recommendation (2013). On establishing a Youth Guarantee. 2013/C 120/01.

Crouch, C. (2009). 'Privatised Keynesianism: an unacknowledged policy regime', *British Journal of Politics and International Relations* 11, 382–99.

Crouch, C. (2011). *The Strange Non-Death of Neo-Liberalism*. Cambridge: Polity Press.

Crouch, C. (2015). *Governing Social Risks in Europe*. Cheltenham: Edward Elgar.

Crouch, C., and Keune, M. (2012). 'The governance of economic uncertainty: beyond "new social risks" analysis'. In G. Bonoli and D. Natali (eds.), *The Politics of the New Welfare State*. Oxford: Oxford University Press, 45–67.

Crouch, C., Streeck, W., Boyer, R., Amable, B., Hall, P. A., and Jackson, G. (2005). 'Dialogue on "Institutional Complementarity and Political Economy"', *Socio-Economic Review* 3(2), 359–82.

Cuhne, F. and Heckman, J. J. (2007). 'The technology of skill formation', *American Economic Review*, 97(2), 31–47.

Cunha, F., Heckman, J. J., Lochner, L., and Masterov, D. V. (2006). 'Interpreting the evidence on life cycle skill formation', *Handbook of the Economics of Education*, 1, 697–812.

Currie, J., and Gahvari, F. (2008). 'Transfers in cash and in-kind: theory meets the data', *Journal of Economic Literature* 46(2), 333–83.

Dalton, R. (2005). 'The social transformation of trust in government', *International Review of Sociology* 15(1), 133–54.

Daly, M. (2011). 'What adult worker model? A critical look at recent social policy reform in Europe from a gender and family perspective', *Social Politics*, 18(1), 1–23.

Daly, M. (2015). 'ESPN thematic report on social investment: Ireland, January, Directorate-General for Employment, Social Affairs and Equal Opportunities'. European Commission, Brussels.

Danforth, B. (2014). 'Worlds of welfare in time: a historical reassessment of the three-world typology', *Journal of European Social Policy*, 24(2), 164–82.

Dang, H.-A., and Rogers, F. H. (2008). 'The growing phenomenon of private tutoring: does it deepen human capital, widen inequalities, or waste resources?' *World Bank Research Observer*, 23(2), 161–200.

Dasgupta, P. (2008). 'Discounting climate change', *Journal of Risk and Uncertainty*, 37, 141–69.

De Brauw, A., Gilligan, D., Hoddinott, J., and Roy, S. (2015). 'The impact of Bolsa Familia on schooling', *World Development* 70, 303–16.

De Búrca, G. (2010). 'The EU in the Negotiation of the UN Disability Convention', *European Law Review*, 35(2), 174–96.

De Deken, J. (2014). 'Identifying the skeleton of the social investment state: defining and measuring patterns of social policy change on the basis of expenditure data'. In B. Cantillon and F. Vandenbroucke (eds.), *Reconciling Work and Poverty Reduction: How Successful are European Welfare States?* Oxford: Oxford University Press, 260–85.

De Deken, J., and Clasen, J. (2011). 'Tracking caseloads: the changing composition of working age benefit recipients in Europe'. In J. Clasen and D. Clegg (eds.), *Regulating the Risk of Unemployment*. Oxford: Oxford University Press, 297–318.

De Deken, J., and Clasen, J. (2013). 'Benefit dependency: the pros and cons of using "caseload" data for national and international comparisons', *International Social Security Review*, 88(2), 53–78.

De la Porte, C., and Heins, E. (2015). 'A new era of European integration? Governance of labour market and social policy since the sovereign debt crisis', *Comparative European Politics*, 13(1), 8–28.

De Mello, L., and Dutz, M. A. (eds.) (2012). *Promoting Inclusive Growth: Challenges and Policies*. Paris: OECD Publishing.

De Ruiter, R., Akerboom, M., and Steunenberg, B. (2014). 'European parliament elections: main issues and positions based on party manifestos', Research Note of the Leiden University Jean Monnet Center of Excellence.

Deakin, S., and Supiot, A. (eds.) (2009). *Capacitas: Contract Law and the Institutional Preconditions of a Market Economy*. Oxford and Portland, OR: Hart.

Dean, H., Bonvin, J-M., and Vielle, P. (2005). 'Developing capabilities and rights in welfare-to-work policies', *European Societies*, 7(1), 3–26.

Deeming, C., and Smyth, P. (2015). 'Social investment after neoliberalism: policy paradigms and political platforms', *Journal of Social Policy*, 44(2), 297–318.

Deeming, C., and Smyth, P. (forthcoming). *Redefining Global Social Policy: Inclusive Growth and the Social Investment Perspective*. Bristol: Policy Press.

Del Boca, D., Mencarini, L., and Pasqua, S. (2012). *Valorizzare le donne conviene. Ruoli di genere nell'economia italiana*. Bologna: Il Mulino.

Deleeck, H., Huybrechs, J., and Cantillon, B. (1983). *Het Matteüseffect*. Antwerp: Kluwer.

Department of the Taoiseach (2006). *Towards 2016: Ten-Year Framework Social Partnership Agreement 2006–2015*. Dublin: Stationery Office.

Dewilde, C. (2008). 'Individual and institutional determinants of multidimensional poverty: A European comparison', *Social Indicators Research*, 86(2), 233–56.

Deyo, F. C. (1992). 'The political economy of social policy formation: East Asia's newly industrialized countries'. In R. P. Appelbaum and J. Henderson (eds.), *States and Development in the Asian Pacific Rim*. Thousand Oaks, CA: Sage, 289–306.

DGB (Deutsche Gewerkschaftsbund) (2000). 'Schriftliche Stellungnahme für die öffentliche Anhörung zum Entwurf eines Gesetzes zur Reform der gesetzlichen Rentenversicherung und zur Förderung eines kapitalgedeckten Altersvorsorgevermögens (BT-Drs. 14/4595) und zum Antrag der CDU/CSU-Fraktion zur Verbesserung der Nachhaltigkeit in der Alterssicherung durch eine gerechte und sozialverträgliche Rentenpolitik (BT-Drs. 14/1310) vom 11. bis 13.12.2000 in Berlin', Deutscher Bundestag, Ausschuss für Arbeit und Sozialordnung, Ausschussdrucksache 14/1092.

DGB (Deutsche Gewerkschaftsbund) (2003). 'Schriftliche Stellungnahme für die Öffentliche Anhörung am 8. September 2003 in Berlin', Deutscher Bundestag, Ausschuss für Wirtschaft und Arbeit, 22, August, Ausschussdrucksache 15(9)561: 30.

Di Monaco, R., and Pilutti, S. (2012). 'L'apprendistato è la soluzione? Dipende', paper presented at the ESPAnet Italia Conference 'Risposte alla crisi. Esperienze, proposte e politiche di welfare in Italia e in Europa', Rome, 20–2 September.

Diris, R., and Vandenbroucke, F. (forthcoming). 'How does early deprivation relate to later-life outcomes? A longitudinal analysis', CES Discussion Paper Series.

Dobrowolsky, A., and Lister, R. (2008). 'Social investment: the discourse and the dimensions of change'. In M. Powell (ed.), *Modernising the Welfare State: The Blair Legacy*. Bristol: Policy Press, 125–42.

Doeringer, P. B., and Piore, M. J. (1971). *Internal Labor Markets and Manpower Analysis*. Lexington, MA: Heath.

Doerrenberg, P., and Peichl, A. (2014). 'The impact of redistributive policies on inequality in OECD countries', *Applied Economics*, 46(17), 2066–86.

Doherty, M. (2014). 'Can the patient survive the cure? Irish labour law in the austerity era', *European Labour Law Journal*, 5, 82–96.

Dolfin, S., and Schochet, P. (2012). 'The benefits and costs of the Trade Adjustment Assistance (TAA) program under the 2002 amendments', *Mathematica Policy Research-Report*, <https://wdr.doleta.gov/research/FullText_Documents/ETAOP_2013_09.pdf>, accessed 26 October 2016.

Dølvik, J. E., Fløtten, T., Hippe, J. M., and Jordfald, B. (2015). 'The Nordic model towards 2030: a new chapter?' Fafo report 2015:07, Oslo.

Drobnic, S., and León, M. (2014). 'Agency freedom for worklife balance in Germany and Spain'. In B. Hobson (ed.), *Work–Life Balance: The Agency and Capabilities Gap across European and Asian Societies*. Oxford: Oxford University Press, 126–52.

Duncan, G. J. and Murnane, R. J. (eds.) (2011). *Whither Opportunity? Rising Inequality, Schools, and Children's Life Chances*. New York: Russell Sage Foundation.

Ebbinghaus, B. (ed.) (2011). *The Varieties of Pension Governance: Pension Privatization in Europe*. Oxford: Oxford University Press.

ECLAC (Economic Commission for Latin America and the Caribbean) (2010). *Social Panorama of Latin America 2010*. Santiago: ECLAC.

ECLAC (Economic Commission for Latin America and the Caribbean) (2014). *Social Panorama of Latin America 2014*. Santiago: ECLAC.

ECLAC (Economic Commission for Latin America and the Caribbean) (2015). Social Expenditure Database, <http://estadisticas.cepal.org/cepalstat/web_cepalstat/estadisticasIndicadores.asp?idioma=i>, accessed 10 October 2015.

Egelund, N. (2012). 'PISA 2012—Danske unge i en international sammenligning', <http://www.kora.dk>, accessed 26 October 2016.

EIF (European Investment Fund) (2012). *Progress for Microfinance in Europe*, EIF Working Paper 2012/13. Luxembourg: European Investment Fund.

Emmenegger, P., Häusermann, S., Palier, B., and Seeleib-Kaiser, M. (eds.) (2012). *The Age of Dualization: The Changing Face of Inequality in Deindustrializing Societies*. New York and Oxford: Oxford University Press.

EMN (European Microfinance Network) (2014). *Overview of the Microcredit Sector in the European Union 2012–2013*. Brussels: European Microfinance Network.

EPSC (European Political Strategy Centre) (2015). 'Europe 2020: from indicators and targets to performance and delivery', *EPCS Strategy Notes*, 6, 1–9.

Erikson, R., and Goldthorpe, J. (1992). *The Constant Flux: A Study of Class Mobility in Industrial Societies*. New York: Oxford University Press.

Erikson, R., and Goldthorpe, J. H. (2002). 'Intergenerational inequality: a sociological perspective', *The Journal of Economic Perspectives*, 16(3), 31–44.

Erturk, I., Froud, J., Johal, S., Leaver, A., and Williams, K. (2007). 'The democratization of finance? Promises, outcomes and conditions', *Review of International Political Economy*, 14, 553–75.

Esping-Andersen, G. (1990). *The Three Worlds of Welfare Capitalism*. Cambridge: Polity Press.

Esping-Andersen, G. (1999). *Social Foundations of Postindustrial Economies*. Oxford and New York: Oxford University Press.

Esping-Andersen, G. (2001). 'A welfare state for the 21st century'. In A. Giddens (ed.), *The Global Third Way Debate*. Cambridge: Polity Press, 134–56.

Esping-Andersen, G. (2002a). 'A child-centered social investment strategy'. In G. Esping-Andersen, D. Gallie, A. Hemerijck, and J. Myles (eds.), *Why We Need a New Welfare State*. Oxford: Oxford University Press, 26–67.

Esping-Andersen, G. (2002b). 'Towards the good society, once again?' In G. Esping-Andersen, D. Gallie, A. Hemerijck, and J. Myles (eds.), *Why We Need a New Welfare State*. Oxford: Oxford University Press, 1–25.

Esping-Andersen, G. (2008). 'Childhood investments and skill formation', *International Tax and Public Finance*, 15(1), 19–44.

Esping-Andersen, G. (2009). *The Incomplete Revolution: Adapting to Women's New Roles*. Cambridge: Polity Press.

Esping-Andersen, G., Garfinkel, I., Han, W. J., Magnuson, K., Wagner, S., and Waldfogel, J. (2012). 'Child care and school performance in Denmark and the United States', *Children and Youth Services Review*, 34(3), 576–89.

Esping-Andersen, G. (2015a). 'Investing in early childhood', *Revue Belge de Sécurité Sociale*, 2015(1), 99–112.

Esping-Andersen, G. (2015b). 'Welfare regimes and social stratification', *Journal of European Social Policy*, 25(1), 124–34,

Esping-Andersen, G., and Myles, J. (2009). 'Economic inequality and the welfare state'. In W. Salverda, B. Nolan, and T. Smeeding (eds.), *Oxford Handbook of Economic Inequality*. Oxford: Oxford University Press, 639–64.

Esping-Andersen, G., Gallie, D., Hemerijck, A., and Myles, J. (2002). *Why We Need a New Welfare State*. Oxford: Oxford University Press.

ESPN (European Social Policy Network) (2015a). *ESPN Thematic Report on Social Investment*. Netherlands: European Commission.

Estévez-Abe, M. (2008). *Welfare and Capitalism in Postwar Japan*. Cambridge: Cambridge University Press.

Estévez-Abe, M., Iversen, T., and Soskice, D. (2001). 'Social Protection and the formation of skills'. In P. A. Hall and D. Soskice (eds.), *Varieties of Capitalism: The Institutional Foundations of Comparative Advantage*. Oxford: Oxford University Press, 145–83.

Etzemüller, T. (2014). *Alva and Gunnar Myrdal: Social Engineering in the Modern World*. London: Lexington Books.

EU Network of Independent Experts on Social Inclusion (2014). *Investing in Children: Breaking the Cycle of Disadvantage: A Study of National Policies*. Sweden: European Union.

Eurofound (2012). 'NEETs—Young people not in employment, education or training: Characteristics, costs and policy responses in Europe'. Luxembourg: Publications Office of the European Union.

European Commission (2009). *The Provision of Childcare Services: A Comparative Review of 30 European Countries*. Luxembourg: European Commission.

European Commission (2011a). Agenda for the rights of the child. COM(2011) 60 final. Brussels: Publications Office of the European Union.

European Commission (2011b). Early Childhood Education and Care: Providing all our children with the best start for the world of tomorrow. COM(2011) 66 final. Brussels: Publications Office of the European Union.

European Commission (2012a). *Assessment of the 2012 National Reform Programme and Stability Programme for the Czech Republic*, Commission Staff Working Document, SWD(2012) 303 final. Brussels: European Commission.

European Commission (2012b). *White Paper: An Agenda for Adequate, Safe and Sustainable Pensions*, COM(2012) 55 final. Brussels: European Commission.

European Commission (2013a). *Commission Recommendation: Investing in Children: Breaking the Cycle of Disadvantage*, C(2013) 778 final. Brussels: European Commission.

European Commission (2013b). *Investing in Social Europe*. Luxembourg: Publications Office of the European Union.

European Commission (2013c). *Paper on Automatic Stabilisers*. Brussels: Publications Office of the European Union.

European Commission (2013d). *Towards Social Investment for Growth and Cohesion— Including Implementing the European Social Fund 2014–2020*, COM(2013) 83 final. Brussels: European Commission.

European Commission (2013e). *Evidence on Demographic and Social Trends. Social Policies' Contribution to Inclusion, Employment and the Economy*, SWD(2013) 38 final. Brussels: European Commission.

European Commission (2014a). *Assessment of the 2014 National Reform Programme and Convergence Programme for Czech Republic*, Commission Staff Working Document, SWD(2014) 404 final. Brussels: European Commission.

European Commission (2014b). *Assessment of the 2014 National Reform Programme and Stability Programme for the Netherlands*, Commission Staff Working Document, SWD (2014) 420 final. Brussels: European Commission.

European Commission (2014c). *Assessment of the 2014 National Reform Programme and Convergence Programme for Poland*, Commission Staff Working Document, SWD (2014) 422 final. Brussels: European Commission.

European Commission (2014d). *Assessment of the 2014 National Reform Programme and Convergence Programme for United Kingdom*, Commission Staff Working Document, SWD(2014) 429 final. Brussels: European Commission.

European Commission (2014e). *Taking Stock of the Europe 2020 Strategy for Smart, Sustainable and Inclusive Growth*. COM(2014) 130 final/2. Brussels: European Commission.

European Commission (2015a). *Annual Growth Survey 2016: Strengthening the Recovery and Fostering Convergence*, COM(2015) 690 final. Brussels: European Commission.

European Commission (2015c). 'Policy roadmap for the implementation of the Social Investment Package', August.

European Commission (2015d). 'Proposal for a regulation of the European Parliament and of the Council on the establishment of the Structural Reform Support Programme for the period 2017 to 2020 and amending Regulations (EU) No 1303/2013 and (EU) No 1305/2013'.

European Commission (2015e). *Seventh Report on Economic, Social and Territorial Cohesion*. Brussels: Publications Office of the European Union.

European Commission/EACEA/Eurydice/Eurostat (2014). *Key Data on Early Childhood Education and Care in Europe: Eurydice and Eurostat Report*. Luxembourg: Publications Office of the European Union.

European Commission and SPC (Social Protection Committee) (2014). Adequate social protection for long-term care needs in an ageing society. 10406/14 ADD 1. Luxembourg: Publications Office of the European Union.

European Commission and SPC (Social Protection Committee) (2015a). The 2015 Pension Adequacy Report: current and future income adequacy in old age in the EU. Luxembourg: Publications Office of the European Union.

European Commission and SPC (Social Protection Committee) (2015b). Social Protection Systems in the EU: Financing Arrangements and the Effectiveness and Efficiency of Resource Allocation. 6140/15 ADD 1. Luxembourg: Publications Office of the European Union.

European Council (2000). Presidency Conclusions, Lisbon European Council, 23–24 March. SN 100/00. Available at: <http://www.europarl.europa.eu/summits/lis1_en.htm>, accessed 27 October 2016.

Eurostat (2015). 'Total fertility rate', <http://ec.europa.eu/eurostat/tgm/table.do?tab=table&init=1&language=en&pcode=tsdde220&plugin=1>, accessed 15 May 2015.

Eurydice (2012). *Key Data on Education in Europe 2012*. Brussels: Education, Audiovisual and Culture Executive Agency.

Eurydice (2013). *Key Data on Teachers and School Leaders in Europe. 2013 Edition*. Eurydice Report. Luxembourg: Publications Office of the European Union.

Eurydice (2014). *The Structure of the European Education Systems 2014/15: Schematic Diagrams*. Brussels: European Commission.

Evans, P., and Rauch, J. E. (1999). 'Bureaucracy and growth: a cross-national analysis of the effects of "Weberian" state structures on economic growth', *American Sociological Review*, 64(5), 748–65.

Fage Hedegaard, T. (2015). 'The dynamics of stability: how processes of policy feedback help reproduce support for the Nordic welfare model', Dissertation, Aalborg University, Denmark.

FAZ (Frankfurter Allgemeine Zeitung) (1997). 'Arbeitgeber unzufrieden mit den Sozialreformen', *Frankfurter Allgemeine Sonntagszeitung*, 26 March.

FAZ (Frankfurter Allgemeine Zeitung) (2004). 'Kritik der Gewerkschaften an Hartz IV: "Soziale Schieflage"', *Frankfurter Allgemeine Zeitung*, 1 July.

FAZ (Frankfurter Allgemeine Zeitung) (2005). 'Das "familienfreundlichste Land in Europa"', *Frankfurter Allgemeine Zeitung*, 13 April.

Featherstone, D., Ince, A., Mackinnon, D., Strauss, K., and Cumbers, A. (2012). 'Progressive localism and the construction of political alternatives', *Transactions of the Institute of British Geographers*, 37(2), 177–82.

Feinstein, J. S. (1993). 'The relationship between socioeconomic status and health: a review of the literature', *Milbank Memorial Fund Quarterly*, 71, 279–322.

Fenwick, T. (2014). 'Bringing the state(s) back in: from Lula's Bolsa Familia to Dilma's Sem Miseria', paper presented at the International Sociological Association's World Congress, Yokohama, 13–19 July.

Ferragina, E., and Seeleib-Kaiser, M. (2011). 'Thematic review: welfare regime debate: past, present, futures?' *Policy and Politics*, 39(4), 583–611.

Ferrera, M. (2005). *The Boundaries of Welfare: European Integration and the New Spatial Politics of Social Protection*. Oxford: Oxford University Press.

Ferrera, M. (2013). *Liberal New Welfarism, New Perspectives for the European Social Model*, Opinion Paper n°14. Brussels: OSE.

Ferrera, M., Hemerijck, A., and Rhodes, M. (2000). *The Future of Social Europe: Recasting Work and Welfare in the New Economy. Report prepared for the Portuguese Presidency of the EU*. Oeiras: Celta Editora.

Fertig, M., and Osiander, C. (2012). *Selektivität beim Zugang in Weiterbildungsmaßnahmen Die Bedeutung individueller und struktureller Faktoren am Beispiel der 'Initiative zur Flankierung des Strukturwandels'*. Nürnberg: IAB.

Finansministeriet (2010). 'Aftale mellem regeringen og Dansk Folkeparti om genopretning af dansk økonomi', <http://www.fm.dk>, accessed 27 October 2016.

Finansministeriet (2012). 'Aftale om skattereform', <http://www.fm.dk>, accessed 27 October 2016.

Fine, M., and Glendinning, C. (2005). 'Dependence, independence or interdependence? Revisiting the concepts of "care" and dependency', *Ageing and Society* 25(4), 601–21.

Fishkin, J. (2014). *Bottlenecks: A New Theory of Equal Opportunity*. Oxford: Oxford University Press.

Fiszbein, A., and Schady, N. (2009). *Conditional Cash Transfers: Reducing Present and Future Poverty*. Washington, DC: World Bank.

Fleckenstein, T. (2010). 'Party politics and childcare: comparing the expansion of service provision in England and Germany', *Social Policy & Administration*, 44(7), 789–807.

Fleckenstein, T. (2011). 'The politics of ideas in welfare state transformations: Christian Democracy and the reform of family policy in Germany', *Social Politics*, 18(4), 543–71.

Fleckenstein, T., and Lee, S. C. (2014). 'The politics of post-industrial social policy: family policy reforms in Britain, Germany, South Korea, and Sweden', *Comparative Political Studies*, 47(4), 601–30.

Fleckenstein, T., and Seeleib-Kaiser, M. (2011). 'Business, skills and the welfare state: the political economy of employment-oriented family policies in Britain and Germany', *Journal of European Social Policy*, 21(2) 136–49.

Foley, K., and Green, D. (2015). 'Why more education will not solve rising inequality (and may make it worse)'. In D. Green, C. Riddell, and F. St.-Hilaire (eds.), *Income Inequality: The Canadian Story*. Montreal: Institute for Research on Public Policy, 347–98.

Förster, M., and Verbist, G. (2012). *Money or Kindergarten: What Is the Optimal Mix? A Comparative Analysis of the Distributive Effects of Family Cash Transfers and Childcare Services*, OECD Social, Employment and Migration Working Papers 135. Paris: OECD Publishing.

Förster, M., Llena-Nozal, A., and Nafilyan, V. (2014). *Trends in Top Incomes and their Taxation in OECD Countries*, OECD Society, Employment and Migration Working Papers 159. Paris: OECD.

Fortin, P. (2011). 'Quebec Quiet Revolution, 50 years later', *Inroads*, 29, summer, 90–9.

Fraser, N. (1994). 'After the family wage: gender equity and the welfare state' *Political Theory*, 44(4), 591–618.

Frenette, M., Green, D. A., and Milligan, K. (2009). 'Taxes, transfers, and income inequality', *Canadian Public Policy*, 35(4), 389–411.

Freund, C., and Weinhold, D. (2002). 'The internet and international trade in services', *American Economic Review*, 92(2), 236–40.

Friendly, M., Grady, B., Macdonald, L., and Forer, B. (2015). Early Childhood Education and Care in Canada 2014. Toronto: Childcare Resource and Research Unit.

Fugate, M., Kinicki, A. J., and Ashforth, B. E. (2004). 'Employability: a psycho-social construct, its dimensions, and applications', *Journal of Vocational Behavior*, 65(1), 14–38.

Gaarder, M., Glassman, A., and Todd, J. (2010). 'Conditional cash transfers and health: unpacking the causal chain', *Journal of Development Effectiveness*, 2(1), 6–50.

Gallie, D., and Russell, H. (2009). 'Work–family conflict and working conditions in Western Europe', *Social Indicators Research*, 93(3), 445–67.

Gambardella, D., Pavolini, E., and Arlotti, M. (2015). 'Il social investment alle prese con disuguaglianze sociali e territoriali'. In U. Ascoli, C. Ranci, and G. B. Sgritta (eds.), *Investire nel sociale. La difficile innovazione del welfare italiano*. Bologna: Il Mulino, 45–73.

Gangl, M. (2003). *Unemployment Dynamics in the United States and West Germany: Economic Restructuring, Institutions, and Labor Market Processes*. Heidelberg and New York: Springer.

Gangl, M. (2006). 'Scar effects of unemployment: an assessment of institutional complementarities', *American Sociological Review*, 71(6): 986–1013.

Garcia da Rosa, S., Guadalupe, C., and Pozuelo, J. (2015). *The Latin America Learning Barometer: Moving Forward in Access, Lagging Behind in Learning*, Working Paper 93, Global Economy and Development. Washington, DC: The Brookings Institution.

Garfinkel, I., Rainwater, L., and Smeeding, T. M. (2006). 'A re-examination of welfare states and inequality in rich nations: how in-kind transfers and indirect taxes change the story', *Journal of Policy Analysis and Management*, 25(4), 897–919.

Garfinkel, I., Rainwater, L., and Smeeding, T. (2010). *Wealth and Welfare States: Is America a Laggard or a Leader?* Oxford: Oxford University Press.

Garland, D. (2016). *The Welfare State: A Very Short Introduction*. Oxford: Oxford University Press.

Gauthier, A. (2007). 'The impact of family policies on fertility', *Population Research and Policy Review*, 26, 323–46.

Gazier, B. (2007). '"Making Transitions Pay": The Transitional Labour Markets' Approach to "Flexicurity"'. In H. Jørgensen and P. K. Madsen (eds.), *Flexicurity and Beyond: Finding a New Agenda for the European Social Model*. Copenhagen: DJØF Publishing, 99–130.

Gemeente Rotterdam (2014). Beleidsplan Nieuw Rotterdams Jeugdstelsel, 2015–2018, Rotterdam, July, <http://www.rotterdam.nl/nieuwjeugdstelsel>, accessed 28 October 2016.

Gensicke, M., Hartmann, J., and Tschersich, N. (2014). *INVEDUC (Investing in Education in Europe: Attitudes, Politics and Policies): Final Report*. Munich: TNS Infratest Sozialforschung.

Ghysels, J., and van Lancker, W. (2011). 'The unequal benefits of activation: an analysis of the social distribution of family policy among families with young children', *Journal of European Social Policy*, 21(5), 472–85.

Giannelli, G. C., Jaenichen, U., and Rothe, T. (2013). *Doing Well in Reforming the Labour Market? Recent Trends in Job Stability and Wages in Germany*, IZA Discussion Paper 7580. Bonn: IZA.

Giddens, A. (1998). *The Third Way: The Renewal of Social Democracy*. Cambridge: Polity Press.

Giese, D. (1986). '25 Jahre Bundessozialhilfegesetz. Entstehung, Ziele, Entwicklung', *Zeitschrift für Sozialhilfe und Sozialgesetzbuch*, 25, part I, 249–58, part II, 305–14, part III, 374–82.

Gilbert, N. (1995). *Welfare Justice: Restoring Social Equity*. New Haven, CT: Yale University Press.

Gilbert, N., and Gilbert, B. (1989). *The Enabling State Modern Welfare Capitalism in America*. New York: Oxford University Press.

Gingrich, J., and Häusermann, S. (2015). 'The decline of the working class vote, the reconfiguration of the welfare support coalition and consequences for the welfare state', *Journal of European Social Policy*, 25, 50–75.

Glaeser, E., La Porta, R., Lopez-de-Silanes, F., and Shleifer, A. (2004). 'Do institutions cause growth?' *Journal of Economic Growth*, 9, 271–303.

Glassman, A., Duran, D., and Koblinsky, M. (2013). *Impact of Conditional Cash Transfers on Maternal and Newborn Health*, CGD Policy Paper 19. Washington, DC: Center for Global Development.

Glotz, P. (1985). *Manifest für eine Europäische Linke*. Berlin: Siedler.

Goldin, C. (2006). 'The Quiet Revolution that transformed women's employment, education, and family', *American Economic Review, Papers and Proceedings*, 96(May), 1–21.

Goldin, C. D., and Katz, L. F. (2008). *The Race between Education and Technology*. Boston, MA: Bellknap Press of Harvard University Press.

Goldstein, J., and Keohane, R. O. (1993). 'Ideas and Foreign Policy: An Analytical Framework'. In J. Goldstein and R. O. Keohane (eds.), *Ideas and Foreign Policy: Beliefs, Institutions, and Political Change*. Ithaca, NY, and London: Cornell University Press, 3–30.

González de la Rocha, M. (2008). 'Programas de transferencias condicionadas. Sugerencias para mejorar su operación e impacto'. In I. Arriagada (ed.), *Futuro de las familias a desafríos para las políticas*. Santiago: ECLAC, 139–50.

Goos, M., Manning, A., and Salomons, A. (2010). *Explaining Job Polarization in Europe: The Role of Technology, Globalization, and Institutions*, Centre for Economic Performance (LSE) Discussion Paper (1026). <https://ideas.repec.org/p/cep/cepdps/dp1026.html>, accessed 28 October 2016.

Gore, C. (2000). 'The rise and fall of the Washington Consensus as a paradigm for developing countries', *World Development*, 28(5), 789–804.

Gornick, J., and Jäntti, M. (2012). 'Child poverty in cross-national perspective: lessons from the Luxembourg Income Study', *Children and Youth Services Review*, 34, 558–68.

Gough, I. (2001). 'Social assistance regimes: a cluster analysis', *Journal of European Social Policy*, 11(2), 165–70.

Gough, I., Bradshaw, J., Ditch, J., Eardley, T., and Whiteford, P. (1997). 'Social assistance in OECD countries', *Journal of European Social Policy*, 7(1), 17–43.

Government of the Republic of Korea (2006). Vision 2030, Seoul. <http://investpool.go.kr/kor/section/vision2030/info06/view.jsp>, accessed 4 November 2016.

Government of the Republic of Korea (2009). 'The first national plan for low-fertility and ageing society', revised version (in Korean), Seoul. <http://www.mohw.go.kr/front_new/jb/sjb030301vw.jsp?PAR_MENU_ID=03&MENU_ID=0319&CONT_SEQ=315669&page=1>, accessed 4 November 2016.

Governor General (1997). 'Speech from the Throne', presented at 36th Parliament, 1st Session, House of Commons, Canada, 23 September, <http://www.parl.gc.ca/HousePublications/Publication.aspx?Language=E&Mode=1D&Parl=36&Ses=1&DocId=2332706>, accessed 29 October 2016.

Graham, M. (2011). 'Changing paradigms and conditions of childhood: implications for the social professions and social work', *British Journal of Social Work*, 41, 1532–47.

Granovetter, M. S. (1973). 'The strength of weak ties', *American Journal of Sociology*, 78(6), 1360–80.

Greve, B. (2014). 'Free movement as a threat for universal welfare states?' *European Review*, 22(3), 388–402.

Guillemard, A. M. (2008). 'Un cours de vie plus flexible, de nouveaux profils de risques, enjeux pour la protection sociale'. In A. M. Guillemard (ed.), *Où va la protection sociale?* Paris: Presses Universitaires de France, 25–48.

Hacker, J. (2002). *The Divided Welfare State: The Battle over Public and Private Social Benefits in the US*. Cambridge: Cambridge University Press.

Hacker, J. (2004). 'Privatizing risk without privatizing the welfare state: the hidden politics of social policy retrenchment in the United States', *American Political Science Review*, 98, 243–60.

Hacker, J. (2006). *The Great Risk Shift*. New York: Oxford University Press.

Haddow, R. (2013). 'Labour market income transfers and redistribution: national themes and provincial variations'. In K. Banting and J. Myles (eds.), *Inequality and the Fading of Redistributive Politics*. Vancouver: UBC Press, 381–409.

Haddow, R. (2014). 'Power resources and the Canadian welfare state: unions, partisanship and interprovincial differences in inequality and poverty reduction', *Canadian Journal of Political Science*, 47(4), December, 717–39.

Haddow, R. (2015). *Comparing Quebec and Ontario: Political Economy and Public Policy at the Turn of the Millennium*. Toronto, University of Toronto Press.

Haffert, L. (2015). *Freiheit von Schulden—Freiheit zum Gestalten? Die Politische Ökonomie von Haushaltsüberschüssen [Growing Capacity or Shrinking Ambition? The Political Economy of Budget Surpluses]*. Frankfurt and New York: Campus.

Haffert, L., and Mehrtens, P. (2015). 'From austerity to expansion? Consolidation, budget surpluses, and the decline of fiscal capacity', *Politics & Society*, 43(1), 119–48.

Hagglund, P. (2007). *Are there Pre-Programme Effects of Swedish Active Labour Market Policies? Evidence from Three Randomized Experiments*, Swedish Institute for Social Research Working Paper No. 2/2007. Stockholm: Stockholm University Press.

Hall, A. (2007). 'Social policies in the World Bank: paradigms and challenges', *Global Social Policy*, 7(2), 151–75.

Hall, A. (2008). 'Brazil's Bolsa Família: A double-edged sword?' *Development and Change*, 39(5), 799–822.

Hall, A. (2015). 'More of the same: the World Bank's social policy response to global economic crisis', *Global Social Policy*, 15(1), 89–90.

Hall, P. A. (1989). *The Political Power of Economic Ideas: Keynesianism across Nations*. Princeton, NJ: Princeton University Press.

Hall, P. A. (1993). 'Policy paradigms, social learning, and the state: the case of economic policy making in Britain', *Comparative Politics*, 25(3), 275–96.

Hall, P. A., and Soskice, D. (2001). 'An introduction to varieties of capitalism'. In A. Hall and D. Soskice, (eds.), *Varieties of Capitalism: The Institutional Foundations of Comparative Advantage*. Oxford: Oxford University Press, 1–70.

Halleröd, B. (2015). 'ESPN thematic report on social investment, Sweden'. European Commission's European Social Policy Network, <http://ec.europa.eu/social>, accessed 14 October 2015.

Handa, S., and Davis, B. (2006). 'The experience of conditional cash transfers in Latin America and the Caribbean', *Development Policy Review*, 24(5), 513–36.

Hansen, M. H. (2014). 'Kvinders fertilitet har ikke været så lav siden 1989', *Berlingske*, <http://www.b.dk>, accessed 14 October 2015.

Harding, D. J. (2003). 'Counterfactual models of neighborhood effects: the effect of neighborhood poverty on dropping out and teenage pregnancy', *American Journal of Sociology*, 109(3), 676–719.

Harel, L. (2015). 'Les déficits zéro de 1995 et 2015, même combat? Il y a vingt ans, l'opération s'était faite sous le signe de la concertation', *Le Devoir*, 1 May.

Harsløf, I., and Ulmestig, R. (2013). 'Introduction: changing social risks and social policy responses in the Nordic welfare states'. In I. Harsløf and R. Ulmestig (eds.), *Changing Social Risks and Social Policy Responses in the Nordic Welfare States*. Basingstoke: Palgrave Macmillan, 1–24.

Hasmath, R. (ed.) (2015). *Inclusive Growth, Development, and Welfare Policy: A Critical Assessment*. New York: Routledge.

Hassel, A. (2015). 'Trade unions and the future of democratic capitalism'. In P. Beramendi, S. Häusermann, H. Kitschelt, and H. Kriesi (eds.), *The Politics of Advanced Capitalism*. Cambridge: Cambridge University Press, 231–58.

Hassel, A., and Palier, B. (2015). 'National growth strategies and welfare state reforms', paper presented at the CES Annual Conference, Paris, July.

Häusermann, S. (2010). *The Politics of Welfare State Reform in Continental Europe: Modernization in Hard Times*. Cambridge: Cambridge University Press.

Häusermann, S. (2012). 'The politics of old and new social policies'. In G. Bonoli and D. Natali (eds.), *The Politics of the New Welfare State*. Oxford and New York: Oxford University Press, 111–32.

Häusermann, S., and Kübler, D. (2011). 'Policy frames and coalition dynamics in the recent reforms of Swiss family policy', *German Policy Studies*, 6(3), 163–94.

Häusermann, S., and Zollinger, C. (2014). 'Familienpolitik'. In P. Knoepfel, Y. Papadopoulos, P. Scarini, A. Vatter, and S. Häusermann (eds.), *Handbuch der Schweizer Politik*. Zürich: NZZ Verlag, 911–35.

Häusermann, S., and Zollinger, C. (2016). 'The multidimensional politics of social investment: family policy modernization in continental welfare regimes'. Unpublished manuscript.

Hay, C. (2013). *The Failure of Anglo-Liberal Capitalism*. Basingstoke: Palgrave Macmillan.

Heckman, J. J. (2000). 'Policies to foster human capital', *Research in Economics*, 54(1), 3–56.

Heckman, J. J. (2006). 'Skill formation and the economics of investing in disadvantaged children', *Science*, 312(5782), 1900–2.

Heckman, J. J. and Jacobs, B. (2010). *Policies to Create and Destroy Human Capital in Europe*, NBER Working Paper (15742). Cambridge, MA: National Bureau of Economic Research.

Heckman, J. J., LaLonde, R. J., and Smith, J. A. (1999). 'The economics and econometrics of active labor market programs', *Handbook of Labor Economics*, 3, 1865–2097.

Heckman, J., Pinto, R., and Savelyev, P. (2013). 'Understanding the mechanisms through which an influential early childhood program boosted adult outcomes', *The American Economic Review*, 103(6), 2052–86.

Hegelich, S. (2006). *Reformkorridore des deutschen Rentensystems*. Wiesbaden: Verlag für Sozialwissenschaften.

Heinze, R. G. (1998). *Die blockierte Gesellschaft*. Wiesbaden: Westdeutscher Verlag.

Hemerijck, A. (2002). 'The self-transformation of the European social model(s)'. In G. Esping-Andersen, D. Gallie, A. Hemerijck, and J. Myles (eds.), *Why We Need a New Welfare State*. Oxford: Oxford University Press, 173–213.

Hemerijck, A. (2012a). 'When changing welfare states and the Eurocrisis meet', *Sociologica*, 1/2012, 1–49.

Hemerijck, A. (2012b). 'Two or three waves of welfare state transformation'. In N. Morel, B. Palier, and J. Palme (eds.), *Towards a Social Investment Welfare State*. Bristol: The Policy Press, 33–60.

Hemerijck, A. (2013). *Changing Welfare States*. Oxford: Oxford University Press.

Hemerijck, A. (2014a). 'The social investment package and the Europe 2020 policy agenda', *Social Europe*, 17 July, <http://www.socialeurope.eu/2014/07/social-investment-package>, accessed 29 October 2016.

Hemerijck, A. (2014b). 'Social investment: "stocks", "flows" and "buffers"', *Politiche Sociali*, 1(1), 9–26.

Hemerijck, A. (2015). 'The quiet paradigm revolution of social investment', *Social Politics: International Studies in Gender, State & Society*, 22(2), 242–56.

Hemerijck, A. (2016). 'Making social investment happen for the Eurozone', *Intereconomics. Review of European Economic Policy*, 51(6), 341–7.

Hemerijck, A., and Vandenbroucke, F. (2012). 'Social investment and the euro crisis: the necessity of a unifying social policy concept', *Intereconomics*, 47(4), 200–6.

Hemerijck, A., Burgoon, B., di Pietro, A., and Vydra, S. (2017). *Assessing Social Investment Synergies*. Brussels: European Commission.

Hieda, T. (2013). 'Politics of childcare policy beyond the left-right scale: post-industrialisation, transformation of party systems and welfare state restructuring', *European Journal of Political Research*, 52(4), 483–511.

Hills, J. (2011). 'The changing architecture of the UK welfare state', *Oxford Review of Economic Policy*, 27(4), 589–607.

Hills, J. (2014). *Good Times, Bad Times: The Welfare Myth of Them and Us*. Bristol: Policy Press.

Hirsch, F. (1976). *Social Limits to Growth*. Cambridge, MA: Harvard University Press.

Hobson, B. (2011). 'The agency gap in work–life balance: applying Sen's capabilities framework within European contexts', *Social Politics*, 18(2), 147–67.

Hobson, B. (ed.) (2014). *Work–Life Balance: The Agency and Capabilities Gap across European and Asian Societies*. Oxford: Oxford University Press.

Hobson, B., and Fahlén, S. (2009). *Applying Sen's Capabilities Framework to Work Family Balance within a European Context: Theoretical and Empirical Challenges*, Recwowe Working Paper 03/2009, Edinburgh: Recwowe.

Holliday, I. (2000). 'Productivist welfare capitalism: social policy in East Asia', *Political Studies*, 48(4), 706–23.

Holliday, I., and Wilding, P. (2003a). *Welfare Capitalism in East Asia: Social Policy in the Tiger Economies*. Basingstoke: Palgrave Macmillan.

Holliday, I., and Wilding, P. (2003b). *Welfare Capitalism in East Asia: Social Policy in the Tiger Economies*. Basingstoke: Palgrave Macmillan.

Hort, S. E. O. (2014). *Social Policy, Welfare State, and Civil Society in Sweden*, vol. 1: *History, Policies, and Institutions 1884–1988*. Lund: Arkiv Forlag.

Hsu, J. W., Matsa, D. A., and Melzer, B. T. (2014). *Positive Externalities of Social Insurance: Unemployment Insurance and Consumer Credit*, NBER Working Paper No. 20353. Boston, MA: NBER.

Huber, E., and Stephens, J. D. (2001). *Development and Crisis of the Welfare State: Parties and Policies in Global Markets*. Chicago and London: University of Chicago Press.

Huber, E., and Stephens, J. D. (2012). *Democracy and the Left: Social Policy and Inequality in Latin America*. Chicago: University of Chicago Press.

Huber, E., and Stephens, J. D. (2015). 'Pre-distribution or redistribution'. In P. Diamond and R. Liddle (eds.), *The Pre-Distribution Agenda: Tackling Inequality and Supporting Sustainable Growth*. Bristol: Policy Press, 67–78.

Hughes, J. J., Peoples, J., and Perlman, R. (1996). 'The differential impact of unemployment insurance on unemployment duration by income level', *International Journal of Manpower*, 17(2), 18–33.

Hütti, P., Wilson, K., and Wolff, G. (2015). 'The growing intergenerational divide in Europe. What role for the welfare state?' Vision Europe Summit. Redesigning European Welfare States–Ways Forward, Gütersloh, 78–97.

IDB (Inter-American Development Bank) (2011). *Evaluación Externa de Impacto del Programa de Transferencias Monetarias Condicionadas Mi Familia Progresa*. Guatemala City: Inter-American Development Bank.

IDB (Inter-American Development Bank) (2013a). 'Despite progress, learning gaps still exist', <http://www.iadb.org/en/topics/education/student-learning-is-still-unequal, 8306.html>, accessed 29 October 2013).

IDB (Inter-American Development Bank) (2013b). 'Why do students in Latin America drop out of school?', <http://www.iadb.org/en/topics/education/infographics-why-do-students-drop-out-of-school,7290.html>, accessed 22 September 2013.

IEG (Independent Evaluation Group) (2011). *Social Safety Nets: An Evaluation of World Bank Support, 2000–2010*. Washington, DC: The Independent Evaluation Group, World Bank.

IG Metall Vorstand (2014). 'Arbeit: sicher und fair! Die Befragung', Frankfurt, <http://www.arbeitsicherundfair.de/w/files/igm26/130617_themenheft_ergebnis-befragung.pdf>, accessed 29 October 2016.

ILO (International Labour Organization) (2013). *Labour Overview Latin America and the Caribbean*. Lima: ILO.

IMF (International Monetary Fund) (2002). *IMF Increases Stand-By Credit to Uruguay by US1.5 Billion, News Brief No. 0254*. Washington, DC: International Monetary Fund.

IMF (International Monetary Fund) (2003a). *Brazil—Letter of Intent, November 21*. Washington, DC: International Monetary Fund.

IMF (International Monetary Fund) (2003b). *IMF Approves 15-Month Extension, and US6.6 Billion Augmentation of Brazil's Stand-By Credit, Press Release No. 03217*. Washington, DC: International Monetary Fund.

IMF (International Monetary Fund) (2009). *Fiscal Rules: Anchoring Expectations for Sustainable Public Finances*. Washington, DC: International Monetary Fund.

Immervoll, H., and Scarpetta, S. (2012). 'Activation and employment support policies in OECD countries: an overview of current approaches', *IZA Journal of Labor Policy*, 1(1), 1–20.

Indire (2013a). Alternanza scuola-lavoro: Binomio impossibile. Florence: Indire.

Indire (2013b). Alternanza scuola-lavoro: lo stato dell'arte. Rapporto di monitoraggio 2012. Florence: Indire.

Ingold, J., and Etherington, D. (2013). 'Work, welfare and gender inequalities: an analysis of activation strategies for partnered women in the UK, Australia and Denmark', *Work, Employment & Society*, 27(4), 621–38.

Isfol-Inps (2012). 'Monitoraggio sull'apprendistato. XIII rapporto', Rome, December, <http://goo.gl/faKkzq>, accessed 20 January 2015.

Isfol-Inps (2013). 'Monitoraggio sull'apprendistato. XIV rapporto', Rome, December, <http://goo.gl/losmRj>, accessed 20 January 2015.

Istat (2013). 'L'offerta comunale di asili nido e altri servizi socio-educativi per la prima infanzia. Anno scolastico 2011/2012', <http://www.istat.it>, accessed 29 October 2016.

Iversen, T., and Soskice, D. (2010). 'Real exchange rates and competitiveness: the political economy of skill formation, wage compression, and electoral systems', *American Political Science Review*, August, 1–23.

Iversen, T., and Soskice, D. (2013). 'A political-institutional model of real exchange rates, competitiveness, and the division of labor'. In A. Wren (ed.), *The Political Economy of the Service Transition*. Oxford: Oxford University Press, 73–107.

Iversen, T., and Soskice, D. (2015). 'Democratic limits to redistribution: inclusionary versus exclusionary coalitions in the knowledge economy', *World Politics*, 67(2), April, 185–335.

Iversen, T., and Stephens, J. D. (2008). 'Partisan politics, the welfare state, and the three worlds of human capital formation', *Comparative Political Studies*, 41, 600–37.

Iversen, T., and Wren, A. (1998). 'Equality, employment, and budgetary restraint: the trilemma of the service economy', *World Politics*, 50(4), 507–74.

Jacobs, A. (2011). *Governing for the Long Term: Democracy and the Politics of Investment*. Cambridge: Cambridge University Press.

James, A., and Prout, A. (2005). *Constructing and Reconstructing Childhood. Contemporary Issues in the Sociological Study*, 2nd edn. London: Falmer Press.

Jantti, M., Sierminska, E., and Smeeding, T. (2008). *The Joint Distribution of Household Income and Wealth: Evidence from the Luxembourg Wealth Study*, OECD Social, Employment and Migration Working Papers No. 65. Paris: OECD.

Jenkins, A., Vignoles, A., Wolf, A., and Galindo-Rueda, F. (2003). 'The determinants and labour market effects of lifelong learning', *Applied Economics*, 35(16), 1711–21.

Jenson, J. (2001). 'Canada's shifting citizenship regime: investing in children'. In T. C. Salmon and M. Keating (eds.), *The Dynamics of Decentralization: Canadian Federalism and British Devolution*. Montreal and Kingston: McGill-Queen's University Press, 107–24.

Jenson, J. (2008). 'Children, new social risks and policy change: a Lego future?' In A. Leira and C. Saraceno (eds.), *Childhood: Changing Contexts*, Comparative Social Research, vol. 25. Bingley: Emerald Group Publishing, 357–82.

Jenson, J. (2009a). 'Lost in translation: the social investment perspective and gender equality', *Social Politics* 16(4), 446–83.

Jenson, J. (2009b). 'Redesigning citizenship regimes after neoliberalism: moving towards social investment'. In N. Morel, B. Palier, and J. Palme (eds.), *What Future for Social Investment?* Stockholm: Institute for Future Studies, 27–44.

Jenson, J. (2010). 'Diffusing ideas for after neoliberalism: the social investment perspective in Europe and Latin America', *Global Social Policy*, 10, 59–84.

Jenson, J. (2012). 'Redesigning citizenship regimes after neoliberalism: moving towards social investment'. In N. Morel, B. Palier, and J. Palme (eds.), *Towards a Social Investment Welfare State?* Bristol: The Policy Press, 61–90.

Jenson, J. (2013). 'Historical transformations of Canada's social architecture: institutions, instruments, and ideas'. In K. Banting and J. Myles (eds.), *Inequality and the Fading of Redistributive Politics.* Vancouver: UBC Press, 43–64.

Jenson, J. (2015). 'The "social" in inclusive growth: the social investment perspective'. In R. Hasmath (ed.), *Inclusive Growth, Development, and Welfare Policy: A Critical Assessment.* New York: Routledge, 108–23.

Jenson, J., and Saint-Martin, D. (2003). 'New routes to social cohesion? Citizenship and the social investment state', *Canadian Journal of Sociology*, 28(1), 77–99.

Jenson, J., and Saint-Martin, D. (2006). 'Building blocks for a new social architecture: the LEGO™ paradigm of an active society', *Policy & Politics*, 34(3), 429–51.

Jesuit, D. K., and Mahler V. A. (2010). 'Comparing government redistribution across countries: the problem of second-order effects', *Social Science Quarterly*, 91(5), 1390–404.

Johansson, H., and Hvinden, B. (2016). 'Concluding remarks: exploring the consequences of scale and place for local active inclusion strategies'. In H. Johansson and A. Panican (eds.), *Combating Poverty in Local Welfare Systems: Active Inclusion Strategies in European Cities.* Basingstoke: Palgrave Macmillan, 261–75.

Johansson, S. (1970). *The Level of Living Approach.* Stockholm: Fritzes.

Johnstone, D. B., and Marcucci, P. N. (2010). *Financing Higher Education Worldwide: Who Pays? Who Should Pay?* Baltimore, MD: Johns Hopkins University Press.

Jones, C. (1993). 'The Pacific challenge: Confucian welfare states'. In C. Jones (ed.), *New Perspectives on the Welfare State in Europe.* London: Routledge, 184–203.

Jones, E. (2013). 'The collapse of the Brussels–Frankfurt consensus and the structure of the euro'. In V. A. Schmidt and M. Thatcher (eds.), *Resilient Liberalism in Europe's Political Economy.* Cambridge: Cambridge University Press, 145–70.

Jorgenson, D., Mun, W., Ho, S., and Stiroh, K. J. (2005). 'Growth of U.S. industries and investments in information technology and higher education'. In J. Haltiwanger, C. Corrado, and D. Sichel (eds.), *Measuring Capital in the New Economy.* Chicago: University of Chicago Press, 403–78.

Kabeer, N., Piza, C., and Taylor, L. (2012). *What are the Economic Impacts of Conditional Cash Transfer Programmes? A Systematic Review of the Evidence.* London: DFID.

Kalwij, A. S., Machin, S., Blow, L., van Deelen, M., Gardes, F., Luengo-Prado, M., Ruiz-Castillo, J., Schmitt, J., and Starzec, C. (2007). 'Comparative service consumption in six countries'. In M. Gregory, W. Salverda, and R. Schettkat (eds.), *Services and Employment: Explaining the US–European Gap.* Princeton, NJ: Princeton University Press, 109–38.

Kamerman, S. B., and Moss, P. (2009). *The Politics of Parental Leave Policies: Children, Parenting, Gender and the Labour Market.* Bristol: Policy Press.

Kangas, O. (2000). 'Distributive justice and social policy: some reflections on Rawls and income distribution', *Social Policy & Administration*, 34, 510–28.

Kap, H., and Palme, J. (2010). 'Social citizenship and social inclusion: assessing the social situation in the EU', paper presented at the EQUALSOC Final Conference, Amsterdam, 4–5 June.

Karoly, L. A., Kilburn, M. R., and Cannon, J. S. (2006). Early childhood interventions: proven results, future promise. Rand Corporation.

Kasza, G. J. (2002). 'The illusion of welfare "regimes"', *Journal of Social Policy*, 31(2), 271–87.

Katzenstein, P. (1987). *Policy and Politics in West Germany: The Growth of a Semisovereign State*. Philadelphia, PA: Temple University Press.

Kaufmann F.-X. (2003). 'Sichereit: Das Leitbild beherrschbarer Komplexität'. In S. Lessenich (ed.), *Wohlfahrtsstaatliche Grundbegriffe, Historische und actuelle Diskurse*. Frankfurt am Main: Campus Verlag, 73–104.

Kautto, M. (2002). 'Investing in services in West European welfare states', *Journal of European Social Policy*, 12(1), 53–65.

Kazepov, Y. (2008). 'The subsidiarisation of social policies: actors, processes and impacts. Some reflections on the Italian case from a European perspective', *European Societies*, 10(2), 247–73.

Keman, H. (2010). 'Cutting back public investment after 1980: collateral damage, policy legacies and political adjustment', *Journal of Public Policy*, 30(2), 163–82.

Kenworthy, L. (2004). *Egalitarian Capitalism*. New York: Russell Sage Foundation.

Kenworthy, L. (2008). *Jobs with Equality*. Oxford: Oxford University Press.

Kenworthy, L. (2011a). 'How should we measure the poverty rate? Consider the evidence', <http://www.wp.me/p8wob-1DG>, accessed 4 November 2016.

Kenworthy, L. (2011b). *Progress for the Poor*. Oxford: Oxford University Press.

Kenworthy, L. (2015a). 'A decent and rising income floor', *The Good Society*, <http://www.wp.me/P8wob-2vH>, accessed 4 November 2016.

Kenworthy, L. (2015b). 'Public insurance and the least well-off', *The Good Society*, <http://www.wp.me/P8wob-2xN>, accessed 4 November 2016.

Kenworthy, L. (2015c). 'Shared prosperity', *The Good Society*, <http://www.wp.me/P8wob-2Dx>, accessed 4 November 2016.

Kersbergen, K., and Hemerijck, A. (2012). 'Two decades of change in Europe: the emergence of the social investment state', *Journal of Social Policy*, 41(3), 475–92.

Keynes, J. M. (1936) [1973]. *The General Theory of Employment, Interest and Money*. London: Macmillan for the Royal Economic Society.

Kildal, N., and Kuhnle, S. (2014). 'The principle of universalism challenged: towards an ideational shift in the Norwegian welfare state?' In P. Kettunen, S. Kuhnle, and Y. Ren (eds.), *Reshaping Welfare Institutions in China and the Nordic Countries*. Helsinki: NordWel, 122–38.

Kilpatrick, C., and de Witte, B. (2014). 'A comparative framing of fundamental rights challenges to social crisis measures in the Eurozone', SIEPS working paper, October.

Kim, I.-K. (2012). *The Shortcomings of and Solutions to Childcare Policy*. Seoul: Korea Development Institute.

Kim, S.-K., Park, J.-S., Kim, Y.-K., Kim, Y.-W., Choi, Y.-J., Sohn, C.-G., and Yoon, A.-R. (2012). *Marriage and Birth Trend Survey*. Seoul: Ministry of Health and Welfare.

Kitschelt, H., and Rehm, P. (2014). 'Occupations as a site of political preference formation', *Comparative Political Studies*, 47(12), 1670–1706.

Kitschelt, H., and Streeck, W. (2003). 'From stability to stagnation: Germany at the beginning of the twenty-first century', *West European Politics*, 26(4), 1–34.

Kittay Eva, F. (1999). *Love's Labor: Essay on Women, Equality and Dependency*. New York: Routledge.

Klitgaard, M. B. (2008). 'School vouchers and the new politics of the welfare state', *Governance: An International Journal of Policy, Administration, and Institutions*, 21(4), 479–98.

Kluve, J. (2010). 'The effectiveness of European active labor market programs', *Labour Economics*, 17(6), 904–18.

Knijn, T., and Kremer, M. (1997). 'Gender and the caring dimension of welfare states: toward inclusive citizenship', *Social Politics* 4(3), 328–61.

Knijn, T., and Smit, A. (2009). 'Investing, facilitating or individualizing the reconciliation of work and family life: three paradigms and ambivalent policies', *Social Politics*, 16(4), 484–518.

Knuth, M. (2013). 'Labour market reforms and the "jobs miracle" in Germany, Bruxelles', paper for the European Economic and Social Committee (Workers' Group), <http://www.eesc.europa.eu/gr2>, accessed 2 November 2016.

Knuth, M. (2014). 'Broken hierarchies, quasi-markets and supported networks: a governance experiment in the second tier of Germany's public employment service', *Social Policy & Administration*, 48(2), 240–61.

Knuth, M., Stegmann, T., and Zink, L. (2014). 'Die Wirkungen des Bundesprogramms "Perspektive 50plus": Chancen für ältere Langzeitarbeitslose'. IAQ-Report 2014-01, University of Duisburg-Essen, <http://www.iaq.uni-due.de/iaq-report/2014/report2014-01.php>, accessed 2 November 2016.

Kohl, J. (2011). 'Comments to Claus Offe: what, if anything, might we mean by "progressive" politics today?', paper presented at the Social Indicators Conference, Villa Vigoni, March.

Kongsrud, P. M., and Wanner, I. (2005). *The Impact of Structural Policies on Trade-Related Adjustment and the Shift to Services*, OECD Economics Department Working Paper (427), <http://dx.doi.org/10.1787/605814347080>, accessed 2 November 2016.

Korpi, W. (1983). *The Democratic Class Struggle*. London: Routledge.

Korpi, W. (2000). 'Faces of inequality: gender, class, and patterns of inequalities in different types of welfare states', *Social Politics*, 7(2), 127–91.

Korthouwer, G. H. P. (2010). *Party Politics As We Knew It? Failure to Dominate Government, Intraparty Dynamics and Welfare Reforms in Continental Europe*. Oisterwijk: Uitgeverij BOXPress.

Krippner, G. R. (2011). *Capitalizing on Crisis: The Political Origins of the Rise of Finance*. Cambridge, MA: Harvard University Press.

Krishnaratne, S., White, H., and Carpenter, E. (2013). *Quality Education for All Children? What Works in Education in Developing Countries*, Working Paper 20. New Delhi: International Initiative for Impact Evaluation (3ie).

Kuipers, S. (2006). *The Crisis Imperative: Crisis Rhetoric and Welfare State Reform in Belgium and the Netherlands in the Early 1990s*. Amsterdam: Amsterdam University Press.

Kuivalainen, S., and Nelson, K. (2012). 'Eroding minimum income protection in the Nordic countries'. In J. Kvist, J. Fritzell, B. Hvinden, and O. Kangas (eds.), *Changing Social Equality: The Nordic Welfare Model in the 21st Century*. Bristol: Policy Press, 69–88.

Kuivalainen, S., and Niemelä, M. (2010). 'From universalism to selectivism: the ideational turn of the anti-poverty policies in Finland', *Journal of European Social Policy*, 20(3), 263–76.

Kvist, J. (2013). 'The post-crisis European social model: developing or dismantling social investments?' *Journal of International and Comparative Social Policy*, 29(1), 91–107.

Kvist, J. (2015a). 'ESPN thematic report on social investment, Denmark', report by the European Commission's European Social Policy Network, <http://ec.europa.eu/social>, accessed 14 October 2015.

Kvist, J. (2015b). 'A framework for social investment strategies: integrating generational, life course and gender perspectives in the EU Social Investment Strategy', *Comparative European Politics*, 13, 131–49.

Kvist, J., and Greve, B. (2011). 'Has the Nordic welfare model been transformed?', *Social Policy & Administration* 45(2), 146–60.

Kwon, H.-J. (1997). 'Beyond European welfare regimes: comparative perspectives on East Asian welfare systems', *Journal of Social Policy*, 26(4), 467–84.

Kwon, H.-J. (2005). *Transforming the Developmental Welfare State in East Asia*. Basingstoke: Palgrave Macmillan.

Kwon, H.-J. (2009). 'The reform of the developmental welfare state in East Asia', *International Journal of Social Welfare*, 18, 12–21.

Lalive, R., Landais, C., and Zweimüller, J. (2013). *Market Externalities of Large Unemployment Insurance Extension Programs*, IZA-Discussion Paper 7650. Bonn: IZA.

Lalonde, R. J. (1995). 'The promise of public sector-sponsored training programs', *Journal of Economic Perspectives*, 9(2), 149–68.

Lavinas, L. (2015). 'Latin America: anti-poverty schemes instead of social protection', *Contemporary Readings in Law and Social Justice*, 7(1), 112–71.

Layard, R. (2005). *Happiness*. London: Penguin.

Le Grand, J. (1982). *The Strategy for Equality: Redistribution and the Social Services*. London: Allen & Unwin.

Lee, D. J., and Turner, B. S. (1996). *Conflicts about Class: Debating Inequality in Late Industrialism*. London: Routledge.

Lee, S.-S., Jung, Y.-S., Kim, H.-K., Choi, E.-Y., Park, S.-K., Cho, N.-H., Shin, I.-C., Doh, S.-R., Cho, S.-K., and Kang, J.-H. (2005). *Marriage and Birth Trend Survey*. Seoul: Ministry of Health and Welfare.

Leibfried, S., and Obinger, H. (2003). 'The state of the welfare state: German social policy between macroeconomic retrenchment and microeconomic recalibration', *West European Politics*, 26(4), 199–218.

Leibfried, S., and Tennstedt, F. (eds.) (1985). *Politik der Armut und die Spaltung des Sozialstaats*. Frankfurt am Main: Suhrkamp.

Leira, A. (2002). *Working Parents and the Welfare State*. Cambridge: Cambridge University Press.

Leira, A., and Saraceno, C. (2002). 'Care: actors, relationships and contexts'. In B. Hobson, J. Lewis, and B. Siim (eds.), *Contested Concepts in Gender and Social Politics*. Cheltenham: Edward Elgar, 55–83.

Leisering, L. (2009). 'Germany: a centrist welfare state at the crossroads'. In P. Alcock and G. Craig (eds.), *International Social Policy*, 2nd edn. Basingstoke: Palgrave Macmillan, 148–70.

León, M. (ed.) (2014). *The Transformation of Care in European Societies*. Basingstoke: Palgrave Macmillan.

León, M., and Pavolini, E. (2014). 'Social investment or back to familialism? The impact of the economic crisis on family policies in southern Europe', *South European Society and Politics*, 3, 353–69.

León, M., Ranci, C., and Rostgaard, T. (2014a). 'Actors, discourses and institutional adaptations: explaining convergence and divergence in European care regimes'. In M. León (ed.), *The Transformation of Care in European Societies*. Basingstoke: Palgrave Macmillan, 11–33.

León, M., Pavolini, E., and Rostgaard, T. (2014b). 'Cross-national variations in care'. In M. León (ed.), *The Transformation of Care in European Societies*, Basingstoke: Palgrave Macmillan 34–61.

Lessenich, S. (2003). 'Wohlfahrtsstaatliche Semantiken: Politik im Wohlfahrtsstaat'. In S. Lessenich (ed.), *Wohlfahrtsstaatliche Grundbegriffe, Historische und actuelle Diskurse*. Frankfurt am Main: Campus Verlag, 419–26.

Levine, M. V. (1997). *La reconquête de Montréal*. Montreal: vlb éditeur.

Levy, F., and Murnane, R. J. (2005). *The New Division of Labor: How Computers are Creating the Next Job Market*. Princeton, NJ: Princeton University Press.

Levy, J. D. (1999). 'Vice into virtue? Progressive politics and welfare reform in continental Europe', *Politics & Society*, 27(2), June, 239–73.

Levy, S. (2006). *Progress against Poverty: Sustaining Mexico's Progresa-Oportunidades Program*. Washington, DC: Brookings Institution Press.

Levy, S. (2008). *Good Intentions, Bad Outcomes: Social Policy, Informality, and Economic Growth in Mexico*. Washington, DC: Brookings Institution Press.

Lewis, J. (1992). 'Gender and the development of welfare regimes', *Journal of European Social Policy*, 2(3), 159–73.

Lewis, J. (2009). *Work–Family Balance, Gender and Policy*. Cheltenham: Edward Elgar.

Lewis, J. (2010). 'Book review: Gosta Esping-Andersen (2009), The incomplete revolution. Adapting to women's new roles', *Journal of Social Policy*, 39(3), 485–7.

Lewis, J., and Giullari, S. (2005). 'The adult worker model family, gender equality and care: the search for new policy principles and the possibilities and problems of a capabilities approach', *Economy and Society*, 34, 76–104.

Liechti, F. (2015). 'Matthew effects in active labour market policies', unpublished paper, University of Lausanne.

Lierse, H. (2011). *The Evolution of the European Economic Governance System*. Baden-Baden: Nomos.

Lindbeck, A., and Snower, D. J. (1989). *The Insider–Outsider Theory of Employment and Unemployment*. Cambridge, MA: The MIT Press.

Lindh, T. (2009). 'The future needs for social investment in ageing populations: Sweden as a pilot case'. In N. Morel, B. Palier, and J. Palme (eds.), *What Future for Social Investment?* Stockholm: Institute for Future Studies, 131–42.

Lindvall, J., and Rueda, D. (2014). 'The insider–outsider dilemma', *British Journal of Political Science*, 44(2), 460–75.

Lister, R. (2003). 'Investing in the citizen-workers of the future: transformations in citizenship and the state under New Labour', *Social Policy and Administration*, 37(5), 427–43.

Lister, R. (2004). 'The Third Way's social investment state'. In J. Lewis and R. Surender (eds.), *Welfare State Change: Towards a Third Way?* Oxford: Oxford University Press, 157–81.

Lowi, T. (1972). 'Four systems of policy, politics and choice', *Public Administration Review*, July/August, 298–309.

Mclanahan, S. (2004). 'Diverging destinies: how children are faring under the second demographic transition', *Demography* 41(4), 607–27.

Madsen, P. K. (2014). Danish Flexicurity: Still a Beautiful Swan?, Brussels, DG Employment, Social Affairs and Inclusion: Host Country Comments Paper—Denmark.

Maestripieri, L., and Ranci, C. (2015). 'Non è un paese per laureati. La sovra-qualificazione occupazionale dei lavoratori italiani', paper presented at the AIS-ELO Conference, University of Cagliari, 15–17October, <http://goo.gl/LvpSqd>, accessed 3 November 2016.

Mahon, R. (2009). 'The OECD's discourse on the reconciliation of work and family life', *Global Social Policy*, 9(2), 182–203.

Mahon, R. (2010). 'After neo-liberalism? The OECD, the World Bank and the child', *Global Social Policy*, 10(2), 172–92.

Mahon, R. (2013). 'Social investment according to the OECD/DELSA: a discourse in the making', *Global Policy*, 4(2), 150–9.

Mahoney, J. (2012). 'The logic of process tracing tests in the social sciences', *Sociological Methods and Research*, 41(4), 570–97.

Mares, I. (2003). *The Politics of Social Risk*. Cambridge: Cambridge University Press.

Marical, F., Mira d'Ercole, M., Vaalavuo, M., and Verbist, G. (2008). 'Publicly-provided services and the distribution of households' economics resources', *OECD Economic Studies*, 44(1), 9–47.

Marshall, T. H. (1950). *Citizenship and Social Class*. Cambridge: Cambridge University Press.

Martin, J. P. (2014). *Activation and Active Labour Market Policies in OECD Countries: Stylized Facts and Evidence on their Effectiveness*, IZA Policy Paper No. 84. Bonn: IZA.

Martin, J. P., and Grubb, D. (2001). 'What works and for whom: a review of OECD countries' experiences with active labour market policies', *Swedish Economic Policy Review*, 8, 9–56.

Marx, I., and Nolan, B. (2014). 'In-work poverty'. In B. Cantillon and F. Vandenbroucke (eds.), *Reconciling Work and Poverty Reduction: How Successful are European Welfare States?* Oxford: Oxford University Press, 131–57.

Marx, I., Salanauskaite, L., and Verbist, G. (2013). *The Paradox of Redistribution Revisited: And that It May Rest in Peace?*, IZA Discussion Paper 7414. Bonn: IZA.

Matsaganis, M., and Verbist, G. (2009). 'Distributional effects of publicly funded childcare'. In T. Ward, O. Lelkes, H. Sutherland, and I. Toth (eds.), *European Inequalities: Social Inclusion and Income Distribution in the European Union*. Budapest: Tarki, 177–86.

Mätzke, M., and Ostner, I. (2010). 'Introduction: change and continuity in recent family policies', special issue of *Journal of European Social Policy*, 20(5), 387–98.

Meidner, R. (1974). *Coordination and Solidarity: An Approach to Wages Policy*. Stockholm: Bokforlaget Prisma.

Merkel, A. (2013). Speech given at the World Economic Forum Annual Meeting, Davos, <https://www.bundesregierung.de/ContentArchiv/EN/Archiv17/Reden/2013/2013-01-24-merkel-davos.html>, accessed 3 November 2016.

Merton, R. K. (1968). 'The Matthew effect in science', *Science*, 159(3810), 56–63.

Michaels, G., Aswhwini N., and Van Reenan, J. (2010). *Has ICT Polarized Skill Demand? Evidence from Eleven Countries over 25 Years*, Centre for Economic Performance (LSE) Discussion Paper (987). London: Centre for Economic Performance.

Micossi, S., and Peirce, F. (2014). 'Flexibility clauses in the Stability and Growth Pact: no need for revision', *CEPS Policy Brief*, 31(9), 1–14.

Midgley, J. (1999). 'Growth, redistribution, and welfare: toward social investment', *Social Service Review*, 73(1), 3–21.

Midgley, J. (2005). 'Assets in historical and international perspective'. In M. Sherraden (ed.), *Inclusion in the American Dream: Assets, Poverty and Public Policy*. New York: Oxford University Press, 42–58.

Mincer, J. (1958). 'Investment in human capital and personal income distribution', *Journal of Political Economy*, 66(4), 281–302.

Ministère du Travail, de l'Emploi et de la Solidarité sociale (2016). 'Rapport statistique sur la clientèle des programmes d'assistance sociale', Ministère du Travail, de l'Emploi et de la Solidarité sociale, Québec, January.

Ministero degli Affari Esteri (2013). 'Terzi: micro finance to prevent social fragility', press release, 1 February, <http://www.esteri.it/mae/en/sala_stampa/archivionotizie/approfondimenti/2013/02/20130201_puntare_microfinanza.html?LANG=EN>, accessed 3 November 2016.

Ministry of Employment and Labour (2012). 'White Paper 2012' (in Korean), Seoul.

Ministry of Gender Equality and Family (2006). *Annual Report on Women's Policy (in Korean)*, Seoul, <http://www.mogef.go.kr/korea/view/policy/policy02_01d.jsp?func=view&currentPage=4&key_type=&key=&search_start_date=&search_end_date=&class_id=0&idx=1639>, accessed 4 November 2016.

Ministry of Gender Equality and Family (2011). 'Annual report on women's policy' (in Korean), Seoul.

Ministry of Health and Welfare (1997). 'Annual health and welfare statistics' (in Korean), Seoul.

Ministry of Health and Welfare (2002). 'Annual health and welfare statistics' (in Korean), Seoul.

Ministry of Health and Welfare (2006). 'Future-oriented health and social policy: directions and core tasks', press brief (in Korean), Seoul, 21 August.

Ministry of Health and Welfare (2010). 'White Paper 2010' (in Korean), Seoul.

Ministry of Health and Welfare (2013). 'White Paper 2013' (in Korean), Seoul.

Ministry of Health and Welfare (2014). 'Childcare statistics', Seoul.

Ministry of Labour (1997). 'Annual labour statistics' (in Korean), Seoul.

Ministry of Labour (2002a). 'Annual labour statistics' (in Korean), Seoul.

Ministry of Labour (2002b). 'White Paper 2002' (in Korean), Seoul.

Ministry of Labour (2008). 'White Paper 2008' (in Korean), Seoul.

Mintz, S. (2015). *The Prime of Life: A History of Modern Adulthood*. Cambridge, MA: Harvard University Press.

Miura, M., and Hamada, E. (2014). 'A failed attempt? Social investment strategy in Japan', paper presented at ISA World Congress, Yokohama, Japan.

Morel, N. (2007). 'From subsidiarity to "free choice": child- and elder-care policy reforms in France, Belgium, Germany and the Netherlands', *Social Policy and Administration*, 41(6), 618–37.

Morel, N., Palier, B., and Palme, J. (2012a). 'Beyond the welfare state as we knew it?' In N. Morel, B. Palier, and J. Palme (eds.), *Towards a Social Investment Welfare State? Ideas, Policies and Challenges*. Bristol: Policy Press, 1–32.

Morel, N., Palier, B., and Palme, J. (2012b). 'Social investment: a paradigm in search of a new economic model and political mobilisation', In N. Morel, B. Palier, and J. Palme (eds.), *Towards a Social Investment Welfare State? Ideas, Policies and Challenges*. Bristol: Policy Press, 353–76.

Morel, N., Palier, B., and Palme, J. (eds.) (2012c). *Towards a Social Investment State? Ideas, Policies and Challenges*. Bristol: Policy Press.

Morgan, K. J. (2012). 'Promoting social investment through work–family policies: which nations do it and why?' In N. Morel, B. Palier, and J. Palme (eds.), *Towards a Social Investment Welfare State? Ideas, Policies and Challenges*. Bristol: Policy Press, 153–80.

Morgan, K. J. (2013). 'Path shifting of the welfare state: electoral competition and the expansion of work–family policies in Western Europe', *World Politics*, 65(1), 73–115.

Morissette, R., and Johnson, A. (2004). *Earnings of Couples with High and Low Levels of Education, 1980–2000*, Research Paper No. 230, Analytical Studies Branch. Ottawa: Statistics Canada.

Morissette, R., Zhang, X., and Drolet, M. (2002). *The Evolution of Wealth Inequality in Canada, 1984–1999*, Research Paper No. 187, Analytical Studies Branch. Ottawa: Statistics Canada.

Mosher, J. (2015). 'Education state, welfare capitalism regimes, and politics', *Comparative European Politics*, 13, 240–62.

Murmann, K. (1995). 'Blüm hat recht', *Frankfurter Allgemeine Sonntagszeitung*, 23 July.

Myles, J. (2000). 'The maturation of Canada's retirement income system: income levels, income inequality and low income among older persons', *Canadian Journal on Aging* 19(3), 287–316.

Myles, J. (2002). 'A new social contract for the elderly'. In G. Esping-Andersen, D. Gallie, A. Hemerijck, and J.Myles (eds.), *Why We Need a New Welfare State*. Oxford: Oxford University Press, 130–72.

Myles, J. (2010). 'The inequality surge: changes in the family life course are the main cause'. The Free Library (1 January), <https://www.thefreelibrary.com/The inequality surge: changes in the family life course are the main...-a0215786568>, accessed 25 October 2016.

Naczyk, M., and Seeleib-Kaiser, M. (2015). 'Solidarity against all odds: trade unions and the privatization of pensions in the age of dualization', *Politics and Society*, 43, 361–84.

National Advisory Council of Economy (2007). 'New vision and strategy for mutual growth' (in Korean), Seoul.

Nelson, M. (2010). 'The adjustment of national education systems to a knowledge-based economy: a new approach', *Comparative Education*, 46(4), 463–86.

Nelson, M., and Sandberg, J. (2016). 'From perspectives to policy contingencies: conditional cash transfers as social investments', *Global Social Policy*, 1468018116633560.

Nelson, M., and Stephens, J. D. (2012). 'Do social investment policies produce more and better jobs?' In N. Morel, B. Palier, and J. Palme (eds.), *Towards a Social Investment Welfare State? Ideas, Policies and Challenges*. Bristol: Policy Press, 205–34.

Nelson, M., and Stephens, J. D. (2013). 'The service transition and women's employment'. In A. Wren (ed.), *The Political Economy of the Service Transition*. New York: Oxford University Press, 147–70.

NESC (National Economic and Social Council) (2002). *An Investment in Quality: Services, Inclusion and Enterprise, Overview, Conclusions and Recommendations*. Dublin: National Economic and Social Council.

NESC (National Economic and Social Council) (2005). *The Developmental Welfare State*. Dublin: National Economic and Social Council.

NESC (National Economic and Social Council) (2009). *Ireland's Five-Part Crisis: An Integrated National Response*. Dublin: National Economic and Social Council.

NESC (National Economic and Social Council) (2013). *Five Part Crisis, Five Years On: Deepening Reform and Institutional Innovation*. Dublin: National Economic and Social Council.

NESF (National Economic and Social Forum) (1997). *A Framework for Partnership: Enriching Strategic Consensus through Partnership*. Dublin: National Economic and Social Forum.

Neumayer, E. (2007). 'A missed opportunity: the Stern Review on climate change fails to tackle the issue of non-substitutable loss of natural capital', *Global Environmental Change*, 17(3), 297–301.

Newman, K. (2012). *The Accordion Family: Boomerang Kids, Anxious Parents, and the Private Toll of Global Competition*. Boston, MA: Beacon Press.

Nieuwenhuis, R., Need, A., and Van Der Kolk, H. (2012). 'Institutional and demographic explanations of women's employment in 18 OECD countries, 1975–1999', *Journal of Marriage and Family*, 74(3), 614–30.

Nieuwenhuis, R., van Lancker, W., Collado, D., and Cantillon, B. (2016). *Has the Potential for Compensating Poverty by Women's Employment Growth Been Depleted?*, LIS Working Paper No. 664, Luxembourg Income Study, <http://www.lisdatacenter.org/wps/liswps/664.pdf>, accessed 3 November 2016.

Nikolai, R. (2012). 'Towards social investment? Patterns of public policy in the OECD world'. In N. Morel, B. Palier, and J. Palme (eds.), *Towards a Social Investment Welfare State? Ideas, Policies and Challenges*. Bristol: Policy Press, 91–116.

Noël, A. (2008). 'Fédéralisme d'ouverture et pouvoir de dépenser au Canada', *Revista d'Estudis Autonòmics i Federals*, 7, October, 10–36.

Noël, A. (2013). 'Quebec's new politics of redistribution'. In K. Banting and J. Myles (eds.), *Inequality and the Fading of Redistributive Politics*. Vancouver: UBC Press, 256–82.

Noël, A. (2015). 'Quebec: the ambivalent politics of social solidarity'. In D. Béland and P.-M. Daigneault (eds.), *Welfare Reform in Canada: Provincial Social Assistance in Comparative Perspective*. Toronto: University of Toronto Press, 127–41.

Nolan, B. (2013). 'What use is "social investment"?' *Journal of European Social Policy*, 23(5), 459–68.

Nordhaus, W. D. (2007). 'A review of the Stern Review on the economics of climate change', *Journal of Economic Literature*, 45, 686–702.

Nussbaum, M. C. (2001). *Women and Human Development: The Capabilities Approach*. New York: Cambridge University Press.

Nussbaum, M. C. (2002). 'Bisogni di cura e diritti umani'. In M. C. Nussbaum, *Giustizia sociale e dignità umana*. Bologna: Il Mulino, 27–50.

Nussbaum, M. C., and Sen, A. (eds.) (1993). *The Quality of Life*. Oxford: Clarendon Press.

Obama, B. (2015). 2015 State of the Union Speech, delivered 20 January 2015. <https://www.whitehouse.gov/blog/2015/01/20/watch-president-obamas-2015-state-union>, accessed 14 December 2016.

Oberhuemer, P. (2011). 'The early childhood education workforce in Europe between divergencies and emergencies', *International Journal of Child Care and Education Policy*, 5(1), 55–63.

Ocampo, J. (2004). 'Latin America's growth and equity frustrations during structural reforms', *Journal of Economic Perspectives*, 18(2), 67–88.

O'Connor, J. (1973). *The Fiscal Crisis of the State*. New York: St. Martin's Press.

O'Donnell, R. (2008). 'The partnership state: building the ship at sea'. In M. Adshead, P. Kirby, and M. Millar (eds.), *Contesting the State: Lessons from the Irish Case*. Manchester: Manchester University Press, 73–99.

O'Donnell, R., Adshead, M., and Thomas, D. (2011). 'Ireland: two trajectories of institutionalisation'. in S. Avdagic, M. Rhodes, and J. Visser (eds.), *Social Pacts in Europe: Emergence, Evolution, and Institutionalization*. Oxford: Oxford University Press, 89–117.

O'Donnell, R., Cahill, N., and Thomas, D. (2010). 'Ireland: the evolution of social pacts in the EMU era'. in P. Pochet, M. Keune, and D. Natali (eds.), *After the Euro and Enlargement: Social Pacts in the EU*. Brussels: ETUI aisbl, 191–222.

OECD (Organisation for Economic Co-operation and Development) (1994). *The OECD Jobs Study*. Paris: OECD.

OECD (Organisation for Economic Co-operation and Development) (1997). *Beyond 2000: The New Social Policy Agenda*, OECD Working Papers, vol. V: #43. Paris: OECD.

OECD (Organisation for Economic Co-operation and Development) (2001). *The Well-Being of Nations: The Role of Human and Social Capital*. Paris: OECD.

OECD (Organisation for Economic Co-operation and Development) (2005). *Education at a Glance: OECD Indicators*. Paris: OECD.

OECD (Organisation for Economic Co-operation and Development) (2006a). *OECD Employment Outlook: Boosting Jobs and Wages*. Paris: OECD.

OECD (Organisation for Economic Co-operation and Development) (2006b). *OECD Work on Education*. Paris: OECD.

OECD (Organisation for Economic Co-operation and Development) (2007). *Babies and Bosses, Reconciling Work and Family Life: A Synthesis of Findings for OECD Countries*. Paris: OECD.

OECD (Organisation for Economic Co-operation and Development) (2008). *Growing Unequal? Income Distribution and Poverty in OECD Countries*. Paris, OECD.

OECD (Organisation for Economic Co-operation and Development) (2009). *Regions at a Glance*. Paris: OECD.

OECD (Organisation for Economic Co-operation and Development) (2011a). *Divided We Stand: Why Inequality Keeps Rising*. Paris: OECD.

OECD (Organisation for Economic Co-operation and Development) (2011b). *Doing Better for Families*. Paris: OECD.

OECD (Organisation for Economic Co-operation and Development) (2012a). *Education at a Glance: Country Note Korea*. Paris: OECD.

OECD (Organisation for Economic Co-operation and Development) (2012b). *Perspectives on Global Development: Social Cohesion in a Shifting World*. Paris: OECD.

OECD (Organisation for Economic Co-operation and Development). (2012c). *What are the Returns on Higher Education for Individuals and Countries? Education Indicators in Focus, 2012/06 (June)*. Paris: OECD.

OECD (Organisation for Economic Co-operation and Development) (2013a). *Activation Strategies for Stronger and More Inclusive Labour Markets in G20 Countries: Key Policy Challenges and Good Practices*. Paris: OECD.

OECD (Organisation for Economic Co-operation and Development) (2013b). *Education Reform in Korea*, OECD Economics Department Working Papers, No. 1067. Paris: OECD.

OECD (Organisation for Economic Co-operation and Development) (2013c). *Italy. Country Note, Education at a Glance, 2013*. Paris: OECD.

OECD (Organisation for Economic Co-operation and Development) (2014a). *All on Board: Making Inclusive Growth Happen*. Paris: OECD.

OECD (Organisation for Economic Co-operation and Development) (2014b). *Education at a Glance 2014: OECD Indicators*. Paris: OECD.

OECD (Organisation for Economic Co-operation and Development) (2014c). *Education at a Glance 2014: OECD Indicators, Country Note Sweden*. Paris: OECD.

OECD (Organisation for Economic Co-operation and Development) (2014d). *Resources, Policies and Practices in Sweden's Schooling System: An In-Depth Analysis of Pisa 2012 Results*. Paris: OECD.

OECD (Organisation for Economic Co-operation and Development) (2015a). *Better Life Initiative: Measuring Well-Being and Progress*. Paris: OECD.

OECD (Organisation for Economic Co-operation and Development) (2015b). 'Income distribution and poverty', OECD, <https://stats.oecd.org/Index.aspx?DataSetCode=IDD>, accessed 15 May 2015.

OECD (Organisation for Economic Co-operation and Development) (2015c). *In It Together: Why Less Inequality Benefits All*. Paris: OECD.

OECD (Organisation for Economic Co-operation and Development) (2015d). 'Labour force statistics by sex and age: indicators', OECD, <http://stats.oecd.org/Index.aspx?DataSetCode=LFS_SEXAGE_I_R>, accessed 15 May 2015.

OECD (Organisation for Economic Co-operation and Development) (2015e). 'OECD family database', OECD, <http://www.oecd.org/social/family/database.htm>, accessed 15 May 2015.

OECD (Organisation for Economic Co-operation and Development) (2015f). *OECD Skills Outlook 2015: Youth, Skills and Employability*. Paris: OECD.

OECD (Organisation for Economic Co-operation and Development) (2016a). Social Expenditure Database (SOCX), <http://stats.oecd.org/>, accessed 3 November 2016.

OECD (Organisation for Economic Co-operation and Development) (2016b). Social and Welfare Statistics: Income Distribution, <http://stats.oecd.org/>, accessed 3 November 2016.

OECD (Organisation for Economic Co-operation and Development) (2016c). Social Protection and Wellbeing database: Full-time equivalent employment rate, by sex, <http://stats.oecd.org/>, accessed 3 November 2016.

OECD (Organisation for Economic Co-operation and Development) (n.d.). Inclusive Growth: About, <http://www.oecd.org/inclusive-growth/about.htm>, accessed 4 November 2016.

Oesch, D. (2015). 'Welfare regimes and change in the employment structure: Britain, Denmark and Germany since 1990', *Journal of European Social Policy*, 25(1), 94–110.

Offe, C. (1991). 'Smooth consolidation in the West German welfare state: structural change, fiscal policies, and populist politics'. In F. F. Piven (ed.), *Labor Parties in Postindustrial Societies*. New York and Oxford: Oxford University Press, 124–46.

Offe, C. (2011). 'What, if anything, might we mean by 'progressive' politics today?', paper presented at the Social Indicators Conference, Villa Vigoni, March.

Office of the President (1999). 'Way to productive welfare for the new millennium' (in Korean), Seoul.

Økonomi- og Indenrigsministeriet. (2015). 'Kommunale nøgletal', <http://www.noegletal.dk/>, accessed 6 May 2015.

Okun, A. M. (1975). *Equality and Efficiency: The Big Trade Off*. Washington, DC: The Brookings Institution.

O'Neill, D., and Sweetman, O. (1998). 'Intergenerational mobility in Britain: evidence from unemployment patterns', *Oxford Bulletin of Economics and Statistics*, 60(4), 431–47.

Orloff, A. S. (2010). 'Gender'. In F. G. Castles, S. Leibfried, J. Lewis, H. Obinger, and C. Pierson (eds.), *The Oxford Handbook of the Welfare State*. Oxford: Oxford University Press.

Orton, M. (2011). 'Flourishing lives: the capabilities approach as a framework for new thinking about employment, work and welfare in the 21st century', *Work, Employment & Society*, 25, 352.

Paananen, M., Kumpulainen, K., and Lipponen, L. (2015). 'Quality drift within a narrative of early childhood education', *European Early Childhood Education Research Journal*, 23(5), 690–705.

Pakulski, J., and Waters, M. (1996). *The Death of Class*. London: Sage.

Palier, B. (2005). 'Ambiguous agreement, cumulative change: French social policy in the 1990s'. In W. Streeck and K. Thelen (eds.), *Beyond Continuity: Institutional Change in Advanced Political Economies*. Oxford: Oxford University Press, 127–44.

Palier, B. (2006). 'The re-orientation of Europe social policies towards social investment', *International Journal of Politics, Culture and Society*, 1, 105–16.

Palier, B. (2010). *A Long Goodbye to Bismarck? The Politics of Welfare Reforms in Continental Europe*. Amsterdam: Amsterdam University Press.

Palier, B., and Thelen, K. (2010). 'Institutionalising dualism: complementarities and change in France and Germany', *Politics & Society*, 38(1), 119–48.

Palme, J., and Cronert, A. (2015). *Trends in the Swedish Social Investment Welfare State*, ImPRovE Working Paper 15-12. Antwerp: Herman Deleeck Centre for Social Policy, University of Antwerp.

Palme, J., Bergmark, A., Bäckman, O., Estrada, F., Fritzell, J., Lundberg, O., Sjöberg, O., Sommestad, L., and Szebehely, M. (2003). 'A welfare balance sheet for the 1990s: final report of the Swedish Welfare Commission', *Scandinavian Journal of Public Health*, 63, 7–143.

Park, D.-Y. (2011). 'Korean policies on secondary vocatiobal education: efforts to overcome skills mismatch and labor force shortage', *Berufsbildung in Wissenschaft and Praxis*, 40(3), 30–3.

Paulus, A., Sutherland, H., and Tsakloglou, P. (2010). 'The distributional impact of in-kind public benefits in European countries', *Journal of Policy Analysis and Management*, 29(2), 243–66.

Pavolini, E., and Arlotti, M. (2015). 'Growing unequal: child care policies in Italy and the social class divide', paper presented at the 22nd International Conference of Europeanists, organized by the Council for European Studies (CES), Paris, 8–10 July.

Pavolini, E., León, M., Guillén, A. M., and Ascoli, U. (2015). 'From austerity to permanent strain? The EU and welfare state reform in Italy and Spain', *Comparative European Politics*, 13(1), 56–76.

Pearson, M., and Scherer, P. (1997). 'Balancing security and sustainability in social policy', *OECD Observer*, 205, April–May, 6–9.

Peng, I. (2002). 'Social care in crisis: gender, demography, and welfare state restructuring in Japan', *Social Politics: International Studies in Gender, State & Society*, 9(3), 411–43.

Peng, I. (2011). 'Social investment in Canada, Australia, Japan and South Korea', *International Journal of Child Care and Education Policy*, 5(1), 41–53.

Peng, I. (2012a). 'Economic dualization in Japan and South Korea'. In P. Emmenegger, S. Häusermann, B. Palier, and M. Seeleib-Kaiser (eds.), *The Age of Dualization: The Changing Face of Inequality in Deindustrializing Societies*. New York: Oxford University Press, 226–52.

Peng, I. (2012b). 'Social and political economy of care in Japan and South Korea', *International Journal of Sociology and Social Policy*, 32(11/12), 636–49.

Peng, I. (2015). 'The "new" social investment policies in Japan and South Korea'. In R. Hasmath (ed.), *Inclusive Growth, Development and Welfare Policy*. Oxford: Routledge, 142–60.

Peng, I., and Wong, J. (2010). 'East Asia'. In F. G. Castles, S. Leibfried, J. Lewis, H. Obinger, and C. Pierson (eds.), *The Oxford Handbook of the Welfare State*. Oxford: Oxford University Press, 656–70.

Pestoff, V., Brandsen T., and B. Verscheure (eds.) (2012). *New Public Governance, the Third Sector and Co-Production*. London: Routledge.

Petmesidou, M., and Guillén, A. M. (2014). 'Can the welfare state as we know it survive? A view from the crisis-ridden south European periphery', *South European Society and Politics*, 19(3), 295–307.

Pettersen, S. V., and Østby, L. (2013). Immigrants in Norway, Sweden and Denmark, Samfunnsspeilet 5/2013. Statistisk sentralbyrå. <https://www.ssb.no/en/befolkning/artikler-og-publikasjoner/_attachment/204333?_ts=1497ab86428>, accessed 3 November 2016.

Pierson, P. (1996). 'The new politics of the welfare state', *World Politics*, 48, 143–79.

Pierson, P. (1998). 'Irresistible forces, immovable objects: post-industrial welfare states confront permanent austerity', *Journal of European Public Policy*, 5, 539–60.

Pierson, P. (2000). 'Increasing returns, path dependence, and the study of politics', *American Political Science Review*, 94(2), 251–67.

Pierson, P. (ed.) (2001). *The New Politics of the Welfare State*. Oxford and New York: Oxford University Press.

Pierson, P. (2004). *Politics in Time: History, Institutions and Social Analysis*. Princeton, NJ, and Oxford: Princeton University Press.

Pigou, A. C. (1928). *A Study in Public Finance*. London: Macmillan.

Piketty, T. (2014). *Capital in the Twenty-First Century*. Cambridge, MA, and London: Belknap Press of Harvard University Press.

Pintelon, O., Cantillon, B., Van den Bosch, K., and Whelan, C. T. (2013). 'The social stratification of social risks: the relevance of class for social investment strategies', *Journal of European Social Policy*, 23(1), 52–67.

Plantenga, J., and Remery, C. (2013). *Childcare Services for School Age Children*. Luxembourg: Publications Office of the European Union.

Polanyi, K. (1957). *The Great Transformation*. Boston, MA: Beacon Press.

Portes, A. (2010). *Economic Sociology: A Systematic Inquiry*. Princeton, NJ: Princeton University Press.

Posner, P. L., and Sommerfeld, M. (2013). 'The politics of fiscal austerity: democracies and hard choices', *OECD Journal on Budgeting*, 2013 (1), 141–74.

Psacharopoulos, G. (1995). *Building Human Capital for Better Lives*. Washington, DC: World Bank.

Putnam, R. (2015). *Our Kids: The American Dream in Crisis*. New York: Simon & Schuster.

Radice, H. (2014). 'Enforcing austerity in Europe: the structural deficit as a policy target', *Journal of Contemporary European Studies*, 22(3), 318–28.

Radner, D. (1997). 'Non-cash income, equivalence scales and the measurement of economic well-being', *Review of Income and Wealth*, 43(1), March, 71–88.

Ramsey, F. P. (1928). 'A mathematical theory of saving', *Economic Journal*, 38(4), 543–9.

Ranci, C., and Sabatinelli, S. (2014). 'Long term and child care in Italy between familism and privatisation'. In M. Leon (ed.), *Care Regimes in Transitional European Societies*. Basingstoke: Palgrave Macmillan, 233–55.

Ranganathan, M., and Lagarde, M. (2012). 'Promoting healthy behaviours and improving health outcomes in low and middle income countries: a review of the impact of conditional cash transfer programmes', *Preventive Medicine*, 55, 95–105.

Rawls, J. (1971). *A Theory of Justice*. Cambridge, MA: Harvard University Press.

Rehn, G. (1985). 'Swedish active labour market policy: retrospect and prospect', *Industrial Relations: A Journal of Economy and Society*, 24(1), 62–89.

Rice, D. (2015). *Building Active Welfare States: How Policy Shapes Caseworker Practice*. Amsterdam: VU University Press.

Richardson, D., and Patana, P. (2012). *Integrating Service Delivery: Why, for Who, and How*. Paris: OECD.

Rocher, F. (2009). 'The Quebec-Canada dynamic or the negation of the ideal of federalism'. In A. G. Gagnon (ed.), *Contemporary Canadian Federalism: Foundations, Traditions, Institutions*. Toronto, University of Toronto Press, 81–131.

Rodríguez-Oreggia, E., and Freije, S. (2012). *Long Term Impact of a Cash-Transfer Program on Labor Outcomes of the Rural Youth*, CID Working Paper No. 230. Cambridge, MA: Harvard University Press.

Rodrik, D. (2006). 'Goodbye Washington Consensus, hello Washington confusion? A review of the World Bank's economic growth in the 1990s: learning from a decade of reform', *Journal of Economic Literature*, 44(4), 973–87.

Rothstein, B. (1996). 'The moral logic of the universal welfare state'. In E. O. Erikson and J. Loftager (eds), *The Rationality of the Welfare State*. Oslo: Scandinavian University Press.

Rothstein, B. (1998). *Just Institutions Matter*. Cambridge: Cambridge University Press.

Rovny, A. E. (2014). 'The capacity of social policies to combat poverty among new social risk groups', *Journal of European Social Policy*, 21(4), 335–47.

Rueda, D. (2007). *Social Democracy Inside Out: Partisanship and Labor Market Policy in Advanced Industrialized Democracies*. Oxford: Oxford University Press.

Rueda, D. (2015). 'The state of the welfare state: unemployment, labor market policy and inequality in the age of workfare', *Comparative Politics*, 47(3), 296–314.

Rueda, D., Wibbels, E., and Altamirano, M. (2015). 'The origins of dualism'. In P. Beramendi, S. Häusermann, H. Kitschelt, and H. Kriesi (eds.), *The Politics of Advanced Capitalism*. Cambridge: Cambridge University Press, 89–111.

Sabel, C. F. (2012). 'Individualized service provision and the new welfare state: are there lessons from northern Europe for developing countries?' In L. de Mello and M. A. Dutz (eds.), *Promoting Inclusive Growth, Challenges and Policies*. Paris: OECD, 75–111.

Sabel, C. F. (2006). 'A real-time revolution in routines'. In C. Heckscher and P. Alder (eds.), *The Firm as a Collaborative Community*. New York: Oxford University Press, 106–56.

Sabel, C. F., and Victor, D. (2015). 'Governing global problems under uncertainty: making bottom-up climate policy work', *Climatic Change* (October), 1–13.

Sabel, C. F., Saxenian, A., Miettinen, R., Kristensen, P. H., and Hautamäki, J. (2011). 'Individualized service provision in the new welfare state: lessons from special education in Finland'. Report prepared for SITRA, Helsinki, December, <http://www2.law.columbia.edu/sabel/papers.html>, accessed 3 November 2016.

Sacchi, S., and Vesan, P. (2015). 'Employment policy: segmentation, deregulation and reforms in the Italian labour market'. In U. Ascoli and E. Pavolini (eds.), *The Italian Welfare State in a European Perspective*. Bristol: Policy Press, 71–99.

Sahlberg, P. (2011). *Finnish Lessons*. New York: Teachers' College Press.

Saint-Martin, D. (2000). 'De l'État-providence à l'État d'investissement social: un nouveau paradigme pour enfant-er l'économie du savoir?' In L. A. Pal (ed.), *How Ottawa Spends 2000–2001: Past Imperfect, Future Tense*. Don Mills, Ontario: Oxford University Press, 33–57.

Salais, R. (2003). 'Work and welfare: toward a capability approach'. In J. Zeitlin and D. Trubek (eds.), *Governing Work and Welfare in a New Economy: European and American Experiments*. Oxford: Oxford University Press, 317–44.

Samans, R., Blanke, J., Corrigan, G., and Drzeniek, M. (2015). *The Inclusive Growth and Development Report 2015*. Geneva: World Economic Forum.

Sandberg, J. (2012). 'Conditional cash transfers and social mobility: the role of asymmetric structures and segmentation processes', *Development and Change*, 43(6), 1337–59.

Sandberg, J. (2015). 'Between poor relief and human capital investments: paradoxes in hybrid social assistance', *Social Policy & Administration*. 50(3), 316–35.

Sandberg, J., and Tally, E. (2015). 'Politicisation of conditional cash transfers: the case of Guatemala', *Development Policy Review*, 3(4), 503–22.

Saraceno, C. (2011). 'Childcare needs and childcare policies: a multidimensional issue', *Current Sociology*, 79(1), 78–96.

Saraceno, C. (2015). 'A critical look to the social investment approach from a gender perspective', *Social Politics*, 22(2), 257–69.

Saraceno, C., and Keck, W. (2010). 'Can we identify intergenerational policy regimes in Europe?' *European Societies*, 12(5), 675–96.

Sauve, P. (2001). *The Trade Policy Implications of the New Economy*. Paris: OECD.

Scharpf, F. W. (1991). *Crisis and Choice in European Social Democracy*. Ithaca, NY: Cornell University Press.

Scharpf, F. W. and Schmidt, V. A. (eds.) (2000). *Welfare and Work in the Open Economy*. Oxford: Oxford University Press.

Schelkle, W. (2012a). 'In the spotlight of crisis: how social policies create, correct, and compensate financial markets', *Politics & Society*, 40(1), 3–8.

Schelkle, W. (2012b). 'Policymaking in hard times: French and German responses to the Eurozone crisis'. In N. Bermeo and J. Pontusson (eds.), *Coping with Crisis: Government Reactions to the Great Recession*. New York: Russell Sage, 130–61.

Schindler, H. S., Kholoptseva, J., Oh, S. S., Yoshikawa, H., Duncan, G. J., Magnuson, K. A., and Shonkoff, J. P. (2015). 'Maximizing the potential of early childhood education to prevent externalizing behavior problems: a meta-analysis', *Journal of School Psychology*, 53(3), 243–63.

Schmid, G. (2008). *Full Employment in Europe. Managing Labour Market Transitions and Risks*. Cheltenham and Northampton, MA: Edward Elgar.

Schmid, G. (2011). 'Non-standard employment in europe: its development and consequences for the European employment strategy', *German Policy Studies*, 7(1), 171–210.

Schmid, G. (2015). 'Sharing risks of labour market transitions: towards a system of employment insurance', *British Journal of Industrial Relations*, 63(1), 70–93.

Schmidt, M. G. (2002). 'Germany: the grand coalition state'. In J. M. Colomer (ed.), *Political Institutions in Europe*. London: Routledge, 55–93.

Schmidt, V. A. (2008). 'Discursive institutionalism: the explanatory power of ideas and discourse', *Political Science*, 11(1), 303.

Schmidt, V. A. (2010). 'Taking ideas and discourse seriously: explaining change through discursive institutionalism as the fourth "new institutionalism"', *European Political Science Review*, 2(1), 1–25.

Schmidt, V. A. and Thatcher, M. (eds.) (2013). *Resilient Liberalism in Europe's Political Economy*. Cambridge: Cambridge University Press.

Schultz, T. W. (1961). 'Investment in human capital', *American Economic Review*, 51, 1–17.

Scott, J. (1996). Class: critical concepts (vol. 1). Abingdon: Taylor & Francis.

Seeleib-Kaiser, M. (1993). *Amerikanische Sozialpolitik*. Opladen: Leske & Budrich.

Seeleib-Kaiser, M. (2001). *Globalisierung und Sozialpolitik*. Frankfurt am Main: Campus.

Seeleib-Kaiser, M. (2002). 'A dual transformation of the German welfare state?' *West European Politics*, 24(4), 25–48.

Seeleib-Kaiser, M. (2010). 'Socio-economic change, party competition and intra-party conflict: the family policy of the grand coalition', *German Politics*, 19(3–4), 416–28.

Seeleib-Kaiser, M. (2014). 'Welfare state reform and social policy'. In S. Padgett, W. E. Paterson, and R. Zohlnhöfer (eds.), *Developments in German Politics*. Basingstoke: Palgrave Macmillan, 227–40.

Seeleib-Kaiser, M. (2016). 'The end of the conservative German welfare state model', *Social Policy & Administration*, 50(2), 219–40.

Seeleib-Kaiser, M., and Fleckenstein, T. (2007). 'Discourse, learning and welfare state change: the case of German labour market reforms', *Social Policy & Administration*, 41(5), 427–48.

Seeleib-Kaiser, M., Saunders, A., and Naczyk, M. (2012). 'Shifting the public–private mix: a new dualization of welfare?' In P. Emmenegger, S. Häusermann, B. Palier, and M. Seeleib-Kaiser (eds.), *The Age of Dualization: The Changing Face of Inequality in Deindustrializing Societies*. New York and Oxford: Oxford University Press, 151–75.

Sen, A. (1985). *Commodities and Capabilities*. Amsterdam: North Holland.

Sen, A. (2001). *Development as Freedom*. Oxford: Oxford University Press.

Sen, A. (2009). *The Idea of Justice*. Cambridge, MA: Harvard University Press.

Serra, N., Spiegel, S., and Stiglitz, J. (2008). 'Introduction: from the Washington Consensus towards a new global governance'. In N. Serra and J. Stiglitz (eds.), *The Washington Consensus Reconsidered: Towards a New Global Governance*. Oxford: Oxford University Press, 3–13.

Seth, M. J. (2002). *Education Fever: Society, Politics, and the Pursuit of Schooling in South Korea*. Honolulu: University of Hawai'i Press.

Sharp, C. (2002). 'School starting age: European policy and recent research', paper presented at the LGA Seminar 'When Should Our Children Start School?', LGA Conference Centre, Smith Square, London.

Shavit, Y., and Blossfeld, H.-P. (eds.) (1993). *Persistent Inequality: Changing Educational Attainment in Thirteen Countries*. Boulder, CO: Westview Press.

Sinn, H. W. (1996). 'Social insurance, incentives and risk-taking', *International Tax and Public Finance*, 3(3), 259–80.

Skolverket (2012). *Educational Equity in the Swedish School System? A Quantitative Analysis of Equity over Time*. Stockholm: National Agency for Education.

Skoufias, E., Davis, B., and De la Vega, S. (2001). 'Targeting the poor in Mexico: an evaluation of the selection of households for Progresa', *World Development*, 29(10), 1769–84.

Smeeding, T. M. (1977). 'The antipoverty effectiveness of in-kind transfers', *Journal of Human Resources*, 12, 360–78.

Smeeding, T. M. (1982). *Alternative Methods for Valuing Selected In-Kind Transfer Benefits and Measuring their Effect on Poverty*, U.S. Bureau of Census Technical Paper No. 50. Washington, DC: US Government Printing Office.

Smeeding, T. M., Saunders, P., Coder, J., Jenkins, S. P., Fritzell, J., Hagenaars, A. J. M., Hauser, R., and Wolfson, M. (1993). 'Poverty, inequality, and family living standards impact across seven nations: the effect of noncash subsidies for health, education and housing', *Review of Income and Wealth*, 39(3), 229–56.

Smyth, P. (2015). 'Social investment for inclusive growth in Australia'. In R. Hasmath (ed.), *Inclusive Growth, Development and Welfare Policy: A Critical Assessment*. London: Routledge, 179–94.

Soares, F., and Britto, T. (2007). *Confronting Capacity Constraints on Conditional Cash Transfers in Latin America: The Cases of El Salvador and Paraguay*, Working Paper No. 38. Brasilia: International Poverty Centre.

Soares, S., Osorio, R. G., Soares, F. V., Medeiros, M., and Zepeda, E. (2009). 'Conditional cash transfers in Brazil, Chile and Mexico: impacts upon inequality', *Estudios Económicos*, 1, 207–24.

Soares, S., Osório, R., Soares, F., Medeiros, M., and Zepeda, E. (2007). *Conditional Cash Transfers in Brazil, Chile and Mexico: Impacts upon Inequality*, Working Paper No. 35. International Poverty Centre. <https://www.researchgate.net/profile/Eduardo_Zepeda/publication/5129056_Conditional_Cash_Transfers_in_Brazil_Chile_and_Mexico_Impacts_Upon_Inequality/links/0deec536ba7846eb35000000.pdf>, accessed 3 November 2016.

Soederberg, S. (2014). *Debtfare States and the Poverty Industry: Money, Discipline and the Surplus Population*. London and New York: Routledge.

Solga, H. (2014). 'Education, economic inequality and the promises of the social investment state', *Socio-Economic Review*, 12, 269–97.

Staab, S. (2010). 'Social investment policies in Chile and Latin America: towards equal opportunities for women and children?' *Journal of Social Policy*, 39(4), 607–26.

Standing, G. (2014). *A Precariat Charter: From Denizens to Citizens*. London: Bloomsbury Academic.

Statistics Denmark (2014). 'Indvandrere i Danmark, Copenhagen: Danmarks Statistik', <http://www.dst.dk/publ/indvandrereidk>, accessed 3 November 2016.

Statistics Sweden (2005). 'Trends and forecasts 2005: population, education and labour market in Sweden, outlook to 2020'. Stockholm: Prognosinstitutet.

Statistics Sweden (2013). 'Youth unemployment: comparability in statistics between a number of European countries', Stockholm.

Statistics Sweden (2014). 'Women and men in Sweden 2014', Örebro.

Steinmo, S. (2003). 'The evolution of policy ideas: tax policy in the 20th century', *British Journal of Politics and International Relations*, 5(2), 206–36.

Stern, N. H. (2006). *Stern Review: The Economics of Climate Change* (vol. 30). Cambridge: Cambridge University Press.

Stern, N. H. (2015). *Why are We Waiting? The Logic, Urgency, and Promise of Tackling Climate Change*. Cambridge, MA: The MIT Press.

Stevenson, A. (ed.) (2010). *Oxford Dictionary of English*. Oxford: Oxford University Press.

Stiglitz, J., Sen, A., and Fitoussi, J.-P. (2009). 'Report by the Commission on the Measurement of Economic Performance and Social Progress', <http://www.stiglitz-sen-fitoussi.fr>, accessed 3 November 2016.

Stiller, S. (2010). *Ideational Leadership in German Welfare State Reform*. Amsterdam: Amsterdam University Press.

Stiroh, K. J. (2002). 'Information technology and the U.S. productivity revival: what do the industry data say?' *American Economic Review*, 92(5), 1559–76.

Stoesz, D. (2016). *The Dynamic Welfare State*. New York: Oxford University Press.

Streeck, W. (2011). *Skills and Politics: General and Specific*, MPIfG Discussion Paper 11/1, <http://dx.doi.org/10.2139/ssrn.1781042>, accessed 3 November 2016.

Streeck, W. (2014). *Buying Time: The Delayed Crisis of Democratic Capitalism*. New York: Verso.

Streeck, W. (2015). *The Rise of the European Consolidation State*, MPIfG Discussion Paper 1/15. Cologne: Max Planck Institute for the Study of Societies.

Streeck, W., and Mertens, D. (2011). *Fiscal Austerity and Public Investment: Is the Possible the Enemy of the Necessary?* MPIfG Discussion Paper, 11/12. <https://ssrn.com/abstract=1894657>, accessed 3 November 2016.

Streeck, W., and Mertens, D. (2013). 'Public finance and the decline of state capacity in democratic capitalism'. In A. Schäfer and W. Streeck (eds.), *Politics in the Age of Austerity*. Cambridge: Polity Press, 26–58.

Streeck, W., and Thelen, K. (2005). *Beyond Continuity: Institutional Change in Advanced Political Economies*. Oxford: Oxford University Press.

Sundhedsstyrelsen (2012). *Fertilitetsbehandlinger 2010*. Copenhagen: Sundhedsstyrelsen, <http://www.sst.dk>, accessed 3 November 2016.

Sung, S., and Pascall, G. (2014). *Gender and Welfare Stares in East Asia: Confucianism or Gender Equality?* Basingstoke: Palgrave Macmillan.

Sweeney, J. (2015). 'Raising the status of FET: the labour market as an ally', ETBI, <http://www.etbi.ie/wp-content/uploads/2015/02/ETBI_Spring15_final_low-res.pdf>, accessed 3 November 2016.

Sweeney, J., Barr, J., and Pyne, L. (2014). *Employment and Skills Strategies in Ireland*. Brussels: OECD.

Sylwester, K. (2002). 'Can education expenditures reduce income inequality?', *Economics of Education Review*, 21, 43–52.

Tatsimaros, K. (2006). *Unemployment Insurance in Europe: Unemployment Duration and Subsequent Employment Stability*, IZA Discussion Paper No. 2280. Bonn: IZA.

Taylor, T. K., Schmidt, F., Pepler, D., and Hodgins, C. (1998). 'A comparison of eclectic treatment with Webster-Stratton's parents and children series in a children's mental health center: a randomized controlled trial', *Behavior Therapy*, 29(2), 221–40.

Taylor-Gooby, P. (ed.) (2004). *New Risks, New Welfare: The Transformation of the European Welfare State*. Oxford: Oxford University Press.

Taylor-Gooby, P. (2008). 'The new welfare state settlement in Europe', *European Societies*, 10(1), 3–24.

Taylor-Gooby, P. (2013). *The Double Crisis of the Welfare State and What We Can Do About It*. Basingstoke: Palgrave Macmillan.

Taylor-Gooby, P. (2014). 'Can "new welfare" address poverty through more and better jobs?' *Journal of Social Policy*, 44(1), January, 83–104.

Teichman, J. (2008). 'Redistributive conflict and social policy in Latin America', *World Development*, 36(3), 446–60.

Thelen, K. (2014). *Varieties of Liberalization and the New Politics of Social Solidarity*. Cambridge: Cambridge University Press.

Theodoropoulou, S. (2015). 'National social and labour market policy reforms in the shadow of EU bail-out conditionality: the cases of Greece and Portugal', *Comparative European Politics*, 13(1), 29–55.

Théret B. (2002). *Protection sociale et fédéralisme, l'Europe dans le miroir de l'Amérique du Nord*. Brussels: PIE Peter Lang.

Tilly, C. (1998). *Durable Inequality*. Berkeley, CA: University of California Press.

Tinbergen, J. (1975). *Income Distribution: Analysis and Policies*. Amsterdam: North Holland Publishing Co.

Triplett, J. E., and Bosworth, B. (2004). *Productivity in the U.S. Services Sector: New Sources of Economic Growth*. Washington, DC: Brookings Institution Press.

Tsai, P.-Y. (2011). *The Transformation of Social Risks: A Case Study of Work-Family Balance Policies in Taiwan*. Oxford: University of Oxford.

Tsakalotos, E. (2005). 'Homo Economicus and the reconstruction of political economy: six theses on the role of values in economics', *Cambridge Journal of Economics*, 29, 893–908.

Tsebelis, G. (2002). *Veto Players: How Political Institutions Work*. Princeton, NJ: Princeton University Press.

UNDP (United Nations Development Programme) (2010). *Acting on the Future: Breaking the Intergenerational Transmission of Inequality*. Regional Human Development Report for Latin America and the Caribbean. San José: UNDP.

UNDP (United Nations Development Programme) (2014). *Human Development Report 2014. Sustaining Human Progress: Reducing Vulnerabilities and Building Resilience*. New York: UNDP.

UNESCO (United Nations Educational, Scientific and Cultural Organization) (2013). *The State of Education in Latin America and the Caribbean: Towards a Quality Education for All—2015*. Santiago: UNESCO.

Urban, M., Vandenbroek, M., Lazzari, A., Peeters, J., and van Laere, K. (2011). 'Competence requirements in early childhood education and care', London and Ghent, September, <http://bookshop.europa.eu/en/competence-requirements-in-early-childhood-education-and-care-pbNC3113958/>, accessed 26 October 2016.

Usher, A. (2005). *Global Debt Patterns: An International Comparison of Student Loan Burdens and Repayment Conditions*. Toronto: Educational Policy Institute.

Vaalavuo, M. (2011). 'Towards an improved measure of income inequality: the impact of public services in income distribution: an international comparison', PhD Thesis, European University Institute, Florence, Italy.

Vaillancourt, Y. (2003). 'The Quebec model in social policy and its interface with Canada's social union'. In S. Fortin, A. Noël, and F. St-Hilaire (eds.), *Forging the Canadian Social Union: SUFA and Beyond*. Montreal: Institute for Research on Public Policy, 157–95.

Valencia Lomelí, E. (2008). 'Conditional cast transfers as social policy in Latin America: an assessment of their contributions and limitations', *Annual Review of Sociology*, 34, 475–99.

Van Arum, S., and Schoorl, R. (2015). 'Sociale (wijk)teams in vogelvlucht: State of the art najaar 2014'. Report commissioned by the Vereniging van Nederlandse Gemeenten (VNG), Utrecht, Movisie, February, <https://www.movisie.nl/publicaties/sociale-wijkteams-vogelvlucht>, accessed 3 November 2016.

Vandecasteele, L. (2010). 'Poverty trajectories after risky life course events in different European welfare regimes', *European Societies*, 12(2), 257–78.

Vandell, D. L., Belsky, J., Burchinal, M., Steinberg, L., and Vandergrift, N. (2010). 'Do effects of early child care extend to age 15 years? Results from the NICHD study of early child care and youth development', *Child Development*, 81(3), 737–56.

Vandenbroucke, F. (2015). 'The case of a European social union: from muddling through to a sense of common purpose'. In B. Marin (ed.), *The Future of Welfare in a Global Europe*. Aldershot: Ashgate, 433–64.

Vandenbroucke, F., and Rinaldi, D. (2015). Social inequalities in Europe—the challenge of convergence and cohesion. <http://hdl.handle.net/11245/1.493924>, accessed 14 December 2016.

Vandenbroucke, F., with Vanhercke, B. (2014). *A European Social Union: 10 Tough Nuts to Crack*. Brussels: Friends of Europe.

Vandenbroucke, F., and Vleminckx, K. (2011). 'Disappointing poverty trends: is the social investment state to blame?' *Journal of European Social Policy*, 21(5), 450–71.

Vandenbroucke, F., Diris, R., and Verbist, G. (2013). *Excessive Social Imbalances and the Performance of Welfare States in the EU*. KU Leuven: Euroforum.

Vandenbroucke, F., Hemerijck, A., and Palier, B. (2011). *The EU Needs a Social investment Pact*, Ose Opinion Paper N°5. Brussels: Ose.

Vanhercke, B., and Lelie, P. (2012). 'Benchmarking social Europe a decade on: demystifying the OMC's learning tools'. In A. Fenna and F. Knuepling (eds.), *Benchmarking in Federal Systems: Australian and International Experiences*. Melbourne: Productivity Commission, 145–84.

Vanhercke, B., Zeitlin J., and Zwinkels A. (2015). 'Further Socializing the European Semester: moving forward for the "Social Triple A"?', Working Paper, Brussels, Observatoire Social Europeen (OSE).

Van Hooren, F., and Becker, U. (2012). 'One welfare state, two care regimes: understanding developments in child and elderly care policies in the Netherlands', *Social Policy & Administration*, 46(1), 83–107.

Van Kersbergen, K., and Hemerijck, A. (2012). 'Two decades of change in Europe: the emergence of the social investment state', *Journal of Social Policy*, 41, 475–92.

Van Kersbergen, K., and Vis, B. (2014). *Comparative Welfare State Politics: Development, Opportunities, and Reform*. Cambridge: Cambridge University Press.

Van Lancker, W. (2013). 'Putting the child-centred investment strategy to the test: evidence for EU27', *European Journal of Social Security*, 15(1), 4–27.

Van Lancker, W. (2014). 'To whose benefit? An empirical and comparative investigation into the (un)intended consequences of family policy in the social investment state', Doctoral dissertation, University of Antwerp.

Van Lancker, W., and Ghysels, J. (2012). 'Who benefits? The social distribution of subsidized childcare in Sweden and Flanders', *Acta Sociologica*, 55, 125–42.

Van Lancker, W., and Van Mechelen, N. (2014). *Universalism under Siege? Exploring the Association between Targeting, Child Benefits and Child Poverty across 26 Countries*, CSB Working Paper 14(1). Antwerp: Herman Deleeck Centre for Social Policy.

Van Oorschot, W. (2004). 'Balancing work and welfare: activation and flexicurity policies in the Netherlands, 1980–2000', *International Journal of Social Welfare*, 13(1), 15–27.

Verbist, G., and Matsaganis, M. (2014). 'The redistributive capacity of services in the European Union'. In B. Cantillon and F. Vandenbroucke (eds.), *Reconciling Work and Poverty Reduction: How Successful are European Welfare States?* Oxford: Oxford University Press, 185–211.

Verbist, G., Förster, M., and Vaalavuo, M. (2012). *The Impact of Publicly Provided Services on the Distribution of Resources: A Review of New Results and Methods*, OECD Social, Employment and Migration Working Paper, No. 130. Paris: OECD Publishing.

Verbist, G., Roggeman, A., and De Lathauwer, L. (2007). 'Labour market activation policies: a comparison of the use of tax credits in Belgium, the UK and the US'. In J. de Koning (ed.), *Evaluation of Active Labour Market Policies: Measures, Public Private Partnerships and Benchmarking*. Cheltenham: Edward Elgar Publishing, 46–75.

Villani, C. (2015). 'I dati sull'apprendistato e le tendenze nel tempo'. In U. Ascoli, C. Ranci, and G. B. Sgritta (eds.), *Investire nel sociale. La difficile innovazione del welfare italiano*. Bologna: Il Mulino, 171–204.

Vossensteyn, H., Cremonini, L., Epping, E., Laudel, G., and Leisyte, L. (2013). *International Experiences with Student Financing Tuition Fees and Student Financial Support in Perspective*. Twente: Centre for Higher Education Policy Studies.

Wallerstein, M. (1990). 'Centralized bargaining and wage restraint', *American Journal of Political Science*, 33(4), 982–1004.

Watson, D., and Maître, B. (2013). *Social Transfers and Poverty Alleviation in Ireland: An Analysis of the Survey on Income and Living Conditions 2004–2011*. Dublin: Department of Social Protection and Economic and Social Research Institute.

Weishaupt, J. T. (2011). *From the Manpower Revolution to the Activation Paradigm: Explaining Institutional Continuity and Change in an Integrated Europe*. Amsterdam: Amsterdam University Press.

Wenzelburger, G. (2011). 'Political strategies and fiscal retrenchment: evidence from four countries', *West European Politics*, 34(6), 1151–84.

Whelan, C. T., Layte, R., and Maître, B. (2003). 'Poverty, deprivation and time: a comparative analysis of the structuring of disadvantage'. Institute for Social and Economic Research, University of Essex.

White, L. A. (2012). 'Must we all be paradigmatic? Social investment policies and liberal welfare states', *Canadian Journal of Political Science*, 45(3), 657–83.

Wilson, K. (2014). 'New investment approaches for addressing social and economic challenges', OECD Science, Technology and Industry Policy Papers. Paris: OECD Publishing.

Won, S.-Y., and Pascall, G. (2004). 'A Confucian war over childcare? Practice and policy in childcare and their implications for understanding the Korean gender regime', *Social Policy & Administration*, 38(3), 270–89.

Wong, J. (2004). *Healthy Democracies: Welfare Politics in Taiwan and South Korea*. Ithaca, NY: Cornell University Press.

World Bank (1995). *Investing in People: The World Bank in Action*. Washington, DC: World Bank.

World Bank (2001). *Colombia: Human Capital Protection (Cash Transfers) Project*. Washington, DC: World Bank.

Wren, A. (2013a). 'Introduction: the political economy of post-industrial societies'. In A. Wren (ed.), *The Political Economy of the Service Transition*. Oxford: Oxford University Press, 1–72.

Wren, A. (2013b). *The Political Economy of the Service Transition*. Oxford: Oxford University Press.

Wren, A., Fodor, M., and Theodoropoulou, S. (2013). 'The trilemma revisited: institutions, inequality, and employment creation in an era of ICT-intensive service expansion'. In A. Wren (ed.), *The Political Economy of the Service Transition*. Oxford: Oxford University Press, 108–46.

Zeitlin, J., and Vanhercke, B. (2014). 'Socializing the European Semester? Economic governance and social policy coordination in Europe 2020'. Report prepared for the Swedish Institute of European Studies (SIEPS), 1 October.

Index